READINGS IN PERSONALITY

READINGS IN PERSONALITY
CLASSIC THEORIES AND MODERN RESEARCH

Edited and with Commentary by

HOWARD S. FRIEDMAN
University of California, Riverside

MIRIAM W. SCHUSTACK
California State University, San Marcos

ALLYN AND BACON
Boston • London • Toronto • Sydney • Tokyo • Singapore

Executive Editor: Carolyn Merrill
Editorial Assistant: Lara Zeises
Marketing Manager: Caroline Croley
Editorial Production Service: Chestnut Hill Enterprises, Inc.
Manufacturing Buyer: Megan Cochran
Cover Administrator: Kristina Mose-Libon
Electronic Composition: Omegatype Typography, Inc.

Internet: www.abacon.com

Between the time Website information is gathered and published, some sites may have closed. Also, the transcription of URLs can result in typographical errors. The publisher would appreciate notification where these occur so that they may be corrected in subsequent editions.

Library of Congress Cataloging-in-Publication Data

Readings in personality: classic theories and modern research / edited and with commentary by Howard S. Friedman, Miriam W. Schustack.
    p. cm.
  Includes bibliographical references and index.
  ISBN 0-205-32149-6
   1. Personality.   I. Friedman, Howard S.   II. Schustack, Miriam W.
  BF698 .R346 2000
  155.2—dc21

                                           00-064606

Printed in the United States of America
10 9 8 7 6 5 4 3 2   05 04 03 02 01

Contents

UNIT FOUR
BEHAVIORIST AND LEARNING ASPECTS
OF PERSONALITY

UNIT FIVE
COGNITIVE ASPECTS OF PERSONALITY

UNIT SIX
TRAIT AND SKILL ASPECTS OF PERSONALITY

UNIT SEVEN
HUMANISTIC AND EXISTENTIAL ASPECTS
OF PERSONALITY

UNIT EIGHT
PERSON-SITUATION INTERACTIONIST ASPECTS
OF PERSONALITY

UNIT NINE
APPLICATIONS TO INDIVIDUAL DIFFERENCES

PREFACE

In many ways, the best introduction to the brilliance of influential personality theorists and researchers is through their own words. A verbal and eloquent group, personality theorists are not shy about stating their views of human nature in a forceful and direct manner. In the context of a course that provides orientation and framework to students, excerpts from theorists' writings can be a powerful tool for learning.

We have selected articles and excerpts that give the student a taste of the perspective offered by key theorists from the major traditions. Although not intended to be fully comprehensive, the articles provide an excellent sampling of the core concepts with which any well-educated personality psychologist is familiar. More basically, the selections provide a set of answers to the question, What does it mean to be a person? *Readings in Personality: Classic Theories and Modern Research* can thus be used in a wide variety of courses.

Each selection begins with a brief description of the author and the author's theoretical perspective. The selection is followed by a list of *Key Points,* to help the student review the highlights. Finally, each selection concludes with some *Questions to Think About.*

The book is organized into nine units, which correspond to nine basic perspectives on personality. Although this reader is designed to stand on its own, the units are also set up to correspond loosely to our personality textbook, *Personality: Classic Theories and Modern Research* (Allyn and Bacon, Publishers). That textbook is coordinated with a Website with quizzes, links, and other resources for student learning.

We want to thank Kathleen Clark, Paavai Jayaraman, Aarti Kulkami, Joya Paul, and Sophia Rath for their assistance in preparing this book. We also thank the authors of the selected contributions.

Howard S. Friedman

Miriam W. Schustack

READINGS IN PERSONALITY

My Views on the Role of Sexuality in the Etiology of the Neuroses*

SIGMUND FREUD

Sigmund Freud (1856–1939) was the son of Jacob Freud and his third wife Amalie. He was raised in a Jewish family, but later in life Freud, interested in biology, would become antireligious. Like many scientists of his time, Freud saw himself as discarding old superstitions and developing a science of the mind. Building on Charles Darwin's ideas of evolution, Freud saw the sex drive as fundamental.

Freud's mother was young and attractive. Freud and his two adult stepbrothers adored her. Freud remembered his brothers flirting with his mother, and recalled a memorable moment from childhood when he saw his mother naked.

When the 26-year-old Freud fell in love with Martha Bernays, he had to wait four long years to marry her. Around that time, Freud began developing his psychosexual theories of the human psyche, which had a profound influence on twentieth-century thought, as they popularized notions of repressed psychosexual conflict. The following reading lays out one of the core ideas of the psychoanalytic perspective, namely that sexuality, especially infantile sexuality, lies at the heart of people's psychological problems.

I am of the opinion that my theory on the etiological significance of the sexual moment in the neuroses can be best appreciated by following its development. I will by no means make any effort to deny that it passed through an evolution during which it underwent a change. My colleagues can find the assurance in this admission that this theory is nothing other than the result of continued and painstaking experiences. In contradistinction to this whatever originates from speculation can certainly appear complete at one go and continue unchanged.

Originally the theory had reference only to the morbid pictures comprehended as "neurasthenia," among which I found two types which occasionally appeared pure, and which I described as "actual neurasthenia" and "anxiety neurosis." For it was always known that sexual moments could play a part in the causation of these forms, but they were found neither regularly effective, nor did one think of conceding to them a precedence over other etiological influences. I was above all surprised at the frequency of coarse disturbances in the vita sexualis of nervous patients. The more I was in quest of such disturbances, during which I remembered that all men conceal the truth in things sexual, and the more skillful I became in continuing the

*Freud, S. (1912). My views on the role of sexuality in the etiology of the neuroses. In S. Freud, *Selected papers on hysteria and other psychoneuroses*, pp. 186–193. (Translation by A. A. Brill.) New York: The Journal of Nervous and Mental Diseases Publishing Company.

examination despite the incipient negation, the more regularly such disease-forming moments were discovered in the sexual life, until it seemed to me that they were but little short of universal. But one must from the first be prepared for similar frequent occurrences of sexual irregularities under the stress of the social relations of our society, and one could therefore remain in doubt as to what part of the deviation from the normal sexual function is to be considered as a morbid cause. I could therefore only place less value on the regular demonstration of sexual noxas than on other experiences which appeared to me to be less equivocal. It was found that the form of the malady, be it neurasthenia or anxiety neurosis, shows a constant relation to the form of the sexual injury. In the typical cases of neurasthenia we could always demonstrate masturbation or accumulated pollutions, while in anxiety neurosis we could find such factors as coitus interruptus, "frustrated excitement," etc. The moment of insufficient discharge of the generated libido seemed to be common to both. Only after this experience, which is easy to gain and very often confirmed, had I the courage to claim for the sexual influences a prominent place in the etiology of the neurosis. It also happened that the mixed forms of neurasthenia and anxiety neurosis occurring so often, showed the admixture of the etiologies accepted for both, and that such a bipartition in the form of the manifestations of the neurosis seemed to accord well with the polar characters of sexuality (male and female).

At the same time, while I assigned to sexuality this significance in the origin of the simple neurosis, I still professed for the psychoneuroses (hysteria and obsessions) a purely psychological theory in which the sexual moment was no differently considered than any other emotional sources. Together with J. Breuer, and in addition to observations which he has made on his hysterical patients fully a decade before, I have studied the mechanism of the origin of hysterical symptoms by the awakening of memories in hypnotic states. We obtained information which permitted us to cross the bridge from Charcot's traumatic hysteria to the common non-traumatic hysteria. We reached the conception that the hysterical symptoms are permanent results of psychic traumas, and that the amount of affect belonging to them was pushed away from conscious elaboration by special determinations, thus forcing an abnormal road into bodily innervation. The terms "strangulated affect," "conversion," and "ab-reaction," comprise the distinctive characteristics of this conception.

In the close relations of the psychoneuroses to the simple neuroses, which can go so far that the diagnostic distinction is not always easy for the unpracticed, it could happen that the cognition gained from one sphere has also taken effect in the other. Leaving such influences out of the question, the deep study of the psychic traumas also leads to the same results. If by the "analytic" method we continue to trace the psychic traumas from which the hysterical symptoms are derived, we finally reach to experiences which belong to the patient's childhood, and concerns his sexual life. This can be found even in such cases where a banal emotion of a non-sexual nature has occasioned the outburst of the disease. Without taking into account these sexual traumas of childhood we could neither explain the symptoms, find their determination intelligible, nor guard against their recurrence. The incomparable significance of sexual experiences in the etiology of the psychoneuroses seems therefore firmly established, and this fact remains until today one of the main supports of the theory.

If we represent this theory by saying that the course of the life long hysterical neurosis lies in the sexual experiences of early childhood which are usually trivial in themselves, it surely would sound strange enough. But if we take cognizance of the historical development of the theory, and transfer the main content of the same into the sentence: hysteria is the expression of a special behavior of the sexual function of the individual, and that this behavior was already decisively determined by the first effective influences and experiences of childhood, we will perhaps be poorer in a paradox but richer in a motive for directing our attention to a hi[t]herto very neglected and most significant after-effect of infantile impressions in general.

As I reserve the question whether the etiology of hysteria (and compulsion neurosis) is to be found in the sexual infantile experiences for a later more thorough discussion, I now return to the construction of the theory expressed in some small preliminary publications in the years 1895–1896. The bringing into prominence of the assumed etiological moments permitted us at the time to contrast the common neuroses which are maladies with an actual etiology, with the psychoneuroses which etiology was in the first place to be sought in the sexual experiences of remote times. The theory culminates in the sentence: In a normal vita sexualis no neurosis is possible.

If I still consider today this sentence as correct it is really not surprising that after ten years labor on the knowledge of these relations I passed a good way beyond my former point of view, and that I now think myself in a position to correct by detailed experience the imperfections, the displacements, and the misconceptions, from which this theory then suffered. By chance my former rather meagre material furnished me with a great number of cases in which infantile histories, sexual seduction by grown-up persons or older children, played the main role. I overestimated the frequency of these (otherwise not to be doubted) occurrences, the more so because I was then in no position to distinguish definitely the deceptive memories of hysterical patients concerning their childhood, from the traces of the real processes, whereas, I have since then learned to explain many a seduction fancy as an attempt at defense against the reminiscences of their own sexual activity (infantile masturbation). The emphasis laid on the "traumatic" element of the infantile sexual experience disappeared with this explanation, and it remained obvious that the infantile sexual activities (be they spontaneous or provoked) dictate the course of the later sexual life after maturity. The same explanation which really corrects the most significant of my original errors perforce also

changed the conception of the mechanism of the hysterical symptoms. These no longer appeared as direct descendants of repressed memories of sexual infantile experiences, but between the symptoms and the infantile impressions there slipped in the fancies (confabulations of memory) of the patients which were mostly produced during the years of puberty and which on the one hand, are raised from and over the infantile memories, and on the other, are immediately transformed into symptoms. Only after the introduction of the element of hysterical fancies did the structure of the neurosis and its relation to the life of the patient become transparent. It also resulted in a veritable surprising analogy between these unconscious hysterical fancies and the romances which became conscious as delusions in paranoia.

After this correction the "infantile sexual traumas" were in a sense supplanted by the "infantilism of sexuality." A second modification of the original theory was not remote. With the accepted frequency of seduction in childhood there also disappeared the enormous emphasis of the accidental influences of sexuality to which I wished to shift the main role in the causation of the disease without, however, denying constitutional and hereditary moments. I even hoped to solve thereby the problem of the selection of the neurosis, that is, to decide by the details of the sexual infantile experience, the form of the psychoneurosis into which the patient may merge. Though with reserve I thought at that time that passive behavior during these scenes results in the specific predisposition for hysteria, while active behavior results in compulsion neurosis. This conception I was later obliged to disclaim completely though some facts of the supposed connection between passivity and hysteria, and activity and compulsion neurosis, can be maintained to some extent. With the disappearance of the accidental influences of experiences, the elements of constitution and heredity had to regain the upper hand, but differing from the view generally in vogue I placed the "sexual constitution" in place of the general neuropathic predisposition. In my recent work, "Three Contributions to the Sexual Theory," I have attempted to discuss the varieties of this sexual constitution, the components of the sexual impulse in general, and its origin from the contributory sources of the organism.

Still in connection with the changed conception of the "sexual infantile traumas," the theory continued to develop in a course which was already indicated in the publications of 1894-1896. Even before sexuality was installed in its proper place in the etiology, I had already stated as a condition for the pathogenic efficaciousness of an experience that the latter must appear to the ego as unbearable and thus evoke an exertion for defense. To this defense I have traced the psychic splitting—or as it was then called the splitting of consciousness—of hysteria. If the defense succeeded, the unbearable experience with its resulting affect was expelled from consciousness and memory; but under certain conditions the thing expelled which was now unconscious, developed its activity, and with the aid of the symptoms and their adhering affect it returned into consciousness, so that the disease corresponded to a failure of the defense. This conception had the merit of entering into the play of the psychic forces, and hence approximate the psychic processes of hysteria to the normal instead of shifting the characteristic of the neurosis into an enigmatic and no further analyzable disturbance.

Further inquiries among persons who remained normal furnished the unexpected result, that the sexual histories of their childhood need not differ essentially from the infantile life of neurotics, and that especially the role of seduction is the same in the former, so the accidental influences receded still more in comparison to the moments of "repression" (which I began to use instead of "defense"). It really does not depend on the sexual excitements which an individual experiences in his childhood but above all on his reactions towards these experiences, and whether these impressions responded with "repression" or not. It could be shown that spontaneous sexual manifestations of childhood were frequently interrupted in the course of development by an act of repression. The sexual maturity of neurotic individuals thus regularly brings with it a fragment of "sexual repression" from childhood which manifests itself in the requirements of real life. Psychoanalysis of hysterical individuals show[s] that the malady is the result of the conflict between the libido and the sexual repression, and that their symptoms have the value of a compromise between both psychic streams.

Without a comprehensive discussion of my conception of repression I could not explain any further this part of the theory. It suffices to refer here to my "Three Contributions to the Sexual Theory," where I have made an attempt to throw some light on the somatic processes in which the essence of sexuality is to be sought. I have stated there that the constitutional sexual predisposition of the child is more irregularly multifarious than one would expect, that it deserves to be called "polymorphousperverse," and that from this predisposition the so called normal behavior of the sexual functions results through a repression of certain components. By referring to the infantile character of sexuality, I could form a simple connection among normal, perversions, and neurosis. The normal resulted through the repression of certain partial impulses and components of the infantile predisposition, and through the subordination of the rest under the primacy of the genital zones for the service of the function of procreation. The perversions corresponded to disturbances of this connection due to a superior compulsive-like development of some of the partial impulses, while the neurosis could be traced to a marked repression of the libidinous strivings. As almost all perversive impulses of the infantile predisposition are demonstrable as forces of symptom formation in the neurosis, in which, however, they exist in a state of repression, I could designate the neurosis as the "negative" of the perversion.

I think it worth emphasizing that with all changes my ideas on the etiology of the psychoneuroses still never disavowed or abandoned two points of view, to wit, the estimation of sexuality and infantilism. In other respects we have in place of the accidental influences the constitutional moments, and instead of the pure psychologically intended defense we have the organic "sexual repression." Should anybody ask where a cogent proof can be found for the asserted etiological significance of sexual factors in the psychoneuroses, and argue that since an outburst of these diseases can result from the most banal emotions, and even from somatic causes, a specific etiology in the form of special experiences of childhood must therefore be disavowed; I mention as an answer for all these arguments the psychoanalytic investigation of neurotics as the source from which the disputed conviction emanates. If one only makes use of this method of investigation he will discover that the symptoms represent the whole or a partial sexual manifestation of the patient from the sources of the normal or perverse partial impulses of sexuality. Not only does a good part of the hysterical symptomatology originate directly from the manifestations of the sexual excitement, not only are a series of erogenous zones in strengthening infantile attributes raised in the neurosis to the importance of genitals, but even the most complicated symptoms become revealed as the converted representations of fancies having a sexual situation as a content. He who can interpret the language of hysteria can understand that the neurosis only deals with the repressed sexuality. One should, however, understand the sexual function in its proper sphere as circumscribed by the infantile predisposition. Where a banal emotion has to be added to the causation of the disease, the analysis regularly shows that the sexual components of the traumatic experience, which are never missing, have exercised the pathogenic effect.

We have unexpectedly advanced from the question of the causation of the psychoneuroses to the problem of its essence. If we wish to take cognizance of what we discovered by psychoanalysis we can only say that the essence of these maladies lies in disturbances of the sexual processes, in those processes in the organism which determine the formation and utilization of the sexual libido. We can hardly avoid perceiving these processes in the last place as chemical, so that we can recognize in the so-called actual neuroses the somatic effects of disturbances in the sexual metabolism, while in the psychoneuroses we recognize besides the psychic effects of the same disturbances. The resemblance of the neuroses to the manifestations of intoxication and abstinence following certain alkaloids, and to Basedow's and Addison's diseases, obtrudes itself clinically without any further ado, and just as these two diseases should no more be described as "nervous diseases," so will the genuine "neuroses" soon have to be removed from this class despite their nomenclature.

Everything that can exert harmful influences in the processes serving the sexual function therefore belongs to the etiology of the neurosis. In the first place we have the noxas directly affecting the sexual functions insofar as they are accepted as injuries by the sexual constitution which is changeable through culture and breeding. In the second place, we have all the different noxas and traumas which may also injure the sexual processes by injuring the organism as a whole. But we must not forget that the etiological problem in the neuroses is at least as complicated as in the causation of any other disease. One single pathogenic influence almost never suffices, it mostly requires a multiplicity of etiological moments reinforcing one another, and which can not be brought in contrast to one another. It is for that reason that the state of neurotic illness is not sharply separated from the normal. The disease is the result of a summation, and the measure of the etiological determinations can be completed from any one part. To seek the etiology of the neurosis exclusively in heredity or in the constitution would be no less one sided than to attempt to raise to the etiology the accidental influences of sexuality alone, even though the explanations show that the essence of this malady lies only in a disturbance of the sexual processes of the organism.

REFERENCE

Freud, S. (1910). *Three contributions to the sexual theory* (A. A. Brill, Trans.). New York: The Journal of Nervous and Mental Disease Publishing Co.

KEY POINTS

1. Freud believes that hysterical symptoms in adults can be traced back to psychic trauma, and that these traumas always turn out to be based on sexual experiences from childhood.

2. A normal adult sexual life (*vita sexualis*) is not possible in the presence of neurosis.

3. Repression of the memory of childhood sexual experience is part of the development of the later neurosis.

QUESTIONS TO THINK ABOUT

1. What are some alternatives to Freud's focus on childhood sexual trauma that might also explain adult psychological difficulties?

2. In terms of its effect on the person later in life, does it matter whether a childhood sexual experience was one of fantasy or one that actually occurred?

3. Freud believed that both deep love and suppressed sadism exist within every adult. What could be some factors that determine which is suppressed and which dominates?

4. Freud's view was that normal sexual behavior in adults could develop only if many aspects of the child's "polymorphously perverse" sexual predispositions were repressed. How else could the development of healthy adult sexuality be explained, with alternative theoretical perspectives?

2

Psychoanalytic "Evidence": A Critique Based on Freud's Case of Little Hans*

JOSEPH WOLPE AND STANLEY RACHMAN

In this classic response to Freud's classic case of Little Hans, Joseph Wolpe (1915–1997) and Stanley Rachman used learning theory to present an alternative explanation of Hans's phobia. This in turn launched a dispute with psychoanalytic psychotherapists about whether it is necessary to search for deep, hidden conflicts when attempting to help people with anxiety and related dysfunctions. This dispute continues to this day. Further explanation of the behaviorist and learning approaches to personality is found later in this book in the selections by Watson and Rayner and by B. F. Skinner.

Wolpe and Rachman are best known for using behaviorist principles (of learning) to treat anxiety. For example, they helped develop systematic desensitization, a technique for treating anxiety in which people learn relaxation techniques, and then learn to relax in situations of steadily increasing provocation. In the selection that follows, they claim that their approach is more scientific than Freud's and suggest that psychoanalysts and their patients search for evidence to support their theories (and thus are biased).

Beginning with Wohlgemuth's trenchant monograph, the factual and logical bases of psychoanalytic theory have been the subject of a considerable number of criticisms. These have generally been dismissed by psychoanalysts, at least partly on the ground that the critics are oblivious of the "wealth of detail" provided by the individual case. One way to examine the soundness of the analysts' position is to study fully-reported cases that they themselves regard as having contributed significantly to their theories. We have undertaken to do this, and have chosen as our subject matter one of Freud's most famous cases,

given in such detail that the events of a few months occupy 140 pages of the *Collected Papers*.

In 1909, Freud published "The Analysis of a Phobia in a Five-year old Boy." This case is commonly referred to as "The case of Little Hans." Ernest Jones, in his biography of Freud, points out that it was "the first published account of a child analysis," and states that "the brilliant success of child analysis" since then was "indeed inaugurated by the study of this very case." The case also has special significance in the development of psychoanalytic theory because Freud believed himself to have found in it "a more direct

*Wolpe, J., & Rachman, S. (1960). Psychoanalytic "evidence": A critique based on Freud's case of Little Hans. *Journal of Nervous & Mental Disease, 131,* 135–148. Reprinted by permission. [Ed. note: Citations in the text of this selection and the sources to which they point have been edited to leave only those that are the most relevant and important. Readers wishing to see the full reference list can consult the original work.]

and less roundabout proof" of some fundamental psychoanalytic theorems. In particular, he thought that it provided a direct demonstration of the essential role of sexual urges in the development of phobias. He felt his position to have been greatly strengthened by this case and two generations of analysts have referred to the evidence of Little Hans as a basic substantiation of psychoanalytic theories. As an example, Glover may be quoted.

> In its time the analysis of Little Hans was a remarkable achievement and the story of the analysis constitutes one of the most valued records in psychoanalytical archives. Our concepts of phobia formation, of the positive Oedipus complex, of ambivalence, castration anxiety and repression, to mention but a few, were greatly reinforced and amplified as the result of this analysis.

In this paper we shall re-examine this case history and assess the evidence presented. We shall show that although there are manifestations of sexual behavior on the part of Hans, there is no scientifically acceptable evidence showing any connection between this behavior and the child's phobia for horses; that the assertion of such connection is pure assumption; that the elaborate discussions that follow from it are pure speculation; and that the case affords no factual support for any of the concepts listed by Glover above. Our examination of this case exposes in considerable detail patterns of thinking and attitudes to evidence that are well-nigh universal among psychoanalysts. It suggests the need for more careful scrutiny of the bases of psychoanalytic "discoveries" than has been customary; and we hope it will prompt psychologists to make similar critical examinations of basic psychoanalytic writings.

The case material on which Freud's analysis is based was collected by Little Hans's father, who kept Freud informed of developments by regular written reports. The father also had several consultations with Freud concerning Little Hans's phobia. During the analysis, Freud himself saw the little boy only once.

The following are the most relevant facts noted of Hans's earlier life. At the age of three,

he showed "a quite peculiarly lively interest in that portion of his body which he used to describe as his widdler." When he was three and a half, his mother found him with his hand to his penis. She threatened him in these words, "If you do that, I shall send for Dr. A. to cut off your widdler. And then what will you widdle with?" Hans replied, "With my bottom." Numerous further remarks concerning widdlers in animals and humans were made by Hans between the ages of three and four, including questions directed at his mother and father asking them if they also had widdlers. Freud attaches importance to the following exchange between Hans and his mother. Hans was "looking on intently while his mother undressed."

MOTHER: "What are you staring like that for?"
HANS: "I was only looking to see if you'd got a widdler, too."
MOTHER: "Of course. Didn't you know that?"
HANS: "No, I thought you were so big you'd have a widdler like a horse."

When Hans was three and a half his sister was born. The baby was delivered at home and Hans heard his mother "coughing," observed the appearance of the doctor and was called into the bedroom after the birth. Hans was initially "very jealous of the new arrival" but within six months his jealousy faded and was replaced by "brotherly affection." When Hans was four he discovered a seven-year-old girl in the neighborhood and spent many hours awaiting her return from school. The father commented that "the violence with which this 'long-range love' came over him was to be explained by his having no play-fellows of either sex." At this period also, "he was constantly putting his arms round" his visiting boy cousin, aged five, and was once heard saying, "I *am* so fond of you" when giving his cousin "one of these tender embraces." Freud speaks of this as the "first trace of homosexuality."

At the age of four and a half, Hans went with his parents to Gmunden for the summer holidays. On holiday Hans had numerous playmates including Mariedl, a fourteen-year-old girl. One evening Hans said, "I want Mariedl to sleep with me." Freud says that Hans's wish was an expression of his desire to have Mariedl as part of his family. Hans's parents occasionally took him into their bed and Freud claims that, "there can be no doubt that lying beside them had aroused erotic feelings in him; so that his wish to sleep with Mariedl had an erotic sense as well."

Another incident during the summer holidays is given considerable importance by Freud, who refers to it as Hans's attempt to seduce his mother. It must be quoted here in full.

Hans, four and a quarter. This morning Hans was given his usual daily bath by his mother and afterwards dried and powdered. As his mother was powdering round his penis and taking care not to touch it, Hans said, "Why don't you put your finger there?"

MOTHER: "Because that'd be piggish."
HANS: "What's that? Piggish? Why?"
MOTHER: "Because it's not proper."
HANS (laughing): "But it's great fun."

Another occurrence prior to the onset of his phobia was that when Hans, aged four and a half, laughed while watching his sister being bathed and was asked why he was laughing, he replied, "I'm laughing at Hanna's widdler." "Why?" "Because her widdler's so lovely." The father's comment is, "Of course his answer was a disingenuous one. In reality her widdler seemed to him funny. Moreover, this is the first time he has recognized in this way the distinction between male and female genitals instead of denying it."

In early January, 1908, the father wrote to Freud that Hans had developed "a nervous disorder." The symptoms he reported were: fear of going into the streets; depression in the evening; and a fear that a horse would bite him in the street. Hans's father suggested that "the ground was prepared by sexual over-excitation due to his mother's tenderness" and that the fear of the horse "seems somehow to be connected with his having been frightened by a large penis." The first signs appeared on January 7th, when Hans was being taken to the park by his nursemaid as usual.

He started crying and said he wanted to "coax" (caress) with his mother. At home "he was asked why he had refused to go any further and had cried, but he would not say." The following day, after hesitation and crying, he went out with his mother. Returning home Hans said ("after much internal struggling"), *"I was afraid a horse would bite me"* (original italics). As on the previous day, Hans showed fear in the evening and asked to be "coaxed." He is also reported as saying, "I know I shall have to go for a walk again tomorrow," and "The horse'll come into the room." On the same day he was asked by his mother if he put his hand to his widdler. He replied in the affirmative. The following day his mother warned him to refrain from doing this.

At this point in the narrative, Freud provided an interpretation of Hans's behavior and consequently arranged with the boy's father "that he should tell the boy that all this nonsense about horses was a piece of nonsense and nothing more. The truth was, his father was to say, that he was very fond of his mother and wanted to be taken into her bed. The reason he was afraid of horses now was that he had taken so much interest in their widdlers." Freud also suggested giving Hans some sexual enlightenment and telling him that females "had no widdler at all."

"After Hans had been enlightened there followed a fairly quiet period." After an attack of influenza which kept him in bed for two weeks the phobia got worse. He then had his tonsils out and was indoors for a further week. The phobia became "very much worse."

During March, 1908, after his physical illnesses had been cured, Hans apparently had many talks with his father about the phobia. On March 1, his father again told Hans that horses do not bite. Hans replied that white horses bite and related that while at Gmunden he had heard and seen Lizzi (a playmate) being warned by her father to avoid a white horse lest it bite. The father said to Lizzi, *"Don't put your finger to the white horse"* (original italics). Hans's father's reply to this account given by his son was, "I say, it strikes me it isn't a horse you mean, but a widdler, that one mustn't put one's hand to." Hans answered, "But a widdler doesn't bite." The father: "Perhaps it does, though." Hans then "went on eagerly to try to prove to me that it was a white horse." The following day, in answer to a remark of his father's, Hans said that his phobia was "so bad because I still put my hand to my widdler every night." Freud remarks here that, "Doctor and patient, father and son, were therefore at one in ascribing the chief share in the pathogenesis of Hans's present condition to his habit of onanism." He implies that this unanimity is significant, quite disregarding the father's indoctrination of Hans the previous day.

On March 13, the father told Hans that his fear would disappear if he stopped putting his hand to his widdler. Hans replied, "But I don't put my hand to my widdler any more." Father: "But you still want to." Hans agreed, "Yes, I do." His father suggested that he should sleep in a sack to prevent him from wanting to touch his widdler. Hans accepted this view and on the following day was much less afraid of horses.

Two days later the father again told Hans that girls and women have no widdlers. "Mummy has none, Anna has none and so on." Hans asked how they managed to widdle and was told "They don't have widdlers like yours. Haven't you noticed already when Hanna was being given her bath." On March 17 Hans reported a phantasy in which he saw his mother naked. On the basis of this phantasy and the conversation related above, Freud concluded that Hans had not accepted the enlightenment given by his father. Freud says, "He regretted that it should be so, and stuck to his former view in phantasy. He may also perhaps have had his reasons for refusing to believe his father at first." Discussing this matter subsequently, Freud says that the "enlightenment" given a short time before to the effect that women really do not possess a widdler was bound to have a shattering effect upon his self-confidence and to have aroused his castration complex. For this reason he resisted the information, and for this reason it had no therapeutic effect.

For reasons of space we shall recount the subsequent events in very brief form. On a visit to the Zoo Hans expressed fear of the giraffe, elephant and all large animals. Hans's father said to him, "Do you know why you're afraid of big animals? Big animals have big widdlers and you're really afraid of big widdlers." This was denied by the boy.

The next event of prominence was a dream (or phantasy) reported by Hans. "In the night there was a big giraffe in the room and a crumpled one; and the big one called out because I took the crumpled one away from it. Then it stopped calling out; and then I sat down on the top of the crumpled one."

After talking to the boy the father reported to Freud that this dream was "a matrimonial scene transposed into giraffe life. He was seized in the night with a longing for his mother, for her caresses, for her genital organ, and came into the room for that reason. The whole thing is a continuation of his fear of horses." The father infers that the dream is related to Hans's habit of occasionally getting into his parents' bed in the face of his father's disapproval. Freud's addition to "the father's penetrating observation" is that sitting down on the crumpled giraffe means taking possession of his mother. Confirmation of this dream interpretation is claimed by reference to an incident which occurred the next day. The father wrote that on leaving the house with Hans he said to his wife, "Good-bye, big giraffe." "Why giraffe?" asked Hans. "Mummy's the big giraffe," replied the father. "Oh, yes," said Hans, "and Hanna's the crumpled giraffe, isn't she?" The father's account continues, "In the train I explained the giraffe phantasy to him, upon which he said 'Yes, that's right.' And when I said to him that I was the big giraffe and that its long neck reminded him of a widdler, he said 'Mummy has a neck like a giraffe too. I saw when she was washing her white neck'."

On March 30, the boy had a short consultation with Freud who reports that despite all the enlightenment given to Hans, the fear of horses continued undiminished. Hans explained that he was especially bothered "by what horses wear in front of their eyes and the black round their mouths." This latter detail Freud interpreted as meaning a moustache. "I asked him whether he meant a moustache," and then, "disclosed to him that he was afraid of his father precisely because he was so fond of his mother." Freud pointed out that this was a groundless fear. On April 2, the father was able to report "the first real improvement." The next day Hans, in answer to his father's inquiry, explained that he came into his father's bed when he was frightened. In the next few days further details of Hans's fear were elaborated. He told his father that he was most scared of horses with "a thing on their mouths," that he was scared lest the horses fall, and that he was most scared of horse-drawn buses.

HANS: "I'm most afraid too when a bus comes along."

FATHER: "Why? Because it's so big?"

HANS: "No. Because once a horse in a bus fell."

FATHER: "When?"

Hans then recounted such an incident. This was later confirmed by his mother.

FATHER: "What did you think when the horse fell down?"

HANS: "Now it will always be like this. All horses in buses'll fall down."

FATHER: "In all buses?"

HANS: "Yes. And in furniture vans too. Not often in furniture vans."

FATHER: "You had your nonsense already at that time?"

HANS: "*No* (italics added). I only got it then. When the horse in the bus fell down, it gave me such a fright really: That was when I got the nonsense."

The father adds that, "all of this was confirmed by my wife, as well as the fact that *the anxiety broke out immediately afterwards*" (italics added).

Hans's father continued probing for a meaning of the black thing around the horses' mouths.

Hans said it looked like a muzzle but his father had never seen such a horse "although Hans asseverates that such horses do exist." He continues, "I suspect that some part of the horse's bridle really reminded him of a moustache and that after I alluded to this the fear disappeared." A day later Hans observing his father stripped to the waist said, "Daddy you are lovely! You're so white."

FATHER: "Yes. Like a white horse."

HANS: "The only black thing's your moustache. Or perhaps it's a black muzzle."

Further details about the horse that fell were also elicited from Hans. He said there were actually two horses pulling the bus and that they were both black and "very big and fat." Hans's father again asked about the boy's thoughts when the horse fell.

FATHER: "When the horse fell down, did you think of your daddy?

HANS: "Perhaps. Yes. It's possible."

For several days after these talks about horses Hans's interests, as indicated by the father's reports, "centered upon lumf (feces) and widdle, but we cannot tell why." Freud comments that at this point "the analysis began to be obscure and uncertain."

On April 11 Hans related this phantasy. "I was in the bath and then the plumber came and unscrewed it. Then he took a big borer and stuck it into my stomach." Hans's father translated this phantasy as follows: "I was in bed with Mamma. Then Pappa came and drove me away. With his big penis he pushed me out of my place by Mamma."

The remainder of the case history material, until Hans's recovery from the phobia early in May, is concerned with the lumf theme and Hans's feelings towards his parents and sister. It can be stated immediately that as corroboration for Freud's theories all of this remaining material is unsatisfactory. For the most part it consists of the father expounding theories to a boy who occasionally agrees and occasionally disagrees. The following two examples illustrate the nature of most of this latter information.

Hans and his father were discussing the boy's slight fear of falling when in the big bath.

FATHER: "But Mamma bathes you in it. Are you afraid of Mamma dropping you in the water?"

HANS: "I am afraid of her letting go and my head going in."

FATHER: "But you know Mummy's fond of you and won't let you go."

HANS: "I only just thought it."

FATHER: "Why?"

HANS: "I don't know at all."

FATHER: "Perhaps it was because you'd been naughty and thought she didn't love you any more?"

HANS: "Yes."

FATHER: "When you were watching Mummy giving Hanna her bath perhaps you wished she would let go of her so that Hanna should fall in?"

HANS: "Yes."

On the following day the father asks, "Are you fond of Hanna?"

HANS: "Oh, yes, very fond."

FATHER: "Would you rather that Hanna weren't alive or that she were?"

HANS: "I'd rather she weren't alive."

In response to close, direct questioning Hans voiced several complaints about his sister. Then his father proceeded again:

FATHER: "If you'd rather she weren't alive, you can't be fond of her, at all."

HANS: (assenting) "Hm, well."

FATHER: "That's why you thought when Mummy was giving her her bath if only she'd let go, Hanna would fall in the water. . ."

HANS: (taking me up) " . . . and die."

FATHER: "and then you'd be alone with Mummy. A good boy doesn't wish that sort of thing, though."

On April 24, the following conversation was recorded.

FATHER: "It seems to me that, all the same, you do wish Mummy would have a baby."

HANS: "But I don't want it to happen."

FATHER: "But you wish for it?"

HANS: "Oh, yes, *wish*."

FATHER: "Do you know why you wish for it? It's because you'd like to be Daddy."

HANS: "Yes. How does it work?"

FATHER: "You'd like to be Daddy and married to Mummy; you'd like to be as big as me and have a moustache; and you'd like Mummy to have a baby."

HANS: "And Daddy, when I'm married I'll have only one if I want to, when I'm married to Mummy, and if I don't want a baby, God won't want it either when I'm married."

FATHER: "Would you like to be married to Mummy?"

HANS: "Oh yes."

THE VALUE OF THE EVIDENCE

Before proceeding to Freud's interpretation of the case, let us examine the value of the evidence presented. First, there is the matter of selection of the material. The greatest attention is naturally paid to material related to psychoanalytic theory and there is a tendency to ignore other facts. The father and mother, we are told by Freud, "were both among my closest adherents." Hans himself was constantly encouraged, directly and indirectly, to relate material of relevance to the psychoanalytic doctrine.

Second, we must assess the value to be placed on the testimony of the father and of Hans. The father's account of Hans's behavior is in several instances suspect. For example, he twice presents his own interpretations of Hans's remarks as observed facts. This is the father's report of a conversation with Hans about the birth of his sister Hanna.

FATHER: "What did Hanna look like?"

HANS (hypocritically): "All white and lovely. So pretty."

On another occasion, despite several clear statements by Hans of his affection for his sister (and also the voicing of complaints about her screaming), the father said to Hans, "If you'd rather she weren't alive, you can't be fond of her at all." Hans (assenting): "Hm, well." (See above.)

The comment in parenthesis in each of these two extracts is presented as observed fact. A third example has also been quoted above. When Hans observes that Hanna's widdler is "so lovely" the father states that this is a "disingenuous" reply and that "in reality her widdler seemed to him funny." Distortions of this kind are common in the father's reports.

Hans's testimony is for many reasons unreliable. Apart from the numerous lies which he told in the last few weeks of his phobia, Hans gave many inconsistent and occasionally conflicting reports. Most important of all, much of what purports to be Hans's views and feelings is simply the father speaking. Freud himself admits this but attempts to gloss over it. He says, "It is true that during the analysis Hans had to be told many things which he could not say himself, that he had to be presented with thoughts which he had so far shown no signs of possessing and that his attention had to be turned in the direction from which his father was expecting something to come. This detracts from the evidential value of the analysis but the procedure is the same in every case. For a psychoanalysis is not an impartial scientific investigation but a therapeutic measure." To sum this matter up, Hans's testimony is subject not only to "mere suggestion" but contains much material that is not his testimony at all!

From the above discussion it is clear that the "facts of the case" need to be treated with considerable caution and in our own interpretation of Hans's behavior we will attempt to make use only of the testimony of direct observation.

FREUD'S INTERPRETATION

Freud's interpretation of Hans's phobia is that the boy's oedipal conflicts formed the basis of the illness which "burst out" when he underwent "a time of privation and the intensified sexual excitement." Freud says, "These were tendencies in Hans which had already been suppressed and which, so far as we can tell, had never been able to find uninhibited expression: hostile and jealous feelings against his father, and sadistic impulses (premonitions, as it were, of copulation) towards his mother. These early suppressions may perhaps have gone to form the predisposition for his subsequent illness. These aggressive propensities of Hans's found no outlet, and as soon as there came a time of privation and of intensified sexual excitement, they tried to break their way out with reinforced strength. It was then that the battle which we call his 'phobia' burst out."

This is the familiar oedipal theory, according to which Hans wished to replace his father "whom he could not help hating as a rival" and then complete the act by "taking possession of his mother." Freud refers for confirmation to the following: "Another symptomatic act, happening as though by accident, involved a confession that he had wished his father dead; for, just at the moment that his father was talking of his death-wish Hans let a horse that he was playing with fall down—knocked it over, in fact." Freud claims that, "Hans was really a little Oedipus who wanted to have his father 'out of the way' to get rid of him, so that he might be alone with his handsome mother and sleep with her." The predisposition to illness provided by the oedipal conflicts is supposed to have formed the basis for "the transformation of his libidinal longing into anxiety." During the summer prior to the onset of the phobia, Hans had experienced "moods of mingled longing and apprehension" and had also been taken into his mother's bed on occasions. Freud says, "We may assume that since then Hans had been in a state of intensified sexual excitement, the object of which was his mother. The intensity of this excitement was shown by his two attempts at seducing his mother (the second of which occurred just before the outbreak of his anxiety); and he found an incidental channel of discharge for it by masturbating. . . . Whether the sudden exchange of this excitement into anxiety took place spontaneously, or as a result of his mother's rejection of his advances, or owing to the accidental revival of earlier impressions by the 'exciting cause' of his illness . . . this we cannot decide. The fact remains that his sexual excitement suddenly changed into anxiety."

Hans, we are told, "transposed from his father on to the horses." At his sole interview with Hans, Freud told him "that he was afraid of his father because he himself nourished jealous and hostile wishes against him." Freud says of this, "In telling him this, I had partly interpreted his fear of horses for him: the horse must be his father—whom he had good internal reasons for fearing." Freud claims that Hans's fear of the black things on the horses' mouths and the things in front of their eyes was based on moustaches and eye-glasses and had been "directly transposed from his father on to the horses." The horses "had been shown to represent his father."

Freud interprets the agoraphobic element of Hans's phobia thus. "The content of his phobia was such as to impose a very great measure of restriction upon his freedom of movement, and that was its purpose . . . After all, Hans's phobia of horses was an obstacle to his going into the street, and could serve as a means of allowing him to stay at home with his beloved mother. In this way, therefore, his affection for his mother triumphantly achieved its aim."

Freud interprets the disappearance of the phobia as being due to the resolution by Hans of his oedipal conflicts by "promoting him (the father) to a marriage with Hans's grandmother . . . instead of killing him." This final interpretation is based on the following conversation between Hans and his father.

On April 30, Hans was playing with his imaginary children.

FATHER: "Hullo, are your children still alive? You know quite well a boy can't have any children."

HANS: "I know. I was their Mummy before, *now I'm their Daddy*" (original italics).

FATHER: "And who's the children's Mummy?"

HANS: "Why, Mummy, and you're their *Granddaddy* (original italics).

FATHER: "So then you'd like to be as big as me, and be married to Mummy, and then you'd like her to have children."

HANS: "Yes, that's what I'd like, and then my Lainz Grandmamma" (paternal side) "will be their Grannie."

CRITIQUE OF FREUD'S CONCLUSIONS

It is our contention that Freud's view of this case is not supported by the data, either in its particulars or as a whole. The major points that he regards as demonstrated are these: (1) Hans had a sexual desire for his mother, (2) he hated and feared his father and wished to kill him, (3) his sexual excitement and desire for his mother were transformed into anxiety, (4) his fear of horses was symbolic of his fear of his father, (5) the purpose of the illness was to keep near his mother and finally (6) his phobia disappeared because he resolved his Oedipus complex.

Let us examine each of these points:

1. That Hans derived satisfaction from his mother and enjoyed her presence we will not even attempt to dispute. But nowhere is there any evidence of his wish to copulate with her. Yet Freud says that, "if matters had lain entirely in my hands . . . I should have confirmed his instinctive premonitions, by telling him of the existence of the vagina and of copulation." The "instinctive premonitions" are referred to as though a matter of fact, though no evidence of their existence is given.

The only seduction incident described (see above) indicates that on *that particular occasion* Hans desired contact of a sexual nature with his mother, albeit a sexual contact of a simple, primitive type. This is not adequate evidence on which to base the claim that Hans had an Oedipus complex which implies a sexual desire for the mother, a wish to possess her and to replace the father. The most that can be claimed for this "attempted seduction" is that it provides a small degree of support for the assumption that Hans had a desire for sexual stimulation by some other person (it will be recalled that he often masturbated). Even if it is assumed that stimulation provided by his mother was especially desired, the two other features of an Oedipus complex (a wish to possess the mother and replace the father) are not demonstrated by the facts of the case.

2. Never having expressed either fear or hatred of his father, Hans was told by Freud that he possessed these emotions. On subsequent occasions Hans denied the existence of these feelings when questioned by his father. Eventually, he said "Yes" to a statement of this kind by his father. This simple affirmative obtained after considerable pressure on the part of the father and Freud is accepted as the true state of affairs and all Hans's denials are ignored. The "symptomatic act" of knocking over the toy horse is taken as further evidence of Hans's aggression towards his father. There are three assumptions underlying this "interpreted fact"—first, that the horse represents Hans's father; second, that the knocking over of the horse is not accidental; and third, that this act indicates a wish for the removal of whatever the horse symbolized.

Hans consistently denied the relationship between the horse and his father. He was, he said, afraid of horses. The mysterious black around the horses' mouths and the things on their eyes were later discovered by the father to be the horses' muzzles and blinkers. This discovery undermines the suggestion (made by Freud) that they were transposed moustaches and eye-glasses. There is no other evidence that the horses represented Hans's father. The assumption that the knocking over of the toy horse was meaningful in that it was prompted by an unconscious motive is, like most similar examples, a moot point. Freud himself (3) does not state that *all* errors are provoked by unconscious motives and in this sense "deliberate." This is understandable for it is easy to compile numerous instances of errors which can be accounted for in other, simpler terms without recourse to unconscious motivation or indeed motivation of any kind. Despite an examination of the literature we are unable to find a categorical statement

regarding the frequency of "deliberate errors." Furthermore, we do not know how to recognize them when they do occur. In the absence of positive criteria the decision that Hans's knocking over of the toy horse was a "deliberate error" is arbitrary.

As there is nothing to sustain the first two assumptions made by Freud in interpreting this "symptomatic act," the third assumption (that this act indicated a wish for his father's death) is untenable; and it must be reiterated that there is no independent evidence that the boy feared or hated his father.

3. Freud's third claim is that Hans's sexual excitement and desire for his mother were transformed into anxiety. This claim is based on the assertion that "theoretical considerations require that what is today the object of a phobia must at one time in the past have been the source of a high degree of pleasure." Certainly such a transformation is not displayed by the facts presented. As stated above, there is no evidence that Hans sexually desired his mother. There is also no evidence of any change in his attitude to her before the onset of the phobia. Even though there is some evidence that horses were to some extent previously a source of pleasure, in general the view that phobic objects must have been the source of former pleasures is amply contradicted by experimental evidence. Apart from the numerous experiments on phobias in animals which disprove this contention, the demonstrations of Watson and Rayner and Jones have clearly shown how phobias may be induced in children by a simple conditioning process. The rat and rabbit used as the conditioned stimuli in these demonstrations can hardly be regarded as sources of "a high degree of pleasure," and the same applies to the generalized stimulus of cotton wool.

4. The assertion that Hans's horse phobia symbolized a fear of his father has already been criticized. The assumed relationship between the father and the horse is unsupported and appears to have arisen as a result of the father's strange failure to believe that by the "black around their mouths" Hans meant the horses' muzzles.

5. The fifth claim is that the purpose of Hans's phobia was to keep him near his mother. Aside from the questionable view that neurotic disturbances occur for a purpose, this interpretation fails to account for the fact that Hans experienced anxiety even when he was out walking *with his mother.*

6. Finally, we are told that the phobia disappeared as a result of Hans's resolution of his oedipal conflicts. As we have attempted to show, there is no adequate evidence that Hans had an Oedipus complex. In addition, the claim that this assumed complex was resolved is based on a single conversation between Hans and his father (see above). This conversation is a blatant example of what Freud himself refers to as Hans having to "be told many things he could not say himself, that he had to be presented with thoughts which he had so far *shown* no signs of possessing, and that his attention had to be turned in the direction that his father was expecting something to come."

There is also no satisfactory evidence that the "insights" that were incessantly brought to the boy's attention had any therapeutic value. Reference to the facts of the case shows only occasional coincidences between interpretations and changes in the child's phobic reactions. For example, "a quiet period" early followed the father's statement that the fear of horses was a "piece of nonsense" and that Hans really wanted to be taken into his mother's bed. But soon afterwards, when Hans became ill, the phobia was worse than ever. Later, having had many talks without effect, the father notes that on March 13 Hans, after agreeing that he still *wanted* to play with his widdler, was "much less afraid of horses." On March 15, however, he was frightened of horses, after the information that females have no widdlers (though he had previously been told the opposite by his mother). Freud asserts that Hans resisted this piece of enlightenment because it aroused castration fears, and therefore no therapeutic success was to be observed. The "first real improvement" of April 2

is attributed to the "moustache enlightenment" of March 30 (later proved erroneous), the boy having been told that he was "afraid of his father precisely because he was so fond of his mother." On April 7, though Hans was constantly improving, Freud commented that the situation was "decidedly obscure" and that "the analysis was making little progress."

Such sparse and tenuous data do not begin to justify the attribution of Hans's recovery to the bringing to consciousness of various unacceptable unconscious repressed wishes. In fact, Freud bases his conclusions entirely on deductions from his theory. Hans's latter improvement appears to have been smooth and gradual and unaffected by the interpretations. In general, Freud infers relationships in a scientifically inadmissible manner: if the enlightenments or interpretations given to Hans are followed by behavioral improvements, then they are automatically accepted as valid. If they are not followed by improvement we are told the patient has not accepted them, and not that they are invalid. Discussing the failure of these early enlightenments, Freud says that in any event therapeutic success is not the primary aim of the analysis, thus sidetracking the issue; and he is not deflected from claiming an improvement to be due to an interpretation even when the latter is erroneous, *e.g.,* the moustache interpretation.

No systematic follow-up of the case is provided. However, fourteen years after the completion of the analysis, Freud interviewed Hans, who "declared that he was perfectly well and suffered from no troubles or inhibitions" (!). He also said that he had successfully undergone the ordeal of his parents' divorce. Hans reported that he could not remember anything about his childhood phobia. Freud remarks that this is "particularly remarkable." The analysis itself "had been overtaken by amnesia!"

AN ALTERNATIVE VIEW OF HANS'S PHOBIA

In case it should be argued that, unsatisfactory as it is, Freud's explanation is the only available one, we shall show how Hans's phobia can be understood in terms of learning theory, in the theoretical framework provided by Wolpe. This approach is largely Hullian in character and the clinical applications are based on experimental findings.

In brief, phobias are regarded as conditioned anxiety (fear) reactions. Any "neutral" stimulus, simple or complex, that happens to make an impact on an individual at about the time that a fear reaction is evoked acquires the ability to evoke fear subsequently. If the fear at the original conditioning situation is of high intensity or if the conditioning is many times repeated, the conditioned fear will show the persistence that is characteristic of *neurotic* fear; and there will be generalization of fear reactions to stimuli resembling the conditioned stimulus.

Hans, we are told, was a sensitive child who "was never unmoved if someone wept in his presence" and long before the phobia developed became "uneasy on seeing the horses in the merry-go-round being beaten." It is our contention that the incident to which Freud refers as merely the exciting cause of Hans's phobia was in fact the cause of the entire disorder. Hans actually says, "No. I only got it [the phobia] then. When the horse in the bus fell down, it gave me such a fright, really! That was when I got the nonsense." The father says, "All of this was confirmed by my wife, as well as the fact that the anxiety broke out immediately afterwards." The evidence obtained in studies on experimental neuroses in animals and the studies by Watson and Rayner, Jones and Woodward on phobias in children indicate that it is quite possible for one experience to induce a phobia.

In addition, the father was able to report two other unpleasant incidents which Hans had experienced with horses prior to the onset of the phobia. It is likely that these experiences had sensitized Hans to horses or, in other words, he had already been partially conditioned to fear horses. These incidents both occurred at Gmunden. The first was the warning given by the father of Hans's friend to avoid the horse lest it bite, and the second when another of Hans's friends injured himself (and bled) while they were playing horses.

Just as the little boy Albert (in Watson's classic demonstration) reacted with anxiety not only to the original conditioned stimulus, the white rat, but to other similar stimuli such as furry objects, cotton wool and so on, Hans reacted anxiously to horses, horse-drawn buses, vans and features of horses, such as their blinkers and muzzles. In fact he showed fear of a wide range of generalized stimuli. The accident which provoked the phobia involved two horses drawing a bus and Hans stated that he was more afraid of large carts, vans or buses than small carts. As one would expect, the less close a phobic stimulus was to that of the original incident the less disturbing Hans found it. Furthermore, the last aspect of the phobia to disappear was Hans's fear of large vans or buses. There is ample experimental evidence that when responses to generalized stimuli undergo extinction, responses to other stimuli in the continuum are the less diminished the more closely they resemble the original conditional stimulus.

Hans's recovery from the phobia may be explained on conditioning principles in a number of possible ways, but the actual mechanism that operated cannot be identified, since the child's father was not concerned with the kind of information that would be of interest to us. It is well known that especially in children many phobias decline and disappear over a few weeks or months. The reason for this appears to be that in the ordinary course of life generalized phobic stimuli may evoke anxiety responses weak enough to be inhibited by other emotional responses simultaneously aroused in the individual. Perhaps this process was the true source of Little Hans's recovery. The interpretations may have been irrelevant, or may even have retarded recovery by adding new threats and new fears to those already present. But since Hans does not seem to have been greatly upset by the interpretations, it is perhaps more likely that the therapy was actively helpful, for phobic stimuli were again and again presented to the child in a variety of emotional contexts that may have inhibited the anxiety and in consequence diminished its habit strength. The *gradualness* of Hans's recovery is consonant with an explanation of this kind.

CONCLUSIONS

The chief conclusion to be derived from our survey of the case of Little Hans is that it does not provide anything resembling direct proof of psychoanalytic theorems. We have combed Freud's account for evidence that would be acceptable in the court of science, and have found none. In attempting to give a balanced summary of the case we have excluded a vast number of interpretations but have tried not to omit any material facts. Such facts, and they alone, could have supported Freud's theories. For example, it it had been observed after Gmunden that Hans had become fearful of his father, and that upon the development of the horse phobia the fear of the father had disappeared, this could reasonably have been regarded as presumptive of a displacement of fear from father to horse. This is quite different from observing a horse phobia and then asserting that it must be a displaced father-fear without ever having obtained any direct evidence of the latter; for then that which needs to be demonstrated is presupposed. To say that the father-fear was repressed is equally no substitute for evidence of it.

Freud fully believed that he had obtained in Little Hans a direct confirmation of his theories, for he speaks towards the end of "the infantile complexes that were revealed behind Hans's phobia." It seems clear that although he wanted to be scientific Freud was surprisingly naive regarding the requirements of scientific evidence. Infantile complexes were not *revealed* (demonstrated) behind Hans's phobia: they were merely hypothesized.

It is remarkable that countless psychoanalysts have paid homage to the case of Little Hans, without being offended by its glaring inadequacies. We shall not here attempt to explain this, except to point to one probable major influence—a tacit belief among analysts that Freud possessed a kind of unerring insight that absolved him from the obligation to obey rules applicable to ordinary men. For example, Glover, speaking of other analysts who arrogate to themselves the right Freud claimed to subject his material to "a touch of revision," says, "No doubt when someone of Freud's calibre appears in our midst he will be freely accorded . . . this privilege." To accord such a privilege to anyone is to violate the spirit of science.

It may of course be argued that some of the conclusions of Little Hans are no longer held and that there is now other evidence for other of the conclusions; but there is no evidence that in general psychoanalytic conclusions are based on any better logic than that used by Freud in respect of Little Hans. Certainly no analyst has ever pointed to the failings of this account or disowned its reasoning, and it has continued to be regarded as one of the foundation stones on which psychoanalytic theory was built.

SUMMARY

The main facts of the case of Little Hans are presented and it is shown that Freud's claim of "a more direct and less roundabout proof" of certain of his theories is not justified by the evidence presented. No confirmation by direct observation is obtained for any psychoanalytic theorem, though psychoanalysts have believed the contrary for 50 years. The demonstrations claimed are really interpretations that are treated as facts. This is a common practice and should be checked, for it has been a great encumbrance to the development of a science of psychiatry.

REFERENCES

Freud, S. *Collected Papers,* Vol. 3. Hogarth Press, London, 1950.

Glover, E. *On the Early Development of Mind.* International Universities Press, New York, 1956.

Glover, E. Research methods in psychoanalysis. *International Journal of Psychoanylsis,* 33: 403–409, 1952.

Jones, E. *Sigmund Freud: Life and Work,* Vol. 2. Hogarth Press, London, 1955.

Watson, J. B. and Rayner, P. Conditioned emotional reactions. *Journal of Experimental Psychology,* 3: 1–14, 1920 [Editor's note: This article is included as Chapter 15 of this reader.]

Wohlgemuth, A. *A Critical Examination of Psychoanalysis.* Allen Unwin, London, 1923.

KEY POINTS

1. Wolpe and Rachman claim that there is no independent verification of Freud's claim that Oedipal conflict was the source of Hans's phobia.

2. They claim that psychoanalytic methods of collecting evidence are biased and not objective, but depend on prior acceptance of psychoanalytic theory.

3. They argue that anxiety should be approached in terms of conditioning, not in terms of repressed psychosexual drives.

QUESTIONS TO THINK ABOUT

1. Freud has proposed a deep, complex theory of human nature. What do we lose by discarding it and turning instead to simple notions of conditioning? What do we gain?

2. Freud believed that underlying most human conflicts and distresses are issues of unresolved, repressed sexuality and aggression. Behaviorists view such notions as unscientific. How can Freud's theories best be tested, since by their very nature the repressed sexual conflicts are difficult to access?

3

The Interpretation of Dreams*

SIGMUND FREUD

Sigmund Freud made sure to publish his exciting new book, *The Interpretation of Dreams,* in the year 1900, hoping that it would have a great influence on his new science of the mind in the new century. Although dream interpretation was well established by biblical times, several thousand years ago, Freud viewed dream interpretation based on his new theories as a scientific tool, a royal road to the unconscious. He began interpreting his own dreams as well as those of other people to figure out what was going on in the hidden recesses of a person's psyche. As a biologist, Freud saw himself as well acquainted with the biological structures and laws that underlie his psychological views.

According to Freud, a pointed object like a clarinet could represent a phallus, and a fur bag could represent a vagina. In dreams, hidden thoughts that we cannot normally access can slip out, represented by symbols.

I shall, therefore, select one of my own dreams and use it to elucidate my method of interpretation. Every such dream necessitates a preliminary statement. I must now beg the reader to make my interests his own for a considerable time and to become absorbed with me in the most trifling details of my life, for an interest in the hidden significance of dreams imperatively demands such transference.

Preliminary statement: In the summer of 1895 I had psychoanalytically treated a young lady who stood in close friendship to me and those near to me. It is to be understood that such a complication of relations may be the source of manifold feelings for the physician, especially for the psychotherapist. The personal interest of the physician is greater, his authority is less. A failure threatens to undermine the friendship with the relatives of the patient. The cure ended with partial success, the patient got rid of her hysterical fear, but not of all her somatic symptoms. I was at that time not yet sure of the criteria marking the final settlement of a hysterical case, and expected her to accept a solution which did not seem acceptable to her. In this disagreement, we cut short the treatment on account of the summer season. One day a younger colleague, one of my best friends, who had visited the patient—Irma—and her family in their country resort, came to see me. I asked him how he found her, and received the answer: "She is better, but not altogether well." I realise that those words of my friend Otto, or the tone of voice in which they were spoken, made me angry. I thought I heard a reproach in the words, perhaps to the effect that I had promised the patient too much, and rightly or wrongly I traced Otto's supposed siding against me to the influence of the relatives of the

*Freud, S. (1915). *The interpretation of dreams.* (Translation by A. A. Brill of 3rd edition.) London: George Allen & Unwin, Ltd. (Selection is from Dream of July 23–24, 1895, pp. 88–102.)

patient, who, I assume, had never approved of my treatment. Moreover, my disagreeable impression did not become clear to me, nor did I give it expression. The very same evening, I wrote down the history of Irma's case, in order to hand it, as though for my justification, to Dr. M., a mutual friend, who was at that time a leading figure in our circle. During the night following this evening (perhaps rather in the morning) I had the following dream, which was registered immediately after waking:—

DREAM OF JULY 23–24, 1895

A great hall—many guests whom we are receiving— among them Irma, whom I immediately take aside, as though to answer her letter, to reproach her for not yet accepting the " solution." I say to her: "If you still have pains, it is really only your own fault." She answers: "If you only knew what pains I now have in the neck, stomach, and abdomen; I am drawn together." I am frightened and look at her. She looks pale and bloated; I think that after all I must be overlooking some organic affection. I take her to the window and look into her throat. She shows some resistance to this, like a woman who has a false set of teeth. I think anyway she does not need them. The mouth then really opens without difficulty and I find a large white spot to the right, and at another place I see extended grayish-white scabs attached to curious curling formations, which have obviously been formed in the turbinated bone—I quickly call Dr. M., who repeats the examination and confirms it. . . . Dr. M.'s looks are altogether unusual; he is very pale, limps, and has no beard on his chin. . . . My friend Otto is now also standing next to her, and my friend Leopold percusses her small body and says: "She has some dulness on the left below," and also calls attention to an infiltrated portion of the skin on the left shoulder (something which I feel as he does, in spite of the dress). . . . M. says: "No doubt it is an infection, but it does not matter; dysentery will develop too, and the poison will be excreted. . . . We also have immediate knowledge of the origin of the infection. My friend Otto has recently given her an injection with a propyl preparation when she felt ill, propyls. . . . Propionic acid . . . Trimethylamine (the formula of which I see printed before me in heavy type). . . . Such injections are not made so rashly. . . . Probably also the syringe was not clean.

This dream has an advantage over many others. It is at once clear with what events of the preceding day it is connected, and what subject it treats. The preliminary statement gives information on these points. The news about Irma's health which I have received from Otto, the history of the illness upon which I have written until late at night, has occupied my psychic activity even during sleep. In spite of all this, no one, who has read the preliminary report and has knowledge of the content of the dream, has been able to guess what the dream signifies. Nor do I myself know. I wonder about the morbid symptoms, of which Irma complains in the dream, for they are not the same ones for which I have treated her. I smile about the consultation with Dr. M. I smile about the nonsensical idea of an injection with propionic acid, and at the consolation attempted by Dr. M. Towards the end the dream seems more obscure and more terse than at the beginning. In order to learn the significance of all this, I am compelled to undertake a thorough analysis.

ANALYSIS

The hall—many guests, whom we are receiving.

We were living this summer at the Bellevue, in an isolated house on one of the hills which lie close to the Kahlenberg. This house was once intended as a place of amusement, and on this account has unusually high, hall-like rooms. The dream also occurred at the Bellevue, a few days before the birthday of my wife. During the day, my wife had expressed the expectation that several friends, among them Irma, would come to us as guests for her birthday. My dream, then, anticipates this situation: It is the birthday of my wife, and many people, among them Irma, are received by us as guests in the great hall of the Bellevue.

I reproach Irma for not having accepted the solution. I say: "If you still have pains, it is your own fault."

I might have said this also, or did say it, while awake. At that time I had the opinion (recognised later to be incorrect) that my task was limited to informing patients of the hidden meaning of their symptoms. Whether they then accepted or did not accept the solution upon which success depended—for that I was not responsible. I am thankful to this error, which fortunately has now been overcome, for making life easier for me at a time when, with all my unavoidable ignorance, I was to produce successful cures. But I see in the speech which I make to Irma in the dream, that above all things I do not want to be to blame for the pains which she still feels. It is Irma's own fault, it cannot be mine. Should the purpose of the dream be looked for in this quarter?

Irma's complaints; pains in the neck, abdomen, and stomach; she is drawn together.

Pains in the stomach belonged to the symptom-complex of my patient, but they were not very prominent; she complained rather of sensations of nausea and disgust. Pains in the neck and abdomen and constriction of the throat hardly played a part in her case. I wonder why I decided upon this choice of symptoms, nor can I for the moment find the reason.

She looks pale and bloated.

My patient was always ruddy. I suspect that another person is here being substituted for her.

I am frightened at the thought that I must have overlooked some organic affection.

This, as the reader will readily believe, is a constant fear with the specialist, who sees neurotics almost exclusively, and who is accustomed to ascribe so many manifestations, which other physicians treat as organic, to hysteria. On the other hand, I am haunted by a faint doubt—I know not whence it comes—as to whether my fear is altogether honest. If Irma's pains are indeed of organic origin, I am not bound to cure

them. My treatment, of course, removes only hysterical pains. It seems to me, in fact, that I wish to find an error in the diagnosis; in that case the reproach of being unsuccessful would be removed.

I take her to the window in order to look into her throat. She resists a little, like a woman who has false teeth. I think she does not need them anyway.

I had never had occasion to inspect Irma's oral cavity. The incident in the dream reminds me of an examination made some time before, of a governess who at first gave an impression of youthful beauty, but who upon opening her mouth took certain measures for concealing her teeth. Other memories of medical examinations and of little secrets which are discovered by them, unpleasantly for both examiner and examined, connect themselves with the case. "She does not need them anyway," is at first perhaps a compliment for Irma; but I suspect a different meaning. In careful analysis one feels whether or not the "background thoughts" which are to be expected have been exhausted. The way in which Irma stands at the window suddenly reminds me of another experience. Irma possesses an intimate woman friend, of whom I think very highly. One evening on paying her a visit I found her in the position at the window reproduced in the dream, and her physician, the same Dr. M., declared that she had a diphtheritic membrane. The person of Dr. M. and the membrane return in the course of the dream. Now it occurs to me that during the last few months, I have been given every reason to suppose that this lady is also hysterical. Yes, Irma herself has betrayed this to me. But what do I know about her condition? Only the one thing, that like Irma she suffers from hysterical choking in dreams. Thus in the dream I have replaced my patient by her friend. Now I remember that I have often trifled with the expectation that this lady might likewise engage me to relieve her of her symptoms. But even at the time I thought it improbable, for she is of a very shy nature. *She resists,* as the dream shows. Another explanation might be that *she does not need it;* in fact, until now she has shown herself strong enough to master her condition without outside help. Now only a few features remain, which I can assign neither to Irma nor to her friend: *Pale, bloated, false teeth.* The false teeth lead me to the governess; I now feel inclined to be satisfied with bad teeth. Then another person, to whom these features may allude, occurs to me. She is not my patient, and I do not wish her to be my patient, for I have noticed that she is not at her ease with me, and I do not consider her a docile patient. She is generally pale, and once, when she had a particularly good spell, she was bloated. I have thus compared my patient Irma with two others, who would likewise resist treatment. What can it mean that I have exchanged her for her friend in the dream? Perhaps that I wish to exchange her; either the other one arouses in me stronger sympathies or I have a higher opinion of her intelligence. For I consider Irma foolish because she does not accept my solution. The other one would be more sensible, and would thus be more likely to yield. *The mouth then really opens without difficulty;* she would tell more than Irma.

What I see in the throat; a white spot and scabby nostrils.

The white spot recalls diphtheria, and thus Irma's friend, but besides this it recalls the grave illness of my eldest daughter two years before and all the anxiety of that unfortunate time. The scab on the nostrils reminds me of a concern about my own health. At that time I often used cocaine in order to suppress annoying swellings in the nose, and had heard a few days before that a lady patient who did likewise had contracted an extensive necrosis of the nasal mucous membrane. The recommendation of cocaine, which I had made in 1885, had also brought grave reproaches upon me. A dear friend, already dead in 1895, had hastened his end through the misuse of this remedy.

I quickly call Dr. M., who repeats the examination.

This would simply correspond to the position which M. occupied among us. But the word "quickly" is striking enough to demand a special explanation. It reminds me of a sad medical experience. By the continued prescription of a remedy (sulfonal) which was still at that time considered harmless, I had once caused the severe intoxication of a woman patient, and I had turned in great haste to an older, more experienced colleague for assistance. The fact that I really had this case in mind is confirmed by an accessory circumstance. The patient, who succumbed to the intoxification, bore the same name as my eldest daughter. I had never thought of this until now; now it seems to me almost like a retribution of fate—as though I ought to continue the replacement of the persons here in another sense; this Matilda for that Matilda; an eye for an eye, a tooth for a tooth. It is as though I were seeking every opportunity to reproach myself with lack of medical conscientiousness.

Dr. M. is pale, without a beard on his chin, and he limps.

Of this so much is correct, that his unhealthy appearance often awakens the concern of his friends. The other two characteristics must belong to another person. A brother living abroad occurs to me, who wears his chin clean-shaven, and to whom, if I remember aright, M. of the dream on the whole bears some resemblance. About him the news arrived some days before that he was lame on account of an arthritic disease in the hip. There must be a reason why I fuse the two persons into one in the dream. I remember that in fact I was on bad terms with both of them for similar reasons. Both of them had rejected a certain proposal which I had recently made to them.

My friend Otto is now standing next to the sick woman, and my friend Leopold examines her and calls attention to a dulness on the left below.

My friend Leopold is also a physician, a relative of Otto. Since the two practise the same specialty, fate has made them competitors, who are continually being compared with each other. Both of them assisted me for years, while I was still directing a public dispensary for nervous children. Scenes like the one reproduced in the dream have often taken place there. While I was debating with Otto about the diagnosis of a case, Leopold had examined the child anew and had made an unexpected contribution towards the decision. For there was a difference of character between the two similar to that between Inspector Brassig and his friend Charles. The one was distinguished for his brightness, the other was slow, thoughtful, but thorough. If I contrast Otto and the careful Leopold in the dream, I do it, apparently, in order to extol Leopold. It is a comparison similar to the one above between the disobedient patient Irma and her friend who is thought to be more sensible. I now become aware of one of the tracks along which the thought association of the dream progresses; from the sick child to the children's asylum. The dulness to the left, below, recalls a certain case corresponding to it, in every detail in which Leopold astonished me by his thoroughness. Besides this, I have a notion of something like a metastatic affection, but it might rather be a reference to the lady patient whom I should like to have instead of Irma. For this lady, as far as I can gather, resembles a woman suffering from tuberculosis.

An infiltrated portion of skin on the left shoulder.

I see at once that this is my own rheumatism of the shoulder, which I always feel when I have remained awake until late at night. The turn of phrase in the dream also sounds ambiguous; something which I feel . . . in spite of the dress. "Feel on my own body " is intended. Moreover, I am struck with the unusual sound of the term "infiltrated portion of skin." "An infiltration behind on the upper left " is what we are accustomed to; this would refer to the lung, and thus again to tuberculosis patients.

In spite of the dress.

This, to be sure, is only an interpolation. We, of course, examine the children in the clinic undressed; it is some sort of contradiction to the manner in which grown-up female patients must be examined. The story used to be told of a prominent clinician that he always examined his patients physically only through the clothes. The rest is obscure to me; I have, frankly, no inclination to follow the matter further.

Dr. M. says: "It is an infection, but it does not matter. Dysentery will develop, and the poison will be excreted.

This at first seems ridiculous to me; still it must be carefully analysed like everything else. Observed more closely, it seems, however, to have a kind of meaning. What I had found in the patient was local diphtheritis. I remember the discussion about diplitheritis and diphtheria at the time of my daughter's illness. The latter is the general infection which proceeds from local diphtheritis. Leopold proves the existence of such general infection by means of the dulness which thus suggests a metastatic lesion. I believe, however, that just this kind of metastasis does not occur in the case of diphtheria. It rather recalls pyæmia.

It does not matter, is a consolation. I believe it fits in as follows: The last part of the dream has yielded a content to the effect that the pains of the patient are the result of a serious organic affection. I begin to suspect that with this I am only trying to shift the blame from myself. Psychic treatment cannot be held responsible for the continued presence of diphtheritic affection. But now, in turn, I am disturbed at inventing such serious suffering for Irma for the sole purpose of exculpating myself. It seems cruel. I need (accordingly) the assurance that the result will be happy, and it does not seem ill-advised that I should put the words of consolation into the mouth of Dr. M. But here I consider myself superior to the dream, a fact which needs explanation.

But why is this consolation so nonsensical?

Dysentery:

Some sort of far-fetched theoretical notion that pathological material may be removed through the intestines. Am I in this way trying to make fun of Dr. M.'s great store of far-fetched explanations, his habit of finding curious pathological relationships? Dysentery suggests something else. A few months ago I had in charge a young man suffering from remarkable pains during evacuation of the bowels, a case which colleagues had treated as "anæmia with malnutrition." I realized that it was a question of hysteria; I was unwilling to use my psychotherapy on him, and sent him off on a sea voyage. Now a few days before I had received a despairing letter from him from Egypt, saying that while there he had suffered a new attack, which the physician had declared to be dysentery. I suspect, indeed, that the diagnosis was only an error of my ignorant colleague, who allows hysteria to make a fool of him; but still I cannot avoid reproaching myself for putting the invalid in a position where he might contract an organic affection of the bowels in addition to his hysteria. Furthermore, dysentery sounds like diphtheria, a word which does not occur in the dream.

Indeed it must be that, with the consoling prognosis; "Dysentery will develop, etc.," I am making fun of Dr. M., for I recollect that years ago he once jokingly told a very similar story of another colleague. He had been called to consult with this colleague in the case of a woman who was very seriously ill and had felt obliged to confront the other physician, who seemed very hopeful, with the fact that he found albumen in the patient's urine. The colleague, however, did not let this worry him, but answered calmly: "That does not matter, doctor; the albumen will without doubt be excreted." Thus I can no longer doubt that derision for those colleagues who are ignorant of hysteria is contained in this part of the dream. As though in confirmation, this question now arises in my mind: "Does Dr. M. know that the symptoms of his patient, of our friend Irma, which give cause for fearing tuberculosis, are also based on hysteria? Has he recognised this hysteria, or has he stupidly ignored it?"

But what can be my motive in treating this friend so badly? This is very simple: Dr. M. agrees with my solution as little as Irma herself. I have thus already in this dream taken revenge on two persons, on Irma in the words, "If you still have pains, it is your own fault," and on Dr. M. in the wording of the nonsensical consolation which has been put into his mouth.

We have immediate knowledge of the origin of the infection.

This immediate knowledge in the dream is very remarkable. Just before we did not know it, since the infection was first demonstrated by Leopold.

My friend Otto has recently given her an injection when she felt ill.

Otto had actually related that in the short time of his visit to Irma's family, he had been called to a neighbouring hotel in order to give an injection to some one who fell suddenly ill. Injections again recall the unfortunate friend who has poisoned himself with cocaine. I had recommended the remedy to him merely for internal use during the withdrawal of morphine, but he once gave himself injections of cocaine.

With a propyl preparation . . . propyls . . . propionic acid.

How did this ever occur to me? On the same evening on which I had written part of the history of the disease before having the dream, my wife opened a bottle of cordial labelled "Ananas," (which was a present from our friend Otto. For he had a habit of making presents on every possible occasion; I hope he will some day be cured of this by a wife.) Such a smell of fusel oil arose from this cordial that I refused to taste it. My wife observed: "We will give this bottle to the servants," and I, still more prudent, forbade it, with the philanthropic remark: "They mustn't be poisoned either." The smell of fusel oil (amyl . . .) has now apparently awakened in my memory the whole series, propyl, methyl, &c., which has furnished the propyl preparation of the dream. In this, it is true, I have employed a substitution; I have dreamt of propyl, after smelling amyl, but substitutions of this kind are perhaps permissible, especially in organic chemistry.

Trimethylamin. I see the chemical formula of this substance in the dream, a fact which probably gives evidence of a great effort on the part of my memory, and, moreover, the formula is printed in heavy type, as if to lay special stress upon something of particular importance, as distinguished from the context. To what does this trimethylamin lead, which has been so forcibly called to my attention? It leads to a conversation with another friend who for years has known all my germinating activities, as I have his. At that time he had just informed me of some of his ideas about sexual chemistry, and had mentioned, among others, that he thought he recognized in trimethylamin one of the products of sexual metabolism. This substance thus leads me to sexuality, to that factor which I credit with the greatest significance for the origin of the nervous affections which I attempt to cure. My patient Irma is a young widow; if I am anxious to excuse the failure of her cure, I suppose I shall best do so by referring to this condition, which her admirers would be glad to change. How remarkably too, such a dream is fashioned! The other woman, whom I take as my patient in the dream instead of Irma, is also a young widow.

I suspect why the formula of trimethylamin has made itself so prominent in the dream. So many important things are gathered up in this one word: Trimethylamin is not only an allusion to the overpowering factor of sexuality, but also to a person whose sympathy I remember with satisfaction when I feel myself forsaken in my opinions. Should not this friend, who plays such a large part in my life, occur again in the chain of thoughts of the dream? Of course, he must;

he is particularly acquainted with the results which proceed from affections of the nose and its adjacent cavities, and has revealed to science several highly remarkable relations of the turbinated bones to the female sexual organs (the three curly formations in Irma's throat). I have had Irma examined by him to see whether the pains in her stomach might be of nasal origin. But he himself suffers from suppurative rhinitis, which worries him, and to this perhaps there is an allusion in pyæmia, which hovers before me in the metastases of the dream.

Such injections are not made so rashly. Here the reproach of carelessness is hurled directly at my friend Otto. I am under the impression that I had some thought of this sort in the afternoon, when he seemed to indicate his siding against me by word and look. It was perhaps: "How easily he be can be influenced; how carelessly he pronounces judgment." Furthermore, the above sentence again points to my deceased friend, who so lightly took refuge in cocaine injections. As I have said, I had not intended injections of the remedy at all. I see that in reproaching Otto I again touch upon the story of the unfortunate Matilda, from which arises the same reproach against me. Obviously I am here collecting examples of my own conscientiousness, but also of the opposite.

Probably also the syringe was not clean. Another reproach directed at Otto, but originating elsewhere. The day before I happened to meet the son of a lady eighty-two years of age whom I am obliged to give daily two injections of morphine. At present she is in the country, and I have heard that she is suffering from an inflammation of the veins. I immediately thought that it was a case of infection due to contamination from the syringe. It is my pride that in two years I have not given her a single infection; I am constantly concerned, of course, to see that the syringe is perfectly clean. For I am conscientious. From the inflammation of the veins, I return to my wife, who had suffered from emboli during a period of pregnancy, and now three related situations come to the surface in my memory, involving my wife, Irma, and the deceased Matilda, the identity of which three persons plainly justifies my putting them in one another's place.

I have now completed the interpretation of the dream. In the course of this interpretation I have taken great pains to get possession of all the notions to which a comparison between the dream content and the dream thoughts hidden behind it must have given rise. Meanwhile, the "meaning" of the dream has dawned upon me. I have become conscious of a purpose which is realized by means of the dream, and which must have been the motive for dreaming. The dream fulfills several wishes, which have been actuated in me by the events of the preceding evening (Otto's news, and the writing down of the history of the disease). For the result of the dream is that I am not to blame for the suffering which Irma still has, and that Otto is to blame for it. Now Otto has made me angry by his remark about Irma's imperfect cure; the dream avenges me upon him by turning the reproach back upon him. The dream acquits me of responsibility for Irma's condition by referring it to other causes, which indeed furnish a great number of explanations. The dream represents a certain condition of affairs as I should wish it to be; *the content of the dream is thus the fulfilment of a wish; its motive is a wish.*

This much is apparent at first sight. But many things in the details of the dream become intelligible when regarded from the point of view of wish-fulfilment. I take revenge on Otto, not only for hastily taking part against me, in that I accuse him of a careless medical operation (the injection), but I am also avenged on him for the bad cordial which smells like fusel oil, and I find an expression in the dream which unites both reproaches; the injection with a preparation of propyl. Still I am not satisfied, but continue my revenge by comparing him to his more reliable competitor. I seem to say by this: "I like him better than you." But Otto is not the only one who must feel the force of my anger. I take revenge on the disobedient patient by exchanging her for a more sensible and more docile one. Nor do I leave the contradiction of Dr. M. unnoticed, but express my opinion of him in an obvious allusion, to the effect that his relation to the question is that of an *ignoramus* (*"dysentery will develop," etc.*).

It seems to me, indeed, as though I were appealing from him to someone better informed (my friend, who has told me about trimethylamin); just as I have turned from Irma to her friend, I turn from Otto to Leopold. Rid me of these three persons, replace them by three others of my own choice, and I shall be released from the reproaches which I do not wish to have deserved! The unreasonableness itself of these reproaches is proved to me in the dream in the most elaborate way. Irma's pains are not charged to me, because she herself is to blame for them, in that she refuses to accept my solution. Irma's pains are none of my business, for they are of an organic nature, quite impossible to be healed by a psychic cure. Irma's sufferings are satisfactorily explained by her widowhood (trimethylamin!); a fact which, of course, I cannot alter. Irma's illness has been caused by an incautious injection on the part of Otto, with an ill-suited substance—in a way I should never have made an injection. Irma's suffering is the result of an injection made with an unclean syringe, just like the inflammation of the veins in my old lady, while I never do any such mischief with my injections. I am aware, indeed, that these explanations of Irma's illness, which unite in acquitting me, do not agree with one another; they even exclude one another. The whole pleading—this dream is nothing else—recalls vividly the defensive argument of a man who was accused by his neighbour of having returned a kettle to him in a damaged condition. In the first place, he said, he had returned the kettle undamaged; in the second, it already had holes in it when he borrowed it; and thirdly, he had never borrowed the kettle from his neighbour at all. But so much the better; if even one of these three methods of defence is recognised as valid, the man must be acquitted.

Still other subjects mingle in the dream, whose relation to my release from responsibility for Irma's illness is not so transparent: the illness of my daughter and that of a patient of the same name, the harmfulness of cocaine, the illness of my patient travelling in Egypt, concern about the health of my wife, my brother, of Dr. M., my own bodily troubles, and concern about the absent friend who is suffering from suppurative rhinitis. But if I keep all these things in view, they combine into a single train of thought, labelled perhaps: concern for the health of myself and others—professional conscientiousness. I recall an undefined disagreeable sensation, as Otto brought me the news of Irma's condition. I should like to note finally the expression of this fleeting sensation which is part of this train of thought that is mingled into the dream. It is as though Otto had said to me: "You do not take your physicians's duties seriously enough, you are not conscientious, do not keep your promises." Thereupon this train of thought placed itself at my service in order that I might exhibit proof of the high degree in which I am conscientious, how intimately I am concerned with the health of my relatives, friends, and patients. Curiously enough, there are also in this thought material some painful memories, which correspond rather to the blame attributed to Otto than to the accusation against me. The material has the appearance of being impartial, but the connection between this broader material, upon which the dream depends, and the more limited theme of the dream which gives rise to the wish to be innocent of Irma's illness, is nevertheless unmistakable.

I do not wish to claim that I have revealed the meaning of the dream entirely, or that the interpretation is flawless.

I could still spend much time upon it; I could draw further explanations from it, and bring up new problems which it bids us consider. I even know the points from which further thought associations might be traced; but such considerations as are connected with every dream of one's own restrain me from the work of interpretation. Whoever is ready to condemn such reserve, may himself try to be more straightforward than I. I am content with the discovery which has been just made. If the method of dream interpretation here indicated is followed, it will be found that the dream really has meaning, and is by no means the expression of fragmentary brain activity, which the authors would have us believe. *When the work of interpretation has been completed the dream may be recognised as the fulfilment of a wish.*

KEY POINTS

1. "The dream fulfilled certain wishes which were started in me by the events of the previous evening." Freud sees dreams as motivated by wishes, influenced by past events. Freud also interprets certain parts of his dream as expressions of his true feelings.

2. " . . . dreams really have a meaning and are far from being the expression of a fragmentary activity of the brain, as the authors would have us believe." Freud claims that dreams are important components of expression, including unconscious conflicts, past experiences, and repressed erotic feelings.

3. Freud viewed dreams as products of the unconscious, and claimed that the study of dreams could lead to an understanding of a person's hidden memories, urges, and ideas. He tried to figure out the latent content (hidden meaning) of his own dream.

QUESTIONS TO THINK ABOUT_____

1. According to Freud's interpretation of his dream, what were his feelings for Irma? What conclusions did Freud reach about her diagnosis? Why did Freud say, "If you still get pains, it's your own fault"?

2. Freud continually stresses the fact that dreams fulfill certain wishes and desires. What are some of the wishes and motives that Freud fulfilled through his dream?

3. Recall a dream you have had recently. Try to use Freud's psychoanalytic approach to interpret your dream. Describe the manifest and, more importantly, the *latent* content of your dream.

4

The Assault on Truth:
Freud's Suppression
of the Seduction Theory*

JEFFREY MOUSSAIEFF MASSON

J. M. Masson (1941–) was the provisional Projects Director to the Freud Archives. He undertook the responsibility of putting together a complete record of all of Freud's letters and other materials. It was during this task that he found correspondence and papers on the seduction theory that Freud had proposed and then abandoned. Masson tried to expose this theory and the controversy surrounding it to the public, but he was met with disapproval from the psychoanalytic establishment and was soon dismissed from his position at the Freud Archives.

In classic Freudian theory, personality is formed as the child struggles with unconscious sexual urges. For example, little boys feel sexual attraction to their mothers and little girls feel sexual attraction to their fathers, but these dangerous desires cannot be realized. Psychological tension results. According to Freud, adult neuroses result from unresolved sexual conflicts in childhood. Psychoanalysis was built on the idea that children's memories and perceptions are unreliable conglomerations, influenced by struggles between unacceptable impulses and the demands of society. However, what if many adult neuroses arise not from imagined sexual conflicts but from real sexual abuse? That is, what if sexual abuse of young children is common and is really the cause of many neuroses? Masson asserts in this introductory chapter that Freud considered this possibility but was pressured to abandon the idea because it would cause public outrage that would threaten the position of psychoanalysis.

In 1970, I became interested in the origins of psychoanalysis and in Freud's relationship with Wilhelm Fliess, the ear, nose, and throat physician who was his closest friend during the years Freud was formulating his new theories.

For some time I had been corresponding with Anna Freud about the possibility of preparing a complete edition of Freud's letters to Fliess, an abridged version of which had been published in 1950 in German and in 1954 in English as *The Origins of Psychoanalysis* (New York: Basic Books). This edition had been edited by Anna Freud, Ernst Kris, and Marie Bonaparte. In 1980, I met with Dr. K. R. Eissler, the head of the Freud

*Masson, J. M. (1984). *The assault on truth: Freud's suppression of the seduction theory.* New York: Farrar, Straus and Giroux. Reprinted with permission of Pocket Books, a division of Simon & Schuster. Copyright © 1984, 1985, 1992, 1998 by Jeffrey Moussaieff Masson. (Selection is from Introduction, pp. xv–xxiii.)

Archives and Anna Freud's trusted adviser and friend, and with Anna Freud in London, and Miss Freud agreed to a new edition of the Freud/Fliess letters. As a result, I was given access to this sealed correspondence (the originals are in the Library of Congress), which constitutes our most important source of information concerning the beginnings of psychoanalysis.

In addition to including all the letters and passages which previously had been omitted (which amounted to more than half the text), I thought it necessary to annotate the book fully. I would thus need access to other relevant material. Anna Freud offered her complete cooperation, and I was given the freedom of Maresfield Gardens, where Freud spent the last year of his life.

Freud's magnificent personal library was there, and many of the volumes, especially from the early years, were annotated by Freud. In Freud's desk I discovered a notebook kept by Marie Bonaparte after she purchased Freud's letters to Fliess in 1936, in which she comments on Freud's reactions to these letters, which he had written years before. I also found a series of letters concerned with Sándor Ferenczi, who was in later years Freud's closest analytic friend and colleague, and with the last paper Ferenczi delivered to the 12th International Psycho-Analytic Congress in Wiesbaden. This paper dealt with the sexual seduction of children, a topic that had engrossed Freud during the years of his friendship with Fliess.

In a large black cupboard outside Anna Freud's bedroom, I found many original letters to and from Freud written during this same period, letters that were previously unknown—a letter from Fliess to Freud, letters from Charcot to Freud, letters from Freud to Josef Breuer, to his sister-in-law Minna Bernays, to his wife Martha, and to former patients.

A short time later, Dr. Eissler asked me if I would be willing to succeed him as director of the Freud Archives. I agreed and was appointed provisional Projects Director. The Archives had purchased Freud's house in Maresfield Gardens,

and I was to convert the house into a museum and research center. Anna Freud gave me access to the restricted material she had already donated to the Library of Congress, to enable me to prepare a catalogue of all the Freud material at the Library (most of it from the Archives), which came to nearly 150,000 documents. The Library agreed to supply copies of these documents to the projected museum. I also became one of the four directors of Sigmund Freud Copyrights, which allowed me to negotiate with Harvard University Press for the publication of Freud's letters in scholarly, annotated, complete editions.

As I was reading through the correspondence and preparing the annotations for the first volume of the series, the Freud/Fliess letters, I began to notice what appeared to be a pattern in the omissions made by Anna Freud in the original, abridged edition. In the letters written after September 1897 (when Freud was supposed to have given up his "seduction" theory), all the case histories dealing with sexual seduction of children were excised. Moreover, every mention of Emma Eckstein, an early patient of Freud and Fliess who seemed connected in some way with the seduction theory, was deleted. I was particularly struck by a section of a letter written in December 1897 that brought to light two previously unknown facts: Emma Eckstein was herself seeing patients in analysis (presumably under Freud's supervision); and Freud was inclined to lend credence, once again, to the seduction theory.

I asked Anna Freud why she had deleted this section from the December 1897 letter. She said she no longer knew why. When I showed her an unpublished letter from Freud to Emma Eckstein, she said that she could well understand my interest in the subject, as Emma Eckstein had indeed been an important part of the early history of psychoanalysis, but the letter should nevertheless not be published. In subsequent conversations, Miss Freud indicated that, since her father eventually abandoned the seduction theory, she felt it would only prove confusing to readers to be exposed to his early hesitations and doubts. I, on the other hand, felt that these passages not only were of great historical importance, they might well represent the truth. Nobody, it seemed to me, had the right to decide for others, by altering the record, what was truth and what was error. Moreover, whatever Freud's ultimate decision, it was evident that he was haunted by this theory all his life.

I showed Miss Freud the 1932 correspondence I found in Freud's desk concerning his close friend Sándor Ferenczi's last paper, which dealt with this very topic. Clearly, I thought, it was her father's continued preoccupation with the seduction theory that explained his otherwise mysterious turning away from Ferenczi. Miss Freud, who was very fond of Ferenczi, found these letters painful reading and asked me not to publish them. But the theory, I insisted, was not one that Freud had dismissed lightly as an early and insignificant error, as we had been led to believe.

Anna Freud urged me to direct my interests elsewhere. In conversations with other analysts close to the Freud family, I was given to understand that I had stumbled upon something that was better left alone. Perhaps, if the seduction theory had really been only a detour along the road to truth, as so many psychoanalysts believe, it would have been possible for me to turn my attention to other matters. But the seduction hypothesis, in my opinion, was the very cornerstone of psychoanalysis. In 1895 and 1896 Freud, in listening to his women patients, learned that something dreadful and violent lay in their past. The psychiatrists who had heard these stories before Freud had accused their patients of being hysterical liars and had dismissed their memories as fantasy. Freud was the first psychiatrist who believed his patients were telling the truth. These women were sick, not because they came from "tainted" families, but because something terrible and secret had been done to them as children.

Freud announced his discovery in a paper which he gave in April 1896 to the Society for Psychiatry and Neurology in Vienna, his first major public address to his peers. The paper—Freud's most brilliant, in my opinion—met with total silence. Afterwards, he was urged never to publish it, lest his reputation be damaged beyond repair. The silence around him deepened, as did his loneliness. But he defied his colleagues and published "The Aetiology of Hysteria," an act of great courage. Eventually, however, for reasons which I will attempt to elucidate in this book, Freud decided that he had made a mistake in believing his women patients. This, Freud later claimed, marked the beginning of psychoanalysis as a science, a therapy, and a profession.

It had never seemed right to me, even as a student, that Freud would not believe his patients. I did not agree that the seduction scenes represented as memories were only fantasies, or memories of fantasies. But I had not thought to doubt Freud's historical account (often repeated in his writings) of his motives for changing his mind. Yet, when I read the Fliess letters without the omissions (of which Freud, by the way, would undoubtedly have approved), they told a very different, agonizing story. Moreover, wherever I turned, even in Freud's later writing, I encountered cases in which seduction or abuse of children played a role.

Muriel Gardiner, a psychoanalyst and a friend of both Anna Freud and Kurt Eissler, supported my work both financially and by giving me every possible encouragement. She asked me to go through the unpublished material she had in her home concerning the Wolf-Man, one of Freud's most famous later patients, who had been financially supported by Dr. Gardiner and Dr. Eissler. There I found some notes by Ruth Mack Brunswick for a paper she never published. At Freud's request, she had re-analyzed the Wolf-Man and was astonished to learn that as a child he had been anally seduced by a member of his family—and that Freud did not know this. She never told him. Why? Did Freud not know because he did not want to know? And did Ruth Mack Brunswick not tell him because she sensed this?

In my search for further data, I tried to learn more about Freud's trip to Paris in 1885–1886. I visited the library of his early teacher, Charcot, in the Salpêtriére, and that led me to the Paris morgue, for I knew that Freud had attended autopsies performed there by a friend and collaborator of Charcot's, Paul Brouardel. Hints dropped by Freud indicated that he had seen something at the morgue "of which medical science preferred to take no notice." At the morgue, I learned that a whole literature of legal medicine existed in French devoted to the topic of child abuse (especially rape), and Freud had this material in his personal library, though he did not refer to it in his writings. I discovered, moreover, that some of the autopsies attended by Freud may have been autopsies done on children who had been raped and murdered.

I found myself in a strange position. When I became a psychoanalyst, I believed that Freud had fearlessly pursued truth, that he wanted to help his patients face their personal histories, and the wrongs inflicted on them, no matter how unpleasant. My analytic training taught me early on that these ideals were not shared by the profession at large. But I did not think they had altogether vanished from the science; surely there were still people who uncompromisingly sought out truth. That is why, I argued to myself, I had been encouraged in my research; no restrictions had been placed on it.

The information I was uncovering, I felt, was vital to an understanding of how psychoanalysis had developed, and I reported the results of my research to those responsible for it in the first place, Anna Freud, Dr. Eissler, and Dr. Gardiner. I thought that although they might not agree with my interpretations, they would not discount the significance of my discoveries.

My disappointment with psychoanalysis as I knew it was well known, and in fact it was shared by many of my colleagues. In this connection, one meeting with Anna Freud seems to me important enough to merit recounting. Generally, my relations with Miss Freud were formal, confined to discussions of research matters. One afternoon, however, we both began to talk more personally. I told her how disillusioned I was with my training in Toronto, and said that I had not found much improvement in San Francisco and I doubted it would be different anywhere

else. I asked her whether, if her father were alive today, he would want to be part of the psychoanalytic movement, or even would want to be an analyst. "No," she replied, "he would not." Anna Freud, then, understood my criticism of psychoanalysis as it is practiced today, and seemed to support me in this criticism. However, when my research carried me further back, to Freud himself, this support ceased.

Indeed, what I was finding pointed back to Freud's early period, 1897–1903, as the time when fundamental changes set in that would, in my opinion, undermine psychoanalysis. With the greatest reluctance, I gradually came to see Freud's abandonment of the seduction hypothesis as a failure of courage. If I was wrong in my view, surely I would meet with intelligent rebuttal and serious criticisms of my interpretation of the documents. Wherever it lay, the truth had to be faced, and the documents I found had to be brought out into the open.

At the invitation of Anna Freud, I presented a preliminary account of my findings to a meeting of psychoanalysts at the Hampstead Clinic in London in 1981. The participants had been invited by Anna Freud to a conference on "Insight in Psychoanalysis," and many of the leading analysts from around the world were present. The negative response to my paper alerted me to the political overtones of my research, to the possibility that it would have an adverse effect on the profession. But I dismissed such considerations as not worthy of attention by a serious researcher.

In June 1981 I was asked to make a more detailed presentation of the documents and their implications before a closed meeting of the Western New England Psychoanalytic Society in New Haven. The paper I gave was entitled "The Seduction Hypothesis in the Light of New Documents." The anger aroused by this paper, most of it directed at me rather than focused on the documents I had uncovered, brought home the realization that my views would not be treated simply as one man's attempt to come closer to the historical truth behind Freud's abandonment of the seduction theory. The truth or falsity of my research was not questioned, only the wisdom of making the material available to the public. My interpretations, the critics seemed to feel, put in jeopardy the very heart of psychoanalysis.

It was my conviction that what Freud had uncovered in 1896—that, in many instances, children are the victims of sexual violence and abuse within their own families—became such a liability that he literally had to banish it from his consciousness. The psychoanalytic movement that grew out of Freud's accommodation to the views of his peers holds to the present day that Freud's earlier position was simply an aberration. Freud, so the accepted view goes, had to abandon his erroneous beliefs about seduction before he could discover the more basic truth of the power of internal fantasy and of spontaneous childhood sexuality. Every first-year resident in psychiatry knew that simple fact, yet I seemed incapable of understanding it. And I now claimed that this accepted view actually represented a travesty of the truth. The prevalent opinion in psychotherapy was that the victim fashioned his or her own torture. In particular, violent sexual crimes could be attributed to the victim's imagination, a position held by Freud's pupil Karl Abraham and enthusiastically accepted by Freud himself. It was a comforting view for society, for Freud's interpretation—that the sexual violence that so affected the lives of his women patients was nothing but fantasy—posed no threat to the existing social order. Therapists could thus remain on the side of the successful and the powerful, rather than of the miserable victims of family violence. To question the basis of that accommodation was seen as something more than a historical investigation; it threatened to call into question the very fabric of psychotherapy.

When a series of articles in *The New York Times* in August 1981 reported on my findings, the resulting wave of protest culminated in a demand for my removal from the Archives. I was dismissed, to the evident relief of the analytic community; the reason offered was that I had shown "poor judgment" in expressing opinions before a non-professional audience.

Here, then, is the story of Freud's abandonment of the seduction theory, including the documents and my interpretations. My pessimistic conclusions may possibly be wrong. The documents may in fact allow a very different reading. However they are evaluated, I believe that anybody who reads them will come away with a new understanding of psychoanalysis.

KEY POINTS

1. The author, Masson, discovered some letters between Freud and his close friend, Fliess, discussing the topic of the seduction theory. Masson soon found more material on this topic in letters written between Freud and Ferenczi. Masson also discovered that Freud had taken trips to France and found evidence to support the seduction theory.

2. Masson discovered that the seduction theory, in Freud's time, was met with serious disapproval and disregarded by the professional psychoanalytic community.

3. Masson himself was ostracized by the modern psychoanalytic establishment as a consequence of his publicizing Freud's correspondence.

QUESTIONS TO THINK ABOUT

1. Why did Freud initially develop his seduction theory and why did he later drop it? Was it social pressure that forced him to drop the theory or did he find solid evidence to the contrary?

2. What would happen to psychoanalytic theory and practice if neuroses were found to be mostly caused by actual sexual abuse rather than by sexual conflict and repression?

5

The Conception of the Unconscious*

CARL G. JUNG

Carl Gustav Jung (1875–1961) grew up in a religious home in Switzerland. His father, the Reverend Paul Jung, was a country minister, and his mother, Emilie, was a minister's daughter. Jung's theories of personality were focused on the more mystical and spiritual aspects of personality and the roots of his approach can be traced to thoughts and experiences from his own childhood.

Jung was interested in the deepest universal aspects of personality. He expanded ideas of the unconscious to include emotionally charged images and quasi-instincts that seem characteristic of all generations. In particular, he was interested in beliefs that we all share and in how our many similarities develop. Jung described personality as being comprised of competing forces, pulling one against another to reach equilibrium. According to the Jungian theory, the mind or psyche is divided into three parts: the conscious ego, the personal unconscious, and the collective (or universal, impersonal) unconscious. Jung introduced the concepts of archetypes (powerful emotional symbols) and complexes (emotionally charged thoughts and feelings on a particular theme). Most significantly, it was Jung who challenged Freud and broke new conceptual ground about motivation and the ego, allowing other approaches to flourish.

Since the breach with the Viennese school upon the question of the fundamental explanatory principle of analysis—that is, the question if it be sexuality or energy—our concepts have undergone considerable development. After the prejudice concerning the explanatory basis had been removed by the acceptance of a purely abstract view of it, the nature of which was not anticipated, interest was directed to the concept of the unconscious.

According to Freud's theory the contents of the unconscious are limited to infantile wish-tendencies, which are repressed on account of the incompatibility of their character. Repression is a process which begins in early childhood under the moral influence of environment; it continues throughout life. These repressions are done away with by means of analysis, and the repressed wishes are made conscious. That should theoretically empty the unconscious, and, so to say, do away with it; but in reality the production of infantile sexual wish-fantasies continues into old age.

According to this theory, the unconscious contains only those parts of the personality which might just as well be conscious, and have really only been repressed by the processes of civilisation. According to Freud the essential content of the unconscious would therefore be *personal*. But although, from such a view-point the infantile tendencies of the unconscious are the more prominent, it would be a mistake to estimate or

*Jung, C. G. (1917). The conception of the unconscious. In C. G. Jung, *Collected papers on analytical psychology*. New York: Moffat Yard & Company. (Selection is excerpted from pp. 445–474.)

define the unconscious from this alone, for it has another side.

Not only must the repressed materials be included in the periphery of the unconscious, but also all the psychic material that does not reach the threshold of consciousness. It is impossible to explain all these materials by the principle of repression, for in that case by the removal of the repression a phenomenal memory would be acquired, one that never forgets anything. As a matter of fact repression exists, but it is a special phenomenon. If a so-called bad memory were only the consequence of repression, then those persons who have an excellent memory should have no repression, that is, be incapable of being neurotic. But experience teaches us that this is not the case. There are, undoubtedly, cases with abnormally bad memories, where it is clear that the main cause must be attributed to repression. But such cases are comparatively rare.

We therefore emphatically say that the unconscious contains all that part of the psyche that is found under the threshold, including subliminal sense-perceptions, in addition to the repressed material. We also know—not only on account of accumulated experience, but also for theoretical reasons—that the unconscious must contain all the material that has *not yet* reached the level of consciousness. These are the germs of future conscious contents. We have also every reason to suppose that the unconscious is far from being quiescent, in the sense that it is inactive, but that it is probably constantly busied with the formation and re-formation of so-called unconscious phantasies. Only in pathological cases should this activity be thought of as comparatively autonomous, for normally it is coordinated with consciousness.

It may be assumed that all these contents are of a personal nature in so far as they are acquisitions of the individual life. As this life is limited, the number of acquisitions of the unconscious must also be limited, wherefore an exhaustion of the contents of the unconscious through analysis might be held to be possible. In other words, by

the analysis of the unconscious the inventory of unconscious contents might be completed, possibly in the sense that the unconscious cannot produce anything besides what is already known and accepted in the conscious. Also, as has already been said, we should have to accept the fact that the unconscious activity had thereby been paralysed, and that by the removal of the repression we could stop the conscious contents from descending into the unconscious. Experience teaches us that is only possible to a very limited extent. We urge our patients to retain their hold upon repressed contents that have been brought to consciousness, and to insert them in their scheme of life. But, as we may daily convince ourselves, this procedure seems to make no impression upon the unconscious, inasmuch as it goes on producing apparently the same phantasies, namely, the so-called infantile-sexual ones, which according to the earlier theory were based upon personal repressions. If in such cases analysis be systematically continued, an inventory of incompatible wish-phantasies is gradually revealed, whose combinations amaze us. In addition to all the sexual perversions every conceivable kind of crime is discovered, as well as every conceivable heroic action and great thought, whose existence in the analysed person no one would have suspected. . . .

We now come to a problem the overlooking of which would cause the greatest confusion.

As I said before, the immediate result of the analysis of the unconscious is that additional personal portions of the unconscious are incorporated into the conscious. I called those parts of the unconscious which are repressed but capable of being made conscious, *the personal unconscious*. I showed moreover that through the annexation of the deeper layers of the unconscious, which I called the *impersonal unconsciousness,* an extension of the personality is brought about which leads to the state of God-Almightiness ("Gottähnlichheit"). This state is reached by a continuation of the analytical work, by means of which we have already reintroduced what is repressed to consciousness. By continuing analysis further we incorporate some distinctly impersonal universal basic qualities of humanity with the personal consciousness, which brings about the aforesaid enlargement, and this to some extent may be described as an unpleasant consequence of analysis.

From this standpoint, the conscious personality seems to be a more or less arbitrary excerpt of the collective psyche. It appears to consist of a number of universal basic human qualities of which it is *a priori* unconscious, and further of a series of impulses and forms which might just as well have been conscious, but were more or less arbitrarily repressed, in order to attain that excerpt of the collective psyche, which we call personality. The term *persona* is really an excellent one, for persona was originally the mask which an actor wore, that served to indicate the character in which he appeared. For if we really venture to undertake to decide what psychic material must be accounted personal and what impersonal, we shall soon reach a state of great perplexity; for, in truth, we must make the same assertion regarding the contents of the personality as we have already made with respect to the impersonal unconscious, that is to say that it is *collective*, whereas we can only concede *individuality to the bounds of the persona*, that is to the particular choice of personal elements, and that only to a very limited extent. It is only by virtue of the fact that the persona is a more or less accidental or arbitrary excerpt of the collective psyche that we can lapse into the error of deeming it to be *in toto* individual, whereas as its name denotes, it is only a mask of the collective psyche *a mask which simulates individuality*, making others and oneself believe that one is individual, whilst one is only acting a part through which the collective psyche speaks.

If we analyse the persona we remove the mask and discover that what appeared to be individual is at bottom collective. We thus trace "the Little God of the World" back to his origin, that is, to a personification of the collective psyche. Finally, to our astonishment, we realise that the persona was only the mask of the collective psyche. Whether we follow Freud and reduce the primary impulse to sexuality, or Adler and reduce it to the elementary desire for power, or reduce it to the general principle of the collective psyche which contains the principles of both Freud and Adler, we arrive at the same result; namely, the dissolution of the personal into the collective. Therefore in every analysis that is continued sufficiently far, the moment arrives when the aforesaid God-Almightiness must be realised. This condition is often ushered in by peculiar symptoms; for instance, by dreams of flying through space like a comet, of being either the earth, the sun, or a star, or of being either extraordinarily big or small, of having died, etc. Physical sensations also occur, such as sensations of being too large for one's skin, or too fat; or hypnagogic feelings of endless sinking or rising occur, of enlargement of the body or of dizziness. This state is characterised psychologically by an extraordinary loss of orientation about one's personality, about what one really is, or else the individual has a positive but mistaken idea of that which he has just become. Intolerance, dogmatism, self-conceit, self-depreciation, contempt and belittling of "not analysed"' fellow-beings, and also of their opinions and activities, all very frequently occur. An increased disposition to physical disorders may also occasionally be observed, but this occurs only if pleasure be taken therein, thus prolonging this stage unduly.

The wealth of the possibilities of the collective psyche is both confusing and dazzling. The dissolution of the persona results in the release of phantasy, which apparently is nothing else but the functioning of the collective psyche. This release brings materials into consciousness of whose existence we had no suspicion before. A rich mine of mythological thought and feeling is revealed. It is very hard to hold one's own against such an overwhelming impression. That is why this phase must be reckoned one of the real dangers of analysis, a fact that should not be concealed.

As may easily be understood, this condition is hardly bearable, and one would like to put an end to it as soon as possible, for the analogy with a mental derangement is too close. The essence of the most frequent form of derangement—dementia praecox or schizophrenia—consists, as is well known, in the fact that the unconscious to a large extent ejects and replaces the conscious. The unconscious is given the value of reality, being substituted for the reality function. The unconscious thoughts become audible as voices, or visible as visions, or perceptible as physical hallucinations, or they become fixed ideas of a kind that supersede reality. In a similar, although not in the same way, by the resolution of the persona of the collective psyche, the unconscious is drawn into the conscious. The difference between this state of mind and that of mental derangement consists in the fact that the unconscious is brought up by the help of the conscious analysis; at least that is the case in the beginning of analysis, when there are still strong cultural resistances against the unconscious to be overcome. Later on, after the removal of the barriers erected by time and custom, the unconscious usually proceeds, so to say, in a peremptory manner, sometimes even discharging itself in torrents into the consciousness. In this phase the analogy with mental derangement is very close. But it would only be a real mental disorder should the content of the unconscious *take the place of the conscious reality*, that is, in other words, if the contents of the unconscious were believed absolutely and without reserve. . . .

SUMMARY

A. *Psychological Material must be divided into* CONSCIOUS *and* UNCONSCIOUS *Contents.*

1. The *conscious contents* are partly *personal*, in so far as their universal validity is not recognised; and partly *impersonal*, that is, collective, in so far as their universal validity is recognised.

2. The *unconscious contents* are partly *personal*, in so far as they concern solely repressed materials of a personal nature, that have once been relatively conscious and whose universal validity is therefore not recognised when they are made conscious; partly *impersonal*, in so far as the materials concerned are recognised as *impersonal* and of purely universal validity, of whose earlier even relative consciousness we have no means of proof.

B. *The Composition of the Persona.*

1. The conscious personal contents constitute the conscious personality, the conscious ego.
2. The unconscious personal contents constitute the *self*, the unconscious or subconscious ego.
3. The conscious and unconscious contents of a personal nature constitute the persona.

C. *The Composition of the Collective Psyche.*

1. The conscious and unconscious contents of an *impersonal* or collective nature compose the psychological *non-ego*, the *image of the object*. These materials can appear analytically as projections of feeling or of opinion, but they are *a priori* collectively identical with the object-imago, that is they appear as qualities of the object, and are only *a posteriori* recognised as subjective psychological qualities.

2. The persona is that grouping of conscious and unconscious contents which is opposed as ego to the non-ego. The general comparison of personal contents of different individuals establishes their far-reaching similarity, extending even to identity, by which the *individual* nature of personal contents, and therewith of the persona, is for the most part suspended. To this extent the persona must be considered an excerpt of the collective psyche, and also a component of the collective psyche.

3. The collective psyche is therefore composed of the object-imago and the persona.

D. *What is Individual.*

1. What is individual appears partly as the principle that decides the selection and limitation of the contents that are accepted as personal.

2. What is individual is the principle by which an increasing differentiation from the collective psyche is made possible and enforced.

3. What is individual manifests itself partly as an impediment to collective accomplishment, and as a resistance against collective thinking and feeling.

4. What is individual is the uniqueness of the combination of universal (collective) psychological elements.

E. *We must divide the Conscious and Unconscious Contents into Individualistic and Collectivistic.*

1. A content is individualistic whose developing tendency is directed towards the differentiation from the collective.

2. A content is collectivistic whose developing tendency aims at universal validity.

3. There are insufficient criteria by which to designate a given content as simply individual or collective, for uniqueness is very difficult to prove, although it is a perpetually and universally recurrent phenomenon.

4. The life-line of an individual is the resultant of the individualistic and collectivistic tendency of the psychological process at any given moment.

KEY POINTS

1. The unconscious contains both personal content and impersonal (collective, universal) content.

2. Analysis of the unconscious cannot bring forth anything besides what is already accepted in the conscious.

3. The parts of the unconscious that are repressed but capable of being made conscious are termed the *personal unconscious.*

4. The "conscious personality" is derived from the *conscious* personal contents whereas the *unconscious* personal contents constitute the "self."

QUESTIONS TO THINK ABOUT

1. Both Freud and Jung acknowledged an important association between repressed thoughts and psychological analysis. How did their views of repression differ?

2. How is the "impersonal unconscious" an extension of the personality?

3. Jung says that the "persona" is only a mask of the collective psyche suggesting a lack of individuality. Discuss the existence of a universal, collective personality and whether or not individual differences are merely a result of masks people wear to simulate individuality.

4. Jung suggests that schizophrenia may result when the unconscious ejects and replaces the conscious, hence the unconscious is given the value of reality. What might Freud say about this explanation for schizophrenia?

6

The Neurotic Constitution:
The Origin and Development
of the Feeling of Inferiority*

ALFRED ADLER

Alfred Adler (1870–1937) was born in Vienna, and was frail as a child, coming close to death on several occasions. Adler felt powerless and fearful due to his childhood frailty and his flirtations with death. He decided to become a physician to learn to defeat death. He studied medicine at the University of Vienna, graduated in 1895, and started his own practice soon thereafter. In 1902, Adler was a member of the Vienna Psychoanalytic Society and he attended some small, informal seminars with Freud. However, by 1911, disagreements between Adler and Freud became so intense that Adler resigned from his position as president of the society and began his own society, called the Society for Free Psychoanalysis. The debates with Freud and other Freudian psychoanalysts helped Adler to think through his own emerging theory of personality.

Adler titled his theory *Individual Psychology* because he firmly believed in the unique motivations of individuals and the importance of each person's perceived niche in society. Adler believed that striving for superiority is a central core of personality. He coined the terms *inferiority complex* and *superiority complex*, claiming that physical problems in early life engender feelings of inferiority that lead to later neurosis. Adler also developed a personality typology based loosely on ancient Greek notions of the bodily humors, but he is perhaps best known as someone who firmly believed in the positive, goal-oriented nature of humankind.

The facts established through my study of somatic inferiority concerned themselves with the causes, the behavior, the manifestations and altered mode of activity of inferiorily developed organs and has led me to assume the idea of "compensation through the central nervous system" with which were linked certain discussions of the subject of psychogenesis.

There came to light a remarkable relationship between somatic inferiority and psychic overcompensation, so that I gained a fundamental viewpoint, namely, that the realization of somatic inferiority by the individual becomes for him a permanent impelling force for the development of his psyche. . . .

The psychic phase of this compensation and overcompensation can only be disclosed by means of psychologic investigation and analysis.

As I have given a detailed description of organ-inferiority as the etiology of the neuroses

*Adler, A. (1917). The origin and development of the feeling of inferiority. In A. Adler, *The neurotic constitution* (pp. 1–34), (B. Glueck & J. E. Lind, Trans.). New York: Moffat, Yard and Co. (Selection is excerpted from the chapter.)

in my former contributions,. . . . I may in the present description confine myself to those points which promise a further elucidation of the relationship between somatic-inferiority and psychic compensation and which are of importance in the study of the neurotic character.

Summarizing, I lay stress on the fact that organ-inferiority, as described by me, includes the incompleteness in such organs, the frequently demonstrable arrests of development or functional maturity, the functional failure in the post-fetal period and the fetal character of organs and systems of organs; on the other hand the accentuation of their developmental tendency in the presence of compensatory and coördinating forces and the frequent bringing about of increased functional activity. One may easily detect in every instance from observation of the child and from the anamneses of the adult that the possession of definitely inferior organs is reflected upon the psyche—and in such a way as to lower the self-esteem, to raise the child's psychological uncertainty; but it is just out of this lowered self-esteem that there arises the struggle for self-assertion which assumes forms much more intense than one would expect. As the compensated inferior organ gains in the scope of activity both qualitatively and quantitatively and acquires protective means from itself as well as from the entire organism, the predisposed child in his sense of inferiority selects out of his psychic resources expedients for the raising of his own value which are frequently striking in nature and among which may be noted as occupying the most prominent places those of a neurotic and psychotic character. . . .

Concerning the nature of the predisposition to disease dependent upon organ-inferiority there exists a unanimity of opinion. The standpoint assumed by me emphasizes more strongly than does that of other authors, the assurance of an adjustment through compensation. With the release from the maternal organism there begins for these inferior organs or systems of organs the struggle with the outside world, which must of necessity ensue and which is initiated with

greater vehemence than in the more normally developed apparatus. This struggle is accompanied by greater mortality and morbidity rates. This fetal character, however, at the same time furnishes the increased possibility for compensation and over-compensation, increases the adaptability to ordinary and extraordinary resistances and assures the attainment of new and higher forms, new and higher accomplishments.

Thus the inferior organs furnish the inexhaustible material by means of which the organism continuously seeks to reach a better accord with the altered conditions of life through adaptation, repudiation, and improvement. Its hypervalency is deeply rooted in the compulsion of a constant training, in the variability and greater tendency to growth, frequently associated with inferior organs, and in the more facile evolution of the appertaining nervous and psychic complexes, on account of the introspection and concentration bestowed on them. The evils of constitutional inferiority manifest themselves in the most varied diseases and predispositions to disease. . . .

The inferior organ constantly endeavors to make a very special demand upon the interest and attention. I was able to prove in this and other contributions to what extent inferiority of an organ constantly shows its influence on the psyche in action, in thought, in dreams, in the choice of a vocation and in artistic inclinations and capabilities.

The existence of an inferior organ demands a kind of training on the part of the appertaining nerve tracts and on the part of the psychic superstructure which would render the latter active in a compensatory manner when a possibility for compensation exists. In such an event, however, we must likewise find a reënforcement in the psychic superstructure of certain allied points of contact which the inferior organ has with the outside world. . . .

The neurotic individual is derived from this sphere of uncertainty and in his childhood is under the pressure of his constitutional inferiority. In most cases this may be easily detected. In other cases the patient behaves as if he were inferior. In all cases, however, his striving and thinking are built upon the foundation of the feeling of inferiority. This feeling must always be understood in a relative sense, as the outgrowth of the individual's relation to his environment or to his strivings. He has constantly been drawing comparisons between himself and others, at first with his father, as the strongest in the family, sometimes with his mother, his brothers and sisters, later with every person with whom he comes into contact. Upon closer analysis, one finds that every child, especially the one less favored by nature, has made a careful estimate of his own value. The constitutionally inferior child, the unattractive child, the child too strictly reared, the pampered child, all of whom we may align as being predisposed to the development of a neurosis, seek more diligently than does the normal child to avoid the evils of their existence. They soon long to banish into a distant future the fate which confronts them. In order to bring this about, he, the defective child, requires an expedient which enables him to keep before his eyes a fixed picture in the vicissitudes of life and the uncertainty of his existence. He turns to the construction of this expedient. He sums up in his self-estimation all evils, considers himself incompetent, inferior, degraded, insecure. And in order to find a guiding principle he takes as a second fixed point his father or mother who endowed him with all the attributes of life.

And in adjusting this guiding principle to his thinking and acting, in his endeavors to raise himself to the level of his (all-powerful) father, even to the point of surpassing the latter, he has quite removed himself with one mighty bound from reality and is suspended in the meshes of a fiction.

Similar observations may also be made in a lesser degree among normal children. They too desire to be great, to be strong, to rule as the father, and are guided by this objective. Their conduct, their psychical and physical attitude is constantly directed towards this goal, so that one may almost detect a true imitation, an identical psychic gesture.

Example becomes the guide to the "masculine" goal, so long as the masculinity is not doubted. Should the idea of "the masculine goal" become unacceptable to girls, then there takes place a change of form of this "masculine" guiding principle. One can scarcely evaluate this phenomenon in a more correct way than by assuming that the necessary denial of the gratification of certain organic functions forces the child from the first hour of his extrauterine life into assuming a combative attitude towards his environment. . . .

In the temporary denials and discomforts which the first years of childhood bring with them, one must seek the impulse for the development of a host of common traits of character. Above all the child learns in his weakness and helplessness, in his anxiety and manifold shortcomings to value an expedient which assures him of the help and support of his relatives and guarantees their concern. In his negativistic behavior, in his obstinacy and refractoriness he often finds a gratification of his consciousness of his own powers, thus ridding himself of the painful realization of his inferiority. Both mainsprings of the child's behavior, obstinacy and obedience, guarantee to him an accentuation of his feeling of ego-consciousness and assist him in groping his way towards the masculine goal or, as we wished to adduce before, towards the equivalent of this. The awakening self-consciousness is always being suppressed in constitutionally inferior children, their self-esteem is lowered because their capacity for gratification is much more limited. . . .

The child usually explains his difficulty by the assumption of a neglect, a slight by the parents, especially as it occurs in later children or in the youngest, occasionally even in the first born. This hostile aggression, reinforced and accentuated in constitutionally inferior children, becomes confluent with his effort to become as great and strong as the strongest and thrusts forward activities which lie at the bottom of the infantile ambition. All later trains of thought and activities of the neurotic are constructed similarly with his childhood wish phantasy. The "recurrence of the identical" (Nietzsche) is nowhere so well illustrated as in the neurotic. His feeling of inferiority in the presence of men and things, his uncertainty in the world force him to an accentuation of his guiding principles. To these he clings throughout life in order to orient himself in existence by means of his beliefs and superstitions, in order to overcome his feeling of inferiority, in order to rescue his sense of ego-consciousness, in order to possess a subterfuge to avoid a much-dreaded degradation. Never has he succeeded so well in this as during his childhood. His guiding fiction which makes him behave as if he surpassed all others may therefore, also bring about a form of conduct identical with that of the child. . . .

An individual of this type will as a rule manifest a carefully adjusted mode of behavior, exactness and pedantry, first of all, in order not to increase the great difficulties of life and secondly and principally, in order to distinguish himself from others in dress, in work, in morals, and thus acquire for himself a feeling of superiority. . . .

The egoism of neurotics, their envy, their greed, frequently unconscious, their tendency to undervalue men and things, originate in their feeling of uncertainty and serve the purpose of assuring them, of guiding them and of spurring them on. . . .

Therefore from constitutional inferiority there arises a feeling of inferiority which demands a compensation in the sense of a maximation of the ego-consciousness. From this circumstance the fiction which serves as a final purpose acquires an astonishing influence and draws all the psychic forces in its direction. Itself an outgrowth of the striving for security, it organizes psychic preparatory measures for the purpose of guaranteeing security, among which the neurotic character as well as the functional neurosis are noticeable as prominent devices.

The guiding fiction has a simple, infantile scheme, and influences the apperception and the mechanism of memory.

KEY POINTS

1. Somatic inferiority (some bodily problem) in the infant or child has an important impact on psychological development.

2. Constitutional inferiority leads to neurosis.

3. Neurotics strive for a sense of superiority to compensate for their sense of inferiority.

QUESTIONS TO THINK ABOUT

1. Are people who suffer from various physical problems in childhood doomed to suffer from psychological difficulties throughout their lives as well? How would Adler's view affect our treatment of those who are handicapped or disabled?

2. To what extent do notions of superiority as an overcompensation for inferiority apply to people in general rather than just to the physically impaired people on whom Adler focuses?

3. Other than the inferiority complex, are there other explanations that account for the behavior of people who are consistently overbearing, hostile, greedy, and egoistic?

7

The Goals of Analytic Therapy*

KAREN HORNEY

Karen Horney (1885–1952) was a leading neo analyst who challenged many of Freud's views about a world centered around the male. She proposed a theory of womb envy, which stated that rather than females' being envious of the male penis, males were unconsciously envious of the female's ability to give birth. She also put much more emphasis on the role of culture and society in shaping personality.

Karen Danielson Horney grew up in Hamburg, Germany at the end of the nineteenth century. Her world was filled with interpersonal struggles. She believed that her father did not love her as he loved his sons. She felt that she was unattractive and spent her life becoming intelligent instead. She grew up at a time when women had limited opportunities and yet she was one of the first women admitted into medical school. In 1901 she married Oskar Horney and had three daughters. She was always distant with her daughters, because she wanted to instill in them a sense of independence, but her child-rearing style might have lacked appropriate warmth and interest. It is now generally accepted that children struggle with their social worlds to develop their identities, but the ideal paths to self-realization are still a subject of great debate.

The goals of psychoanalysis have changed in recent years. When Freud made the astonishing discovery that symptoms, such as the paralysis of an arm or anxiety, could be eliminated by calling back to mind the traumatic experience the patient had forgotten, or, as we say, had not gotten over at the time, it was of course the aim of therapy to remove the symptoms. The next discovery Freud made was that this simple method of removing symptoms did not always work. In some cases, no individual experience could be found that was responsible for a specific physical disorder, and it seemed necessary to make a long detour and learn a great deal about the patient's life and his entire personality in order to understand the symptom and help the patient to overcome it. Freud gradually realized the fact that symptoms do not simply vanish but can only be removed if we understand the human personality, and especially neurosis. The goal was therefore redefined as removing symptoms through an understanding of the personality. But the emphasis was still on the symptom.

The next development was that several progressive analysts noticed with surprise that there are neuroses without symptoms. It was Franz Alexander who rather naively named this discovery "character neurosis," a formulation we feel to be totally wrong today, since every neurosis is a character neurosis; but at the time, the

*Horney, K. (1991). The goals of analytic therapy. *American Journal of Psychoanalysis, 51* (3), 219–226. (Translation by Andrea Dlaska of Horney's 1951 paper published in German in *Psyche*.) Reprinted by permission.

discovery was a considerable advance. What Alexander was trying to say was that neurosis is not only a matter of symptoms but is a disorder of the personality.

We have still not overcome the focus on the symptom, however. Because an enormous number of people suffer from neuroses, it is only natural that the doctor should look for a short way to free patients from desperate situations, from depression, insomnia, alcoholism, or whatever the symptom may be. It gives him the feeling, justified to a certain extent, that at least he did help. The fact that short-term therapy plays such an enormous role is due to a genuine need, but it reflects a widespread ignorance among both doctors and patients.

I can illustrate this with an example. A patient who started an analysis at age 40 told me that she was engaged at the age of 21 and had suffered from such severe symptoms of fatigue that she was unable to do anything at all. It was quite natural that her doctor told her that she was simply weak and needed some rest, although this did not improve her exhaustion. Then a friend appeared who had just become acquainted with analysis, was full of enthusiasm, and said, "This is all psychological; your tiredness has to do with your doubts about your fiancé. You have some reservations with regard to marriage." Her fatigue ceased instantly, and she could climb a mountain.

This is impressive, of course, and, like short-term therapy, it helped the patient to master an obstacle. But it ignored a great many questions. Where did the ambivalent feelings toward her fiancé come from? Why was she not aware of them? Why did she never raise the question of whether she should marry that man? These would have been reasonable questions at the time. Or the question of whether her reservations only related to this specific man or would arise with every man or with every human being.

When I later analyzed this patient, deep traits of self-denial emerged behind the reservations, which appeared to have been produced by a current situation. After her marriage was dissolved, she took up a relationship of typical morbid dependence, a self-denying relationship in which she had deep feelings of being sacrificed.

This example shows that a symptom cannot be understood unless one enters more deeply into the personality. As soon as one starts asking very simple questions—Why didn't she become conscious of the conflict right away? What was the conflict? Why did she want to get married at all? Why didn't she have any doubts?—as soon as one does this one gets involved in the deep entanglements of the personality. When we understand that the hidden traits of the overall structure contribute to this patient's symptoms, we realize that symptoms are not isolated but that a neurosis is a disorder of the personality as a whole. The goal of therapy increasingly shifts to an embracing of the entire personality.

In other areas of medicine the doctor is usually not contented with the removal of a symptom. He will hardly be satisfied to get rid of a cough without trying to cure its cause. Therefore, the objection that the personality is not the concern of analysis cannot really be sustained, unless one clearly contends that the task of the doctor and of modern psychoanalytic therapy merely lies in achieving a symptomatic cure. We realize that our conception of the goals of therapy depends on our understanding not only of neurosis but also on our Weltanschauung, i.e., our conception of our profession.

When we realized that neurosis basically is a process in which human relationships are disturbed, the goal of therapy emerged as the improvement of human relationships. This was a much more complex goal than relieving symptoms, since human relationships are decidedly the most important part of life. But what does improvement of human relationships mean? We can say, for instance, that a person who is either too dependent, or too dominating, or too aggressive, or who exploits other people can be considered improved if we can help him to view relationships with others on a basis of mutual respect and to learn to give something. Similarly, a patient who is defensively aggressive toward others and to whom we open the possibility of friendly feelings and common goals can be considered improved. It would be an improvement if a person whose relationships are mainly determined by habitual intimidation of others, habitual friendliness, habitual praise, or distancing through politeness—all compulsive strategies—could be helped again to spontaneous feelings. By improvement we mean, then, turning such relationships into something more constructive.

Probing deeper, we realize that such disorders in human relationships are more or less determined by conflicts. A person feels a strong need to distance himself from others but he may also desire affection. Or, a person feels that he has to fight and subject everybody, but he also needs warmth. We see the goal of therapy as helping people to resolve conflicts of this kind and to achieve a harmony of feelings and a sense of inner integration. If we try to help a person to have direct and wholehearted feelings for others, to replace deliberate or automatic strategies with spontaneity, we say that we are helping the person to find himself.

We end up with three objectives: reorientation, constructive integration, and finding oneself. This leads to the fourth concern, which is a person's relationship with himself. In a way, of course, this was included when we talked of a person's relationships with others, since no dividing line can be drawn between a person's relationships with others and with himself. They are connected with each other and inseparable, but the emphasis may lie on the one side or the other. We are gradually beginning to examine intrapsychic processes more closely. I have to condense here considerably.

What we see on the surface are a person's feelings toward himself, which usually vary considerably. At times, someone may feel that he is the most brilliant and generous person ever, but at other times he may feel just as profoundly that he is a complete idiot. He can consider himself the most glorious lover and feel it to be the utmost cruelty to reject a woman who approaches him because it deprives her of the unique experience of himself; but he may also feel that a girl who loves him can only be despicable, or he may feel safe only with strumpets. Such waverings may be conscious with some people, hidden with others, but they are always there.

In neurosis a process sets in regularly in which a person despairs because he feels lost, divided, inferior, and takes refuge in fantasy. He begins to glorify himself and feels that, like a personified god, he is, or should be, equipped with infinite power and perfection, that he is as good as St. Francis or has absolute courage. If he does not possess absolute courage, he considers himself a downright coward. In other words, by building his pedestal so high, by idealizing himself in such a fantastic way, by raising his standard to an impossible level, he is beginning to turn against himself as he really is. He begins to hate and despise himself the way he happens to be. If this self-hate and self-contempt get the upper hand, he does indeed feel guilty, stupid, depraved, hopeless, whereas the minute the self-glorification gets the upper hand he feels on top of the world.

We can summarize this process with the titles of two books: *Man Against Himself* by Menninger, and *Man for Himself* by Fromm. Man turns against himself with the whole bitterness of his worst enemy. If I am not capable of writing a brilliant article on a subject I haven't even thought about, I am simply good for nothing. If my child is ill and I do not devote every minute to him without thinking of anything else, I am simply a miserable mother. As Rashkolnikov says, "If I am not as ruthless as Napoleon who could kill without qualms, if I cannot slay one poor pawnbroker, I am good for nothing and a damned coward."

One might expect that at this point the goals of therapy should be to help a person surrender such illusions and realize that, in reality, he is claiming to be like god, and at the same time, to make him aware of his self-hate, so that he finally can see and accept himself as the person he is. One cannot simply attack the patient's illusions, however. If one treated a patient in this way, showed him outright where his illusions lay, and told him that he had to surrender them in order to be happy, he might say, if he is the more arrogant type, "I don't know, are you crazy or am I?" There would even be some validity in this question, for if he really accepted what the doctor told him, he might break down immediately and fall into an abyss of self-contempt. If he takes the suggestions of the analyst seriously there is also the possibility that the patient will fall prey to something I call "insincere resignation." "All right, I realize I'm not exactly a genius, at least not without effort; it seems I have to accept myself on a lower level." This means, in effect, that he is settling for a "swallow the bitter pill" attitude. "Of course I would like to live these wonderful ideals, but since you tell me that they are not realistic, well, I'll simply give them up."

We should ask ourselves why a direct approach is not possible. I found an answer to this question in O'Neill's play *The Ice Man Cometh,* in which a man meets some drunks in an inn and tells them, "These are all illusions, you would like to give them up yourselves; show us what you can do, lead an active life." But they cannot do it and only feel even more miserable. For these illusions are not simply phantoms. The patient cannot give them up before he has become much stronger without doing damage to himself.

I would like to cite an old German fairytale to illustrate this process from a slightly different angle. It describes a little fir tree who wants to have golden leaves. It gets them, but in the night they are stolen by robbers. The tree thinks that his idea was no good and wishes for glass leaves. He gets them, but a storm breaks them all. This wasn't right either, says the tree, and now I wish for leaves like a maple's, but in no event my own. So he gets the green leaves, but a goat eats them all. Finally, the little tree decides that it was best to simply be a fir tree.

Here you have a glorification of the gold and glass leaves, which the tree believes he wants to have because they are something better. He wants to be something different from what he really is, for in reality he happens to be a fir tree,

and only as a fir tree can he grow. Even without the robbers, the goats, the storms, a fir tree with golden leaves would perish as a fir tree. His real self would be destroyed in the process.

In our own words, this means that if we begin to idealize ourselves, if we consider ourselves outstanding, godlike, more important than befits us, if we want to be something we are not, without knowing it, we lose our own self. From the perspective of this understanding of the neurotic process, it is the goal of therapy to help a person to find his own self, to rediscover his own feelings, his wishes, what he really believes—to help him to make his own decisions; for only if he finds himself has he a chance to grow and fulfill himself.

If we suggest this to the patient in general terms, he will probably say, "Right, that's exactly what I want, to be myself." But this would again be a deception. Remember Peer Gynt who constantly talks about being "himself," while in reality he is only chasing the phantom of his self-glorification. He becomes emperor of the Sahara, where he solves the enigmas of the Sphinx, but he ends up in the madhouse, having destroyed his whole life. It is right that one should wish to be oneself, but one has to wish for the right thing. Initially no neurotic can achieve that; he mainly lives on his neurotic pride and his illusions. The way to his real self is painful, for it is not only full of obstacles and disruptions but is also full of confusing and diverting delusions.

The neurotic has to do a number of things simultaneously in order to gradually reach himself. First, he has to experience and understand all the false values on which his pride is founded. Then he has to realize what he can and cannot do. He has to understand, for instance, that he has talents for real achievements, but that he has to develop his abilities before he can do very much with them. In the past, he has neglected to recognize his real capacities and to develop them, but now their discovery and development must become genuinely desirable for him.

He must also realize through analysis that he does not recognize his own feelings and never has recognized them, that he only feels what he thinks he ought to feel, and that this has made him insecure, has deprived him of vitality, and has robbed his feelings of intensity and depth. He must come to understand that nothing in life is more desirable than genuinely experiencing his real feelings in all their intensity. He has only believed what others believed and has never asked himself, "What do I really believe?" He must discover that finding out what he really believes is an important part of his growth. He may also realize that he was too proud ever to ask for anything. He may originally have called that modesty, but he now understands that this was not a good method, since this way one never learns from one's experiences. To profit from one's experiences it is necessary to admit to one's needs and imperfections. He may have believed that he only reproached himself, condemned himself, and had guilty feelings in order to demonstrate the loftiness of his moral standards. But now he has to realize that he has not really recognized his imperfections and that he has never attempted to overcome them in a constructive way.

This process gradually undermines false pride while making clear what the self lacked so far: real emotions, real beliefs, and personal decisions. The patient recognizes that real emotions or the effort to achieve them are the really desirable thing. False positions are slowly surrendered and a genuine insight into the self takes their place; there is now strength of feeling, a knowledge of what he wants, and the ability to take responsibility. The patient no longer considers it a loss to detach himself from his illusions, for now he knows that striving to be his real self is the only productive way of living.

I would like to illuminate the same issue from another perspective. One may ask whether one should really say with Socrates that the goal of analysis is to know yourself. I would argue that this depends on what one means by self-knowledge. We can shed some light on this, if we differentiate between the actual self and what

William James calls the real self. The actual self is everything I am, my aggressions, my false pride, my vindictiveness. At first, the patient cannot see this, since he will admit to certain traits he is proud of, according to his type, while he will deny others. An arrogant person will admit to his vindictiveness, which he will call a sense of justice, while he will deny his need for sympathy or affection and his great vulnerability. The dependent type will admit to self-denying traits with comparative ease, will gladly take the part of a martyr, a victim, or assume the dependent attitude in a love relationship; but he will refuse to own up to vindictiveness, pride, ambition, or competitive feelings: "Oh no, that's not like me." Some patients do this on a large scale. What they like is their self, and the rest is their neurosis. One patient said, "The idealized image is I, the rest is unconscious."

The patient must learn to recognize what he is really like, but it is *not* enough to know about oneself without taking a firm viewpoint or reorienting oneself. In reality, this never happens anyway, for the more a person knows about himself, the more he is forced to differentiate between good and evil. The more he knows, the more unconditionally he has to decide for the constructive forces of his real self. One might say in brief, "For the patient, the goal of analysis is to learn to know himself as he is (actual self) in order to reorient himself and to make finding his real self a possibility." It is difficult to describe the nature of the real self. It is something one can only describe from experience; something within us that can decide, accept, and discard, that can want something, have spontaneous feelings, and exercise willpower. We can call it constructive energy—something that holds us together.

Every neurotic is aware of certain aspects of himself and unaware of others. Because he denies certain parts of himself, according to the nature of his disease, he only lives a part of himself. One patient expressed it as follows: "I might be compared to a person whose one lung does not function at all, while three quarters of the other is ill."

It is always surprising to see with how little a person can still function—but only as long as things go smoothly. Any situation that taxes the patient can lead to a severe and unexpected breakdown.

A neurotic does not perceive himself as a whole organism, as a unity, but tends to feel painfully divided. He manages, in one way or other, to create a pseudosolution in order not to feel this division constantly, a pseudofeeling of unity that allows him to live. Pseudosolutions can be of very different kinds. One solution is seclusion—I am thinking here of people who live tolerably well, who seem to lack nothing as long as they keep their distance from others and, I would like to add, from themselves. This is one of the neurotic solutions that allows a partial functioning without the person being aware of how divided he really is. Others find their neurotic solution in "love," which in this case means a dependent relationship. The person expects love to provide all the answers to his problems and worries, to provide an integration through merger with another. Others look for their solution in ambition, yet others simply in fantasy. We must not make light of these solutions, for while they lead the person deeper and deeper into neurosis, they at least allow him to function. The fact that such pseudosolutions can develop also shows that a constructive force is at work that aims at integration. It is not very useful in this form, since it leaves the neurotic divided into compulsive traits; but it is there and is a powerful drive that we can use in therapy. If we try again to define the goals of our work when we have realized that the neurotic lives only in a divided way and not with his whole self, we may say, "The goal of psychoanalysis is integration and unity."

Integration, finding oneself, and the ability for growth are constructive forces. They are extremely strong drives in our selves, maybe the strongest, the only ones that really count. Therapy depends on these strong constructive drives, and even the most skilled analyst would get nowhere without them. It is a goal and a means of therapy to mobilize and strengthen these forces, for only with their help can a person overcome the retarding forces within himself. If the analyst tries to bring the patient closer to himself, he is basically doing no more and, in a way, even less than the somatic doctor, who has the means of the clinic at his disposal, while in analysis the actual healing forces lie in the patient himself. This is a fact of which by no means every analyst is aware. I cannot bring about the growth of the patient myself, any more than he can bring about mine. The analyst can make suggestions here and there, he can make the patient aware of things, he can foster the patient's wish to be himself, but the patient must do the growing.

In conclusion, let us return to Ibsen's Peer Gynt, a man who shouts from every roof top that he is "himself," that he wants to be "himself" all his life. But Peer Gynt only wants to be self-sufficient, which, to him, implies a godlike self-sufficiency, a perfection without any needs. Ibsen shows very clearly that this is not human. Peer Gynt never was himself, for in that case he would have had another goal. "Be true to yourself" does not mean "be self-sufficient," for self-sufficiency is at once too much and too little for a human being.

KEY POINTS

1. Horney asserts that originally the goal of psychoanalysis was to treat symptoms and to remove symptoms, but the neo-analysts developed the idea that the whole personality should be evaluated in a social context, broadening the focus beyond symptoms and pathology.

2. Horney thus defines neurosis as a "process in which human relationships are disturbed." This is in keeping with the neo-analytic view,

which is interpersonal (and ego-focused) and less drive-oriented (and id-focused).

3. Horney defines the goals of therapy as reorienting, constructive integration, and finding oneself. She believes that these objectives will eventually lead a person to have a good relationship with himself or herself. She believes that once a neurotic person has learned to do this, then he or she will have good relationships with others.

4. Horney feels that sometimes a neurotic person creates a fantasy image of himself, because he "feels lost, divided, [and] inferior." She feels that the best way to treat this is by having the patient realize what he or she can and cannot do; the patient must come to understand that the idealized values of self-perfection are false. Once a patient has learned to experience real emotions and personal decisions, he or she will better understand his or her real self. The goal of therapy should be to enable a person to accept his or her real self.

QUESTIONS TO THINK ABOUT

1. Horney states that her goal in therapy and Freud's goal in therapy have different objectives. What are the modern implications?

2. Is there any empirical evidence or can there be any empirical evidence showing that all neurotic behavior stems from persons' loss of their real self?

3. What are the implications for women of viewing psychological development as centered around the penis, as Freud asserted? What are the implications for understanding personality of focusing more on the culture, as Horney suggests?

8

The Life Cycle: Epigenesis of Identity*

ERIK H. ERIKSON

With his focus on identity, Erik Erikson (1902–1994) worked squarely within the neo-analytic (ego) perspective on personality. Erikson faced his own identity challenges in childhood. His Scandinavian birthfather abandoned Erik before he was born, and Erik was raised by his mother and Jewish stepfather. His stepfather was a physician and hoped that Erik would follow in his footsteps, but Erik first became an artist, and then became interested in psychoanalysis. He underwent psychoanalytic training with Sigmund Freud's daughter, Anna Freud. When the Nazis came to power in Germany, Erik moved to the United States and changed his name from Erik Homburger to Erik H. Erikson.

Building on certain psychoanalytic views but rejecting others, Erikson believed that each of us must struggle with the demands of our emotions and the pressures of the environment. Erikson was among the first to propose a life-long, developmental theory of self-identity. He thus moved psychoanalytic thought beyond childhood, and opened the theoretical possibility of identity crises in adulthood. In this selection, Erikson describes his idea that identity emerges in stages through the successful negotiation of a series of conflicts or crises.

Among the indispensable co-ordinates of identity is that of the life cycle, for we assume that not until adolescence does the individual develop the prerequisites in physiological growth, mental maturation, and social responsibility to experience and pass through the crisis of identity. We may, in fact, speak of the identity crisis as the psychosocial aspect of adolescing. Nor could this stage be passed without identity having found a form which will decisively determine later life.

Let us, once more, start out from Freud's far-reaching discovery that neurotic conflict is not very different in content from the "normative" conflicts which every child must live through in his childhood, and the residues of which every adult carries with him in the recesses of his personality. For man, in order to remain psychologically alive, constantly re-resolves these conflicts just as his body unceasingly combats the encroachment of physical deterioration. However, since I cannot accept the conclusion that just to be alive, or not to be sick, means to be healthy, or, as I would prefer to say in matters of personality, *vital*, I must have recourse to a few concepts which are not part of the official terminology of my field.

I shall present human growth from the point of view of the conflicts, inner and outer, which the vital personality weathers, re-emerging from each crisis with an increased sense of inner unity, with an increase of good judgment, and an increase in the capacity "to do well" according to

*Erikson, E. (1968). The life cycle: Epigenesis of identity. In E. Erikson, *Identity, youth, and crisis.* New York: W. W. Norton. Copyright © 1968 by W. W. Norton & Company, Inc. Used by permission of W. W. Norton & Company, Inc. (Selection is pp. 91–96.)

his own standards and to the standards of those who are significant to him. The use of the words "to do well" of course points up the whole question of cultural relativity. Those who are significant to a man may think he is doing well when he "does some good" or when he "does well" in the sense of acquiring possessions; when he is doing well in the sense of learning new skills and new knowledge or when he is not much more than just getting along; when he learns to conform all around or to rebel significantly; when he is merely free from neurotic symptoms or manages to contain within his vitality all manner of profound conflict.

There are many formulations of what constitutes a "healthy" personality in an adult. But if we take up only one—in this case, Marie Jahoda's definition, according to which a healthy personality *actively masters* his environment, shows a certain *unity of personality,* and is able to *perceive the world and himself correctly*—it is clear that all of these criteria are relative to the child's cognitive and social development. In fact, we may say that childhood is defined by their initial absence and by their gradual development in complex steps of increasing differentiation. How, then, does a vital personality grow or, as it were, accrue from the successive stages of the increasing capacity to adapt to life's necessities—with some vital enthusiasm to spare?

Whenever we try to understand growth, it is well to remember the *epigenetic principle* which is derived from the growth of organisms *in utero.* Somewhat generalized, this principle states that anything that grows has a ground plan, and that out of this ground plan the parts arise, each part having its time of special ascendancy, until all parts have arisen to form a functioning whole. This, obviously, is true for fetal development where each part of the organism has its critical time of ascendance or danger of defect. At birth the baby leaves the chemical exchange of the womb for the social exchange system of his society, where his gradually increasing capacities meet the opportunities and limitations of his culture. How the maturing organism continues to

unfold, not by developing new organs but by means of a prescribed sequence of locomotor, sensory, and social capacities, is described in the child-development literature. As pointed out, psychoanalysis has given us an understanding of the more idiosyncratic experiences, and especially the inner conflicts, which constitute the manner in which an individual becomes a distinct personality. But here, too, it is important to realize that in the sequence of his most personal experiences the healthy child, given a reasonable amount of proper guidance, can be trusted to obey inner laws of development, laws which create a succession of potentialities for significant interaction with those persons who tend and respond to him and those institutions which are ready for him. While such interaction varies from culture to culture, it must remain within "the proper rate and the proper sequence" which governs all epigenesis. Personality, therefore, can be said to develop according to steps predetermined in the human organism's readiness to be driven toward, to be aware of, and to interact with a widening radius of significant individuals and institutions.

It is for this reason that, in the presentation of stages in the development of the personality, we employ an epigenetic diagram analogous to the one employed in *Childhood and Society* for an analysis of Freud's psychosexual stages. It is, in fact, an implicit purpose of this presentation to bridge the theory of infantile sexuality (without repeating it here in detail) and our knowledge of the child's physical and social growth.

The diagram is presented on p. 53. The double-lined squares signify both a sequence of stages and a gradual development of component parts; in other words, the diagram formalizes a progression through time of a differentiation of parts. This indicates (1) that each item of the vital personality to be discussed is systematically related to all others, and that they all depend on the proper development in the proper sequence of each item; and (2) that each item exists in some form before "its" decisive and critical time normally arrives.

	1	2	3	4	5	6	7	8
VIII								INTEGRITY vs. DESPAIR
VII							GENERATIVITY vs. STAGNATION	
VI						INTIMACY vs. ISOLATION		
V	Temporal Perspective vs. Time Confusion	Self-Certainty vs. Self-Consciousness	Role Experimentation vs. Role Fixation	Apprenticeship vs. Work Paralysis	IDENTITY vs. IDENTITY CONFUSION	Sexual Polarization vs. Bisexual Confusion	Leader- and Followership vs. Authority Confusion	Ideological Commitment vs. Confusion of Values
IV				INDUSTRY vs. INFERIORITY	Task Identification vs. Sense of Futility			
III			INITIATIVE vs. GUILT		Anticipation of Roles vs. Role Inhibition			
II		AUTONOMY vs. SHAME, DOUBT			Will to Be Oneself vs. Self-Doubt			
I	TRUST vs. MISTRUST				Mutual Recognition vs. Autistic Isolation			

If I say, for example, that a sense of basic trust is the first component of mental vitality to develop in life, a sense of autonomous will the second, and a sense of initiative the third, the diagram expresses a number of fundamental relations that exist among the three components, as well as a few fundamental facts for each.

Each comes to its ascendance, meets its crisis, and finds its lasting solution in ways to be described here, toward the end of the stages mentioned. All of them exist in the beginning in some form, although we do not make a point of this fact, and we shall not confuse things by calling these components different names at earlier or later stages. A baby may show something like "autonomy" from the beginning, for example, in the particular way in which he angrily tries to wriggle his hand free when tightly held. However, under normal conditions, it is not until the second year that he begins to experience the whole critical alternative between being an autonomous creature and being a dependent one, and it is not until then that he is ready for a specifically new encounter with his environment. The environment, in turn, now feels called upon to convey to him its particular ideas and concepts of autonomy in ways decisively contributing to his personal character, his relative efficiency, and the strength of his vitality.

It is this encounter, together with the resulting crisis, which is to be described for each stage. Each stage becomes a crisis because incipient growth and awareness in a new part function go together with a shift in instinctual energy and yet also cause a specific vulnerability in that part. One of the most difficult questions to decide, therefore, is whether or not a child at a given stage is weak or strong. Perhaps it would be best to say that he is always vulnerable in some respects and completely oblivious and insensitive in others, but that at the same time he is unbelievably persistent in the same respects in which he is vulnerable. It must be added that the baby's weakness gives him power; out of his very dependence and weakness he makes signs to which his environment, if it is guided well by a responsiveness combining "instinctive" and traditional patterns, is peculiarly sensitive. A baby's presence exerts a consistent and persistent domination over the outer and inner lives of every member of a household. Because these members must reorient themselves to accommodate his presence, they must also grow as individuals and as a group. It is as true to say that babies control and bring up their families as it is to say the converse. A family can bring up a baby only by being brought up by him. His growth consists of a series of challenges to them to serve his newly developing potentialities for social interaction.

Each successive step, then, is a potential crisis because of a radical change in perspective. Crisis is used here in a developmental sense to connote not a threat of catastrophe, but a turning point, a crucial period of increased vulnerability and heightened potential, and therefore, the ontogenetic source of generational strength and maladjustment. The most radical change of all, from intrauterine to extrauterine life, comes at the very beginning of life. But in postnatal existence, too, such radical adjustments of perspective as lying relaxed, sitting firmly, and running fast must all be accomplished in their own good time. With them, the interpersonal perspective also changes rapidly and often radically, as is testified by the proximity in time of such opposites as "not letting mother out of sight" and "wanting to be independent." Thus, different capacities use different opportunities to become full-grown components of the ever-new configuration that is the growing personality.

REFERENCES

Jahoda, M. (1950). Toward a social psychology of mental health. In M. J. E. Benn (Ed.), *Symposium on the healthy personality.* New York: Josiah Macy, Jr. Foundation.

Erikson, Erik H. (1963). *Childhood and society* (2nd ed.). New York: W. W. Norton.

KEY POINTS

1. Erikson believed that adolescence and other transition periods are an important time to develop and refine an identity.

2. He claimed that personality develops through steps or stages rather than continuously.

3. Erikson believed that even mentally "healthy" persons must engage in conflicts and inner crises, which help them develop a stronger personality. As we move from stage to stage throughout life, the psychologically healthy, successful person becomes more and more mature.

QUESTIONS TO THINK ABOUT

1. How important are inner motivations compared to environmental factors in the successful movement through the stages of life? For example, would a child be able to develop an autonomous self if the caregiver was very protective and controlling?

2. Is it possible for a person to move on to start a new stage of development without having completed a prior stage?

3. What are some key factors in the completion of one stage and the starting of a new one?

9

Self-Monitoring of Expressive Behavior*

MARK SNYDER

Mark Snyder has worked to relate social psychology, social skills, and personality. In particular, he has examined how individuals tend to create their own social worlds. Concerned with the basic issue of personal identity, Snyder works in the field first laid out by the ego and neo-analytic psychologists, but with modern concepts, measures, and study designs.

Snyder (1947–) received his Ph.D. from Stanford University in 1972, and has long been a professor at the University of Minnesota. In this selection, Snyder presents his idea of self-monitoring, which merges personality and social psychology with a focus on self-presentation. Note the modern views on the meaning of identity.

A common observation in literature and cultural folklore has been that certain nonlanguage behaviors, such as voice quality, body motion, touch, and the use of personal space appear to play a prominent role in communication. Furthermore, laboratory and field research clearly indicates that much information about a person's affective states, status and attitude, cooperative and competitive nature of social interaction, and interpersonal intimacy is expressed and accurately communicated to others in nonverbal expressive behavior (e.g., Ekman, 1971).

Much interest in nonverbal expressive behavior stems from a belief that it may not be under voluntary control and might function as a pipeline or radarscope to one's true inner "self" (e.g., Freud, 1959). Although nonverbal behavior may often escape voluntary attempts at censorship (Ekman & Friesen, 1969), there have been numerous demonstrations that individuals can voluntarily express various emotions with their vocal and/or facial expressive behavior in such a way that their expressive behavior can be accurately interpreted by observers. In fact, some social observers have proposed that the ability to manage and control expressive presentation is a prerequisite to effective social and interpersonal functioning. Thus Goffman (1955) has likened social interaction to a theatrical performance or "line" of verbal and nonverbal self-expressive acts which are managed to keep one's line appropriate to the current situation. Such self-management requires a repertoire of face-saving devices, an awareness of the interpretations which others place on one's acts, a desire to maintain social approval, and the willingness to use this repertoire of impression management tactics. Within the more restricted domain of facial expressions of emotional affect, Ekman (1971) has suggested that individuals typically exercise control over their, facial expressions to intensify, deintensify, neutralize, or mask the ex-

*Snyder, M. (1974). Self-monitoring of expressive behavior. *Journal of Personality and Social Psychology, 30*(4), 526–537. Copyright © 1974 by the American Psychological Association. Reprinted by permission. [Ed. note: Citations in the text of this selection and the sources to which they point have been edited to leave only those that are the most relevant and important. Readers wishing to see the full reference list can consult the original work.]

pression, of a felt affect, according to various norms of social performance.

There are, however, striking and important individual differences in the extent to which individuals can and do monitor their self-presentation, expressive behavior, and non-verbal affective display. Clearly, professional stage actors can do what I cannot. Politicians have long known how important it is to wear the right face for the right constituency. LaGuardia learned the expressive repertoires of several different cultures in New York and became "chameleon-like" the son of whatever people he was facing. Yet little research has directly concerned such individual differences in the self-control of expressive behavior. At best, some dispositional correlates of spontaneous and natural expression of emotion have been reported.

A Concept of Self-Monitoring of Expressive Behavior

How might individual differences in the self-control of expressive behavior arise? What might be the developmental, historical, and current motivational origins of self-control ability and performance? Perhaps some individuals have learned that their affective experience and expression are either socially inappropriate or lacking. Such people may *monitor* (observe and control) their self-presentation and expressive behavior. The goals of self-monitoring may be (a) to communicate accurately one's true emotional state by means of an intensified expressive presentation; (b) to communicate accurately an arbitrary emotional state which need not be congruent with actual emotional experience; (c) to conceal adoptively an inappropriate emotional state and appear unresponsive and unexpressive; (d) to conceal adaptively an inappropriate emotional state and appear to be experiencing an appropriate one; (e) to appear to be experiencing some emotion when one experiences nothing and a nonresponse is inappropriate.

An acute sensitivity to the cues in a situation which indicate what expression or self-presentation is appropriate and what is not is a corollary ability to self-monitoring. One such set of cues for guiding self-monitoring is the emotional expressive behavior of other similar comparison persons in the same situation.

There is some evidence of an acute version of this process. When persons are made uncertain of their emotional reactions, they look to the behavior of others for cues to define their emotional states and model the emotional expressive behavior of others in the same situation who appear to be behaving appropriately (Schachter & Singer, 1962).

On the other hand, persons who have not learned a concern for appropriateness of their self-presentation would not have such well-developed self-monitoring skills and would not be so vigilant to social comparison information about appropriate patterns of expression and experience. This is not to say that they are not emotionally expressive or even that they are less so than those who monitor their presentation. Rather, their self-presentation and expressive behavior seem, in a functional sense, to be controlled from within by their affective states (they express it as they feel it) rather than monitored, controlled, and molded to fit the situation.

Self-Monitoring and Consistency in Expression: Between Modalities and across Situations

Do people, as Freud (1959) believed, say one thing with their lips and another with their fingertips? More specifically, what governs the consistency between expression in different channels of expression, such as vocal and facial, and the consistency between nonverbal and verbal expression? The self-monitoring approach provides one perspective on differences and consistencies across channels of expression, including verbal self-presentation.

It is likely that when one is monitoring, various channels are monitored differentially, and perhaps some forgotten. Thus, what may be communicated by one channel may differ from what is communicated by another. For example, I may cover my sadness by putting on a happy face but forget to use a happy voice.

Ekman and Friesen (1969) have demonstrated with psychiatric patients and student nurses that in deception situations people are more likely to monitor their facial than body presentation, with the result that the deception is more likely to be detected from an examination of body cues than facial cues. Thus, the information encoded in monitored channels should differ from that encoded in nonmonitored channels. However, it is likely that great consistency characterizes that set of channels of expressive (verbal or nonverbal) behaviors which are simultaneously monitored according to the same criteria. Furthermore, self-monitored expressive behavior should vary more from situation to situation than nonmonitored expressive behavior. Self-monitoring individuals should be most likely to monitor and control their expression in situations which contain reliable cues to social appropriateness. Thus, such a person would be more likely to laugh at a comedy when watching it with amused peers than when watching it alone. The laughing behavior of the non-self-monitoring person should be more invariant across those two situations and more related to how effectively amused he himself actually is. The expressive behavior of self-monitoring individuals should be more reflective of an internal affect state when it is generated in a situation with minimal incentives for, and cues to, self-monitoring.

The cross-situational variability of the self-monitoring versus the consistency of the non-self-monitoring individuals is similar to the "traits versus situations" issue: Is behavior controlled by situational factors and hence predictable from characteristics of the surrounding situation, or is it controlled by internal states and dispositions which produce cross-situational consistency and facilitate prediction from characteristics of the person, measures of internal states, or dispositions (Mischel, 1968; Moos, 1968)? Bem (1972) has proposed that the issue be redirected from an "either traits or situations for all behavior of all people" debate to a search for moderating variables which would allow the specification for an individual of equivalence classes of situations and responses across which he monitors his behavior with re-

spect to a particularly central self-concept. In these areas he would show trait-like cross-situational and interresponse mode consistency; in others he would not. In the domain of expressive behavior, individual differences in self-monitoring are a moderating variable which identifies individuals who demonstrate or fail to demonstrate consistency across channels of expression and between situations differing in monitoring properties.

In Search of a Measure of Individual Differences in Self-Monitoring

How can we capture individual differences in self-monitoring? A review of the literature suggests at least one currently available measure which might serve to identify individuals who differ in self-monitoring.

The self-monitoring individual is one who, out of a concern for social appropriateness, is particularly sensitive to the expression and self-presentation of others in social situations and uses these cues as guidelines for monitoring his own self-presentation. Is there then any difference between this person and the individual with a high "need for approval" as measured by the Marlowe-Crowne Social Desirability Scale? In a wide variety of situations, individuals who have a high need for approval give socially desirable responses. They conform more than low-need-for-approval individuals in an Asch situation; they verbally condition better; they do not show overt hostility toward one who has insulted and double-crossed them; and they are less likely to report dirty words in a perceptual defense task. All of this would suggest that the high-need-for-approval person is one who modifies his behavior from situation to situation. However, other evidence suggests that this ability to alter behavior may be severely limited to contingencies of social approval (Bem, 1972).

In addition, it may be only the social approval of adult experimenters which is reinforcing and sought after. In a sociometric study, fraternity members with a high need for approval were described by their peers as individuals who spend most of their time alone rather than with other people, do not go out of their way to make friends, are not very conversational, and do not act friendly toward other fraternity members.

In another study on verbal conditioning, high- and low-need-for-approval subjects did not differ in the extent to which they modeled the behavior of a peer (actually a confederate) they had previously observed perform the experimental task appropriately. Furthermore, and particularly relevant to the self-monitoring of expressive behavior, this self-control ability may not extend into the domain of expressive behavior. Individuals who scored high on the Need for Approval Scale were actually less able to communicate either positive or negative affect facially or vocally than were low-need-for-approval subjects. In this experimental situation, the socially desirable response and the one which would gain the approval of the experimenter would clearly be the accurate expression and communication of affect. Thus, although high-need-for-approval individuals may be motivated to modify their expressive self-presentation in order to gain approval, they may lack necessary self-control abilities and skills.

Self-monitoring would probably best be measured by an instrument specifically designed to discriminate individual differences in concern for social appropriateness, sensitivity to the expression and self-presentation of others in social situations as cues to social appropriateness of self-expression, and use of these cues as guidelines for monitoring and managing self-presentation and expressive behavior. Accordingly, an attempt was made to transpose the self-monitoring concept into a self-report scale which reliably and validly measures it.

The convergence between diverse methods of measuring self-monitoring was examined according to the strategy of construct validation. To demonstrate discriminant validity, comparisons were made between self-monitoring and need for approval in the prediction of each external criterion in the validation strategy. Need for approval was chosen for these critical comparisons for two reasons. Its conceptual relationship to self-monitoring has already been discussed. Naturally, this procedure also further individuates

the type of person identified by the Need for Approval Scale. In addition, Campbell (1960) has recommended that in view of the general response tendency of some individuals to describe themselves in a favorable manner, and the close relationship between probability of endorsement of personality statements and their social desirability, all tests of the voluntary self-descriptive sort should be demonstrated to predict their criterion measures better than a measure of the general social desirability factor.

CONSTRUCTION OF THE SELF-MONITORING SCALE

Forty-one true–false self-descriptive statements were administered to 192 Stanford University undergraduates. The set included items which describe (a) concern with the social appropriateness of one's self-presentation (e.g., "At parties and social gatherings, I do not attempt to do or say things that others will like"); (b) attention to social comparison information as cues to appropriate self-expression (e.g., "When I am uncertain how to act in social situations, I look to the behavior of others for cues"); (c) the ability to control and modify one's self-presentation and expressive behavior (e.g., "I can look anyone in the eye and tell a lie with a straight face [if for a right end]"); (d) the use of this ability in particular situations (e.g, "I may deceive people by being friendly when I really dislike them"); and (e) the extent to which the respondent's expressive behavior and self-presentation is cross-situationally consistent or variable (e.g., "In different situations and with different people, I often act like very different persons").

The individual items were scored in the direction of high self-monitoring. For approximately half the items, agreement was keyed as high SM; for the remainder, disagreement was keyed as high SM.

An item analysis was performed to select items to maximize internal consistency. In this procedure, the top and bottom thirds in total test scores of persons were found. Then the percentages of persons in each group who responded in the manner keyed as high SM were determined. Finally, the percentage in the bottom group was subtracted from the percentage in the top group. This difference (*D*) served as an index of item validity to discriminate total test scores. *D* is directly proportional to the difference between the number of "correct" and "incorrect" total score discriminations made by an item. *D* values are not independent of item difficulty and are biased in favor of items of intermediate difficulty level. *D* is, then, an appropriate criterion for selecting items according to both discriminative power and intermediate difficulty level.

Items were discarded on the basis of low *D* scores until a set of 25 items remained which maximized the internal consistency of the scale. The Self-Monitoring Scale has a Kuder-Richardson 20 reliability of .70, and a test–retest reliability of .83 (*df* = 51, *p* < .001, one-month time interval). Cross-validation on an independent sample of 146 University of Minnesota undergraduates yielded a Kuder-Richardson 20 reliability coefficient of .63.

TABLE 1   Instructions, Items, Scoring Key, Difficulty, and Discrimination Indexes for the Self-Monitoring Scale[a]

ITEM AND SCORING KEY[b]	DIFFICULTY[c]	Discrimination			
		D[d]	x^{2e}	*p*	r_{pb}[f]
1. I find it hard to imitate the behavior of other people. (F)	.63	.50	32.07	.0005	.33
2. My behavior is usually an expression of my true inner feelings, attitudes, and beliefs. (F)	.67	.23	7.26	.01	.13
3. At parties and social gatherings, I do not attempt to do or say things that others will like. (F)	.17	.21	8.29	.005	.34
4. I can only argue for ideas which I already believe. (F)	.43	.29	8.91	.005	.22
5. I can make impromptu speeches even on topics about which I have almost no information. (T)	.69	.21	6.41	.025	.32
6. I guess I put on a show to impress or entertain people. (T)	.65	.44	26.5	.0005	.45
7. When I am uncertain how to act in a social situation, I look to the behavior of others for cues. (T)	.20	.19	6.55	.025	.24
8. I would probably make a good actor. (T)	.69	.36	17.8	.0005	.43
9. I rarely need the advice of my friends to choose movies, books, or music. (F)	.64	.24	6.78	.01	.15
10. I sometimes appear to others to be experiencing deeper emotions than I actually am. (T)	.57	.20	4.78	.05	.39
11. I laugh more when I watch a comedy with others than when alone. (T)	.33	.23	6.51	.025	.29
12. In a group of people I am rarely the center of attention. (F)	.64	.32	13.09	.0005	.40
13. In different situations and with different people, I often act like very different persons. (T)	.40	.22	5.54	.025	.40

Note. T = true; F = false; SM = Self-Monitoring Scale.

[a] Directions for Personal Reaction Inventory were: The statements on the following pages concern your personal reactions to a number of different situations. No two statements are exactly alike, so consider each statement carefully before answering. If a statement is *TRUE* or *MOSTLY TRUE* as applied to you, blacken the space marked *T* on the answer sheet. If a statement is *FALSE* or *NOT USUALLY TRUE* as applied to you, blacken the space marked *F*. Do not put your answers on this test booklet itself.

It is important that you answer as frankly and as honestly as you can. Your answers will be kept in the strictest confidence.

The 25 items of the SM, proportions of respondents answering the item in the low-SM-scored direction, their D values, and item total point-biserial correlations calculated for the University of Minnesota sample are presented in Table 1.

Correlations with Other Scales

Correlations between the SM and related but conceptually distinct individual differences measures provide some evidence for its discriminant validity. There is a slight negative relationship ($r = -.1874$, $df = 190$, $p < .01$) between the SM and the Marlowe-Crowne Social Desirability Scale (M-C SDS). Individuals who report that they observe, monitor, and manage their self-presentation are unlikely to report that they engage in rare but socially desirable behaviors.

There is a similarly low negative relationship ($r = -.2002$, $df = 190$, $p < .01$) between the SM and the Minnesota Multiphasic Personality Inventory Psychopathic Deviate scale. High-SM subjects

ITEM AND SCORING KEY[b]	DIFFICULTY[c]	Discrimination			
		D[d]	χ^{2}[e]	p	r_{pb}[f]
14. I am not particularly good at making other people like me. (F)	.30	.27	10.12	.005	.22
15. Even if I am not enjoying myself, I often pretend to be having a good time. (T)	.61	.21	5.67	.025	.24
16. I'm not always the person I appear to be. (T)	.26	.23	7.17	.01	.33
17. I would not change my opinions (or the way I do things) in order to please someone else or win their favor. (F)	.61	.34	15.5	.0005	.34
18. I have considered being an entertainer. (T)	.79	.28	12.64	.0005	.46
19. In order to get along and be liked, I tend to be what people expect me to be rather than anything else. (T)	.79	.25	9.96	.005	.29
20. I have never been good at games like charades or improvisational acting. (F)	.52	.45	25.96	.0005	.31
21. I have trouble changing my behavior to suit different people and different situations. (F)	.36	.38	19.35	.0005	.45
22. At a party I let others keep the jokes and stories going. (F)	.65	.24	6.80	.01	.36
23. I feel a bit awkward in company and do not show up quite so well as I should. (F)	.54	.21	11.05	.001	.32
24. I can look anyone in the eye and tell a lie with a straight face (if for a right end). (T)	.58	.38	19.25	.0005	.33
25. I may deceive people by being friendly when I really dislike them. (T)	.46	.35	15.07	.0005	.32

[b] Items keyed in the direction of high SM.

[c] Difficulty = proportion of individuals not responding in SM-keyed direction.

[d] Discrimination = difference between proportions of individuals in upper and lower thirds of total scores responding in high-SM direction.

[e] χ^{2} calculated from the contingency table relating frequencies of T, F for each item and upper third, lower third for *total* SM score (including that item).

[f] Point-biserial correlations between individual items and total scores with that item excluded.

are unlikely to report deviant psychopathological behaviors or histories of maladjustment.

There is a small and nonsignificant negative relationship ($r = -.25$, $df = 24$, ns) between the SM and the c scale of the Performance Style Test. The c scale was designed to identify a person who is knowledgeable about the kind of social performance required in a wide range of situations and who seeks social approval by becoming whatever kind of person the situation requires. He is literally a chameleon. Clearly the SM and c do not identify the same individuals.

The SM was also found to be unrelated to Christie and Geis's Machiavellianism ($r = -.0931$, $df = 51$, ns), Alpert-Haber Achievement Anxiety Test ($r = +.1437$, $df = 51$, ns), and Kassarjian's inner-other directedness ($r = -.1944$, $df = 54$, ns).

It thus appears that SM is relatively independent of the other variables measured.

VALIDATION. SELF-MONITORING AND PEER RATINGS

As a first source of validity evidence for the SM, a sociometric study of peer rating was conducted. In choosing this method, it was assumed that a person who has good control of his self-presentation and expressive behavior and who is sensitive to social appropriateness cues should be seen as such a person by others who have had the opportunity for repeated observation of his self-presentation in a wide variety of social situations.

Method

Subjects

The subjects in this study were 16 members of a male fraternity living group at Stanford University who agreed to participate in an investigation of person perception.

Procedure

Each subject completed the SM and the M-C SDS and then participated in a sociometric person perception task.

Each subject indicated for each of six other members of the fraternity specified for him by the experimenter whether the following self-monitoring attributes were very true, mostly true, somewhat true, or not at all true:

1. Concerned about acting appropriately in social situations;
2. Openly expresses his true inner feelings, attitudes, and beliefs;
3. Has good self-control of his behavior. Can play many roles;
4. Is good at learning what is socially appropriate in new situations;
5. Often appears to lack deep emotions; and
6. Has good self-control of his emotional expression. Can use it to create the impression he wants.

In addition, two other judgments were required: "Is ingratiating. Attempts to do or say things designed to make others like him more" (same 4-point scale as above) and "How much do you like this person?" (very much, moderately, somewhat, not at all).

Results and Discussion

Each subject in the experiment served as a judge of six others and was in turn judged by six other members of his living group. For each person as a stimulus, ratings of him were summed across his six judges to form a single score on each dimension which could range from 0 (six ratings of not at all true) to 18 (six ratings of very true). For each person, a single "peer rating of self-monitoring" score was computed by summing across the six self-monitoring dimensions.

The group of 16 subjects was then dichotomized at the median to form a high-SM group ($n = 8$) and a low-SM group ($n = 8$).

Self-monitoring characteristics were seen as more true of high-SM ($M = 50.5$) than of low-SM ($M = 40.2$) individuals ($t = 2.69$, $df = 14$, $p < .02$, two-tailed test). No differences were observed between high-SM and low-SM individuals on ingratiation or liking ($t = .49$ and $.20$, respectively, $df = 14$, ns).

Mean peer rating of self-monitoring, ingratiation, and liking for high M-C SDS (above the median, $n = 8$) and low M-C SDS (below the median, $n = 8$) were also calculated. In contrast to SM scores, M-C SDS scores were unrelated to peer rating of self-monitoring (high M-C SDS $M = 54.0$, low M-C SDS $M = 56.7$, $t = .59$, $df = 14$, ns).

The relationship between the SM, M-C SDS, and peer rating of self-monitoring may be examined in terms of product-moment correlations. There is a significant relationship between the SM and peer rating of self-monitoring ($r = .45$, $df = 14$, $p < .05$). The higher an individual's score on the SM, the more frequently self-monitoring characteristics were attributed to him. The M-C SDS and peer rating of self-monitoring are not related ($r = -.14$, $df = 14$, ns).

An image emerges of the high-SM individual as perceived by his peers. He is a person who, out of a concern for acting appropriately in social situations, has become particularly skilled at controlling and modifying his social behavior and emotional expression to suit his surroundings on the basis of cues in the situation which indicate what attitudes and emotions are appropriate. The low-SM individual, as perceived by his peers, is less able and/or less likely to control and modify his self-presentation and expressive behavior to keep it in line with situational specifications of appropriateness. He is also less vigilant to such cues.

High and low scorers on the M-C SDS, by contrast, do not differ in these characteristics. In fact, the evidence suggests that if in fact the M-C SDS is a measure of need for approval, this need is not related to the ability (as perceived by one's peers) to control and monitor one's self-presentation and emotional expressive behavior on the basis of situation-to-situation variation in contingencies of social appropriateness.

VALIDATION: SELF-MONITORING, STAGE ACTORS, AND PSYCHIATRIC WARD PATIENTS

Another means of establishing the validity of an instrument is by predicting how predetermined groups of individuals would score when the instrument is administered to them. According to this strategy, SM scores of criterion groups chosen to represent extremes in self-monitoring were compared with the unselected sample of Stanford University undergraduates.

Professional Stage Actors

Groups of individuals known to be particularly skilled at controlling their expressive behavior (e.g., actors, mime artists, and politicians) should score higher on the SM than an unselected sample. The SM was administered to a group of 24 male and female dramatic actors who were appearing in professional productions at Stanford and in San Francisco.

Their average score on the SM was 18.41 with a standard deviation of 3.38. This is significantly higher than the mean SM score for the Stanford sample ($t = 8.27$, $df = 555$, $p < .001$).

Thus, stage actors do score higher than nonactors on the SM. Actors probably do have particularly good self-control of their expressive behavior and self-presentation while on stage. It is not clear that actors are any more concerned about monitoring their expressive presentation in other situations.

Hospitalized Psychiatric Ward Patients

The behavior of hospitalized psychiatric patients is less variable across situations than that of "normals." Moos (1968) investigated the reactions of patients and staff in a representative sample of daily settings in a psychiatric inpatient ward in order to assess the relative amount of variance accounted for by settings and individual differences. The results indicated that for patients, individual differences accounted for more variance than setting differences; whereas for staff, individual differences generally accounted for less variance than setting differences. One interpretation of this finding is that psychiatric ward patients are unable or unwilling to monitor their social behavior and self-presentation to conform to variations in contingencies of social appropriateness between situations. In fact, diagnoses of "normal" and "psychopathological" may be closely related to cross-situational plasticity or rigidity. Situational factors play an increasingly potent role in the behavior of institutionalized individuals as therapy progresses.

Accordingly, it was expected that a sample of hospitalized psychiatric ward patients should score lower on the SM than nonhospitalized normals.

The SM was administered to 31 male hospitalized psychiatric patients at the Menlo Park Veterans Administration Hospital. Their psychiatric diagnoses varied, and most had been previously institutionalized. Each patient's cumulative length of hospitalization varied from several months to several years.

The average SM score for this group was 10.19 with a standard deviation of 3.63. This is significantly lower than the mean SM score for the Stanford sample ($t = 3.44$, $df = 562$, $p < .001$).

VALIDATION: SELF-MONITORING AND THE EXPRESSION OF EMOTION

If the SM discriminates individual differences in the self-control of expressive behavior, this should be reflected behaviorally. In a situation in which individuals are given the opportunity to communicate an arbitrary affective state by means of nonverbal expressive behavior, a high-SM individual should be able to perform this task more accurately, easily, and fluently than a low SM.

Method

Subjects: Expression of Emotion

Male and female students whose SM scores were above the 75th percentile (SM > 15) or below the 25th percentile (SM < 9) were recruited by telephone from the pool of pretested introductory psychology students. In all, 30 high-SM and 23 low-SM subjects participated in the study and received either course credit or $1.50.

Procedure: Expression of Emotion

Each subject was instructed to read aloud an emotionally neutral three-sentence paragraph (e.g., "I am going out now. I won't be back all af-

ternoon. If anyone calls, just tell him I'm not here.") in such a way as to express each of the seven emotions anger, happiness, sadness, surprise, disgust, fear, and guilt or remorse using their vocal and facial expressive behavior. The order of expression was determined randomly for each subject. The subject's facial and upper-body expressive behavior was filmed and his voice tape-recorded. It was suggested that he imagine he was trying out for a part in a play and wanted to give an accurate, convincing, natural, and sincere expression of each emotion—one that someone listening to the tape or watching the film would be able to understand as the emotion the subject had been instructed to express....

These filmed and taped samples of expressive behavior were scored by judges who indicated which of the seven emotions the stimulus person was expressing. Accuracy of the judges was used as a measure of the expressive self-control ability of the stimulus subjects.

Judgments of Expressive Behavior: Subjects

The films and tapes of expressive behavior were scored by a group of 20 high-SM (SM > 15, or top 25%) and 13 low-SM (SM < 9, or bottom 25%) naive judges who were paid $2.00 an hour.

Judgments of Emotional Expressive Behavior: Procedure

Judges participated in small groups of both high- and low-SM judges who watched films for approximately one fourth of the subjects in the expression experiment and listened to the tapes of approximately another one fourth of the subjects. For each stimulus segment, judges indicated which of the seven emotions had been expressed.

Results and Discussion

Accuracy of Expression and SM Scores

Accuracy of the judges in decoding the filmed and taped expressive behavior for each stimulus person was used as a measure of his self-control of expressive behavior ability. For each of the 53 subjects in the expression task, the

TABLE 2   SM and Accuracy of Expression of Emotion: Naive Judges

STIMULUS	High-SM Judge		Low-SM Judge	
	FACE	VOICE	FACE	VOICE
High SM				
($n = 30$)				
M[a]	3.353	4.047	3.196	3.564
Variance	.718	.636	1.117	1.769
Low SM				
($n = 23$)				
M	2.518	2.957	2.493	3.094
Variance	1.348	.982	1.479	2.102

Note. SM = Self-Monitoring Scale.

[a]Average accuracy computed for each stimulus across all judges who rated him and then averaged across *n* stimulus persons; range = 0–7.

average accuracy of his judges was computed separately for films and tapes and high- and low-SM judges. Table 2 represents these accuracy scores as a function of stimulus (expresser) SM scores, facial or vocal channel of expression, and judge SM score for naive judges. Each stimulus person expressed seven emotions. Therefore, mean accuracy scores can range from 0 to 7.

The average accuracy scores for each stimulus person's facial and vocal expressive behavior, as judged by high-SM and low-SM judges, were entered into an analysis of variance. Expresser SM score (high SM or low SM) was a between-stimulus-persons factor; channel of expression (face or voice) and judge SM score (high SM or low SM) were within-stimulus-persons factors.

The following pattern of results emerges. Individuals who scored high on the SM were better able to communicate accurately an arbitrarily chosen emotion to naive judges than were individuals who scored low on the SM. That is, judges were more often accurate in judging both the facial and vocal expressive behavior generated in this emotion communication task by high-SM stimuli than by low-SM stimuli ($F = 11.72$, $df = 1/51$, $p < .01$). For both high- and low-SM stimuli, accuracy was greater in the vocal

than the facial channel ($F = 19.12$, $df = 1/153$, $p < .001$). Finally, there was a tendency for high-SM judges to be better judges of emotion than low-SM judges ($F = 1.69$, $df = 1/153$, $p < .25$). In addition, high-SM judges may have been more differentially sensitive to the expressive behavior of high- and low-SM stimuli. That is, the difference in accuracy for judging high-SM and low-SM stimuli for high-SM judges was greater than the corresponding difference for low-SM judges. However, once again the differences are not significant ($F = 2.41$, $df = 1/153$, $p < .25$).

Discriminant Validation: SM versus M-C SDS

In the sample of 192 from which the subjects for the expression task were selected, scores on the SM and M-C SDS were very slightly correlated ($r = -.1874$). However, in the sample of 53 subjects chosen for this experiment, the correlation was $-.3876$ ($df = 51$, $p < .01$). Furthermore, individuals who scored below the median on the M-C SDS were better able than those who scored above the median to voluntarily communicate emotion in this experimental task ($F = 4.426$, $df = 1/51$, $p < .05$). These differences present a rival explanation of the differences observed in self-control of expressive behavior between high-SM and low-SM groups.

To discriminate between the SM and M-C SDS as predictors of self-control of expression ability, two analyses of covariance were performed. In the first, accuracy scores for naive judges collapsed across judge SM score and channel were examined as a function of stimulus SM scores as the independent variable and stimulus M-C SDS scores as the covariate. After removing the effects of the covariate (M-C SDS), there is still a highly significant treatment (SM) effect ($F = 7.13$, $df = 1/50$, $p < .01$). That is, individuals who scored high on the SM were better able than low-SM scorers to accurately express and communicate arbitrary emotions independent of their M-C SDS scores.

In the second analysis of covariance, accuracy scores for naive judges collapsed across judge SM score and channel were examined as a function of stimulus M-C SDS as the independent variable and stimulus SM scores as the covariate. The results of this analysis are quite conclusive. After removing the effects of the covariate (SM), there is no remaining relationship between the independent variable (M-C SDS) and expression accuracy ($F = .75$, $df = 1/50$, ns). That is, whatever relationship exists between M-C SDS scores and self-control of expression ability is entirely accounted for by the slight negative correlation between the M-C SDS and SM.

Thus, the results of this experiment clearly indicate that scores on the SM are related to the self-control of expressive behavior. High-SM individuals were better able than low-SM individuals to express arbitrary emotional states in facial and vocal behavior.

VALIDATION: SELF-MONITORING AND ATTENTION TO SOCIAL COMPARISON INFORMATION

It has been proposed that out of a concern for social appropriateness of his behavior, a high-SM individual is particularly attentive to social comparison information and uses this information as guidelines to monitor and manage his self-presentation and expressive behavior.

Consistent with this formulation, high-SM individuals are seen by their peers as better able to learn what is socially appropriate in new situations than are low-SM. Two SM items which best predict performance in the emotion expression task are: "When I am uncertain how to act in a social situation, I look to the behavior of others for cues," and "I laugh more when I watch a comedy with others than when alone."

All of this suggests that, given the opportunity in a self-presentation situation, a high-SM individual should be more likely to seek out relevant social comparison information.

Method

Subjects

Subjects were recruited from the pretested introductory psychology subject pool on the basis of high-SM scores (SM > 15) or low-SM scores (SM < 9). A total of 14 high-SM and 13 low-SM subjects participated in the experiment and were paid $1.00.

Procedure

Each subject performed a self-presentation task in a situation designed to facilitate self-monitoring. He was asked to respond to a series of true–false self-descriptive personality test items in preparation for a discussion of how test-takers decide how to respond to ambiguously worded questionnaire items. During the task he was given the opportunity to consult a "majority response sheet" which listed the modal response of his introductory psychology class for each item in order to consider possible alternative interpretations of the items in preparation for the discussion.

Pretesting had indicated that the task was interpreted as neither social pressure to consult the information nor a test of resistance to temptation to cheat. Rather it appears that a situation was created in which the subjects knew that normative social comparison information was available to them and they could consult it or not as they wished in preparation for a later discussion of their self-descriptions on the questionnaire items.

Unknown to the subject who performed this task alone, an observer in the next room recorded the frequency with which the subject consulted the majority response sheet and timed each look. The sheet had been left by the experimenter at the far corner of the subject's table so that consulting it required observable but not effortful behavior by the subject. It was expected that a high-SM subject would look more often, as measured by frequency and duration of looking, at this social comparison information than would a low-SM subject.

Results and Discussion

Results on the dependent measures of seeking out of social comparison information were analyzed as a function of both SM and M-C SDS scores ($r_{SM, M–C SDS} = -.067$, $df = 25$, ns) in a 2×2 (High SM, Low SM × High M-C SDS, Low M-C SDS) unweighted means analysis of variance.

There were three measures of seeking out social comparison information during the self-presentation task: (a) frequency of looking at the majority response sheet as recorded by the observer; (b) frequency of looking at the majority response sheet as measured by the subject's retrospective self-report; and (c) total duration of looking at the majority response sheet as timed by the observer. These three measures are highly intercorrelated ($r_{12} = .92$, $r_{13} = .90$, $r_{23} = .83$, $df = 25$, $p < .001$). The means for each of these measures are presented in Table 3.

For frequency of looking as recorded by an observer, a high-SM subject looked more frequently than a low-SM at the majority response sheet ($F = 4.70$, $df = 1/23$, $p < .05$). Given the opportunity to consult social comparison information in a self-presentation situation in which they expected to justify their self-descriptions, high self-monitors did so more frequently than did low self-monitors. There was no systematic relationship between M-C SDS and looking behavior ($F = .122$, $df = 1/23$, ns), nor was there any interaction between SM and M-C SDS scores ($F = .011$, $df = 1/23$, ns). Thus, there was no relationship between the tendency to describe oneself in socially desirable fashion and consulting social comparison information in this self-presentation situation.

Analyses of subjects' self-report of looking behavior and total time looking measured by the observer result in identical conclusions. For either measure, high-SM subjects were more likely than low-SM to seek out social comparison information.

CONCLUSIONS

Individuals differ in the extent to which they monitor (observe and control) their expressive behavior and self-presentation. Out of a concern for social appropriateness, the self-monitoring individual is particularly sensitive to the expression and self-presentation of others in social situations and uses these cues as guidelines for monitoring and managing his own self-presentation and expressive behavior. In contrast, the non-self-monitoring person has little concern for the appropriateness of his presentation and expression, pays less attention to the expression of others, and monitors and controls his presentation to a lesser extent. His presentation and expression appear to be controlled from within by his experience rather than by situational interpersonal specifications of appropriateness.

A self-report measure of individual differences in self-monitoring was constructed. The Self-Monitoring Scale is internally consistent,

TABLE 3 Three Measures of Looking at Social Comparison Information

MEASURE	n	FREQUENCY OF LOOKING[a]	FREQUENCY OF LOOKING[b]	TOTAL DURATION OF LOOKING (IN SECONDS)
High SM, low M-C SDS	6	14.67	15.83	20.83
High SM, high M-C SDS	8	12.25	12.25	19.38
Low SM, low M-C SDS	7	5.14	5.83	5.43
Low SM, high M-C SDS	6	4.83	4.13	4.83

Note. SM = Self-Monitoring Scale; M-C SDS = Marlowe-Crowne Social Desirability Scale.
[a] Recorded by observer.
[b] Subject's self-report.

temporally stable, and uncorrelated with self-report measure of related concepts.

Four studies were conducted to validate the Self-Monitoring Scale. According to peers, individuals with high SM scores are good at learning what is socially appropriate in new situations, have good self-control of their emotional expression, and can effectively use this ability to create the impressions they want. Theater actors scored higher and hospitalized psychiatric ward patients scored lower than university students. Individuals with high SM scores were better able than those with low SM scores to intentionally express and communicate emotion in both the vocal and facial channels of expressive behavior. In a self-presentation task, individuals with high SM scores were more likely than those with low scores to seek out and consult social comparison information about their peers. Self-monitoring and need for approval were compared as predictors of each external criterion to demonstrate the discriminant validity of the SM.

REFERENCES

Bem, D. J. Constructing cross-situational constituencies in behavior: Some thoughts on Alker's critique of Mischel. *Journal of Personality*, 1972, *40*, 17–26.

Campbell, D. J. Recommendations for APA test standards regarding construct, trait, and discriminant validity. *American Psychologist*, 1960, *15*, 546–553.

Ekman, P. Universals and cultural differences in facial expressions of emotion. In J. Cole (Ed.), *Nebraska Symposium on Motivation: 1971*. Lincoln: University of Nebraska Press, 1971.

Ekman, P., & Friesen, W. V. Nonverbal leakage and clues to deception. *Psychiatry*, 1969, *32*, 88–105.

Freud, S. Fragment of an analysis of a case of hysteria (1905). In, *Collected Papers*. Vol. 3. New York: Basic Books, 1959.

Goffman, E. On face work: An analysis of ritual elements in social interaction. *Psychiatry*, 1955, *18*, 213–221.

Mischel, W. *Personality and assessment*. New York: Wiley, 1968.

Moos, R. H. Situational analysis of a therapeutic community milieu. *Journal of Abnormal Psychology*, 1968, *73*, 49–61.

Schachter, S., & Singer, J. Cognitive, social, and physiological determinants of emotional state. *Psychological Review*, 1962, *69*, 379–399.

KEY POINTS

1. People high on self-monitoring are willing and able to observe themselves and control their expressive behavior, guided by situational cues to social appropriateness.

2. Self-monitoring can account for individual differences in cross-situational consistency of behavior.

3. The self-report Self-monitoring Scale is a reasonably valid tool for assessing ability and willingness to control one's expressive behavior.

QUESTIONS TO THINK ABOUT

1. What kinds of careers and environments are appropriate for people who score very high on self-monitoring? Very low?

2. What happens if people are willing and able to control their own expressive behaviors, but are unable to read the demands of the situation and the social expectations of others?

3. If identity is a function of both individuals and their situations, what implications does this have for our conceptions of ego?

10

Dimensions of Personality: The Biosocial Approach to Personality*

HANS J. EYSENCK

Some of the most interesting evidence for the effects of biological temperament on personality comes from this British psychologist. Eysenck (1916–1997) developed a nervous system-based theory of personality. The basic idea of Eysenck's theory is that extroverts have a relatively low level of brain arousal that leads them to seek stimulation. Conversely, introverts are thought to have a higher level of central nervous system arousal, so they tend to shy away from stimulating social environments.

Eysenck's research led him to believe that the basis of personality was accounted for by three personality dimensions. He viewed all traits as deriving from three biological systems: extraversion, neuroticism, and psychoticism. Psychoticism includes a tendency toward psychopathology involving impulsivity and cruelty, tough-mindedness, shrewdness, low agreeableness, and low conscientiousness. Neuroticism is an emotional instability.

Eysenck, born in Germany, fled to England in 1934 where he became an important voice in psychology. Eysenck's parents were actors and he himself became an extremely passionate and outspoken psychologist and intellectual. Thus, it is not surprising Eysenck asked intriguing questions such as whether extroversion runs in families.

A PARADIGM OF PERSONALITY DESCRIPTION

It would seem difficult to doubt the truth of the proposition that man is a biosocial animal (Eysenck, 1980b). There is no longer any doubt about the strong determination of individual differences in personality by genetic factors (Eaves, Eysenck, & Martin, 1989), and much progress has been made in the study of physiological, neurological, and biochemical-hormonal factors in mediating this influence (Eysenck, 1981; Zuckerman, Ballenger, & Post, 1984; Stelmack, 1981). It has been suggested that the biological aspects of personality should be identified with the concept of *temperament* (Strelau, 1983) and this may prove an acceptable use, although the dictionary defines the term as equivalent to personality ("the characteristic way an individual behaves, especially towards other people"). What is not in doubt is the importance of considering individual differences as an important part of scientific psychology (Eysenck, 1984) and, indeed, it has been fundamental for any proper understanding of human behavior (Eysenck, 1983). Personality

*Eysenck, H. J. (1991). Dimensions of personality: The biosocial approach to personality. In J. Strelau & A. Angleitner (Eds.), *Explorations in temperament* (pp. 87–103). New York: Plenum. Reprinted by permission. (Selection is excerpted from pp. 87–99.) [Ed. note: All citations in the text of this selection have been left intact from the original, but the list of references includes only those sources that are the most relevant and important. Readers wishing to follow any of the other citations can find the full references in the original work or in an online database.]

is more than superficial behavioral characteristics, easily acquired and easily abandoned; it is an indispensable part of any meaningful scientific investigation in educational, industrial, clinical, social or experimental psychology (Eysenck & Eysenck, 1985).

Concepts like values, interests, and attitudes are related to personality but do not usually form part of its central core. Undoubtedly they too are influenced by biological factors as shown, for instance, by the high heritabilities for social attitudes and interests (Eaves *et al.*, 1989); but too little work has been published on such determinants to deserve extended treatment here.

The multiplicity of approaches to the descriptive analysis of personality should not mislead psychologists into thinking there is no agreement; Eysenck (1983) has argued that there is a paradigm in personality research, and Royce and Powell (1983), in a reanalysis of all large-scale psychometric analyses of personality to date have found that there are three major dimensions in this field. They appear again and again, and are very similar to the three major dimensions suggested by Eysenck, namely Psychoticism (P), Extraversion (E), and Neuroticism (N). There are several reasons for asserting that these three dimensions are firmly linked with biological determinants. These reasons are as follows:

1. As already noted, regardless of instrument of measurement or method of analysis, these three dimensions emerge from practically all large-scale investigations into personality, a result unlikely if environmental factors alone determined a person's position on these dimensions (Eysenck & Eysenck, 1985; Royce & Powell, 1983).

2. These same three dimensions are found cross-culturally in all parts of the world where studies have been carried out to investigate this universality (Barrett & Eysenck, 1984). Using the Eysenck Personality Questionnaire (EPQ; Eysenck & Eysenck, 1975), these authors analyzed results from 25 countries as diverse as Nigeria and Uganda in Africa, mainland China and Japan, European and Scandinavian countries, South American countries, Socialist countries like the USSR, Hungary, and Poland, as well as the former British colonies (USA, Canada, and Australia), testing 500 males and 500 females in each country with a translation of the EPQ, and carrying out factor analyses separately for males and females. It was found that, overall, practically identical factors emerged, showing indices of factor comparison which averaged .98. This identity of personality dimensions in fundamentally different cultures suggests a biological foundation.

3. Individuals tend to retain their position on these three dimensions with remarkable consistency (Conley, 1984a, b, 1985). This suggests that the events of everyday life have little influence on a person's temperament, and that biological causes are predominant in determining disposition.

4. Work on the genetics of personality (Eaves *et al.*, 1989) has powerfully reinforced this argument, as already pointed out; genetic factors determine at least half the phenotypic variance of the major dimensions of personality, and there is little if any evidence for between family environmental variance. This finding alone would seem to contradict all the major theories of personality advanced in psychological textbooks!

Clearly, genetic factors cannot act directly on behavior; there must be an intervening link between genes and chromosomes on the one hand, and social behavior on the other. This intervening link may be looked for in physiological factors, neurological structure, biochemical and hormonal determinants or other biological features of the organism. The proper theory of personality requires some knowledge of the relationships between social behavior, on the one hand, which gives rise to the descriptions of the major dimensions of personality, based on patterns of behavior, and specific biological features of the organism on the other. It is unlikely that simple heuristic findings will establish a convincing link; what is needed clearly is a set of theories relating the various dimensions of personality. Eysenck (1990) has given a detailed review of the theories and studies available to date in this very large and complex field; here we can only discuss some of the issues in question, with particular reference to the theory of "arousal" in relation to extraversion-introversion.

BIOLOGICAL THEORIES OF PERSONALITY

Eysenck (1967) originally suggested a link between cortical arousal and extraversion-introversion. This was based essentially on the findings of Moruzzi and Magoun (1949) of the ascending reticular activating system (ARAS), the system activation of which elicited a general activation pattern in the cortical EEG. Collaterals from the ascending sensory pathways produce activity in the ARAS, which subsequently relays the excitation to numerous sites in the cerebral cortex. It was this excitation which produced the EEG synchronization observed by Moruzzi and Magoun. Much research has since shown that the reticular formation is implicated in the initiation and maintenance of motivation, emotion, and conditioning by way of excitatory and inhibitory control of autonomic and postural adjustments, and by way of cortical coordination of activity serving attention, arousal, and orienting behavior.

The link suggested by Eysenck (1967) between personality and the ARAS amounted to the suggestion that the extraversion-introversion dimension is identified largely with differences in level of activity in the cortico-reticular loop, introverts being characterized by higher levels of activity than extroverts, and thus being chronically more cortically aroused. In addition, Eysenck suggested that neuroticism was closely related to the activity of the visceral brain, which consists of the hippocampus-amygdala, singulum, septum, and hypothalamus. These two systems are independent, hence we have an orthogonal relation between extraversion-introversion and neuroticism-stability. However, this independence is only partial. One of the ways in which cortical arousal can be produced is through activity in the visceral brain which reaches the reticular formation through collaterals. Activity in the visceral brain produces autonomic arousal, and Eysenck has used the term *activation* to distinguish this form of arousal from that produced by

reticular activity. Thus in a condition of high activation, we would expect high arousal; a person who is strongly affected by anger, or fear, or some other emotion will certainly also be in a state of high cortical arousal. Fortunately, such states of strong emotional involvement are relatively rare, but they do indicate that the independence of the two systems is only relative (Routtenberg, 1966).

A detailed discussion of the concept of arousal by many authors is given in a book edited by Strelau and Eysenck (1987). Clearly, the concept of general physiological arousal that was a core construct in Duffy's (1957) early theory and Hebb's (1955) optimal arousal approach does not seem viable any longer. The reticulo-cortical system of Moruzzi and Magoun (1949) now appears to be only one of several arousal systems (Zuckerman & Como, 1983), probably including the limbic arousal system, suggested by recent work (Aston-Jones & Bloom, 1981), as well as a monoamine oxidase system, the diffuse thalamocortical system and the pituitary-adrenocortical system (Zuckerman, 1983). This apparent diversity may not prevent the systems from operating in a relatively unitary fashion. Clearly, the way from the "conceptual nervous system" of Hebb to the "central nervous system" of the neurosciences is a hard one!

PROBLEMS IN THEORIES TESTING

At first sight it may seem relatively easy to test theories of this kind by taking groups of extroverts and introverts, or high and low N scorers, and submitting them to physiological tests of one kind or another. However, note the following:

1. There is no single measure of arousal or excitation in the neurophysiological field. As Lacey and Lacey (1958) have emphasized repeatedly, the underlying systems show *response specificity*, in that different systems are primarily activated by suitable stimulation in different people. Thus one person may react to emotional stimuli primarily through an increase in heart rate, another through increase in the conductivity of the skin, a third through more rapid breathing, etc. No single measure is adequate to portray the complexity of reactions; the recommended solution is to take measures of as many systems as possible, and score changes in the system maximally involved. But few experimenters have followed this advice, so that failure to support the theory may be due to faulty or too restricted choice of measuring instrument.

2. There is also *stimulus specificity,* in the sense that different people may be sensitive to different stimuli. Saltz (1970) has shown that failure, or the threat of failure, produces more anxiety among N+ subjects, whereas shocks generate greater anxiety among N– than N+ subjects. Genetic factors predispose individuals to condition anxiety responses to quite specific stimuli (Eysenck & Martin, 1987). Thus the usual stimuli chosen by experimenters, e.g., shocks, may result in quite different relationships between stimulus and response than some other stimuli.

3. Relations between stimulus and response are usually nonlinear. Both the Yerkes-Dodson Law (1908) and Pavlov's (1927) Law of Transmarginal Inhibition show that as stimuli get stronger, responses at first increase in strength, then they decline, producing a curvilinear regression. This leads to complex theoretical formulation which makes precise prediction difficult. We can predict that the high arousal of introverts will lead to a reversal of the stimulus-response correlation at a lower point of stimulus intensity than would be true of extroverts, but the precise point is difficult to establish. Nevertheless, the Law has shown impressive predictive powers in relation to a variety of behavioral responses (Eysenck, 1976; Eysenck & Eysenck, 1985).

4. Threshold and ceiling effects may make choice of measure difficult. Looking at the electrodermal response (EDR) as a measure of N, we could use as our response measure: (a) Size of response; (b) latency of response; or (c) duration of response, i.e., time to return to base-line. Only (c) seems to give useful correlations, but that could not have been predicted from what little we know of the EDR.

5. Resting levels are ill-defined, and are influenced powerfully by uncontrolled preexperi-

mental variables. Subjects coming into our laboratories may have suffered an emotional shock quite recently, may have smoked or drunk alcohol heavily, have been frightened by rumors about the experiments to be performed, or may have been annoyed by being kept waiting; these and many other factors may determine decisively their reactions in the test. Eysenck (1981) has discussed in detail how anticipation in subjects produced quite contradictory results in two series of experiments. Spence had postulated, and found, that eyeblink conditioning was correlated with N, not with E. Eysenck had postulated, and found, that eyeblink conditioning was correlated with E, but not N. Kimble visited both laboratories and discovered that while Eysenck reassured his subjects, told them explicitly that they would not receive electric shock, hid all the threatening apparatus, and avoided mechanical links with the eyelid, Spence went to the opposite extreme and thoroughly frightened his subjects. As a consequence, N played an important part in Spence's experiments, differences in activation drowning out differences in arousal, while activation played no part in Eysenck's experiment, allowing arousal to determine the observed correlations. Note that these preexperimental conditions were not discussed in the presentation of the experiments in question!

6. Neurological and hormonal systems interact in complex ways, and so do the dimensions of personality; it is never safe to assume that E+ and E– subjects are not influenced in their reactions by differences in P, or N, or intelligence, or whatever. At best these extraneous influences balance out, but they obviously constitute a goodly background of noise against which the signal may not be all that strong. The effects of such interactions deserve more detailed study than they have received hitherto. These difficulties are particularly critical in relation to neuroticism, because of the added complication that it is very difficult to manipulate experimentally states of depression, anxiety, guilt feelings, etc. Laboratory experiments are very restricted in what can and cannot be done ethically, and the very minor and weak manipulations of mood possible in the labora-

tory pay little relation to the very strong feelings elicited in a normal life. Cortical arousal, on the other hand, is much more manipulable, and hence work with the arousal theory of extraversion has been much more successful.

EEG STUDIES AND PERSONALITY

Of the many different ways in which cortical arousal has been studied in relation to extraversion-introversion, the most prominent and indeed also the most obvious has of course been that of using electroencephalography. High levels of arousal are linked with low-amplitude, high-frequency activity in the alpha range of the EEG, and if it were found that extroverts showed low-amplitude and high-frequency alpha activity, this would certainly speak very strongly against the theory. It can of course be objected that the EEG, being recorded from the outside of the skull, represents a kind of composite amalgam of electrical energy generated from different parts of the cortex, and may thus produce a misleading impression of the actual activity in any specific area of the brain. In spite of this complication, evidence has consistently tended to support the hypothesis.

Gale (1983) has reviewed 33 studies containing a total of 38 experimental comparisons. Results are far from uniform, but nevertheless on this criterion extroverts were less aroused than introverts in 22 comparisons, while introverts were less aroused than extroverts in only five comparisons, no significant effects being reported in the remaining studies. The ratio of 22 to 5 in favor of the hypothesis is certainly a very positive finding, but one would like to be able to account for the 5 studies failing to show the predicted relationship.

Gale suggested that the effects of extraversion of the EEG were influenced by the level of arousal induced by the experimental conditions; in particular, he suggested that introverts are most likely to be more aroused than extroverts in moderately arousing conditions, with the differences between introverts and extroverts either disappearing or being reversed with conditions producing either very low or very high levels of arousal. These suggestions follow from the general theory, with high levels of arousal and introversion producing the paradoxical lowering of arousal postulated by Pavlov's Law of Transmarginal Inhibition. Conditions of very low arousal would paradoxically produce strong feelings of boredom in extroverts, which have been shown to lead to attempts at disinhibition.

Gale classified all the relevant EEG studies according to whether the test conditions were minimally, moderately, or highly arousing; he found that introverts appeared to be more aroused than extroverts in all eight of the studies using moderately arousing conditions that reported significant effects of extraversion; but the expected result was found in only 9 out of 12 significant studies using low-arousal conditions, and 5 out of 7 using high-arousal conditions. This result certainly suggests that in testing the hypothesis we should avoid extreme low arousal and high arousal situations, although even under such conditions likely to produce failure of the hypothesis, we still have 14 experiments supporting it, and only 5 giving the opposite result.

Later studies (O'Gorman & Mallise, 1984; O'Gorman & Lloyd, 1987; and Venturini, Pascalis, Imperiali, & Martini, 1981) found results which on the whole were in confirmity with the hypothesis. They also added new measures, such as the alpha attenuation response, which demonstrated that extroverts sometimes reacted to the auditory stimuli, while introverts did not. This greater responsivity to stimulation of introverts is of course in line with the theory.

Cortical evoked potentials furnish us with another possible way of testing the theory. Stelmack, Achorn, and Michaud (1977) found that introverts obtained greater amplitude of the average evoked response (AER) than extroverts with low-frequency stimulation, both with 55 dB and with 80 dB, while observing no differences between groups with high-frequency stimulation. This finding is explicable in terms of the known tendency of greater interindividual variability of the AER at low-frequency than at high-frequency levels (Davis & Zerlin, 1966; Rothman, 1970), as an increase in variance would obviously increase the possibility of obtaining significant covariance. The study is instructive in demonstrating the need to control details of the experimental manipulation, and pay attention to known features of the variables in question.

Another approach using evoked potentials is the augmenting/reducing effect, which relies on the assessment of cortical responses to stimuli of varying intensities. Increasing intensity of stimulation may produce corresponding increases or decreases in the amplitude of particular EP components recorded from different subjects. Augmenters are called such because increased stimulation produces increased amplitude, while for reducers increased stimulation produces decreased amplitude. The theory would predict an increase in amplitude with increases in stimulus intensity, up to a point where transmarginal inhibition would set in to lead to a reduction in amplitude. The point where reduction would be expected to set in would be expected to occur at lower levels of stimulus intensity for introverts than for extroverts. Thus introverts should be reducers, extroverts augmenters. This, indeed, has been the pattern in earlier studies (Friedman & Mears, 1979; Soskis & Shagass, 1974), and in studies using sensation-seeking measures, especially disinhibition, which is most closely related to extraversion (von Knorring, 1980; Zuckerman, Murtaugh, & Siegel, 1974). The only study out of line is one published by Haier, Robinson, Braden and Williams (1984). This only dealt with 11 augmenters and 10 reducers, which is a very small number, but nevertheless the results were significant and counter to the theory. Clearly, what is needed are more analytical studies to give us more information. . . .

ELECTRODERMAL STUDIES OF PERSONALITY

Studies of electrodermal responses are almost as numerous as those using the EEG. In particular, relations have been studied to the orienting response (Lynn, 1966; Sokolov, 1963). Eysenck's theory would predict that introverts would show a stronger OR, and slower habituation. A large number of studies has been referenced by Eysenck (1990), most supporting the hypothesis, but many giving insignificant or contrary results. It can be noted that greater intensity of stimulation tends to produce differences where less intense stimulation does not. Thus, as far as auditory stimulation is concerned, which has been most widely used, studies using sounds in the region of 60–75 dB typically fail to differentiate introverts and extroverts, whereas stimuli in the 75 90 dB range tend to do so. As mentioned, in terindividual variability of the auditory-evoked response has been found to be greater under low-frequency conditions, which also favor the differentiation of extroverts and introverts; similarly, low-frequency stimulation seems to be more effective in differentiating extroverts and introverts in the OR paradigm. . . .

MISCELLANEOUS MEASURES OF PERSONALITY

In addition to EEG and electrodermal studies, there are a number of miscellaneous measures which ought at least to be mentioned. The first of these concerns stimulated salivation in its relation to extraversion. Eysenck's theory predicts that introverts would react more strongly than extroverts to stimulation, such as drops of lemon juice on the tongue, producing a greater flow of saliva. Deary, Ramsay, Wilson, and Riad (1988) have summarized details on nine studies; they abstract their results as follows:

> The negative relation between extraversion and acid-stimulated salivation holds: for both male and female Ss with different saliva collection procedures; whether fresh or synthetic lemon juice or citric acid is used as a stimulus, (although fresh lemon juice appears the most reliable); whether the stimulus is dropped or swabbed onto the tongue and whether the saliva is collected for ten seconds or ten minutes. There is, however, some evidence that the correlation is more robust when testing is performed in the morning when arousal differences are at their greatest. Swallowing the stimulus also appears to reduce the correlation. (p. 906)

S. P. G. and H. J. Eysenck (1967), tested the hypothesis that swallowing the stimulus, and thus increasing its intensity, would evoke transmarginal inhibition preferentially in introverts, and found that it in fact reversed the correlation. Overall results are certainly favorable to the hypothesis. In their own study, Deary, *et al.,* (1988) used 24 subjects, and reported replication of the findings outlined above.

Pupillometry is the next topic to be discussed in this section. In recent years there has been an increased interest in the use of the pupillary response as a psychophysiological measure relating to personality. Pupillary dilation is due primarily to sympathetic activity, whereas constriction reflects parasympathetic activity. We can thus use pupillometry to measure individual differences in responsiveness to stimulation, and tonic pupil size in the absence of specific stimulation can provide an index of general or autonomic arousal. In the first of this line of studies, Holmes (1967) measured speed of pupillary constriction to the onset of a light. The fast dilators tended to be extraverted, whereas the fast constrictors were introverted. Holmes argued that the rapid pupillary constriction of introverts indicated that they had greater amounts of acetylcholine at cholinergic synapses than extroverts.

Frith (1977) confirmed some of Holmes' findings, reporting that high scorers of the impulsivity component of extraversion showed less pupillary constriction than low impulsives in responses to a light flash, perhaps because they were less reactive to stimulation. He also found that impulsivity was negatively correlated with pupil size during an initial interval of no stimulation. This suggests that the more impulsive subjects (high P?) were less aroused than the less impulsive subjects.

The most important study in this field was reported by Stelmack and Mandelzys (1975); they also found that introverts had larger pupils than extroverts in the absence of specific stimulation, suggesting that the introverted subjects were more aroused throughout the experiment. As regards phasic pupillary responses to auditorily presented neutral, affective, and taboo words, they found that introverts showed significantly more pupillary dilation to these stimuli than extroverts, especially in response to taboo

words. In other words, introverts responded more strongly than extroverts to the auditory stimuli. Altogether this line of research seems promising, and should be pursued in the future.

Studies of physique and constitution, as reviewed by Eysenck (1990), are also relevant to the concept of extraversion, although, because of a failure to link theoretically the work on body build, blood groups, etc. with the concept of arousal, these data will not be discussed in detail here. Suffice it to say that extroverts tend to be relatively broad, introverts elongated in body build (Eysenck, 1970; Rees, 1973), and that introversion is found to be significantly more frequent among persons having the AB blood group (Angst & Maurer-Groeli, 1974; Maurer-Groeli, 1974a, b). Eysenck (1977) has reported on national differences in personality as related to ABO blood group polymorphism.

BIOCHEMICAL DETERMINANTS OF PERSONALITY

As a final group of studies relating biological mechanisms to personality we must turn to biochemical influences, a group of determinants which have been studied more and more frequently in recent years, and work which has been surveyed in some detail by Zuckerman, Ballenger, and Post (1984). Of the more obvious hormones here we may mention the gonadal hormones, particularly testosterone. It is of course *prenatal* androgenization which has been shown to be particularly effective in producing masculine-type behaviors (Eysenck & Wilson, 1979), and there are obvious problems with correlational studies of testosterone and behavior, as well as with other biochemicals that show day-to-day fluctuations in level. Nevertheless, Daitzman, Zuckerman, Sammelwitz, and Ganjam (1978) found significant correlations between plasma androgen levels and the Disinhibition subscale of the Sensation-Seeking Scale, i.e., the scale most closely related to extraversion. In their later and more comprehensive study, Daitzman and Zuckerman (1980) again found high scorers on the Disinhibition scale to have higher levels of testosterone, and of estradiol and estrogen, than those with lower scores. They also used other indices of hormonal influence, and carried out a factor analysis too complex to be discussed here.

Another important biochemical agent is the enzyme MAO, which is present in all tissues including brain, with highest brain concentrations being found in the hypothalamus. MAO plays a role in the degradation of the monoamines norepinephrine, dopamine, and serotonin. The review by Zuckerman *et al.* (1984) indicates that MAO levels relate *negatively* to extraversion and sensation-seeking; these findings are consistent with behavioral observations of high- and low-MAO monkeys, and humans (Coursey, Buchsbaum, & Murphy, 1979). High-MAO monkeys in colony tended to be solitary, inactive, and passive; low-MAO monkeys tended to be active, to make many social contacts, and engage frequently in play. In rodents, too, MAO inhibitors produce hyperactivity and increase activity in a novel environment. Later studies by Schalling, Edman, Asberg, and Oreland, (1988), Calhoon (1988), Klinteberg, Schalling, Edman, Oreland, and Asberg (1987), and von Knorring, Oreland, and Wimblad (1984) bear out these major findings. Correlations have also been found between measures of impulsivity and CSF levels of the serotonin metabolite, 5-HIAA (Schalling, Asberg, Edman, & Levander, 1984), which is interesting in view of the associations assumed to exist between low-platelet MAO activity and central serotonergic hyperactivity. These results form a fairly congruent whole centering on the concept of impulsivity, and hence implicating P as well as E. Others have used the monoamine system (e.g., Ballenger, Post, Jimmerson, Lake, Murphy, Zuckerman, & Cronin, 1983), showing that CSF calcium correlated positively with extraversion and negatively with neurotic introversion and general neuroticism. Another interesting finding is that cortisol assayed from CSF correlated negatively with the Disinhibition scale from the Sensation-Seeking Scale.

Finally, we must mention the sedation threshold (Krishnamoorti & Shagass, 1963; Shagass & Jones, 1958; Shagass & Kerenyi, 1958). In these studies we start out with a group of introverts, ambiverts and extraverts who are administered some form of depressant or sedative, usually one of the barbiturates; also defined is a "sedation threshold," i.e., a point at which qualitative differences in behavior occur as a function of drug administration. Extraverts being characterized by lower arousal (or higher inhibition) than introverts, according to the theory, should require less of the drug to reach this threshold. The early studies certainly supported the hypothesis quite strongly, but later studies (e.g., Claridge, Donald, & Birchall, 1981) found that differences in neuroticism disturbed this clear-cut picture. The highest drug tolerance was shown by introverts with smallest neuroticism, and the lowest drug tolerance occurred among neurotic extraverts. Thus the hypothesis that introverts have higher sedation thresholds than extraverts was supported among those of medium neuroticism, whereas the opposite tendency was present among those of low neuroticism. While on the whole the data supports the hypothesis, it clearly requires amplification.

This rapid overview will suffice to show that there are meaningful and significant relationships between biological features of the organism and observable behavior patterns in social life. No doubt the arousal theory is simplistic, not sufficiently detailed, and certainly oversimplified; nevertheless it has given rise to large numbers of positive findings. Making a rough-and-ready calculation of all the available studies in this field, we may say that the ratio of successes to failures is roughly 4 or 5 to 1. This would seem to argue that while the theory is clearly along the right lines, it requires a good deal of modification, amplification, and explication, particularly with respect to the details of experimental manipulation. Predictions from the personality theory to behavioral indices and laboratory studies of memory, conditioning, vigilance, reminiscence, perception, and many other areas, have on the whole been somewhat more successful than predictions in the physiological, neurological, and hormonal fields (Eysenck, 1976, 1981), for reasons already given. Nevertheless, at the moment there is no alternative theory which could account for the facts anything like as well as that of cortical arousal.

It should perhaps be noted, if only as a final comment, that the arrow of causality does not necessarily always go from the biological to the behavioral side. Taking testosterone as an example, aggressive and sexual behavior can significantly change the level of testosterone, as well as being itself influenced by that level (Eysenck, 1990). This is not true of all the variables discussed (e.g., blood type polymorphisms are not affected by behavior), but it would be simpleminded to assume that the relationship is completely one-sided. The biosocial approach to human behavior, and to personality in particular, must take all possibilities into account. Nevertheless, it is clear that in the majority of cases genetic factors determine physiological, neurological and hormonal patterns, and these in turn affect behavior. This simple lesson is absolutely fundamental to an understanding of personality differences in particular, and behavior in general.

REFERENCES

Eysenck, H. J. (1967). *The biological basis of personality.* Springfield, IL: Thomas.

Eysenck, H. J. (1990). Biological dimensions of personality. In L. A. Pervin (Ed.), *Handbook of personality theory and research.* New York: Guilford Press.

Haier, R. J., Robinson, D. L., Braden, W., & Williams, D. (1984). Evoked potential augmenting-reducing and personality differences. *Personality and Individual Differences, 5,* 293–301.

Klinteberg, B., Schalling, D. Edman, G., Oreland, L., & Asberg, H. E. (1987). Personality correlates of platelet monamine oxidase (MAO) activity in female and male subjects. *Neuropsychology, 18,* 89–96.

Stelmack, R. M. (1981). The psychophysiology of extraversion and neuroticism. In H. J. Eysenck (Ed.), *A model for personality.* New York: Springer.

Strelau, J., & Eysenck, H. J. (Eds.). (1987). *Personality dimensions and arousal.* New York: Plenum.

Zuckerman, M. (Ed.). (1983). *Biological bases of sensation seeking, impulsivity and anxiety.* Hillsdale, NJ: Erlbaum.

KEY POINTS

1. A comprehensive personality theory, in Eysenck's view, requires the consideration of social behavior, which provides information based on patterns of behavior, as well as specific biological features.

2. Brain function, such as the function of the ascending reticular activating system (ARAS), may be linked to the extraversion-introversion dimensions of personality.

3. The process of testing biological theories poses numerous problems such as response specificity, stimulus specificity, a nonlinear relationship between stimulus and response, threshold and ceiling effects, and the fact that neurological and hormonal systems interact in complex ways as do the dimensions of personality.

4. Biochemical influences, such as the enzyme monoamine oxidase (MAO), need to be considered in relationship to behavior patterns of social life as a means of understanding personality.

QUESTIONS TO THINK ABOUT

1. What are some of the advantages of considering both the biology and environment of an individual when assessing personality?

2. Could a person's personality be biologically designed by altering biochemical and/or biological functions? What are some possible consequences of creating an "artificial personality"?

3. How useful are such biological measures as heart rate, blood, pupil dilation, and physique to personality assessment?

11

My Genes Made Me Do It*

STANTON PEELE AND RICHARD DEGRANDPRE

Stanton Peele is a psychologist who is an expert on research on addiction. He received his Ph.D. from the University of Michigan, and has spent many years talking to the public about the bases of drug use and social compulsions. Richard DeGrandpre, who worked with Peele on this article, is known for his opposition to the overuse of drugs, especially Ritalin, to treat Attention Deficit Disorder.

Peele has been forceful in arguing that people increasingly have a tendency to over-attribute and overexplain their behavior in terms of genetic and other biological causes. As this selection points out, growing interest in the biological bases of behavior raises many old issues of freedom versus determinism, and blame versus responsibility, that are so important for understanding personality psychology and are often hidden or embedded within the theories.

Just about every week now, we read a newspaper headline about the genetic basis for breast cancer, homosexuality, intelligence, or obesity. In previous years, these stories were about the genes for alcoholism, schizophrenia, and manic-depression. Such news stories may lead us to believe our lives are being revolutionized by genetic discoveries. We may be on the verge of reversing and eliminating mental illness, for example. In addition, many believe, we can identify the causes of criminality, personality, and other basic human foibles and traits.

But these hopes, it turns out, are based on faulty assumptions about genes and behavior. Although genetic research wears the mantle of science, most of the headlines are more hype than reality. Many discoveries loudly touted to the public have been quietly refuted by further research. Other scientifically valid discoveries—like the gene for breast cancer—have nonetheless fallen short of initial claims.

Popular reactions to genetic claims can be greatly influenced by what is currently politically correct. Consider the hubbub over headlines about a genetic cause for homosexuality and by the book *The Bell Curve,* which suggested a substantial genetic basis for intelligence. Many thought the discovery of a "gay gene" proved that homosexuality is not a personal choice and should therefore not lead to social disapproval. *The Bell Curve,* on the other hand, was attacked for suggesting differences in IQ measured among the races are inherited.

The public is hard pressed to evaluate which traits are genetically inspired based on the validity of scientific research. In many cases, people are motivated to accept research claims by the hope of finding solutions for frightening problems, like breast cancer, that our society has failed to solve. At a personal level, people wonder about how much actual choice they have in their lives. Accepting genetic causes for their

*Peele, S., & DeGrandpre, R. (1995). My genes made me do it! *Psychology Today, 28*(4), (July/August), 50–53, 62, 64, 66, 68. Reprinted by permission.

traits can relieve guilt about behavior they want to change, but can't.

These psychological forces influence how we view mental illnesses like schizophrenia and depression, social problems like criminality, and personal maladies like obesity and bulimia. All have grown unabated in recent decades. Efforts made to combat them, at growing expense, have made little or no visible progress. The public wants to hear that science can help, while scientists want to prove that they have remedies for problems that eat away at our individual and social well-being.

Meanwhile, genetic claims are being made for a host of ordinary and abnormal behaviors, from addiction to shyness and even to political views and divorce. If who we are is determined from conception, then our efforts to change or to influence our children may be futile. There may also be no basis for insisting that people behave themselves and conform to laws. Thus, the revolution in thinking about genes has monumental consequences for how we view ourselves as human beings.

THE HUMAN GENOME PROJECT

Today scientists are mapping the entire genome—the DNA contained in the 23 human chromosomes. This enterprise is enormous. The chromosomes of each person contain 3 billion permutations of four chemical bases arrayed in two interlocking strands. This DNA may be divided into between 50,000 and 100,000 genes. But the same DNA can function in more than one gene, making the concept of individual genes something of a convenient fiction. The mystery of how these genes, and the chemistry underlying them, cause specific traits and diseases is a convoluted one.

The Human Genome Project has, and will continue to, advance our understanding of genes and suggest preventive and therapeutic strategies for many diseases. Some diseases, like Huntington's, have been linked to a single gene. But the search for single genes for complex human traits, like sexual orientation or antisocial behavior, or mental disorders like schizophrenia or depression, is seriously misguided.

Most claims linking emotional disorders and behaviors to genes are *statistical* in nature. For example, differences in the correlations in traits between identical twins (who inherit identical genes) and fraternal twins (who have half their genes in common) are examined with the goal of separating the role of environment from that of genes. But this goal is elusive. Research finds that identical twins are treated more alike than fraternal twins. These calculations are therefore insufficient for deciding that alcoholism or manic-depression is inherited, let alone television viewing, conservatism, and other basic, everyday traits for which such claims have been made.

THE MYTH OF MENTAL ILLNESS

In the late 1980s, genes for schizophrenia and manic-depression were identified with great fanfare by teams of geneticists. Both claims have now been definitively disproved. Yet, while the original announcements were heralded on TV news and front pages of newspapers around the country, most people are unaware of the refutations.

In 1987, the prestigious British journal *Nature* published an article linking manic-depression to a specific gene. This conclusion came from family linkage studies, which search for gene variants in suspect sections on the chromosomes of families with a high incidence of a disease. Usually, an active area of DNA (called a genetic marker) is observed to coincide with the disease. If the same marker appears only in diseased family members, evidence of a genetic link has been established. Even so, this does not guarantee that a gene can be identified with the marker.

One genetic marker of manic-depression was identified in a single extended Amish family. But this marker was not apparent in other families that displayed the disorder. Then, further evaluations placed several members of the family without the marker in the manic-depressive category. Another marker detected in several Israeli families was subjected to more detailed genetic analysis, and a number of subjects were switched between the marked and unmarked categories. Ultimately, those with and without the putative markers had similar rates of the disorder.

Other candidates for a manic-depression gene will be put forward. But most researchers no longer believe a single gene is implicated, even within specific families. In fact, genetic research on manic-depression and schizophrenia has rekindled the recognition of the role of environment in emotional disorders. If distinct genetic patterns can't be tied to the disorders, then personal experiences are most likely crucial in their emergence.

Epidemiologic data on the major mental illnesses make it clear that they can't be reduced to purely genetic causes. For example, according to psychiatric epidemiologist Myrna Weissman, Ph.D., Americans born before 1905 had a 1 percent rate of depression by age 75. Among Americans born a half century later, 6 percent become depressed *by age 24!* Similarly, while the average age at which manic-depression first appears was 32 in the mid 1960s, its average onset today is 19. Only social factors can produce such large shifts in incidence and age of onset of mental disorders in a few decades.

GENES AND BEHAVIOR

Understanding the role of our genetic inheritance requires that we know how genes express themselves. One popular conception is of genes as templates stamping out each human trait whole cloth. In fact, genes operate by instructing the developing organism to produce sequences of biochemical compounds.

In some cases, a single, dominant gene *does* largely determine a given trait. Eye color and Huntington's disease are classic examples of such Mendelian traits (named after the Austrian monk, Gregor Mendel, who studied peas). But the problem for behavioral genetics is that complex human attitudes and behavior—and even most disease—are not determined by single genes.

Moreover, even at the cellular level, environment affects the activity of genes. Much active genetic material does not code for any kind of trait. Instead it regulates the speed and direction of the expression of other genes; it modulates the unfolding of the genome. Such regulatory DNA reacts to conditions inside and outside the womb, stimulating different rates of biochemical activity and cellular growth. Rather than forming a rigid template for each of us, most genes form part of a lifelong give-and-take process with the environment.

The inextricable interplay between genes and environment is evident in disorders like alcoholism, anorexia, or overeating that are characterized by abnormal behaviors. Scientists spiritedly debate whether such syndromes are more or less biologically driven. If they are mainly biological—rather than psychological, social, and cultural—then there may be a genetic basis for them.

Therefore, there was considerable interest in the announcement of the discovery of an "alcoholism gene" in 1990. Kenneth Blum, Ph.D., of the University of Texas, and Ernest Noble, M.D., of the University of California, Los Angeles, found an allele of the dopamine receptor gene in 70 percent of a group of alcoholics—these were cadavers—but in only 20 percent of a nonalcoholic group. (An allele is one form of gene.)

The Blum-Noble discovery was broadcast around the country after being published in the *Journal of the American Medical Association* and touted by the AMA on its satellite news service. But, in a 1993 *JAMA* article, Joel Gelernter, M.D., of Yale and his colleagues surveyed all the studies that examined this allele and alcoholism. Discounting Blum and Noble's research, the combined results were that 18 percent of nonalcoholics, 18 percent of problem drinkers, and 18 percent of severe alcoholics *all* had the allele. There was simply no link between this gene and alcoholism!

Blum and Noble have developed a test for the alcoholism gene. But, since their own data indicate that the majority of people who have the target allele are not alcoholics, it would be foolhardy to tell those who test positive that they have an "alcoholism gene."

The dubious state of Blum and Noble's work does not disprove that a gene—or set of genes—could trigger alcoholism. But scientists already know that people do not inherit loss-of-control-drinking whole cloth. Consider this: Alcoholics do not drink uncontrollably when they are unaware that they are drinking alcohol—if it is disguised in a flavored drink, for example.

A more plausible model is that genes may affect how people experience alcohol. Perhaps drinking is more rewarding for alcoholics. Perhaps some people's neurotransmitters are more activated by alcohol. But although genes can influence reactions to alcohol, they cannot explain why some people continue drinking to the point of destroying their lives. Most people find orgasms rewarding, but hardly any engage in sex uncontrollably. Rather, they balance their sexual urges against other forces in their lives.

Jerome Kagan, Ph.D., a Harvard developmental psychologist, was speaking about more than genes when he noted, "we also inherit the human capacity for restraint."

OF (FAT) MICE AND MEN

Public interest was aroused by the 1995 announcement by Rockefeller University geneticist Jeffrey Friedman, M.D., of a genetic mutation in obese mice. The researchers believe this gene influences development of a hormone that tells the organism how fat or full it is. Those with the mutation may not sense when they have achieved satiety or if they have sufficient fatty tissue, and thus can't tell when to stop eating.

The researchers also reported finding a gene nearly identical to the mouse obesity gene in humans. The operation of this gene in humans has not yet been demonstrated, however. Still, professionals like University of Vermont psychologist Esther Rothblum, Ph.D., reacted enthusiastically. "This research indicates that people really are born with a tendency to have a certain weight, just as they are to have a particular skin color or height."

Actually, behavioral geneticists believe that less than half of total weight variation is programmed in the genes, while height is almost entirely genetically determined. Whatever role genes play, America is getting fatter. A survey by the Center for Disease Control found that obesity has increased greatly over the last 10 years. Such rapid change underlines the role of environmental factors, like the abundance of rich foods in America's overeating. The CDC has also found that teens are far less physically active than they were even a decade ago.

Certainly people metabolize food differently and some gain weight more easily than others. Nonetheless, anyone placed in a food-rich environment that encourages inactivity will gain weight, whatever fat genes the person has. But, in nearly all environments, highly motivated people can maintain lower weight levels. We thus see that social pressure, self-control, specific situations—even seasonal variations—combine with physical make-up to influence diet and determine weight.

Accepting that weight is predetermined can relieve guilt for overweight people. But people's belief that they cannot control their weight can itself contribute to obesity. No test will ever be performed that can tell you how much you must weigh. Personal choices will always influence the equation. And anything that inspires positive efforts at weight control can help people lose weight, or avoid gaining more.

The case of obesity—along with schizophrenia, depression, and alcoholism—raises a striking paradox. At the same time that we now view these conditions as diseases that should be treated medically, their prevalence is growing precipitously. The very reliance on drugs and other medical treatments has created a cultural milieu that seeks external solutions for these problems. Relying on external solutions may itself be exacerbating matters; it may be teaching us a helplessness that is at the root of many of our problems. Instead of reducing the incidence of these problems, this seems to have fueled their growth.

HARNESSING DISCOVERIES

In 1993, the gene that determines the occurrence of Huntington's disease, an irreversible degeneration of the nervous system, was discovered. In 1994, a gene was identified that leads to some cases of breast cancer. Utilizing these discoveries, however, is proving more difficult than anticipated.

Finding a gene for breast cancer was cause for elation. But of all the women with breast cancer, only a tenth have family histories of the disease. Furthermore, only half of this group has the gene mutation. Scientists also hoped that breast cancer victims without family histories would show irregularities at this same site on the DNA. But only a small minority do.

The section of the DNA involved in inherited breast cancer is enormously large and complex. There are probably several hundred forms of the gene. The task of determining which variations in the DNA cause cancer, let alone developing therapies to combat the disease, is tremendous. Right now, women who learn that they have the gene defect know they have a high (85 percent) likelihood of developing the disease. But the only decisive response available to them is to have their breasts removed before the disease appears. And even this does not eliminate the possibility of cancer.

The failure to translate genetic discoveries into treatments has also been true for Huntington's disease. Scientists have been unable to detect how the flawed gene switches on dementia and palsy. These difficulties with a disease created by an individual gene show the monumental complexity involved in unraveling how genes determine human traits.

When a distinct gene is not involved, linking genes to traits may well be an absurdity. Any possible link between genes and traits is exponentially more complex with elaborate behavior patterns like overdrinking, personality characteristics like shyness or aggressiveness, or social attitudes such as political conservatism and religiousness. Many genes might be involved in all such traits. It is impossible to separate the contributions environment and DNA make to attitudes and behaviors.

BEHAVIORAL GENETICS: METHODS AND MADNESS

The research discussed so far searches for genes implicated in specific problems. But research relating behavior and genetics rarely involves actual examination of the genome. Instead, psychologists, psychiatrists, and other nongeneticists calculate a heritability statistic by comparing the similarity in behaviors among different sets of relatives. This statistic expresses the old nature–nurture division by representing the percentage of a behavior due to genetic inheritance versus the percentage due to environmental causes.

Such research purports to show a substantial genetic component to alcoholism. For example, some studies have compared the incidence of alcoholism in adopted children with that of their adoptive parents and with their natural parents. When the similarities are greater between the offspring and absent biologic parents, the trait is thought to be highly heritable.

But children are often adopted by relatives or people from the same social background as the parents. The very social factors related to placement of a child—particularly ethnicity and social class—are also related to drinking problems, for example, thus confusing efforts to separate nature and nurture. A team led by University of California sociologist Kaye Fillmore, Ph.D., incorporated social data on adoptive families in the reanalysis of two studies claiming a large genetic inheritance for alcoholism. Fillmore found that the educational and economic level of the receiving families had the greater influence, statistically erasing the genetic contribution from the biological parents.

Another behavioral genetics methodology compares the prevalence of a trait in monozygotic (identical) twins and dizygotic (fraternal) twins. On average, fraternal twins have only half their genes in common. If the identical twins are more alike, it is believed that genetic inheritance is, more important, because the two types of twins are supposedly brought up in identical environments. (To eliminate the confounding influence of gender differences, only same-sex fraternal twins are compared.)

But if people treat identical twins more similarly than they treat fraternal twins, the assumptions of the heritability index dissolve. Much research shows that physical appearance affects how parents, peers, and others react to a child. Thus, identical twins—who more closely resemble one another—will experience a more similar environment than fraternal twins. University of Virginia psychologist Sandra Scarr, Ph.D., has shown that fraternal twins who resemble one another enough to be *mistaken* for identical twins have more similar personalities than other such twins.

Heritability figures depend upon a number of factors, such as the specific population being studied and where. For example, there will be less variation in weight in a food-deprived environment. Studying the inheritance of weight in deprived settings rather than an abundant food environment can greatly influence the heritability calculation.

Heritability figures in fact vary widely from study to study. Matthew McGue, Ph.D., and his colleagues at the University of Minnesota calculated a zero heritability of alcoholism in women, while at the same time a team led by Kenneth Kendler, M.D., at Virginia Medical College calculated a 60 percent heritability with a different group of female twins! One problem is that the number of female alcoholic twins is small, which

is true of most abnormal conditions we study. As a result, the high heritability figure Kendlier's team found would be reduced to nothing with a shift in the diagnoses of as few as four twins.

Shifting definitions also contribute to variations in the heritability measured for alcoholism. Alcoholism may be defined as any drinking problems, or only physiological problems such as DTs, or various combinations of criteria. These variations in methodology explain why heritability figures for alcoholism in different studies vary from zero to almost 100 percent!

THE INHERITANCE OF HOMOSEXUALITY

In the debate over homosexuality, the data supporting a genetic basis are similarly weak. One study by Michael Bailey, Ph.D., a Northwestern University psychologist, and Richard Piliard, M.D., a psychiatrist at Boston University, found that about half the identical twins (52 percent) of homosexual brothers were homosexual themselves, compared with about a quarter (22 percent) of fraternal twins of homosexuals. But this study recruited subjects through ads in gay publications. This introduces a bias toward the selection of overtly gay respondents, a minority of all homosexuals.

Moreover, other results of their study do not support a genetic basis for homosexuality. Adopted brothers (11 percent) had as high a "concordance rate" for homosexuality as ordinary brothers (9 percent). The data also showed that fraternal twins were more than twice as likely as ordinary brothers to share homosexuality, although both sets of siblings have the same genetic relationship. These results suggest the critical role of environmental factors.

One study that focused on a supposed homosexual gene was conducted by Dean Hamer, Ph.D., a molecular biologist at the National Cancer Institute. Hamer found a possible genetic marker on the X chromosome in 33 of 40 brothers who were both gay (the number expected by chance was 20). Earlier Simon LeVay, M.D., a neurologist at the Salk Institute, noted an area of the brain's hypothalamus that was smaller among gay than heterosexual men.

Although both these findings were front-page stories, they provide quite a slender basis for the genetics of homosexuality. Hamer did not check for the frequency of the supposed marker in heterosexual brothers, where it could conceivably be as prevalent as in gay siblings. Hamer has noted that he doesn't know how the marker he found could cause homosexuality, and LeVay likewise concedes he hasn't found a brain center for homosexuality.

But for many, the politics of a homosexual gene outweigh the science. A genetic explanation for homosexuality answers bigots who claim homosexuality is a choice that should be rejected. But to accept that nongenetic factors contribute to homosexuality does not indicate prejudice against gays. David Barr, of the Gay Men's Health Crisis, puts the issue this way. "It doesn't really matter why people are gay. . . . What's really important is how they're treated."

EVERYDAY PSYCHOLOGICAL TRAITS

By assigning a simple percentage to something very complex and poorly understood, behavioral geneticists turn heritability into a clear-cut measurement. Behavioral geneticists have employed these same statistical techniques with ordinary behaviors and attitudes. The resulting list of traits for which heritability has been calculated extends from such well known areas as intelligence, depression, and shyness to such surprising ones as television viewing, divorce, and attitudes like racial prejudice and political conservatism.

Such heritability figures may seem quite remarkable, even incredible. Behavioral geneticists report that half of the basis of divorce, bulimia, and attitudes about punishing criminals is biologically inherited, comparable to or higher than the figures calculated for depression, obesity, and anxiety. Almost any trait seemingly yields a min-

imum heritability figure around 30 percent. The heritability index acts like a scale that reads 30 pounds when empty and adds 30 pounds to everything placed on it!

Believing that basic traits are largely predetermined at birth could have tremendous implications for our self conceptions and public policies. Not long ago, an announcement of a government conference, for example, suggested that violence could be prevented by treating with drugs children with certain genetic profiles. Or parents of children with an alcoholic heritage may tell the children never to drink because they're destined to be alcoholics. But such children, in expecting to become violent or drink excessively, may enact a self-fulfilling prophecy. Indeed, this is known to be the case. People who believe they are alcoholic drink more when told a beverage contains alcohol—even if it doesn't.

Believing the heritability figures developed by behavioral geneticists leads to an important conclusion: Most people must then be overestimating how much daily impact they have on important areas of children's development. Why ask Junior to turn off the TV set if television viewing is inherited, as some claim? What, exactly, can parents accomplish if traits such as prejudice are largely inherited? It would not seem to matter what values we attempt to convey to our children. Likewise, if violence is mostly inbred, then it doesn't make much sense to try to teach our kids to behave properly.

FROM FATALISM TO DEPRESSION

The vision of humanity generated by statistical research on behavioral genetics seems to enhance the passivity and fatalism many people are already saddled with. Yet evidence gathered by University of Pennsylvania psychologist Martin Seligman, Ph.D., and others indicates that "learned helplessness"—or believing one can't influence one's destiny—is a major factor in depression. The opposite state of mind occurs when people believe they control what happens to them. Called self-efficacy, it is a major contributor to psychological well-being and successful functioning.

Is there a connection between the increase in depression and other emotional disorders in 20th-century America and our outlook as a society? If so, then the growing belief that our behavior is not ours to determine could have extremely negative consequences. As well as attacking our own sense of personal self-determination, it may make us less able to disapprove of the misbehavior of others. After all, if people are born to be alcoholic or violent, how can they be punished when they translate these dispositions into action?

Jerome Kagan, whose studies provide a close-up of the interaction of nature and nurture and how it plays out in real life, worries that Americans are too quick to accept that behavior is predetermined. He has studied the temperaments of infants and children and found distinctive differences from birth—and even before. Some babies are outgoing, seemingly at home in the world. And some recoil from the environment; their nervous systems are overly excitable in response to stimulation. Do such findings mean children born with a highly reactive nervous system will grow into withdrawn adults? Will extremely fearless children grow into violent criminals?

In fact, less than half of the reactive infants (those who more frequently fret and cry) are fearful children at the age of two. It all depends on the actions parents take in response to their infant.

Kagan fears people may read too much into children's supposedly biological dispositions, and make unwarranted predictions about how they will develop: "It would be unethical to tell parents that their three-year-old son is at serious risk for delinquent behavior." People who are more fearful or fearless than average have choices about the paths their lives will take, like everyone else.

NATURE, NURTURE: LET'S CALL THE WHOLE THING OFF

How much freedom each person has to develop returns us to the issue of whether nature and nurture can be separated. Thinking of traits as being either environmentally or genetically caused cripples our understanding of human development. As Kagan puts it, "To ask what proportion of personality is genetic rather than environmental is like asking what proportion of a blizzard is due to cold temperature rather than humidity."

A more accurate model is one in which chains of events split into further layers of possible paths. Let's return to alcoholism. Drinking produces greater mood change for some people. Those who find alcohol to serve a strong palliative function will be more likely to use it to calm themselves. For example, if they are highly anxious, alcohol may tranquilize them. But even this tranquilizing effect, we should recognize, is strongly influenced by social learning.

Among drinkers who are potentially vulnerable to alcohol's addictive effects, most will nonetheless find alternatives to drinking to deal with anxiety. Perhaps their social group disapproves of excessive drinking, or their own values strongly rule out drunkenness. Thus, although people who find that alcohol redresses their anxiety are more likely to drink addictively than others, they are not programmed to do so.

MIRROR, MIRROR

The goal of determining what portion of behavior is genetic and environmental will always elude us. Our personalities and destinies don't evolve in this straightforward manner. Behavioral genetics actually shows us how the statistical plumbing of the human spirit has reached its limits. Claims that our genes cause our problems, our misbehavior, even our personalities are more a mirror of our culture's attitudes than a window for human understanding and change.

KEY POINTS

1. The search for single genes for complex human traits like antisocial behavior is seriously misguided. Relevant research designs are inherently weak, and possible causal pathways are often oversimplified.

2. Conditions like depression vary dramatically across time and subpopulations, precluding a simple explanation involving genes.

3. Although people may vary in how they perceive and react to alcohol, or how they taste and metabolize food, such biologically-based variations do not mean that overeating or overdrinking are biological addictions.

QUESTIONS TO THINK ABOUT

1. Why are so many people and so many counselors eager to explain alcoholism, obesity, and mental disturbances in terms of genetic endowment?

2. People clearly vary in certain biological temperaments. Think about more complex models that explain how these temperaments unfold in different environments.

3. Why does it matter if a tendency to overeat and gain weight is 31-percent influenced by our biological makeup or 46-percent so influenced?

12

Violence Against Stepchildren*

MARTIN DALY AND MARGO WILSON

Martin Daly (1944–) and Margo I. Wilson (1942–) take a Darwinian view of parental love. They specialize in researching the evolutionary psychology of violence. Within this field of research, they have studied family homicide, child abuse, and step-relationships. They thus view complex human behaviors as having been selected for by eons of survival pressures.

Working for a while at the University of California, Riverside, and then for many years at McMaster University in Canada, Daly and Wilson use human epidemiological data (the distribution of disease and health in populations), but they also study animal ecosystems, including desert rodents. Daly is a past-president of the Human Behavior and Evolution Society.

On February 20th, 1992, 2-year-old Scott M. died in a Montreal hospital of massive internal injuries caused by one or more abdominal blows. At the manslaughter trial of his mother's 24-year-old live-in boyfriend, doctors testified that Scott's body displayed "all the symptoms of a battered child," mainly because of "numerous bruises of varying ages." The accused, who portrayed himself as Scott's primary caretaker, admitted assaulting the mother and other adults, but "I don't hurt kids." According to an acquaintance, however, the accused had admitted striking the child with his elbow because Scott was "bothering him while he was trying to watch television." The trial outcome was conviction.

A reader of any major newspaper is likely to have encountered similar stories, and may even have noticed that the victims are often the progeny of their killers' predecessors. Is step-relationship really a significant risk factor for lethal assaults on children? (Persons who reside with a partner and the partner's child or children of prior unions are here deemed stepparents regardless of marital registration.)

This issue has been obscured by a scarcity of relevant information in official records. In the United States, for example, the census has not distinguished between genetic parenthood and stepparenthood, and the national archive of homicide cases (the Federal Bureau of Investigation's *Supplementary Homicide Reports*) is also incomplete in this regard. But local data sets can be more informative. We examined the Chicago police department's homicide records, for example, and found that 115 children under 5 years of age were killed by their putative fathers in 1965 through 1990, while 63 were killed by stepfathers or (more or less co-resident) mothers' boyfriends. Most of these children were less than 2 years old, and because very few babies reside with substi-

*Daly, M., & Wilson, M. I. (1996). Violence against stepchildren. *Current Directions in Psychological Science, 5*, 77–81. Reprinted by permission. [Ed. note: Citations in the text of this selection and the sources to which they point have been edited to leave only those that are the most relevant and important. Readers wishing to see the full reference list can consult the original work.]

tute fathers, the numbers imply greatly elevated risk to such children. Just how great that risk might be cannot be determined, however, without better information on the living arrangements of Chicago children.

Canadian data permit somewhat more precise comparisons. A national homicide archive maintained by Statistics Canada from 1974 to 1990 included the relevant distinctions among parental relationships, and recent national probability sample surveys provide estimates of the age-specific distribution of such relationships in the population at large. Estimated rates of homicide by stepfathers versus genetic fathers in Canada are portrayed in Figure 1. Because step-relationships were in fact increasing from 1974 to 1990, the use of recent surveys for population-at-large estimation ensures a conservative comparison: It is virtually certain that estimated numbers of stepfathers in the population are higher than actually prevailed over the 17-year period, and that the estimated homicide rates by stepfathers are therefore low. Nevertheless, the differential is immense.

VIOLENCE IN STEPFAMILIES

Research on child abuse proliferated after Henry Kempe and colleagues' 1962 proclamation of a battered-child syndrome. However, no study addressed the incidence of child maltreatment in step- versus genetic-parent homes until 1980, when we reported that stepchildren constituted a much higher proportion of U.S. child abuse cases than their numbers in the population at large would warrant. This excess could not be dismissed as an artifact of biased detection or reporting because it was most extreme in the fatal cases, for which such biases should be minimal: Whereas young children incurred about seven

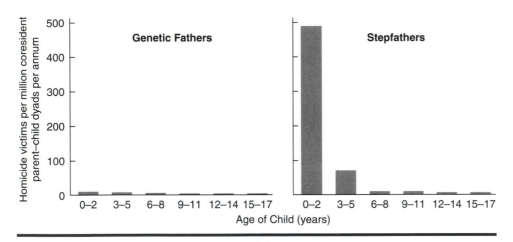

FIGURE 1   Estimated rates of homicide by genetic fathers versus stepfathers in Canada, 1974–1990. Rate numerators are based on a Statistics Canada national archive of all homicides known to Canadian police. Denominators are age-specific estimates of the numbers of Canadian children residing with each type of father, based on census information on the numbers of Canadian children in each age class in each year and age-specific proportions living with genetic fathers versus stepfathers averaged across two national surveys, conducted in 1984 (Statistics Canada's *Family History Survey*) and 1990 (Statistics Canada's *General Social Survey*). Homicide rates for stepfathers are probably underestimates, for reasons explained in the text.

times higher rates of physical abuse in step-plus-genetic-parent homes than in two-genetic-parent homes, the differential in fatal abuse was on the order of 100-fold. Canadian and British data tell much the same story, with a large excess of stepchildren among reported child abuse victims and an even larger excess among children fatally abused.

Genetic parents kill children, too, but recent analyses indicate that the motives in these cases tend to be different. Whereas filicidal parents are often deeply depressed and may even construe murder-suicide as a humane act of rescue, homicidal stepparents are seldom suicidal and typically manifest their antipathy to their victims in the relative brutality of their lethal acts. In Canada, 44 of 155 men (28%) who slew their preschool-age children during a 17-year period did so in the context of a completed suicide, compared with just 1 of 66 men who killed stepchildren, and whereas 82% of the victims of stepfathers were beaten to death, the majority of children slain by genetic fathers were killed by less assaultive means. These contrasts are replicated in British cases.

Given that the rate of abuse and murder is greatly elevated in stepfamilies, one may still question whether step-relationship is itself germane. Might it not be an incidental correlate of other risk factors? Several possible confounds have been examined, but none seems to account for the differential risks among family types. Poverty, for example, is an important risk factor in its own right, but is virtually uncorrelated with the incidence of step-relationship in two-parent families in the United States or Canada and thus cannot explain away the family composition effects. Large family size and maternal youth are additional factors with effects on abuse risk that are apparently distinct from the effects of step-relationship.

Finally, excess risk in stepfamilies might be due to excess numbers of violent personalities among remarried persons, but this hypothesis is refuted by evidence that abusive stepparents typically spare their own children. Step-relationship itself remains the single most important risk factor for severe child maltreatment yet discovered.

DISCRIMINATIVE PARENTAL SOLICITUDE AND STEPPARENTAL INVESTMENT

Elevated risk at the hands of stepparents has been abundantly confirmed, in a range of societies and with respect to the gamut of forms of child maltreatment. But conflict in stepfamilies is not confined to these extremes. Research on nonviolent stepfamilies is a growth industry with a single focus: how people cope with the problems characteristic of step-relationships. It is important to emphasize that many people do indeed cope very well. Nevertheless, the research consistently indicates that step-relationships are, on average, less investing, more distant, more conflictual, and less satisfying than the corresponding genetic parent–child relationships.

These results gibe with popular belief. Undergraduates impute unfair treatment and hostility to persons merely labeled stepfather or stepmother, negative attributions that are mitigated but not eliminated in people who have actually been stepchildren. Folk tales of stepparental antipathy and mistreatment are cross-culturally ubiquitous and familiar to everyone. Given these facts and the prominence of stepfamilies in a typical child protection worker's caseload, it is remarkable that almost two decades of intensive child abuse research elapsed before anyone asked whether stepparent households are really more dangerous than genetic-parent households, and, if so, to what degree.

It was neither folklore nor familiarity with case materials that inspired us to address these questions. We were stimulated by evolutionary logic and by the results of research on nonhuman animals. Current theory implies that natural selection shapes social motives and behavior to function nepotistically on behalf of blood kin, and animals have demonstrably evolved a variety of psychological mechanisms functioning to protect parents against parasitism by unrelated young. Parental care is costly, and animals usually avoid expending it on behalf of young other than their own. But then why is the human animal so willing to enter into step-relationships that may entail prolonged, costly pseudoparental investments?

One hypothesis is that stepparenthood was simply not a recurring adaptive problem for ancestral humans, so people never evolved any psychological defenses against it. Nonnutritive saccharin, an evolutionarily unforeseen component of novel environments, tickles an evolved system for the recognition of nutritive sugars. Might substitute parenthood constitute a sort of social saccharin: an evolutionarily novel circumstance in which the evolved psychology of parenthood is activated in a context slightly different from that for which it evolved? We consider this hypothesis implausible because step-relationship is assuredly not a modern novelty. Mortality levels in contemporary tribal foragers suggest that remarriage and stepparenthood must have been common for as long as people have formed marital bonds with biparental care. Moreover, the available evidence indicates that half-orphans who entered the perilous status of stepchild in a nonstate society faced a major diminution in the quality and quantity of parental care, and an elevated risk of death. In one study of a contemporary South American foraging people, for example, 43% of children raised by a mother and stepfather died before their 15th birthdays, compared with just 19% of those raised by two genetic parents.

An alternative explanation for stepparental investment that is more plausible than the social-saccharin hypothesis derives from comparative studies. Although animals usually avoid caring for their mates' offspring of prior unions, exceptions have been observed in certain species of fish, birds, and mammals. In each case, stepparental investment has been interpreted as *mating effort*, that is, as part of the cost of courting a single parent who, despite the burden of dependent young, remains an attractive prospective mate in a limited mating market. This explanation fits the human case, too. Stepparents assume their obligations in the context of a web of reciprocities with the genetic parent, who is likely to recognize more or less explicitly that stepparental tolerance and investment constitute benefits bestowed on the genetic parent and the child, entitling the stepparent to reciprocal considerations.

In this light, the existence of stepparental investment is not so surprising. But the fact of such investment cannot be taken to imply that stepparents ordinarily (or indeed ever) come to feel the sort of commitment commonly felt by genetic parents. Evolutionary thinking suggests that stepparental affection will tend to be restrained. Indulgence toward a mate's children may have had some social utility for many millennia, but it must rarely have been the case that a stepchild's welfare was as valuable to one's expected fitness as one's own child's welfare. We would therefore expect evolved mechanisms of parental feeling to be buffered against full activation when one merely assumes a parental role, and the empirical literature on stepfamily life confirms this expectation.

PARENTAL LOVE IS MORE THAN JUST A ROLE

Even within the history of Western nations, step-relationships are no novelty. In fact, they were more prevalent in Europe in recent centuries than they are now, thanks to higher death rates of parents whose children were still dependent. In premodern Germany, the age-specific mortality of children was elevated if one parent died and, more remarkably, was further elevated if the surviving parent remarried. It seems that Cinderella was more than a fairy tale.

The cross-cultural ubiquity of Cinderella stories reflects basic, recurring tensions in human society. Stepparental obligations are seldom attractive, and dependent children decrease a widowed or forsaken parent's value in the marriage market. In remarriages, pre-existing children remain a focus and a source of marital conflict, including marital violence. People in all societies face these problems, and they deal with them in various ways. One solution is for remarrying parents to leave children in the care of post-menopausal female relatives. Another is for a widow to retain her children and marry her dead husband's brother, a practice widely perceived as reducing the likelihood or severity of exploitation and mistreatment, because the stepfather is an uncle who may be expected to have some benevolent interest in his brother's children. In the absence of such practices, children have been obliged to tag along as best they can, hoping that their welfare will remain a high priority of the surviving genetic parent. Sometimes the genetic parent has to choose between the new mate and the child, and may even become complicit in the exploitation and abuse of the latter.

American social scientists have interpreted stepparenthood as a role, only partly coincident with that of genetic parenthood. The role concept has usefully directed attention to the importance of socialization and scripts, but it is at best a limited metaphor that has diverted attention away from motivational and emotional aspects of the social psyche. There is more to social action than mere familiarity with the relevant roles. Why are people motivated to embrace certain roles and to shun others? Parents are profoundly concerned for their children's well-being and future prospects, but human concerns have no part in role theorists' explanations of human action.

As Donald Symons has argued, it is especially in the domain of social motives and feelings that psychology needs Darwinism. Some aspects of human physiological and mental adaptations may be elucidated without consideration of how natural selection works, but the investigation of social motives and feelings gains crucial guidance from the recognition that it is genetic posterity, rather than happiness or life span or self-esteem, that has been the arbiter of their evolution. As any evolutionist might have anticipated, it appears that stepparents do not typically experience the same child-specific love and commitment, nor reap the same emotional rewards from unreciprocated parental investment, as genetic parents. Enormous differentials in the risk of violence are one particularly dramatic result of this predictable difference in feelings.

REFERENCES

Daly, M. and Wilson, M. I. (1996). Evolutionary psychology and marital conflict: The relevance of stepchildren. In D. M. Buss and N. Malamuth (Eds.), *Sex, power, conflict: Feminist and evolutionary perspectives*. New York; Oxford.

Lightcap, J. L., Kurland, J. A., and Burgess, R. L. (1982). Child abuse: A test of some predictions from evolutionary theory. *Ethology and Sociobiology, 3,* 61–67.

Symons, D. (1987). If we're all Darwinians, what's the fuss about? In C. Crawford, M. Smith, and D. Krebs (Eds.), *Sociobiology and psychology*. Hillsdale, NJ: Erlbaum.

KEY POINTS

1. Steprelationships have been found to be significant risk factors for child abuse. Child mortality rates are significantly higher within stepfamilies than in genetic-parent families.

2. Current evolutionary theory suggests a Cinderella phenomenon: that we naturally tend to give blood kin greater priority in terms of investment and care. In this way, our genes are more likely to be perpetuated.

3. Despite the common view that stepfamilies are becoming more prevalent because of higher divorce rates, steprelationships were even more prevalent in past centuries due to higher parental death rates.

QUESTIONS TO THINK ABOUT_____

1. How and why might child homicides differ between genetic parents and stepparents?

2. What factors may promote solidarity or discord within stepfamilies?

3. How might stepparenthood serve as a mating effort?

4. When do stepparents experience the same child-specific love and commitment, and reap the same emotional rewards from unreciprocated parental investment, as genetic parents? Why would many stepparents give their lives for their stepchildren?

5. What are the dangers of an oversimplified, evolutionary view of stepparenthood?

6. What are the limits of generalizing from the social behavior of rodents to the social behavior of humans?

13

Sex Differences in Jealousy:
Evolution, Physiology, and Psychology*

DAVID M. BUSS, RANDY J. LARSEN, DREW WESTEN, AND JENNIFER SEMMELROTH

Although basic evolutionary theory has been known to psychologists since the late 1800s, few direct applications to personality psychology have been attempted until recent years. In part, this is due to new developments in the theory. Evolutionary approaches to personality represent one of the few new "grand," wide-ranging approaches to personality to emerge in a long time. This approach has encountered a substantial amount of criticism as well.

David Buss, Randy Larsen, Drew Westen, and Jennifer Semmelroth are active and influential modern-day personality researchers, whose work has ranged over a variety of important topics. In this article, they make an interesting and provocative argument about how and why men and women may differ in what makes them jealous.

In species with internal female fertilization and gestation, features of reproductive biology characteristic of all 4,000 species of mammals, including humans, males face an adaptive problem not confronted by females—uncertainty in their paternity of offspring. Maternity probability in mammals rarely or never deviates from 100%. Compromises in paternity probability come at substantial reproductive cost to the male—the loss of mating effort expended, including time, energy, risk, nuptial gifts, and mating opportunity costs. A cuckolded male also loses the female's parental effort, which becomes channeled to a competitor's gametes. The adaptive problem of paternity uncertainty is exacerbated in species in which males engage in some postzygotic parental investment (Trivers, 1972). Males risk investing resources in putative offspring that are genetically unrelated.

These multiple and severe reproductive costs should have imposed strong selection pressure on males to defend against cuckoldry. Indeed, the literature is replete with examples of evolved anticuckoldry mechanisms in lions (Bertram, 1975), bluebirds (Power, 1975), doves (Erickson & Zenone, 1976), numerous insect species (Thornhill & Alcock, 1983), and nonhuman primates (Hrdy, 1979). Since humans arguably show more paternal investment than any other of the 200 species of primates (Alexan-

*Buss, D. M., Larsen, R. J., Westen, D., & Semmelroth, J. (1992). Sex differences in jealousy: Evolution, physiology, and psychology. *Psychological Science, 3,* 251–255. Reprinted by permission. [Ed. note: All citations in the text of this selection have been left intact from the original, but the list of references includes only those sources that are the most relevant and important. Readers wishing to follow any of the other citations can find the full references in the original work or in an online database.]

der & Noonan, 1979), this selection pressure should have operated especially intensely on human males. Symons (1979); Daly, Wilson, and Weghorst (1982); and Wilson and Daly (in press) have hypothesized that male sexual jealousy evolved as a solution to this adaptive problem (but see Hupka, 1991, for an alternative view). Men who were indifferent to sexual contact between their mates and other men presumably experienced lower paternity certainty, greater investment in competitors' gametes, and lower reproductive success than did men who were motivated to attend to cues of infidelity and to act on those cues to increase paternity probability.

Although females do not risk maternity uncertainty, in species with biparental care they do risk the potential loss of time, resources, and commitment from a male if he deserts or channels investment to alternative mates (Buss, 1988; Thornhill & Alcock, 1983; Trivers, 1972). The redirection of a mate's investment to another female and her offspring is reproductively costly for a female, especially in environments where offspring suffer in survival and reproductive currencies without investment from both parents.

In human evolutionary history, there were likely to have been at least two situations in which a woman risked losing a man's investment. First, in a monogamous marriage, a woman risked having her mate invest in an alternative woman with whom he was having an affair (partial loss of investment) or risked his departure for an alternative woman (large or total loss of investment). Second, in polygynous marriages, a woman was at risk of having her mate invest to a larger degree in other wives and their offspring at the expense of his investment in her and her offspring. Following Buss (1988) and Mellon (1981), we hypothesize that cues to the development of a deep emotional attachment have been reliable leading indicators to women of potential reduction or loss of their mate's investment.

Jealousy is defined as an emotional "state that is aroused by a perceived threat to a valued relationship or position and motivates behavior aimed at countering the threat. Jealousy is 'sexual' if the valued relationship is sexual" (Daly et al., 1982, p. 11; see also Salovey, 1991; White & Mullen, 1989). It is reasonable to hypothesize that jealousy involves physiological reactions (autonomic arousal) to perceived threat and motivated action to reduce the threat, although this hypothesis has not been examined. Following Symons (1979) and Daly et al. (1982), our central hypothesis is that the events that activate jealousy physiologically and psychologically differ for men and women because of the different adaptive problems they have faced over human evolutionary history in mating contexts. Both sexes are hypothesized to be distressed over both sexual and emotional infidelity, and previous findings bear this out (Buss, 1989). However, these two kinds of infidelity should be weighted differently by men and women. Despite the importance of these hypothesized sex differences, no systematic scientific work has been directed toward verifying or falsifying their existence (but for suggestive data, see Francis, 1977; Teismann & Mosher, 1978; White & Mullen, 1989).

STUDY 1: SUBJECTIVE DISTRESS OVER A PARTNER'S EXTERNAL INVOLVEMENT

This study was designed to test the hypothesis that men and women differ in which form of infidelity—sexual versus emotional—triggers more upset and subjective distress, following the adaptive logic just described.

Method

After reporting age and sex, subjects ($N = 202$ undergraduate students) were presented with the following dilemma:

Please think of a serious committed romantic relationship that you have had in the past, that you currently have, or that you would like to have. Imagine that you discover that the person with whom you've been seriously involved became interested in someone else. What would distress or upset you more (*please circle only one*):

(A) Imagining your partner forming a deep emotional attachment to that person.

(B) Imagining your partner enjoying passionate sexual intercourse with that other person.

Subjects completed additional questions, and then encountered the next dilemma, with the same instructional set, but followed by a different, but parallel, choice:

(A) Imagining your partner trying different sexual positions with that other person.

(B) Imagining your partner falling in love with that other person.

Results

Shown in Figure 1 (upper panel) are the percentages of men and women reporting more distress in response to sexual infidelity than emotional infidelity. The first empirical probe, contrasting distress over a partner's sexual involvement with distress over a partner's deep emotional attachment, yielded a large and highly significant sex difference ($\chi^2 = 47.56$, $df = 3$, $p < .001$). Fully 60% of the male sample reported greater distress over their partner's potential sexual infidelity; in contrast, only 17% of the female sample chose that option, with 83% reporting that they would experience greater distress over a partner's emotional attachment to a rival.

This pattern was replicated with the contrast between sex and love. The magnitude of the sex difference was large, with 32% more men than women reporting greater distress over a partner's sexual involvement with someone else, and the majority of women reporting greater distress over a partner's falling in love with a rival ($\chi^2 = 59.20$, $df = 3$, $p < .001$).

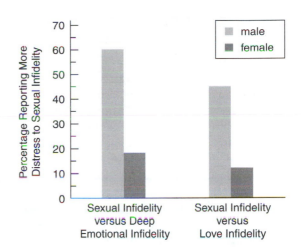

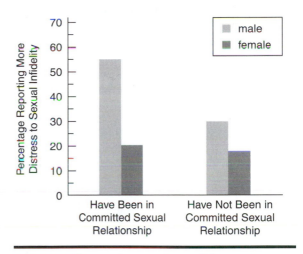

FIGURE 1   Reported comparisons of distress in response to imagining a partner's sexual or emotional infidelity. The upper panel shows results of Study 1—the percentage of subjects reporting more distress to the sexual infidelity scenario than to the emotional infidelity (left) and the love infidelity (right) scenarios. The lower panel shows the results of Study 3—the percentage of subjects reporting more distress to the sexual infidelity scenario than to the emotional infidelity scenario, presented separately for those who have experienced a committed sexual relationship (left) and those who have not experienced a committed sexual relationship (right).

STUDY 2: PHYSIOLOGICAL RESPONSES TO A PARTNER'S EXTERNAL INVOLVEMENT

Given the strong confirmation of jealousy sex linkage from Study 1, we sought next to test the hypotheses using physiological measures. Our central measures of autonomic arousal were electrodermal activity (EDA), assessed via skin conductance, and pulse rate (PR). Electrodermal activity and pulse rate are indicators of autonomic nervous system activation (Levenson, 1988). Because distress is an unpleasant subjective state, we also included a measure of muscle activity in the brow region of the face—electromyographic (EMG) activity of the *corrugator supercilii* muscle. This muscle is responsible for the furrowing of the brow often seen in facial displays of unpleasant emotion or affect (Fridlund, Ekman, & Oster, 1987). Subjects were asked to image two scenarios in which a partner became involved with someone else—one sexual intercourse scenario and one emotional attachment scenario. Physiological responses were recorded during the imagery trials.

Subjects

Subjects were 55 undergraduate students, 32 males and 23 females, each completing a 2-hr laboratory session.

Physiological Measures

Physiological activity was monitored on the running strip chart of a Grass Model 7D polygraph and digitized on a laboratory computer at a 10-Hz rate, following principles recommended in Cacioppo and Tassinary (1990).

Electrodermal Activity. Standard Beckman Ag/AgCl surface electrodes, filled with a .05 molar NaCl solution in a Unibase paste, were placed over the middle segments of the first and third fingers of the right hand. A Wheatstone bridge applied a 0.5-V voltage to one electrode.

Pulse Rate. A photoplethysmograph was attached to the subject's right thumb to monitor the pulse wave. The signal from this pulse transducer was fed into a Grass Model 7P4 cardiotachometer to detect the rising slope of each pulse wave, with the internal circuitry of the Schmitt trigger individually adjusted for each subject to output PR in beats per minute.

Electromyographic activity. Bipolar EMG recordings were obtained over the *corrugator supercilii* muscle. The EMG signal was relayed to a wide-band AC-preamplifier (Grass Model 7P3), where it was band-pass filtered, full-wave rectified, and integrated with a time constant of 0.2 s.

Procedure

After electrode attachment, the subject was made comfortable in a reclining chair and asked to relax. After a 5-min waiting period, the experiment began. The subject was alone in the room during the imagery session, with an intercom on for verbal communication. The instructions for the imagery task were written on a form which the subject was requested to read and follow.

Each subject was instructed to engage in three separate images. The first image was designed to be emotionally neutral: "Imagine a time when you were walking to class, feeling neither good nor bad, just neutral." The subject was instructed to press a button when he or she had the image clearly in mind, and to sustain the image until the experimenter said to stop. The button triggered the computer to begin collecting physiological data for 20 s, after which the experimenter instructed the subject to "stop and relax."

The next two images were infidelity images, one sexual and one emotional. The order of presentation of these two images was counterbalanced. The instructions for sexual jealousy imagery were as follows: "Please think of a serious romantic relationship that you have had in the past, that you currently have, or that you would like to have. Now imagine that the person with whom you're seriously involved becomes interested in someone else. *Imagine you find out that your partner is having sexual intercourse with this other person. Try to feel the feelings You would have if this happened to you."*

The instructions for emotional infidelity imagery were identical to the above, except the italicized sentence was replaced with *"Imagine that your partner is falling in love and forming an emotional attachment to that person."* Physiological data were collected for 20 s following the subject's button press indicating that he or she had achieved the image. Subjects were told to "stop and relax" for 30 s between imagery trials.

Results

Physiological Scores. The following scores were obtained: (a) the amplitude of the largest EDA response occurring during each 20-s trial; (b) PR in beats per minute averaged over each 20-s trial; and (c) amplitude of EMG activity over the *corrugator supercilii* averaged over each 20-s trial. Difference scores were computed between the neutral imagery trial and the jealousy induction trials. Within-sex *t* tests revealed no effects for order of presentation of the sexual jealousy image, so data were collapsed over this factor.

Jealousy Induction Effects. Table 1 shows the mean scores for the physiological measures for men and women in each of the two imagery conditions. Differences in physiological responses to the two jealousy images were examined using paired-comparison *t* tests for each sex separately for EDA, PR, and EMG. The men showed significant increases in EDA during the sexual imagery compared with the emotional imagery ($t = 2.00$, $df = 29$, $p < .05$). Women showed significantly greater EDA to the emotional infidelity image than to the sexual infidelity image ($t = 2.42$, $df = 19$, $p < .05$). A similar pattern was observed with PR. Men showed a substantial increase in PR to both images, but significantly more so in response to the sexual infidelity image ($t = 2.29$, $df =$

TABLE 1   Means and Standard Deviations on Physiological Measures during Two Imagery Conditions

MEASURE	IMAGERY TYPE	MEAN	SD
	Males		
EDA	Sexual	1.30	3.64
	Emotional	−0.11	0.76
Pulse rate	Sexual	4.76	7.80
	Emotional	3.00	5.24
Brow EMG	Sexual	6.75	32.96
	Emotional	1.16	6.60
	Females		
EDA	Sexual	−0.07	0.49
	Emotional	0.21	0.78
Pulse rate	Sexual	2.25	4.68
	Emotional	2.57	4.37
Brow EMG	Sexual	3.03	8.38
	Emotional	8.12	25.60

Note. Measures are expressed as changes from the neutral image condition. EDA is in microsiemen units, pulse rate is in beats per minute, and EMG is in microvolt units.

31, $p < .05$). Women showed elevated PR to both images, but not differentially so. The results of the *corrugator* EMG were similar, although less strong. Men showed greater brow contraction to the sexual infidelity image, and women showed the opposite pattern, although results with this nonautonomic measure did not reach significance ($t = 1.12$, $df = 30$, $p < .14$, for males; $t = −1.24$, $df = 22$, $p < .12$, for females). The elevated EMG contractions for both jealousy induction trials in both sexes support the hypothesis that the affect experienced is negative.

STUDY 3: CONTEXTS THAT ACTIVATE THE JEALOUSY MECHANISM

The goal of Study 3 was to replicate and extend the results of Studies 1 and 2 using a larger sample. Specifically, we sought to examine the effects of having been in a committed sexual relationship versus not having been in such a relationship on the activation of jealousy. We hypothesized that men who had actually experienced a committed sexual relationship would report greater subjective distress in response to the sexual infidelity imagery than would men who had not experienced a high-investing sexual relationship, and that women who had experienced a committed sexual relationship would report greater distress to the emotional infidelity image than women who had not been in a committed sexual relationship. The rationale was that direct experience of the relevant context during development may be necessary for the activation of the sex-linked weighting of jealousy activation.

Subjects

Subjects for Study 3 were 309 undergraduate students, 133 men and 176 women.

Procedure

Subjects read the following instructions:

Please think of a serious or committed romantic relationship that you have had in the past, that you currently have, or that you would like to have. Imagine that you discover that the person with whom you've been seriously involved became interested in someone else. What would distress or upset you more (*please circle only one*):

(A) Imagining your partner falling in love and forming a deep emotional attachment to that person.

(B) Imagining your partner having sexual intercourse with that other person.

Alternatives were presented in standard forced-choice format, with the order counterbalanced across subjects. Following their responses, subjects were asked: "Have you ever been in a serious or committed romantic relationship? (yes or no)" and "If yes, was this a sexual relationship? (yes or no)."

Results

The results for the total sample replicate closely the results of Study 1. A much larger proportion of men (49%) than women (19%) reported that they would be more distressed by their partner's sexual involvement with someone else than by their partner's emotional attachment to, or love for, someone else ($\chi^2 = 38.48$, $df = 3$, $p < .001$).

The two pairs of columns in the bottom panel of Figure 1 show the results separately for those subjects who had experienced a committed sexual relationship in the past and those who had not. For women, the difference is small and not significant. Women reported that they would experience more distress about a partner's emotional infidelity than a partner's sexual infidelity, regardless of whether or not they had experienced a committed sexual relationship ($\chi^2 = 0.80$, $df = 1$, ns).

For men, the difference between those who had been in a sexual relationship and those who had not is large and highly significant. Whereas 55% of the men who had experienced committed sexual relationships reported that they would be more distressed by a partner's sexual than emotional infidelity, this figure drops to 29% for men who had never experienced a committed sexual relationship ($\chi^2 = 12.29$, $df = 1$, $p < .001$). Sexual jealousy in men apparently becomes increasingly activated upon experience of the relevant relationship.

DISCUSSION

The results of the three empirical studies support the hypothesized sex linkages in the activators of jealousy. Study 1 found large sex differences in reports of the subjective distress individuals would experience upon exposure to a partner's sexual infidelity versus emotional infidelity. Study 2 found a sex linkage in autonomic arousal to imagined sexual infidelity versus emotional infidelity; the results were particularly strong for the EDA and PR. Study 3 replicated the large sex differences in reported distress to sexual versus emotional infidelity, and found a strong effect for men of actually having experienced a committed sexual relationship.

These studies are limited in ways that call for additional research. First, they pertain to a single age group and culture. Future studies could explore the degree to which these sex differences transcend different cultures and age groups. Two clear evolutionary psychological predictions are (a) that male sexual jealousy and female commitment jealousy will be greater in cultures where males invest heavily in children, and (b) that male sexual jealousy will diminish as the age of the male's mate increases because her reproductive value decreases. Second, future studies could test the alternative hypotheses that the current findings reflect (a) domain-specific psychological adaptations to cuckoldry versus potential investment loss or (b) a more domain-general mechanism such that any thoughts of sex are more interesting, arousing, and perhaps disturbing to men whereas any thoughts of love are more interesting, arousing, and perhaps disturbing to women, and hence that such responses are not specific to jealousy or infidelity. Third, emotional and sexual infidelity are clearly correlated, albeit imperfectly, and a sizable percentage of men in Studies 1 and 3 reported greater distress to a partner's emotional infidelity. Emotional infidelity may signal sexual infidelity and vice versa, and hence both sexes should become distressed at both forms (see Buss, 1989). Future research could profitably explore in greater detail the correlation of these forms of infidelity as well as the sources of within-sex variation. Finally, the intriguing finding that men who have experienced a committed sexual relationship differ dramatically from those who have not, whereas for women such experiences appear to be irrelevant to their selection of emotional infidelity as the more distressing event, should be examined. Why do such ontogenetic experiences matter for men, and why do they appear to be irrelevant for women?

Within the constraints of the current studies, we can conclude that the sex differences found here generalize across both psychological and physiological methods—demonstrating an empirical robustness in the observed effect. The degree to which these sex-linked elicitors correspond to the hypothesized sexlinked adaptive problems lends support to the evolutionary psychological framework from which they were derived. Alternative theoretical frameworks, including those that invoke culture, social construction, deconstruction, arbitrary parental socialization, and structural powerlessness, undoubtedly could be molded post hoc to fit the findings—something perhaps true of any set of findings. None but the Symons (1979) and Daly et al. (1982) evolutionary psychological frameworks, however, generated the sex-differentiated predictions in advance and on the basis of sound evolutionary reasoning. The recent finding that male sexual jealousy is the leading cause of spouse battering and homicide across cultures worldwide (Daly & Wilson, 1988a, 1988b) offers suggestive evidence that these sex differences have large social import and may be species-wide.

REFERENCES

Daly, M., & Wilson, M. (1988a). Evolutionary social psychology and family violence. *Science, 242,* 519–524.

Daly, M., & Wilson, M. (1988b). *Homicide.* Hawthorne, NY: Aldine.

Hrdy, S. B. G. (1979). Infanticide among animals: A review, classification, and examination of the implications for the reproductive strategies of females. *Ethology and Sociobiology, 1,* 14–40.

Hupka, R. B. (1991). The motive for the arousal of romantic jealousy: Its cultural origin. In P. Salovey (Ed.), *The psychology of jealousy and envy* (pp. 252–270). New York: Guilford Press.

Salovey, P. (Ed.). (1991). *The psychology of jealousy and envy.* New York: Guilford Press.

Trivers, R. (1972). Parental investment and sexual selection. In B. Campbell (Ed.), *Sexual selection and the descent of man, 1871–1971* (pp. 136–179). Chicago: Aldine.

Wilson, M., & Daly, M. (1992). The man who mistook his wife for a chattel. In J. Barkow, L. Cosmides, & J. Tooby (Eds.), *The adapted mind: Evolutionary psychology and the generation of culture.* New York: Oxford University Press.

KEY POINTS

1. It is proposed that sex differences in jealousy emerged in humans as solutions to the respective adaptive problems faced by each sex over human evolutionary history. The central hypothesis is that the events that activate jealousy differ for men versus women.

2. Men who were indifferent to sexual contact between their mates and other men presumably experienced lower paternity certainty, greater "investment" in competitors' gametes, and lower reproductive success than men motivated to attend to cues of infidelity and to act on those cues to increase paternity probability.

3. Cues to the development of a deep emotional attachment to another woman may have been reliable leading indicators to women of potential loss of their mate's investment.

4. There were large sex differences in reports of the subjective distress individuals believed they would experience upon exposure to a partner's sexual infidelity versus emotional infidelity. The difference was especially pronounced for males who had experienced a committed sexual relationship.

5. Autonomic arousal to imagined sexual infidelity versus emotional infidelity differed for males versus females.

QUESTIONS TO THINK ABOUT

1. Derive some predictions and hypotheses for future experiments about jealousy. Using these predictions and hypotheses, propose some new experiments.

2. What are alternative explanations for the findings? What are the limits of an evolutionary approach in drawing strong inferences about human behavior?

3. What does this paper tell us about jealousy in sexually experienced individuals?

14

Exaptation: A Crucial Tool for an Evolutionary Psychology*

STEPHEN JAY GOULD

A paleontologist focused on evolutionary theory, Stephen Jay Gould (1941–) has examined the existence of racism in science. In his book, *The Mismeasure of Man*, Gould tells how even the most eminent scientists were blinded by prejudices while claiming to be engaged in purely scientific assessments. One example of such a prejudice is using skull size to "prove that men are smarter than women and Caucasians are smarter than African Americans." Such biases were especially dangerous because, though many well-intentioned scientists of the nineteenth and twentieth centuries were not conscious of distortions in their data, the fact was that their biases led to inaccurate and incorrect results. Politicians then used these biased findings to help justify racist and sexist social policies.

In the following excerpt, Gould warns against concluding that, just because some characteristic is helpful in today's world, it must have been selected for through natural selection. Rather, he points out that many characteristics that have previously been selected for a specific purpose are now taken over for, that is co-opted for, a new use. It is therefore very difficult to know the selection pressures that have allowed for complex human behaviors, and it is dangerous to assume that people behave the way they do simply because of "natural selection."

In his classic treatise, "On the Nature of Limbs," published in 1849, Richard Owen presented a conundrum for biologists committed to the principle of adaptations—a word and concept of ancient pedigree, long antedating Darwin's later explanation in terms of evolution by natural selection. Mammals, and humans especially, must begin life with a tight squeeze—the passage of the relatively large fetal head through the narrow birth canal. The bones of the skull are not yet fully ossified or sutured together. Consequently, the nonrigid head can be "molded" as the bones alter their positions to allow this first essential adjustment to extrauterine life. If this molding could not occur, birth with such a large head would be impossible. Thus, we seem to have a *prima facie* case for a *vitally important adaptation* in this delayed ossification of skull bones. After all, big heads are a key to human success, and delayed ossification permits big heads. (With limited

*Gould, S. J. (1991). Exaptation: A crucial tool for an evolutionary psychology. *Journal of Social Issues, 47*, 43–65. Reprinted by permission. (Selection is excerpted from the original.) [Ed. note: All citations in the text of this selection have been left intact from the original, but the list of references includes only those sources that are the most relevant and important. Readers wishing to follow any of the other citations can find the full references in the original work or in an online database.]

brain growth after birth, small neonatal heads and later expansion may not represent an option for an alternative pathway.)

Yet Owen, Britain's greatest vertebrate anatomist and first director of the independent natural history branch of the British Museum, denied that delayed ossification could rank as a mammalian adaptation—for the excellent reason that "lower" vertebrates (and mammalian ancestors), which need only to break free from an egg, share this feature with us. Owen wrote, linking the case to a general critique of adaptationism by way of Sir Francis Bacon's famous simile about the barrenness of teleology in general:

> Such a final purpose is indeed readily perceived and admitted in regard to the multiplied points of ossification of the skull of the human fetus, and their relation to safe parturition. But when we find that the same ossific centers are established, and in similar order, in the skull of the embryo kangaroo, which is born when an inch in length, and in that of the callow bird that breaks the brittle egg, we feel the truth of Bacon's comparison of "final causes" to the Vestal Virgins, and perceive that they would be barren and unproductive of the fruits we are laboring to attain. (1849, p. 40)

Charles Darwin, whose strongly adaptationist theory set the problem (by imposing limits to thought) that this paper addresses, took Owen's point and example to heart, and repeated the case in a cautionary note on overindulgence in adaptationist explanation (Darwin, 1859, p. 197):

> The sutures in the skull of young mammals have been advanced as a beautiful adaptation for aiding parturition, and no doubt they facilitate, or may be indispensable for this act; but as sutures occur in the skulls of young birds and reptiles, which have only to escape from a broken egg, we may infer that this structure has arisen from the laws of growth, and has been taken advantage of in the parturition of the higher animals.

This case raises some of the deepest issues in evolutionary theory but, for now, let me pose a question almost laughably trivial in comparison (yet deceptively profound as an opening to the generalities): If the term "adaptation" be inappropriate for reasons given by Owen and Darwin, what shall we call this eminently useful delay of ossification in the human embryo? We cannot maintain a clear concept if we have no name for the primary phenomenon so illustrated.

We might honor the fact that delayed ossification did not arise "for" its current role in parturition by calling it a "nonadaptation" or a "nonaptation" (and such cumbersome terms are in frequent use, by yours truly among others—see Gould, 1984). But such a resolution would be unsatisfactory for at least two reasons beyond infelicity: (a) active concepts should not be defined negatively by what they are not, and (b) "nonaptation" would not get at the heart of the evolutionary meaning of the phenomenon—that a useful structure may arise for other reasons and then be coopted for its present role.

I can imagine two solutions to this terminological problem:

1. We might extend "adaptation"—the great warhorse term of Darwinian evolution—to cover this phenomenon. Delayed ossification is useful in parturition, and "adaptation" is about use—so why not extend a term for a *process of building utility* into a general description for the *state of utility*, whatever its origin? (Insofar as evolutionary biologists have considered the issue at all, they have favored this extension. Nonetheless, most extensions of "adaptation" from process to state do not represent an active decision, consciously devised and defended, but rather a passive oozing forth of a favored term beyond a logical border into a defenseless territory. Many biologists have not even considered the crucial difference between historical origin and current utility. In a thoughtless analog of the contemporary motto "if it feels good, do it," they have simply taken the line, "if it works, call it adaptation.") But this extension should be rejected for two reasons:

(a) *Historical.* Adaptation, throughout the history of English usage in biology, has been a "process term," not a "state term." This definition inheres in etymology, for an adaptation is, literally, something fit (*aptus*) by active construction for (*ad*) its usage. The process meaning conforms with vernacular use; we can adapt a bicycle for a young beginner by installing training wheels, but no one would call a credit card an adaptation for opening certain kinds of locked doors, even though the card works as well for this purpose as does the altered bike for a stable ride. Moreover, and most importantly, the process definition affirms a long tradition of professional usage within evolutionary biology. The previous quotation from Darwin himself clearly supports the "process" definition—for Darwin states that some colleagues have called delayed ossification an adaptation, but they are wrong because this eminently useful feature has been coopted, rather than built for, successful parturition. This usage enjoys an unbroken pedigree, and is explicitly defended in the most important modern work on adaptation—for Williams (1966, p. 6) argues that we should speak of adaptation only if we can "attribute the origin and perfection of this design to a long period of selection for effectiveness in this particular role."

(b) *Conceptual and utilitarian.* For a historical scientist, no conceptual tool can be more important than the clear separation of *historical origin* and *current utility*. The false conceptual passage from present function to initial construction ranks with the post hoc fallacy and the confusion of correlation with cause as primary errors of reasoning about temporal sequences. We all understand this principle in the case of human artifacts: No one would claim that the U.S. Mint made dimes thin so that all Americans could carry surrogate screwdrivers in their change purses. And we all laugh at Voltaire's Dr. Pangloss when he exclaims: "Everything is made for the best purpose. Our noses were made to carry spectacles, so we have spectacles. Legs were clearly intended for breeches, and we wear them."

2. We might recognize a lacuna (favorite fancy word of scholars, though the vernacular "gap" will do nicely) in current terminology and coin a new term for the important phenomenon illustrated by the case of delayed ossification—i.e., vital current utility based on cooptation of structures evolved in other contexts and for other purposes (or perhaps for no purpose at all). We who dwell in the jargon-polluted groves of academe should propose new words only with the greatest caution, in the direst of circumstances, and in the absence of any other reasonable solution to a problem. The most compelling justification for a new term resides in conceptual gaps and persistent errors in thought reasonably connected with the absence of a category in the taxonomy of ideas. For a concept without a name often lies hidden from identification and use.

Elisabeth Vrba and I struggled with this issue in our attempts to formulate theories of large-scale evolutionary change. We finally decided that the absence of a term for "useful structures not evolved for their current function, but coopted from other contexts" had produced a sufficiently long-standing and serious muddle to warrant a new term by the criteria suggested above. We therefore proposed the term "exaptation" for "features that now enhance fitness, but were not built by natural selection for their current role" (Gould & Vrba, 1982, p. 4). The extent of immediate commentary (Lewin, 1982) and later usage and debate (Endler & McLellan, 1988; Gans, 1988; Pierce, 1988; Chatterton & Speyer, 1989; and many others) convinces us that, at the very least, we identified a conceptual weakness not sufficiently appreciated by evolutionary biologists in the past.

In our "taxonomy of fitness" (see Table 1), process, state (character), and usage must be distinguished. In the realm of process, traditional adaptation (Darwin's usage) occurs when natural selection shapes a feature for its current use. If characters are built for other reasons, and then "seized" for an altered utility, we speak (using a vernacular term) of "cooptation." Coopted characters may have been built by natural selection for a different function (e.g., the proto-wing, initially evolved as an adaptation for thermoregulation and later coopted for flight, according to the standard, classic conjecture), or may have arisen for no adaptive purpose at all (e.g., as a sequel or consequence of another adaptation, in

TABLE 1   A Taxonomy of Fitness

PROCESS	CHARACTER		USAGE
Natural selection shapes the character for a current use—adaptation	Adaptation		Function
A character, previously shaped by natural selection for a particular function (an adaptation), is coopted for a new use—cooptation		Aptation	
A character whose origin cannot be ascribed to the direct action of natural selection (a nonaptation) is coopted for current use—cooptation	Exaptation		Effect

what Darwin called "correlation of growth"). In either case, coopted structures will probably undergo some secondary modification—counting as superimposed, true adaptation—for the newly seized function. (The feather, for example, will need some redesign for efficient flight—as we can scarcely imagine that a structure evolved for thermoregulation would be accidentally and optimally suited for something so different as aerial locomotion.) But such secondary tinkering does not alter the primary status of such a structure as coopted rather than adapted.

For current state, we reluctantly permit *stare decisis* in retaining "adaptation" for characters built by selection for their current use. (We assume, for example, that the elaborate plumages and behavioral displays of male birds of paradise are true adaptation for mating success.) We do regret the retention of the same word—adaptation—for both a process and a utility arising by the process, but we bow to entrenched convention here. We then fill the previous gap by coining *exaptation* for useful structures coopted from other contexts—for such structures are fit (*aptus*) not by explicit molding for (*ad*) current use, but as a consequence of (*ex*) properties built for other reasons.

We recognize, of course, that distinction of adaptation from exaptation requires knowledge of historical sequences—and that such evidence is often, probably usually, unavailable. In such cases, we may only know that a structure is currently useful—and we may be unable to identify the source of utility. In such cases, we urge that the neutral term "aptation" (encompassing both ad- and ex-aptation) be used in place of the conventional and falsely inclusive "adaptation." (Vrba and I are delighted that since publication of our revised taxonomy in 1982, this recommendation has been followed by many biologists—see Vermeij, 1987, and Allmon, in press—whatever their feeling about our term "exaptation.")

In the final category of usage, adaptations have functions, but "function" cannot describe the utility of an exaptation. To cite Williams' (1966) amusing but profound example, flying fishes fall back into the water by virtue of gravity, and this descent is essential to their continued existence. But weight, as an inevitable property of matter in Newton's world, is an exaptation for falling back, clearly not an adaptation. In ordinary English usage, we would not call falling back a function of weight. We therefore, following Williams, designate the utility of an exaptation as an "effect" (again choosing vernacular English—falling back is an effect of weight).

One final point on terminology: Evolutionists have always recognized that some currently useful structures must be coopted rather than adapted—if only because cooptation provides the classical solution to the famous "problem of the incipient stages of useful structures." In plain English and concrete form, how can wings evolve for flight if 5% of a wing confers no conceivable aerodynamic benefit? The classical solution argues that wings evolved for something else (thermoregulation, in the most common scenario) and were then coopted.

In standard terminology, the proto-wing is called a "preadaptation" for flight. I doubt that any other evolutionary term has been so widely viewed as misleading and problematical. All teachers introduce "preadaptation" with an apology, disavowing the explicit etymological claim for foreordination, and explaining that the term really does not mean what it plainly says. But we did not decide to coin "exaptation" as a mere etymological nicety. If "preadaptation" had included all that "exaptation" now supplies, we would not have suggested our revision. As its major inadequacy, "preadaptation" covers only one of the two styles of cooptation, and therefore cannot subsume all exaptations. Preadaptations are built for one purpose, and then coopted for another (e.g., wings built for thermoregulation are coopted for flight). But what about the second category?—structures not built as adaptations at all, but later coopted for utilities just as vital (e.g., weight existing by virtue of the physics of matter, is then coopted for falling back into the water). Preadaptation does not cover the large domain of nonaptations later coopted for utility—and "exaptation" is therefore needed to fill a substantial lacuna. I argue in the next section that the concept of coopted nonaptation is the key to a proper evolutionary psychology for the human brain—and exaptation is therefore especially vital in human affairs.

I need hardly mention—for it forms the underlying theme of this paper—that the conceptual incubus of this entire tale is the overreliance on adaptation so characteristic of English evolutionary thought, and the insufficiently critical acceptance of this bias in cognate fields that, however properly, have borrowed evolutionary concepts for their own explanations....

THE HUMAN BRAIN

As the primary point of this paper, I wish to present an argument for regarding the human brain as, *prima facie*, the best available case for predominant exaptation—in other words, for a near

certainty that exaptations must greatly exceed adaptations in number and importance (the proper criterion of relative frequency). Based on this argument, exaptation becomes a crucial concept for an evolutionary psychology. Much of our cultural tradition has been devoted to defining human uniqueness, particularly in terms of brain power and action. We may epitomize the evolutionary version of this massive interdisciplinary effort by stating that the human brain is, *pur excellence*, the chief exemplar of exaptation.

The case can be best developed by recalling a famous episode from the history of evolutionary theory. Charles Darwin drew no boundaries in applying his theory of natural selection to organic nature. He specifically included the human brain—the structure that he had called "the citadel itself" in an early notebook—and he wrote two books (Darwin, 1871, 1872) on the evolution of human bodies, brains, and emotional expressions.

Alfred Russel Wallace, codiscoverer of natural selection, applied the theory (far more rigidly than Darwin, as we shall see) to everything else, but stopped short at the human brain. Our intellect and morality, Wallace argued, could not be the result of natural evolution. Some higher power must have intervened to construct this latest and greatest of evolutionary innovations—natural selection for absolutely everything else; God for the human brain.

Darwin was aghast at his colleague's *volte face* right at the finish line itself. He wrote to Wallace in 1869: "I hope you have not murdered too completely your own and my child" (Marchant, 1916, p. 197). A month later, he added ruefully: "If you had not told me, I should have thought that [your remarks on the brain] had been added by some one else. As you expected, I differ grievously from you, and I am very sorry for it" (Marchant, 1916, p. 199). Wallace, sensitive to the rebuke, thereafter referred to his theory of the human brain as "my special heresy."

The outlines of this tale are well known, but the usual interpretation of Wallace's motives is not only wrong, but backwards. Sources cite Wallace's interest in spiritualism, or simply suggest intellectual cowardice in failing to extend an argument to its most threatening limit. I do not claim to have any insight into Wallace's psyche (where such factors may be relevant), but I can at least report that his explicit logical argument for cerebral uniqueness flowed not from reticence or active theological belief, but (ironically) from a fierce and opposite commitment to the exclusive power of natural selection as an evolutionary agent.

Darwin viewed natural selection as a dominant but not exclusive force. Wallace, ironically, was the hyper-Darwinian of his age. He held that all forms and behaviors, including the most trivial, must be directly built by natural selection for utility. He wrote in 1867 (reprinted in Wallace, 1890):

> No special organ, no characteristic form or marking, no peculiarities of instinct or of habit, no relations between species or between groups of species, can exist but which must now be, or once have been, useful to the individuals or races which possess them.

Wallace would not admit the existence of spandrels [Ed. note: spandrels are coopted nonaptations, or non-adaptation side consequences], or of any nonaptations correlated with features built by natural selection:

> The assertion of "inutility" in the case of any organ is not, and can never be, the statement of a fact, but merely an expression of our ignorance of its purpose or origin.

Paradoxically, this very hyperadaptationism led Wallace to deny that natural selection could have built the human brain—for the following interesting and idiosyncratic reason. Wallace, almost uniquely among 19th-century Western natural scientists, was a genuine nonracist who believed in at least the near intellectual equality of all peoples. Yet he was a cultural chauvinist, who asserted a massive superiority of Western ways over "savage" practices. Consequently, under his hyperadaptationism, an insoluble paradox arises: natural selection can only build for immediate use; savages (surrogates for an-

cestors) have brains as good as ours but do not employ them to nearly their full capacity in devising complex culture. Hence, natural selection did not construct the human brain.

To cite just one example, Wallace argued that the human ability to sing beautifully must have arisen long before any call upon this capacity, and cannot therefore be a product of natural selection. He wrote:

> The habits of savages give no indication of how this faculty could have been developed by natural selection, because it is never required or used by them. The singing of savages is a more or less monotonous howling. . . . This wonderful power . . . only comes into play among civilized people. It seems as if the organ had been prepared in anticipation of the future progress in man, since it contains latent capacities which are useless to him in his earlier condition. (Wallace, 1895, p. 198)

Darwin was dumbfounded, primarily because he did understand the concept of spandrels (and also because he had more appreciation for the complexities of "savage" cultures). Wallace's illogic can be illustrated by the following anachronistic metaphor: If I put a computer in the business office of my small company, its capacities are not limited by the purposes of my installation. My computer, by virtue of its structural complexity and flexibility, maintains latent and unused capacities that must vastly outnumber the explicit reasons for my design or purchase. And the more complex the computing device, the greater the disparity between its field of potential and my explicit purposes (e.g., the calculator attached to my Casio watch may not perform much beyond my needs; but a Cray supercomputer can do more than I could ever even imagine).

Similarly for the evolution of the human brain. For the sake of argument, I will accept the most orthodox of Darwinian positions—that the human brain achieved its enlarged size and capacity by natural selection for some set of purposes in our ancestral state. Large size is therefore an adaptation. Does this mean that everything the enlarged brain can do must be a direct product of the natural selection that built the structure? Wallace certainly thought so, in arguing that "latent capacities" must imply preparation in "anticipation of future progress"—and therefore indicated intelligent design by God. But the principle of exaptation and the concept of spandrels expose Wallace's dilemma as a non-problem. Natural selection built the brain; yet, by virtue of structural complexities so engendered, the same brain can perform a plethora of tasks that may later become central to culture, but that are spandrels rather than targets of the original natural selection— singing Wagner (to cite Wallace's example, though some, even today, regard the *Ring* as monotonous howling), not to mention reading and writing. . . .

THE EXAMPLE OF RELIGION

To choose just one overly broad and oversimplified example, much sociobiological effort has been expended in devising adaptive scenarios for the origin of religion (most center on the importance of tribal order and cohesion). But consider Freud's alternative, an argument based on spandrels. The origin of consciousness in our enlarged brain forced us to deal explicitly with the most frightening of all conceivable facts—the certainty of our personal mortality. To assuage this fear, we devised a great cultural variety of concepts with a central theme of mitigation— from metempsychosis (transmigration of souls), to resurrection of the body, to eternal realms for immaterial souls. These concepts form the core of religion as a cultural institution.

I am not so naive as to imagine that anything so complex and so multifaceted as religion could be fully rendered by either of these monistic propositions, but they do provide alternative approaches to a basis. The recognition of personal mortality is clearly a spandrel of our large brains, for surely no one would seek the adaptive advantage of increased brain size in achievement of this knowledge! If Freud is right, this focal and organizing concept of religion is a spandrel of a brain enlarged for other reasons; and religion did

not arise as an adaptation (whatever its current function, and despite the cogency of a claim that all societies need institutions to promote and maintain group cohesion—for religion need not supply this function).

Go down the list of what you regard as human universals and cultural predictabilities. How many would you putatively assign to adaptation, and therefore view as amenable to sociobiological explanation? Incest avoidance? Such universal gestures as eyebrow flashing? Fine—but how long is your list and how much of our human essence, how much of what really makes culture, will you find? On the other side of the scale place the basis of religion as exaptation; add anything that relies on reading, writing, or any form of mental expression not in the initial repertoire of large-brained populations; add most of the fine and practical arts, the norms of commerce, the practices of war. Exaptation may be historically subsequent to adaptation, and may only coopt the structures and capacities built by adaptation. (But do not be so sure that the brain necessarily became large as an adaptation for more complex conceptualization; other alternatives exist, and consciousness itself may be exaptive.) No matter; the list of exaptations is a mountain to the adaptive molehill. Structural consequences have outstripped original bases. Human uniqueness, human power, human nature itself, lies in the consequences. . . .

FUNDAMENTAL ATTRIBUTES

Those characteristics that we share with other closely related species are most likely to be conventional adaptations. (For example, I accept my colleague Steve Pinker's (1985) argument for the basic mechanics of the visual system, while rejecting his extensions to special properties of human consciousness.) But attributes unique to our species, and constituting the essence of what we call *human* consciousness, are likely to be exaptations by the arguments of the last section.

As an obvious prime candidate, consider the greatest and most contentious of all subjects embodying claims for our uniqueness: human language. The adaptationist and Darwinian tradition has long advocated a gradualistic continuationism—constructing scenarios that language "grew" from gestural and calling systems of other species; trying to teach chimpanzees the rudiments of human linguistic structure, etc. Noam Chomsky, on the other hand, has long advocated a position corresponding to the claim that language is an exaptation of brain structure. (Chomsky, who has rarely written anything about evolution, has not so framed his theory, but he does accept my argument as a proper translation of his views into the language of my field—Chomsky, personal communications.) Many adaptationists have so misunderstood Chomsky that they actually suspect him of being an odd sort of closet creationist. For them, evolution means adaptive continuity, and they just cannot grasp the alternative of exaptive seizure of latent capacity that is present for other reasons.

The spectacular collapse of the chimp language experiments, and their exposure as some combination of wishful thinking and the Clever Hans effect, have made Chomsky's alternative all the more plausible. Cross-species continuity must exist, of course, in the growth of conceptual powers, but why should our idiosyncratic capacity for embodying much of this richness in the unique and highly peculiar mental structure called language be seen as an expression of this continuity? The traits that Chomsky (1986) attributes to language—universality of the generative grammar, lack of ontogeny (for language "grows" more like a programmed organ than like memorizing the kings of England), highly peculiar and decidedly nonoptimal structure, formal analogy to other attributes, including our unique numerical faculty with its concept of discrete infinity—fit far more easily with an exaptive, rather than an adaptive, explanation. The brain, in becoming large for whatever adaptive reasons, acquired a plethora of cooptable fea-

tures. Why shouldn't the capacity for language be among them? Why not seize this possibility as something discrete at some later point in evolution, grafting upon it a range of conceptual capacities that achieve different expression in other species (and in our ancestry)?

EVOLUTIONARY SCENARIOS

Consider everyone's favorite game in evolutionary reconstruction—the spinning of behavioral and ecological scenarios for human origins. We usually consider these efforts as exercises in adaptationism. But, given the cardinal property of adaptation as usually limiting and restricting, and given the need to posit structures that permit flexibility and opportunity in conceptualizing human origins, these scenarios almost always make a claim for *exaptation* at crucial junctions (not, perhaps, in the radical mode of spandrels, but at least in the more conventional style of quirky functional shifts from an original reason to a very different consequence).

As just one example, recently subject to much discussion and debate, consider Falk's (1990) "radiator theory" (so close to Aristotle's old idea that the brain cools the blood). In her theory, gracile (slender) and robust (heavy-boned) australopithecines evolved different adaptations for adequate cranial blood flow in bipedal creatures—robusts via a greatly enlarged occipital/marginal sinus system, graciles via a widespread network of veins becoming more elaborate with time. This network system, an efficient cooling device, may have arisen as an adaptive response to the more intense solar radiation of savanna habitats favored by graciles. But this "radiator" then released a thermal constraint on brain size—allowing a larger brain to cool adequately. The graciles could evolve into the large brained *Homo* lineage; the robusts were stuck. Thus, the radiator system, arising as an ecological adaptation in initially small-brained graciles, became an exaptation for cooling the enlarged brain of their descendants.

If Falk is right, we would not be here today but for this crucial exaptation.

CURRENT UTILITY

If you doubt all the other arguments for exaptation, just make a list of the most important current uses of consciousness. Start with reading, writing, and arithmetic. How many can even be plausibly rendered as adaptations?

Even so committed a hereditarian (and adaptationist) as Bouchard (of the Minnesota twin study) has seen the point, at least for the variability underlying human cognitive differences. Bouchard et al. (1990) write:

> Whatever the ancient origins and functions of genetic variability, its repercussions in contemporary society are pervasive and important. A human species whose members did not vary genetically with respect to significant cognitive and motivational attributes . . . would have created a very different society than the one we know. (p. 228)

They even recognize that most of this variability, in ancestral contexts, might have been "evolutionary debris, unimportant to fitness and perhaps not expressed in prehistoric environments" (p. 228). Bravo, for this is a radical exaptive hypothesis with a vengeance (and almost surely correct)—describing a trait now vital to our social constitution, but so nonaptive at its origin that it achieved no phenotypic expression.

Yet just as these erstwhile adaptationists see the light, they retrogress with a knee-jerk assertion of the orthodox position that they denied in their primary specific interpretation!

> Evolutionary psychologists or sociobiologists attempt to delineate species-typical proclivities or instincts and to understand the relevant evolutionary developments that took place in the Pleistocene epoch and were adaptive in the lives of tribal hunter-gatherers. The genes sing a prehistoric song that today should sometimes be resisted but which it would be foolish to ignore. (1990, p. 228)

And yet, the authors just told us that these particular genes probably were not singing at all back then, despite their crucial role in framing human society today. I interpret this inconsistency as a lovely example of working through the logic of a specific argument correctly (the claim for exaptation of a spandrel), but then missing the implication and spouting a contradictory orthodoxy. Clearly, we need to make the notion of exaptation explicit and available.

An evolutionary psychology properly grounded in the centrality of exaptation would be a very different, and less threatening, construct (for those feeling the breath of biological imperialism) than the conventional Darwinian account of continuity in adaptation, with its implications of gradualism, predictability, and simple transfer from overt cultural expression to underlying biological basis. Exaptation, with its quirky and unpredictable functional shifts (e.g., thermoregulation to flight) and its recruitment of nonadaptive, even invisible structures (e.g., repeated copies of genes providing for future flexibility; the "debris" of unexpressed genetic variability leading to later cultural diversity), produces a cultural history with unanticipated changes in direction, potentially abrupt transitions, and no simply derived status of cultural expressions (for the path from biological substrate to overt manifestation passes through the switches of exaptive shift). The concept of exaptation honors the contingency of history, the unpredictable discontinuity of change in complex systems, and the plurality of legitimate sources of insight from biological substrate through quirky shift to social expression. We can therefore recall Haldane's dictum that "the universe is not only queerer than we suppose, but queerer than we *can* suppose." And lest we be tempted to read this (as Haldane most surely did not) as nihilism or pessimism (rather than as joy for being in such a fascinating place), we should also remember Einstein's equally famous remark that the Lord God is subtle, but not malicious (*Raffiniert ist der Herr Gott, aber boshaft ist er nicht*).

REFERENCES

Bouchard, T. J., Lykken, D. T., McGue, M., Segal, N. L., Jr., & Tellegen, A. (1990). Sources of human psychological differences: The Minnesota study of twins reared apart. *Science, 250,* 223–228.

Darwin, C. (1859). *On the origin of species.* London: John Murray.

Darwin, C. (1871). *The descent of man and selection in relation to sex.* London: John Murray.

Darwin, C. (1872). *On the expression of the emotions in man and animals.* London: John Murray.

Gould, S. J. (1980). *The panda's thumb.* New York: Norton.

Gould, S. J. (1989). A developmental constraint in *Cerion,* with comments on the definition and interpretation of constraint in evolution. *Evolution, 43,* 516–539.

Gould, S. J., & Vrba, E. S. (1982). Exaptation—a mission term in the science of form. *Paleobiology, 8,* 4–15.

Lewin, R. (1982). Adaptation can be a problem for evolutionists. *Science, 216,* 212–213.

Vrba, E. S., & Gould, S. J. (1986). The hierarchical expansion of sorting and selection: Sorting and selection cannot be equated. *Paleobiology, 12,* 217–228.

KEY POINTS

1. Evolutionary theory has lacked a term for a crucial concept—a feature, now useful to an organism, that did not arise as an adaptation for its present role, but was later co-opted for its current function. An "exaptation" (a term coined by Gould) is a feature used for something other than its original application.

2. Exaptation differs from adaptation. Adaptations are features that were refined through natural selection for their current role. Exaptations are features that enhance current fitness but did not evolve for their current role by natural selection. Adaptations have functions: A feature is used for the purpose for which it was selected. Exaptations have effects, not functions: A feature can serve a purpose other than the specific function for which it was selected.

3. The human brain is the chief exemplar of the importance of exaptations. Because our ancestors had brains as big as ours but did not use them to their full capacity in devising a complex culture, many higher level functions cannot be adaptations. Many higher level thinking processes such as those involved in religion, reading, writing, language, fine arts, forms of commerce, and practices of war are all probably exaptations.

QUESTIONS TO THINK ABOUT

1. How do exaptations differ from adaptations?

2. Why can delayed ossification of the human skull be considered an exaptation? Why is the human brain an ideal example of exaptation?

3. What are the dangers of seeing culture-based practices such as the dominance of men (rather than women) in political office as due to the natural way of the world?

15

Conditioned Emotional Reactions*

JOHN B. WATSON AND ROSALIE RAYNER

John B. Watson (1878–1958) was a dominant figure in establishing a key learning approach in psychology called *behaviorism*. Behaviorism emphasizes the study of observable behavior rather than internal thoughts or traits. The environment is key to understanding a person.

A professor at Johns Hopkins University from 1908 to 1919, Watson's basic theories about studying observable behavior were proclaimed in his 1914 book, *Behavior*. Additionally, in 1919, he wrote *Psychology from the Standpoint of a Behaviorist*, which condemned introspectionists and psychoanalysts. Watson's basic perspective on personality was that personality is a function of the environment in which a child is raised; that is, personality is conditioned (learned). In the following selection, Watson and his assistant Rosalie Rayner (1899–1936) show that emotional problems can be conditioned (learned) and, thus, are not necessarily due to any internal conflicts or neuroses.

In recent literature various speculations have been entered into concerning the possibility of conditioning various types of emotional response, but direct experimental evidence in support of such a view has been lacking. If the theory advanced by Watson and Morgan to the effect that in infancy the original emotional reaction patterns are few, consisting so far as observed of fear, rage and love, then there must be some simple method by means of which the range of stimuli which can call out these emotions and their compounds is greatly increased. Otherwise, complexity in adult response could not be accounted for. These authors without adequate experimental evidence advanced the view that this range was increased by means of conditioned reflex factors. It was suggested there that the early home life of the child furnishes a laboratory situation for establishing conditioned emotional responses. The present authors have recently put the whole matter to an experimental test.

Experimental work has been done so far on only one child, Albert B. This infant was reared almost from birth in a hospital environment; his mother was a wet nurse in the Harriet Lane Home for Invalid Children. Albert's life was normal: he was healthy from birth and one of the best developed youngsters ever brought to the hospital, weighing twenty-one pounds at nine months of age. He was on the whole stolid and unemotional. His stability was one of the principal reasons for using him as a subject in this test. We felt that we could do him relatively little harm by carrying out such experiments as those outlined below.

At approximately nine months of age we ran him through the emotional tests that have become a part of our regular routine in determining whether fear reactions can be called out by other stimuli than sharp noises and the sudden removal of support. Tests of this type have been described by the senior author in another place.

*Watson, J. B., & Rayner, R. (1920). Conditioned emotional reactions. *Journal of Experimental Psychology, 3*, 1–14.

In brief, the infant was confronted suddenly and for the first time successively with a white rat, a rabbit, a dog, a monkey, with masks with and without hair, cotton wool, burning newspapers, etc. A permanent record of Albert's reactions to these objects and situations has been preserved in a motion picture study. Manipulation was the most usual reaction called out. *At no time did this infant ever show fear in any situation.* These experimental records were confirmed by the casual observations of the mother and hospital attendants. No one had ever seen him in a state of fear and rage. The infant practically never cried.

Up to approximately nine months of age we had not tested him with loud sounds. The test to determine whether a fear reaction could be called out by a loud sound was made when he was eight months, twenty-six days of age. The sound was that made by striking a hammer upon a suspended steel bar four feet in length and three-fourths of an inch in diameter. The laboratory notes are as follows:

> One of the two experimenters caused the child to turn its head and fixate her moving hand; the other, stationed back of the child, struck the steel bar a sharp blow. The child started violently, his breathing was checked and the arms were raised in a characteristic manner. On the second stimulation the same thing occurred, and in addition the lips began to pucker and tremble. On the third stimulation the child broke into a sudden crying fit. This is the first time an emotional situation in the laboratory has produced any fear or even crying in Albert.

We had expected just these results on account of our work with other infants brought up under similar conditions. It is worth while to call attention to the fact that removal of support (dropping and jerking the blanket upon which the infant was lying) was tried exhaustively upon this infant on the same occasion. It was not effective in producing the fear response. This stimulus is effective in younger children. At what age such stimuli lose their potency in producing fear is not known. Nor is it known whether less placid children ever lose their fear of them. This probably depends upon the training the child gets. It is well known that children eagerly run to be tossed into the air and caught. On the other hand it is equally well known that in the adult fear responses are called out quite clearly by the sudden removal of support, if the individual is walking across a bridge, walking out upon a beam, etc. There is a wide field of study here which is aside from our present point.

The sound stimulus, thus, at nine months of age, gives us the means of testing several important factors. I. Can we condition fear of an animal, *e.g.*, a white rat, by visually presenting it and simultaneously striking a steel bar? II. If such a conditioned emotional response can be established, will there be a transfer to other animals or other objects? III. What is the effect of time upon such conditioned emotional responses? IV. If after a reasonable period such emotional responses have not died out, what laboratory methods can be devised for their removal?

I. The establishment of conditioned emotional responses. At first there was considerable hesitation upon our part in making the attempt to set up fear reactions experimentally. A certain responsibility attaches to such a procedure. We decided finally to make the attempt, comforting ourselves by the reflection that such attachments would arise anyway as soon as the child left the sheltered environment of the nursery for the rough and tumble of the home. We did not begin this work until Albert was eleven months, three days of age. Before attempting to set up a conditioned response we, as before, put him through all of the regular emotional tests. *Not the slightest sign of a fear response was obtained in any situation.*

The steps taken to condition emotional responses are shown in our laboratory notes.

11 Months 3 Days

1. White rat suddenly taken from the basket and presented to Albert. He began to reach for rat with left hand. Just as his hand touched the animal the bar was struck immediately behind his head. The infant jumped violently and fell forward, burying his face in the mattress. He did not cry, however.

2. Just as the right hand touched the rat the bar was again struck. Again the infant jumped violently, fell forward and began to whimper.

In order not to disturb the child too seriously no further tests were given for one week.

11 Months 10 Days

1. Rat presented suddenly without sound. There was steady fixation but no tendency at first to reach for it. The rat was then placed nearer, whereupon tentative reaching movements began with the right hand. When the rat nosed the infant's left hand, the hand was immediately withdrawn. He started to reach for the head of the animal with the forefinger of the left hand, but withdrew it suddenly before contact. It is thus seen that the two joint stimulations given the previous week were not without effect. He was tested with his blocks immediately afterwards to see if they shared in the process of conditioning. He began immediately to pick them up, dropping them, pounding them, etc. In the remainder of the tests the blocks were given frequently to quiet him and to test his general emotional state. They were always removed from sight when the process of conditioning was under way.

2. Joint stimulation with rat and sound. Started, then fell over immediately to right side. No crying.

3. Joint stimulation. Fell to right side and rested upon hands, with head turned away from rat. No crying.

4. Joint stimulation. Same reaction.

5. Rat suddenly presented alone. Puckered face, whimpered and withdrew body sharply to the left.

6. Joint stimulation. Fell over immediately to right side and began to whimper.

7. Joint stimulation. Started violently and cried, but did not fall over.

8. Rat alone. *The instant the rat was shown the baby began to cry. Almost instantly he turned sharply to the left, fell over on left side, raised himself on all fours and began to crawl away so rapidly that he was caught with difficulty before reaching the edge of the table.*

This was as convincing a case of a completely conditioned fear response as could have been theoretically pictured. In all seven joint stimulations were given to bring about the complete reaction. It is not unlikely had the sound been of greater intensity or of a more complex clang character that the number of joint stimulations might have been materially reduced. Experiments designed to define the nature of the sounds that will serve best as emotional stimuli are under way.

II. When a conditioned emotional response has been established for one object, is there a transfer? Five days later Albert was again brought back into the laboratory and tested as follows:

11 Months 15 Days

1. Tested first with blocks. He reached readily for them, playing with them as usual. This shows that there has been no general transfer to the room, table, blocks, etc.

2. Rat alone. Whimpered immediately, withdrew right hand and turned head and trunk away.

3. Blocks again offered. Played readily with them, smiling and gurgling.

4. Rat alone. Leaned over to the left side as far away from the rat as possible, then fell over, getting up on all fours and scurrying away as rapidly as possible.

5. Blocks again offered. Reached immediately for them, smiling and laughing as before.

The above preliminary test shows that the conditioned response to the rat had carried over completely for the five days in which no tests were given. The question as to whether or not there is a transfer was next taken up.

6. Rabbit alone. The rabbit was suddenly placed on the mattress in front of him. The reaction was pronounced. Negative responses began at once. He leaned as far away from the animal as possible, whimpered, then burst into tears. When the rabbit was placed in contact with him he buried his face in the mattress, then got up on all fours and crawled away, crying as he went. This was a most convincing test.

7. The blocks were next given him, after an interval. He played with them as before. It was observed by four people that he played far more energetically with them than ever before. The blocks were raised high over his head and slammed down with a great deal of force.

8. Dog alone. The dog did not produce as violent a reaction as the rabbit. The moment fixation occurred the child shrank back and as the animal came nearer he attempted to get on all fours but did not cry at first. As soon as the dog passed out of his range of vision he became quiet. The dog was then made to approach the infant's head (he was lying down at the moment). Albert straightened up immediately, fell over to the opposite side and turned his head away. He then began to cry.

9. The blocks were again presented. He began immediately to play with them.

10. Fur coat (seal). Withdrew immediately to the left side and began to fret. Coat put close to him on the left side, he turned immediately, began to cry and tried to crawl away on all fours.

11. Cotton wool. The wool was presented in a paper package. At the end the cotton was not covered by the paper. It was placed first on his feet. He kicked it away but did not touch it with his hands. When his hand was laid on the wool he immediately withdrew it but did not show the shock that the animals or fur coat produced in him. He then began to play with the paper, avoiding contact with the wool itself. He finally, under the impulse of the manipulative instinct, lost some of his negativism to the wool.

12. Just in play W. put his head down to see if Albert would play with his hair. Albert was completely negative. Two other observers did the same thing. He began immediately to play with their hair. W. then brought the Santa Claus mask and presented it to Albert. He was again pronouncedly negative.

11 Months 20 Days

1. Blocks alone. Played with them as usual.

2. Rat alone. Withdrawal of the whole body, bending over to left side, no crying. Fixation and following with eyes. The response was much less marked than on first presentation the previous week. It was thought best to freshen up the reaction by another joint stimulation.

3. Just as the rat was placed on his hand the rod was struck. Reaction violent.

4. Rat alone. Fell over at once to left side. Reaction practically as strong as on former occasion but no crying.

5. Rat alone. Fell over to left side, got up on all fours and started to crawl away. On this occasion there was no crying, but strange to say, as he started away he began to gurgle and coo, even while leaning far over to the left side to avoid the rat.

6. Rabbit alone. Leaned over to left side as far as possible. Did not fall over. Began to whimper but reaction not so violent as on former occasions.

7. Blocks again offered. He reached for them immediately and began to play.

All of the tests so far discussed were carried out upon a table supplied with a mattress, located in a small, well-lighted dark-room. We wished to test next whether conditioned fear responses so set up would appear if the situation were markedly altered. We thought it best before making this test to freshen the reaction both to the rabbit and to the dog by showing them at the moment the steel bar was struck. It will be recalled that this was the first time any effort had been made to directly condition response to the dog and rabbit. The experimental notes are as follows:

8. The rabbit at first was given alone. The reaction was exactly as given in test (6) above. When the rabbit was left on Albert's knees for a long time he began tentatively to reach out and manipulate its fur with forefingers. While doing this the steel rod was struck. A violent fear reaction resulted.

9. Rabbit alone. Reaction wholly similar to that on trial (6) above.

10. Rabbit alone. Started immediately to whimper, holding hands far up, but did not cry. Conflicting tendency to manipulate very evident.

11. Dog alone. Began to whimper, shaking head from side to side, holding hands as far away from the animal as possible.

12. Dog and sound. The rod was struck just as the animal touched him. A violent negative reaction appeared. He began to whimper, turned to one side, fell over and started to get up on all fours.

13. Blocks. Played with them immediately and readily.

On this same day and immediately after the above experiment Albert was taken into the large well-lighted lecture room belonging to the laboratory. He was placed on a table in the center of the room immediately under the skylight. Four people were present. The situation was thus very different from that which obtained in the small dark room.

1. Rat alone. No sudden fear reaction appeared at first. The hands, however, were held up and away from the animal. No positive manipulatory reactions appeared.

2. Rabbit alone. Fear reaction slight. Turned to left and kept face away from the animal but the reaction was never pronounced.

3. Dog alone. Turned away but did not fall over. Cried. Hands moved as far away from the animal as possible. Whimpered as long as the dog was present.

4. Rat alone. Slight negative reaction.

5. Rat and sound. It was thought best to freshen the reaction to the rat. The sound was given just as the rat was presented. Albert jumped violently but did not cry.

6. Rat alone. At first he did not show any negative reaction. When rat was placed nearer he began to show negative reaction by drawing back his body, raising his hands, whimpering, etc.

7. Blocks. Played with them immediately.

8. Rat alone. Pronounced withdrawal of body and whimpering.

9. Blocks. Played with them as before.

10. Rabbit alone. Pronounced reaction. Whimpered with arms held high, fell over backward and had to be caught.

11. Dog alone. At first the dog did not produce the pronounced reaction. The hands were held high over the head, breathing was checked, but there was no crying. Just at this moment the dog, which had not barked before, barked three times loudly when only about six inches from the baby's face. Albert immediately fell over and broke into a wail that continued until the dog was removed. The sudden barking of the hitherto quiet dog produced a marked fear response in the adult observers!

From the above results it would seem that emotional transfers do take place. Furthermore it would seem that the number of transfers resulting from an experimentally produced conditioned emotional reaction may be very large. In our observations we had no means of testing the complete number of transfers which may have resulted.

III. The effect of time upon conditioned emotional responses. We have already shown that the conditioned emotional response will continue for a period of one week. It was desired to make the time test longer. In view of the imminence of Albert's departure from the hospital we could not make the interval longer than one month. Accordingly no further emotional experimentation was entered into for thirty-one days after the above test. During the month, however, Albert was brought weekly to the laboratory for tests upon right and left-handedness, imitation, general development, etc. No emotional tests whatever were given and during the whole month his regular nursery routine was maintained in the Harriet Lane Home. The notes on the test given at the end of this period are as follows:

1 Year 21 Days

1. Santa Claus mask. Withdrawal, gurgling, then slapped at it without touching. When his hand was forced to touch it, he whimpered and cried. His hand was forced to touch it two more

times. He whimpered and cried on both tests. He finally cried at the mere visual stimulus of the mask.

2. Fur coat. Wrinkled his nose and withdrew both hands, drew back his whole body and began to whimper as the coat was put nearer. Again there was the strife between withdrawal and the tendency to manipulate. Reached tentatively with left hand but drew back before contact had been made. In moving his body to one side his hand accidentally touched the coat. He began to cry at once, nodding his head in a very peculiar manner (this reaction was an entirely new one). Both hands were withdrawn as far as possible from the coat. The coat was then laid on his lap and he continued nodding his head and whimpering, withdrawing his body as far as possible, pushing the while at the coat with his feet but never touching it with his hands.

3. Fur coat. The coat was taken out of his sight and presented again at the end of a minute. He began immediately to fret, withdrawing his body and nodding his head as before.

4. Blocks. He began to play with them as usual.

5. The rat. He allowed the rat to crawl towards him without withdrawing. He sat very still and fixated it intently. Rat then touched his hand. Albert withdrew it immediately, then leaned back as far as possible but did not cry. When the rat was placed on his arm he withdrew his body and began to fret, nodding his head. The rat was then allowed to crawl against his chest. He first began to fret and then covered his eyes with both hands.

6. Blocks. Reaction normal.

7. The rabbit. The animal was placed directly in front of him. It was very quiet. Albert showed no avoiding reactions at first. After a few seconds he puckered up his face, began to nod his head and to look intently at the experimenter. He next began to push the rabbit away with his feet, withdrawing his body at the same time. Then as the rabbit came nearer he began pulling his feet away, nodding his head, and wailing "da da." After about a minute he reached out tentatively and slowly and touched the rabbit's ear with his right hand, finally manipulating it. The rabbit was again placed in his lap. Again he began to fret and withdrew his hands. He reached out tentatively with his left hand and touched the animal, shuddered and withdrew the whole body. The experimenter then took hold of his left hand and laid it on the rabbit's back. Albert immediately withdrew his hand and began to suck his thumb. Again the rabbit was laid in his lap. He began to cry, covering his face with both hands.

8. Dog. The dog was very active. Albert fixated it intensely for a few seconds, sitting very still. He began to cry but did not fall over backwards as on his last contact with the dog. When the dog was pushed closer to him he at first sat motionless, then began to cry, putting both hands over his face.

These experiments would seem to show conclusively that directly conditioned emotional responses as well as those conditioned by transfer persist, although with a certain loss in the intensity of the reaction, for a longer period than one month. Our view is that they persist and modify personality throughout life. It should be recalled again that Albert was of an extremely phlegmatic type. Had he been emotionally unstable probably both the directly conditioned response and those transferred would have persisted throughout the month unchanged in form.

IV. "Detachment" or removal of conditioned emotional responses. Unfortunately Albert was taken from the hospital the day the above tests were made. Hence the opportunity of building up an experimental technique by means of which we could remove the conditioned emotional responses was denied us. Our own view, expressed above, which is possibly not very well grounded, is that these responses in the home environment are likely to persist indefinitely, unless an accidental method for removing them is hit upon. The importance of establishing some method must be apparent to all. Had the opportunity been at hand we should have tried out several methods, some of which we may mention. (1) Constantly confronting the child with those stimuli which called out the responses in the hopes that habituation would come in corresponding to " fatigue" of reflex when differential reactions are to be set up. (2) By trying to "recondition" by showing objects calling out fear responses (visual) and simultaneously stimulating the erogenous zones (tactual). We should try first the lips, then the nipples and as a final resort the sex organs. (3) By trying to "recondition" by feeding the subject candy or other food just as the animal is shown. This method calls for the food control of the subject. (4) By building up "constructive" activities around the object by imitation and by putting the hand through the motions of manipulation. At this age imitation of overt motor activity is strong, as our present but unpublished experimentation has shown.

INCIDENTAL OBSERVATIONS

(a) Thumb sucking as a compensator device for blocking fear and noxious stimuli. During the course of these experiments, especially in the final test, it was noticed that whenever Albert was on the verge of tears or emotionally upset generally he would continually thrust his thumb into his mouth. The moment the hand reached the mouth he became impervious to the stimuli producing fear. Again and again while the motion pictures were being made at the end of the thirty-day rest period, we had to remove the thumb from his mouth before the conditioned response could be obtained. This method of blocking noxious and emotional stimuli (fear and rage) through erogenous stimulation seems to persist from birth onward. Very often in our experiments upon the work adders with infants under ten days of age the same reaction appeared. When at work upon the adders both of the infants arms are under slight restraint. Often rage appears. They begin to cry, thrashing their arms and legs about. If the finger gets into the mouth crying ceases at once. The organism thus apparently from birth, when under the influence of love stimuli is blocked to all others.[1] This resort to sex stimulation when under the influence of noxious and emotional situations, or when the individual is restless and idle, persists through-

out adolescent and adult life. Albert, at any rate, did not resort to thumb sucking except in the presence of such stimuli. Thumb sucking could immediately be checked by offering him his blocks. These invariably called out active manipulation instincts. It is worth while here to call attention to the fact that Freud's conception of the stimulation of erogenous zones as being the expression of an original "pleasure" seeking principle may be turned about and possibly better described as a compensatory (and often conditioned) device for the blockage of noxious and fear and rage producing stimuli.

(b) Equal primacy of fear, love and possibly rage. While in general the results of our experiment offer no particular points of conflict with Freudian concepts, one fact out of harmony with them should be emphasized. According to proper Freudians sex (or in our terminology, love) is the principal emotion in which conditioned responses arise which later limit and distort personality. We wish to take sharp issue with this view on the basis of the experimental evidence we have gathered. Fear is as primal a factor as love in influencing personality. Fear does not gather its potency in any derived manner from love. It belongs to the original and inherited nature of man. Probably the same may be true of rage although at present we are not so sure of this.

The Freudians twenty years from now, unless their hypotheses change, when they come to analyze Albert's fear of a seal skin coat—assuming that he comes to analysis at that age—will probably tease from him the recital of a dream which upon their analysis will show that Albert at three years of age attempted to play with the pubic hair of the mother and was scolded violently for it. (We are by no means denying that this might in some other case condition it). If the analyst has sufficiently prepared Albert to accept such a dream when found as an explanation of his avoiding tendencies, and if the analyst has the authority and personality to put it over, Albert may be fully convinced that the dream was a true revealer of the factors which brought about the fear.

It is probable that many of the phobias in psychopathology are true conditioned emotional reactions either of the direct or the transferred type. One may possibly have to believe that such persistence of early conditioned responses will be found only in persons who are constitutionally inferior. Our argument is meant to be constructive. Emotional disturbances in adults cannot be traced back to sex alone. They must be retraced along at least three collateral lines—to conditioned and transferred responses set up in infancy and early youth in all three of the fundamental human emotions.

ENDNOTE

1. The stimulus to love in infants according to our view is stroking of the skin, lips, nipples and sex organs, patting and rocking, picking up, etc. Patting and rocking (when not conditioned) are probably equivalent to actual stimulation of the sex organs. In adults of course, as every lover knows, vision, audition and olfaction soon become conditioned by joint stimulation with contact and kinaesthetic stimuli.

REFERENCES

Watson, J. B. (1919). *Psychology, from the standpoint of a behaviorist.* Philadelphia and London: J. B. Lippincott.

Watson, J. B., and Morgan, J. J. (1917). Emotional reactions and psychological experimentation. *American Journal of Psychology, 28,* 163–174.

KEY POINTS

1. A few basic reaction patterns are observed in infants (fear, rage, and love). The range of stimuli which evoke these reactions can be increased through *conditioned* emotional responses, and the early home life of a child is a stable setting for doing so.

2. Experimental work was done on a child named Albert. He was unemotional as an infant and never showed much fear in any situation before experimental work was done. At nine months of age, a loud sound evoked a fear reaction in Albert. The loud sound (unconditioned stimulus) gave the experimenters a way of testing fear conditioning. Fear of a rat was conditioned by repeatedly showing the rat and making the sound.

3. After several rounds of conditioning, fear was produced in Albert by merely seeing the rat. There was then transfer (generalization) of this fear of the rat to fear of a rabbit, dog, fur coat, and other objects resembling the texture of the rat. However, there was no transfer of fear to objects such as blocks or a table. Emotional disturbances in adults can be traced back to conditioned responses established in infancy and early youth.

QUESTIONS TO THINK ABOUT

1. What are conditioned emotional responses? How can they be established?

2. Why was the fear response to the rat by Albert B. transferred to the dog and the rabbit, but not to the blocks or the table?

3. What do these tests on Albert imply about human emotional disturbances in adults? To what might adult emotional disturbances be attributed?

4. How does Watson's explanation of emotional disturbance differ from Freud's? What are the implications for therapy (treatment)?

16

Intellectual Self-Management in Old Age*

B. F. SKINNER

B. F. Skinner was by no means a personality psychologist; indeed, he thought the term *personality* to be meaningless. Notions of internal, nonobservable psychological characteristics were an anathema to him. Rather, Skinner theorized, personality can be located in the environment; the responses that have been rewarded are the ones that are most likely to appear again. For example, to Skinner, a neurotic is someone who has been reinforced for overly emotional behavior.

Skinner (1904–1990) worked for many years at Harvard University, constantly criticizing the idea of internal states and generally being a thorn in the side of traditional personality theorists. Studying rats and pigeons, Skinner deduced laws about the most effective schedules of reinforcement. In this selection, Skinner shows how one can deal with old age by focusing on changing the external environment, rather than worrying about internal biological deterioration.

A quarter of a century ago I presented a paper at the Eastern Psychological Association meeting called "A Case History in Scientific Method." In it I pointed out that my life as a behavioral scientist did not seem to conform to the picture usually painted by statisticians and scientific methodologists. The present article is also a case history but in a very different field. I have heard it said that G. Stanley Hall, one of our founding fathers, wrote a book on each of the stages of his life as he passed through it. I did not have the foresight to begin early enough to do that, but I can still talk about the last stage, and so I now present myself to you behaving verbally in old age as I once presented those pigeons playing Ping-Pong.

Developmentalism is a branch of structuralism in which the form or topography of behavior is studied as a function of time. At issue is how behavior changes as one grows older. *Aging* should be the right word for this process, but it does not mean developing. In accepted usage, *to develop* is not simply to grow older but to unfold a latent structure, to realize an inner potential, to become more effective. *Aging,* on the other hand, usually means growing less effective. For Shakespeare the "ages of man" ranged from the infant mewling and puking, to the schoolboy "creeping like snail unwillingly to school," to lovers sighing and soldiers seeking the bubble reputation, to the justice full of wise saws and modern instances, to a stage in which the "big manly voice . . . pipes and whistles in his sound" and then at last to second childishness and mere oblivion—"sans teeth, sans eyes, sans taste," and in the end, of course, "sans everything." The aged are old people. Aging is growing not merely older but old.

In developmentalism the horticultural metaphor is strong. There are stages of *growth*, and

*Skinner, B. F. (1983). Intellectual self-management in old age. *American Psychologist, 38,* 239–244.

maturity is hailed as a desirable state of completion. But the metaphor then becomes less attractive, for there is a point at which we are glad to stop developing. Beyond maturity lie decay and rot. Fortunately, the developmental account is incomplete, and what is missing is particularly important if we want to do anything about aging. There is no doubt an inexorable biological process, a continuation of the growth of the embryo, which can be hindered or helped but not stopped. In speaking of the development of an *organism*, growth is no metaphor, but *persons* develop in a different way and for different reasons, many of which are not inexorable. Much of what seems to be the unfolding of an inner potential is the product of an unfolding environment; a person's *world* develops. The aging of a person, as distinct from the aging of an organism, depends upon changes in the physical and social environments. We recognize the difference when we say that some young people are old for their years or when, as Shakespeare put it, old people return to childishness. Fortunately, the course of a developing environment can be changed. That kind of aging can be retarded.

If the stages in our lives were due merely to the passage of time, we should have to find a fountain of youth to reverse the direction of change, but if many of the problems of old people are due to shortcomings in their environments, the environments can be improved.

Organism and person do not, of course, develop independently; the biological changes interact with the environmental contingencies. As the senses grow dull, the stimulating environment becomes less clear. As muscles grow slower and weaker, fewer things can be done successfully. Changes in sensory and motor capacities are conspicuous in games and other forms of competition, and athletes retire young just because of aging.

Many remedial steps are, of course, well-known. Eyeglasses compensate for poor vision and hearing aids for poor hearing. These are conspicuous prosthetic devices, but what is needed is a *prosthetic environment* in which, in spite of reduced biological capacities, behavior will be relatively free of aversive consequences and abundantly reinforced. New repertoires may be needed as well as new sources of stimulation. If you cannot read, listen to book recordings. If you do not hear well, turn up the volume on your phonograph (and wear headphones to protect your neighbors). Foods can be flavored for aging palates. Paul Tillich, the theologian, defended pornography on the ground that it extended sexuality into old age. And there is always the possibility, secondhand though it may be, of living the highly reinforcing lives of others through literature, spectator sports, the theater and movies, and television.

There is nothing particularly new in all this, but there is a special problem to which little attention has, I think, been given. One of the inexorable effects of biological aging is particularly important for those engaged in intellectual work—in writing, inventing, composing, painting, having ideas—in a word, thinking. It is characteristic of old people not to think clearly, coherently, logically, or, in particular, creatively. In physiological terms we should have to say that deterioration occurs not only in sense organs and effectors but in central processes. The changes are certainly central if we are talking about the nervous system, but changes in behavior are changes in the body as a whole.

Forgetting is a classical problem. It is most conspicuous in forgetting names because names have so little going for them by way of context. I have convinced myself that names are very seldom wholly forgotten. When I have time—and I mean something on the order of half an hour—I can almost always recall a name if I have already recalled the occasion for using it. I work with thematic and formal prompts, in the latter case going through the alphabet, testing for the initial letter. But that will not work in introducing your wife to someone whose name you have forgotten. My wife and I use the following strategy: If there is any conceivable chance that she could have met the person, I simply say to her, "Of course, you remember . . . ?" and she grasps the outstretched hand and says, "Yes, of course. How are you?" The acquaintance may not remember meeting my wife, but is not sure of his or her memory, either.

The failure to produce a name at the right moment, as in making an introduction, can be especially punishing, and the punishment is part of the problem. Stutterers are all the more likely to stutter because they have failed to speak fluently in the past, and an emotional state called "anxiety" has been conditioned. Similarly, we may fail to recall a name when making an introduction in part because of past failings. We are, as we say, afraid we are going to forget. Some help may come from making such situations as free from aversive consequences as possible. Graceful ways of explaining your failure may help. Appeal to your age. Flatter your listener by saying that you have noticed that the more important the person, the easier it is to forget the name. Recall the amusing story about forgetting your own name when you were asked for it by a clerk. If you are skillful at that sort of thing, forgetting may even be a pleasure. Unfortunately, there is no similar strategy when you are suffering from a diminished access to verbal behavior while writing a paper. Nevertheless, a calm acceptance of deficiencies and a more careful observance of good intellectual self-management may have a comparable effect.

The problem is raised by the way in which we make use of past experience, the effects of which seem to fade too quickly. A special set of techniques is needed for its solution. Practical examples may be helpful before turning to comparable intellectual behavior.

Ten minutes before you leave your house for the day you hear a weather report: It will probably rain before you return. It occurs to you to take an umbrella (the sentence means quite literally what it says: The behavior of taking an umbrella occurs to you), but you are not yet able to execute it. Ten minutes later you leave without the umbrella. You can solve that kind of problem by executing as much of the behavior as possible when it occurs to you. Hang the umbrella on the doorknob, or put it through the handle of your briefcase, or in some other way start the process of taking it with you.

Here is a similar intellectual problem: In the middle of the night it occurs to you that you can clarify a passage in the paper you are writing by making a certain change. At your desk the next day you forget to make the change. Again, the solution is to make the change when it occurs to you, using, say, a notepad or tape recorder kept beside your bed. The problem in old age is not so much how to have ideas as how to have them when you can use them. A written or dictated record, consulted from time to time, has the same effect as the umbrella hung on the doorknob. A pocket notebook or recorder helps to maximize one's intellectual output by recording one's behavior when it occurs. The practice is helpful at any age but particularly so for the aging scholar. In place of memories, memoranda.

Another symptom of the same failing is to forget what you were going to say. In a conversation you wait politely until someone else finishes, and your own clever comment has then vanished. One solution is to keep saying it to yourself; another is to appeal to the privilege of old age and interrupt the speaker; another is to make a note (perhaps pretending it is about what the other person is saying). The same problem arises when *you* are speaking and digress. You finish the digression and cannot remember why you embarked on it or where you were when you did so. The solution is simply not to digress—that is, not to interrupt yourself. A long sentence always raises that kind of problem: The last part is not likely to agree with the first because the first has passed out of reach. The effect is especially clear in speaking a language you do not speak well, where it is always a mistake to embark upon complex sentences. You will do much better if you speak only simple sentences, and the same remedy is available to the aging scholar who is giving an impromptu address in his or her own language. Short sentences are also advisable when you are talking to yourself—in other words, thinking.

A different kind of problem is solved by skillful prompting. You are going to attend a class reunion and are taking someone with you whom you must introduce to old friends. How can you remember their names? Before you go, look in your alumni register for a list of those who will be there, visualizing them if you can. The textual stimuli will prompt names that must otherwise be emitted, if at all, simply in response to the appearances of your friends.

Forgetting a name is only a conspicuous example of the essential failing. In writing a paper or thinking about a problem, there are relevant responses that would occur sooner or in greater abundance to a younger person. Their absence is not as conspicuous as a forgotten name, but it must be acknowledged and dealt with. One way to increase the probability that relevant responses will occur while you are writing a paper or solving a problem is to read relevant material and reread what you have written. Reference books within easy reach will supply prompts for names, dates, and other kinds of information. A thesaurus can be used, not to find a new word, but to prompt an old one. Even in extemporaneous speaking it is possible to prepare yourself in advance. You may "put yourself in better possession" of the verbal behavior you will be emitting by rehearsing your speech just one more time.

Old age is like fatigue, except that its effects cannot be corrected by relaxing or taking a vacation. Particularly troublesome is old age *plus* fatigue, and half of that can be avoided. It may be necessary to be content with fewer good working hours per day, and it is particularly necessary to spend the rest of the time in what the Greeks called *eutrapelia*—the productive use of leisure. Leisure should be relaxing. Possibly you like complicated puzzles, or chess, or other intellectual games. Give them up. If you want to continue to be intellectually productive you must

risk the contempt of your younger acquaintances and freely admit that you read detective stories or watch Archie Bunker on TV.

The kind of fatigue that causes trouble has been called mental, perhaps because it has so little to do with the physical fatigue of labor. You can be fully rested in a physical sense yet tired of what you are doing intellectually. To take appropriate steps one needs some measure of fatigue. Curiously enough, Adolf Hitler can be of help. In a report to the Nieman Foundation, William Lederer has called attention to relevant documents in the Harvard library. Toward the end of the Second World War, Hitler asked the few social scientists left in Germany to find out why people made bad decisions. When they reported that it was when they were mentally exhausted, he asked them for a list of the signs of mental fatigue. Then he issued an order: Any officer showing signs of mental fatigue should immediately be sent on vacation. Fortunately for the world, he did not apply the order to himself.

Among the signs on Hitler's list are several I find helpful. One is an unusual use of profanity or blasphemy. According to that principle, at least two of our recent presidents must have been mentally exhausted. When I find myself saying "damn," I know it is time to relax. (That mild expletive is a sign of my age as well as of my fatigue; I have never felt right about the scatological language of young people.) Other signs on Hitler's list include an inclination to blame others for mistakes, procrastinating on making decisions, an inclination to work longer hours than normally, an inclination to feel sorry for oneself, a reluctance to take exercise and relax, and dietary extremes—either gluttonous appetite or almost none at all. Clues not on Hitler's list that I have found useful are especially bad handwriting and mistakes in playing the piano.

Effects on my thinking are much harder to spot, but I have learned to watch for a few of them. One is verbal padding. The ancient troubador sang or spoke standard lines that allowed time to remember what to say next. Phrases like

"At this point it is interesting to note . . . " or "Let us now turn to another aspect of the problem . . . " serve the same function. They hold the floor until you have found something to say. Fatigued verbal behavior is also full of clichés, inexact descriptions, poorly composed sentences, borrowed sentences, memorized quotations, and Shakespeare's "wise saws." These are the easy things to say and they come out when you are tired. They can be avoided, if at all, only by avoiding fatigue.

I could have doubled my audience by calling my article "Cognitive Self-Management in Old Age." *Cognitive* means so many things that it could scarcely fail to apply here. But I could have described the field much more accurately by speaking of *verbal* self-management, because the problems are primarily verbal. I have discussed some of them in an article called "How to Discover What You Have to Say," recently published in the *Behavior Analyst*. At any given moment we are in possession of a latent repertoire of verbal behavior, every item of which presumably has a resting probability of "occurring to us." As a layperson might put it, there are lots of ideas waiting to be had. Some of them have occurred many times, are strengthened by common features of our daily life, and hence are the ideas that it is easiest to have as we think about or write about a problem, but they generally yield hackneyed, shopworn stuff. What is worth saying—the idea that is possibly unique to us because of the uniqueness of our experience and hence more likely to be called original—is least likely to occur. In short, in old age special difficulties arise because verbal behavior becomes less and less accessible. Perhaps we can do nothing about the accessibility, but we can improve the conditions under which verbal behavior occurs.

It helps to make the behavior as easy as possible; there are no crutches or wheelchairs for the verbally handicapped, but some prosthetic support is available—convenient pens, pencils, and paper, a good typewriter (a word processor, if possible), dictating equipment, and a convenient filing system.

I find it harder to "think big thoughts" in the sense of moving easily from one part of a paragraph to another or from one part of a chapter to another. The intraverbal connections are weak, and inconsistencies are therefore likely. The prosthetic remedy is to use outlines—spatial arrangements of the materials of a paragraph, chapter, or book. Decimal notation is helpful, with successive digits indicating chapter, section, paragraph, and sentence, in that order. This may look like constraint, but it is constraint against senile nattering and inconsistencies and repetition. You remain free to change the outline as a paragraph or chapter develops. An index, constructed as you write, will help in answering questions like "Now where did I take *that* up?" or "Have I already said that?"

It is commonly believed that those who have passed their prime can have nothing new to say. Jorge Luis Borges exclaimed, "What can I do at 71 except plagiarize myself!" Among the easiest things to say are things that have already been said, either by others or, especially, by ourselves. What we have already said most closely resembles what we now have to say. One of the more disheartening experiences of old age is discovering that a point you have just made—so significant, so beautifully expressed—was made by you in something you published a long time ago.

But one *can* say something new. Creative verbal behavior is not produced by exercising creativity; it is produced by skillful self-management. The creation of behavior raises the same issues as the creation of species. It is a selective process, and the appearance of something new—the *origin* of Darwin's title—can be promoted by introducing variations. You are also less likely to plagiarize yourself if you move into a new field or a new style.

One problem is often called a lack of motivation. Aging scholars lose interest; they find it hard to get to work; they work slowly. It is easy to attribute this to a change in *them*, but we should not overlook a change in their world. For *motivation* read *reinforcement*. In old age, behavior is not so strongly reinforced. Biological aging weakens reinforcing consequences. Behavior is more and more likely to be followed by aches and pains and quick fatigue. Things tend to become "not worth doing" in the sense that the aversive consequences exact too high a price. Positive reinforcers become less common and less powerful. Poor vision closes off the world of art, faulty hearing the enjoyment of highly fidelitous music. Foods do not taste as good, and erogenous tissues grow less sensitive. Social reinforcers are attenuated. Interests and tastes are shared with a smaller and smaller number of people.

In a world in which our behavior is not generously reinforced we are said to lack zest, joie de vivre, interest, ambition, aspirations, and a hundred other desirable "states of mind" and "feelings." These are really the by-products of changed contingencies of reinforcement. When the occasion for strong behavior is lacking or when reinforcing consequences no longer follow, we are bored, discouraged, and depressed. But it is a mistake to say that we suffer from such feelings. We suffer from the defective contingencies of reinforcement responsible for the feelings. Our environment is no longer maintaining strong behavior.

Our culture does not generously reinforce the behavior of old people. Both affluence and welfare destroy reinforcing contingencies, and so does retirement. Old people are not particularly important to younger people. Cicero made the point in his *De Senectute:* "Old age is honored only on condition that it defends itself, maintains its rights, is subservient to no one, and to its last breath rules over its own domain." We neglect that sage advice when we turn things over to another generation; we lose our position in the world and destroy important social reinforcers. Parents who turn their fortunes over to their children and then complain of neglect are the classical example, and aging scholars often do something of the same as they bring their work

to an end in the expectation that they will be satisfied with well-deserved kudos. They find themselves out of date as the world moves forward.

A common reinforcer affects old age in a different, though equally destructive way. Aging scholars come into possession of a unique stock-in-trade—their memories. They learn that they can hold a restless audience with personal reminiscences. "Thorndike? Oh, I knew him well." I have been guilty of a bit of that name-dropping myself when other reinforcers were in short supply, and I have been wallowing in reminiscence lately in writing my autobiography. The trouble is that it takes you backward. You begin to live your life in the wrong direction.

There are other things than memories to be exploited by the aged, and a careful assessment of one's possessions may be helpful. Harvey Lehman found that in certain fields—theoretical physics, for example—the best work was done well before the age of 40. What should theoretical physicists do with the rest of their lives? Some 20 years ago I asked Lehman that question about myself (I trust that my personal reference to Lehman has gripped you). I felt that my science was fairly rigorous, and perhaps I was near the end of a productive life as an experimentalist. What should I do with myself? "Administration," Lehman said. But I had been a department chairman, and that was not an attractive alternative. I turned instead to broader issues in the design of a culture, culminating in the publication of *Beyond Freedom and Dignity.*

Something more than subject matter is involved. The whole repertoire we call intellectual is acquired when one is young. It survives as a lifestyle when one grows old, when it is much harder to execute. If intellectual behavior were as conspicuous as baseball, we would understand the problem. The solution may simply be to replace one repertoire with another. People who move from one city to another often suffer a brief depression, which appears to be merely the result of an old repertoire of behavior having become useless. The old stores, restaurants, theaters, and friends are no longer there. The depression is relieved by acquiring a new repertoire. It may be necessary in old age to acquire new ways of thinking, to adopt a new intellectual style, letting the size of the repertoire acquired in a long life offset the loss of skill in making use of it.

We should ask what we have written papers or books *for*. In the world of scholarship the answer is seldom money (if we exclude writers of pot-boiling textbooks), and in any case, economic circumstances in old age are not easily improved. If the answer is commendation or fame, the problem may be extinction if commendation no longer follows, or satiation if there is a surfeit of commendation. Not much can be done about that, but a more likely explanation, and one which suggests helpful action, is that the scholar at his or her desk is not receiving the previously accustomed, immediate reinforcements: Sentences are not saying what they should say; solutions to problems remain out of reach; situations are not being effectively characterized; sequences are not in the right order; *sequiturs* are too often *non*. Something can be done about that, as I have suggested in the article mentioned earlier.

Reinforcers need not occur too frequently if we are fortunate enough to have been reinforced on a good schedule. A "stretched variable-ratio schedule" refers to a process you have all experienced as you acquired a taste for good literature, in which the reinforcing moments occur much less often than in cheap literature. In a comic strip you laugh at the end of every four frames, and in cheap literature something interesting happens on almost every page. Learning to enjoy good literature is essentially learning to read for longer and longer periods of time before coming upon a moving passage—a passage all the more moving for having required a long preparation. Gambling is reinforced on a variable-ratio schedule, and pathological gamblers show the effect of a history in which they began with reasonable success and only later exhausted their resources. Many of the reinforcers in old age tend to be on a stretched variable-ratio schedule. The Marquis de Sade described many interesting examples. The same process may explain the persistence of the aging scholar. If your achievements as a thinker have been spaced on a favorable schedule, you will have no difficulty in remaining active even though current achievements are spaced far apart. Like the hooked gambler, you will enjoy your life as a thinker in spite of the negative utility.

An audience is a neglected, independent variable. What one says is determined in a very important way by whom one is talking to. But the retired teacher no longer talks with students, the retired scientist no longer discusses work with colleagues. Old people find themselves spending time with others who are not interested in their fields. They may receive fewer invitations to speak or find it harder to accept them. Those who will read the papers or books they are writing are much too far removed in time to serve as an audience. An appropriate measure of intellectual self-management is to organize discussions, if only in groups of two. Find someone with similar interests. Two heads together are better than both apart. In talking with another person we have ideas that do not occur when we are alone at our desks. Some of what we say may be borrowed from what the other says, but the mere effect of having someone to say it to is usually conspicuous.

In searching for an audience, beware of those who are trying to be helpful and too readily flatter you. Second childishness brings you back within range of those kindergarten teachers who exclaim, "But *that* is very *good!*" Except that now, instead of saying, "My, you are really growing up!" they will say, "You are not really getting old!" As I have pointed out elsewhere, those who help those who can help themselves work a sinister kind of destruction by making the good things in life no longer properly contingent on behavior. If you have been very successful, the most sententious stupidities will be received as pearls of wisdom, and your standards will instantly fall.

If you are still struggling to be successful, flattery will more often than not put you on the wrong track by reinforcing useless behavior.

Well, there you have it. I have been batting that Ping-Pong ball back and forth long enough. I have reported some of the ways in which I have tried to avoid growing old as a thinker, and in addition I have given you a sample of the result. You may wish to turn to another comparison with a different species and conclude, if I may so paraphrase Dr. Johnson, "Sir, an aged lecturer is like a dog walking on his hinder legs. It is not done well; but you are surprised to find it done at all."

KEY POINTS

1. The organism does not exist in isolation. Biological changes constantly interact with environmental contingencies.

2. In old age, a useful strategy is to act on one's ideas when one thinks of them so as not to forget them later. Changing the environment (in various ways) changes the individual's success.

3. Positive reinforcements on a stretched variable-ratio schedule will encourage and maintain intellectual behavior. Eliminating the possibility of rewards will likely diminish the likelihood of desirable behaviors; thus retirement can be harmful.

QUESTIONS TO THINK ABOUT

1. Does aging occur mostly as a result of deteriorating environmental contingencies rather than deteriorating biological abilities?

2. Why is positive reinforcement in a stretched variable-ratio schedule favored over constant reinforcement?

3. Could Skinner's tools for intellectual self-management apply for young people and middle-aged people, as well as for the aged?

17

The Steep and Thorny Way
to a Science of Behavior*

B.F. SKINNER

In this second selection by Skinner, he lays out his basic approach to a science of behavior. He pleads for a focus on the relationship between behavior and the environment, asserting that we have been misled by a tendency to look inside the person for an explanation of behavior.

A critic contends that a recent book of mine does not contain anything new, that much the same thing was said more than four centuries ago in theological terms by John Calvin. You will not be surprised, then, to find me commending to you the steep and thorny way to that heaven promised by a science of behaviour. But I am not one of those ungracious pastors, of whom Ophelia complained, who 'recking not their own rede themselves tread the primrose path of dalliance'. No, I shall rail at dalliance, and in a manner worthy, I hope, of my distinguished predecessor. If I do not thunder or fulminate, it is only because we moderns can more easily portray a truly frightening hell. I shall merely allude to the carcinogenic fallout of a nuclear holocaust. And no Calvin ever had better reason to fear his hell, for I am proceeding on the assumption that nothing less than a vast improvement in our understanding of human behaviour will prevent the destruction of our way of life or of mankind.

Why has it been so difficult to be scientific about human behaviour? Why have methods which have been so prodigiously successful almost everywhere else failed so ignominiously in this one field? Is it because human behaviour presents unusual obstacles to a science? No doubt it does, but I think we are beginning to see how they may be overcome. The problem, I submit, is digression. We have been drawn off the straight and narrow path, and the word *diversion* serves me well by suggesting not only digression but dalliance. In this lecture I shall analyse some of the diversions peculiar to the field of human behaviour which seem to have delayed our advance towards the better understanding we desperately need.

I must begin by saying what I take a science of behaviour to be. It is, I assume, part of biology. The organism that behaves is the organism that breaths, digests, conceives, gestates, and so on. As such, it will eventually be described and explained by the anatomist and physiologist. So far as behaviour is concerned, they will give us an account of the genetic endowment of the species and tell us how that endowment changes during

*Skinner, B. F. (1975). The steep and thorny way to a science of behavior. In R. Harré (Ed.), *Problems of scientific revolution: The Herbert Spencer lectures 1973*, pp. 58–71. Oxford: Oxford University Press. © Oxford University Press 1975. Reprinted by permission of Oxford University Press.

the lifetime of the individual and why, as a result, the individual then responds in a given way upon a given occasion. Despite remarkable progress, we are still a long way from a satisfactory account in such terms. We know something about the chemical and electrical effects of the nervous system and the location of many of its functions, but the events which actually underlie a single instance of behaviour—as a pigeon picks up a stick to build a nest, or a child a block to complete a tower, or a scientist a pen to write a paper—are still far out of reach.

Fortunately, we need not wait for further progress of that sort. We can analyse a given instance of behaviour in its relation to the current setting and to antecedent events in the history of the species and the individual. Thus, we do not need an explicit account of the anatomy and physiology of genetic endowment in order to describe the behaviour, or the behavioural processes, characteristic of a species, or to speculate about the contingencies of survival under which they might have evolved, as the ethologists have convincingly demonstrated. Nor do we need to consider anatomy and physiology in order to see how the behaviour of the individual is changed by his exposure to contingencies of reinforcement during his lifetime and how as a result he behaves in a given way on a given occasion. I must confess to a predilection here for my own speciality, the experimental analysis of behaviour, which is a quite explicit investigation of the effects upon individual organisms of extremely complex and subtle contingencies of reinforcement.

There will be certain temporal gaps in such an analysis. The behaviour and the conditions of which it is a function do not occur in close temporal or spatial proximity, and we must wait for physiology to make the connection. When it does so, it will not invalidate the behavioural account (indeed, its assignment could be said to be specified by that account), nor will it make its terms and principles any the less useful. A science of behaviour will be needed for both theoretical and practical purposes even when the behaving organism is fully understood at another level, just as much of chemistry remains useful even though a detailed account of a single instance may be given at the level of molecular or atomic forces. Such, then, is the science of behaviour from which I suggest we have been diverted—by several kinds of dalliance to which I now turn.

Very little biology is handicapped by the fact that the biologist is himself a specimen of the thing he is studying, but that part of the science with which we are here concerned has not been so fortunate. We seem to have a kind of inside information about our behaviour. It may be true that the environment shapes and controls our behaviour as it shapes and controls the behaviour of other species—but *we* have feelings about it. And what a diversion they have proved to be! Our loves, our fears, our feelings about war, crime, poverty, and God—these are all basic, if not ultimate, concerns. And we are as much concerned about the feelings of others. Many of the great themes of mythology have been about feelings—of the victim on his way to sacrifice or of the warrior going forth to battle. We read what poets tell us about their feelings, and we share the feelings of characters in plays and novels. We follow regimens and take drugs to alter our feelings. We become sophisticated about them in, say, the manner of La Rochefoucauld, noting that jealousy thrives on doubt, or that the clemency of a ruler is a mixture of vanity, laziness, and fear. And with some psychiatrists we may even try to establish an independent science of feelings in the intrapsychic life of the mind or personality.

And do feelings not have some bearing on our formulation of a science of behaviour? Do we not strike because we are angry and play music because we feel like listening? And if so, are our feelings not to be added to those antecedent events of which behaviour is a function? This is not the place to answer such questions in detail, but I must at least suggest the kind of answer that may be given. William James questioned the causal order: perhaps we do not strike because we are angry but feel angry because we strike. That does not bring us back to the environment, however, although James and others were on the right track. What we feel are conditions of our bodies, most of them closely associated with behaviour and with the circumstances in which we behave. We both strike *and* feel angry for a common reason, and that reason lies in the environment. In short, the bodily conditions we feel are *collateral products* of our genetic and environmental histories. They have no explanatory force; they are simply additional facts to be taken into account.

Feelings enjoy an enormous advantage over genetic and environmental histories. They are warm, salient, and demanding, where facts about the environment are easily overlooked. Moreover, they are *immediately* related to behaviour, being collateral products of the same causes, and have therefore commanded more attention than the causes themselves, which are often rather remote. In doing so, they have proved to be one of the most fascinating attractions along the path of dalliance.

A much more important diversion has for more than 2000 years made any move towards a science of behaviour particularly difficult. The environment acts upon an organism at the surface of its body, but when the body is our own, we seem to observe its progress beyond that point—for example, we seem to see the real world become experience, a physical presentation become a sensation or a percept. Indeed, this second stage may be all we see. Reality may be merely an inference, and according to some authorities a bad one. What is important may not be the physical world on the far side of the skin, but what that world means to us on this side.

Not only do we seem to see the environment on its way in, we seem to see behaviour on its way out. We observe certain early stages—wishes, intentions, ideas, and acts of will—before

they have, as we say, found expression in behaviour. And as for our environmental history, that can also be viewed and reviewed inside the skin for we have tucked it all away in the storehouse of our memory. Again this is not the place to present an alternative account, but several points need to be made. The behaviouristic objection is not primarily to the metaphysical nature of mind stuff. I welcome the view, clearly gaining in favour among psychologists and physiologists and by no means a stranger to philosophy, that what we introspectively observe, as well as feel, are states of our bodies. But I am not willing to give introspection much of a toehold even so, for there are two important reasons why we do not discriminate precisely among our feelings and states of mind and hence why there are many different philosophies and psychologies.

In the first place, the world within the skin is private. Only the person whose skin it is can make certain kinds of contact with it. We might expect that the resulting intimacy should make for greater clarity, but there is a difficulty. The privacy interferes with the very process of coming to know. The verbal community which teaches us to make distinctions among things in the world around us lacks the information it needs to teach us to distinguish events in our private world. It cannot teach us the difference between diffidence and embarrassment, for example, as readily or as accurately as that between red and blue or sweet and sour.

Secondly, the self-observation which leads to introspective knowledge is limited by anatomy. It arose very late in the evolution of the species, because it is only when a person begins to be asked about his behaviour and about why he behaves as he does that he becomes conscious of himself in this sense. Self-knowledge depends upon language and in fact upon language of a rather advanced kind, but when questions of this sort first began to be asked, the only nervous systems available in answering them were those which had evolved for entirely different reasons. They had proved useful in the internal economy of the organism, in the co-ordination of movement, and in operating upon the environment, but there was no reason why they should be suitable in supplying information about those very extensive systems which mediate behaviour. To put it crudely, introspection cannot be very relevant or comprehensive because the human organism does not have nerves going to the right places.

One other problem concerns the nature and location of the knower. The organism itself lies, so to speak, between the environment that acts upon it and the environment it acts upon, but what lies between those inner stages—between, for example, experience and will? From what vantage point do we watch stimuli on their way into the storehouse of memory or behaviour on its way out to physical expression? The observing agent, the knower, seems to contract to something very small in the middle of things.

In the formulation of a science with which I began, it is the *organism as a whole* that behaves. It acts in and upon a physical world, and it can be induced by a verbal environment to respond to some of its own activities. The events observed as the life of the mind, like feelings, are *collateral products*, which have been made the basis of many elaborate metaphors. The philosopher at his desk asking himself what he really knows, about himself or the world, will quite naturally begin with his experiences, his acts of will, and his memory, but the effort to understand the mind from that vantage point, beginning with Plato's supposed discovery, has been one of the great diversions which have delayed an analysis of the role of the environment.

It did not, of course, take inside information to induce people to direct their attention to what is going on inside the behaving organism. We almost instinctively look inside a system to see how it works. We do this with clocks, as with living systems. It is standard practice in much of biology. Some early efforts to understand and explain behaviour in this way have been de-

scribed by Onians in his classic *Orgins of European thought*.[1] It must have been the slaughterhouse and the battlefield which gave man his first knowledge of anatomy and physiology. The various functions assigned to parts of the organism were not usually those which had been introspectively observed. If Onians is right, the *phrénes* were the lungs, intimately associated with breathing and hence, so the Greeks said, with thought and, of course, with life and death. The *phrénes* were the seat of *thumós*, a vital principle whose nature is not now clearly understood, and possibly of ideas, in the active sense of Homeric Greek. (By the time an idea had become an object of quiet contemplation, interest seems to have been lost in its location.) Later, the various fluids of the body, the humours, were associated with dispositions, and the eye and the ear with sense data. I like to imagine the consternation of that pioneer who first analysed the optics of the eyeball and realized that the image on the retina was upside down!

Observation of a behaving system from without began in earnest with the discovery of reflexes, but the reflex arc was not only not the seat of mental action, it was taken to be a usurper, the spinal reflexes replacing the *Rückenmarkseele* or soul of the spinal cord, for example. The reflex arc was essentially an anatomical concept, and the physiology remained largely imaginary for a long time. Many years ago I suggested that the letters CNS could be said to stand, not for the central nervous system, but for the conceptual nervous system. I had in mind the great physiologists Sir Charles Sherrington and Ivan Petrovich Pavlov. In his epoch-making *Integrative action of the nervous system*[2] Sherrington had analysed the role of the synapse, listing perhaps a dozen characteristic properties. I pointed out that he had never seen a synapse in action and that all the properties assigned to it were inferred from the behaviour of his preparations. Pavlov had offered his researches as evidence of the activities of the cerebral cortex though he had never observed the cortex in action but had merely inferred its processes from the behaviour of his experimental animals. But Sherrington, Pavlov, and many others were moving in the direction of an instrumental approach, and the physiologist is now, of course, studying the nervous system directly.

The conceptual nervous system has been taken over by other disciplines—by information theory, cybernetics, systems analyses, mathematical models, and cognitive psychology. The hypothetical structures they describe do not depend upon confirmation by direct observation of the nervous system for that lies too far in the future to be of interest. They are to be justified by their internal consistency and the successful prediction of selected facts, presumably not the facts from which the constructions were inferred.

These disciplines are concerned with how the brain or the mind must work if the human organism is to behave as it does. They offer a sort of thermodynamics of behaviour without reference to molecular action. The computer with its apparent simulation of Thinking Man supplies the dominant analogy. It is not a question of the physiology of the computer—how it is wired or what type of storage it uses—but of its behavioural characteristics. A computer takes in information as an organism receives stimuli, and processes it according to an inbuilt program as an organism is said to do according to its genetic endowment. It encodes the information, converting it to a form it can handle, as the organism converts visual, auditory, and other stimuli into nerve impulses. Like its human analogue it stores the encoded information in a memory, tagged to facilitate retrieval. It uses what it has stored to process information as received, as a person is said to use prior experience to interpret incoming stimuli, and later to perform various operations—in short, to compute. Finally, it makes decisions and behaves: it prints out.

There is nothing new about any of this. The same things were done thousands of years ago with clay tiles. The overseer or tax collector kept a record of bags of grain, the number, quality,

and kind being appropriately marked. The tiles were stored in lots as marked; additional tiles were grouped appropriately; the records were eventually retrieved and computations made; and a summary account was issued. The machine is much swifter, and it is so constructed that human participation is needed only before and after the operation. The speed is a clear advantage, but the apparent autonomy has caused trouble. It has seemed to mean that the mode of operation of a computer resembles that of a person. People do make physical records which they store and retrieve and use in solving problems, but it does not follow that they do anything of the sort in the mind. If there were some exclusively subjective achievement, the argument for the so-called higher mental processes would be stronger, but, so far as I know, none has been demonstrated. True, we say that the mathematician sometimes intuitively solves a problem and only later, if at all, reduces it to the steps of a proof, and in doing so he seems to differ greatly from those who proceed step by step, but the differences could well be in the evidence of what has happened, and it would not be very satisfactory to define thought simply as unexplained behaviour.

Again, it would be foolish of me to try to develop an alternative account in the time available. What I have said about the introspectively observed mind applies as well to the mind that is constructed from observations of the behaviour of others. The *accessibility* of stored memories, for example, can be interpreted as the *probability* of acquired behaviours, with no loss in the adequacy of the treatment of the facts, and with a very considerable gain in the assimilation of this difficult field with other parts of human behaviour.

I have said that much of biology looks inside a living system for an explanation of how it works. But not all of biology. Sir Charles Bell could write a book on the hand as evidence of design. The hand was evidence; the design lay elsewhere. Darwin found the design, too, but in a different place. He could catalogue the creatures he discovered on the voyage of the *Beagle* in terms of their form or structure, and he could classify barnacles for years in the same way, but he looked beyond structure for the principle of natural selection. It was *the relation of the organism to the environment* that mattered in evolution. And it is the relation to environment which is of primary concern in the analysis of behaviour. Hence, it is not enough to confine oneself to organization or structure, even of the most penetrating kind. That is the mistake of most of phenomenology, existentialism, and the structuralism of anthropology and linguistics. When the important thing is a relation to the environment, as in the phylogeny and ontogeny of behaviour, the fascination with an inner system becomes a simple digression.

We have not advanced more rapidly to the methods and instruments needed in the study of behaviour precisely because of the diverting preoccupation with a supposed or real inner life. It is true that the introspective psychologist and the model builder have investigated environments, but they have done so only to throw some light on the internal events in which they are interested. They are no doubt well-intentioned helpmates, but they have often simply misled those who undertake the study of the organism as a behaving system in its own right. Even when helpful, an observed or hypothetical inner determiner is no explanation of behaviour until it has itself been explained, and the fascination with an inner life has allayed curiosity about the further steps to be taken.

I can hear my critics: 'Do you really mean to say that all those who have inquired into the human mind, from Plato and Aristotle through the Romans and scholastics, to Bacon and Hobbes, to Locke and the other British empiricists, to John Stuart Mill, and to all those who began to call themselves psychologists—that they have all been wasting their time' Well, not all their time, fortunately. Forget their purely psychological speculations, and they were still remarkable people. They would have been even more remarkable, in my opinion, if they could have forgotten that speculation themselves. They were careful observers of human behaviour, but the intuitive wisdom they acquired from their contact with real people was flawed by their theories.

It is easier to make the point in the field of medicine. Until the present century very little was known about bodily processes in health and disease from which useful therapeutic practices could be derived. Yet it should have been worthwhile to call in a physician. Physicians saw many ill people and should have acquired a kind or wisdom—unanalysed perhaps, but still of value in prescribing simple treatments. The history of medicine, however, is largely the history of barbaric practices—blood-lettings, cuppings, poultices, purgations, violent emetics—which much of the time must have been harmful. My point is that these measures were not suggested by the intuitive wisdom acquired from familiarity with illness; they were suggested by *theories*, theories about what was going on inside an ill person. Theories of the mind have had a similar effect—less dramatic, perhaps, but quite possibly far more damaging. The men I have mentioned made important contributions in government, religion, ethics, economics, and many other fields. They could do so with an intuitive wisdom acquired from experience. But philosophy and psychology have had their bleedings, cuppings, and purgations too, and they have obscured simple wisdom. They have diverted wise people from a path which would have led more directly to an eventual science of behaviour. Plato would have made far more progress towards the good life if he could have forgotten those shadows on the wall of his cave.

Still another kind of concern for the self distracts us from the programme I have outlined. It has to do with the individual, not as an object of self-knowledge, but as an agent, an initiator, a creator. I have developed this theme in *Beyond freedom and dignity*.[3] We are more likely to give a person credit for what he does if it is not obvious that it can be attributed to his physical or social environment, and we are likely to feel that truly great achievements must be inexplicable. The more derivative a work of art, the less creative; the more conspicuous the personal gain, the less heroic an act of sacrifice. To obey a well-enforced law is not to show civic virtue. We see a concern for the aggrandizement of the individual, for the maximizing of credit due him, in the self-actualization of so-called humanistic psychology, in some versions of existentialism, in Eastern mysticism and certain forms of Christian mysticism in which a person is taught to reject the world in order to free himself for union with a divine principle or with God, as well as in the simple structuralism which looks to the organization of behaviour rather than to the antecedent events responsible for that organization. The difficulty is that, if the credit due a person is infringed by evidences of the conditions of which his behaviour is a function, then a scientific analysis appears to be an attack on human worth or dignity. Its task is to explain the hitherto inexplicable and hence to reduce any supposed inner contribution which has served in lieu of explanation. Freud moved in this direction in explaining creative art, and it is no longer just the cynic who traces heroism and martyrdom to powerful indoctrination. The culminating achievement of the human species has been said to be the evolution of man as a moral animal, but a simpler view is that it has been the evolution of cultures in which people behave morally although they have undergone no inner change of character.

Even more traumatic has been the supposed attack on freedom. Historically, the struggle for freedom has been an escape from physical restraint and from behavioural restraints exerted through punishment and exploitative measures of other kinds. The individual has been freed from features of his environment arranged by governmental and religious agencies and by those who possess great wealth. The success of that struggle, though it is not yet complete, is one of man's great achievements, and no sensible person would challenge it. Unfortunately, one of its by-products has been the slogan that 'all control of human behaviour is wrong and must be resisted'. Nothing in the circumstances under which man has struggled for freedom justifies this extension of the attack on controlling measures, and we should have to abandon all the advantages of a well-developed culture if we were to relinquish all practices involving the control of human behaviour. Yet new techniques in education, psychotherapy, incentive systems, penology, and the design of daily life are currently subject to attack because they are said to threaten personal freedom, and I can testify that the attack can be fairly violent.

The extent to which a person is free or responsible for his achievements is not an issue to be decided by rigorous proof, but I submit that what we call the behaviour of the human organism is no more free than its digestion, gestation, immunization, or any other physiological process. Because it involves the environment in many subtle ways it is much more complex, and its lawfulness is, therefore, much harder to demonstrate. But a scientific analysis moves in that direction, and we can already throw some light on traditional topics, such as free will or creativity, which is more helpful than traditional accounts, and I believe that further progress is imminent.

The issue is, of course, determinism. Slightly more than a hundred years ago in a famous paper Claude Bernard raised with respect to physiology the issue which now stands before us in the behavioural sciences. The almost insurmountable obstacle to the application of scientific method in biology was, he said, the belief in 'vital spontaneity'. His contemporary, Louis Pasteur, was responsible for a dramatic test of the theory of spontaneous generation, and I suggest that the spontaneous generation of behaviour in the guise of ideas and acts of will is now at the stage of the spontaneous generation of life in the form of maggots and micro-organisms a hundred years ago.

The practical problem in continuing the struggle for freedom and dignity is not to destroy controlling forces but to change them, to create a world in which people will achieve far more than they have ever achieved before in art, music, literature, science, technology, and above all the enjoyment of life. It could be a world in which people feel freer than they have ever felt before, because they will not be under aversive control. In building such a world, we shall need all the help a science of behaviour can give us. To misread the theme of the struggle for freedom and dignity and to relinquish all efforts to control would be a tragic mistake.

But it is a mistake that may very well be made. Our concern for the individual as a creative agent is not dalliance; it is clearly an obstacle rather than a diversion. For ancient fears are not easily allayed. A shift in emphasis from the individual to the environment, particularly to the social environment, is reminiscent of various forms of totalitarian statism. It is easy to turn from what may seem like an inevitable movement in that direction and to take one's chances with libertarianism. But much remains to be analysed in that position. For example, we may distinguish between liberty and license by holding to the right to do as we please provided we do not infringe similar rights in others, but in doing so we conceal or disguise the public sanctions represented by private rights. Rights and duties, like a moral or ethical sense, are examples of hypothetical internalized environmental sanctions.

In the long run, the aggrandizement of the individual jeopardizes the future of the species and the culture. In effect it infringes the so-called rights of billions of people still to be born, in whose interests only the weakest of sanctions are now maintained. We are beginning to realize the magnitude of the problem of bringing human behaviour under the control of a projected future, and we are already suffering from the fact that we have come very late to recognize that mankind will have a future only if it designs a vi-

able way of life. I wish I could share the optimism of both Darwin and Herbert Spencer that the course of evolution is necessarily towards perfection. It appears, on the contrary, that that course must be corrected from time to time. But, of course, if the intelligent behaviour that corrects it is also a product of evolution, then perhaps they were right after all. But it could be a near thing.

Perhaps it is now clear what I mean by diversions and obstacles. The science I am discussing is the investigation of the relation between behaviour and the environment—on the one hand, the environment in which the species evolved and which is responsible for the facts investigated by the ethologists and, on the other hand, the environment in which the individual lives and in response to which at any moment he behaves. We have been diverted from, and blocked in, our inquiries into the relations between behaviour and those environments by an absorbing interest in the organism itself. We have been misled by the almost instinctive tendency to look inside any system to see how it works, a tendency doubly powerful in the case of behaviour because of the apparent inside information supplied by feelings and introspectively observed states. Our only recourse is to leave that subject to the physiologist, who has, or will have, the only appropriate instruments and methods. We have also been encouraged to move in a centripetal direction because the discovery of controlling forces in the environment has seemed to reduce the credit due us for our achievements and to suggest that the struggle for freedom has not been as fully successful as we had imagined. We are not yet ready to accept the fact that the task is to change, not people, but rather the world in which they live.

We shall be less reluctant to abandon these diversions and to attack these obstacles, as we come to understand the possibility of a different approach. The role of the environment in human affairs has not, of course, gone unnoticed. Historians and biographers have acknowledged influences on human conduct, and literature has made the same point again and again. The Enlightenment advanced the cause of the individual by improving the world in which he lived—the Encyclopedia of Diderot and D'Alembert was designed to further changes of that sort—and by the nineteenth century, the controlling force of the environment was clearly recognized. Bentham and Marx have been called behaviourists, although for them the environment determined behaviour only after first determining consciousness, and this was an unfortunate qualification because the assumption of a mediating state clouded the relation between the terminal events.

The role of the environment has become clearer in the present century. Its selective action in evolution has been examined by the ethologists, and a similar selective action during the life of the individual is the subject of the experimental analysis of behaviour. In the current laboratory, very complex environments are constructed and their effects on behaviour studied. I believe this work offers consoling reassurance to those who are reluctant to abandon traditional formulations. Unfortunately, it is not well known outside the field. Its practical uses are, however, beginning to attract attention. Techniques derived from the analysis have proved useful in other parts of biology—for example, physiology and psychopharmacology—and have already led to the improved design of cultural practices, in programmed instructional materials, contingency management in the classroom, behavioural modification in psychotherapy and penology, and many other fields.

Much remains to be done, and it will be done more rapidly when the role of the environment takes its proper place in competition with the apparent evidences of an inner life. As Diderot put it, nearly two hundred years ago, 'Unfortunately it is easier and shorter to consult oneself than it is to consult nature. Thus the reason is inclined to dwell within itself.' But the problems we face are not to be found in men and women but in the world in which they live, especially in those social environments we call cultures. It is an important and promising shift in emphasis because, unlike the remote fastness of the so-called human spirit, the environment is within reach and we are learning how to change it.

And so I return to the role that has been assigned to me as a kind of twentieth-century Calvin, calling upon you to forsake the primrose path of total individualism, of self-actualization, self-adoration, and self-love, and to turn instead to the construction of that heaven on earth which is, I believe, within reach of the methods of science. I wish to testify that, once you are used to it, the way is not so steep or thorny after all.

REFERENCES

Onians, R. D. (1951). *The origins of European thought.* Cambridge, UK: Cambridge University Press.

Sherrington, C. S. (1906). *Integrative action of the nervous system.* New Haven, CT: Yale University Press.

Skinner, B. F. (1971). *Beyond freedom and dignity.* New York: Knopf.

KEY POINTS

1. Feelings are inadequate explanations of behavior. Rather, we must look to environmental contingencies that reinforced previous actions.

2. It is the organism as a whole that behaves. Only behavior can be a scientific unit of analysis.

3. To improve the world, we should try to change reinforcement contingencies rather than trying to change some internal personality processes.

QUESTIONS TO THINK ABOUT

1. What are the implications of the view of human nature that eliminates the need for studying thoughts, feelings, and motivations, but instead focuses on how we are shaped by the environment?

2. Is Skinner working in the iconoclastic tradition of Charles Darwin and Claude Bernard as he implies?

3. Because all behavior is determined, should we move beyond ideas of freedom?

18

Personal Construct Theory and the Psychotherapeutic Interview*

GEORGE A. KELLY

George A. Kelly (1905–1966), best known for his psychology of "Personal Constructs," was born in Kansas. After receiving his Ph.D. from Iowa State University, Kelly focused his early work on issues of diagnostic testing. Throughout his career Kelly pursued his interest in training and providing clinical psychological services that utilized his theories.

It was, however, Kelly's personal construct theory that had a large impact on approaches to personality and on clinical practice. Kelly used the model of the scientific method to describe human behavior, claiming that every person is, in his or her own particular way, a scientist. Importantly, Kelly's major work was published in 1955, years before cognitive psychology became firmly established as a field of study within psychology. Nevertheless, Kelly's work helped lay the groundwork for the cognitive social learning theories that followed.

BIOGRAPHY OF A THEORY

A good many years ago when I first set for myself the task of writing a manual of clinical procedures it was with the idea that psychologists needed to get their feet on the ground, and I was out to help them do it. Other scientists had gotten their feet on the ground; why couldn't we? Elsewhere all about us there were those hardy breeds who had penetrated the frontiers of reality with boldness and forthrightness. Practical men they were who, with each bedrock discovery, discredited all those generations of anemic philosophers who never dared venture beyond the comforts of their own redundancies. And yet here was the gloomiest vista of all, the mind of man, only one step away—a deep cavern so close behind our very own eyes and still enshadowed in Delphian mystery. And here we were, psychologists, standing on one foot wanting very much to be scientists—and more than a little defensive about it, too—chattering away and so frightened of what we might see that we never dared take a close look.

Fancying myself thus as a practical man and seeing science as something which was, above all things, practical, it seemed that whatever I could do to bring psychologists into contact with human beings, novel as that might be, would help extricate psychology from the mishmash of its abstruse definitions. So I proposed to write as much as I knew about how to come to terms with living persons. I took as my prototypes the ones who confided in me, particularly those who were in trouble, because, as I saw it, when a per-

*Kelly, G. A. (1969). Personal construct theory and the psychotherapeutic interview. In B. Maher (Ed.), *Clinical psychology and personality: The selected papers of George Kelly* (pp. 224–232). New York: Wiley. Copyright © 1969, John Wiley & Sons. Reprinted by permission of John Wiley & Sons, Inc. (Original work published 1958.)

son is in trouble he acts more like what he is and less like something dangling from the strings of social convention. Out of such an undertaking, if enough psychologists were willing to join in, I could envision a gradual awakening of the ancient half-conscious mind of man and the ultimate fruition of its vast potentialities. It should be obvious that all this fantasy took place when I was very young.

That manual was never written, at least not that kind of manual. The business of being practical turned out to be not as simple as I thought. After more delay than should have been necessary, even for one short of wits, the notion finally struck me that, no matter how close I came to the man or woman who sought my help, I always saw him through my own peculiar spectacles, and never did he perceive what I was frantically signaling to him, except through his. From this moment I ceased, as I am now convinced every psychotherapist does whether he wants to admit it or not, being a realist. More important, I could now stop representing psychology to clients as packaged reality, warranted genuine and untouched by human minds.

Perhaps "realism" is not a good term for what I am talking about. It is obvious, of course, that I am not talking about Platonic realism. Nobody talks about that any more. The realism from which my clients and I are always trying to wriggle loose might possibly be called "materialistic realism." At least it is the hardheaded unimaginative variety nowadays so popular among scientists, businessmen, and neurotics.

REALISM AND DOGMATISM

What happened was this. Like most therapists with a background of liberal scholarship rather than strictly professional training, I soon became aware that dogmatic interpretations of clients' problems often did more harm than good. It was not only the client who suffered; therapists were affected in much the same way he was. Dogmatism produces a kind of mental rigidity that replaces thoughts with word, stifles the zest for free inquiry, and tries to seal the personality up tight at the conclusion of the last psychotherapeutic interview.

Understand, I am not yet ready to say that dogmatism has no place whatsoever in psychotherapy, especially when weighed against certain grimmer alternatives. It may even prove valuable to all of us as a firm point from which to rebel. But these are other matters.

What actually jarred me loose was the observation that clients who felt themselves confronted with down-to-earth realities during the course of psychotherapy became much like those who were confronted with downright dogmatic interpretations of either the religious or psychological variety. On the heels of this observation came the notion that dogmatism—the belief that one has the word of truth right from the horse's mouth—and modern realism—the belief that one has the word of truth right from nature's mouth—add up to the same thing. To go even further, I now suspect that neither of these assumptions about the revealed nature of truth is any more useful to scientists than it is to clients. But especially I am sure that both assumptions get square in the way of that supreme ontological venture we call psychotherapy and that they serve only to perpetuate its present unhappy captivity to fee-based medical materialism.

While my original views of ontology—and I am insisting that it is the same ontological process that runs its course whether the man is in the role of a client, a psychotherapist, a physicist, or an artist—have changed in some respects with the years, one of my original convictions remains with me. It still seems important for the psychologist to deal directly with persons on the most forthright terms possible. This is why I think of clinical psychology, not as an applied field of psychology, but as a focal and essential area and method of scientific inquiry. On the other hand, traditional psychology, it seems to me, is still much too self-consciously scientific and still much too peripheral to its subject matter. Instead of being so careful to do nothing that a scientist would not do, it would be more appropriate for the psychologist to get on with his job of understanding human nature. To the extent that he is successful, "Science" will eventually be only too glad to catch up and claim his methods as its own.

As for dogmatism, I certainly am not the first to say that it often works badly in therapy. Nor am I the first to recognize that the client has a point of view worth taking into account. But if one is to avoid dogmatism entirely he needs to alert himself against realism also, for realism, as I have already implied, is a special form of dogmatism and one which is quite as likely to stifle the client's creative efforts. A client who is confronted with what are conceded to be stark realities can be as badly immobilized as one confronted with a thickheaded therapist. Even the presumed realism of his own raw feelings can convince a client that he has reached a dead end.

ALTERNATIVISM

As my client's therapist I can temporarily avoid pushing him over the brink of reality by being passive or by accepting as nonjudgmentally as possible anything and everything he says or does. There is no doubt but that in this atmosphere of intimate ambiguity many clients will figure out sensible things to do in spite of a therapist's short-sightedness. This is good and, for a therapist who thinks he has to act like a realist, it is about as far as one can go without betraying the dogmatism implicit in his realism. But I am not a realist—not anymore—and I do not believe either the client or the therapist has to lie down and let facts crawl over him. Right here is where the theoretical viewpoint I call *the psychology of personal constructs* stakes out its basic philosophical claim.

There is nothing so obvious that its appearance is not altered when it is seen in a different light. This is the faith that sustains the troubled person when he undertakes psychotherapy seriously. It is the same as the faith expressed in the *Book of Job*—not so much in the overwritten poetic lines as in the development of the theme. To state this faith as a philosophical premise: *What-*

ever exists can be reconstrued. This is to say that none of today's constructions—which are, of course, our only means of portraying reality—is perfect and, as the history of human thought repeatedly suggests, none is final.

Moreover, this is the premise upon which most psychotherapy has to be built, if not in the mind of the therapist, at least in the mind of the client. To be sure, one may go to a therapist with his facts clutched in his hand and asking only what he ought to do with them. But this is merely seeking technical advice, not therapy. Indeed, what else would one seek unless he suspected that the obstacles now shaping up in front of him are not yet cast in the ultimate form of reality? As a matter of fact, I have yet to see a realistic client who sought the help of a therapist in changing his outlook. To the realist, outlook and reality are made of the same inert stuff. On the other hand, a client who has found his therapeutic experience helpful often says, "In many ways things are the same as they were before, but how differently I see them!"

This abandonment of realism may alarm some readers. It may seem like opening the door to wishful thinking, and to most psychologists wishful thinking is a way of coming unhinged. Perhaps this is why so many of them will never admit to having any imagination, at least until after they suppose they have realistically demonstrated that what they secretly imagined was there all the time, waiting to be discovered. But for me to say that *whatever exists can be reconstrued* is by no manner or means to say that it makes no difference how it is construed. Quite the contrary. It often makes a world of difference. Some reconstructions may open fresh channels for a rich and productive life. Others may offer one no alternative save suicide.

A THEORETICAL POSTULATE

Here, then, is where one takes the next step, a step that leads him from a philosophical premise—called *constructive alternativism*—to a psychological postulate. Put it this way: *A person's processes are psychologically channelized by the ways in which he anticipates events.* Next, combining this statement with the gist of some of its ensuing corollaries, we can say simply: *A person lives his life by reaching out for what comes next and the only channels he has for reaching are the personal constructions he is able to place upon what may actually be happening.* If in this effort he fails, by whatever criterion, the prudence of his constructions is laid open to question and his grasp upon the future is shaken.

Let us make no mistake; here we come to the exact point where we all have trouble. If our misleading construction is based on dogmatic belief, that is to say it is held to be true because someone like God or the Supreme Soviet said so, we are not likely to have the audacity to try to revise it. Similarly, if it is believed to have had its origin in nature rather than in our own noggin—the position of "realism" I have been talking about—we are left with no choice except to adjust and make the best of matters as they stand. Or if realizing that it was altogether our own mistaken notions that led us afield, if it seems now that there is nothing left to do except to scrap our convictions, one and all, then utter chaos will start closing in on all sides. Any of these is bad. Fortunately, there are always other alternatives when predictions go awry. For the person who does not see any of them—psychotherapy!

VIEW OF PSYCHOTHERAPY

We have ruled out the notion of psychotherapy as the confrontation of the client with stark reality, whether it is put to him in the form of dogma, natural science, or the surges of his own feelings. Instead, we see him approaching reality in the same ways that all of us have to approach it if we are to get anywhere. The methods range all the way from those of the artist to those of the scientist. Like them both and all the people in between, the client needs to assume that something can be created that is not already known or is not already there.

In this undertaking the fortunate client has a partner, the psychotherapist. But the psychotherapist does not know the final answer either—so they face the problem together. Under the circumstances there is nothing for them to do except for both to inquire and both to risk occasional mistakes. So that it can be a genuinely cooperative effort, each must try to understand what the other is proposing and each must do what he can to help the other understand what he himself is ready to try next. They formulate their hypotheses jointly. They even experiment jointly and upon each other. Together they take stock of outcomes and revise their common hunches. Neither is the boss, nor are they merely well-bred neighbors who keep their distance from unpleasant affairs. It is, as far as they are able to make it so, a partnership.

The psychotherapy room is a protected laboratory where hypotheses can be formulated, test-tube sized experiments can be performed, field trials planned, and outcomes evaluated. Among other things, the interview can be regarded as itself an experiment in behavior. The client says things to see what will happen. So does the therapist. Then they ask themselves and each other if the outcomes confirmed their expectations.

Often a beginning therapist finds it helpful to close his cerebral dictionary and listen primarily to the subcortical sounds and themes that run through his client's talk. Stop wondering what the words literally mean. Try to recall, instead, what it is they sound like. Disregard content for the moment; attend to theme. Remember that a client can abruptly change content—thus throwing a literal-minded therapist completely off the scent—but he rarely changes the theme so easily. Or think of these vocal sounds, not as words, but as preverbal outcries, impulsive sound gestures, stylized oral grimaces, or hopelessly mumbled questions.

But at other times the therapist will bend every effort to help the client find a word, the precise word, for a newly emerged idea. Such an exact labeling of elusive thoughts is, at the proper time, crucial to making further inquiries and to the experimental testing of hypotheses. Particularly is this true when the team—client and therapist—is elaborating personal constructs. But before we can discuss this matter further we need to say something about the nature of personal constructs from the point of view of the theory.

PERSONAL CONSTRUCTS

We have said that a person lives his life by reaching out for what comes next and the only channels through which he can reach are the personal constructions he is able to place upon what appears to be going on. One deals with the events of life, not as entirely strange and unique occurrences but as recurrences. There is a property, a human quality of our own manufacture, that makes today seem like yesterday and leads us to expect that tomorrow may be another such day. To see this is to construe similarity among one's days. Without this view the future would seem chaotic indeed.

But to say that one's days are all alike, and nothing more, is to lose them amidst the hours and the years. What makes days seem alike is also precisely what sets them apart. We construe, then, by ascribing some property that serves both to link an event with certain other events and to set it in contrast to those with which it might most likely become confused. This construed dimension, embodying both likeness and difference, this reference axis, is what we call a construct. And constructs are personal affairs; regardless of the words he uses, each person does his own construing.

In this world—past, present, and future—ordered by each of us in his own way, constructs and events are interwoven so that events give definition to constructs and constructs give meaning to events. Take the client. The events, for example, that he recalls from childhood during the course of a psychotherapeutic interview serve to define the constructs that often he can otherwise express only through "intellectualization" or by "acting out." But constructs, on the other hand, give current meaning both to his memories and to his future plans and, particularly when they are precisely verbalized, they lay the ground for profitable experimentation.

The constructs one applies to himself and his interpersonal relationships have particular importance. Psychotherapy finds itself mainly concerned with them. While always fewer in number than one might wish, they nevertheless set the pattern of human resources available to the client and, when they are applied to his own changes of mood or behavior, they become wide-open pathways for shifting his position and altering the course of his life. Knowledge of them helps the therapist predict and control the client's possible reactions to threat, including the implicit threat that, to some extent, is always implied by psychotherapy itself.

THE VARYING TECHNIQUES OF PSYCHOTHERAPY

The team of client and therapist can go about their task in a variety of ways. Essentially these are the same ways that, on one kind of occasion or another, man has always employed for dealing with perplexities. (1) The two of them can decide that the client should reverse his position with respect to one of the more obvious reference axes. Call this slot rattling, if you please. It has its place. (2) Or they can select another construct from the client's ready repertory and apply it to matters at hand. This, also, is a rather straightforward approach. Usually the client has already tried it. (3) They can make more explicit those preverbal constructs by which all of us order our lives in considerable degree. Some think of this as dredging the unconscious. The figure is one that a few have found useful, but I would prefer not to use it. (4) They can elaborate the construct system to test it for internal consistency. (5) They can test constructs for their predictive validity. (6) They can increase the range of convenience of certain constructs, that is, apply them more generally. They can also decrease the range of convenience and thus reduce a construct to a kind of obsolescence. (7) They can alter the meaning of certain constructs; rotate the reference axes. (8) They can erect new reference axes. This is the most ambitious undertaking of all.

Alteration or replacement of constructs—the last two methods mentioned—is essentially a creative kind of effort. Both involve first a loosening of the client's constructions, either by the use of fantasy, dreams, free association, or the introduction of varied and illusive content into the therapeutic interview. But creativity is not a single mode of thought; it follows a cycle. The second phase of the cycle involves tightening and validation of the newly placed or newly formed constructs.

I have summarized what goes on in therapy under eight headings. More might have been used. It is necessary only that I offer some sketch of how psychotherapy can be envisioned in terms of personal construct theory, that I try to make clear that what I am talking about is not restricted to the process tradition calls "cognition" (a term for which I find little practical use lately), that psychotherapy runs the gamut of man's devices for coming to grips with reality, and that the client and his therapist embark together as shipmates on the very same adventure.

KEY POINTS

1. Realism and dogmatism in therapy can do more harm than good by creating mental constraints that can stifle a patient's creative efforts.

2. Personal construct theory postulates that whatever exists can be reconstrued. That is, reality as we see it is not rigid and unchangeable.

3. The only channels a person has for reaching out to the world are the personal constructs he or she places upon what may actually be happening. That is, a person lives in anticipation of events, and reacts relative to what he or she expects to happen.

QUESTIONS TO THINK ABOUT

1. What is materialistic realism? Why should therapists wriggle loose from this view?

2. What is personal construct theory?

3. Describe the components of the ideal client/therapist relationship from the viewpoint of a theorist.

19

External Control and Internal Control*

JULIAN B. ROTTER

Julian Rotter (1916–) was an important bridge between traditional social learning theories and the modern ideas that have come to be called social-cognitive theory. He believes that our behavior depends both on how strongly we expect that our performance will have a positive result and on how much we value the expected reinforcement. Expectancy is key but expectancy is not necessarily so simple.

Rotter was born in New York to Jewish immigrants, and he was influenced by the situational pressures he observed during the Great Depression of the 1930s. Rotter is perhaps best known for his ideas about internal and external locus of control. This has turned out to be a powerful and popular approach to individual differences and he describes it in the following selection.

Some social scientists believe that the impetus behind campus unrest is youth's impatient conviction that they can control their own destinies, that they can change society for the better.

My research over the past 12 years has led me to suspect that much of the protest, outcry and agitation occurs for the opposite reason—because students feel they *cannot* change the world, that the system is too complicated and too much controlled by powerful others to be changed through the students' efforts. They feel more powerless and alienated today than they did 10 years ago, and rioting may be an expression of their hostility and resentment.

Dog. One of the most pervasive laws of animal learning is that a behavior followed by a reward tends to be repeated, and a behavior followed by a punishment tends not to be repeated. This seems to imply that reward and punishment act directly on behavior, but I think this formulation is too simplistic to account for many types of human behavior.

For example, if a dog lifts its leg at the exact moment that someone throws a bone over a fence, the dog may begin to lift its leg more often than usual when it is in the same situation—whether or not anyone is heaving a bone. Adult human beings are usually not so superstitious—a person who finds a dollar bill on the sidewalk immediately after stroking his hair is not likely to stroke his hair when he returns to the same spot.

It seemed to me that, at least with human beings who have begun to form concepts, the important factors in learning were not only the strength and frequency of rewards and punishments but also whether or not the person believed his behavior produced the reward or punishment.

*Rotter. J. (1971). External control and internal control. *Psychology Today, 5* (June), pp. 37, 38, 40, 42, 58–59. Reprinted with permission from Psychology Today Magazine, copyright © 1971 Sussex Publishers, Inc.

According to the social-learning theory that I developed several years ago with my colleagues and students, rewarding a behavior strengthens an *expectancy* that the behavior will produce future rewards.

In animals, the expectation of reward is primarily a function of the strength and frequency of rewards. In human beings, there are other things that can influence the expectation of reward—the information others give us, our knowledge generalized from a variety of experiences, and our perceptions of causality in the situation.

Consider the ancient shell game. Suppose I place a pea under one of three shells and quickly shuffle the shells around the table. A player watches my movements carefully and then, thinking that he is using his fine perceptual skills, he tells me which shell the pea is under. If his choice is correct, he will likely choose the same shell again the next time he sees me make those particular hand movements. It looks like a simple case of rewarding a response.

But suppose I ask the subject to turn his back while I shuffle the shells. This time, even if his choice is rewarded by being correct, he is not so likely to select the same shell again, because the outcome seems to be beyond his control—just a lucky guess.

Chips. In 1957, E. Jerry Phares tried to find out if these intuitive differences between chance-learning and skill-learning would hold up in the laboratory. Phares would give each subject a small gray-colored chip and ask him to select one of 10 standard chips that had exactly the same shade of gray. The standards were all different but so similar in value that discrimination among them was very difficult. Phares told half of his subjects that matching the shades required great skill and that some persons were very good at it. He told the rest that the task was so difficult that success was a matter of luck. Before the experiment began, Phares arbitrarily decided which trials would be "right" and which would be "wrong"; the schedule was the same for everyone. He found that because of the difficulty of the task all subjects accepted his statements of right and wrong without question.

Phares gave each subject a stack of poker chips and asked him to bet on his accuracy before each trial as a measure of each subject's expectancy of success.

The subjects who thought that success depended on their own skills shifted and changed frequently—their bets would rise after success and drop after failure, just as reinforcement-learning theory would predict. But subjects who thought that a correct match was a matter of luck reacted differently. In fact, many of them raised their bets after failure and lowered them after success—the "gambler's fallacy." Thus, it appeared that traditional laws of learning could not explain some types of human behavior.

Guess. Another well-established law of learning states that behavior learned by partial reinforcement takes longer to extinguish than behavior learned by constant reinforcement. In other words, when rewards cease, a behavior becomes weaker and eventually stops—but it takes longer for a behavior to die out if it was learned with intermittent rewards than if it had been rewarded every time it occurred.

William H. James and I tested this proposition. We told some subjects that an ESP guessing task was a matter of skill; we told other subjects that the same task was purely chance. We told some subjects they were correct on half their guesses. At a predetermined point we began to call all guesses incorrect. The subjects who believed they were in a skill task lowered their expectancy of success sooner than the subjects who thought that successful guesses were a matter of luck. Other subjects had been told they were correct on every trial. In this condition it was the chance subjects who lost their expectancy of success soonest.

In these early studies we gave one task to all subjects and told some that it was a skill task and others it was a chance task. To discover how subjects behaved when no such instructions were given, Douglas Crowne, Shephard Liverant and

I repeated the study using two different tasks and no special instructions. We found that the "law" of partial reinforcement held true only when subjects thought their successes were the result of chance. Subjects who thought their rewards were due to skill actually took longer to extinguish their responses after constant (100 per cent) reinforcement than after partial (50 per cent) reinforcement. This is the opposite of what one would expect from the laws of animal learning. In this experiment half of the subjects guessed at hidden cards in an ESP test in which cultural expectancies led most of them to assume that success was primarily a matter of luck. The other subjects tried, by pulling a string, to raise a platform with a ball balanced on it—a task that is easily assumed to be a skill.

Actually, the experimenter could control the ball—keep it on the platform or let it fall off—so that both chance and skill subjects had the same sequence of success and failure.

Several other experiments have confirmed that, under skill conditions, constant-reward learning may take longer to extinguish than partial-reward learning. It has become increasingly clear that in chance situations other laws as well are quantitatively and qualitatively different from the laws that apply to skill learning.

I decided to study internal and external control (I-E), the beliefs that rewards come from one's own behavior or from external sources. The initial impetus to study internal-external control came both from an interest in individual differences and from an interest in explaining the way human beings learn complex social situations. There seemed to be a number of attitudes that would lead a person to feel that a reward was not contingent upon his own behavior, and we tried to build all of these attitudes into a measure of individual differences. A person might feel that luck or chance controlled what happened to him. He might feel that fate had preordained what would happen to him. He might feel that powerful others controlled what happened to him or he might feel that he simply could not predict the effects of this behavior because the world was too complex and confusing.

Scale. Phares first developed a test of internal-external control as part of his doctoral dissertation, and James enlarged and improved on Phares' scale as part of his doctoral dissertation. Later scales were constructed with the important help of several of my colleagues including Liverant, Melvin Seeman and Crowne. In 1962 I developed a final 29-item version of the I-E scale and published it in *Psychological Monographs* in 1966. This is a forced-choice scale in which the subject reads a pair of statements and then indicates with which of the two statements he more strongly agrees. The scores range from zero (the consistent belief that individuals can influence the environment—that rewards come from *internal* forces) to 23 (the belief that all rewards come from *external* forces).

A recent bibliography of studies of internal versus external control contains over 300 references. Most of these that deal with high-school or college students or adults use the 29-item scale. This test has also been translated into at least six other languages. Other successful methods of measuring I-E control have been devised and there are now four children's scales in use.

Degree. One conclusion is clear from I-E studies: people differ in the tendency to attribute satisfactions and failures to themselves rather than to external causes, and these differences are relatively stable. For the sake of convenience most investigators divide their subjects into two groups—internals and externals—depending on which half of the distribution a subject's score falls into. This is not meant to imply that there are two personality types and that everyone can be classified as one or the other, but that there is a continuum, and that persons have varying degrees of internality or externality.

Many studies have investigated the differences between internals and externals. For example, it has been found that lower-class children tend to be external; children from richer,

TABLE 1   Internal Control—External Control, A Sampler

Julian B. Rotter is the developer of a forced-choice 29-item scale for measuring an individual's degree of internal control and external control. This I-E test is widely used. The following are sample items taken from an earlier version of the test, but not, of course, in use in the final version. The reader can readily find for himself whether he is inclined toward internal control or toward external control, simply by adding up the choices he makes on each side.

I more strongly believe that:	**OR**
Promotions are earned through hard work and persistence.	Making a lot of money is largely a matter of getting the right breaks.
In my experience I have noticed that there is usually a direct connection between how hard I study and the grades I get.	Many times the reactions of teachers seem haphazard to me.
The number of divorces indicates that more and more people are not trying to make their marriages work.	Marriage is largely a gamble.
When I am right I can convince others.	It is silly to think that one can really change another person's basic attitudes.
In our society a man's future earning power is dependent upon his ability.	Getting promoted is really a matter of being a little luckier than the next guy.
If one knows how to deal with people they are really quite easily led.	I have little influence over the way other people behave.
In my case the grades I make are the results of my own efforts; luck has little or nothing to do with it.	Sometimes I feel that I have little to do with the grades I get.
People like me can change the course of world affairs if we make ourselves heard.	It is only wishful thinking to believe that one can really influence what happens in society at large.
I am the master of my fate.	A great deal that happens to me is probably a matter of chance.
Getting along with people is a skill that must be practiced.	It is almost impossible to figure out how to please some people.

better-educated families tend to have more belief in their own potential to determine what happens to them. The scores do not seem to be related to intelligence, but young children tend to become more internal as they get older.

Esther Battle and I examined the attitudes of black and white children in an industrialized Ohio city. The scale we used consisted of five comic-strip cartoons; the subjects told us what they thought one of the children in the cartoon would say. We found the middle-class blacks were only slightly more external in their beliefs than middle-class whites but that among children from lower socioeconomic levels blacks were significantly more external than whites. Herbert Lefcourt and Gordon Ladwig also found that among young prisoners in a Federal reformatory, blacks were more external than whites.

Ute. It does not seem to be socioeconomic level alone that produces externality, however. Theodore Graves, working with Richard and Shirley L. Jessor, found that Ute Indians were more external than a group of Spanish-Americans, even though the Indians had higher average living standards than the Spanish-Americans. Since Ute tradition puts great emphasis on fate and unpredictable external forces, Graves concluded that internality and externality resulted from cultural training. A group of white subjects in the same community were more internal than either the Indians or the Spanish-Americans.

A measure of internal-external control was used in the well-known Coleman Report on Equality of Educational Opportunity. The experimenters found that among disadvantaged children in the sixth, ninth and 12th grades, the students with high scores on an achievement test had more internal attitudes than did children with low achievement scores.

One might expect that internals would make active attempts to learn about their life situations. To check on this, Seeman and John Evans gave the I-E scale to patients in a tuberculosis hospital. The internal patients knew more details about their medical conditions and they questioned doctors and nurses for medical feedback more often than did the external patients. The experimenters made sure that in their study there were no differences between the internals and externals in education, occupational status or ward placement.

Rules. In another study, Seeman found that internal inmates in a reformatory learned more than external inmates did about the reformatory rules, parole laws, and the long-range economic

facts that would help one get along in the outside world. These subjects did not differ from one another in intelligence—only in the degree of belief in internal or external control.

At a Negro college in Florida, Pearl Mayo Gore and I found that students who made civil-rights commitments to march on the state capitol during a vacation or to join a Freedom-Riders group were clearly and significantly more internal than the students who would only attend a rally or who were not interested at all. The willingness to be an activist seems to be related to previous experiences and the generalized expectation that one can influence his environment.

Studying a Negro church group in Georgia, Bonnie Strickland found that activists were significantly more internal than were nonactivists of similar educational and socioeconomic status.

Smoke. Phares wanted to see if internals really were more effective than externals in influencing their environments. He instructed his subjects to act as experimenters and try to change other college students' attitudes toward fraternities and sororities. Using a before-and-after questionnaire to assess these attitudes, Phares found that the internal subjects were much more successful than the external subjects in persuading students to change their minds.

It is not surprising that persons who believe that they can control their environments also believe that they can control themselves. Two studies have shown that nonsmokers are significantly more internal than smokers. After the Surgeon General's report, one study showed that male smokers who successfully quit smoking were more internal than other male smokers who believed the report but did not quit smoking. The difference was not significant with females, who apparently were motivated by other variables including, for example, one's tendency to gain weight after quitting.

Bet. Highly external persons feel that they are at the mercy of the environment, that they are being manipulated by outside forces. When they *are* manipulated, externals seem to take it in stride. Internals are not so docile. For example, Crowne and Liverant set up an experiment to see how readily their subjects would go along with a crowd. In a simple Asch-type conformity experiment in which there is one true subject plus several stooges posing as subjects, Crowne and Liverant found that neither internals nor externals were more likely to yield to an incorrect majority judgement. But when the experimenters gave money to the subjects and allowed them to bet on their own judgments, the externals yielded to the majority much more often than did the internals. When externals did vote against the majority they weren't confident about their independence—they bet less money on being right than they did when they voted along with the crowd.

Strickland also studied the way people react to being manipulated. In a verbal-conditioning experiment, she handed each subject a series of cards. On each card were four words—two nouns, a verb and an adjective. The subject simply picked one of the words. Strickland would say "good" whenever a subject picked the verb, for example, which was intended as a subtle social reward to get the subjects to pick more verbs.

In a thorough postexperiment interview she found out which subjects had caught on to the fact that she was dispensing praise ("good") systematically. There were no important differences among subjects who said they did not notice her system. But among subjects who were aware of her attempt to manipulate them, those who actually chose the verbs more often tended to be external—the internal subjects actively resisted being conditioned.

TATs. But internals are negative only when they think they are victims of hidden manipulation. If a manipulative system is out in the open—as in a typical student-teacher relationship—internals may choose to go along readily. Gore clarified this issue in a study in which she asked subjects to tell stories about TAT cards. She told them she was trying to test her theory about which cards produce the longest stories. In one group she told each subject which card she

thought was best, and in this case there was no significant difference between the stories of internals and those of externals—the stories all tended to be a little longer than those of a control group that was not given biasing instructions.

But with another group she indicated her favorite picture more subtly—when she presented it to a subject she would smile and say, "Now let's see what you do with *this* one." In this condition, the internals made up much shorter stories than did either externals or control subjects who got no special suggestions. Internals actively resist subtle pressure.

Suspicion. Some externals, who feel they are being manipulated by the outside world, may be highly suspicious of authorities. With Herbert Hamsher and Jesse Geller, I found that male subjects who believed that the Warren Commission Report was deliberately covering up a conspiracy were significantly more external than male subjects who accepted the report.

To some degree externality may be a defense against expected failure but internals also have their defenses. In investigating failure defenses, Jay Efran studied high-school students' memories for tasks they had completed or failed. He found that the tendency to forget failures was more common in internal subjects than in external ones. This suggests that external subjects have less need to repress past failures because they have already resigned themselves to the defensive position that failures are not their responsibility. Internals, however, are more likely to forget or repress their failures.

Today's activist student groups might lead one to assume that our universities are filled with internals—people with strong belief in their ability to improve conditions and to control their own destinies. But scores on the same I-E test involving large numbers of college students in many localities show that between 1962 and 1971 there was a large increase in externality on college campuses. Today the average score on the I-E scale is about 11. In 1962 about 80 per cent of college students had more internal scores than this. The increase in externality has been somewhat less in Midwest colleges than in universities on the coasts, but there is little doubt that, overall, college students feel more powerless to change the world and control their own destinies now than they did 10 years ago.

Clearly, we need continuing study of methods to reverse this trend. Our society has so many critical problems that it desperately needs as many active, participating internal-minded members as possible. If feelings of external control, alienation and powerlessness continue to grow, we may be heading for a society of dropouts—each person sitting back, watching the world go by.

KEY POINTS

1. Learning theory is a powerful tool for understanding behavior, but people are especially influenced by the rewards they get from other people.

2. Knowing people's *expectations* about the effects of their behaviors helps us to better understand how behaviors are shaped by environmental contingencies.

3. Highly external people feel that they are at the mercy of their environments, but internals have a strong belief in their ability to control their own destinies.

4. A person's internal versus external locus of control is predictive of many aspects of the person's beliefs and behaviors.

QUESTIONS TO THINK ABOUT

1. What are the various factors that determine whether someone has an internal or external locus of control?

2. Do you think personality differences about issues of control have an effect on social activism and other social movements?

3. To what extent can a person's locus of control be modified by training or experience?

20

Social Foundations of Thought and Action: A Social Cognitive Theory*

ALBERT BANDURA

Albert Bandura (1925–) is a social cognitive personality theorist whose work focuses on observational learning processes, including how we interpret what we see. The individual is affected not only by external processes of reinforcement, but also by expectations, anticipated reinforcement, thoughts, plans, and goals. Behavior, cognition, and the environment all affect one another.

Trained in learning theory at the University of Iowa, Bandura first made his mark trying to understand aggression. A psychology professor at Stanford University, Bandura's approach to personality is especially distinctive because it not only accepts the importance of social learning, but also emphasizes that people think about their prospective (future) actions, setting goals and plans for themselves. As this selection illustrates, he widened the learning theory perspective to allow cognitive factors.

In the social cognitive view people are neither driven by inner forces nor automatically shaped and controlled by external stimuli. Rather, human functioning is explained in terms of a model of triadic reciprocality in which behavior, cognitive and other personal factors, and environmental events all operate as interacting determinants of each other. The nature of persons is defined within this perspective in terms of a number of basic capabilities. These are discussed briefly below and analyzed fully in the chapters that follow.

SYMBOLIZING CAPABILITY

The remarkable capacity to use symbols, which touches virtually every aspect of people's lives, provides them with a powerful means of altering and adapting to their environment. Through symbols people process and transform transient experiences into internal models that serve as guides for future action. Through symbols they similarly give meaning, form, and continuance to the experiences they have lived through.

By drawing on their knowledge and symbolizing powers, people can generate innovative courses of action. Rather than solving problems solely by enacting options and suffering the costs of missteps, people usually test possible solutions symbolically and discard or retain them on the basis of estimated outcomes before plunging into action. An advanced cognitive capability coupled with the remarkable flexibility of symbolization enables people to create ideas that transcend their sensory experiences. Through the medium of symbols, they can communicate

*Bandura, A. (1986). *Social foundations of thought and action: A social cognitive theory.* Englewood Cliffs, NJ: Prentice-Hall. Reprinted by permission of Prentice-Hall, Inc., Upper Saddle River, NJ. (Selection is pp. 18–22.)

with others at almost any distance in time and space. Other distinctive human characteristics to be discussed shortly are similarly founded on symbolic capability.

To say that people base many of their actions on thought does not necessarily mean they are always objectively rational. Rationality depends on reasoning skills which are not always well developed or used effectively. Even if people know how to reason logically, they make faulty judgments when they base their inferences on inadequate information or fail to consider the full consequences of different choices. Moreover, they often missample and misread events in ways that give rise to erroneous conceptions about themselves and the world around them. When they act on their misconceptions, which appear subjectively rational, given their errant basis, such persons are viewed by others as behaving in an unreasoning, if not downright foolish, manner. Thought can thus be a source of human failing and distress as well as human accomplishment.

FORETHOUGHT CAPABILITY

People do not simply react to their immediate environment, nor are they steered by implants from their past. Most of their behavior, being purposive, is regulated by forethought. The future time perspective manifests itself in many ways. People anticipate the likely consequences of their prospective actions, they set goals for themselves, and they otherwise plan courses of action for cognized futures, for many of which established ways are not only ineffective but may also be detrimental. Through exercise of forethought, people motivate themselves and guide their actions anticipatorily. By reducing the impact of immediate influences, forethought can support foresightful behavior, even when the present conditions are not especially conducive to it.

The capability for intentional and pursive action is rooted in symbolic activity. Future events cannot serve as determinants of behavior, but their cognitive representation can have a strong causal impact on present action. Images of desirable future events tend to foster the behavior most likely to bring about their realization. By representing foreseeable outcomes symbolically, people can convert future consequences into current motivators and regulators of foresightful behavior. Forethought is translated into action through the aid of self-regulating mechanisms.

In analyses of telic or purposive mechanisms through goals and outcomes projected forward in time, the future acquires causal efficacy by being represented cognitively in the present. Cognized futures thus become temporally antecedent to actions. Some writers have misinterpreted the acknowledgment that experience influences thought to mean that thoughts are nothing more than etchings of environmental inputs in the host organism (Rychlak, 1979). When thought is miscast as mechanical mediationism, it is imprinted histories, rather than cognized futures, that impel and direct behavior. This is clearly not the view of cognition and personal agency to which social cognitive theory subscribes. Forethought is the product of generative and reflective ideation.

VICARIOUS CAPABILITY

Psychological theories have traditionally assumed that learning can occur only by performing responses and experiencing their effects. Learning through action has thus been given major, if not exclusive, priority. In actuality, virtually all learning phenomena, resulting from direct experience, can occur vicariously by observing other people's behavior and its consequences for them. The capacity to learn by observation enables people to acquire rules for generating and regulating behavioral patterns without having to form them gradually by tedious trial and error.

The abbreviation of the acquisition process through observational learning is vital for both development and survival. Because mistakes can produce costly, or even fatal consequences, the prospects for survival would be slim indeed if one could learn only from the consequences of trial and error. For this reason, one does not teach children to swim, adolescents to drive automobiles, and novice medical students to perform surgery by having them discover the requisite behavior from the consequences of their successes and failures. The more costly and hazardous the possible mistakes, the heavier must be the reliance on observational learning from competent exemplars. The less the behavior patterns draw on inborn properties, the greater is the dependence on observational learning for the functional organization of behavior.

Humans come with few inborn patterns. This remarkable plasticity places high demand on learning. People must develop their basic capabilities over an extended period, and they must continue to master new competencies to fulfill changing demands throughout their life span. It therefore comes as no surprise that humans have evolved an advanced vicarious learning capability. Apart from the question of survival, it is difficult to imagine a social transmission system in which the language, life styles, and institutional practices of the culture are taught to each new member just by selective reinforcement of fortuitous behaviors, without the benefit of models to exemplify these cultural patterns.

Some complex skills can be mastered only through the aid of modeling. If children had no exposure to the utterances of models, it would be virtually impossible to teach them the linguistic skills that constitute a language. It is doubtful that one could ever shape intricate words, let alone grammatical rules, by selective reward of random vocalization. In other behavior patterns that are formed by unique combinations of elements selected from numerous possibilities, there is little, if any, chance of producing the novel patterns spontaneously, or something even resembling them. Where novel forms of behavior can be conveyed effectively only by social cues, modeling is an indispensable aspect of learning. Even when it is possible to establish new patterns of behavior through other means, the acquisition process can be considerably shortened through modeling.

Most psychological theories were cast long before the advent of enormous advances in the technology of communication. As a result, they give insufficient attention to the increasingly powerful role that the symbolic environment plays in present-day human lives. Indeed, in many aspects of living, televised vicarious influence has dethroned the primacy of direct experience. Whether it be thought patterns, values, attitudes, or styles of behavior, life increasingly models the media.

SELF-REGULATORY CAPABILITY

Another distinctive feature of social cognitive theory is the central role it assigns to self-regulatory functions. People do not behave just to suit the preferences of others. Much of their behavior is motivated and regulated by internal standards and self-evaluative reactions to their own actions. After personal standards have been adopted, discrepancies between a performance and the standard against which it is measured activate evaluative self-reactions, which serve to influence subsequent behavior. An act, therefore, includes among its determinants self-produced influences.

Self-directedness is exercised by wielding influence over the external environment as well as enlisting self-regulatory functions. Thus, by arranging facilitative environmental conditions, recruiting cognitive guides, and creating incentives for their own efforts, people make causal contribution to their own motivation and actions. To be sure, self-regulatory functions are fashioned from, and occasionally supported by, external influences. Having some external origins and supports, however, does not refute the fact that the exercise of self-influence partly determines the course of one's behavior.

SELF-REFLECTIVE CAPABILITY

If there is any characteristic that is distinctively human, it is the capability for reflective self-consciousness. This enables people to analyze their experiences and to think about their own thought processes. By reflecting on their varied experiences and on what they know, they can derive generic knowledge about themselves and the world around them. People not only gain understanding through reflection, they evaluate and alter their own thinking. In verifying thought through self-reflective means, they monitor their ideas, act on them or predict occurrences from them, judge the adequacy of their thoughts from the results, and change them accordingly. While such metacognitive activities usually foster veridical thought (Flavell, 1978a), they can also produce faulty thought patterns through reciprocal causation. Forceful actions arising from erroneous beliefs often create social effects that confirm the misbeliefs (Snyder, 1980).

Among the types of thoughts that affect action, none is more central or pervasive than people's judgments of their capabilities to deal effectively with different realities. It is partly on the basis of self-percepts of efficacy that they choose what to do, how much effort to invest in activities, how long to persevere in the face of disappointing results, and whether tasks are approached anxiously or self-assuredly (Bandura, 1982a). In the self-appraisal of efficacy, there are many sources of information that must be processed and weighed through self-referent thought. Acting on one's self-percepts of efficacy brings successes or missteps requiring further self-reappraisals of operative competencies. The self-knowledge which underlies the exercise of many facets of personal agency is largely the product of such reflective self-appraisal.

Self-reflectivity entails shifting the perspective of the same agent, rather than reifying different internal agents or selves regulating each other. Thus, in their daily transactions, people act on their thoughts and later analyze how well their thoughts have served them in managing events. But it is the one and the same person who is doing the thinking and then later evaluating the adequacy of his or her knowledge, thinking skills, and action strategies. The shift in perspective does not transform one from an agent to an object. One is just as much an agent reflecting on one's experiences as in executing the original courses of action. The same self performing mul-

tiple functions does not require positing multiple selves pursuing different roles.

THE NATURE OF HUMAN NATURE

Seen from the social cognitive perspective, human nature is characterized by a vast potentiality that can be fashioned by direct and observational experience into a variety of forms within biological limits. To say that a major distinguishing mark of humans is their endowed plasticity is not to say that they have no nature or that they come structureless (Midgley, 1978). The plasticity, which is intrinsic to the nature of humans, depends upon neurophysiological mechanisms and structures that have evolved over time. These advanced neural systems for processing, retaining, and using coded information provide the capacity for the very characteristics that are distinctly human—generative symbolization, forethought, evaluative self-regulation, reflective self-consciousness, and symbolic communication.

Plasticity does not mean that behavior is entirely the product of post-natal experience. Some innately organized patterns of behavior are present at birth; others appear after a period of maturation. One does not have to teach infants to cry or suck, toddlers to walk, or adolescents how to copulate. Nor does one have to teach somatic motivators arising from tissue deficits and aversive events or to create somatically-based rewards. Infants come equipped with some attentional selectivity and interpretive predilections, as well (von Cranach, Foppa, Lepenies, & Ploog, 1979). This neural programming for basic physiological functions is the product of accumulated ancestral experiences that are stored in the genetic code.

Most patterns of human behavior are organized by individual experience and retained in neural codes, rather than being provided ready-made by inborn programming. While human thought and conduct may be fashioned largely through experience, innately determined factors enter into every form of behavior to some degree. Genetic factors affect behavioral potentialities. Both experiential and physiological factors interact, often in intricate ways, to determine behavior. Even in behavioral patterns that are formed almost entirely through experience, rudimentary elements are present as part of the natural endowment. For example, humans are endowed with basic phonetic elements which may appear trivial compared to complex acquired patterns of speech, but the elements are, nevertheless, essential. Similarly, even action patterns regarded as instinctual, because they draw heavily on inborn elements, require appropriate experience to be developed. The level of psychological and physiological development, of course, limits what can be acquired at any given time. Because behavior contains mixtures of inborn elements and learned patterns, dichotomous thinking, which separates activities neatly into innate and acquired categories, is seriously inaccurate.

REFERENCES

Bandura, A. (1982). Self-efficacy mechanism in human agency. *American Psychologist, 37*, 747–755.

Flavell, J. H. (1978). Metacognitive development. In J. M. Scandura & C. J. Brainerd (Eds.), *Structural-process theories of complex human behavior* (pp. 213–245). Alphen a.d. Rijn, Netherlands: Sijithoff and Noordhoff.

Midgley, M. (1978). *Beast and man: The roots of human nature.* Ithaca, NY: Cornell University Press.

Rychlak, J. F. (1979). A nontelic teleology? *American Psychologist, 34*, 435–438.

Snyder, M. (1980). Seek, and ye shall find: Testing hypotheses about other people. In E. T. Higgins, C. P. Herman, and M. P. Zanna (Eds.), *Social cognition: The Ontario symposium on personality and social psychology* (Vol. 1, pp. 105–130). Hillsdale, NJ: Erlbaum.

von Cranach, M., Foppa, K., Lepenies, W., & Ploog, D. (Eds.). (1979) *Human ethology: Claims and limits of a new discipline.* Cambridge, UK: Cambridge University Press.

KEY POINTS

1. Human beings are complex organisms who can think, remember, observe, and plan.

2. The environment, our thought processes, and behavior all mutually and reciprocally interact to affect each other.

3. People have plans, and they think about how their behaviors may or may not affect their outcomes.

QUESTIONS TO THINK ABOUT

1. Bandura cites the capacity to use symbols as a key element of the social cognitive approach. Why are symbols so important?

2. Bandura is well-known for his emphasis on vicarious learning—the ability to learn through observation. How is this different from more traditional learning approaches?

3. Bandura's theory is full of complex notions like self-regulation, self-efficacy, and planning. Can these concepts be assessed and applied in a clear and meaningful way?

21

Catastrophizing and Untimely Death*

*CHRISTOPHER PETERSON, MARTIN E. P. SELIGMAN,
KAREN H. YURKO, LESLIE R. MARTIN, AND HOWARD S. FRIEDMAN*

Christopher Peterson (1950–) is a psychology professor at the University of Michigan. With his colleague Karen H. Yurko, and with Martin E. P. Seligman, a professor at the University of Pennsylvania, Peterson has conducted research on optimism and learned helplessness, and their long-term effects. For this study, they joined forces with Leslie R. Martin, a professor at La Sierra University, and Howard S. Friedman, a professor at the University of California, Riverside. Friedman and his team have been studying how personality relates to mortality risk.

The paper that follows illustrates how the social–cognitive approach to personality psychology can be applied to health psychology. The researchers scored people's explanatory style from answers they had given about bad events in 1936 and 1940. These characteristics were used to predict their likelihood of dying each year through 1991.

Explanatory style is a cognitive personality variable that reflects how people habitually explain the causes of bad events (Peterson & Seligman, 1984). Among the dimensions of explanatory style are

- internality ("it's me") versus externality
- stability ("it's going to last forever") versus instability
- globality ("it's going to undermine everything") versus specificity

These dimensions capture tendencies toward self-blame, fatalism, and catastrophizing, respectively. Explanatory style was introduced in the attributional reformulation of helplessness theory to explain individual differences in response to bad events (Abramson, Seligman, & Teasdale, 1978). Individuals who entertain internal, stable, and global explanations for bad events show emotional, motivational, and cognitive disturbances in their wake.

Explanatory style has been examined mainly with regard to depression, and all three dimensions are consistent correlates of depressive symptoms (Sweeney, Anderson, & Bailey, 1986). More recent studies have looked at other outcomes (notably, physical well-being), and researchers have also begun to examine the dimensions separately. Stability and globality—but not internality—predict poor health (Peterson & Bossio,

*Peterson, C., Seligman, M. E. P., Yurko, K. H., Martin, L. R., & Friedman, H. S. (1998). Catastrophizing and untimely death. *Psychological Science, 9*, 127–130. Reprinted by permission. [Ed. note: All citations in the text of this selection have been left intact from the original, but the list of references includes only those sources that are the most relevant and important. Readers wishing to follow any of the other citations can find the full references in the original work or in an online database.]

1991). This is an intriguing finding, but questions remain.

First, do these correlations mean that explanatory styles are risk factors for early death? Previous studies are equivocal either because of small samples or because research participants were already seriously ill.

Second, is the link between explanatory style and health the same or different for males versus females? Again, previous studies are equivocal because they often included only male or only female research participants.

Third, what mediates the link between ways of explaining bad events and poor health? The path is probably overdetermined, but one can ask if fatalism and catastrophizing predict differentially to particular illnesses. These explanatory styles, as cognates of hopelessness, may place one at special risk for cancer, implying an immunological pathway (Eysenck, 1988). Alternatively, these explanatory tendencies, because of their link with stress, may place one at special risk for heart disease, suggesting a cardiovascular pathway (Dykema, Bergbower, & Peterson, 1995). Or perhaps fatalism and catastrophizing predispose one to accidents and injuries and thus point to an incautious lifestyle as a mediator. Once again, previous studies are equivocal either because illness was deliberately operationalized in nonspecific terms or because only one type of illness was studied.

We attempted to answer these questions by investigating explanatory style and mortality among participants in the Terman Life-Cycle Study (Terman & Oden, 1947). The original sample of more than 1,500 preadolescents has been followed from the 1920s to the present, with attrition (except by death) of less than 10% (Friedman et al., 1995). For most of those who have died (about 50% of males and 35% of females as of 1991), year of death and cause of death are known. In 1936 and 1940, the participants completed open-ended questionnaires about difficult life events, which we content-analyzed for explanatory style. We determined the associations between dimensions of explanatory style on the one hand and time of death and cause of death on the other.

METHOD

Sample

The Terman Life-Cycle Study began in 1921–1922, when most of the 1,528 participants were in public school. Terman's original objective was to obtain a reasonably representative sample of bright California children (IQs of 135 or greater) and to examine their lives. Almost every public school in the San Francisco and Los Angeles areas was searched for intelligent children. The average birth date for children in the sample was 1910 (SD = 4 years). Most of the children were preadolescents when first studied; those still living are now in their 80s. Data were collected prospectively, without any knowledge of eventual health or longevity.

In young adulthood, the participants were generally healthy and successful. In middle age, they were productive citizens, but none was identifiable as a genius. The sample is homogeneous on dimensions of intelligence (above average), race (mostly white), and social class (little poverty).

Content Analysis of Causal Explanations

We scored explanatory style of the responses to the 1936 and 1940 questionnaires using the CAVE (content analysis of verbatim explanations) technique (Peterson, Schulman, Castellon, & Seligman, 1992). A single researcher read through all responses in which bad events were described. Examples of questions that elicited such responses include

> (from 1936): Have any disappointments, failures, bereavements, uncongenial relationships with others, etc., exerted a prolonged influence upon you?

> (from 1940): What do you regard as your most serious fault of personality or character?

When a bad event was accompanied by a causal explanation, the event and the attribution were written down. These events, each with its accompanying attribution, were then presented in a nonsystematic order to eight judges who blindly and independently rated each explanation on a 7-point scale according to its stability, its globality, and its internality. The researchers (supervised by Peterson) who identified and rated attributions were independent of the researchers (supervised by Friedman) who collected and coded mortality information (see the next section).

A total of 3,394 attributions was obtained from 1,182 different individuals, an average of 2.87 attributions per person, with a range of 1 to 13. Each of these attributions was rated by each of the eight judges along the three attributional dimensions. We estimated coding reliability by treating the judges as "items" and calculating Cronbach's (1951) alpha for each dimension; alphas were satisfactory: .82, .73, and .94, for stability, globality, and internality, respectively. Ratings were averaged across raters and across different attributions for the same participant. These scores were intercorrelated (mean $r = .52$), as previous research has typically found (Peterson et al., 1982). The means (and standard deviations) were 4.52 (0.86) for stability, 4.46 (0.64) for globality, and 4.49 (1.29) for internality.

Cause of Death

Death certificates for deceased participants were obtained from the relevant state bureaus and coded for underlying cause of death by a physician-supervised certified nosologist using the criteria of the ninth edition of the International Classification of Diseases (U.S. Department of Health and Human Services, 1980) to distinguish among deaths by cancer, cardiovascular disease, accidents or violence, and other causes. For approximately 20% of the deceased, death certificates were unavailable; whenever possible, cause of death was assigned from information provided by next of kin. Among the 1,182 participants for whom explanatory style scores were available,

mortality information was known for 1,179. The numbers of deaths as of 1991 were 148 from cancer (85 men, 63 women), 159 from cardiovascular disease (109 men, 50 women), 57 from accidents or violence (40 men, 17 women), 87 from other (known) causes (50 men, 37 women), and 38 from unknown causes (24 men, 14 women).

RESULTS

Explanatory Styles and Mortality

To investigate the association between explanatory styles and mortality (through 1991), we used Cox Proportional Hazards regressions and checked them with logistic regressions. The Cox approach is nonparametric and assumes that the ratio of hazard functions for individuals with differing values of the covariates (stability, globality, and internality) is invariant over time. We used Tuma's (1980) RATE program for the Cox models, and LOGIST of SAS for the logistic regressions. When all three attributional dimensions were examined simultaneously for the entire sample, only globality was associated with mortality, with a risk hazard (rh) of 1.26 ($p < .01$). Results from the logistic regression analyses (predicting to a dichotomous variable of survival to at least age 65 vs. not) were consistent with this finding; only the odds ratio associated with globality was significant (rh = 1.25, $p < .05$).

Figure 1 depicts the probability of a 20-year-old in this sample dying by a given age as a function of sex and globality (top vs. bottom quartiles of scores). The point at which each curve crosses the .50 probability line represents the "average" age of death of individuals in the group. As can be seen, males with a global explanatory style were at the highest risk for early death.

To test whether the effects of globality were due to individuals being seriously ill or suicidal at the time of assessment, we conducted additional survival analyses that excluded individuals who died before 1945. The effects of globality remained for males.

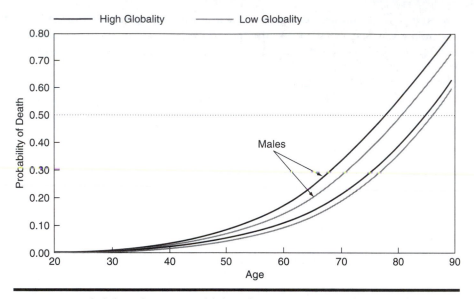

FIGURE 1   Probability of a 20-year-old dying by a given age as a function of sex and globality (upper vs. lower quartiles).

Globality of Explanatory Style and Cause of Death

Next we investigated whether globality was differentially related to causes of death (cancer, cardiovascular disease, accidents or violence, other, and unknown) by comparing Gompertz models (see Table 1). When comparing a model with both sex and globality as predictors but constraining the effects of globality to predict equally across all causes of death (Model 2) with an unconstrained model in which globality was allowed to predict differentially to separate causes of death (Model 3), we found that the unconstrained model fit the data better than did the constrained model. This finding was also obtained when participants who did not survive until at least 1945 were excluded, $\Delta\chi^2(4, N = 1, 157) = 13.29, p < .01$.

Globality best predicted deaths by accident or violence ($rh = 1.98, p < .01$) and deaths from unknown causes ($rh = 2.08, p < .01$). The risk ratios associated with other causes were 1.03 for cardiovascular disease (n.s.), 1.18 for cancer (n.s.), and 1.22 for other (known) causes (n.s.).

Finally, we computed a Cox model for prediction from globality specifically to suicide

(which had been included in the accident-violence group). The result was marginally significant ($rh = 1.84, p < .06$), but only 25 individuals in the sample with globality scores available were known to have committed suicide. When these

TABLE 1   Goodness of Fit for Gompertz Models Predicting (Age-Adjusted) Cause of Death from Sex and Globality of Explanatory Style ($n = 1,179$)

MODEL	$\Delta\chi^2$	df
Model 1: predicting mortality from sex	705.44**	10
Model 2: predicting mortality from sex and globality, constraining the effect of globality to be equal across all causes of death	715.83**	11
Model 3: predicting mortality from sex and globality, not constraining the effects of globality to be equal across all causes of death	726.62**	15
Model 2 vs. Model 1	10.39**	1
Model 3 vs. Model 1	21.18**	5
Model 3 vs. Model 2	10.79*	4

*$p < .05$.   **$p < .001$.

25 individuals were excluded, along with individuals who died of accidents (some of which may have been suicides), and the analyses already described were repeated, the same results were obtained: Globality predicted mortality for the entire sample ($rh = 1.20$, $p < .05$), especially for males ($rh = 1.31$, $p < .05$).

Additional Analyses

How might we explain the finding that globality of explanatory style predicted untimely death? In terms of simple correlations, men who had years earlier made global attributions experienced more mental health problems in 1950 ($r = .14$, $p < .001$), had lower levels of adjustment at this time ($r = -.11$, $p < .02$), and reported that they drank slightly more ($r = .07$, $p < .08$) than men who had made more specific attributions (see Martin et al., 1995). We examined other variables such as education, risky hobbies, and physical activity from 1940 through 1977, but none of the simple associations with globality was significant. The subsample of individuals for whom we had smoking data available was substantially smaller than the original sample because these data were collected in 1990–1991; however, within this group, no associations with globality were found.

Additional survival analyses were conducted, controlling for mental health and psychological adjustment. In these analyses, the association between globality and mortality risk remained stable and significant. When mental health was controlled, the relative hazard associated with globality was 1.27 ($p < .05$). When level of adjustment was controlled, the relative hazard was 1.29 ($p < .01$). A final model controlling for both mental health and adjustment resulted in a relative hazard of 1.24 ($p < .05$). Globality, although related to these aspects of psychological well-being, was distinct, and its association with mortality was not substantially mediated by these other factors.

Finally, globality of explanatory style was inversely related to a measure of neuroticism constructed from 1940 data ($r = -.15$, $p < .001$) (Martin, 1996). This finding seems to rule out confounding of our measures by response sets involving complaints or exaggeration.

DISCUSSION

The present results extend past investigations of explanatory style and physical well-being. They represent the first evidence from a large sample of initially healthy individuals that a dimension of explanatory style—globality—is a risk factor for early death, especially among males. Because globality scores were the least reliably coded of the three attributional dimensions and had the most restricted range, the present results may underestimate the actual association between globality and mortality. In any event, our findings were not due to confounding by neuroticism, suicide, or psychological maladjustment. Stability per se did not predict mortality, perhaps because it involves a belief that is circumscribed, that is, relevant in certain situations but not others.

In contrast, globality taps a pervasive style of catastrophizing about bad events, expecting them to occur across diverse situations. Such a style can be hazardous because of its link with poor problem solving, social estrangement, and risky decision making across diverse settings (Peterson, Maier, & Seligman, 1993). Supporting this interpretation is the link between globality and deaths due to accident or violence. Deaths like these are often not random. "Being in the wrong place at the wrong time" may be the result of a pessimistic lifestyle, one more likely among males than females. Perhaps deaths due to causes classified as unknown may similarly reflect an incautious lifestyle.

Explanatory style, at least as measured in this study, showed no specific link to death by cancer or cardiovascular disease. Speculation concerning explanatory style and poor health has often centered on physiological mechanisms, but behavioral and lifestyle mechanisms are probably more typical and more robust. We were unable to identify a single behavioral mediator, however, which implies that there is no simple set of health mediators set into operation by globality.

Previous reports on the health of the Terman Life-Cycle Study participants found that childhood personality variables predicted mortality (Friedman et al., 1993). Specifically, a variable identified as "cheerfulness" was inversely related to longevity. Its components involved parental judgments of a participant's "optimism" and "sense of humor." Because a hopeless explanatory style is sometimes described as pessimistic and its converse as optimistic, these previous reports appear to contradict the present results. However, in this sample, cheerfulness in childhood was unrelated to explanatory style in adulthood. If cheerfulness and explanatory style tap the same sense of optimism, then this characteristic is discontinuous from childhood to adulthood. It is also possible, perhaps likely, that these two variables measure different things: An optimistic explanatory style is infused with agency: the belief that the future will be pleasant because one can control important outcomes.

In summary, a cognitive style in which people catastrophize about bad events, projecting them across many realms of their lives, foreshadows untimely death decades later. We suggest that a lifestyle in which an individual is less likely to avoid or escape potentially hazardous situations is one route leading from pessimism to an untimely death.

REFERENCES

Friedman, H. S., Tucker, J. S., Schwartz, J. E., Tomlinson-Keasey, C., Martin, L. R., Wingard, D. L., & Criqui, M. H. (1995). Psychosocial and behavioral predictors of longevity: The aging and death of the "Termites." *American Psychologist, 50,* 69–78.

Peterson, C., & Boggio, L. M. (1991). *Health and optimism.* New York: Free Press.

Peterson, C., Maier, S. F., & Seligman, M. E. P. (1993). *Learned helplessness: A theory for the age of personal control.* New York: Oxford University Press.

Peterson, C., & Seligman, M. E. P. (1984). Causal explanations as a risk factor for depression: Theory and evidence. *Psychological Review, 91,* 347–374.

Terman, L. M., & Oden, M. H. (1947). *Genetic studies of genius: IV. The gifted child grows up: Twenty-five years follow-up of a superior group.* Palo Alto, CA: Stanford University Press.

KEY POINTS

1. Explanatory style involves the ways in which people describe and explain events and causes of events in their lives. There are three dimensions of explanatory style. The first is internality, the tendency to blame one's self. The second is stability, a person's belief that the problem or issue is going to last forever. The third is globality, the sense that the one problem or issue will affect everything. A person high on globality catastrophizes bad events.

2. This study found that the explanatory style of globality for bad events is a risk factor for early death, especially in males. The study also found that this association still exists after accounting for the effects of mental health, serious illness, and suicidal tendencies.

3. A cognitive style in which a person catastrophizes bad events may make the person less likely to avoid or escape potentially hazardous situations.

QUESTIONS TO THINK ABOUT

1. How can it be that factors of global attribution (thought) can affect risk of mortality?

2. How does this approach to health differ from our more usual assumptions about health?

3. Why might it be that males show a higher association of globality to mortality then females?

22

Traits Revisited*

GORDON W. ALLPORT

When he was a young boy, Gordon W. Allport (1897–1967) was accused by callous schoolmates of swallowing a dictionary, so enthralled was he with the details of language. This childhood fascination would later prove crucial when he constructed his trait theories of personality. Allport believed that common traits (general internal organizing structures) and personal dispositions (neuropsychic structures peculiar to the individual) intertwine to shape our lives and direct us to behave the ways we do. He viewed personality as a "dynamic organization within the individual of those psychophysical systems that determine his characteristic behavior and thought."

In this selection, Allport defends the concept of traits from two sorts of attacks. The first criticism is the behaviorist one, which argues that we should not label someone as "aggressive," but rather focus directly on the aggressive acts. The second attack is the interactionist one, which argues that because behavior varies from situation to situation, it is difficult to speak of a stable personality. In response, Allport argues that we do gain tremendous utility in understanding people's behavior by using a summary concept like traits, and that people do have tendencies to behave in certain ways, even if they do not always follow these tendencies in every given situation.

Years ago I ventured to present a paper before the Ninth International Congress at New Haven (G. W. Allport, 1931). It was entitled "What Is a Trait of Personality?" For me to return to the same topic on this honorific occasion is partly a sentimental indulgence, but partly too it is a self-imposed task to discover whether during the past 36 years I have learned anything new about this central problem in personality theory.

In my earlier paper I made eight bold assertions. A trait, I said,

1. Has more than nominal existence.
2. Is more generalized than a habit.
3. Is dynamic, or at least determinative, in behavior.
4. May be established empirically.
5. Is only relatively independent of other traits.
6. Is not synonymous with moral or social judgment.
7. May be viewed either in the light of the personality which contains it, or in the light of its distribution in the population at large.

To these criteria I added one more:

8. Acts, and even habits, that are inconsistent with a trait are not proof of the nonexistence of the trait.

While these propositions still seem to me defensible they were originally framed in an age of psychological innocence. They now need

*Allport, G. W. (1966). Traits revisited. *American Psychologist, 21,* 1–10. Copyright © 1966 by the American Psychological Association. Reprinted with permission. [Ed. note: All citations in the text of this selection have been left intact from the original, but the list of references includes only those sources that are the most relevant and important. Readers wishing to follow any of the other citations can find the full references in the original work or in an online database.]

reexamination in the light of subsequent criticism and research.

CRITICISM OF THE CONCEPT OF TRAIT

Some critics have challenged the whole concept of trait. Carr and Kingsbury (1938) point out the danger of reification. Our initial observation of behavior is only in terms of adverbs of action: John behaves aggressively. Then an adjective creeps in: John has an aggressive disposition. Soon a heavy substantive arrives, like William James' cow on the doormat: John has a trait of aggression. The result is the fallacy of misplaced concreteness.

The general positivist cleanup starting in the 1930s went even further. It swept out (or tried to sweep out) all entities, regarding them as question-begging redundancies. Thus Skinner (1953) writes:

> When we say that a man eats because he is hungry, smokes a great deal because he has the tobacco habit, fights because of the instinct of pugnacity, behaves brilliantly because of his intelligence, or plays the piano well because of his musical ability, we seem to be referring to causes. But on analysis these phrases prove to be merely redundant descriptions [p. 31].

It is clear that this line of attack is an assault not only upon the concept of trait, but upon all intervening variables whether they be conceived in terms of expectancies, attitudes, motives, capacities, sentiments, or traits. The resulting postulate of the "empty organism" is by now familiar to us all, and is the scientific credo of some. Carried to its logical extreme this reasoning would scrap the concept of personality itself—an eventuality that seems merely absurd to me.

More serious, to my mind, is the argument against what Block and Bennett (1955) called "traitology" arising from many studies of the variability of a person's behavior as it changes from situation to situation. Every parent knows that an offspring may be a hellion at home and an angel when he goes visiting. A businessman may be hardheaded in the office and a mere marshmallow in the hands of his pretty daughter.

Years ago the famous experiment by La Piere (1934) demonstrated that an innkeeper's prejudice seems to come and go according to the situation confronting him.

In recent months Hunt (1965) has listed various theories of personality that to his mind require revision in the light of recent evidence. Among them he questions the belief that personality traits are the major sources of behavior variance. He, like Miller (1963), advocates that we shift attention from traits to interactions among people, and look for consistency in behavior chiefly in situationally defined roles. Helson (1964) regards trait as the residual effect of previous stimulation, and thus subordinates it to the organism's present adaptation level.

Scepticism is likewise reflected in many investigations of "person perception." To try to discover the traits residing within a personality is regarded as either naive or impossible. Studies, therefore, concentrate only on the *process* of perceiving or judging, and reject the problem of validating the perception and judgment. (Cf. Tagiuri & Petrullo, 1958.)

Studies too numerous to list have ascribed chief variance in behavior to situational factors, leaving only a mild residue to be accounted for in terms of idiosyncratic attitudes and traits. A prime example is Stouffer's study of *The American Soldier* (Stouffer et al., 1949). Differing opinions and preferences are ascribed so far as possible to the GI's age, martial status, educational level, location of residence, length of service, and the like. What remains is ascribed to "attitude." By this procedure personality becomes an appendage to demography (see G. W. Allport, 1950). It is not the integrated structure within the skin that determines behavior, but membership in a group, the person's assigned roles—in short, the prevailing situation. It is especially the sociologists and anthropologists who have this preference for explanations in terms of the "outside structure" rather than the "inside structure" (cf. F. H. Allport, 1955, Ch. 21).

I have mentioned only a few of the many varieties of situationism that flourish today. While not denying any of the evidence adduced I would point to their common error of interpretation. If a child is a hellion at home, an angel outside, he obviously has two contradictory tendencies in his nature, or perhaps a deeper genotype that would explain the opposing phenotypes. If in studies of person perception the process turns out to be complex and subtle, still there would be no perception at all unless there were something out there to perceive and to judge. If, as in Stouffer's studies, soldiers' opinions vary with their marital status or length of service, these opinions are still their own. The fact that my age, sex, social status help form my outlook on life does not change the fact that the outlook is a functioning part of me. Demography deals with distal forces—personality study with proximal forces. The fact that the innkeeper's behavior varies according to whether he is, or is not, physically confronted with Chinese applicants for hospitality tells nothing about his attitude structure, except that it is complex, and that several attitudes may converge into a given act of behavior.

Nor does it solve the problem to explain the variance in terms of statistical interaction effects. Whatever tendencies exist reside in a person, for a person is the sole possessor of the energy that leads to action. Admittedly different situations elicit differing tendencies from my repertoire. I do not perspire except in the heat, nor shiver except in the cold; but the outside temperature is not the mechanism of perspiring or shivering. My capacities and my tendencies lie within.

To the situationist I concede that our theory of traits cannot be so simpleminded as it once was. We are now challenged to untangle the complex web of tendencies that constitute a person, however contradictory they may seem to be when activated differentially in various situations.

ON THE OTHER HAND

In spite of gunfire from positivism and situationism, traits are still very much alive. Gibson (1941) has pointed out that the "concept of set or attitude is nearly universal in psychological thinking." And in an important but neglected paper—perhaps the last he ever wrote—McDougall

(1937) argued that *tendencies* are the "indispensable postulates of all psychology." The concept of *trait* falls into this genre. As Walker (1964) says trait, however else defined, always connotes an enduring tendency of some sort. It is the structural counterpart of such functional concepts as "expectancy," and "goal-directedness."

After facing all the difficulties of situational and mood variations, also many of the methodological hazards such as response set, halo, and social desirability, Vernon (1964) concludes, "We could go a long way towards predicting behavior if we could assess these stable features in which people differ from one another [p. 181]." The powerful contributions of Thurstone, Guilford, Cattell, and Eysenck, based on factor analysis, agree that the search for traits should provide eventually a satisfactory taxonomy of personality and of its hierarchical structure. The witness of these and other thoughtful writers helps us withstand the pessimistic attacks of positivism and situationism.

It is clear that I am using "trait" as a generic term, to cover all the "permanent possibilities for action" of a generalized order. Traits are cortical, subcortical, or postural dispositions having the capacity to gate or guide specific phasic reactions. It is only the phasic aspect that is visible; the tonic is carried somehow in the still mysterious realm of neurodynamic structure. Traits, as I am here using the term, include long-range sets and attitudes, as well as such variables as "perceptual response dispositions," "personal constructs," and "cognitive styles."

Unlike McClelland (1951) I myself would regard traits (i.e., some traits) as motivational (others being merely stylistic). I would also insist that traits may be studied at two levels: (*a*) dimensionally, that is as an aspect of the psychology of individual differences, and (*b*) individually, in terms of *personal dispositions*. (Cf. G. W. Allport, 1961, Ch. 15.) It is the latter approach that brings us closest to the person we are studying.

As for factors, I regard them as a mixed blessing. In the investigations I shall soon report, factorial analysis, I find, has proved both helpful and unhelpful. My principal question is whether the factorial unit is idiomatic enough to reflect the structure of personality as the clinician, the counselor, or the man in the street apprehends it. Or are factorial dimensions screened so extensively and so widely attenuated—through item selection, correlation, axis manipulation, homogenization, and alphabetical labeling—that they impose an artifact of method upon the personal neural network as it exists in nature?

A HEURISTIC REALISM

This question leads me to propose an eptistemological position for research in personality. Most of us, I suspect, hold this position although we seldom formulate it even to ourselves. It can be called a *heuristic realism.*

Heuristic realism, as applied to our problem, holds that the person who confronts us possesses inside his skin generalized action tendencies (or traits) and that it is our job scientifically to discover what they are. Any form of realism assumes the existence of an external structure ("out there") regardless of our shortcomings in comprehending it. Since traits, like all intervening variables, are never directly observed but only inferred, we must expect difficulties and errors in the process of discovering their nature.

The incredible complexity of the structure we seek to understand is enough to discourage the realist, and to tempt him to play some form of positivistic gamesmanship. He is tempted to settle for such elusive formulations as: "If we knew enough about the situation we wouldn't need the concept of personality"; or "One's personality is merely the way other people see one"; or "There is no structure in personality but only varying degrees of consistency in the environment."

Yet the truly persistent realist prefers not to abandon his commitment to find out what the other fellow is really like. He knows that his attempt will not wholly succeed, owing partly to the complexity of the object studied, and partly to the inadequacy of present methods. But unlike Kant who held that the *Ding an Sich* is doomed to

remain unknowable, he prefers to believe that it is at least partly or approximately knowable.

I have chosen to speak of *heuristic* realism, because to me special emphasis should be placed on empirical methods of discovery. In this respect heuristic realism goes beyond naive realism.

Taking this epistemological point of view, the psychologist first focuses his attention on some limited slice of personality that he wishes to study. He then selects or creates methods appropriate to the empirical testing of his hypothesis that the cleavage he has in mind is a trait (either a dimensional trait or a personal disposition). He knows that his present purposes and the methods chosen will set limitations upon his discovery. If, however, the investigation achieves acceptable standards of validation he will have progressed far toward his identification of traits. Please note, as with any heuristic procedure the process of discovery may lead to important corrections of the hypothesis as originally stated.

Empirical testing is thus an important aspect of heuristic realism, but it is an empiricism restrained throughout by rational considerations. Galloping empiricism, which is our present occupational disease, dashes forth like a headless horseman. It has no rational objective; uses no rational method other than mathematical; reaches no rational conclusion. It lets the discordant data sing for themselves. By contrast heuristic realism says, "While we are willing to rest our case for traits on empirical evidence, the area we carve out for study should be rationally conceived, tested by rational methods; and the findings should be rationally interpreted."

THREE ILLUSTRATIVE STUDIES

It is now time for me to illustrate my argument with sample studies. I have chosen three in which I myself have been involved. They differ in the areas of personality carved out for study, in the methods employed, and in the type of traits established. They are alike, however, in proceeding from the standpoint of heuristic realism. The presentation of each study must of necessity be woefully brief. The first illustrates what might be called *meaningful dimensionalism;* the second *meaningful covariation;* the third *meaningful morphogensis.*

Dimensions of Values

The first illustration is drawn from a familiar instrument, dating almost from the stone age, *The Study of Values* (Allport & Vernon, 1931). While some of you have approved it over the years, and some disapproved, I use it to illustrate two important points of my argument.

First, the instrument rests on an a priori analysis of one large region of human personality, namely, the region of generic evaluative tendencies. It seemed to me 40 years ago, and seems to me now, that Eduard Spranger (1922) made a persuasive case for the existence of six fundamental types of subjective evaluation or *Lebensformen.* Adopting this rational starting point we ourselves took the second step, to put the hypothesis to empirical test. We asked: Are the six dimensions proposed—the *theoretic,* the *economic,* the *esthetic, social, political,* and *religious*—measurable on a multidimensional scale? Are they reliable and valid? Spranger defined the six ways of looking at life in terms of separate and distinct ideal types, although he did not imply that a given person belongs exclusively to one and only one type.

It did not take long to discover that when confronted with a forced-choice technique people do in fact subscribe to all six values, but in widely varying degrees. Within any pair of values, or any quartet of values, their forced choices indicate a reliable pattern. Viewed then as empirical continua, rather than as types, the six value directions prove to be measurable, reproducible, and consistent. But are they valid? Can we obtain external validation for this particular a priori conception of traits? The test's *Manual* (Allport & Vernon, 1931) contains much such evidence. Here I would add a bit more, drawn from occupational studies with women subjects. (The evidence for men is equally good.) The data in Table 1 are derived partly from the *Manual,* partly from Guthrie and McKendry (1963) and partly from an unpublished study by Elizabeth Moses.

For present purposes it is sufficient to glance at the last three columns. For the *theoretic* value we note that the two groups of teachers or teachers in preparation select this value significantly more often than do graduate students of business administration. Conversely the young ladies of business are relatively more *economic* in their choices. The results for the *esthetic* value probably reflect the higher level of liberal arts background for the last two groups. The *social* (philanthropic) value is relatively low for the

TABLE 1   Mean Scores for Occupational Groups of Women: Study of Values

	FEMALE COLLEGIATE NORMS N = 2,475	GRADUATE NURSES TRAINING FOR TEACHING N = 328	GRADUATE STUDENTS OF BUSINESS ADMINISTRATION N = 77	PEACE CORPS TEACHERS N = 131
Theoretical	36.5	40.2	37.3	40.6
Economic	36.8	32.9	40.4	29.9
Esthetic	43.7	43.1	46.8	49.3
Social	41.6	40.9	35.0	41.2
Political	38.0	37.2	41.8	39.7
Religious	43.1	45.7	38.7	39.2

TABLE 2 Significant Deviations of Scores on the Study of Values for Occupational Groups of Wellesley Alumni from Wellesley Mean Scores

OCCUPATIONAL GROUPS	N	THEORETICAL	ECONOMIC	ESTHETIC	SOCIAL	POLITICAL	RELIGIOUS
Business workers	64	Lower	Higher				
Medical workers	42	Higher	Lower			Lower	
Literary workers	40	Higher	Lower	Higher			
Artistic workers	37			Higher	Lower		
Scientific workers	28	Higher		Lower			
Government workers	24	Higher				Lower	Lower
Social workers	26				Higher		
Religious workers	11					Lower	Higher

business group, whereas the *political* (power) value is relatively high. Just why nurses should more often endorse the *religious* value is not immediately clear.

Another study of external validation, showing the long-range predictive power of the test is an unpublished investigation by Betty Mawardi. It is based on a follow-up of Wellesley graduates 15 years after taking the Study of Values.

Table 2 reports the significant deviations (at the 5% level or better) of various occupational groups from the mean scores of Wellesley students. In virtually every case we find the deviation meaningful (even necessary) for the occupation in question. Thus women in business are significantly high in *economic* interests; medical, government, and scientific workers in *theoretical*; literary and artistic workers in *esthetic*; social workers in *social*; and religious workers in *religious* values.

One must remember that to achieve a relatively high score on one value, one must deliberately slight others. For this reason it is interesting to note in the table the values that are systematically slighted in order to achieve a higher score on the occupationally relevant value. (In the case of social workers it appears that they "take away" more or less uniformly from other values in order to achieve a high social value.)

Thus, even at the college age it is possible to forecast in a general way modal vocational activity 15 years hence. As Newcomb, Turner, and Converse (1965) say, this test clearly deals with "inclusive values" or with "basic value postures" whose generality is strikingly broad. An evaluative posture toward life saturates, or guides, or gates (choose your own metaphor) specific daily choices over a long expanse of years.

One reason I have used this illustration of trait research is to raise an important methodological issue. The six values are not wholly independent. There is a slight tendency for theoretic and esthetic values to covary; likewise for economic and political values; and so too with social and religious. Immediately the thought arises, "Let's factor the whole matrix and see what orthogonal dimensions emerge." This step has been taken several times (see *Manual*); but always with confusing results. Some investigators discover that fewer than six factors are needed—some that we need more. And in all cases the clusters that emerge seem strange and unnameable. Here is a case, I believe, where our empiricism should submit to rational restraint. The traits as defined are meaningful, reliably measured, and validated. Why sacrifice them to galloping gamesmanship?

Covariation: Religion and Prejudice

Speaking of covariation I do not mean to imply that in restraining our empirical excesses we should fail to explore the patterns that underlie covariation when it seems reasonable to do so.

Take, for example, the following problem. Many investigations show conclusively that on the broad average church attenders harbor more ethnic prejudice than nonattenders. (Some of the relevant studies are listed by Argyle, 1959, and by Wilson, 1960.) At the same time many ardent workers for civil rights are religiously motivated. From Christ to Gandhi and to Martin Luther King we note that equimindedness has been associated with religious devoutness. Here then is a paradox: Religion makes prejudice; it also unmakes prejudice.

First we tackle the problem rationally and form a hypothesis to account for what seems to be a curvilinear relation. A hint for the needed hypothesis comes from *The Authoritarian Personality* (Adorno, Frenkel-Brunswik, Levinson, & Sanford, 1950) which suggests that acceptance of institutional religion is not as important as the *way* in which it is accepted. Argyle (1959) sharpens the hypothesis. He says, "It is not the genuinely devout who are prejudiced but the conventionally religious."

In our own studies we have tentatively assumed that two contrasting but measurable forms of religious orientation exist. The first form we call the *extrinsic* orientation, meaning that for the churchgoer religious devotion is not a value in its own right, but is an instrumental value serving the motives of personal comfort, security, or social status. (One man said he went to church because it was the best place to sell insurance.) Elsewhere I have defined this utilitarian orientation toward religion more fully (G. W. Allport, 1960, 1963). Here I shall simply mention two items from our scale, agreement with which we assume indicates the extrinsic attitude:

What religion offers me most is comfort when sorrows and misfortune strike.

One reason for my being a church member is that such membership helps to establish a person in the community.

By contrast the *intrinsic* orientation regards faith as a supreme value in its own right. Such faith strives to transcend self-centered needs, takes seriously the commandment of brotherhood that is found in all religions, and seeks a unification of being. Agreement with the following items indicates an intrinsic orientation:

My religious beliefs are what really lie behind my whole approach to life.

If not prevented by unavoidable circumstances, I attend church, on the average (more than once a week) (once a week) (two or three times a month) (less than once a month).

This second item is of considerable interest, for many studies have found that it is the irregular attenders who are by far the most prejudiced (e.g., Holtzmann, 1956; Williams, 1964). They take their religion in convenient doses and do not let it regulate their lives.

Now for a few illustrative results in Table 3. If we correlate the extrinsicness of orientation with various prejudice scales we find the hypothesis confirmed. Likewise, as predicted, intrinsicness of orientation is negatively correlated with prejudice.

TABLE 3   Correlation between Measures of Religious Orientation among Churchgoers and Various Prejudice Scales

DENOMINATIONAL SAMPLE	N	r
Unitarian	50	
Extrinsic—anti-Catholicism		.56
Intrinsic—anti-Catholicism		−.36
Extrinsic—anti-Mexican		.54
Intrinsic—anti-Mexican		−.42
Catholic	66	
Extrinsic—anti-Negro		.36
Intrinsic—anti-Negro		−.49
Nazarene	39	
Extrinsic—anti-Negro		.41
Intrinsic—anti-Negro		−.44
Mixed[a]	207	
Extrinsic—anti-Semitic		.65

[a]From Wilson (1960).

In view of the difficulty of tapping the two complex traits in question, it is clear from these studies that our rationally derived hypothesis gains strong support. We note that the trend is the same when different denominations are studied in relation to differing targets for prejudice.

Previously I have said that empirical testing has the ability to correct or extend our rational analysis of patterns. In this particular research the following unexpected fact emerges. While those who approach the intrinsic pole of our continuum are on the average less prejudiced than those who approach the extrinsic pole, a number of subjects show themselves to be disconcertingly illogical. They accept both intrinsically worded items and extrinsically worded items, even when these are contradictory, such as:

> *My religious beliefs are what really lie behind my whole approach to life.*
>
> *Though I believe in my religion, I feel there are many more important things in my life.*

It is necessary, therefore, to inspect this sizable group of muddleheads who refuse to conform to our neat religious logic. We call them "inconsistently proreligious." They simply like religion; for them it has "social desirability" (cf. Edwards, 1957).

The importance of recognizing this third mode of religious orientation is seen by comparing the prejudice scores for the groups presented in Table 4. In the instruments employed the lowest possible prejudice score is 12, the highest pos-

sible, 48. We note that the mean prejudice score rises steadily and significantly from the intrinsically consistent to the inconsistently proreligious. Thus subjects with an undiscriminated proreligious response set are on the average most prejudiced of all.

Having discovered the covariation of prejudice with both the extrinsic orientation and the "pro" response set, we are faced with the task of rational explanation. One may, I think, properly argue that these particular religious attitudes are instrumental in nature; they provide safety, security, and status—all within a self-serving frame. Prejudice, we know, performs much the same function within some personalities. The needs for status, security, comfort, and a feeling of self-rightness are served by both ethnic hostility and by tailoring one's religious orientation to one's convenience. The economy of other lives is precisely the reverse: It is their religion that centers their existence, and the only ethnic attitude compatible with this intrinsic orientation is one of brotherhood, not of bigotry.

This work, along with the related investigations of Lenski (1963), Williams (1964), and others, signifies that we gain important insights when we refine our conception of the nature of the religious sentiment and its functions. Its patterning properties in the economy of a life are diverse. It can fuse with bigotry or with brotherhood according to its nature.

As unfinished business I must leave the problem of nonattenders. From data available it seems that the unchurched are less prejudiced on

TABLE 4   Types of Religious Orientation and Mean Prejudice Scores

	Mean Prejudice Scores			
	CONSISTENTLY INTRINSIC	**CONSISTENTLY EXTRINSIC**	**MODERATELY INCONSISTENT (PRORELIGION)**	**EXTREMELY INCONSISTENT (PRORELIGION)**
Anti-Negro	28.7	33.0	35.4	37.9
Anti-Semitic	22.6	24.6	28.0	30.1

Note.—$N = 309$, mixed denominations. All differences significant at .01 level.

the average than either the extrinsic or the inconsistent churchgoers, although apparently more prejudiced on the average than those whose religious orientation is intrinsic. Why this should be so must form the topic of future research.

Personal Dispositions: An Idiomorphic Approach

The final illustration of heuristic realism has to do with the search for the natural cleavages that mark an individual life. In this procedure there is no reference to common dimensions, no comparison with other people, except as is implied by the use of the English language. If, as Allport and Odbert (1936) have found, there are over 17,000 available trait names, and if these may be used in combinations, there is no real point in arguing that the use of the available lexicon of a language necessarily makes all trait studies purely nomothetic (dimensional).

A series of 172 published *Letters from Jenny* (G. W. Allport, 1965) contains enough material for a rather close clinical characterization of Jenny's personality, as well as for careful quantitative and computational analysis. While there is no possibility in this case of obtaining external validation for the diagnosis reached by either method, still by employing both procedures an internal agreement is found which constitutes a type of empirical validation for the traits that emerge.

The *clinical* method in this case is close to common sense. Thirty-nine judges listed the essential characteristics of Jenny as they saw them. The result was a series of descriptive adjectives, 198 in number. Many of the selected trait names were obviously synonymous; and nearly all fell readily into eight clusters.

The *quantitative* analysis consisted of coding the letters in terms of 99 tag words provided by the lexicon of the General Inquirer (Stone, Bales, Namenwirth, & Ogilvie, 1962). The frequency with which these basic tag words are associated with one another in each letter forms the basis for a factor analysis (see G. W. Allport, 1965, p. 200).

Table 5 lists in parallel fashion the clusters obtained by clinical judgment based on a careful reading of the series, along with the factors obtained by Jeffrey Paige in his unpublished factorial study.

In spite of the differences in terminology the general paralleling of the two lists establishes some degree of empirical check on both of them. We can say that the direct common-sense perception of Jenny's nature is validated by quantification, coding, and factoring. (Please note that in this case factor analysis does not stand alone, but is tied to a parallel rational analysis.)

TABLE 5   Central Traits in Jenny's Personality as Determined by Two Methods

COMMON-SENSE TRAITS	FACTORIAL TRAITS
Quarrelsome-suspicious ⎫	
Aggressive ⎭	Aggressive
Self-centered (possessive)	Possessiveness
Sentimental	⎰ Need for affiliation
	⎱ Need for family acceptance
Independent-autonomous	Need for autonomy
Esthetic-artistic	Sentience
Self-centered (self-pitying)	Martyrdom
(No parallel)	Sexuality
Cynical-morbid	(No parallel)
Dramatic-intense	("Overstate")

While this meaningful validation is clearly present, we gain (as almost always) additional insights from our attempts at empirical validation of the traits we initially hypothesize. I shall point to one instance of such serendipity. The tag words (i.e., the particular coding system employed) are chiefly substantives. For this reason, I suspect, *sexuality* can be identified by coding as a minor factor; but it is not perceived as an independent quality by the clinical judges. On the other hand, the judges, it seems, gain much from the running style of the letters. Since the style is constant it would not appear in a factorial analysis which deals only with variance within the whole. Thus the common-sense traits *cynical-morbid* and *dramatic-intense* are judgments of a pervading expressive style in Jenny's personality and seem to be missed by factoring procedure.

Here, however, the computer partially redeems itself. Its program assigns the tag "overstate" to strong words such as *always, never, impossible*, etc., while words tagged by "understate" indicate reserve, caution, qualification. Jenny's letters score exceedingly high on overstate and exceedingly low on understate, and so in a skeletonized way the method does in part detect the trait of dramatic intensity.

One final observation concerning this essentially idiomorphic trait study. Elsewhere I have reported a small investigation (G. W. Allport, 1958) showing that when asked to list the "essential characteristics" of some friend, 90% of the judges employ between 3 and 10 trait names, the average number being 7.2. An "essential characteristic" is defined as "any trait, quality, tendency, interest, that you regard as of major importance to a description of the person you select." There is, I submit, food for thought in the fact that in these two separate studies of Jenny, the common-sense and the factorial, only 8 or 9 central traits appear. May it not be that the essential traits of a person are few in number if only we can identify them?

The case of Jenny has another important bearing on theory. In general our besetting sin in personality study is irrelevance, by which I mean that we frequently impose dimensions upon persons when the dimensions fail to apply. (I am reminded of the student who was told to interview women patients concerning their mothers. One patient said that her mother had no part in her problem and no influence on her life; but that her aunt was very important. The student answered, "I'm sorry, but our method requires that you tell about your mother." The *method* required it, but the *life* did not.)

In ascribing a list of traits to Jenny we may seem to have used a dimensional method, but such is not the case. Jenny's traits emerge from her own personal structure. They are not imposed by predetermined but largely irrelevant schedules.

CONCLUSION

What then have I learned about traits in the last 4 decades? Well, I have learned that the problem cannot be avoided—neither by escape through positivism or situationism, nor through statistical interaction effects. Tendencies, as McDougall (1937) insisted, remain the "indispensable postulates of all psychology."

Further, I have learned that much of our research on traits is overweighted with methodological preoccupation; and that we have too few restraints holding us to the structure of a life as it is lived. We find ourselves confused by our intemperate empiricism which often yields unnameable factors, arbitrary codes, unintelligible interaction effects, and sheer flatulence from our computors.

As a safeguard I propose the restraints of "heuristic realism" which accepts the common-sense assumption that persons are real beings, that each has a real neuropsychic organization, and that our job is to comprehend this organization as well as we can. At the same time our profession uniquely demands that we go beyond common-sense data and either establish their validity or else—more frequently—correct their errors. To do so requires that we be guided by theory in selecting our trait slices for study, that we employ rationally relevant methods, and be strictly bound by empirical verification. In the end we return to fit our findings to an improved view of the person. Along the way we regard him as an objectively real being whose tendencies we can succeed in knowing—at least in part—beyond the level of unaided common sense. In some respects this recommended procedure resembles what Cronbach and Meehl (1955) call "construct validation," with perhaps a dash more stress on external validation.

I have also learned that while the major foci of organization in a life may be few in number, the network of organization, which includes both minor and contradictory tendencies, is still elusively complex.

One reason for the complexity, of course, is the need for the "inside" system to mesh with the "outside" system—in other words, with the situation. While I do not believe that traits can be defined in terms of interaction effects (since all tendencies draw their energy from within the person), still the vast variability of behavior cannot be overlooked. In this respect I have learned that my earlier views seemed to neglect the variability induced by ecological, social, and situational factors. This oversight needs to be repaired through an adequate theory that will relate the inside and outside systems more accurately.

The fact that my three illustrative studies are so diverse in type leads me to a second concession: that trait studies depend in part upon the investigator's own purposes. He himself constitutes a situation for his respondents, and what he obtains from them will be limited by his purpose and his method. But this fact need not destroy our belief that, so far as our method and purpose allow, we can elicit real tendencies.

Finally, there are several problems connected with traits that I have not here attempted to revisit. There are, for example, refinements of difference between trait, attitude, habit, sentiment, need, etc. Since these are all inside tendencies of some sort, they are for the present occasion all "traits" to me. Nor am I here exploring the question to what extent traits are motivational, cognitive, affective, or expressive. Last of all, and with special restraint, I avoid hammering on the distinction between common (dimensional, nomothetic) traits such as we find in any standard profile, and individual traits (personal dispositions) such as we find in single lives, e.g., Jenny's. (Cf. G. W. Allport, 1961, Ch. 15, also 1962.) Nevitt Sanford (1963) has written that by and large psychologists are "unimpressed" by my insisting on this distinction. Well, if this is so in spite of 4 decades of labor on my part, and in spite of my efforts in the present paper—I suppose I should in all decency cry "uncle" and retire to my corner.

REFERENCES

Adorno, T. W., Frenkel-Brunswik, E., Levinson, D. J., & Sanford, R. N. (1950). *The authoritarian personality.* New York: Harpers.

Allport, G. W. (1961). *Pattern and growth in personality.* New York: Holt, Rinehart & Winston.

Allport, G. W. (Ed.). (1965). *Letters from Jenny.* New York: Harcourt, Brace & World.

Allport, G. W., & Vernon, P. E. (1931). *A study of values.* Boston: Houghton-Mifflin.

Hunt, J. McV. (1965). Traditional personality theory in the light of recent evidence. *American Scientist, 53,* 80–96.

KEY POINTS

1. Allport's trait theory of personality postulates that an individual possesses certain unique motives, attitudes, and innate tendencies that structure the individual's outlook on life and way of life. It is not possible to understand a person fully without understanding these organizing structures.

2. Allport advocates that psychologists apply a more heuristic approach, coupled with empirical study. That is, it is more productive to

assume that people possess certain specified traits and then go about testing this, rather than to rely solely on galloping empiricism.

3. Although clinical and quantitative scrutiny of *Letters from Jenny* revealed several traits of her character, heuristic realism reinforces the idea that natural cleavages exist that mark an individual life, which are not independent of the person's social interactions.

QUESTIONS TO THINK ABOUT

1. Why do individuals within particular occupations tend to support certain values?

2. What is the purpose of approaching empirical testing with the common sense of heuristic realism?

3. Which personality theories best allow us to delve into such complexities as those arising from the covariation of religion and predudice?

Validation of the Five-Factor Model of Personality across Instruments and Observers*

ROBERT R. MCCRAE AND PAUL T. COSTA, JR.

Robert R. McCrae (1949–) received his Ph.D. in personality psychology from Boston University and has worked for many years at the National Institute on Aging, in collaboration with Paul Costa (1942–). Costa received his Ph.D. in human development from the University of Chicago. They have made many distinguished contributions in the field of personality and aging.

McCrae and Costa have provided much significant evidence that personality traits can be best conceived in terms of five basic factors or dimensions. Always concerned with validity, they have gathered relevant information from a wide range of people, measuring instruments, and tasks. In this selection, they lay out the five-factor model of personality and some significant evidence for its validity.

Perhaps in response to critiques of trait models (Mischel, 1968) and to rebuttals that have called attention to common inadequacies in personality research (Block, 1977), personologists in recent years have devoted much of their attention to methodological issues. Lively discussions have centered on the merits and limitations of idiographic versus nomothetic approaches (Kenrick & Stringfield, 1980; Lamiell, 1981), aggregation and its effects on reliability (Epstein, 1979; Rushton, Brainerd, & Pressley, 1983), and alternative methods of scale construction (Burisch, 1984; Wrobel & Lachar, 1982). The veridicality of traits (beyond the realm of cognitive categories) has been tested by examining the correspondence between traits and behaviors (Mischel & Peake, 1982; Small, Zeldin, & Savin-Williams, 1983) and between self-reports and ratings (Edwards & Klockars, 1981; Funder, 1980; McCrae, 1982). As a body, these studies have simultaneously increased the level of methodological sophistication in personality research and restored confidence in the intelligent use of individual difference models of personality.

In contrast, there has been relatively little interest in the substance of personality—the systematic description of traits. The variables chosen as vehicles for tests of methodolical hypotheses

*McCrae, R. R., & Costa, P. T. (1987). Validation of the five-factor model of personality across instruments and observers. *Journal of Personality & Social Psychology, 52,* 81–90. [Ed. note: All citations in the text of this selection have been left intact from the original, but the list of references includes only those sources that are the most relevant and important. Readers wishing to follow any of the other citations can find the full references in the original work or in an online database.]

often appear arbitrary. Bem and Allen (1974) gave no rationale for the use of conscientiousness and friendliness in their classic paper on moderators of validity. McGowan and Gormly's (1976) decision to examine activity and Small et al.'s (1983) choice of prosocial and dominance behavior appear to have been made to facilitate their research designs. Indeed, Kenrick and Dantchik (1983) complained that "catalogs of convenience" have replaced meaningful taxonomics of personality traits among "most of the current generation of social/personality researchers."

This disregard of substance is unfortunate because substance and method are ultimately interdependent. Unless methodological studies are conducted on well-defined and meaningful traits their conclusions are dubious; unless the traits are selected from a comprehensive taxonomy, it is impossible to know how far or in what ways they can be generalized.

Fortunately, a few researchers have been concerned with the problem of structure and have recognized the need for a consensus on at least the general outlines of a trait taxonomy (H. J. Eysenck & Eysenck, 1984; Kline & Barrett, 1983; Wiggins, 1979). One particularly promising candidate has emerged. The five-factor model—comprising extraversion or surgency, agreeableness, conscientiousness, emotional stability versus neuroticism, and culture—of Tupes and Christal (1961) was replicated by Norman in 1963 and heralded by him as the basis for "an adequate taxonomy of personality." Although it was largely neglected for several years, variations on this model have recently begun to reemerge (Amelang & Borkenau, 1982; Bond, Nakazato, & Shiraishi, 1975; Conley, 1985; Digman & Takemoto-Chock, 1981; Goldberg, 1981, 1982; Hogan, 1983; Lorr & Manning, 1978; McCrae & Costa, 1985b).

Some researchers (Goldberg, 1982; Peabody, 1984) have chiefly been concerned with the representativeness and comprehensiveness of this model with respect to the natural language of traits; others have sought to provide a theoretical basis for the taxonomy (Hogan, 1983). Our major concern has been the convergent and discriminant validity of the dimensions of the model across instruments and observers. If the five-factor model is a reasonable representation of human personality, it should be recoverable from questionnaires as well as from adjectives and from observer ratings as well as from self-reports. This line of research addresses substantive questions from the methodological perspective developed in the past few years.

FIVE FACTORS IN SELF-REPORTS AND RATINGS

One of the strongest arguments in favor of the five-factor model has been its appearance in both self-reports and ratings. Norman (1963) reported the structure in peer ratings. Goldberg (1980) showed parallel structures in both ratings and self-reports. As early as the 1960s, convergence across observers was also demonstrated (Borgatta, 1964; Norman & Goldberg, 1966). However, with a few exceptions (e.g., Norman, 1969), these studies used only adjective-rating scales, and few attempts were made to compare adjective factors with standardized questionnaires that are more widely used in personality research.

In a recent publication (McCrae & Costa, 1985b), we examined the correspondence between adjective and questionnaire formats to see if the same substantive dimensions of personality would be obtained in each. Our adjective-rating instrument was an extension of one devised by Goldberg (1983); our questionnaire was the NEO Inventory (McCrae & Costa, 1983a), which measures three broad dimensions identified in analyses of standard personality measures. Self-reports on five adjective factors were compared with both self-reports and spouse ratings on the inventory dimensions of neuroticism, extraversion, and openness to experience. In brief, the study showed that a version of the five-factor model could be recovered from the adjectives, that there were clear correspondences for neuroticism and extraversion dimensions across the two instruments, that Norman's culture factor was better interpreted as openness to experience, and that validity coefficients above .50 could be obtained with both self-reports and spouse ratings.

Three major questions were left unanswered by that study. As Kammann, Smith, Martin, and McQueen (1984) pointed out, research using spouses as raters differs in some respects from more traditional peer-rating studies. Spouses may "more often disclose their feelings to each other through verbal self-statements," and spouses may be more willing to adopt and support the self-concept thus communicated than would peers. Further, the design of our earlier study allowed comparison only between an observer and a self-report; no comparisons were possible between different external observers. A first question, then, concerned the generalizability of our findings to agreement among peer ratings and between peer ratings and self-reports.

A second question involved the particular five-factor structure observed in our set of 80 adjectives. In most studies the fifth and smallest factor has been labeled *culture* and has been thought to include intelligence, sophistication, and intellectual curiosity. The latter element, in particular, suggested correspondence with the questionnaire factor of openness to experience (McCrae & Costa, 1985a). In Goldberg's 40–item instrument (1983) the terms *curious* and *creative* fell on a factor defined primarily by self-rated intelligence. By adding 40 additional items, including some intended to measure such aspects of openness as preference for variety and imaginativeness, we tested the hypothesis that the fifth factor might better be construed as openness rather than as culture. Results confirmed this expectation by showing a factor with only small loadings from *intelligent* and *cultured* but large loadings from *original, imaginative,* and *creative,* and including other forms of openness (*indepen-*

dent, liberal, daring) that were clearly distinct from intelligence. This factor correlated .57 with the NEO Inventory Openness scale. Because of the conceptual importance of this reformulation of the Norman model, it was essential to replicate the adjective-factor structure among peer ratings—the data source on which Norman (1963) had originally relied.

Finally, the NEO Inventory included no measures of two of the Norman factors: agreeableness and conscientiousness. These two dimensions have occurred less frequently in questionnaire measures, and they have been thought by some to represent merely the respondent's evaluation of the target. Consensual validation across observers is therefore particularly important for these two dimensions. For that purpose we developed questionnaire measures of agreeableness–antagonism and conscientiousness–undirectedness, and we examined agreement for both dimensions across instruments and observers in the present study.

METHOD

Subjects

Individuals who provided self-reports and who were targets for peer ratings were members of the Augmented Baltimore Longitudinal Study of Aging. The Baltimore Longitudinal Study of Aging (BLSA) sample is composed of a community-dwelling, generally healthy group of volunteers who have agreed to return for medical and psychological testing at regular intervals (Shock et al., 1984). The sample has been recruited continuously since 1958, with most new subjects referred by friends or relatives in the study. Among the men, 93% are high school graduates and 71% are college graduates; nearly one fourth have doctorate-level degrees. The Augmented BLSA sample consists of 423 men and 129 women who participate in the BLSA, and it includes 183 wives and 16 husbands who are not themselves BLSA participants but who have agreed to complete questionnaires at home. Some participants chose not to participate in this study, and some provided incomplete data. Results are based on the 156 men and 118 women for whom complete data were available, except for one subject who scored more than five standard deviations below the mean on the conscentiousness adjective factor and whose adjective data were thrown out. Comparison of individuals who chose to participate in the peer-rating study with others showed no significant differences in age or sex. Somewhat surprisingly, there were also no differences in self-reported personality as measured by the five adjective factors. Participating subjects were slightly more open to experience than were others, $F(1, 634) = 4.15$, $p < .05$, when NEO Inventory scores were examined. At the time of the peer ratings, ages ranged from 29 to 93 ($M = 59.9$ years) for men and from 28 to 85 ($M = 53.8$ years) for women.

Peer Raters

Subjects were asked to nominate

> three or four individuals who know you very well as you are now. They can be friends, neighbors, or co-workers, but they should not be relatives. These should be people who have known you for at least one year and have seen you in a variety of situations.

A few subjects nominated more than four raters, and names and addresses for 1,075 raters were obtained, a few of whom were dropped because they were themselves members of the BLSA or had already been nominated by another subject (peers rated only one subject). Of those contacted, 747 (69%) provided rating data. Raters were assured of the confidentiality of their responses and were specifically instructed not to discuss the ratings with the subject.

For purposes of item factor analyses, all rating were pooled. For intraclass and peer/self-report correlations, data were analyzed in four subsamples defined by the number of ratings available for each subject: 49 subjects had exactly one rater, 71 had two raters, 90 had three, and 63 had four or more raters. Too few subjects had five or more raters to allow analyses of these data, and only the first four raters' data were examined in these cases.

A background sheet completed by raters was used to characterize the peers and their relationships to the subjects. As a group, the raters resembled the subjects. They ranged in age from 19 to 87 ($M = 54.2$ years), and the correlation of rater's age with subject's age was 72. Like BLSA participants, the raters were well educated: 78% were high school graduates, 57% were college graduates, and 41% had some graduate or professional education. Most of the raters (91% of the men and 75% of the women) were of the same sex as the subjects they rated. However, when asked if they thought they were similar in "personality, attitudes, temperament, and feelings" to the subject, only 8% of the raters considered themselves very similar, and 51% considered themselves similar; 34% considered themselves different, and 7% considered themselves very different from the subject.

The raters appeared to be well acquainted with the subjects. They reported knowing the subjects for an average of 18.3 years (range = 1 to 74 years). Currently, 57% reported seeing the subject weekly, 27% monthly, and 14% once or twice a year. In addition, 9% of the subjects volunteered the information that they had seen the subject more frequently at some time in the past. Furthermore, raters appeared to have some depth of acquaintance: 61% reported that the subject sometimes shared confidences or personal feelings with them, and 35% said he or she often did. In addition, raters said that the subject sometimes (67%) or often (15%) came to them for advice and support. When asked for their own assessment, 56% said they knew the subject pretty well, 40% said they knew the subject very well.

Most (75%) of the raters described their relationship with the subject as a close personal friend, 29% as a family friend, 28% as a neighbor, and 34% as a coworker. Only 8% listed themselves as an acquaintance. Most raters had seen the subject in a variety of settings: at parties or social events (89%), with same-sex friends (67%), with family (85%), at work (51%), during subject's personal crisis (46%), on vacation (39%), or at religious services (31%).

As a group, these raters seemed particularly well qualified to give personality ratings. They had known the subjects for many years, seen them frequently in a variety of settings, and shared their confidences. The raters themselves believed they could give accurate ratings: 86% believed they were good at understanding others, and 89% thought the subject they rated was straightforward and easy to understand.

Measures and Procedure

Data from two kinds of instruments—adjective-rating scale factors and questionnaire scales—were obtained by mail administration over a period of 4 years. The schedule of administration of the personality measures is given in Table 1.

Adjective factors. On the basis of a series of analyses of English-language trait names, Goldberg (1983) developed a 40-item bipolar[1] adjective-rating scale instrument to measure five major dimensions of personality. In subse-

TABLE 1   Schedule of Administration of Personality Measures

INSTRUMENT	DATE
Self-reports	
NEO inventory	February 1980
Adjective-rating scales, agreeableness and conscientiousness items (preliminary)	March 1983
Peer ratings	
Adjective-rating scales	
NEO Personality Inventory (Form R)	July 1983

quent work (McCrae & Costa, 1985b) we supplemented his list with an additional 40 items. Subjects rated themselves on this 80-item instrument with the use of Goldberg's 9-point scale. Five factors were derived from these self-reports and identified as neuroticism, extraversion, openness, agreeableness, and conscientiousness. Similar factors were found for men and women. Neuroticism, extraversion, and openness factors were validated against NEO Inventory measures of the same constructs from both self-reports and spouse ratings, with convergent correlations ranging from .52 to .65 (McCrae & Costa, 1985b). To examine the factor structure of this instrument in peer ratings is one of the aims of this article.

NEO Personality Inventory. A questionnaire measure of the five-factor model is provided by the NEO Personality Inventory (Costa & McCrae, 1985), which comprises the NEO Inventory (Costa & McCrae, 1980; McCrae & Costa, 1983a) along with newly developed scales to measure agreeableness and conscientiousness. The original NEO Inventory is a 144-item questionnaire developed through factor analysis to fit a three-dimensional model of personality. Eight-item scales are used for each of six facets or specific traits within each of three broad trait dimensions, and overall scores are obtained by summing the scores of the six facets of neuroticism, extraversion, and openness. Item scoring is balanced to control for acquiescence, and socially desirable responding does not appear to bias scores (McCrae & Costa, 1983b). Internal consistency and 6-month retest reliability for the three global scores range from .85 to .93 (McCrae & Costa, 1983a). A third-person form of the NEO Inventory has been developed for use by raters and has shown comparable reliability and validity when spouse ratings are obtained (McCrae, 1982).

Questionnaire scales to measure agreeableness and conscientiousness were developed as part of the present research. Two 24-item rational scales were created, and joint factor analysis of these items with NEO Inventory items led to the identification of the hypothesized five factors. Ten items loading on the agreeableness and conscientiousness factors were tentatively adopted as measures of those factors. These items also correlated more highly with the appropriate adjective factor than with any of the other adjective factors in self-reports.

When the NEO Inventory Rating Form was administered to peers, 60 items intended to measure agreeableness and conscientiousness were interspersed. These included the best items from the pilot study undertaken on self-reports along with new items written subsequently. Two final 18-item scales measuring agreeableness and conscientiousness were derived from analyses of these data. Two criteria were used for item selection. First, joint factor analysis with the NEO items in peer ratings again showed five factors that could be identified as neuroticism, extraversion, openness, agreeableness, and conscientiousness. Items selected for the final scales were required to have their highest loadings on their hypothesized factor. Second, scales were created by using the 10-item preliminary scales developed on self-reports. The 60 proposed items were correlated with these two scales as well as with the three domain scores from the NEO Inventory Rating Form. To be included in the final selection, items were required to show higher correlations with the Agreeableness or Conscientiousness scale than with any of the other four scales. Because the final selection included some items written after the self-report data had been collected, the final self-report scales consisted of only 10 agreeableness and 14 conscientiousness items.

Coefficient alpha for the Conscientiousness scale was .91 within peer ratings and .84 within self-reports; for the Agreeableness scale it was .89 within peer ratings but only .56 within self-reports. In part, this low internal consistency was due to the inclusion of only 10 items in the self-report scale; in part, it was due to lower average interitem correlations. Correlations between questionnaire and adjective measures of agreeableness and conscientiousness in self-reports were .48 and .65, respectively; neither scale correlated over .20 with any of the other adjective factors.

It is essential to note that although the development of the Agreeableness and Conscientiousness scales was conducted in parallel on peers and self-reports, correlations across these two methods did not influence item selection in any way. Thus, the correlation between self-reports and ratings was not inflated by the capitalization on chance inherent in some types of item selection.

RESULTS

The results will be considered in three sections. First, we will examine the factor structure of the 80-item adjective-rating scales in peer ratings and validate the factors by correlation with peer ratings on the NEO Personality Inventory. Second, we will consider agreement among peers on the personality characteristics of the targets they have rated by examining intraclass correlations among raters for both adjective factor and questionnaire measures of the five-factor model. Finally, we will present correlations between self-reports and peer ratings.

Adjective Factors in Peer Ratings

Everett (1983) has recently suggested that the number of factors to be retained and interpreted should be determined by comparing rotated solutions in different samples or subsamples and adopting the solution that can be replicated. Coefficients of factor comparability should be used as the measure of similarity, and Everett suggested that coefficients above .90 be required to consider two factors to be a match. When peer ratings on the 80 adjective scales were submitted to principal components analysis, a scree test suggested that approximately five factors would be needed. Everett's procedure was then used to

TABLE 2   Comparabilities for Varimax-Rotated Principal Components in 738 Peers Using Factor-Scoring Matrices from Ratings and Self-Reports

COMPONENTS ROTATED	Factor Comparabilities After Varimax Rotation							
	1ST	2ND	3RD	4TH	5TH	6TH	7TH	8TH
8	.94	.87	.85	.73	.72	.70	.68	.14
7	.95	.95	.86	.85	.58	.53	.08	
6	.96	.93	.91	.89	.82	.61		
5	.98	.98	.97	.96	.95			
4	.93	.86	.81	.76				
3	.87	.84	.74					

compare solutions in self-reports and peer ratings for the third through eighth factors. Varimax-rotated three-factor solutions were obtained independently in self-report data from 503 subjects (McCrae & Costa, 1985b) and in ratings from 738 peers. Comparability coefficients were calculated by applying the scoring weights derived from both analyses to the data from peers and by correlating the resulting factor scores. This process was repeated for four-, five-, six-, seven-, and eight-factor solutions (results are shown in Table 2). Only the five-factor solution showed replication of all factors, and comparabilities were very high in this case, ranging from .95 to .98. This is clear evidence that the five-factor solution, and only the five-factor solution, was invariant across observers.

Table 3 shows factor loadings for the five-factor solution in peers. The factors in Table 3 have been reordered, and variables are arranged using the structure observed in self-reports (McCrae & Costa, 1985b) for comparison. The match between factors in the two data sets is clear; the great majority of items loaded on the same factor in peer ratings as they did in self-reports. The most notable difference appeared to be in the peer agreeableness–antagonism factor, which included, as definers of the antago-

nistic pole, aspects of dominance (e.g., *dominant, bold*) from the extraversion factor and hostility (e.g., *temperamental, jealous*) from the neuroticism factor.

The similarity of structure was particularly important in the case of the openness factor. In peer ratings, as in self-reports, *broad interests, prefer variety, independent,* and *liberal* were among the definers of this factor, *intelligent* and *cultured* showed small loadings. From this set of 80 items in both data sources, a factor emerged in which concern with rich and varied experience was more central than cognitive ability.

The interpretation of the peer-rating factors were [sic] confirmed by correlating factor scores with scale scores from the NEO Personality Inventory ratings. Convergent correlations between adjective factors and corresponding NEO scales were .73 for neuroticism, .70 for extraversion, .70 for openness, .80 for agreeableness, and .76 for conscientiousness ($N = 722$, $p < .001$). The largest divergent correlation was .33. These findings demonstrate that raters were highly consistent across instruments in the ways in which they described their targets on each of the five dimensions. The findings do not, however, speak to the accuracy of the ratings, as judged against external criteria.

TABLE 3 Varimax-Rotated Factor Loadings for 80 Adjective Items From Peer Ratings

	Factor				
ADJECTIVES	N	E	O	A	C
Neuroticism (N)					
Calm–worrying	**79**	05	–01	–20	05
At ease–nervous	**77**	–08	–06	–21	–05
Relaxed–high-strung	**66**	04	01	–34	–02
Unemotional–emotional	**44**	**40**	14	03	–03
Even-tempered–temperamental	**41**	01	01	**–56**	–21
Secure–insecure	**63**	–16	–08	–07	–39
Self-satisfied–self-pitying	**53**	–17	–07	03	–17
Patient–impatient	**41**	02	–03	**–57**	02
Not envious–envious/jealous	29	01	–10	**–46**	–19
Comfortable–self-conscious	**57**	–30	–17	–16	–16
Not impulse ridden–impulse ridden	20	26	22	–16	–38
Hardy–vulnerable	**50**	–14	–13	23	–26
Objective–subjective	17	10	–31	–20	–36
Extraversion (E)					
Retiring–sociable	–14	**71**	08	08	08
Sober–fun loving	–08	**59**	12	14	–15
Reserved–affectionate	–01	**65**	12	25	–15
Aloof–friendly	–16	**58**	02	**45**	06
Inhibited–spontaneous	–21	**52**	**49**	01	–02
Quiet–talkative	01	**64**	06	–19	00
Passive–active	–26	**42**	28	–23	37
Loner–joiner	–14	**53**	–08	14	12
Unfeeling–passionate	14	**43**	28	31	09
Cold–warm	–05	**57**	09	**54**	06
Lonely–not lonely	**–49**	30	–01	10	11
Task oriented–person oriented	–04	36	09	35	–29
Submissive–dominant	–16	20	20	**–57**	27
Timid–bold	–21	33	31	**–44**	10
Openness (O)					
Conventional–original	–06	12	**67**	08	–04
Down to earth–imaginative	16	03	**54**	–10	–12
Uncreative–creative	–08	09	**56**	11	25
Narrow interests–broad interests	–15	20	**52**	18	27
Simple–complex	16	–13	**49**	–20	08
Uncurious–curious	00	12	**41**	00	24
Unadventurous–daring	–18	31	**55**	–06	08
Prefer routine–prefer variety	–11	30	**43**	14	–21
Conforming–independent	–22	09	**49**	–14	21
Unanalytical–analytical	–15	–13	**43**	–13	30
Conservative–liberal	04	08	**46**	15	–13
Traditional–untraditional	02	–01	**45**	-05	–36
Unartistic–artistic	10	15	36	21	18

Note. These are varimax-rotated principal component loading for 738 raters. The loadings above .40 given in boldface. Decimal points are omitted.

ADJECTIVES	Factor				
	N	E	O	A	C
Aggreeableness vs. antagonism (A)					
Irritable–good natured	−17	34	09	**61**	16
Ruthless–soft hearted	12	27	−01	**70**	11
Rude–courteous	03	18	09	**55**	36
Selfish–selfless	−07	−02	04	**65**	22
Uncooperative–helpful	−01	23	14	**44**	**45**
Callous–sympathetic	04	29	11	**67**	20
Suspicious–trusting	−14	19	15	**62**	08
Stingy–generous	02	24	17	**55**	22
Antagonistic–acquiescent	−02	−06	−09	**66**	−02
Critical–lenient	−13	09	00	**65**	−14
Vengeful–forgiving	−15	11	07	**70**	16
Narrow-minded–open-minded	−14	15	**48**	**54**	16
Disagreeable–agreeable	14	24	06	**59**	26
Stubborn–flexible	−18	08	12	**61**	00
Serious–cheerful	−10	**58**	08	26	02
Cynical–gullible	14	14	−17	**40**	−16
Manipulative–straightforward	−15	06	−02	**47**	31
Proud–humble	01	−18	−09	**45**	−13
Conscientiousness vs. undirectedness (C)					
Negligent–conscientious	−01	02	08	18	**68**
Careless–careful	−08	−07	−01	11	**72**
Undependable–reliable	−07	04	05	23	**68**
Lazy–hardworking	−07	17	14	03	**66**
Disorganized–well organized	14	−02	05	−05	**68**
Lax–scrupulous	05	03	03	10	**53**
Weak willed–self-disciplined	−26	−01	23	−03	**62**
Sloppy–neat	−01	00	−04	12	**59**
Late–punctual	−05	−09	−05	05	**60**
Impractical–practical	−24	01	−04	05	**54**
Thoughtless–deliberate	−03	−08	05	14	**45**
Aimless–ambitious	−09	12	21	−08	**52**
Unstable–emotionally stable	**−57**	09	07	27	**45**
Helpless–self-reliant	−29	19	21	−01	**53**
Playful–businesslike	00	−26	−02	−09	**49**
Unenergetic–energetic	−14	34	27	−06	**46**
Ignorant–knowledgeable	−12	−03	**53**	13	**43**
Quitting–perservering	−09	13	27	00	**62**
Stupid–intelligent	−04	03	**41**	17	**44**
Unfair–fair	−14	04	19	**59**	33
Imperceptive–perceptive	−16	07	**46**	24	39
Uncultured–cultured	01	00	36	15	33

Consensual Validation Across Peer Raters

The extent to which different peers agreed on the attribution of traits to the same individual was calculated by examining the intraclass correlations between factor scores for raters. Intraclass correlations were equivalent to the Pearsonian correlation between all possible pairs of raters (Haggard, 1958). The top half of Table 4 gives intraclass correlations for groups of subjects with two, three, or four raters. All were statistically significant, and values ranged from .30 to .65, with a median of .38. Levels of cross-peer agreement were approximately equal for all five factors. These data provide evidence of consensual validation for all five dimensions in three independent subsamples.

Agreement across observers on questionnaire measures is seen in significant intraclass correlations given in the bottom half of Table 4 for three subsamples. These correlations closely resemble those for adjective factors, and they suggest that peers agreed as well on questionnaire as on adjective checklist descriptions of their friends.

Although the magnitude of correlations seen in Table 4 compares favorably with most in the literature (see McCrae, 1982, for a review), and although virtually all exceed the .3 barrier sometimes thought to set a limit to validity coefficients in personality research, it is also true that there was room for considerable difference of opinion between raters with regard to the same subject.

Agreement Between Self-Reports and Ratings

Agreement among raters was only one piece of evidence for consensual validation. It could be argued that shared stereotypes account for some or all of the agreement among peers (Bourne, 1977). A more rigorous test would compare ratings with self-reports, because it is unlikely that any of the artifacts affecting either of these sources would be shared (McCrae, 1982). The top half of Table 5 presents the correlations between averaged peer ratings and self-reports for each of the five factors. With the exception

TABLE 4   Intraclass Correlations for Peer Ratings

NUMBER OF PEER RATERS	N^a	Factor				
		N	E	O	A	C
		Adjective-Factor Scores				
2	146	30	59	65	43	37
3	267	38	37	37	44	36
4	248	30	42	41	36	41
		NEO Personality Inventory				
2	142	53	52	51	38	47
3	270	30	38	39	38	38
4	252	31	43	40	28	40

Note. N = Neuroticism. E = Extraversion. O = Openness. A = Agreeableness. C = Conscientiousness. All correlations are significant at $p < .01$. Decimal points are omitted.

[a]Refers to number of raters.

TABLE 5   Convergent Correlations Between Self-Reports and Peer Ratings for Adjective-Factor Scores and NEO Personality Inventory

NO. OF PEER RATERS	N^a	Self-Reports				
		N	E	O	A	C
		Adjective-Factor Scores				
1	49	33*	29*	46***	41**	25
2	72	53***	62***	46***	42***	30**
3	85	59***	45***	54***	55***	49***
4	61	51***	48***	52***	59***	50***
		NEO Personality Inventory				
1	45	26	37*	53***	20	21
2	68	47***	60***	53***	34**	33**
3	81	43***	46***	62***	35**	50***
4	54	51***	56***	67***	24	58***

Note. N = Neuroticism. E = Extraversion. O = Openness. A = Agreeableness. C = Conscientiousness. Decimal points are omitted.

[a]Refers to targets, not to raters.

*p < .05.

**p < .01.

***p < .001.

of conscientiousness among subjects having only a single rater, all the correlations were statistically significant and many were substantial in magnitude.

The bottom half of Table 5 gives corresponding correlations for the NEO Personality Inventory for subjects with complete data. Although several correlations were small when only a single rater was used, they increased considerably in magnitude when multiple raters were averaged. Only the Agreeableness scale failed to show the utility of aggregating raters.

Finally, we considered divergent as well as convergent validation of the five factors across instruments and observers. To simplify presentation of the data, the four subsamples were combined by calculating an average peer rating (standardized within subsample) for each adjective-factor and questionnaire scale. Table 6 presents

the correlations of mean peer ratings on both adjective factors and questionnaire scales with self-reports on the same variables. Convergent correlations, given in boldface, were invariably larger than divergent correlations, markedly so for all cases except those involving the self-report questionnaire Agreeableness–Antagonism scale. Because there was good agreement across observers when the agreeableness adjective-factor scores were used, it could be inferred that the problem here lay with the questionnaire scale and not with the construct. This was expected given the low reliability of the preliminary Agreeableness scale used in self-reports. For all five dimensions, the median validity coefficient was .44. When examined by sex, convergent correlations ranged from .19 to .58 for men (median = .35) and from .17 to .56 for women (median = .48).

TABLE 6   Correlations of Self-Reports With Mean Peer Ratings for Adjective Factors and Questionnaire Scales

| MEAN PEER RATING | Self-Reports | | | | | | | | | |
| | Adjective Factors | | | | | NEO Personality Inventory | | | | |
	N	E	O	A	C	N	E	O	A	C
Adjective factors										
N	**50*****	00	02	05	–10	**38*****	06	08	01	–09
E	19**	**48*****	01	09	–07	08	**40*****	16*	04	–03
O	01	–01	**49*****	–01	–08	02	11	**43*****	–06	–11
A	–05	–14*	–18**	**49*****	–20***	–08	–26***	–02	**28*****	–19**
C	–09	–08	–12*	–08	**40*****	–11	–02	–09	11	**40*****
NEO Personality Inventory										
N	**44*****	–03	00	–03	–15*	**42*****	02	02	–11	–14*
E	06	**45*****	16**	00	06	–04	**47*****	25***	02	02
O	07	08	**45*****	13*	–07	03	13*	**57*****	02	–13*
A	–06	–11	–15*	**45*****	–10	–12	–25***	–03	**30*****	–12
C	–11	–05	–10	–09	**39*****	–14*	–02	–08	08	**43*****

Note. N = Neuroticism, E = Extraversion, O = Openness, A = Agreeableness, C = Conscientiousness.
N = 255 to 267. Convergent correlations are shown in boldface. Decimal points are omitted.
*p < .05. **p < .01. ***p < .001.

DISCUSSION

Convergence Across Observers and Instruments

This research examined the correspondence between assessments of five major personality dimensions among peer ratings and between peer ratings and self-reports, using both adjective factors and questionnaire scales. The results are straightforward, showing convergent and discriminant cross-observer and cross-instrument validation for all five factors.

The magnitude of the correlations—generally .4 to .6—deserves some comment, because it was larger than typically reported (e.g., Borgatta, 1964). In part, the higher agreement may be due to reliable and well-constructed measures and, in part, to the nature of the raters. On the whole, raters were very well acquainted with the subjects they rated, having seen them fre-

quently in a variety of circumstances over a period of many years. As Table 5 shows, aggregating across raters also tended to increase agreement. However, as Kammann et al. (1984) noted, there are limits to the improvements in accuracy offered by aggregating. Although the averaged ratings may reflect more accurately the consensus of how the individual is viewed, they may always diverge to some extent from the individual's phenomenological view of himself or herself. Given the qualifications of the raters in this study, it seems likely that the correlations seen here will be near the ceiling for self–other agreement.

It is also worth pointing out that ratings and self-reports differed in another respect as well. When raw scores on the NEO Inventory were compared, ratings were approximately one-half standard deviation higher on extraversion, and one-third lower on neuroticism, than were self-reports. Separate norms would thus be needed to make self-reports and ratings comparable.

The Nature of the Five Factors

These methodological considerations lay the groundwork for the equally important question of substance. A growing body of research has pointed to the five-factor model as a recurrent and more or less comprehensive taxonomy of personality traits. Theorists disagree, however, on precisely how to conceptualize the factors themselves. It seems useful at this point to review each of the factors and attempt to define the clear elements as well as disputed aspects. The factors in Table 3, which so closely parallel factors found in self-reports and which show such clear evidence of convergent and discriminant validity across observers and instruments, can form a particularly useful guide to the conceptual content of the dimensions of personality.

Neuroticism versus emotional stability. There is perhaps least disagreement about neuroticism, defined here by such terms as worrying, insecure, self-conscious, and temperamental. Although adjectives describing neuroticism are relatively infrequent in English (Peabody, 1984), psychologists' concerns with psychopathology have led to the development of innumerable scales saturated with neuroticism. Indeed, neuroticism is so ubiquitous an element of personality scales that theorists sometimes take it for granted.

A provocative view of neuroticism is provided by Tellegen (in press), who views it as negative emotionality, the propensity to experience a variety of negative affects, such as anxiety, depression, anger, and embarrassment. Virtually all theorists would concur in the centrality of negative affect to neuroticism; the question is whether other features also define it. Tellegen himself (in press) pointed out that his construct of negative emotionality has behavioral and cognitive aspects. Guilford included personal relations and objectivity in his emotional health factor (Guil-

ford, Zimmerman, & Guilford, 1976), suggesting that mistrust and self-reference form part of neuroticism. We have found that impulsive behaviors, such as tendencies to overeat, smoke, or drink excessively, form a facet of neuroticism (Costa & McCrae, 1980), and *impulse-ridden* is a definer of the neuroticism factor in self-reports, although not in ratings. Others have linked neuroticism to irrational beliefs (Teasdale & Rachman, 1983; Vestre, 1984) or to poor coping efforts (McCrae & Costa, 1986).

What these behaviors seem to share is a common origin in negative affect. Individuals high in neuroticism have more difficulty than others in quitting smoking because the distress caused by abstinence is stronger for them. They may more frequently use inappropriate coping responses like hostile reactions and wishful thinking because they must deal more often with disruptive emotions. They may adopt irrational beliefs like self-blame because these beliefs are cognitively consistent with the negative feelings they experience. Neuroticism appears to include not only negative affect, but also the disturbed thoughts and behaviors that accompany emotional distress.

Extraversion or surgency. Sociable, fun-loving, affectionate, friendly, and talkative are the highest loading variables on the extraversion factor. This is not Jungian extraversion (see Guilford, 1977), but it does correspond to the conception of H. J. Eysenck and most other contemporary researchers, who concur with popular speech in identifying extraversion with lively sociability.

However, disputes remain about which elements are central and which are peripheral to extraversion. Most writers would agree that sociability, cheerfulness, activity level, assertiveness, and sensation seeking all covary, however loosely. But the Eysencks have at times felt the need to distinguish between sociability and what they call impulsiveness (S. B. G. Eysenck & Eysenck, 1963; Revelle, Humphreys, Simon, & Gilliland, 1980). Hogan (1983) believed that the five-factor model was improved by dividing extraversion into sociability and assertiveness factors. In Goldberg's analyses, surgency (dominance and activity) were the primary definers of extraversion, and terms like warm–cold were assigned to the agreeableness–antagonism factor. Tellegen (in press) emphasized the complementary nature of neuroticism and extraversion by labeling his extraversion factor positive emotionality.

These distinctions do seem to merge at a high enough level of analysis (H. J. Eysenck & Eysenck, 1967; McCrae & Costa, 1983a), and sociability—the enjoyment of others' company—seems to be the core. What is essential to recall, however, is that liking people does not necessarily make one likable. Salesmen, those prototypic extraverts, are generally happier to see you than you are to see them.

Openness to experience. The reinterpretation of Norman's culture as openness to experience was the focus of some of our previous articles (McCrae & Costa, 1985a, 1985b), and the replication of results in peer ratings was one of the purposes of the present article. According to adjective-factor results, openness is best characterized by original, imaginative, broad interests, and daring. In the case of this dimension, however, questionnaires may be better than adjectives as a basis for interpretation and assessment. Many aspects of openness (e.g, openness to feelings) are not easily expressed in single adjectives, and the relative poverty of the English-language vocabulary of openness and closedness may have contributed to confusions about this domain (McCrae & Costa, 1985a). We know from questionnaire studies that openness can be manifest in fantasy, aesthetics, feelings, actions, ideas, and values (Costa & McCrae, 1978, 1980), but only ideas and values are well represented in the adjective factor. Interestingly, questionnaire measures of openness give higher validity coefficients than do adjective-factor measures—indeed, the correlation of .57 between the self-reported NEO Openness scale and the peer-rated NEO Openness scale is the highest of those shown in Table 6.

Perhaps the most important distinction to be made here is between openness and intelligence. Open individuals tend to be seen by themselves and others as somewhat more intelligent, and there are correlations of .30 between psychometric measures of intelligence and openness. However, joint factor analyses using Army Alpha intelligence subtests and either adjectives (McCrae & Costa, 1985b) or NEO Inventory scales (McCrae & Costa, 1985a) show that intelligence scales define a factor clearly separate from openness. Intelligence may in some degree predispose the individual to openness, or openness may help develop intelligence, but the two seem best construed as separate dimensions of individual differences.

Agreeableness verse antagonism. As a broad dimension, agreeableness–antagonism is less familiar than extraversion or neuroticism, but some of its component traits, like trust (Stark, 1978) and Machiavellianism (Christie & Geis, 1970), have been widely researched. The essential nature of agreeableness–antagonism is perhaps best seen by examining the disagreeable pole, which we have labeled antagonism. As the high-loading adjectives in Table 3 and the items in Table 2 show, antagonistic people seem always to set themselves against others. Cognitively they are mistrustful and skeptical; affectively they are callous and unsympathetic; behaviorally they are uncooperative, stubborn, and rude. It would appear that their sense of attachment or bonding with their fellow human beings is defective, and in extreme cases antagonism may resemble sociopathy (cf. H. J. Eysenck & Eysenck's, 1975, psychoticism).

An insightful description of antagonism in its neurotic form is provided by Horney's account of the tendency to move against people (1945, 1950). She theorized that a struggle for mastery is the root cause of this tendency and that variations may occur, including narcissistic, perfectionistic, and arrogant vindictive types. Whereas some antagonistic persons are overtly aggressive, others may be polished manipulators. The drive for mastery and the overt or inhibited hostility of antagonistic individuals suggests a resemblance to some formulations of Type A personality (Dembroski & MacDougall, 1983), and systematic studies of the relations between agreeableness–antagonism and measures of coronary-prone behavior should be undertaken.

Unappealing as antagonism may be, it is necessary to recognize that extreme scores on the agreeable pole may also be maladaptive. The person high in agreeableness may be dependent and fawning, and agreeableness has its neurotic manifestation in Horney's self-effacing solution of moving toward people.

Antagonism is most easily confused with dominance. Amelang and Borkenau (1982), working in German and apparently unaware of the Norman taxonomy, found a factor they called *dominance*. Among its key definers, however, were Hartnäckigkeit (*stubbornness*) and Erregbarkeit (*irritability*); scales that measure agreeableness and cooperation defined the opposite pole in their questionnaire factor. Clearly, this factor corresponds to antagonism. In self-reports (McCrae & Costa, 1985b), submissive–dominant is a weak definer of extraversion; in Table 3, from the peers' point of view, it is a definer of antagonism. The close etymological relationship of *dominant* and *domineering* shows the basis of the confusion.

Agreeableness–antagonism and conscientiousness–undirectedness are sometimes omitted from personality systems because they may seem too value laden. Indeed, the judgment of character is made largely along these two dimensions: Is the individual well or ill intentioned? Is he or she strong or weak in carrying out those intentions? Agreeableness–antagonism, in particular, has often been assumed to be an evaluative factor of others' perceptions rather than a veridical component of personality (e.g., A. Tellegen, personal communication, March 28, 1984).

However, the fact that a trait may be judged from a moral point of view does not mean that it is not a substantive aspect of personality. The consensual validation seen among peers and between peer-reports and self-reports demonstrates that there are some observable consistencies of behavior that underlie attributions of agreeableness and conscientiousness. They may be evaluated traits, but they are not mere evaluations.

Conscientiousness versus undirectedness. Conscientious may mean either governed by conscience or careful and thorough (Morris, 1976), and psychologists seem to be divided about which of these meanings best characterizes the last major dimension of personality. Amelang and Borkenau (1982) labeled their factor self-control versus impulsivity, and Conley (1985) spoke of impulse control. This terminology connotes an inhibiting agent, as Cattell (Cattell, Eber, & Tatsuoka, 1970) recognized when he named his Factor G *superego strength*. A conscientious person in this sense should be dutiful, scrupulous, and perhaps moralistic.

A different picture, however, is obtained by examining the adjectives that define this factor. In addition to conscientious and scrupulous, there are a number of adjectives that suggest a more proactive stance: hardworking, ambitious, energetic, persevering. Digman and Takemoto-Chock (1981) labeled this factor *will to achieve*, and it is notable that one of the items in the questionnaire measure of conscientiousness, "He strives for excellence in all he does," comes close to the classic definition of need for achievement (McClelland, Atkinson, Clark, & Lowell, 1953).

At one time, the purposefulness and adherence to plans, schedules, and requirements suggested the word *direction* as a label for this factor, and we have retained that implication in calling the opposite pole of conscientiousness *undirectedness*. In our view, the individual low in conscientiousness is not so much uncontrolled as undirected, not so much impulse ridden as simply lazy.

It seems probable that these two meanings may be related. Certainly individuals who are well organized, habitually careful, and capable of self-discipline are more likely to be able to adhere scrupulously to a moral code if they choose to—although there is no guarantee that they will be so inclined. An undirected individual may have a demanding conscience and a pervasive sense of guilt but be unable to live up to his or her own standards for lack of self-discipline and energy. In any case, it is clear that this is a dimension worthy of a good deal more empirical attention than it has yet received. Important real-life outcomes such as alcoholism (Conley & Angelides, 1984) and academic achievement (Digman & Takemoto-Chock, 1981) are among its correlates, and a further specification of the dimension is sure to be fruitful.

Some personality theorists might object that trait ratings, in whatever form and from whatever source, need not provide the best foundation for understanding individual differences. Experimental analysis of the psychophysiological basis of personality (H. J. Eysenck & Eysenck, 1984), examination of prototypic acts and act frequencies (Buss & Craik, 1983), psychodynamic formulations (Horney, 1945), or behavioral genetics (Plomin, DeFries, & McClearn, 1980) provide important alternatives. But psychophysiological, behavioral, psychodynamic, and genetic explanations must eventually be related to the traits that are universally used to describe personality, and the five-factor model can provide a framework within which these relations can be systematically examined. The minor conceptual divergences noted in this article suggest the need for additional empirical work to fine-tune the model, but the broad outlines are clear in self-reports, spouse ratings, and peer ratings; in questionnaires and adjective factors; and in English and in German (Amelang & Borkenau, 1982; John, Goldberg, & Angleitner, 1984). Deeper causal analyses may seek to account for the structure of personality, but the structure that must be explained is, for now, best represented by the five-factor model.

REFERENCES

Eysenck, H.J., & Eysenck, M. (1984). *Personality and individual differences.* London: Plenum.

Goldberg, L. R. (1982). From Ace to Zombie: Some explorations in the language of personality. In C. D. Spielberg & J. N. Butcher (Eds.), Advances in personality assessment (Vol. 1, pp. 203–234). Hillsdale, NJ: Erlbaum.

Hogan, R. (1983). A socioanalytic theory of personality. In M. M. Page (Ed.), *Nebraska Symposium on Motivation, 1982: Personality—Current theory and research* (pp. 55–89). Lincoln, NE: University of Nebraska Press.

McCrae, R. R. (1982). Consensual validation of personality traits: Evidence from self-reports and ratings. *Journal of Personality and Social Psychology, 43,* 293–303.

McCrae, R. R., & Costa, P. T. (1985). Openness to experience. In R. Hogan and W. H. Jones (Eds.), *Perspectives in personality* (Vol. 1, pp. 145–172). Greenwich, CT: JAI Press.

Mischel, W. (1968). *Personality and assessment.* New York: Wiley.

Norman, W. T. (1963). Toward an adequate taxonomy of personality attributes: Replicated factor structure in peer nomination personality ratings. *Journal of Abnormal and Social Psychology, 66,* 574–583.

Wiggins, J. S. (1979). A psychological taxonomy of trait-descriptive terms: The interpersonal domain. *Journal of Personality and Social Psychology, 37,* 395–412.

KEY POINTS

1. A five-factor structure of personality traits appears in both self-reports and peer ratings.

2. The five dimensions of personality are: neuroticism, extraversion, openness to experience, agreeableness, and conscientiousness.

3. Neurotic people are worrying, self-conscious, and temperamental. Extroverted people are sociable, fun loving, and talkative. People open to experience are original, imaginative, and daring. Agreeable people are trustful, caring, forgiving, and cooperative. Conscientious people are careful, hardworking, and persevering.

QUESTIONS TO THINK ABOUT_____

1. Does it make sense to summarize human personality in terms of five dimensions? Eysenck has argued for three dimensions, and Cattell has argued for sixteen.

2. Although the five factors do a good job in accounting for the data, they are nowhere near perfect. Why might this be?

3. Does it make sense to rely on basic trait dimensions in explaining personality, or do we need to take into account unconscious drives, other motives, perceptions, situations, goals, and other such elements?

24

Personality Pinned Down*

RAYMOND B. CATTELL

Raymond Cattell, who studied with English and American intelligence researchers, took a mathematical approach to understanding personality. In particular, he used the statistical approach termed "factor analysis" to distill a basic set of dimensions of personality. Factor analysis is a way of reducing or summarizing a large number of correlation coefficients. Cattell's approach was very inductive and data-driven.

Cattell (1905–1998) typically used research designs in which a large number of raters would judge other persons they knew well on a large number of adjectives. Such studies led to what Cattell called "mental factors." Cattell proposed that there are sixteen basic personality traits, which he labeled with letters of the alphabet to be sure that they were objective results of the statistical method, not biased by preconceived notions. In this selection, he describes the Sixteen Personality Factor Questionnaire.

Personality is like love: everyone agrees it exists, but disagrees on what it is. Psychologists have tried to pin down the elusive nature of "personality" in many ways, ranging from the broad intuitive systems of psychoanalysis to the precise but narrow views of behaviorism and learning theory. Still, the substance of personality theory from 1910 to 1960 was Freudian, and novelists and journalists still speak the language of Freud.

In the 1930s, my colleagues and I developed a radical approach to personality based on factor analysis. We discovered that there are certain basic mental factors that can be measured with mathematical precision. Consider the sex drive, presumably an impossible force to quantify (other than "she has a lot of it" or "he has too little of it"). George Kawash and Gerrit De Young used our Motivational Analysis Test to measure the strength of the sex drives of 50 married male graduate students at the University of Illinois. The men rated erotic pictures in terms of how sexually arousing they were. The researchers found that a person's score on our sex drive factor predicted accurately how aroused he would be by the pictures, how much his sex drive would increase after looking at the pictures, and how likely he was to want, or to have, sexual intercourse that evening.

We started our study of personality factors with a conservative goal: to define and measure objectively the basic components of personality before trying to explain, predict, or theorize about them. The history of science demonstrates that breakthroughs always follow this pattern. Isaac Newton pointed out that he could not have tested his theories of motion (forces) if he had

*Cattell, R. B. (1973). Personality pinned down. *Psychology Today, 7* (July), 41–42, 44–46.
Reprinted with permission from Psychology Today Magazine, copyright © 1971 Sussex Publishers, Inc.

not been able to use the exact ways to describe moving objects developed by Galileo. Similarly, without accurate measurement of personality, it was virtually impossible to choose between, say, two theories concerning the origin and cure of neurosis.

Clinicians vs. Experimenters. In the 1930s, when we began our work, many experimental psychologists were turning their attention to the study of reflexes, nerve conduction, laws of perception, and laws of rat-learning. But most clinicians chose to ignore the methods of quantitative science. They felt that the experimental psychologists refused to deal with the full complexity of the mind that they encountered in each patient. To the great clinicians, the experimental psychologist must have seemed like a drunkard who knows that his lost wrist watch is out in the alley but searches for it in the house because there is more light inside.

The approach used by experimental psychologists was based typically on a bivariate (meaning "two-variables" or "two-measurements") design. Two groups use the same toothpaste, for example, which varies only in its amount of fluoride. To assess the effect of that one variable, the experimenter looks at a single second variable, the amount of tooth decay.

Such bivariate methods do not work well for studying the mind because mental traits are broad *patterns* of numerous related behaviors, feelings, and responses. Human beings are so complex, and psychological effects so subtle, that trying to get two groups of persons identical in all respects except one becomes unrealistic. It can be done, at best, only in laboratory settings. Bivariate experimental techniques are about as useful for studying personality as forks are for eating soup.

To get around these complex problems, we turned to a mathematical method called factor analysis, which Charles Spearman and Louis L. Thurstone developed in the '20s and '30s. J. P. Guilford used factor analysis in the '50s to find 15 specific ability factors and John L. Horn and I

used it to locate two general intelligence factors that account for a person's performance on ability tests [see "Are I.Q. Tests Intelligent?" PT, March 1968].

Factor analysis allows us to look simultaneously at any number and kind of measures and determine how they reduce to patterns. Out of some 100 test responses, for example, we may find nine underlying factors that influence them. It makes no difference whether the variables we start with are repeated measurements of chemicals in one person's blood, or intelligence test scores taken from thousands of persons, or the distribution of traits in a given group.

The Patterns of Personality. One of our early factor-analysis experiments used check lists of 171 adjectives. We asked our 208 raters to describe other persons they knew well by checking various adjectives—anxious, friendly, dominating, etc. Any individual who tries to describe a particular person in such words might be substantially off base. But we believed that the patterns of use of the adjectives would point to the mental factors which make-up one's "personality." We believed, to paraphrase Lincoln, that you can fool some of the raters all of the time, and all of the raters some of the time, but you can't fool all the raters all the time. Indeed, our factor analysis showed that when the raters describe other persons they often unknowingly evaluate the strength of some 20 underlying personality factors.

We labeled the resulting factors alphabetically, from A to O. We did not assign them descriptive names for years; in the meantime, we established beyond doubt that they were really mental factors, not mathematical artifacts. We slowly became familiar with the intuitive meanings behind the letters and numbers, and we assigned two names to each: one for a high score and another for a low score. We wanted to emphasize that a low score on factor N (forthrightness), for example, indicated the *presence* of something just as an extremely high score on factor N (shrewdness) does. While the verbal names convey meaning to persons unfamiliar with our tests, we prefer the letter designations. Any verbal label gets tied to a complex of everyday meanings and nuances that are different for different persons; moreover, the labels rarely capture the full meaning and content of the factor.

We also wanted to eliminate any possibility that these factors represented some arbitrary but culturally agreed-upon way of speaking about personalities. If we had found *true* mental factors, whatever their psychological meanings, they should appear when we factor-analyzed *any* measures that personality influences. So next we looked at the way individuals describe themselves.

We asked thousands of persons to answer questions about themselves and again analyzed their responses. We came up with 16 to 20 distinct "introspective" factors; most of them turned out to correspond exactly to the factors that the raters had identified earlier.

The Belated Four. We were now quite certain that we had found the building blocks of personality. But there were four new factors that the older rating method had not picked up (Q_1, conservative-experimenting; Q_2, group-dependent-self-sufficient; Q_3, uncontrolled-controlled, and Q_4, relaxed-tense). At first we wondered if these were artifacts not really related to personality. But two findings kept us from discarding them. First, they recurred with different persons, different questions, and even with different ways of computing the factors; that is, the new factors were too persistent to ignore. Second, and more important, these factors turned out to have strong correlations with our ultimate validation, real life behavior. For example, persons who score very high on factor Q_4 (tense/driven) tend to be accident-prone, and a high score on factor Q_1 (conservative) or Q_3 (controlled) predicts a tendency to succeed in school. [Ed. note: The sixteen factors are shown in Table 1.]

Apparently, our early belief that the basic personality factors were independent of how they

TABLE 1   The 16 Personality Factors

A	reserved	outgoing
B	less intelligent	more intelligent
C	affected by feelings	emotionally stable
E	submissive	dominant
F	serious	happy-go-lucky
G	expedient	conscientious
H	timid	venturesome
I	tough-minded	sensitive
L	trusting	suspicious
M	practical	imaginative
N	forthright	shrewd
O	self-assured	apprehensive
Q_1	conservative	experimenting
Q_2	group-dependent	self-sufficient
Q_3	uncontrolled	controlled
Q_4	relaxed	tense

were measured was only partly correct. The four new factors were clearly real, yet undetectable in a factor analysis of raters' descriptions. They were, in a way, the four occasions on which all of the raters were fooled.

Some of the personality traits, as Thomas Klein has shown, are strongly influenced by heredity. One is factor B, general intelligence. Factor C (ego strength), factor F (serious minded-enthusiastic), factor G (superego strength) and factor I (emotional sensitivity) are fairly strongly affected by heredity. Others, such as factor D (calm-excitable), factor E (submissive-dominant), and factor Q (relaxed-tense), are strongly influenced by the way a person is treated in childhood.

A few of the factors are identical to the intuitive concepts that astute clinicians have developed. Factor G (expedient–conscientious) corresponds to what Freud called the superego, while factor C corresponds to ego strength. Jung's concept of extraversion/introversion is identical to a "second-order factor"—an influence touching several primary factors—in this case affecting factors A (aloof-warm), F (sober-happy), H (shy-venturesome), and M (practical-imaginative). Factor A is remarkably like the dimension that Ernst Kretschmer described and called "cyclothymia" (warm) on one extreme and "schizothymia" (cold) on the other.

In addition to confirming some clinical concepts, we were able to enlarge upon them. For example, where Jung thought that there were at most four parts to extroversion, our analysis revealed that there are at least five. Further, we found that a true neurotic usually differs from a normal person on five or six personality factors. In particular, neurotics always have a low level of what we call "regression–energy-mobilization." Regression is a lack of psychological energy and a lack of persistence and it includes a tendency to fall back to simple, inadequate, ways of coping.

True and False Neurotics. By having clinicians diagnose people who have been tested we find that they often diagnose a neurotic person by sensing his high anxiety. As a result they often put the "neurotic" label on an individual who has high anxiety for reasons not related to any neurosis. He may, for example, be anxious because he has been told that half the employees of his company will be laid off that week. Our regression factor distinguishes persons who have high "situational" anxiety from those who have true neurotic anxiety.

The first general-purpose personality test based on our work is the Sixteen Personality Factor Questionnaire. Its 368 (184 in each of two equivalent forms) multiple-choice questions, selected by factor analysis and not by our subjective choice, measure the level of 16 primary personality factors and eight composite, "secondary," personality factors. This test has very practical, predictive abilities.

For instance, John Nesselroade and I wanted to determine whether "opposites attract" or "like marries like." Some psychologists have proposed that persons with similar temperaments will make compatible marriage partners. Others suggest that persons with different ("complementary") personalities should be more compatible.

We gave our test to two groups of married couples, 100 couples who were stably married, and 80 couples who had come to the counseling center for help with marriage difficulties. We found, basically, that like should marry like if one wants a lasting relationship. Couples in the stable marriages were more likely to have similar personalities than those whose marriages were in trouble.

Several personality factors appear to be especially related to the stability of a marriage: factor A (aloof–warm), factor L (trusting–suspicious), and factor Q (group-dependent–self-sufficient). Persons who are similar in these factors tended to fall in the stably married group. The fourth relevant factor is E (submissive–dominant). Husbands in stable marriages were likely to be more dominant than their wives, but if a husband was *much* more dominant than his wife, that couple generally fell in the unstably married group.

Many researchers have used the Sixteen Personality Factor Questionnaire to explore the relationships between mind and body. A. H. Ismail studied persons in a physical conditioning program and found that exercise is linked with personality changes [see "Jogging the Imagination," PT, March]. A. M. Ostfeld analyzed the factor scores of nearly 2,000 men between 40 and 55 years old, the age bracket in which most heart attacks occur. Fifty of the men later developed heart disease. Ostefeld found that these 50 men were significantly more likely to be suspicious (factor L), self-sufficient (factor Q_2), and low in superego strength (factor G), than the other men.

The Psychosomatic and Creative Personalities. In fact, there is a distinct psychosomatic profile that is different from the general neurotic's profile. The person who tends to get psychosomatic ailments has considerable ego-strength (factor C) and self-assurance (factor O); most of all, he is cool, reserved (factor A) and unsentimental (factor I). He also has an atypically high level of a second-order factor called cortical alertness. The psychosomatic person seems to have the psychological resources that make him ready to meet and cope with stress, but he acts out the stress internally instead of anxiously withdrawing like a typical neurotic.

The Sixteen Personality Factor Questionnaire also has been used to study creative people. John Drevdahl and I found that the personalities of prominent artists and writers were more similar to each other than to the general population. And despite the fact that we often think of scientists and artists as opposite types, the profile of a group of creative scientists was very similar to that of the artists and writers. The psychological concomitants of creativity are apparently fairly constant, no matter what the person's creative area is. The composite profile of a creative person partly confirms the popular picture of him, or her, as a sometimes tactless, autonomous, nonconformist who does not always work well with a group.

From this and other related studies, we have extracted an equation that roughly estimates any person's creative potential from his personality factor scores. Our work suggests that there is much more to creativity than intelligence. If we wish to study or nurture creativity, or if we want to avoid screening creative persons out of positions because of their sometimes unpleasant personalities, we now have the means to do so.

Getting Out of Introspection. There are a number of problems with introspective questionnaires. A person can deliberately or unconsciously distort his responses, out of the desire to appear in a particular light. While attempts at distortion rarely achieve the effect that the person desires, there are no perfect ways to unscramble the distortion. Another disadvantage of questionnaire tests is that they can be taken only by persons who can read, or at least talk. Many of the questions that personality researchers want to answer concern young children or persons from other cultures with different languages. The fact that a particular question may be interpreted differently by different persons makes any questionnaire test fall short of perfection.

With those drawbacks in mind, and to show that our factors were properties of the mind rather than of the test, we began to design objective measures. Objective tests are a diverse collection of techniques. We define a test as objective if the person being measured cannot tell what aspect of himself is being evaluated, or, if he can, he has no way to change or distort the outcome of the measurement.

Some objective measures are physiological variables, such as heart rate, metabolism, respiration rate, muscle tension, levels of various biochemicals in the blood, or changes in the electrical resistance of the skin. Other objective measures are psychophysical, such as reaction speed or ability to pick spoken words out of a noisy background. Further, we can measure a person's actual behavior, for example while he is working on pencil and paper maze puzzles. We observe his speed, the amount of time he spends hesitating at intersections, and his persistence on mazes that he does not know are insoluble. We can even extract objective measures from pencil and paper tests, such as the Gottschaldt and the Gestalt Closure Test, in which a person tries to identify the subject of an incomplete but definite line drawing. We can measure such variables as the number of correct guesses or the number of threatening objects he claims to see. Clinicians have used such responses to put the person into one of two intuitively defined categories—"synthetic type" or "analytic type." Instead, we throw these measures into the computer for correlation and let the mathematics of factor analysis tell us whether they can be explained by underlying factor types. In the case of the Gestalt Closure Test, they can.

As evidence that our personality factors are true constructs, we factor-analyzed thousands of responses to more than 2,000 objective tests. The results supported our findings from the previous rater and questionnaire tests.

Most of our personality factors have proved stable, so we call them "source traits," emphasizing that they are steady traits and constant sources of behavior. One's level of ego strength or intelligence, for instance, is usually about the same from month to month. However, when change measures are factored, such dimensions as tension, regression, and anxiety are revealed to fluctuate with time and situation. We may think of them as mood or "state" factors. We later found seven other very changeable mood factors, including excitement, general fatigue, and effort stress. These factors, which make for the ups and downs of daily life, appear most distinctly when we factor-analyze physiological measures such as pulse rate, amounts of hormones and nutrients in the blood, amounts of sleep, goodness of memory, and time of day.

Predictions from Personality. In predicting behavior, what state a man is in may be as important as what kind of man he is. But practicing psychologists have plenty to do at present in predicting from traits. Personality factors already permit us to calculate equations that predict many behaviors: academic success, the likelihood of being able to tolerate contact lenses, alcoholism or drug addiction, the volume of a salesman's selling. For example, low G (expediency), high M (imaginativeness) and high E (dominance) each contribute to accident proneness. Our tests can identify neurotic or psychotic persons as well as a good team of psychiatrists can, and they do so more consistently than any one psychiatrist.

Clinicians often treat patients with psychoactive drugs, without knowing which patients will experience unexpected and negative reactions. Gary Forrest, Timothy Bortner and Cornelis Bakker found they could use a test of factor E (submissive-dominant) to predict reactions to the tranquilizer chlorpromazine. Highly dominant persons tend to respond to this drug by becoming agitated.

Until 1960 our factors did not include motivations and drives which are different from general personality dimensions, and which, we knew, manifest themselves in a person's attitudes and emotions. Thus, the strength of the person's self-assertion drive might appear in his attitudes toward winning arguments, or toward his salary, or toward leading groups.

Two technical advances need to be emphasized. First, we no longer measure motive strength by check list or subjective appraisal. As psychoanalysis has long known, such methods have been shown to be unreliable. Second, we base the decision as to what human drives actually *exist* on multivariate analysis; we do not postulate X number on an armchair basis, as personality theorists have been wont to do. Unfortunately, most laymen, and even many psychologists untrained in multivariate methods, fail to see that the two procedures (nonarbitrary factor analysis and arbitrary speculation) are as different from each other as modern identification of chemical elements is from the air-earth-fire-water system of the alchemists. The labels and the scales may not look very different superficially, but they belong in a new world relative to previous questionnaire scales.

Ergs and Sentiments. In the realm of dynamic structure factors we soon noticed that we were unearthing two quite distinct kinds of motivational roots:

1) Ergs, which seem to be basic biological drives such as sex, fear (or need for security), parental-prospectiveness, gregariousness, curiosity, self-assertion, and narcissism (self-indulgent sensuality).

2) Sentiments, which are learned drives such as self-sentiment (respect for self-image), career-sentiment, and superego-sentiment (conscience). The sentiments are not distinguishable mathematically from the ergs, but the attitudes that the sentiments affect are directed to cultural objects or events.

Our mathematical analysis showed that each motivation, whether an erg or a sentiment, has two components. One is conscious, and shows up in direct, "inventory" measures of attitudes; the other is unconscious, and shows up in indirect measures, such as word associations, blood pressure, and electrical skin-resistance changes.

Keith Barton, T. E. Dielman and I measured the motivation factors, ability factors and personality factors of 311 sixth- and seventh-grade students. Three months later the students took Educational Testing Service achievement tests in social science, science, mathematics and reading. We found that our factors were significantly related to the student's achievement in each area. For example, high assertiveness was related to good performance in social studies and reading, but had no relation to performance in science or mathematics. High superego and self-sentiment strengths were positively related to all performances. In contrast, high scores on fear, pugnacity (the hostile-destructive drive), were negatively related to the students' achievement. To our surprise, only the *conscious* component of the motivations affected achievement scores. The unconscious component, if anything, inhibited achievement.

As Freud noted years ago, a person's unconscious motivation can be far different from his conscious motivation. It seemed to us, as to Freud, that such disparities would be a source of psychological conflict. But unlike Freud, we could measure the amount of both components for each motivation factor and get numerical overall conflict scores. In 1959, J. R. Williams measured conflict scores for eight mental hospital patients and found them significantly higher than those of persons from the general population. We may be able to detect mental illness before it develops by measuring a person's conflicts and watching for sudden changes or long-term trends. Similarly, a therapist might be able to use conflict scores to see if a particular technique is working for a particular patient.

Measures of the Mind. We can formulate equations that demonstrate the role of each motive in any action. This permits us to find out which methods of teaching will reinforce or punish which motives. We have already shown that a freshman college student's first motivation to learn psychology is usually curiosity; but within one semester, curiosity defers to self-assertion and insecurity (fear).

After three decades of learning to catalog and measure the dimensions of the mind, we have the tools to give specific answers to complicated and practical questions. The interrelations of the mental factors we find are extremely complex. They are going to involve more intricate but more exact mathematical predictions than have been envisaged in the incomplete intuitive schemes of clinicians, or the fragmented truths that come from bivariate experiments. But our precise and integrating approach permits us to recognize and handle a person's uniqueness as well as his common humanity, in a manner that no single-faceted psychological system can surpass.

KEY POINTS

1. Personality is best defined and assessed using factor analysis, in which many ratings or responses by many people are collected and examined for their underlying statistical structure.

2. Personality can be best measured using the Sixteen Personality Factor Questionnaire.

3. It is important to see which behaviors and activities are predicted by the sixteen basic personality traits, and it is worthwhile to relate these empirically derived dimensions to more theoretically derived constructs proposed by other personality theorists.

QUESTIONS TO THINK ABOUT_____

1. What are the advantages of an inductive, data-driven approach to personality? How is such an approach limited?

2. Other personality psychologists argue that there are three basic trait dimensions, or five basic trait dimensions. What do you think of Cattell's claim that we need sixteen?

25

Personality Dimensions in Nonhuman Animals: A Cross-Species Review*

SAMUEL D. GOSLING
AND OLIVER P. JOHN

Modern personality research often uses narrower approaches than the grand theories of the past, but often uses innovative tactics in looking for converging lines of evidence. Although most people believe that their animal pets have personality, the topic has drawn relatively little attention from psychologists. Evolutionary theory, however, suggests that we may gain some insights into the structure of human personality by examining individual consistencies in other animals.

Samuel Gosling and Oliver John conducted this research at the Institute of Personality and Social Research, at the University of California, Berkeley. They have conducted considerable work on the Big Five model that asserts that personality can be best summarized in terms of five major personality dimensions. In this selection, they look for evidence of these basic dimensions in nonhuman animals.

In a recent article in the *Los Angeles Times*, Robert Fagen, a professor of biometry, described Susie as irascible, irritable, grumpy, and manipulative. This is hardly newsworthy, except that Susie is a bear. Scientists have been reluctant to ascribe personality traits, emotions, and cognitions to animals, even though they readily accept that the anatomy and physiology of humans is similar to that of animals. Yet there is nothing in evolutionary theory to suggest that only physical traits are subject to selection pressures, and Darwin (1872/1998) argued that emotions exist in both human and nonhuman animals. Thus, personality traits like Extraversion and Agreeableness may not be as uniquely human as once was thought (Buss, 1988). Early attempts to assess animal personality, including the pioneering studies by Stevenson-Hinde, were conducted in the 1970s, and the 1990s have seen a resurgence of research activity. Our goal in this article is to take stock of what is known about animal personality, focusing

*Gosling, S. D., & John, O. P. (1999). Personality dimensions in nonhuman animals: A cross-species review. *Current Directions in Psychological Science, 8,* 69–75. Reprinted by permission. [Ed. note: All citations in the text of this selection have been left intact from the original, but the list of references includes only those sources that are the most relevant and important. Readers wishing to follow any of the other citations can find the full references in the original work or in an online database.]

on individual differences *within* species. We ask, What are the major dimensions of animal personality?

MAPPING THE LANDSCAPE OF ANIMAL PERSONALITY

Faced with the challenge of integrating the fragmented literature on animal personality, we felt like early cartographers faced with the challenge of constructing a map of the globe. Our task—much like that of the cartographers—was to piece together the isolated reports about the landscape of personality. These reports came in different languages; used a variety of scales, methods, and notations; and varied in their scope and reliability. Our first task was to select the most trustworthy reports; starting with more than 100 potentially relevant studies, we selected those that had sample sizes larger than 20 animals and a reasonably broad coverage of personality traits.

To integrate the many pieces of information provided by the diverse research reports, we used the most widely accepted and complete map of personality structure: the human Five-Factor Model (FFM; John, 1990). The FFM is a hierarchical model with five broad factors (Table 1), which represent personality at the broadest level of abstraction. Each bipolar factor

(e.g., Extraversion vs. Introversion) summarizes several more specific facets (e.g., sociability), which, in turn, subsume a large number of even more specific traits (e.g., talkative, outgoing). Unfortunately, no short labels capture the broad FFM dimensions adequately, so the traditional labels are easily misunderstood; thus, we use the letters N (for *Neuroticism, Nervousness, Negative affectivity*), A (for *Agreeableness, Altruism, Affection*), E (for *Extraversion, Energy, Enthusiasm*), O (for *Openness, Originality, Openmindedness*), and C (for *Conscientiousness, Control, Constraint*).

Are there additional dimensions that might be of special importance for describing the personality of nonhuman animals? In adult human personality, Activity and Dominance are part of the E dimension. In children, however, Activity may form a separate dimension (John, Caspi, Robins, Moffitt, & Stouthamer-Loeber, 1994), and temperament models (Buss & Plomin, 1984) also consider it separate. Moreover, many socially living animal species show individual differences related to status in the dominance hierarchy: Individuals with high status can control others and get their way. To explore whether Activity and Dominance form separate dimensions in animals, we added them to the five FFM dimensions in our preliminary framework (see Table 2).

TABLE 1   The Dimensions of the Five-Factor Model (FFM)

FFM DIMENSION LABEL		EXAMPLES OF FACETS
N	Neuroticism vs. Emotional Stability	Anxiety, depression, vulnerability to stress, moodiness
A	Aggreableness vs. Antagonism	Trust, tendermindedness, cooperation, lack of aggression
E	Extraversion vs. Introversion	Sociability, assertiveness, activity, positive emotions
O	Open vs. Closed to Experience	Ideas/intellect, imagination, creativity, curiosity
C	Conscientiousness vs. Impulsiveness	Deliberation, self-discipline, dutifulness, order

Note. See John (1990) and Costa and McCrae (1992) for details.

TABLE 2 Review of Animal Personality Factors: Factor Labels Organized in Terms of the Five-Factor Model (FFM) Plus Two Potential Additional Dimensions

SPECIES	Trait Dimensions in the Human FFM					Additional Dimensions		STUDY
	NEUROTICISM	AGREEABLENESS	EXTRAVERSION	OPENNESS	CONSCIENTIOUSNESS	DOMINANCE	ACTIVITY	
Chimpanzee	Emotional Stability	Agreeableness	Surgency	Openness	Dependability	Dominance		King and Figueredo (1997)
	Audiovisual Reactivity		Affect-Extraversion		Task Behavior		Activity	Bard and Gardner (1996)
	Excitability-Agitation	Aggression; Affinity[a]	Social Play			Submission		Hooff (1973)
Gorilla	Fearfulness	Understanding	Extroversion			Dominance		Gold and Maple (1994)
Rhesus monkey	Tense-Fearful	Aggressive	Solitary	Curious-Playful				Bolig, Price, O'Neill, and Suomi (1992)
	Excitability		Sociability			Confidence		Stevenson-Hinde and Zunz (1978); Stevenson-Hinde, Stillwell-Barnes, and Zunz (1980)
	Fear	Hostility	Affiliation					Chamove, Eysenck, and Harlow (1972)
Vervet monkey		Opportunistic–Self-Serving	Playful-Curious[b]			Social Competence		McGuire, Raleigh, and Pollack (1994)
Hyena	Excitability	Sociability; Human-Related Agreeableness[a]		Curiousity		Assertiveness		Gosling (1998)

Trait Dimensions in the Human FFM

SPECIES	NEUROTICISM	AGREEABLENESS	EXTRAVERSION	OPENNESS	CONSCIENTIOUSNESS	DOMINANCE	ACTIVITY	STUDY
Dog	Emotional Reactivity	Affection	Energy	Competence[c]				Gosling and John (1998)
	Stability vs. Excitability		Sociability	Learning and Obedience Ability[c]		Dominance-Territoriality		Coren (1998)
	Nerve Stability	Affability; Aggression[a]	Lively Temperament					Wilsson and Sundgren (1997)
		Aggression (Disagreeableness)	Reactivity (Surgency)	Trainability (Openness)				Hart and Hart (1985) (reanalyzed by Draper, 1995)
Cat	Emotional Reactivity	Affection	Energy	Competence[c]				Gosling and John (1998)
Donkey		Obstinancy	Vivacity					French (1993)
Pig		Aggression	Sociability	Exploration-Curiosity				Forkman, Furuhaug, and Jensen (1995)
Rat	Emotionality	Fighting vs. Timidity; Freezing vs. Aggression[a]						Billingslea (1941)
Guppy	Fear-Avoidance		Approach					Budaev (1997)
Octopus	Reactivity		Bold vs. Avoiding				Activity	Mather and Anderson (1993)

Additional Dimensions span the DOMINANCE and ACTIVITY columns.

Note. All studies are based on factor analyses of individual animals, except Coren (1998) and Hart and Hart (1985), who analyzed experts' ratings of breeds. Several studies did not include factor labels at all or included labels too brief to understand without further information; for these cases, we used high-loading items to help name the factors.

[a] These four studies yielded two separate factors related to Agreeableness.

[b] This factor combined both social and imaginative elements and thus reflects both Extraversion and Openness.

[c] These factors combined elements from both Openness and Conscientiousness.

201

Our review includes 19 factor analytic studies and represents 12 different species. We reviewed the items defining each personality factor in each study and compared them with the definitions of the seven potential dimensions in Table 2. If there was a match in item content, we classified the animal factor into one of the seven dimensions and included its label (or a short definition) in the appropriate column of Table 2.

Extraversion, Neuroticism, and Agreeableness: Cross-Species Dimensions?

Three human FFM dimensions—E, N, and A—showed considerable generality across species. Of the 19 studies, 17 identified a factor related to E. The factor labels in the E column in Table 2 range from Surgency in chimpanzees to Sociability in pigs, dogs, and rhesus monkeys; Energy in cats and dogs; Vivacity in donkeys; and a dimension contrasting Bold Approach versus Avoidance in octopuses. The particular labels may differ, but they all reflect core features of the broad E dimension (see Table 1). Factors related to N appeared almost as frequently; again, despite the differences in factor labels, these animal factors capture core elements of N, such as Fearfulness, Emotional Reactivity, Excitability, and low Nerve Stability. Factors related to A appeared in 14 studies, with Affability, Affection, and Affinity capturing the high pole of A, and Aggression, Hostility, and Fighting capturing the low pole.

The evidence indicates that chimpanzees, various other primates, nonprimate mammals, and even guppies and octopuses all show individual differences that can be organized along dimensions akin to E, N, and (with the exception of guppies and octopuses) A. These remarkable commonalities across such a wide range of taxa suggest that general biological mechanisms are likely responsible. The way these personality dimensions are manifested, however, depends on the species. For example, whereas the human scoring low on Extraversion stays at home on Saturday night, or tries to blend into a corner at a large party, the octopus scoring low on Boldness stays in its protective den during feedings and attempts to hide itself by changing color or releasing ink into the water.

Openness: Another Potential Cross-Species Personality Dimension?

Factors related to the O dimension in the FFM were identified in 7 of the 12 species. The two major components defining this dimension were curiosity-exploration (interest in new situations and novel objects) and playfulness (which is associated with E when social, rather than imaginative, aspects of play are assessed). Although these factors are similar to the O dimension known from humans, some core facets are obviously missing; openness to ideas and interest in arts are difficult to observe in animals that lack advanced means of symbolic expression, such as language and music. The O factor in these animal studies resembles the early forms of O observed in human toddlers; lacking advanced language skills, their curiosity is manifested in an intense interest in novel objects and events, and their imagination is shown in perspective taking and role shifts characteristic of pretend play.

The evidence for an O-related factor was not consistent across multiple studies of the same species, pointing to methodological differences, most likely in the traits included in the studies. For example, the two chimpanzee studies that did not find an O factor did not include items clearly relevant to O. Given that forms of curiosity have been observed in a wide range of species, a thorough and focused search should provide more consistent evidence for O.

Conscientiousness: Only in Humans and Chimpanzees?

Although cats and dogs showed a factor that combined C and O, chimpanzees were the only species with a separate C factor. The chimpanzee factor was defined more narrowly than in humans but included lack of attention and goal directedness, as well as erratic, unpredictable, and disorganized behavior—characteristics typical of the low pole of C. Why did we not find separate C factors in any other species? The failure to include relevant items cannot explain this finding: In our own studies of dogs and cats, we included items that define C in humans, but they did not form a separate factor. Considering the "super-ego" aspects of the C factor (following norms and rules, thinking before acting, and other complex cognitive functions involved in the control of impulses), it may not be surprising that we found a separate C factor only in humans and in humans' closest relatives, chimpanzees. These findings suggest C may have appeared relatively recently in the evolution of Homininae, the subfamily comprising humans, chimpanzees, and gorillas.

Dominance and Activity: Two Additional Dimensions?

Dominance emerged as a clear separate factor in 7 of the 19 studies. Although interpreted as Confidence in rhesus monkeys and Assertiveness in hyenas, the factor was essentially the same, correlating substantially with dominance rank. Across studies, the Dominance factor was typically defined by assertiveness or boldness (high E), physical aggression (low A), and low fearfulness (low N). Thus, dominance had more diverse personality implications in animals than in humans, for whom it is related only to the E dimension. Perhaps these differences arise because humans participate in multiple dominance hierarchies that are less clearly defined and involve widely divergent skills: The class

bullies may dominate in the school yard, but the conscientious students will get the grades to advance academically, and the open-minded artists will win prizes for their creations. Future research needs to examine more closely the links between dominance rank and personality traits. Personality may vary even among animals of the same rank, and rather than being viewed as a personality trait, dominance rank may be better conceived as a social outcome determined by both personality and physical traits (Buss, 1988).

Finally, our review uncovered scant evidence for the idea that Activity should be retained as a separate dimension of animal personality, with only 2 of the 19 studies showing support. Of the 3 chimpanzee studies, only the study of infants identified a separate Activity factor. This age difference in chimpanzees parallels findings in humans suggesting that Activity may not become integrated with the E dimension until late adolescence (John et al., 1994).

THE SPECTER OF ANTHROPOMORPHISM

A number of the studies summarized in Table 2 relied on human observers rating animals on trait adjectives defined in brief behavioral terms (e.g., playful was defined as "initiates play and joins in when play is solicited"). Although some researchers argue that observer ratings are the best way to assess personality, others are skeptical and worry that these ratings might be anthropomorphic projections. Three kinds of evidence argue against this concern. First, for a wide range of species, including chimpanzees, rhesus monkeys, and hyenas, studies show that independent observers agree about the relative ordering of individuals on a trait. Second, many of the studies reviewed here used behavioral tests in specific situations or carefully recorded ethological observations. Both types of data yielded similar factors. For example, when piglet behavior was tested in specific situations, the E factor was defined by number of vocalizations, number of nose contacts, and location in the pen; when chimpanzee behavior was observed in naturally occurring settings, the E factor was defined by behavior patterns such as "pull limb" (playful social contact), "grasp and poke" (boisterous but relaxed contact), and "gymnastics" (exuberant locomotory play, such as swinging, dangling, turning somersaults). It is remarkable that such similar factors were discovered using such diverse methods. In fact, studies using multiple methods have demonstrated the validity of trait ratings (Capitanio, 1999). Third, our finding that the factor structures showed meaningful differences across species argues against the operation of general rating biases in observers. For example, in our own work, we found the familiar FFM dimensions for humans but only four factors for dogs, even when we collected personality ratings using the same instrument for both species; the items defining a clear C factor in humans failed to form a separate factor in dogs (Gosling & John, 1998). These differences show that personality structure depends on the individual rated, rather than on the particular items in the rating instrument.

Sex differences are another domain where cross-species differences in the meaning and implications of personality factors can be illustrated. Research on the human FFM has repeatedly shown that women tend to be more emotional and prone to worry (i.e., higher on N) than men (Costa & McCrae, 1992). Does the same sex difference emerge in other species? Not necessarily. To illustrate this point, we collected observer ratings of humans using items previously used in a study of hyenas (Gosling, 1998). In humans, women were described as somewhat higher on N than men; in hyenas, the sex difference was reversed, with males being considerably more high-strung, fearful, and nervous than females (see Fig. 1). What explains this dramatic

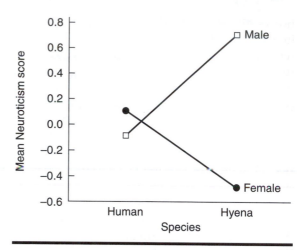

FIGURE 1   Sex differences in standard (z) scores for Neuroticism among humans and hyenas. The ratings for hyenas are from Gosling (1998); the humans (n = 100) were described by peers on the same rating scales used for hyenas.

interaction effect? The key is the difference in social organization: In the hyena clan, dominance rank is transmitted through a matrilineal system, and females are larger than males and more dominant. This example suggests that sex differences in personality may be related to the ecological niches occupied by the two sexes in a species, and illustrates how a comparative approach can offer a fresh perspective on the interplay between social and biological factors in personality.

CONCLUSIONS AND FUTURE DIRECTIONS

The cartographic metaphor serves to highlight some limitations of the initial map of animal personality dimensions presented in Table 2. First, Antarctica will be discovered only if one sails south: The lack of evidence for a dimension does not necessarily prove the factor does not exist; studies may not have included the items relevant for the factor. To show that a dimension does not exist in a species requires that future researchers actively search for that dimension. Equipped with our initial map, we can now conduct hypothesis-driven research. For example, we may hypothesize that solitary species (e.g., orangutans) would not show a separate A dimension, or that O occurs only in species that depend on a great variety of food sources. Second, just as early maps look rough by today's standards, with missing land masses and poorly defined boundaries, we expect that future researchers will refine our rough initial sketch and discover new islands, perhaps even continents. Third, much work remains to be done on the internal geography of the continents. For example, a great many species appear to inhabit the curiosity area of the O continent, but other areas may be inhabited solely by humans and perhaps chimpanzees. Fourth, researchers need to move from mapping personality continents to formulating theories about the movements of tectonic plates, addressing how and why the continents emerged; animal models of personality may be uniquely suited to identify genes for complex traits and to study how these genes work (i.e., functional genomics). Finally, the early sailors knew their maps were not perfect, but imperfect maps were better than no map at all; it is in this spirit that we offer the present classification of animal personality, hoping that future researchers may find this initial sketch helpful in their quest for new discoveries.

REFERENCES

Buss, A. H. (1988). *Personality: Evolutionary heritage and human distinctiveness.* Hillsdale, NJ: Erlbaum.

Darwin, C. (1998). *The expression of emotions in man and animals.* Oxford, England: Oxford University Press. (Original work published 1872).

Draper, T. W. (1995). Canine analogs of human personality factors. *Journal of General Psychology, 122,* 241–252.

King, J. E., & Figueredo, A. J. (1997). The Five-Factor Model plus dominance in chimpanzee personality. *Journal of Research in Personality, 31,* 257–271.

Mather, J. A., & Anderson, R. C. (1993). Personalities of octopuses. (*Octopus rubescens*). *Journal of Comparative Psychology, 107,* 336–340.

McGuire, M. T., Raleigh, M. J., & Pollack, D. B. (1994). Personality features in vervet monkeys: The effects of sex, age, social status, and group composition. *American Journal of Primatology, 33,* 1–13.

Wilsson, E., & Sundgren, P. (1997). The use of a behavior test for the selection of dogs for service and breeding. I: Method of testing and evaluating test results in the adult dog, demands on different kinds of service dogs, sex and breed differences. *Applied Animal Behaviour Science, 53,* 279–295.

KEY POINTS

1. To the extent that animals and humans share certain basic dimensions of personality, animal personality factors can be analyzed in terms of the human five-factor model (Big Five model) of personality.

2. Extraversion, neuroticism, and agreeableness show great generality across different animal species. Openness and conscientiousness seem much less general.

QUESTIONS TO THINK ABOUT_____

1. Do animals really have "personality" traits? Why might this be the case?

2. What are some of the biological and social factors that will affect the development of personality traits in nonhuman animals?

3. Why might some personality dimensions appear only in some animal species?

4. What are anthropomorphic projections, and why are they so dangerous for a scientific approach?

26

What Understanding and Acceptance Mean to Me*

CARL ROGERS

Carl Rogers (1902–1980) believed that people have an inherent tendency toward growth and maturation, but that this maturation is not inevitable. By emphasizing that each person is responsible for his or her own life, Rogers had a tremendous influence on the development of humanistic approaches to personality as well as on the practice of psychotherapy.

Rogers was raised in a strict religious atmosphere with a strong emphasis on ethics. Like many personality theorists, Rogers was influenced by religious and philosophical ideas and was always concerned with the human spirit. In this selection, Rogers makes one of his central points. He emphasizes the value of learning to accept oneself, of accepting others, of dropping masks, and of becoming more open and self-trusting.

This selection is a transcript of a talk Rogers gave in 1956, and was not published until almost forty years later, long after Rogers had died.

When I was invited to address this conference, I debated for some time before accepting the responsibility. It is difficult for me to know what I can offer to the group at this convention. I am no longer in close contact with classroom teachers in the public schools. My experience along those lines is many years in the past. I feel that I have relatively little knowledge of guidance and personnel work in schools and colleges, even though I blush to admit such ignorance. I do have experience, over many years, in personal counseling; but I believe that only a small fraction of this group is primarily engaged in full-time counseling.

In addition to these doubts, there is my feeling that almost anything which might be said in regard to understanding and acceptance has already been said in this conference with its theme of "helping people understand themselves." I suspect that by this time many of you share the feeling of the heroine in *My Fair Lady* when she sings, in the song "Show Me," about how sick she is of words and no action. So it is not without reason that I have questioned myself rather deeply as to what I might have to offer at this point to the conference.

One thing which I fall back upon, one possible point of communication is that we are all individuals who are dealing with people. Each of us is a person dealing with other persons. Furthermore, I suspect that each one of us, in our dealings with these other persons, hopes that as

*Rogers, C. (1995). What understanding and acceptance mean to me. *Journal of Humanistic Psychology*, 35 (4), 7–22. (Transcript of a talk presented to the Illinois Guidance and Personnel Association 12th Annual Conference in 1956.) Copyright © 1995 by Sage Publications. Reprinted by permission of Sage Publications.

a result of our contact, these individuals will become better informed, more independent, wider, better integrated, and more mature.

This realization that we do have this important area in common makes me feel that perhaps there is something of myself that I might share with you, something which might have meaning to you in your work. I have dealt with individuals over a period of many years and, like you, I have hoped that these relationships would prove constructive. Perhaps then, I can voice some of the lessons which I feel I have learned for myself as I have worked with these individuals.

I would like to say in advance that these statements I am going to make, these learnings that have meaning for me, are not intended to be guides for you or for anyone else. It is my strong belief that each one of us has to work out his own way of dealing effectively with others and that it is of no help to copy or imitate or follow the procedures of another. Yet, the experience of another person and his learnings may have meaning for you and may illuminate some of your own experience, may clarify some of the directions which, as individuals, you are taking.

It is with this hope in mind that I shall try to state as simply as I can some of the learnings that have had meaning for me in my experience with working with people.

In the things that I shall say I suppose I am drawing primarily upon my experiences in working with troubled clients, yet I am also drawing upon my experience in working with graduate students, my experience in workshops, seminars, and other educational enterprises. I might start off these several statements of significant learnings with a negative item. *In my relationships with persons I have found that it does not help, in the long run, to act as though I were something that I am not.* It does not help to behave in an understanding way when actually I am trying to manipulate the other person, not understand him. It does not help to act calm and pleasant when actually I am angry and critical. It does not help to act as though I were permis-

sive when I am really feeling that I would like to set limits. It does not help to act as though I know the answers when I do not. It does not help to act as though I were a loving person when actually I am hostile. It does not help to act as though I were acceptant of another person when underneath that exterior I feel rejection of him. It does not help to act as though I were non-evaluative and non-judgmental, if in fact, I am making judgments and evaluations. It does not help for me to act like a conventional, evaluating teacher if, in fact, I am something quite different. Even on a very simple level I have found that this statement seems to hold. It does not help for me to act as though I were well when I feel ill. It does not help for me to act fresh when, in actuality, I feel tired. It does not help me to act as though I were full of assurance, when actually I am frightened and unsure.

What I am saying here, put in another way, is that I have not found it to be helpful or effective in my relationships with other people to try to maintain a facade; to act in one way on the surface when I am experiencing something quite different underneath. It does not, I believe, make me helpful in my attempts to build up constructive relationships with other individuals. I would want to make it clear that while I feel I have learned this to be true, I have, by no means, adequately profited from it. In fact, it seems to me that most of the mistakes I make in personal relationships, most of the times in which I fail to be of help to other individuals, can be accounted for in terms of the fact that I have, for some defensive reason, behaved in one way at a surface level, while in reality my feelings run in a contrary direction.

A second thing which I have learned might be stated as follows: *I have found it effective, in my dealings with people, to be acceptant of myself.* I feel that over the years I have learned to become more adequate in listening to myself; so that I know somewhat more adequately than I used to what I am feeling at any given moment—to be able to realize I *am* angry, or that I *do* feel rejecting toward this person, or that I am uninterested in what is going on, or that I am eager to understand this individual. All of these diverse attitudes are feelings which I think I can listen to in myself. One way of putting this is that I feel I have become more adequate in letting myself be what I am. It becomes easier for me to accept myself in the way in which I would like to function.

This must seem to some like a very strange direction in which to move. It seems to me to have value because the curious paradox is that when I accept myself as I am, then I change. I believe that I have learned this from my clients as well as within my own experience—that we cannot change, we cannot move away from what we are, until we thoroughly *accept* what we are. Then change seems to come about almost unnoticed.

Another result which seems to grow out of self-acceptance is that relationships then become real. Real relationships have an exciting way of being vital and meaningful. If I can accept the fact that I am angry or annoyed at this student, then I am also much more likely to be able to accept his feelings in response. I can also accept the changed experience and the changed feelings which are then likely to occur in me and in him. Real relationships tend to change rather than to remain static.

I am not sure that I can make clear what I am trying to say in regard to this matter of self-acceptance. I think of a foreign student, an advanced graduate student who came into one of my courses and she and others asked me a number of questions, to several of which I simply answered that I did not know. For me, this was simply an acceptance of the fact of my ignorance on these points. To her, it was an utterly incredible experience to hear a professor say he did not know. In all her university work in her own country she had never heard such a statement. This experience challenged her interest to a marked degree and helped her to become a person who is seeking for answers, not simply a person who is a passive receptacle for knowledge. Thus, my acceptance of my ignorance es-

tablished a relationship between us in which she found herself changing.

So I find it effective to let myself be what I am in my attitudes; to know when I have reached my limit of endurance or of tolerance, and to accept that as a fact; to know when I desire to mold or manipulate people, and to accept that as a fact in myself. I would like to be as acceptant of these feelings as of feelings of warmth, interest, permissiveness, kindness, understanding. It is when I do accept all these attitudes as a part of me, then my relationship with the other person becomes what it is and then is able to grow and change most readily.

What I have said up to this point may seem to be somewhat negative in nature, although it does not seem so to me. I come now to a central learning which has had a great deal of significance for me, which I believe comes rather close to the purpose of this conference. I can state this learning as follows: *I have found it of enormous value when I can permit myself to understand another person.*

The way in which I have worded this statement may seem strange to you. Is it necessary to permit oneself to understand another? I think that it is. Our first reaction to most of the statements which we hear from other people is an immediate evaluation, or judgment, rather than an understanding of it. When a pupil speaks up in class expressing some feeling or attitude or belief, our tendency is, almost immediately, to feel "That's good"; "That's right"; or "That's bad"; "That's incorrect." Very rarely do we permit ourselves to understand precisely what the meaning of his statement is to him. Perhaps I can make this even sharper by suggesting that you imagine yourself in conversation with someone who holds a point of view very different from your own on a topic such as segregation, or politics, or the best means of teaching reading. I believe that if you engage in such imaginary conversations for even a few seconds you will not find yourself endeavoring to understand what the person is saying from his point of view, but immediately forming your own judgment of it, or your own argumentative response to it. So I say, it is not an easy thing to permit oneself to understand an individual, to enter thoroughly and completely and empathetically into his frame of reference. I think of one woman in a seminar when I was counseling a client in front of this group. This woman came up to me excitedly after one of the interviews and said:

> I realize now for the first time what it means really to listen to another person without trying to judge or evaluate. I felt that I entered into this client's experience, I really understood another person for the first time in my life.

This, I too, have found to be a valuable and rewarding experience.

To understand is enriching in a double way. I find when I am working with clients in distress that to understand the bizarre world of a partially psychotic individual, or to understand and sense the attitudes of a person who feels that life is too tragic to bear, or to understand a man who feels he is a worthless and inferior individual—each of these understandings somehow enriches me in giving a realization and experience of how other individuals face and meet life. Even more important, perhaps, is the fact that my understanding of these individuals permits them to change. It permits them to accept their own fears and bizarre thoughts and tragic feelings and discouragements as well as their moments of courage and kindness and love and sensitivity; and it is their experience as well as mine that once someone has fully understood those feelings, this has enabled them to accept those feelings in themselves. Then, they find both the feelings and themselves changing. Whether it is understanding a woman who feels that very literally she has a hook in her head by which others lead her about, or understanding a man who feels that no one is as lonely, no one is as separated from others as he, I find these understandings to be of value to me. But also, and perhaps

even more importantly, to be understood has a very positive value to these individuals.

Here I am going to digress a bit and talk about one practical channel for understanding others which I have found extremely helpful in my experience with classes of students. Because I have wanted to know the personal and individual reactions of students in my classes, I frequently set up the policy of asking for individual weekly reaction sheets, as I call them, on which the student can express any feeling he wishes which is relevant to the course. He may talk about the work he is doing; he may express feelings in regard to the class or the instructor; he may quite literally use it in any way he wishes, and he is given my solemn assurance that what he says on these sheets will have no relationship whatsoever to the grade he receives in the course. The use of this simple device has been one of the most meaningful things I have ever done in my teaching. I would like to talk, at some length, about this simple approach.

In the first place, it has caused me to realize that a course is not a course, it is an assemblage of many highly individual perceptions of experience. For example, during this past summer, I taught a course in Personality. I did certain things, I presented certain materials to the group, such as playing tape recordings of interviews. I facilitated discussions. Anyone looking in on the group as an outside observer would say that this was a definite, describable, given experience in which 30 different people were participating. If you ask for the individual reactions of the students, you find that it is not one thing, it is 30 different experiences. The same class can view so differently one and the same situation. I think I would like to read to you some brief excerpts from the reaction sheets which these students turned in. It may help you to realize why I find it of value for myself to permit myself to understand another person.

Let me, for example, take a few excerpts from the statements that were turned in at the end of the first week. One student says,

My immediate thoughts were favorable. I prefer discussions to lectures. I have been able to read without specific assignments. Each member of the class seems to be at a different stage of sophistication regarding personality.

As I understand this person, he is saying, "I am quite comfortable in the way in which the course is starting. Everything is fine." Here is another statement:

I feared that the course might prove too much for a person of my academic standards to cope with. There was only one way that I could find out if this was so; it was necessary for me to register for such a course and find out for myself. I have thus far found the two class sessions interesting, though there were instances that terms referred to were a bit over my head. I keep reminding myself that we all have to start somewhere, and this happens to be that way for me.

Here, if I am understanding him correctly, is a person who is saying, "I feel pretty insecure, but perhaps I can swim in this difficult stream." Here is another reaction:

The first week of class has been one of uncomfortableness and apprehension. These feelings were heightened even more by Friday's session. Even though theory of personality is not an area that is completely foreign to me, it is an area in which I do not have a strong academic background. As I listened to some of the other class members' purposes, projects, etc. I wondered how I could reconcile my very primary needs in this field with their seemingly strongly defined and explicit needs. One of the ways I can see of somewhat removing this apprehension and uncomfortableness is to do some very concentrated reading and thus be better able to share and contribute to class discussions effectively.

To me it is helpful to understand that for such a student this is a frightening new experience in which the main feeling is one of fear. There are also feelings of criticism. Here is one:

The class seems to be lacking in planning and direction.

Here is another:

Since I had looked forward to a fairly rigorous course in personality theory, the first two class meetings have been disappointing. I am sure that in classes such as the last two, one learns something about conducting a class like this, about how other people and I react; but due to the size of the group, it seems to be a bad example even of these things; and these are not what I am primarily interested in. I keep wishing the course would start.

And then one runs across a reaction like this, which also is a reaction to this same first week of this same course:

I couldn't help hearing words beneath words. Everyone spoke to the instructor. To the instructor only; "I want to know you." "I want you to know me." "See my bright shiny mind; see how sharp and clear it is." "I'm no beginner at this; I know plenty." "I don't know but I want to learn." "I hope you'll help me with this." And one person said, "I want to know myself and other people to know themselves. That seems to me the only human use for a personality theory." I liked listening, liked hearing the voices; I liked watching the instructor; but it seems a very long way away. I felt a terrifying distance. I couldn't stay with the voice or the group long. I kept seceding—to interrogate myself. Why was I here? Did I have a speakable purpose? It's all stiff and formal still. I wished my purposes were as clear and keen as some I heard. And persistently, every few minutes, I thought: We are a room full of strangers.

I am sure that this group of students was not unusual. Here is simply a sample of the wide variety of reactions and feelings which occur in every course—favorable reactions, frightened reactions, critical reactions, sensitive reactions. I feel as though I would like to give you many more of their statements, but let me concentrate on two other samples.

I will take one sampling of reactions during the fourth week of the course. I had been teaching the course in quite a free fashion, with a good deal of discussion, with relatively little direction on my part. Here are some of the reactions by the fourth week of the course. Here is one:

My feeling is one of indefinable revulsion with the tone of indecency. As nearly as I can get it, the answer lies somewhere around my dislike of the fuzzy, and my liking for the clear-cut.

I am sure that reactions just as violently negative occur in almost any class we teach. Yet, by our formal structure, we keep ourselves from knowing these reactions. Personally, I have found it of the utmost value to realize how keenly and sharply and negatively people are responding, as well as to understand those who are responding in a much more positive fashion. Here is another reaction from that fourth week:

I was somewhat disturbed by the discussion session wherein several members of the class expressed a desire for a more directive approach from the instructor. I asked myself the question, "Is the atmosphere of this class, which I find so conducive to thought, really so different from the experience of the other members of the class as they expressed?" I found myself questioning whether or not those who were disturbed by the freedom were here to try to find ways and means of understanding human behavior, or whether they desired repetitions from various texts by you through lectures. I could not help but feel that if they desired the latter that they were in the wrong place. The place for texts is the library. I shall have to admit that I am vain enough to believe that I can direct my own readings at this level of education.

Here is another reaction to this same week:

The past week proved to be the most fruitful one for the birth and development of new ideas in a long, long time. The project which I want to carry out for this course was discussed with various people and many new aspects of the problem involved were discovered. This kind of thing seems to happen every time when you share an idea with other people: the more you think that you really have thought of everything, the more you are surprised to find new facets.

Here is one more reaction written by a foreign student and, therefore, rather clumsily worded. He says:

It seems to me that our class follows the best, fruitful and scientific way of learning. But for people who have been taught for a long, long time, as we have, by the lecture type, authoritative method, this new procedure is ununderstandable. People like us are conditioned to hear the instructor, to keep passively our notes and memorize their reading assignments for the exams. There is no need to say that it takes a long time for people to get rid of their habits regardless of whether or not their habits are sterile, infertile and barren

Thus, during this one week, in which they were all exposed to the same situation, I found that the reactions ranged from finding the class utterly revolting to finding it exceptionally fruitful, from experiencing it as just what is wanted to finding it a challenge to old but sterile habits.

As the course continues the reactions become more positive in nature. One student who has evidently been infected by the atmosphere of the class says:

I've been caught up by the idea that "listening is contagious." Or maybe what I want to say is that I've been contaminated by the phenomenon of listening in this class. I want to express the strong feeling I have this week: I like us all so much. To the important thing is not just the positive feeling, but the "all of us." And I think that's where listening comes in. It seems to me as if somehow I have shaken off my rigidity in relating to other people in the class. Now, instead of a categorical response, I can listen, and I hear. I'm rarely without emotional response to this or any other group, but lately I've been quite intellectually stimulated. Suddenly, I'm more realistically aware of the paucity of my formal knowledge. And although I have had glimmers of this lack before, and a thousand "good intentions" for repairing it, I now feel a real intellectual hunger. I think it's because I have now experienced the twofoldedness of communication. It's expression, of course; but it's also listening. I listened. And the experience has forced me to revise my feelings about the omniscience of my wisdom. I feel somehow quite humble, and very grateful.

I believe this student has voiced the same values I feel in listening— that it opens up new vistas of knowledge, it makes me realize how much there is that I have not yet learned.

At the risk of continuing this digression too long, I would like to quote several things from a student who was one of the most quietly resentful and rebellious of any in the course. I must say that if I had not had these reaction sheets, I would have simply assumed that here was a calm quiet girl, who came to nearly all the meetings of the class, sat through them without taking part in the discussion, was quietly learning the material of the course. But her reaction sheets revealed her as being at times almost violently antagonistic. I would like to give three excerpts from her reaction statements toward the end of the course. In one of these reports she says:

> Class this last week has not raised my blood pressure quite as much, but I haven't found it as interesting either. All and all, I'm coming to the realization that in spite of myself I'm getting something from the course.

The following week, however, her whole reaction is taken up with a violent attack upon me. I had played a recording of an interview from another therapeutic orientation and commented on it and she says:

> Your own remarks, which you so carefully stated as being biased—but you needn't have since the whole presentation was—only showed more clearly the weakness of your position. A theory which rests on attacks against other theories is worthless. Only when a theory can show inner consistency is it valid and worthy. Mud-slinging attacks only indicate the weakness of the adherent to a belief; they weaken immeasurably their own stand.

The rest of the reactions were quite sarcastic and equally antagonistic.

One week later she turned in her final reaction to the course. She says:

> This course has been of great interest to me, even though I have maintained a rather consistent silence. I have been angry; I have gone from class filled with fury—fury at first over the fact that the class was so lacking in structure, lacking in unity of purpose, lacking in everything. It all seemed so completely pointless. I would come back solely to see if it actually could go on as it had. Next, I became very angry over your

> biased presentation of psychoanalytic approaches. (I was biased enough myself pro analysis that I couldn't stand your bias!)

> Again and again in my mind these past few days I have found myself thinking about this darn class; I don't seem to be able to escape it. I find myself thinking again and again of a quotation which I cannot remember in its entirety—it's from Walter Whitman, I think, and it goes something like this—"Have you learned lessons only of those who were easy with you . . . have you not also learned great lessons from those who disputed the passionate with you?"

> Well, anyway, that seems to be the way I feel at this point about the course. It has been a battle for me, veiled though it has been. I have come up with no world-shaking conclusions. I doubt that I will know for some time just what I have achieved from this, but one thing is certain, I am not the same as I was prior to this experience.

> Looking back now, I try to remember just what my original purpose was in taking the course. I think it was to find out whether or not my own psychoanalytic bias was correct in its impression of non-directive procedures, and to find out specifically about client-centered theory and practice—mainly to discredit it, to have information with which to continue my own bias and prejudice, to enable me to argue intelligently against it.

> Yet, in my readings, I have found many things which I do like. I have amazed myself. I have come to no final conclusions, however, but, at least the door is open and I have achieved a measure of objectivity about it. Time will tell just what the outcome of this all will be, but no longer is there the closed mind and prejudiced approach. If I gained nothing more from the course, but this standard alone it would be a great contribution to my future learning.

> My only regret is that for so long during the quarter I had not the time nor the energy to devote myself to the readings which I would like to have done. Now, however, there will be time to seek some of the answers to the questions raised in my mind. Perhaps, it would seem that there is great merit to this student-centered teaching. I know that I will not be finished with this course for quite some time to come. So thanks a lot for jolting me out of a certain smug lethargy!

To me it is very enriching indeed to permit myself to understand this wide range variety of reactions to what outwardly is but one course. I find that when I can permit myself to understand these extremely varied reactions, that my contributions to the group are so much richer, so much more personal, so much more responsive to the individuals who compose the group. To put it a slightly different way, I have found that when I can permit myself to understand the students in my classes and their real feelings, the whole interactional experience becomes much more valuable for them and for me. For myself, this is an extension of what I have already learned in counseling with individuals, that to understand another person's private world of feelings is a mutually rewarding experience.

I have talked at considerable length about what understanding another person means to me. There is another very closely related learning which perhaps should already have been part of what I have said. I can voice this learning very briefly: *I have found it highly rewarding when I can accept another person.*

I have found that truly to accept another person and his feelings is by no means an easy thing, any more than is understanding. I think this can be quite well illustrated from the excerpts I have just read to you. Can I really permit a student to feel hostile toward me? Can I accept him when he views life and psychological problems in a way quite different from mine? Can I accept his anger as a real and legitimate part of himself? Can I accept him when he feels very positively toward me, admiring me and wanting to model himself after me?

All this is involved in acceptance and it does not come easy. I believe that it is an increasingly common pattern in our culture for each of us to believe, "Every other person must feel and think and believe the same as I do." We find it very hard to permit our children or our parents or our spouses or other countries to feel differently than we do about particular issues or problems. We cannot permit a student to differ from us or to utilize his experience in his own way and to discover his own meaning in it—the right of the student to enter a course with an instructor and to

see it in his own way—this is one of the most priceless potentialities of life. Each of us is an island unto himself, in a very real sense; and he can only build bridges to other islands if he is first of all content to be himself and permitted to be himself. So I find that when I can accept another person, which means specifically accepting the feelings and attitudes and beliefs that he has as a real and vital part of him, then I am assisting him to become a person; and there seems to me great value in this.

All that I have been saying thus far is very much of one piece. It is only when I can be myself, when I can accept myself, that it is possible for me to understand others and accept others. There are plenty of times and plenty of relationships in which I do not achieve this, and then it seems to me life in these relationships is superficial. My relationship with these individuals is not particularly helpful. I tend either to make these people dependent on me or hostile to me. I do not like the results which ensue when I fail to profit from the learning I have mentioned. On the other hand, in the rather rare experience when these learnings do combine when I am able to accept myself as I am, and to be that self; when I am truly understanding of the way life seems to this other person, and when I can accept him as a separate individual who is not necessarily like me in attitudes or feelings or beliefs, then the relationship seems exceptionally profitable; and both the other person and I gain from it in deep and significant ways. We tend, I think, in such experience, to grow towards being more mature persons. So I have come to prize these learnings because they seem to lead to the development of separate, unique, and creatively different personalities.

I would like to go on to two or three additional learnings, which I will try to state much more briefly. *I have found it of value to be open to the realities of life as they are revealed in me and in other people.* To me, this seems such a personal learning that I am not at all sure that I can communicate it to you. Perhaps I can express a part of it by saying simply that life *is*. It is not something I have to feel responsible for. As Eliza points out to Professor Higgins in *My Fair Lady*, the tide comes in without him pulling it and the earth spins without him twirling it. Somehow, when I can take this attitude of being a part of life, but responsible only for my own small portion of it, responsible really only for me and my reactions, then I find that I enjoy it much more. Then I can appreciate something of the incredible complexity of persons, and can realize that though I categorize them in some of my simple-minded and ignorant classifications, they are far more richly differentiated than any of the pigeonholes into which I can put them. I find that I can appreciate both the delicacy and fragile nature of life and of individuals; but I can also appreciate the strength and ruggedness which is equally evident.

Another learning which has had meaning to me, or perhaps it is the same learning voiced in a somewhat different way, is: *The more I am able to understand myself and others, the more I accept myself and others, the more that I am open to the realities of life, the less do I find myself wishing to rush in.*

What I mean by this is that I have become less and less inclined to hurry in to fix things, to set goals, to mold people, to manipulate and push them in the way that I would like them to go. I am much more content simply to be myself and to let another person be himself. I know very well that this must seem like a strange, almost an Oriental point of view. What is life for if we are not going to do things to people? What is life for if we are not going to mold them to our purposes? What is life for if we are not going to teach them the things that *we* think they should learn? How can anyone hold such a static point of view as the one I am expressing? I am sure that attitudes such as these must be a part of the reaction of many of you.

Yet, the paradoxical aspect of my experience is that the more I am simply willing to be myself, in all this complexity of life, and the more I am willing to understand and accept the realities in myself and in other people, the more change seems to be stirred up. It is a very paradoxical thing—that to the degree that each one of us is willing to be himself, then he finds not only himself changing; but he finds that other people to whom he relates are also changing. At least this is a very vivid part of my experience, and one of the deepest things I think I have learned in my personal and professional life.

There is one final learning about which I should like to speak. It is perhaps basic to all of the things I have said thus far. It has been forced upon me by more than 25 years of trying to be helpful to individuals in personal distress. It is simply this: *It has been my experience that persons have a basically positive direction.* In my deepest contacts with individuals in therapy, even those whose troubles are most disturbing, whose behavior has been most antisocial, whose feelings seem most abnormal, I find this to be true. When I can sensitively understand the feelings which they are expressing, when I am able to accept them as separate persons in their own right, then I find that they tend to move in certain directions. What are these directions in which they tend to move? The words which I believe are most truly descriptive are words such as positive, constructive, moving toward self-actualization, growing toward maturity, growing toward socialization. I have come to feel that the more fully the individual is understood and accepted, the more he tends to drop the false front with which he has been meeting life, and the more he tends to move in a direction which is forward.

I would not want to be misunderstood on this. I do not have a Pollyanna view of human nature. I am quite aware that out of defensiveness and inner fear individuals can and do behave in ways which are horribly destructive, immature, regressive, antisocial, hurtful. Yet, one of the most refreshing and invigorating parts of my experience is to work with such individuals and to discover the strongly positive directional tendencies which exist in them, as in all of us, at the deepest levels.

CONCLUSION

I am a little astonished at the highly personal trend which this talk has taken as I have prepared it. I had not quite anticipated that I would reveal so much. I wonder if I will dare to give it.

Does it have anything at all to do with you and the work in which you are engaged? I am not in the least sure. Yet I can think of two possibilities, each of which leaves me somewhat encouraged. You may find yourself inwardly objecting to almost all that I have said.

You may feel, "This is not at all what my experience has taught me." If so, I shall feel that my remarks have been worthwhile because I believe that in that case you will probably be impelled to formulate more clearly for yourself just what you have learned from your dealings with individuals, what you have learned from your relationships with your students and your clients, as well as your supervisors and administrators; and perhaps you can work out more clearly the meanings that your professional experience has had for you and, consequently, the directions you will want to take.

And if, on the other hand, some of the meanings that I have found in understanding and acceptance, in my own experience, resonate or seem to be in tune with some part of your experience in dealing with the many individuals with whom you work, then perhaps that too, will strengthen you in thinking your own thoughts. It may help you in discovering more sharply the meaning of your experience, learning more clearly the ways in which you have found it helpful to relate to your students and to others; and thus finding more definitely the direction which is meaningful to you in your own life. At any rate, that is my hope.

KEY POINTS

1. It is most helpful to be honest and true to oneself when dealing with others. Pretense holds the seeds of destruction.

2. To have effective dealings with others, one must understand, be true to, and accept oneself. We cannot change until we accept who we are.

3. It is important to listen to another person without trying to judge or evaluate. Each person possesses strong, positive directional tendencies, which will emerge only if they are allowed to come out.

QUESTIONS TO THINK ABOUT

1. How is Rogers's humanistic–existential approach to personality very different from most other personality approaches?

2. Rogers is perhaps best known for emphasizing the importance of "unconditional positive regard." How has this idea been adopted into our common culture?

3. Rogers welcomed systematic testing of his ideas, and in fact demanded evaluations of his type of psychotherapy. How can we validate ideas such as Rogers's notion that a person should "become one's self"?

27

Love and Its Disintegration in Contemporary Western Society*

ERICH FROMM

Erich Fromm (1900–1980) was born in Frankfurt am Main, Germany, to a father whom he described as a moody businessman and a mother who suffered bouts of depression. Despite this childhood environment, Fromm grew up to pursue a doctorate from the University of Heidelberg, study at the University of Munich and the Psycho-Analytic Institute in Berlin, and become a renowned psychoanalyst. Initially a follower of Freud, Fromm eventually developed his own theories that human behavior stems not from unconscious drives, but rather from the needs of a conscious person existing within a network of societal demands. He is thus one of the founders of the existential and humanistic movement. Fromm also disdained the traditional passive and noncommittal role of the psychoanalyst and encouraged the utilization of a more participatory role in treating patients.

In this selection, Fromm bemoans the loss of true love, and notes that in modern society, too many of us are alienated from ourselves, from others, and from nature. We try to overcome this existential alienation of modern society by "having fun." But, alas, it does not work.

If love is a capacity of the mature, productive character, it follows that the capacity to love in an individual living in any given culture depends on the influence this culture has on the character of the average person. If we speak about love in contemporary Western culture, we mean to ask whether the social structure of Western civilization and the spirit resulting from it are conducive to the development of love. To raise the question is to answer it in the negative. No objective observer of our Western life can doubt that love—brotherly love, motherly love, and erotic love—is a relatively rare phenomenon, and that its place is taken by a number of forms of pseudo-love which are in reality so many forms of the disintegration of love.

Capitalistic society is based on the principle of political freedom on the one hand, and of the market as the regulator of all economic, hence social relations, on the other. The commodity market determines the conditions under which commodities are exchanged, the labor market regulates the acquisition and sale of labor. Both useful things and useful human energy and skill are transformed into commodities which are exchanged without the use of force and without fraud under the conditions of the market. Shoes, useful and needed as they may be, have no economic value (exchange value) if there is no demand for them on the market; human energy and skill are without exchange value if there is no demand for them under existing market conditions. The owner of capital can buy labor and command it to work for the profitable investment of his capital. The owner of labor must sell it to capitalists under the existing market conditions, unless he is to starve. This economic structure is reflected in a hierarchy of values. Capital commands labor; amassed things, that which is dead, are of superior value to labor, to human powers, to that which is alive.

This has been the basic structure of capitalism since its beginning. But while it is still characteristic of modern capitalism, a number of factors have changed which give contemporary capitalism its specific qualities and which have a profound influence on the character structure of modern man. As the result of the development of capitalism we witness an ever-increasing process of centralization and concentration of capital. The large enterprises grow in size continuously, the smaller ones are squeezed out. The ownership of capital invested in these enterprises is more and more separated from the function of managing them. Hundreds of thousands of stockholders "own" the enterprise; a managerial bureaucracy which is well paid, but which does not own the enterprise, manages it. This bureaucracy is less interested in making maximum profits than in the expansion of the enterprise, and in their own power. The increasing concentration of capital and the emergence of a powerful managerial bureaucracy are paralleled by the development of the labor movement. Through the unionization of labor, the individual worker does not have to bargain on the labor market by and for himself; he is united in big labor unions, also led by a powerful bureaucracy which represents him vis-à-vis the industrial colossi. The initiative has been shifted, for better or worse, in the fields of capital as well as in those of labor, from the individual to the bureaucracy. An increasing number of people cease to be independent, and become dependent on the managers of the great economic empires.

Another decisive feature resulting from this concentration of capital, and characteristic of modern capitalism, lies in the specific way of the organization of work. Vastly centralized enterprises with a radical division of labor lead to an organization of work where the individual loses his individuality, where he becomes an expendable cog in the machine. The human problem of modern capitalism can be formulated in this way:

Modern capitalism needs men who co-operate smoothly and in large numbers; who want to consume more and more; and whose tastes are standardized and can be easily influenced and anticipated. It needs men who feel free and independent, not subject to any authority or principle or conscience—yet willing to be commanded, to do what is expected of them, to fit into the social machine without friction; who can be guided without force, led without leaders, prompted without aim—except the one to make good, to be on the move, to function, to go ahead.

What is the outcome? Modern man is alienated from himself, from his fellow men, and from nature. He has been transformed into a commodity, experiences his life forces as an investment which must bring him the maximum profit obtainable under existing market conditions. Human relations are essentially those of alienated automatons, each basing his security on staying close to the herd, and not being different in thought, feeling or action. While everybody tries to be as close as possible to the rest, everybody remains utterly alone, pervaded by the deep sense of insecurity, anxiety and guilt which always results when human separateness cannot be overcome. Our civilization offers many palliatives which help people to be consciously unaware of this aloneness: first of all the strict routine of bureaucratized, mechanical work, which helps people to remain unaware of their most fundamental human desires, of the longing for transcendence and unity. Inasmuch as the routine alone does not succeed in this, man overcomes his unconscious despair by the routine of amusement, the passive consumption of sounds and sights offered by the amusement industry; furthermore by the satisfaction of buying ever new things, and soon exchanging them for others. Modern man is actually close to the picture Huxley describes in his *Brave New World:* well fed, well clad, satisfied sexually, yet without self, without any except the most superficial contact with his fellow men, guided by the slogans which Huxley formulated so succinctly, such as: "When the individual feels, the community reels"; or "Never put off till tomorrow the fun you can have today," or, as the crowning statement: "Everybody is happy nowadays." Man's happiness today consists in "having fun." Having fun lies in the satisfaction of consuming and "taking in" commodities, sights, food, drinks, cigarettes, people, lectures, books, movies—all are consumed, swallowed. The world is one great object for our appetite, a big apple, a big bottle, a big breast; we are the sucklers, the eternally expectant ones, the hopeful ones—and the eternally disappointed ones. Our character is geared to exchange and to receive, to barter and to consume; everything, spiritual as well as material objects, becomes an object of exchange and of consumption.

The situation as far as love is concerned corresponds, as it has to by necessity, to this social character of modern man. Automatons cannot love; they can exchange their "personality packages" and hope for a fair bargain. One of the most significant expressions of love, and especially of marriage with this alienated structure, is the idea of the "team." In any number of articles on happy marriage, the ideal described is that of the smoothly functioning team. This description is not too different from the idea of a smoothly functioning employee; he should be "reasonably independent," co-operative, tolerant, and at the same time ambitious and aggressive. Thus, the marriage counselor tells us, the husband should "understand" his wife and be helpful. He should comment favorably on her new dress, and on a tasty dish. She, in turn, should understand when he comes home tired and disgruntled, she should listen attentively when he talks about his business troubles, should not be angry but understanding when he forgets her birthday. All this kind of relationship amounts to is the well-oiled relationship between two persons who remain strangers all their lives, who never arrive at a "central relationship," but who treat each other with courtesy and who attempt to make each other feel better.

In this concept of love and marriage the main emphasis is on finding a refuge from an otherwise unbearable sense of aloneness. In "love" one has found, at last, a haven from aloneness. One forms an alliance of two against the world, and this egoism *à deux* is mistaken for love and intimacy.

The emphasis on team spirit, mutual tolerance and so forth is a relatively recent development. It was preceded, in the years after the First World War, by a concept of love in which mutual sexual satisfaction was supposed to be the basis for satisfactory love relations, and especially for a happy marriage. It was believed that the reasons for the frequent unhappiness in marriage were to be found in that the marriage partners had not made a correct "sexual adjustment"; the reason for this fault was seen in the ignorance regarding "correct" sexual behavior, hence in the faulty sexual technique of one or both partners. In order to "cure" this fault, and to help the unfortunate couples who could not love each other, many books gave instructions and counsel concerning the correct sexual behavior, and promised implicitly or explicitly that happiness and love would follow. The underlying idea was that love is the child of sexual pleasure, and that if two people learn how to satisfy each other sexually, they will love each other. It fitted the general illusion of the time to assume that using the right techniques is the solution not only to technical problems of industrial production, but of all human problems as well. One ignored the fact that the contrary of the underlying assumption is true.

Love is not the result of adequate sexual satisfaction, but sexual happiness—even the knowledge of the so-called sexual technique—is the result of love. If aside from everyday observation this thesis needed to be proved, such proof can be found in ample material of psychoanalytic data. The study of the most frequent sexual problems—frigidity in women, and the more or less severe forms of psychic impotence in men—shows that the cause does not lie in a lack of knowledge of the right technique, but in the inhibitions which make it impossible to love. Fear of or hatred for the other sex are at the bottom of those difficulties which prevent a person from giving himself completely, from acting spontaneously, from trusting the sexual partner in the immediacy and directness of physical closeness. If a sexually inhibited person can emerge from fear or hate, and hence become capable of loving, his or her sexual problems are solved. If not, no amount of knowledge about sexual techniques will help.

But while the data of psychoanalytic therapy point to the fallacy of the idea that knowledge of the correct sexual technique leads to sexual happiness and love, the underlying assumption that love is the concomitant of mutual sexual satisfaction was largely influenced by the theories of Freud. For Freud, love was basically a sexual phenomenon. "Man having found by experience that sexual (genital) love afforded him his greatest gratification, so that it became in fact a prototype of all happiness to him, must have been thereby impelled to seek his happiness further along the path of sexual relations, to make genital eroticism the central point of his life." The experience of brotherly love is, for Freud, an outcome of sexual desire, but with the sexual instinct being transformed into an impulse with "inhibited aim." "Love with an inhibited aim was indeed originally full of sensual love, and in man's unconscious mind is so still." As far as the feeling of fusion, of oneness ("oceanic feeling"),

which is the essence of mystical experience and the root of the most intense sense of union with one other person or with one's fellow men, is concerned, it was interpreted by Freud as a pathological phenomenon, as a regression to a state of an early "limitless narcissism."

It is only one step further that for Freud love is in itself an irrational phenomenon. The difference between irrational love, and love as an expression of the mature personality does not exist for him. He pointed out in a paper on transference love, that transference love is essentially not different from the "normal" phenomenon of love. Falling in love always verges on the abnormal, is always accompanied by blindness to reality, compulsiveness, and is a transference from love objects of childhood. Love as a rational phenomenon, as the crowning achievement of maturity, was, to Freud, no subject matter for investigation, since it had no real existence.

However, it would be a mistake to overestimate the influence of Freud's ideas on the concept that love is the result of sexual attraction, or rather that it is the *same* as sexual satisfaction, reflected in conscious feeling. Essentially the causal nexus proceeds the other way around. Freud's ideas were partly influenced by the spirit of the nineteenth century; partly they became popular through the prevailing spirit of the years after the First World War. Some of the factors which influenced both the popular and the Freudian concepts were, first, the reaction against the strict mores of the Victorian age. The second factor determining Freud's theories lies in the prevailing concept of man, which is based on the structure of capitalism. In order to prove that capitalism corresponded to the natural needs of man, one had to show that man was by nature competitive and full of mutual hostility. While economists "proved" this in terms of the insatiable desire for economic gain, and the Darwinists in terms of the biological law of the survival of the fittest, Freud came to the same result by the assumption that man is driven by a limitless desire for the sexual conquest of all women, and that only the pressure of society prevented man from acting on his desires. As a result men are necessarily jealous of each other, and this mutual jealousy and competition would continue even if all social and economic reasons for it would disappear.

Eventually, Freud was largely influenced in his thinking by the type of materialism prevalent in the nineteenth century. One believed that the substratum of all mental phenomena was to be found in physiological phenomena; hence love, hate, ambition, jealousy were explained by Freud as so many outcomes of various forms of the sexual instinct. He did not see that the basic reality lies in the totality of human existence, first of all in the human situation common to all men, and secondly in the practice of life determined by the specific structure of society. (The decisive step beyond this type of materialism was taken by Marx in his "historical materialism," in which not the body, nor an instinct like the need for food or possession, serves as the key to the understanding of man, but the total life process of man, his "practice of life"). According to Freud, the full and uninhibited satisfaction of all instinctual desires would create mental health and happiness. But the obvious clinical facts demonstrate that men— and women—who devote their lives to unrestricted sexual satisfaction do not attain happiness, and very often suffer from severe neurotic conflicts or symptoms. The complete satisfaction of all instinctual needs is not only not a basis for happiness, it does not even guarantee sanity. Yet Freud's idea could only have become so popular in the period after the First World War because of the changes which had occurred in the spirit of capitalism, from the emphasis on saving to that on spending, from self-frustration as a means for economic success to consumption as the basis for an ever-widening market, and as the main satisfaction for the anxious, automatized individual. Not to postpone the satisfaction of any desire became the main tendency in the sphere of sex as well as in that of all material consumption.

It is interesting to compare the concepts of Freud, which correspond to the spirit of capitalism as it existed, yet unbroken, around the beginning of this century, with the theoretical concepts of one of the most brilliant contemporary psychoanalysts, the late H. S. Sullivan. In Sullivan's psychoanalytic system we find, in contrast to Freud's, a strict division between sexuality and love.

What is the meaning of love and intimacy in Sullivan's concept? "Intimacy is that type of situation involving two people which permits validation of all components of personal worth. Validation of personal worth requires a type of relationship which I call collaboration, by which I mean clearly formulated adjustments of one's behavior to the expressed needs of the other person in pursuit of increasingly identical—that is, more and more nearly mutual satisfactions, and in the maintenance of increasingly similar security operations." If we free Sullivan's statement from its somewhat involved language, the essence of love is seen in a situation of collaboration, in which two people feel: "We play according to the rules of the game to preserve our prestige and feeling of superiority and merit."

Just as Freud's concept of love is a description of the experience of the patriarchal male in terms of nineteenth-century capitalism, Sullivan's description refers to the experience of the alienated, marketing personality of the twentieth century. It is a description of an "egotism *à deux*," of two people pooling their common interests, and standing together against a hostile and alienated world. Actually his definition of intimacy is in principle valid for the feeling of any co-operating team, in which everybody "adjusts his behavior to the expressed needs of the other person in the pursuit of common aims" (it is remarkable that Sullivan speaks here of *expressed* needs, when the least one could say about love is that it implies a reaction to *unexpressed* needs between two people).

Love as mutual sexual satisfaction, and love as "teamwork" and as a haven from aloneness, are the two "normal" forms of the disintegration of love in modern Western society, the socially patterned pathology of love. . . .

REFERENCES

Fromm, E. (1955). *The sane society.* NY: Rinehart.

Freud, S. (1953). *Civilization and its discontents* (J. Riviere, Trans.). London: Hogarth Press.

Sullivan, H. S. (1953). *The Interpersonal theory of psychiatry.* New York: W. W. Norton.

KEY POINTS

1. The position of a person and the person's outlook on life and society is reflective of the socioeconomic structure. An environment that encourages cooperative interaction, not an isolating, mechanized atmosphere, produces workers who are more likely to feel free and independent, thus more satisfied with life and their place in the world.

2. We mask feelings of alienation from ourselves, others, and nature with the facade of having fun. By having fun, we create the illusion of a fulfilling life.

3. It is important that a member of any "team," be it within the workplace or a marriage, retain a sense of independence to achieve goals, yet be tolerant and cooperative to encourage the growth of the relationship.

4. Love is independent from sexual satisfaction and sexual happiness.

5. Fromm disagrees with Freud's belief that all human behavior and emotions, including love, stem from some unconscious, psychological drive. As a result of the disintegration of "real" love in Western society, we have adopted forms of "pseudo-love" to compensate. The capacity to experience "real" love entails gaining understanding through experience and knowledge, breaking from narcissism, and sharing to encourage the growth of others.

QUESTIONS TO THINK ABOUT

1. How and why is love disintegrating in contemporary Western society?

2. Is there anything wrong with having fun?

3. How can "pseudo-love" be differentiated from "real" love?

28

Some Educational Implications of the Humanistic Psychologies*

ABRAHAM H. MASLOW

Abraham Maslow (1908–1970) was born in New York to Russian-Jewish immigrants; he had a difficult childhood with a mother who engaged in bizarre behaviors. As a child, he was shy, bookish, and neurotic. However, he grew up to reach his full potential and become an eminent humanistic psychologist. Maslow believed that the highest form of human need is the need for self-actualization. However, according to his hierarchy of needs, the baser needs such as biological needs, safety needs, belonging, and esteem needs must be met before the higher needs can become important.

Ultimately, as a humanistic psychologist, Maslow expected the best about the potential of human beings, but had to admit that the darker side of humans is perpetually present and cannot be completely eliminated. In this selection, Maslow describes some educational implications of his approach. Contrary to the psychoanalytic approach, which focuses on unconscious motivations, and contrary to the behaviorist approach, which focuses on conditioning and rewards, the humanistic approach urges teachers to help bring out the best of the individual and help him or her to build on existing potential and realize unused talents.

The upshot of the past decade or two of turmoil and change within the field of psychology can be viewed as a local manifestation of a great change taking place in all fields of knowledge. We are witnessing a great revolution in thought, in the Zeitgeist itself: the creation of a new image of man and society and of religion and science (1, 16). It is the kind of change that happens, as Whitehead said, once or twice in a century. This is not an *improvement* of something; it is a real change in direction altogether. It is as if we had been going north and are now going south instead.

Recent developments in psychological theory and research are closely related to the changes in the new image of man which lie at the center of the larger revolution. There are, to oversimplify the situation, two comprehensive theories of human nature which dominate psychology today. The first is the behavioristic, associationistic, experimental, mechanomorphic psychology; the psychology which can be called "classical" because it is in a direct line with the classical conception of science which comes out of astronomy, mechanics, physics, chemistry, and geology; the psychology which can be called "academic" because it has tended to emanate from and flourish in the undergraduate and graduate departments of psychology in our universities. Since its first detailed and testable formulation by Watson (24), Hull (5), and Skinner (21), "classical,"

*Maslow, A. (1968). Some educational implications of the humanistic psychologies. *Harvard Educational Review, 38*, 685–696. Copyright © 1968 by the President and Fellows of Harvard College. All rights reserved. Reprinted by permission.

"academic" psychological theory has been widely applied beyond its original limited focus in such diverse areas as acquisition of motor skills, behavior disorders and therapy, and social psychology. It has answers of a kind to any questions that you may have about human nature. In that sense, it is a philosophy, a philosophy of psychology.

The second philosophy of psychology, the one which dominates the whole field of clinical psychology and social work, emerged essentially from the work of Freud and his disciples and antagonists. In light of its emphasis upon the interplay between unconscious emotional forces and the conscious organization of behavior, I refer to this school of thought as "psychodynamic" or "depth" psychology. It, too, tries to be a comprehensive philosophy of man. It has generated a theory of art, of religion, of society, of education, of almost every major human endeavor.

What is developing today is a third, more inclusive, image of man, which is now already in the process of generating great changes in all intellectual fields and in all social and human institutions (2, 6, 8, 20, 25). Let me try to summarize this development very briefly and succinctly because I want to turn as soon as I can to its meaning for learning and education.

Third Force psychology, as some are calling it, is in large part a reaction to the gross inadequacies of behavioristic and Freudian psychologies in their treatment of the higher nature of man. Classical academic psychology has no systematic place for higher-order elements of the personality such as altruism and dignity, or the search for truth and beauty. You simply do not ask questions about ultimate human values if you are working in an animal lab.

Of course, it is true that the Freudian psychology has confronted these problems of the higher nature of man. But until very recently these have been handled by being very cynical about them, that is to say, by analyzing them away in a pessimistic, reductive manner. Generosity is interpreted as a reaction formation against a stinginess, which is deep down and unconscious, and therefore somehow more real.

Kindliness tends to be seen as a defense mechanism against violence, rage, and the tendency to murder. It is as if we cannot take at face value any of the decencies that we value in ourselves, certainly what I value in myself, what I try to be. It is perfectly true that we do have anger and hate, and yet there are other impulses that we are beginning to learn about which might be called the higher needs of man: "needs" for the intrinsic and ultimate values of goodness and truth and beauty and perfection and justice and order. They are there, they exist, and any attempt to explain them *away* seems to me to be very foolish. I once searched through the Freudian literature on the feeling of love, of wanting love, but especially of giving love. Freud has been called the philosopher of love, yet the Freudian literature contains nothing but the pathology of love, and also a kind of derogatory explaining-away of the finding that people do love each other, as if it could be only an illusion. Something similar is true of mystical or oceanic experiences: Freud analyzes them *away*.

This belief in the reality of higher human needs, motives and capacities, that is, the belief that human nature has been sold short by the dominant psychological theories, is the primary force binding together a dozen or so "splinter groups" into this comprehensive Third Force psychology. All of these groups reject entirely the whole conception of science as being value-free. Sometimes they do this consciously and explicitly, sometimes by implication only. This is a real revolution because traditionally science has been defined in terms of objectivity, detachment, and procedures which never tell you how to find human ends. The discovery of ends and values are turned over to non-scientific, non-empirical sources. The Third Force psychology totally rejects this view of science as merely instrumental and unable to help mankind to discover its ultimate ends and values (11, 18).

Among the many educational consequences generated by this philosophy, to come closer to our topic now, is a different conception of the self. This is a very complex conception, difficult to describe briefly, because it talks for the first time in centuries of an *essence*, of an *intrinsic* nature, of specieshood, of a kind of animal nature (9, 14). This is in sharp contrast with the European existentialists, most especially with Sartre, for whom man is *entirely* his own project, *entirely* and merely a product of his own arbitrary, unaided will. For Sartre and all those whom he has influenced, one's self becomes an arbitrary choice, a willing by fiat to be something or do something without any guidelines about which is better, which is worse, what's good and what's bad. In essentially denying the existence of biology, Sartre has given up altogether any absolute or at least any species-wide conception of values. This comes very close to making a life-philosophy of the obsessive-compulsive neurosis in which one finds what I have called "experiential emptiness," the absence of impulse-voices from within (12, 14).

The American humanistic psychologists and existential psychiatrists are mostly closer to the psychodynamicists than they are to Sartre. Their clinical experiences have led them to conceive of the human being as having an essence, a biological nature, membership in a species. It is very easy to interpret the "uncovering" therapies as helping the person to *discover* his Identity, his Real Self, in a word, his own subjective biology, which he can *then* proceed to actualize, to "make himself," to "choose." The Freudian conception of instincts has been generally discarded by the humanistic psychologists in favor of the conception of "basic needs," or in some cases, in favor of the conception of a single overarching need for actualization or growth (19). In any case, it is implied, if not made explicit, by most of these writers that the organism, in the strictest sense, has *needs* which must be gratified in order to become fully human, to grow well, and to avoid sicknesses (9, 14). This doctrine of a Real Self to be uncovered and actualized is also a total rejection of the *tabula rasa* notions of the behaviorists and associationists who often talk as if *anything* can be learned, *anything* can be taught, as if the human being is a sort of a passive clay to be shaped, controlled, reinforced, modified in any way that somebody arbitrarily decides.

We speak then of a self, a kind of intrinsic nature which is very subtle, which is not necessarily conscious, which has to be sought for, and which has to be uncovered and then built upon, actualized, taught, educated (13). The notion is that something is there but it's hidden, swamped, distorted, twisted, overlayed. The job of the psychotherapist (or the teacher) is to help a person find out what's already in him rather than to reinforce him or shape or teach him into a prearranged form, which someone else has decided upon in advance, *a priori*.

Let me explore what I call "introspective biology" and its relation to new ideas for education. If we accept the notion of the human essence or the core-self, i.e., the constitutional, temperamental, biological, chemical, endocrinological, given raw material, if we do accept the fact that babies come into the world very different from each other (anyone of you who has more than one child knows that), then the job of any helper, and furthermore the first job of each of us for ourselves, is to uncover and discover what we ourselves are. A good example for pedagogical purposes is our maleness and femaleness, which is the most obvious biological, constitutional given, and one which involves all the problems of conflicts, of self-discovery, and of actualization. Practically every youngster, not to mention a good proportion of the older population also, is mixed up about what it means to be a female and what it means to be a male. A lot of time has to be spent on the questions: How do I get to be a good female, or how do I get to be a good male? This involves self-discovery, self-acceptance, and self-making; discoveries about both one's commonness and one's uniqueness, rather than a Sartre-type decision on whether to be a male or a female.

One constitutional difference that I have discovered is that there are differences in triggers to peak-experiences between the sexes. The mystical and peak-experiences, the ultimate, esthetic, poetic experiences of the male, can come from a football game, for example. One subject reported that once when he broke free of the line and got into the open and then ran—that this was a true moment of ecstasy. But Dr. Deborah Tanzer has found women who use the same kinds of words, the same kind of poetry, to describe their feelings during natural childbirth. Under the right circumstances these women have ecstasies which sound just the same as the St. Theresa or Meister Eckhardt kind of ecstasy. I call them peak-experiences to secularize them and to naturalize them, to make them more empirical and researchable.

Individual constitutional differences, then, are an important variable. It continually impresses me that the same peak-experiences come from different kinds of activities for different kinds of people. Mothers will report peak-experiences not only from natural childbirth but also from putting the baby to the breast. (Of course this doesn't happen all the time. These peak-experiences are rare rather than common.) But I've never heard of any man getting a peak-experience from putting his baby to *his* breast. It just doesn't happen. He wasn't constructed right for this purpose. We are confronting the fact that people are biologically different, but have species-wide emotional experiences. Thus I think we should examine individual differences in all of our given biochemical, endocrine, neurological, anatomical systems to see to just what extent they carry along with them psychological and spiritual differences and to what extent there remains a common substratum (14).

The trouble is that the human species is the only species which finds it hard to be a species. For a cat there seems to be no problem about being a cat. It's easy; cats seem to have no complexes or ambivalences or conflicts, and show no signs of yearning to be dogs instead. Their instincts are very clear. But we have no such unequivocal animal instincts. Our biological essence, our instinct-remnants, are weak and subtle, and they are hard to get at. Learnings of the extrinsic sort *are more powerful than our deepest impulses.* These deepest impulses in the human species, at the points where the instincts have been lost almost entirely, where they are extremely weak, extremely subtle and delicate, where you have to dig to find them, *this* is where I speak of introspective biology, of biological phenomenology,

implying that one of the necessary methods in the search for identity, the search for self, the search for spontaneity and for naturalness is a matter of closing your eyes, cutting down the noise, turning off the thoughts, putting away all busyness, just relaxing in a kind of Taoistic and receptive fashion (in much the same way that you do on the psychoanalyst's couch). The technique here is to just wait to see what happens, what comes to mind. This is what Freud called free association, free-floating attention rather than task-orientation, and if you are successful in this effort and learn how to do it, you can forget about the outside world and its noises and begin to hear these small, delicate impulse-voices from within, the hints from your animal nature, not only from your common species-nature, but also from your own uniqueness.

There's a very interesting paradox here, however. On the one hand I've talked about uncovering or discovering your idiosyncrasy, the way in which you are different from everybody else in the whole world. Then on the other hand I've spoken about discovering your specieshood, your humanness. As Carl Rogers has phrased it: "How does it happen that the deeper we go into ourselves as particular and unique, seeking for our own individual identity, the more we find the whole human species?" Doesn't that remind you of Ralph Waldo Emerson and the New England Transcendentalists? Discovering your specieshood, at a deep enough level, merges with discovering your selfhood (13, 14). Becoming (learning how to be) fully human means *both* enterprises carried on simultaneously. You are learning (subjectively experiencing) what you peculiarly are, how you are you, what your potentialities are, what your style is, what your pace is, what your tastes are, what your values are, what direction your body is going, where your personal biology is taking you, i.e., how you are *different* from others. And at the same time it means learning what it means to be a human animal like other human animals, i.e., how you are *similar* to others.

It is such considerations as these that convince me that we are now being confronted with a choice between two extremely different, almost mutually exclusive conceptions of learning. What we have in practically all the elementary and advanced textbooks of psychology, and in most of the brands of "learning theory" which all graduate students are required to learn, is what I want to call for the sake of contrast and confrontation, *extrinsic learning,* i.e., learning of the outside, learning of the impersonal, of arbitrary associations, of arbitrary conditioning, that is, of arbitrary (or at best, culturally-determined) meanings and responses. In this kind of learning, most often it is not the person himself who decides, but rather a teacher or an experimenter who says, "I will use a buzzer," "I will use a bell," "I will use a red light," and most important, "I will reinforce this but not that." In this sense the learning is extrinsic to the learner, extrinsic to the personality, and is extrinsic also in the sense of *collecting* associations, conditionings, habits, or modes of action. It is as if these were *possessions* which the learner accumulates in the same way that he accumulates keys or coins and puts them in his pocket. They have little or nothing to do with the actualization or growth of the peculiar, idiosyncratic kind of person he is.

I believe this is the model of education which we all have tucked away in the back of our heads and which we don't often make explicit. In this model the teacher is the active one who teaches a passive person who gets shaped and taught and who is *given* something which he then accumulates and which he may then lose or retain, depending upon the efficiency of the initial indoctrination process, and of his own accumulation-of-fact process. I would maintain that a good 90% of "learning theory" deals with learnings that have nothing to do with the intrinsic self that I've been talking about, nothing to do with its specieshood and biological idiosyncracy. This kind of learning too easily reflects the goals of the teacher and ignores the values and ends of the learner himself (22). It is also fair, therefore, to call such learning amoral.

Now I'd like to contrast this with another kind of learning, which is actually going on, but is usually unconscious and unfortunately happens more outside the classroom than inside. It often comes in the great personal learning experiences of our lives.

For instance, if I were to list the most important learning experiences in my life, there come to mind getting married, discovering my life work, having children, getting psychoanalyzed, the death of my best friend, confronting death myself, and the like. I think I would say that these were more important learning experiences for me than my Ph.D. or any 15 or 150 credits or courses that I've ever had. I certainly learned more about *myself* from such experiences. I learned, if I may put it so, to throw aside many of my "learnings," that is, to push aside the habits and traditions and reinforced associations which had been imposed upon me. Sometimes this was at a very trivial, and yet meaningful, level. I particularly remember when I learned that I really hated lettuce. My father was a "nature boy," and I had lettuce two meals a day for the whole of my early life. But one day in analysis after I had learned that I carried my father inside me, it dawned on me that it was my father, through my larynx, who was ordering salad with every meal. I can remember sitting there, realizing that *I* hated lettuce and then saying, "My God, take the damn stuff away!" I was emancipated, becoming in this small way me, rather than my father. I didn't eat any more lettuce for months, until it finally settled back to what my body calls for. I have lettuce two or three times each week, which I now enjoy. But *not* twice a day.

Now observe, this experience which I mentioned occurred just once and I could give many other similar examples. It seems to me that we must call into question the generality of repetition, of learning by drilling (4). The experiences in which we uncover our intrinsic selves are apt to be unique moments, not slow accumulations of reinforced bits. (How do you repeat the death of your father?) These are the experiences in which we discover identity (16). These are the experiences in which we learn who we are, what we love, what we hate, what we value, what we are committed to, what makes us feel anxious, what makes us feel depressed, what makes us feel happy, what makes us feel great joy.

It must be obvious by now that you can generate consequences of this second picture of learning by the hundred. (And again I would stress that these hypotheses can be stated in testable, disconfirmable, confirmable form.) One such implication of the point of view is a change in the whole picture of the teacher. If you are willing to accept this conception of two kinds of learning, with the learning-to-be-a-person being more central and more basic than the impersonal learning of skills or the acquisition of habits; and if you are willing to concede that even the more extrinsic learnings are far more useful, and far more effective if based upon a sound identity, that is, if done by a person who knows what he wants, knows what he is, and where he's going and what his ends are; then you *must* have a different picture of the good teacher and of his functions.

In the first place, unlike the current model of teacher as lecturer, conditioner, reinforcer, and boss, the Taoist helper or teacher is receptive rather than intrusive. I was told once that in the world of boxers, a youngster who feels himself to be good and who wants to be a boxer will go to a gym, look up one of the managers and say, "I'd like to be a pro, and I'd like to be in your stable. I'd like you to manage me." In this world, what is then done characteristically is to try him out. The good manager will select one of his professionals and say, "Take him on in the ring. Stretch him. Strain him. Let's see what he can do. Just let him show his very best. Draw him out." If it turns out that the boxer has promise, if he's a "natural," then what the good manager does is to take that boy and train him to be, if this is Joe Dokes, a *better Joe Dokes.* That is, he takes his style as given and builds upon that. He does not start all over again, and say, "Forget all you've learned, and do it this new way," which is like saying, "Forget what kind of body you have," or "Forget what you are good for." He takes him and builds upon his *own* talents and builds him up into the very best Joe Dokes-type boxer that he possibly can.

It is my strong impression that this is the way in which much of the world of education could function. If we want to be helpers, coun-selors, teachers, guiders, or psychotherapists, what we must do is to accept the person and help him learn what kind of person he is already. What is his style, what are his aptitudes, what is he good for, not good for, what can we build upon, what are his good raw materials, his good potentialities? We would be non-threatening and would supply an atmosphere of acceptance of the child's nature which reduces fear, anxiety and defense to the minimum possible. Above all, we would care for the child, that is enjoy him and his growth and self-actualization (17). So far this sounds much like the Rogerian therapist, his "unconditional positive regard," his congruence, his openness and his caring. And indeed there is evidence by now that this "brings the child out," permits him to express and to act, to experiment, and even to make mistakes; to let himself be seen. Suitable feedback at this point, as in T-groups or basic encounter groups, or nondirective counseling, then helps the child to discover what and who he is.

In closing, I would like to discuss briefly the role that peak-experiences can play in the education of the child. We have no systematic data on peak-experiences in children but we certainly have enough anecdotes and introspections and memories to be quite confident that young children have them, perhaps more frequently than adults do. However, they seem at least in the beginning to come more from sensory experiences, color, rhythm, or sounds, and perhaps are better characterized by the words wonder, awe, fascination, absorption, and the like.

In any case, I have discussed the role of these experiences in education in (15), and would refer the reader to that paper for more detail. Using peak-experiences or fascination or wonder experiences as an intrinsic reward or goal at *many* points in education is a very real possibility, and is congruent with the whole philosophy of the humanistic educator. At the very least, this new knowledge can help wean teachers away from their frequent uneasiness with and even disapproval and persecution of these experiences. If they learn to value them as great moments in the learning process, moments in which both cognitive and personal growth take place simultaneously, then this valuing can be transmitted to the child. He in turn is then taught to value rather than to suppress his greatest moments of illumination, moments which validate and make worthwhile the more usual trudging and slogging and "working through" of education.

There is a very useful parallel here with the newer humanistic paradigm for science (11, 18) in which the more everyday cautious and patient work of checking, validating and replicating is seen, not as all there is to science but rather as follow-up work, *subsequent* to the great intuitions, intimations, and illuminations of the creative and daring, innovative, breakthrough scientist. Caution is then seen to *follow* upon boldness and proving comes *after* intuition. The creative scientist then looks more like a gambler than a banker, one who is willing to work hard for seven years because of a dazzling hunch, one who feels certain in the *absence* of evidence, *before* the evidence, and only then proceeds to the hard work of proving or disproving his precious revelation. First comes the emotion, the fascination, the falling in love with a possibility, and *then* comes the hard work, the chores, the stubborn persistence in the face of disappointment and failure.

As a supplement to this conception in which a noetic illumination plays such an important role, we can add the harsh patience of the psychotherapist who has learned from many bitter disappointments that the breakthrough insight doesn't do the therapeutic job all by itself, as Freud originally thought. It needs consolidation, repetition, rediscovery, application to one situation after another. It needs patience, time and hard work—what the psychoanalysts call "working through." Not only for science but also for psychotherapy may we say that the process *begins* with an emotional-cognitive flash but *does not end there!* It is this model of science and therapy that I believe we may now fairly consider for the process of education, if not as an exclusive model, at least as an additional one.

We must learn to treasure the "jags" of the child in school, his fascination, absorptions, his persistent wide-eyed wanderings, his Dionysian enthusiasms. At the very least, we can value his more diluted raptures, his "interests" and hobbies, etc. They can lead to much. Especially can they lead to hard work, persistent, absorbed, fruitful, educative.

And conversely I think it is possible to think of the peak-experience, the experience of awe, mystery, wonder, or of perfect completion, as the goal and reward of learning as well, its end as well as its beginning (7). If this is true for the *great* historians, mathematicians, scientists, musicians, philosophers and all the rest, why should we not try to maximize these studies as sources of peak-experiences for the child as well?

I must say that whatever little knowledge and experience I have to support these suggestions comes from intelligent and creative children rather than from retarded or underprivileged or sick ones. However, I must also say that my experience with such unpromising adults in Synanon, in T-groups (23), in Theory Y industry (10), in Esalen-type educative centers (3), in Grof-type work with psychedelic chemicals, not to mention Laing-type work with psychotics and other such experiences, has taught me never to write *anybody* off in advance.

REFERENCES

1. Braden, W. *The private sea: LSD and the search for God.* Chicago: Quadrangle, 1967.

2. Bugental, J. (ed.) *Challenges of humanistic psychology.* New York: McGraw-Hill, 1967.

3. Esalen Institute. *Residential program brochure.* Big Sur, California, 1966 and subsequent years.

4. Holt, J. *How children fail.* New York: Pitman, 1964.

5. Hull, C. L. *Principles of behavior.* New York: Appleton Century-Crofts, 1943.

6. *Journal of Humanistic Psychology.* (Periodical.) American Association of Humanistic Psychology, Palo Alto, California.

7. Leonard, G. *Education and ecstasy.* New York: Delacorte Press, 1968.

8. *Manas.* (Periodical.) Cunningham Press, South Pasadena, California.

9. Maslow, A. Criteria for judging needs to be instinctoid. In M. R. Jones (ed.), *Human motivation: A symposium.* Lincoln, Neb.: University of Nebraska Press, 1965.

10. Maslow, A. *Eupsychian management: A journal.* New York: Irwin-Dorsey, 1965.

11. Maslow, A. *The psychology of science: A reconaissance.* New York: Harper and Row, 1966.

12. Maslow, A. Neurosis as a failure of personal growth. *Humanitas,* III (1967), 153–169.

13. Maslow, A. Self-actualization and beyond. In J. Bugental (ed.), *Challenges of humanistic psychology.* New York: McGraw-Hill, 1967.

14. Maslow, A. A theory of metamotivation: The biological rooting of the value-life. *Journal of Humanistic Psychology,* I (1967), 93–127.

15. Maslow, A. Music education and peak-experiences. *Music Educators Journal,* LIV (1968), 72–75, 163–171.

16. Maslow, A. *Toward a psychology of being.* (Revised edition) Princeton, N.J.: D. Van Nostrand, 1968.

17. Moustakas, C. *The authentic teacher.* Cambridge, Mass.: Howard A. Doyle Publishing Co., 1966.

18. Polanyi, M. *Personal knowledge.* Chicago: University of Chicago Press, 1958.

19. Rogers, C. *On becoming a person.* Boston: Houghton Mifflin, 1961.

20. Severin, F. (ed.) *Humanistic viewpoints in psychology.* New York: McGraw-Hill, 1965.

21. Skinner, B. F. *Science and human behavior.* New York: Macmillan, 1938.

22. Skinner, B. F. *Walden two.* New York: Macmillan, 1948.

23. Sohl, J. *The lemon eaters.* New York: Simon and Schuster, 1967.

24. Watson, J. B. *Behaviorism.* New York: Norton, 1924 (rev. ed., 1930). Also *Psychology from the standpoint of a behaviorist.* Philadelphia: Lippincott, 1924.

25. Wilson, C. *Introduction to the new existentialism.* Boston: Houghton Mifflin, 1967.

KEY POINTS

1. Third Force psychology focuses on higher human needs, motives, and capacities such as altruism, dignity, and the search for truth and beauty. Third Force psychology rejects the conception of science as purely objective. People can discover ultimate ends and values.

2. One needs to uncover, release, and build upon one's true self. The human being can-not be shaped and modified in an arbitrary way.

3. An effective educational model can be built on the core beliefs of humanistic psychology. Teachers should accept the nature of an individual and help the person build on existing potential, instead of starting from scratch, treating a person like an object, or ignoring individual potential.

QUESTIONS TO THINK ABOUT

1. According to humanistic (Third Force) psychology, what is the role of the teacher?

2. How is the doctrine of a Real Self a rejection of the tabula rasa notion?

3. How can peak experiences be integrated into education?

4. Are humanistic notions of education incompatible with psychoanalytic and behaviorist notions?

29

Existential Bases of Psychotherapy*

ROLLO MAY

Existential psychologists are willing to consider anxiety, dread, and even despair as core elements of human existence. Anxiety has been a particular focus of the existential psychologist Rollo May (1909–1994), who sees anxiety as triggered by a threat to one's core values of existence. May believed that anxiety could be harnessed and used as a positive force for self-fulfillment.

Sometimes considered the father of existential psychotherapy, Rollo May actually bridges the gap between existential and humanistic approaches to personality because he sees the human journey as a dignifying one, albeit soaked with anxiety. Like many in the existential tradition, May was interested in the ministry before turning to psychotherapy. In this selection, May provides a striking example of his approach to both psychotherapy and human nature.

Though the existential approach has been the most prominent in European psychiatry and psychoanalysis for two decades, it was practically unknown in America until a year ago. Since then, some of us have been worried that it might become *too* popular in some quarters, particularly in national magazines. But we have been comforted by a saying of Nietzsche's, "The first adherents of a movement are no argument against it."

We have no interest whatever in importing from Europe a ready-made system. I am, indeed, very dubious about the usefulness of the much-discussed and much-maligned term "Existentialism." But many of us in this country have for years shared this approach, long before we even knew the meaning of that confused term.

On the one hand this approach has a deep underlying affinity for our American character and thought. It is very close, for example, to William James' emphases on the immediacy of experience, the unity of thought and action, and the importance of decision and commitment. On the other hand, there is among some psychologists and psychoanalysts in this country a great deal of hostility and outright anger against this approach. I shall not here go into the reasons for this paradox.

I wish, rather, to *be* existentialist, and to speak directly from my own experience as a person and as a practicing psychoanalytic psychotherapist. Some fifteen years ago, when I was working on my book *The Meaning of Anxiety*, I spent a year and a half in bed in a tuberculosis sanitarium. I had a great deal of time to ponder the meaning of anxiety—and plenty of firsthand data in myself and my fellow patients. In the course of this time I studied the two books written on anxiety up till our day, the one by Freud, *The Problem of Anxiety*, and the one by Kierkegaard, *The Concept of Dread*. I valued highly Freud's formulations: namely, his first theory, that anxiety is the reemergence of repressed libido, and his second, that anxiety is the ego's reaction to the threat of the loss of the loved object.

*May, R. (1960). Existential bases of psychotherapy. *American Journal of Orthopsychiatry, 30*, 685–695.

Kierkegaard, on the other hand, described anxiety as the struggle of the living being against non-being which I could immediately experience there in my struggle with death or the prospect of being a lifelong invalid. He went on to point out that the real terror in anxiety is not this death as such but the fact that each of us within himself is on both sides of the fight, that "anxiety is a desire for what one dreads," as he put it; thus like an "alien power it lays hold of an individual, and yet one cannot tear one's self away."

What powerfully struck me then was that Kierkegaard was writing about *exactly what my fellow patients and I were going through*. Freud was not; he was writing on a different level, giving formulations of the psychic mechanisms by which anxiety comes about. Kierkegaard was portraying what is immediately experienced by human beings in crisis—the crisis specifically of life against death which was completely real to us patients, but a crisis which I believe is not in its essential form different from the various crises of people who come for therapy, or the crises all of us experience in much more minute form a dozen times a day even though we push the ultimate prospect of death far from our minds. Freud was writing on the technical level, where his genius was supreme; perhaps more than any man up to his time, he *knew about* anxiety. Kierkegaard, a genius of a different order, was writing on the existential, ontological level; he *knew anxiety*.

This is not a value dichotomy; obviously both are necessary. Our real problem, rather, is given us by our cultural-historical situation. We in the Western world are the heirs of four centuries of technical achievement in power over nature, and now over ourselves; this is our greatness and, at the same time, it is also our greatest peril. We are not in danger of repressing the technical emphasis (of which Freud's tremendous popularity in this country were proof if any were necessary). But rather we repress the opposite. If I may use terms which I shall be discussing more fully presently, we repress the *sense of being*, the ontological sense. One consequence of this repression of the sense of being is that modern man's image of himself, his experience of himself as a responsible individual, his experience of his own humanity, have likewise disintegrated.

The existential approach, as I understand it, does not have the aim of ruling out the technical discoveries of Freud or those from any other branch of psychology or science. It does, however, seek to place these discoveries on a new basis, a new understanding or rediscovery, if you will, of the nature and image of man.

I make no apologies in admitting that I take very seriously the dehumanizing dangers in our tendency in modern science to make man over into the image of the machine, into the image of the techniques by which we study him. This tendency is not the fault of any "dangerous" men or "vicious" schools; it is rather a crisis brought upon us by our particular historical predicament. Karl Jaspers, both psychiatrist and existentialist philosopher, holds that we in the Western world are actually in process of losing self-consciousness and that we may be in the last age of historical man. William Whyte in his *Organization Man* cautions that modern man's enemies may turn out to be a "mild-looking group of therapists, who . . . would be doing what they did to help you." He refers here to the tendency to use the social sciences in support of the social ethic of our historical period; and thus the process of helping people may actually make them conformist and tend toward the destruction of individuality. We cannot brush aside the cautions of such men as unintelligent or antiscientific; to try to do so would make *us* the obscurantists.

You may agree with my sentiments here but cavil at the terms "being" and "non-being" and many of you may already have concluded that your suspicion was only too right, that this so-called existential approach in psychology is hopelessly vague and muddled. Carl Rogers remarked in his paper at the American Psychological Association convention last September in Cincinnati that many American psychologists must find these terms abhorrent because they sound so general, so philosophical, so untestable. Rogers went on to point out, however, that he had no difficulty at all in putting the existential principles in therapy into empirically testable hypotheses.

But I would go further and hold that *without* some concepts of "being" and "non-being," we cannot even understand our most commonly used psychological mechanisms. Take for example, *repression, resistance* and *transference*. The usual discussions of these terms hang in mid-air, without convincingness or psychological reality, precisely because we have lacked an underlying structure on which to base them. The term "repression," for example, obviously refers to a phenomenon we observe all the time, a dynamism which Freud clearly described in many forms. We generally explain the mechanism by saying that the child represses into unconsciousness certain impulses, such as sex and hostility, because the culture in the form of parental figures disapproves, and the child must protect his own security with these figures. But this culture which assumedly disapproves is made up of the very same people who do the repressing. Is it not an illusion, therefore, and much too simple, to speak of the culture over against the individual in such fashion and make it our whipping boy? Furthermore, where did we get the ideas that child or adult are so much concerned with security and libidinal satisfactions? Are these not a carry-over from our work with the *neurotic, anxious* child and adult?

Certainly the neurotic, anxious child is compulsively concerned with security, for example; and certainly the neurotic adult, and we who study him, read our later formulations back into the unsuspecting mind of the child. But is not the normal child just as truly interested in moving out into the world, exploring, following his curiosity and sense of adventure—going out "to learn to shiver and to shake," as the nursery rhyme puts it? And if you block these needs of the child, you get a traumatic reaction from him just as you do when you take away his security. I, for one, believe we vastly overemphasize the human being's concern with security and survival satisfactions because they so neatly fit our cause-and-effect way of thinking. I believe Nietzsche and Kierkegaard were more accurate when they described man as the organism who makes certain values—prestige, power, tenderness—more important than pleasure and even more important than survival itself.

My implication here is that we can understand repression, for example, only on the deeper level of the meaning of the human being's potentialities. In this respect, "being" is to be defined as the individual's "pattern of potentialities." These potentialities will be partly shared with other persons but will in every case form a unique pattern in each individual. We must ask the questions: What is this person's relation to his own potentialities? What goes on that he chooses or is forced to choose to block off from his awareness something which he knows, and on another level *knows that he knows?* In my work in psychotherapy there appears more and more evidence that anxiety in our day arises not so much out of fear of lack of libidinal satisfactions or security, but rather out of the patient's fear of his own powers, and the conflicts that arise from that fear. This may be the particular "neurotic personality of our time"—the neurotic pattern of contemporary "outer-directed," organizational man.

The "unconscious," then, is not to be thought of as a reservoir of impulses, thoughts, wishes which are culturally unacceptable; I define it rather as *those potentialities for knowing and experiencing which the individual cannot or will not actualize.* On this level we shall find that the simple mechanism of repression is infinitely less simple than it looks; that it involves a complex struggle of the individual's *being* against the possibility of *non-being;* that it cannot be adequately comprehended in "ego" and "not-ego" terms, or even "self" and "not-self"; and that it inescapably raises the question of the human being's margin of freedom with respect to his potentialities, a margin in which resides his responsibility for himself which even the therapist cannot take away.

Let us now come back from theory to more practical matters. For a number of years as a practicing therapist and teacher of therapists, I have been struck by how often our concern with trying to understand the patient in terms of the mechanisms by which his behavior takes place blocks our understanding of what he really is experiencing. Here is a patient, Mrs. Hutchens (about whom I shall center some of my remarks this morning) who comes into my office for the first time, a suburban woman in her middle thirties who tries to keep her expression poised and sophisticated. But no one could fail to see in her eyes something of the terror of a frightened animal or a lost child. I know, from what her neurological specialists have already told me, that her presenting problem is hysterical tenseness of the larynx, as a result of which she can talk only with a perpetual hoarseness. I have been given the hypothesis from her Rorschach that she has felt all her life, "If I say what I really feel, I'll be rejected; under these conditions it is better not to talk at all." During this first hour, also, I get some hints of the genetic *why* of her problem as she tells me of her authoritarian relation with her mother and grandmother, and how she learned to guard firmly against telling any secrets at all. But if as I sit here I am chiefly thinking of these *why's* and *how's* concerning the way the problem came about, I will grasp everything except the most important thing of all (indeed the only real source of data I have), namely, this person now existing, becoming, emerging, this experiencing human being immediately in the room with me.

There are at present in this country several undertakings to systematize psychoanalytic theory in terms of forces, dynamisms and energies. The approach I propose is the exact opposite of this. I hold that our science must be relevant to the distinctive characteristics of what we seek to study, in this case the human being. We do not deny dynamisms and forces—that would be nonsense—but we hold that they have meaning only in the context of the existing, living person; that is to say, in the *ontological* context.

I propose, thus, that we take the one real datum we have in the therapeutic situation, namely, the *existing person* sitting in a consulting room with a therapist. (The term "existing person" is used here as our European colleagues use *Dasein*.) Note that I do not say simply "individual" or "person"; if you take individuals as units in a group for the purposes of statistical prediction—certainly a legitimate use of psychological science—you are exactly *defining out of the picture* the characteristics which make this individual an existing person. Or when you take him as a com-

posite of drives and deterministic forces, you have defined for study everything except *the one to whom these experiences happen,* everything except the existing person himself. Therapy is one activity, so far as I can see, in which we cannot escape the necessity of taking the subject as an existing person.

Let us therefore ask, What are the essential characteristics which constitute this patient as an existing person in the consulting room? I wish to propose six characteristics which I shall call principles, which I find in my work as a psychotherapist. Though these principles are the product of a good deal of thought and experience with many cases, I shall illustrate them with episodes from the case of Mrs. Hutchens.

First, Mrs. Hutchens like every existing person *is centered in herself,* and an attack on this center is an attack on her existence itself. This is a characteristic which we share with all living beings; it is self-evident in animals and plants. I never cease to marvel how, whenever we cut the top off a pine tree on our farm in New Hampshire, the tree sends up a new branch from heaven knows where to become a new center. But this principle has a particular relevance to human beings and gives a basis for the understanding of sickness and health, neurosis and mental health. Neurosis is not to be seen as a deviation from our particular theories of what a person should be. *Is not neurosis, rather, precisely the method the individual uses to preserve his own center, his own existence?* His symptoms are ways of shrinking the range of his world (so graphically shown in Mrs. Hutchens' inability to let herself talk) in order that the centeredness of his existence may be protected from threat; a way of blocking off aspects of the environment that he may then be adequate to the remainder. Mrs. Hutchens had gone to another therapist for half a dozen sessions a month before she came to me. He told her, in an apparently ill-advised effort to reassure her, that she was too proper, too controlled. She reacted with great upset and immediately broke off the treatment. Now technically he was entirely correct; existentially he was entirely wrong. What he did not see, in my judgment, was that this very properness, this over-control, far from being things Mrs. Hutchens wanted to get over, were part of her desperate attempt to preserve what precarious center she had. As though she were saying, "If I opened up, if I communicated, I would lose what little space in life I have." We see here, incidentally, how inadequate is the definition of neurosis as a failure of adjustment. *An adjustment is exactly what neurosis is; and that is just its trouble.* It is a necessary adjustment by which centeredness can be preserved; a way of accepting *non-being,* if I may use this term, in order that some little *being* may be preserved. And in most cases it is a boon when this adjustment breaks down.

This is the only thing we can assume about Mrs. Hutchens, or about any patient, when she comes in: that she, like all living beings, requires centeredness, and that this has broken down. At a cost of considerable turmoil she has taken steps, that is, come for help. Our second principle thus, is: *every existing person has the character of self-affirmation, the need to preserve its centeredness.* The particular name we give this self-affirmation in human beings is "courage." Paul Tillich's emphasis on the "courage to be" is very cogent and fertile for psychotherapy at this point. He insists that in man being is never given automatically but depends upon the individual's courage, and without courage one loses being. *This makes courage itself a necessary ontological corollary.* By this token, I as a therapist place great importance upon expressions of the patients which have to do with willing, decisions, choice. I never let little remarks the patient may make such as "maybe I can," "perhaps I can try," and so on slip by without my making sure he knows I have heard him. It is only a half truth that the will is the product of the wish; I wish to emphasize rather the truth that the wish can never come out in its real power except with will.

Now as Mrs. Hutchens talks hoarsely, she looks at me with an expression of mingled fear and hope. Obviously a relation exists between us not only here but already in anticipation in the waiting room and ever since she thought of coming. She is struggling with the possibility of participating with me. Our third principle is, thus: *all existing persons have the need and possibility of going out from their centeredness to participate in other being.* This always involves risk; if the organism goes out too far, it loses its own centeredness—its identity—a phenomenon which can easily be seen in the biological world. If the neurotic is so afraid of loss of his own conflicted center that he refuses to go out but holds back in rigidity and lives in narrowed reactions and shrunken world space, his growth and development are blocked. This is the pattern in neurotic repressions and inhibitions, the common neurotic forms in Freud's day. But it may well be in our day of conformism and the outer-directed man, that the most common neurotic pattern takes the opposite form, namely, the dispersing of one's self in participation and identification with others until one's own being is emptied. At this point we see the rightful emphasis of Martin Buber in one sense and Harry Stack Sullivan in another, that the human being cannot be understood as a self if participation is omitted. Indeed, if we are successful in our search for these ontological principles of the existing person, it should be true that the omission of any one of the six would mean we do not then have a human being.

Our fourth principle is: *the subjective side of centeredness is awareness.* The paleontologist Pierre Teilhard de Chardin has recently described brilliantly how this awareness is present in ascending degrees in all forms of life from amoeba to man. It is certainly present in animals. Howard Liddell has pointed out how the seal in its natural habitat lifts its head every ten seconds even during sleep to survey the horizon lest an Eskimo hunter with poised bow and arrow sneak up on it. This awareness of threats to being in animals Liddell calls *vigilance,* and he identifies it as the primitive, simple counterpart in animals of what in human beings becomes anxiety.

Our first four characteristic principles are shared by our existing person with all living beings; they are biological levels in which human beings participate. The fifth principle refers now to a distinctively human characteristic, self-consciousness. *The uniquely human form of awareness is self-consciousness.* We do not identify awareness and consciousness. We associate awareness, as Liddell indicates above, with vigilance. This is supported by the derivation of the term—it comes from the Anglo-Saxon *gewaer, waer,* meaning knowledge of external dangers and threats. Its cognates are *beware* and *wary.* Awareness certainly is what is going on in an individual's neurotic reaction to threat, in Mrs. Hutchens' experience in the first hours, for example, that I am also a threat to her. Consciousness, in contrast, we define as not simply my awareness of threat from the world, but *my capacity to know myself as the one being threatened,* my experience of myself as the subject who has a world. Consciousness, as Kurt Goldstein puts it, is man's capacity to transcend the immediate concrete situation, to live in terms of the possible; and it underlies the human capacity to use abstractions and universals, to have language and symbols. This capacity for consciousness underlies the wide range of possibility which man has in relating to his world, and it constitutes the foundation of psychological freedom. Thus human freedom has its ontological base and I believe must be assumed in all psychotherapy.

In his book *The Phenomenon of Man,* Pierre Teilhard de Chardin, as we have mentioned, describes awareness in all forms of evolutionary life. But in man, a new function arises, namely, this self-consciousness. Teilhard de Chardin undertakes to demonstrate something I have always believed, that when a new function emerges the whole previous pattern, the total gestalt of the organism, changes. Thereafter the organism can be understood only in terms of the new function. That is to say, it is only a half truth to hold that the organism is to be understood in terms of the simpler elements below it on the evolutionary scale; it is just as true that every new function forms a new complexity which conditions all the simpler elements in the organism. *In this sense, the simple can be understood only in terms of the more complex.*

This is what self-consciousness does in man. All the simpler biological functions must now be understood in terms of the new function. No one would, of course, deny for a moment the old functions, nor anything in biology which man shares with less complex organisms. Take sexuality for example, which we obviously share with all mammals. But given self-consciousness, sex becomes a new gestalt as is demonstrated in therapy all the time. Sexual impulses are now conditioned by the *person* of the partner; what we think of the other male or female, in reality or fantasy or even repressed fantasy, can never be ruled out. The fact that the subjective person of the other to whom we relate sexually makes least difference in *neurotic* sexuality, say in patterns of compulsive sex or prostitution, only proves the point the more firmly; for such requires precisely the blocking off, the checking out, the distorting of self-consciousness. Thus when we talk of sexuality in terms of sexual *objects,* as Kinsey does, we may garner interesting and useful statistics; but we simply are not talking about human sexuality.

Nothing in what I am saying here should be taken as antibiological in the slightest; on the contrary, I think it is only from this approach that we *can* understand human biology without distorting it. As Kierkegaard aptly put it, "The natural law is as valid as ever." I argue only against the uncritical acceptance of the assumption that the organism is to be understood solely in terms of those elements below it on the evolutionary scale, an assumption which has led us to overlook the self-evident truth that what makes a horse a horse is not the elements it shares with the organisms below it but what constitutes distinctively "horse." *Now what we are dealing with in neurosis are those characteristic and functions which are distinctively human.* It is these that that have gone awry in our disturbed patients. The condition for these functions is self-consciousness—which accounts for what Freud rightly discovered, that the neurotic pattern is characterized by repression and blocking off of consciousness.

It is the task of the therapist, therefore, not only to help the patient become aware; but even more significantly to help him to *transmute this awareness into consciousness.* Awareness is his knowing that something is threatening from outside in his world—a condition which may, as in paranoids and their neurotic equivalents, be correlated with a good deal of acting-out behavior.

But self-consciousness puts this awareness on a quite different level; it is the patient's seeing that *he is the one who is threatened*, that he is the being who stands in this world which threatens, he is the subject who *has* a world. And this gives him the possibility of *in-sight*, of "inward sight," of seeing the world and its problems in relation to himself. And thus it gives him the possibility of doing something about the problems.

To come back to our too-long silent patient: After about 25 hours of therapy Mrs. Hutchens had the following dream. She was searching room by room for a baby in an unfinished house at an airport. She thought the baby belonged to someone else, but the other person might let her take it. Now it seemed that she had put the baby in a pocket of her robe (or her mother's robe) and she was seized with anxiety that it would be smothered. Much to her joy, she found that the baby was still alive. Then she had a strange thought, "Shall I kill it?"

The house was at the airport where she at about the age of 20 had learned to fly solo, a very important act of self-affirmation and independence from her parents. The baby was associated with her youngest son, whom she regularly identified with herself. Permit me to omit the ample associative evidence that convinced both her and me that the baby stood for herself. The dream is an expression of the emergence and growth of self-consciousness, a consciousness she is not sure is hers yet, and a consciousness which she considers killing in the dream.

About six years before her therapy, Mrs. Hutchens had left the religious faith of her parents, to which she had had a very authoritarian relation. She had then joined a church of her own belief. But she had never dared tell her parents of this. Instead, when they came to visit, she attended their church in great tension lest one of her children let the secret out. After about 35 sessions, when she was considering writing her parents to tell them of this change of faith, she had over a period of two weeks spells of partially fainting in my office. She would become suddenly weak, her face would go white, she would feel empty and "like water inside," and would have to lie down for a few moments on the couch. In retrospect she called these spells "grasping for oblivion."

She then wrote her parents informing them once and for all of her change in faith and assuring them it would do no good to try to dominate her. In the following session she asked in considerable anxiety whether I thought she would go psychotic. I responded that whereas anyone of us might at some time have such an episode, I saw no more reason why she should than any of the rest of us; and I asked whether her fear of going psychotic was not rather anxiety coming out of her standing against her parents, as though genuinely being herself she felt to be tantamount to going crazy. I have, it may be remarked, several times noted this anxiety at being one's self experienced by the patient as tantamount to psychosis. This is not surprising, for consciousness of one's own desires and affirming them involves accepting one's originality and uniqueness, and it implies that one must be prepared to be isolated not only from those parental figures upon whom one has been dependent, but at that instant to stand alone in the entire psychic universe as well.

We see the profound conflicts of the emergence of self-consciousness in three vivid ways in Mrs. Hutchens, whose chief symptom, interestingly enough, was the denial of that uniquely human capacity based on consciousness, namely, talking: 1) the temptation to kill the baby; 2) the grasping at oblivion by fainting, as though she were saying, "If only I did not have to be conscious, I would escape this terrible problem of telling my parents"; and 3) the psychosis anxiety.

We now come to the sixth and last ontological characteristic, *anxiety*. Anxiety is the state of the human being in the struggle against what would destroy his being. It is, in Tillich's phrase, the state of a being in conflict with non-being, a conflict which Freud mythologically pictured in his powerful and important symbol of the death instinct. One wing of this struggle will always be against something outside one's self; but even more portentous and significant for psychotherapy is the inner side of the battle, which we saw in Mrs. Hutchens, namely, the conflict within the person as he confronts the choice of whether and how far he will stand against his own being, his own potentialities.

From an existential viewpoint we take very seriously this temptation to kill the baby, or kill her own consciousness, as expressed in these forms by Mrs. Hutchens. We neither water it down by calling it "neurotic" and the product merely of sickness, nor do we slough over it by reassuring her, "O.K., but you don't need to do it." If we did these, we would be helping her adjust at the price of surrendering a portion of her existence, that is, her opportunity for fuller independence. The self-confrontation which is involved in the acceptance of self-consciousness is anything but simple: it involves, to identify some of the elements, accepting the hatred of the past, her mother's against her and hers of her mother; accepting her present motives of hatred and destruction; cutting through rationalizations and illusions about her behavior and motives, and the acceptance of the responsibility and aloneness which this implies; the giving up of childhood omnipotence, and acceptance of the fact that though she can never have absolute certainty of choices, she must choose anyway. But all of these specific points, easy enough to understand in themselves, must be seen in the light of the fact that *consciousness itself implies always the possibil-*

ity of turning against one's self, denying one's self. The tragic nature of human existence inheres in the fact that consciousness itself involves the possibility and temptation at every instant of killing itself. Dostoevski and our other existential forebears were not indulging in poetic hyperbole or expressing the aftereffects of immoderate vodka when they wrote of the agonizing burden of freedom.

I trust that the fact that existential psychotherapy places emphasis on these tragic aspects of life does not at all imply it is pessimistic. Quite the contrary. The confronting of genuine tragedy is a highly cathartic experience psychically, as Aristotle and others through history have reminded us. Tragedy is inseparably connected with man's dignity and grandeur, and is the accompaniment, as illustrated in the dramas of Oedipus and Orestes *ad infinitum,* of the human being's moments of greatest insight.

I hope that this analysis of ontological characteristics in the human being, this search for the basic principles which constitute the existing person, may give us a structural basis for our psychotherapy. Thus the way may be opened for the developing of sciences of psychology and psychoanalysis which do not fragmentize man while they seek to study him, and do not undermine his humanity while they seek to help him.

KEY POINTS

1. People should be taken as they are, not as some therapist or theory might expect them to be.
2. Neurosis and anxiety serve a purpose. The self needs to preserve its centeredness.
3. The uniquely human form of awareness is self-consciousness.

QUESTIONS TO THINK ABOUT

1. For existentialists, the anxiety of being ignored by one's parents or being alienated from one's religion can be the essence of who we are and why we behave as we do. What are the implications of this for understanding human nature?
2. How does the existential explanation of anxiety differ from that offered by other personality psychologists?
3. How can Rollo May's concern with philosophy and existentialism become part of a personality psychology that is heavily scientific?

30

A Note on Formulating the Relationship of the Individual and the Group*

HARRY STACK SULLIVAN

Harry Stack Sullivan (1892–1949) believed that the essence of personality involves enduring patterns of human relationships. Life is a series of interpersonal processes. Influenced by social psychology and the idea of the social self, Sullivan took issue with the idea that each person has a single, fixed personality. Rather, we have as many personalities as we have recurring interpersonal situations.

Sullivan was born in upstate New York, was trained in medicine, and spent much time dealing with people with psychiatric problems. Because people need to learn healthy interpersonal interactions, Sullivan thought that it was often more harmful than helpful to lock away the mentally "ill" in mental sanitariums. Because of this belief, Sullivan often spent time interacting with his patients as chums.

We think conventionally of ourself as a person and of others as individual persons or individuals. This is a convention of reference strongly entrenched in our language and widely disseminated in our culture. It seems to derive immediately from our observations of gross biological phenomena, and any other view would seem to be nothing short of absurd. I am here and not elsewhere. This is my hand, the expression of my thought. It is true that I must maintain recurrent communion with the environing supply of oxygen, water, and other substances. It may even be true that I cannot continue very long to manifest essentially human traits unless I maintain recurrent communion with other people. But my individuality as a concrete human being does not seem to be impaired by these perduring necessities which affect everyone in exactly the same way and to much the same degree that they affect me.

I may go farther and describe myself in generic terms: white, American, denizen of the Western culture in its transitional phase from the Industrial Era. I agree that I would not be myself if I were a Negro—American or African. I have no difficulty in understanding that as I, myself, I am largely a product of acculturation and as such not particularly different in many culturally controlled respects from a great many white Americans of approximately my somatic age and educational background. But, I shall insist that, however like some average people I may be in many respects, I am nonetheless the product of a unique course of acculturation; I have undergone a unique series of events many of which have left their impress in my own personal memory. I know that I have come to have a relatively durable congeries of traits or characteristics (which I call my personality) which singles me

*Sullivan, H. S. (1939). A note on formulating the relationship of the individual and the group. *American Journal of Sociology, 44,* 932–937. Copyright © 1939 University of Chicago Press. Reprinted by permission of The University of Chicago Press, publisher.

out from everyone else. In a word, I am a person of some, however little, distinction; and there are at least a few other people who would be emphatic in supporting this judgment. They know me; they can tell you exactly what to expect if you have dealings with me. Should you confuse me with some other stranger about whom you have been told, you will gradually realize your error as you talk with me. You will see that my personality is different from the one with which you erroneously believed yourself to be dealing.

One may pause here to consider how often one has actually failed to observe these presumably specific differences of personality, has carried on serious conversation with the wrong person without any realization of the error in identification. These instances may not seem to have been at all numerous; this, however, in all likelihood is sheer illusion of memory. Most people would learn a great deal if they could study the negative instances of their identifying a stranger in terms of his reputed personality. So strongly ingrained in us is the conviction that we ought to be able to perceive the "personal traits" of other people that our feeling of personal security is involved in this norm of the "knower of men." In fact, the less secure one feels, the greater a comfort one derives from a facile classifying of other people among various patterns of projection of one's own presumptively static traits— and their verbal opposites.

From infancy each of us is trained to think in this way. If one was fortunately born, the parents have been fairly consistent in their expressed appraisals, and one has elaborated a dependable self. However absurdly it may be related to one's manifest behavior, one is relatively secure in dealing with others. If one's parents have been less reassuring or if experience subsequent to childhood has demonstrated the serious deficiency of a once-trusted illusion as to one's personality, the case is quite otherwise. "I did not think you were *that* kind of a person" comes to be a very painful remark the deeper implications of which do not engage one's attention. One becomes as realistically as possible a member of the group made up of the right kind of people and

acts as rightly as possible in those restricted interpersonal contexts in which one still has freedom to participate.

The traits with which one believes one's self characterized are often amazingly fluid, if one's serious statements are to be taken as evidence. Discussing one's self with one person, one reports one perhaps only moderately consistent set. In an equally serious discussion with a different auditor the account is different. Some people are consistent in referring to certain outstanding traits about which a consensus could be obtained; some are consistent only in the breach—the traits that they generally claim are those which come near being merely ideal; the statements express wishful rather than factual data. Some know that their accounts vary with different auditors and can even rationalize noted differences—usually on the basis of the attitude of the auditor and one's wanting to make as good an impression as possible. The traits with which we endow others are also of varying certainty and sometimes subject to radical change under pressure of divergent opinion. The shift may not appear in the course of the particular controversy but may become evident in subsequent discussions. About all that seems perfectly certain about personal traits as subjects of opinion is that the having of such opinions seems important.

The interpretation of behavior is generally regarded as of a higher probability than is the analysis of conversation about one's self. It is easier to say the right thing than to keep on doing the right thing. This truism is not to be taken too seriously, however, for some people show high consistency over long periods in behavior that expresses a role which they feel is incongruous to them but demanded by the other person. Success in "acting like" this incongruous person does not excite them to much speculation about their "real" personality, perhaps for the good reason that it is but a particular, a clearly noticed, instance of something that has been going on from very early years.

The psychiatrist has to regard each personality (individual, unique person) as an indeterminate entity some significant characteristics of which may be inferred from the processes that occur in the group of persons—real and fantastic—in which the subject-individual participates. Participation is a pattern of processes and, in seeking to delimit the universe of interpersonal relations, the psychiatrist may begin with those psychobiological states in which interpersonal processes do not occur. These are chiefly two: deep sleep and panic. Panic is that condition which is beyond or in excess of complete insecurity. Deep sleep is antithetic in that it can appear only in the absence of insecurity or after neutralization of all insecurity-provoking factors. Behavior is impossible in either state, and the appearance of implicit (mental) activity marks the change alike from panic or from deep sleep toward a more characteristically human condition. Panic is the extreme of a series of states that grades through insecurity and fear to mild anxiety. Deep sleep is the extreme of a series including various levels of what may be called "active" sleep, somnolent detachment, and inattentive reverie states.

The reality of relevant other people is vestigial in severe insecurity and in all the sleep-states. Interpersonal phenomena are present, but the people concerned are largely fantastic, complexly related to real people. Characteristics of related real people have been magnified or minimized, moved from one personality to another, combined in poignantly artificial patterns. Experiences from long ago involving people but remotely related to those seemingly involved contribute elements to the fantastic personalizations. The novel and unreal are created out of items of actual experience, but the items are combined into patterns that reveal little about anyone except the subject-individual, himself in a state bordering on the primitive, if not, in fact, on the infra-human, type of integration.

These are the minimal limits of interpersonal relations. What are the maximal? To find these limits of his field, the psychiatrist organizes his observations of the most durable and the most effective interpersonal situations. Duration is a directional function in time. Effectiveness is less easy to define but must, too, have some reference to vector quality. Remembering that only interpersonal phenomena can be observed, an effective situation must be one that shows directional change in the interpersonal processes and hence in the series of interpersonal situations in which the subject-individual is involved. Maximal interpersonal relations must then be those that approach the span of a lifetime in duration and those that most powerfully alter the integrating tendencies of the person chiefly concerned.

Integrating tendencies are conceived to be the psychobiological substrata of the corresponding integrated interpersonal situations. Person A tends to integrate with Person B a situation to the more or less clearly envisaged end of improving his social status, thus relieving felt insecurity. Provisionally, we assume that, if any incipent A-B situation appears, Person B also tended to integrate a situation with a person such as Person A is apprehended to be. We need not assume that the integrating tendencies respectively of A toward B and of B toward A are in any sense complementary. If they happen to be complementary—if B tends to integrate a situation of the vassalage type with A—and if there are no stronger integrating tendencies that conflict, the A-B situation is consolidated and endures until its tensional aspect shall have been resolved. If the integrating tendencies that coincided in the incipient A-B situation are not complementary, B's integrating tendency is powerful, and there is no strong conflicting tendency, there will develop a B-A situation which will have value to A, but is not likely to relieve the insecurity about status and deference. The incipient A-B situation will in any other case disintegrate promptly, generally with increased feeling of insecurity on the part of A, who will tend somewhat more urgently to integrate a presumably reassuring situation with some other person apprehended by him as in the same class as B; that is, useful in improving A's status. The B-A situation, on the other hand, may be effective in significantly changing this particular integrating tendency in A, so that his insecurity about status disappears.

One must observe that interpersonal situations may have multiple integration, and that durable situations may include more transient multiply integrated phases. Love situations often show recurrent episodes of lust and are not quite the same when there is mutual sexual excitement, "untimely" excitement of one partner, and in the intervals. The tendencies to integrate lustful-erotic situations should not be confused with those which eventuate in love situations. The latter may survive indefinitely the loss of prospective sexual satisfactions or the integration of sexual situations with persons not in the love relationship.

I have now presented in extreme abstract the conceptual framework of the psychiatric study of interpersonal relations, which would seem to have relevance to the sociopsychological study of the relations of the individual and the various groups with which he is more or less identified. I hope that it is clear that the psychiatrist must usually confine his exploration to (1) situations in which he himself takes part—in which his trained alertness may help him to analyze the incipient situations—and (2) those other situations concerned in the life of his subject-individual which have been either very durable or clearly effective in changing the course of the individu-al's manifest interpersonal living. Verbal report and collateral evidence are useful in establishing the second category of data. In actual practice certainty is greatest in working back from the first type of data through the second. Without what we may call the immediate experimental situation and the historic view it is often extremely difficult to get access to a particular group relationship. Durable associations in the general interest of beauty, truth, or humanity—security, love, lust, income, deference—may readily be mistaken one for another by the investigator. The subject-individual, if the relationship to the psychiatrist is not explicit, may also "mislead himself" almost endlessly.

It is clear that the study of interpersonal relations in contrast to the study of persons and group has validity. The demarcation of the field is made difficult by the conventions of speech and thought and by other aspects of the controlling culture. The new type of orientation that can be obtained by this type of approach is quite certain to be fruitful both in social theory and practice. It has some fundamental implications for the field of education.

REFERENCES

Sullivan, H. S. (1937). A note on the implications of psychiatry, the study of interpersonal relations, for investigations in the social sciences. *American Journal of Sociology, 42,* 848–861.

Sullivan, H. S. (1938). Psychiatry: Introduction to the study of interpersonal relations. *Psychiatry, 1,* 121–134.

Sullivan, H. S. (1939). Intuition, reason, and faith. *Psychiatry, 2,* 129–132.

KEY POINTS

1. Living is a series of interpersonal processes.

2. Personality is fluid, changing as a function of the persons with whom one is interacting.

QUESTIONS TO THINK ABOUT

1. If the focus of personality study should be on the interpersonal situation, not on the person, then how could we go about assessing personality?

2. It is clear that the individual has some self-contained psychobiological characteristics. How can this fact be integrated with the idea that personality involves enduring patterns of relationships?

3. Is it only an illusion that a person has a single, fixed personality?

31

Convergences and Challenges in the Search for Consistency*

WALTER MISCHEL

Walter Mischel (1930–) has long been interested in the interactionist approach to personality. Not believing that personality could be broken into broad personality traits, he argued that personality was much more complicated than that. Since a person's behavior varies so much from situation to situation, it may not make sense to think in terms of broad personality traits. Rather, a person's cognitive personality characteristics are learned during experiences with situations and their rewards.

Mischel, born in Vienna, was an undergraduate at City College of New York, and a graduate student in clinical psychology at Ohio State University, where he worked with psychologists who took both a cognitive and a learning approach to personality. He worked for many years at Stanford University, where he was influenced by the social learning theories of Albert Bandura, and he then moved to Columbia University in New York. In this selection, he explains his approach to taking both the person and the situation into account.

Current research in personality psychology is, in many ways, a constructive and exciting response to critiques of traditional trait and psychodynamic approaches of the 1960s (e.g., Mischel, 1968; Peterson, 1968; Vernon, 1964). To understand the direction of current work, it helps first to recall the critiques. I begin with a brief glimpse of the field's history; then I will present some of my own work that grew out of that history and indicate some routes that seem especially exciting to pursue in the future.

SOME BACKGROUND FOR THE CURRENT AGENDA

In the late 1960s the convergence of several forces produced a radical reexamination of the traditional trait and psychodynamic approaches to the study of personality. This created something of a paradigm crisis because these orientations were then the dominant establishment views; they had long provided the core assumptions for personality and clinical psychology, as well as for other areas of social science. The nature of the dissatisfactions with these global dispositional approaches are well known (e.g., Bandura, 1969; Mischel, 1968; Peterson, 1968; Vernon, 1964). Rather than reiterate them, I will only recall some of their essentials. Critics took aim at the utility of global dispositional approaches for the planning of specific individual treatment programs, for the design of social change programs, for the prediction of what individuals will do in specific contexts, and for the conceptualization of persons.

Other criticisms were directed at the failure to recognize systematic judgmental errors both by the professional and by the layperson that are especially relevant to personality assessment. Soon these errors began to be interpreted as reflecting the operation of "cognitive economics" (or heuristics) through which complex information tends to be reduced and sometimes oversimplified, often with serious consequences for inference, judgment, and prediction (e.g., Kahneman & Tversky, 1973; Mischel, 1973, 1979; Nisbett & Ross, 1980). The total platform of mounting criticisms thus ranged from the limitations of global dispositional approaches for specific treatment and assessment applications with the individual case to the theoretical inadequacy of substituting broad labeling and naming for deeper, psychological explaining. It also spread to questioning the nature of the social and clinical judgment process itself.

What were the roots of these challenges, the concerns that led to them? Criticisms of the trait and psychodynamic approaches, including my own monograph, *Personality and Assessment* in 1968, began in large part as a defense of each person's individuality. The defense was against the then-prevailing tendency to use a few behavioral signs to assign individuals to fixed positions on the assessor's favorite nomothetic trait dimensions. In the 1960s it was not uncommon to assume that these categories were sufficiently informative to predict not just average levels within the same behavior domain but the person's specific behavior in many other new situations. It was commonplace to attempt extensive decision making about a person's life and future on the basis of a relatively limited sampling of personological trait indicators. Often these indicators were only indirectly connected with the behaviors for which they were the ostensible signs.

These critiques in the 1960s were fed by common practices in personality assessment and clinical psychology at that time (described in detail, for example, by Hunt, 1965; Mischel, 1968; Peterson, 1968; Vernon, 1964). There were, of course, more cautious practitioners. But it was assumed not infrequently that one could go from a few indicators to extensive predicting and decision making about what the individual will do in new situations far removed ecologically and psychologically from the original observed behavior sample. It was not unusual to predict such remote outcomes as criminal recidivism, parole violations, or psychiatric hospitalization from responses to ambiguous stimuli (such as inkblots) or from the way the individual drew a house, a tree, and a person.

I do not mean to exempt myself from these practices. For example, I tried to predict success for Peace Corps teachers in Nigeria on the basis of their responses to diverse measures while they were in training in the U.S. (Mischel, 1965). This effort, I think, was representative of the expectations and strategies of its time in personality assessment. And the findings point to the concerns that arose from such efforts. To summarize the essentials briefly, global ratings of the trainees made by the faculty, by the assessment board for the project, and by an interviewer were widely shared and significantly intercorrelated. (For example, the assessment board and the interview ratings correlated .72.) Thus, the assessors had similar impressions of the candidates in training. Field performance in Nigeria was assessed independently on six criterion subscales (all of which were highly intercorrelated) that were aggregated into a multiple scale criterion. To illustrate the main results, consider the predictive value of behavior in the interviews for total criterion performance in Nigeria. The correlation turned out to be .13.

To try to broaden the data sources, a three-person subcommittee of the assessment board based its pooled recommendations of each candidate on their discussion and review of all data from all observer sources during training (faculty evaluations, academic records, peer ratings, and interviews). These recommendations were discussed by a larger final assessment review board, representing a variety of disciplines and reflecting diverse assessment experiences. The final review board discussed each candidate individually and had available for each a descriptive summary prepared by the subcommittee. The resulting aggregated evaluations of each candidate by the total assessment board predicted aggregated performance outcomes in the field with a nonsignificant correlation of .20. None of the separate predictions made by the training staff correlated significantly with criterion performance. I was not the only one who was surprised at the time.

Findings of this sort began to accumulate at a time when even small samples of behavior had seemed to promise a diagnostic X-ray to illuminate the core personality, to allow quick leaps from a few subtle signs observed by experts to broad, general inferences about what the person was like "on the whole," and then to predict specific outcomes from those inferences. And even cautious and sophisticated assessors, trying to predict diverse criteria in "real life" contexts, drawing on multiple data sources and a variety of both clinical and statistical combinatorial strategies, were surprised to find their own results weak, costly, and subject to risky errors (e.g., Hunt, 1965; Mischel, 1965; Peterson, 1968; Vernon, 1964; Wiggins, 1973). These concerns revitalized those expressed by Hartshorne and May (1928) and others (e.g., Dudycha, 1936; Newcomb, 1929) about the nonunitary structure of dispositions decades earlier. Now the criticisms were aimed both at the theoretical limitations and at the practical constraints of a personality psychology committed to global, homogeneous, and readily revealable dispositions as its basic units.

In reaction to the personality assessment practices of the 1960s, a search began for some alternatives. This search was guided by a commitment to attend more to what people actually do, to their actions and cognitions in the particular situations central to the theoretical or clinical problem of interest. It was not undertaken to rejuvenate an atomistic behaviorism, nor to elevate situations into the prime causes of behavior. Instead, the aim was to move away from relatively indirect signs on tests to more direct behavioral samples and reports relevant to the particular

problem, outcome, or domain of interest and anchored to the specific social and psychological context. The goal was to base assessment on more circumscribed and direct data, such as peoples' past behavior in similar situations and on analyses that relate the target behavior to the situational conditions in which it occurs (Mischel, 1981a). Direct self-reports and self-statements by the subjects were favored over more indirect inferences by experts (Mischel, 1972). The intention was to try to link these more direct data—these samples and reports of relevant behavior—to the conditions and psychological processes in which they were rooted and to the design of specific treatment programs.

At the same time, an effort began to reconceptualize personality and situation constructs and the processes that underlie person–situation interactions in ways that would bring them into alignment with promising developments in cognitive psychology and in social learning theory. One direction consisted of reanalyzing person characteristics in cognitive and social learning terms (Mischel, 1973, in press-a). This approach to person variables emphasized the discriminativeness of behavior and thus the role of context at relatively molecular levels of observation and analysis, but it stressed at more molar levels the perceived coherence and unity of behavior. It also was hypothesized that cognitive and social competencies provide an important element of stability and unity, serving as basic foundations of coherence in the person. The approach distinguishes between these relatively stable competencies, which underlie the capacity to construct behaviors and social cognitions, and the encodings, expectations, goals and values, and self-regulatory systems and plans that guide the individual's choices. Collectively, such a set of person variables allows one to describe discriminative, adaptive, contextually responsive functioning at the level of specific behavior from situation to situation. At the same time, it allows a sense of unity and identity to be achieved over time and at more superordinate, molar levels (Mischel, 1973, in press-a). Individual differences in behavior are seen as reflecting differences in these person variables and in their interactions with each other and with the particular context.

AN EXAMPLE: DELAY OF GRATIFICATION AS PROCESS AND AS PERSON VARIABLE

To try to understand basic competencies important for personality development from a cognitive social learning perspective, some of my own efforts continue to concentrate on one fundamental human quality—the ability to purposefully defer immediate gratification for the sake of delayed, contingent but more desired future outcomes. These investigations seek to clarify the ability to defer gratification both as a psychological process and as a basic human competence. They analyze the mechanisms that allow self-control (e.g., Mischel, 1974; in press-b) both in terms of the psychology of the situation and of the person, pursuing concurrently an experimental and a correlational strategy to study two sides of the same problem (Cronbach, 1957). An enduring general concern underlying the research is to try to understand how persons can overcome "stimulus control"—the power of situations—and achieve increasing volitional control over their own behavior even when faced with compelling situational pressures. In this effort, it is important to illuminate both the process that underlies this achievement and the competencies in the person that permit it.

The critique of global dispositions in the 1960s became the fuel for a set of extremist oversimplifications. Perhaps most unfortunately, a preemptive dichotomy between the person and the situation was created, with much debate about which one is more important (e.g., Alker, 1972; Bowers, 1973; Magnusson & Endler, 1977). Indeed, considerable personality theorizing in the last decade took such a form. Now consider this competition between the power of the situation versus the power of the person in the context of the research on how attention moderates the effects of rewards in the delay of gratification situation (e.g., Mischel & Ebbesen, 1970; Mischel,

Ebbesen, & Zeiss, 1972; Mischel, 1981b). By covering the rewards or by exposing them during the delay period, one can potently influence how long people are willing to wait for them. Do such results demonstrate the power of situational variables in self-control? They do, in so far as they show how specific changes in the situation can make delay either very difficult or very easy. But at the same time our findings also show that what a situation does to people depends on just how they think about it, on their ideation more than on what they are actually facing. Even preschoolers can transform the identical situation in ways that dramatically reverse its impact. To clarify this transformational process has been the goal of much of my research.

Illustrative results from three experiments are shown in Figure 1. The data are the number of minutes for which preschoolers (mean age about four years) were willing to wait by themselves for a preferred but delayed gratification. (For example, they could have two marshmallows when they wait until the experimenter returns of her own accord or one marshmallow immediately whenever the child decides to terminate the delay.) In this situation when the rewards are unavailable for attention (obscured from view during the delay) the children wait more than 10 times longer on average, than when the rewards are exposed and available for attention. Compare the two "no ideation" conditions in which predelay instructions were not provided to encourage any type of ideation. It might reasonably be concluded that in this situation exposure to the rewards powerfully reduces self-control, presumably by increasing the frustrativeness of the delay (Mischel, 1974). But also note that the impact of the available rewards in the situation hinges on what the children are doing mentally. Ideation about the rewards (as a result of predelay instructions) readily reverses the situational impact; thinking about the rewards, even when they are not physically exposed (last column in Figure 1) makes waiting for them just as difficult as if they were in view (first column). Conversely, the debilitating effects

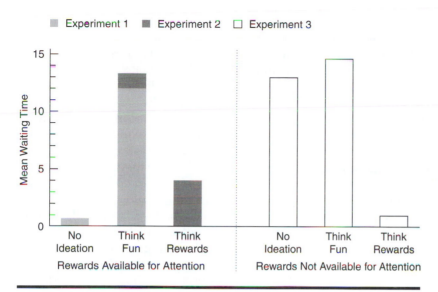

FIGURE 1   Mean Waiting Time in Each Condition

Note. From "Cognitive and Attentional Mechanisms in Delay of Gratification" by W. Mischel, E. B. Ebbesen, and A. R. Zeiss, 1972, *Journal of Personality and Social Psychology, 21,* p. 214. Copyright 1972 by the American Psychological Association.

of the visual presence of the rewards can be overcome through cognitive distraction (as seen in the second column, "think fun"). When children are given predelay instructions to "think fun" if they want to while waiting (ideating about mommy swinging them, for example), they can wait as long on average when facing the exposed rewards as when the rewards are obscured.

Subsequent studies have helped to specify just how the mental representation of the outcomes influences delay regardless of the objective stimulus situation facing the child at the moment. The subject's selective attention to either the consummatory or the more abstract nonconsummatory features of the rewards exerts opposite effects on delay time, respectively making waiting for them either difficult or easy. For example, if the preschoolers ideate about the rewards for which they are waiting in consummatory or "hot" ways (focusing on their taste, for instance, by thinking how crunchy and salty the pretzels are), they cannot delay long (Mischel & Baker, 1975). But if they focus on the nonconsummatory

or "cool" qualities of the rewards (on their abstract features, thinking of the pretzels as if they were sticks or tiny logs, for example), they can wait for them easily. Indeed, under such circumstances they can wait even longer than if they distract themselves from the rewards altogether (Mischel, 1974; Mischel & Moore, 1980). Whereas arousal-generating cognitions about the objects in the contingency significantly impede delay, cognitions about the nonconsummatory (nonmotivational) qualities or about their abstract representations enhance delay (Mischel & Moore, 1980; Moore, Mischel, & Zeiss, 1976). Thus, *how* people ideate about the outcomes (rather than what they face in the situation) is crucial. The more the children focus on the arousing qualities of the blocked goals, the more frustrating and aversive the choice conflict and the delay seem to become and the sooner they terminate the situation. Conversely, cognitive representations of the same objects that focus on their nonconsummatory (more abstract, less arousing) qualities appear to facilitate the maintenance of goal-directed behavior, presumably by allowing the person to keep the goal in mind without becoming too aroused and frustrated to continue to wait for it (Mischel, 1974, 1981b).

Because ideation can readily transform the objective external situation to produce opposite results, the predictability of behavior hangs by a precariously thin thread. That implies a person–situation interaction that makes psychology more interesting and challenging and less simple than either an unmoderated trait theory or an unmoderated situationism would suggest. What people do depends on how they construe their situation at any given moment, but those constructions in turn depend on the particular situation as well as on the construer. The result is both freedom and constraint—many alternative possibilities but also some significant predictability.

A child's momentary mental representation of the outcomes in the delay paradigm influences his or her waiting time and allows us to predict it from knowledge of the psychological conditions and how they operate to influence behavior. Nevertheless, individual differences in waiting time in the delay paradigm, regardless of condition, are not trivial matters; they are, instead, robust prototypic features of an important and enduring personal competence. We see that from related studies in which we are pursuing the personality correlates, the cross-situational consistency, and the temporal stability of delay behavior. Here we find evidence both for the discriminativeness of behavior across contexts and for the temporal stability of the person even over many years. Perhaps most impressive, we see significant continuity between the preschoolers' delay time while waiting for a couple of pretzels or marshmallows and independent ratings of their perceived cognitive and social competence made by their parents a dozen years later (Mischel, 1983; Mischel, Peake, & Zeiss, in preparation).

To illustrate, we know that the preschool child who delays effectively in some contexts may not do so in other even slightly different situations, showing much cross-context discrimi-

nativeness (Mischel & Peake, 1982). However, we also are finding significant continuities linking the preschooler's delay time in our experiments to indices of his or her cognitive and social competence, coping skills, and school performance years later (Mischel, in press-b). For example, the number of seconds preschoolers delayed the first time they had a chance to do so in our 1967–1974 preschool studies, regardless of the specific delay situation they encountered, significantly predicted their social competence as high school juniors and seniors as rated by their parents ($r = .34$, $N = 99$, $p < .001$, Mischel, in press-b). This is not an isolated finding: A clear picture seems to be emerging of adolescent correlates significantly associated with preschool delay in our experimental situation a decade earlier. Table 1 shows significant relations between preschool delay time and mother's and father's composited Q-sort ratings years later. (These children's mean age at first delay was 4 years, 6 months; it was 16 years, 8 months at the time of the parental ratings).

The correlations give a general picture of the child who delayed in preschool developing into an adolescent who is seen as attentive and able to concentrate, able to express ideas well, responsive to reason, competent, skillful, able to plan and think ahead, and able to cope and deal with stress maturely. The magnitude of these relations is modest, leaving most of the variance unexplained. Likewise, the mechanisms through which the obtained coherences develop await clarification. But these correlations seem impressive given that they span a lengthy period of development and are based on the child's preschool behavior (on an average of only 1.65 occasions) objectively assessed in seconds of delay time. Therefore the correlations cannot be attributed merely to stability in the rater's theories. Perhaps most encouraging, the attributes suggested by the adolescent ratings are congruent with the cognitive competencies essential for delay revealed by the experimental research. The experimental analysis of the delay process provided a more specific but highly complementary

TABLE 1   Adolescent Ratings Correlated with Preschool Delay Time ($N = 77$)

ITEM	r	ITEM	r
Positive		*Negative*	
Is attentive and able to concentrate	.49	Tends to go to pieces under stress, becomes rattled	−.49
Is verbally fluent, can express ideas well	.40		
Uses and responds to reason	.38	Reverts to more immature behavior under stress	−.39
Is competent, skillful	.38		
Is planful, thinks ahead	.35	Appears to feel unworthy, thinks of himself as bad	−.33
Is self-reliant, confident, trusts own judgment	.33		
		Is restless and fidgety	−.32
Is curious and exploring, eager to learn, open	.32	Is shy and reserved, makes social contacts slowly	−.31
Is resourceful in initiating activities	.29	Tends to withdraw and disengage himself under stress	−.30
Is self-assertive	.29		
Appears to have high intellectual capacity	.28	Shows specific mannerisms or behavioral rituals	−.27
Has high standards of performance for self	.27	Is stubborn	−.25
Can be trusted, is dependable	.25	Turns anxious when his environment is unpredictable	−.25
Becomes strongly involved in what he does	.25	Is unable to delay gratification	−.25
Is creative in perception, thought, work, or play	.24	Attempts to transfer blame to others	−.24
		Teases other children	−.22
Is persistent in his activities	.23	Tends to be indecisive and vacillating	−.22

Note. Mother-father ratings were obtained and composited on 100 items; correlations significant at $p < .05$ are shown. For $r > .38$, $p < .001$; $r > .27$, $p < .01$; $r > .21$, $p < .05$. Delay scores are mean delay time, with a mean of 1.65 delay situations. Delay scores for computing the correlations are based on z transformations within conditions within each delay study. (Adapted from "Delay of Gratification as Process and as Person Variable in Development" by W. Mischel in *Interactions in Human Development* by D. Magnussen and V. P. Allen (Eds.), in press-b, New York: Academic Press. Copyright 1983 by Academic Press. Adapted by permission).

view of the essential ingredient for effective delay in the waiting paradigm: the ability to divert and control attention, focusing it away from the frustrativeness of the waiting situation and the "hot" arousing stimulus pull of the rewards while maintaining a more abstract "cool" representation of the rewards in the contingency for which one is waiting (Mischel, 1981b).

In juxtaposition, the experimental and correlational efforts yield a more complete view both of the psychological process that allows waiting in the delay situation and of the qualities of the children who are likely to meet the demands of that situation effectively. These qualities are likely to be major ingredients of the "cognitive social competence" proposed as a basic person variable in the cognitive social learning approach (Mischel, 1973). They also converge with elements of the "ego resiliency" construct proposed in related developmental investigations (e.g., Block & Block, 1980; Mischel, 1966). Taken collectively, these findings from our experimental and correlational studies with the same subjects and the same behavioral measures indicate the conjoint operation of contextual and cognitive-personological determinants in self-regulation and the tenuousness of a rigid person–situation dichotomy. Process-oriented experimental studies in conjunction with investigations of correlated individual differences can allow a glimpse of both facets of the situation–person interaction in a complementary fashion. The challenge is to illuminate with increasing precision the competence suggested both by the experimental and the correlational data, simultaneously as a process and as a person variable.

THE COGNITIVE PROTOTYPE APPROACH TO PERSONS AND SITUATIONS

Recognition of the limitations of traditional global trait and state theories does not imply that people have no dispositions; it does require alternative ways to conceptualize those dispositions and to characterize both the discriminativeness and the consistency found in social behavior (Mischel, 1973). In that effort, Nancy Cantor and I began exploring a cognitive prototype approach for the categorization of persons (Cantor & Mischel, 1979) and of situations (Cantor, Mischel, & Schwartz, 1982). This approach appreciates the reality and stability of individual differences, but it tries to reconceptualize them in an interactional framework, guided by cognitive theories of the categorization of everyday objects (e.g., Rosch, Mervis, Gray, Johnson, & Boyes-Braem, 1976). The cognitive prototype approach to personality recognizes the especially "fuzzy" nature of natural categories along the lines first articulated by Wittgenstein (1953). Category knowledge about persons and situations is represented by a loose set of features that are correlated, but only imperfectly, with membership in that category. The approach implies that categorization decisions (e.g., about who is a prototypic extrovert or used car salesman type) will be probabilistic and that members of a category will vary in degree of membership. There will be many ambiguous borderline cases that yield overlapping, fuzzy boundaries between the categories. To study such fuzzy sets, one seeks the clearest and best exemplars (the most prototypic members), omitting the less prototypic, borderline instances. The prototype approach both to persons and to situations lends itself readily to the construction of orderly taxonomies containing categories at different levels of abstraction or inclusiveness that range from superordinate, to middle, to subordinate. Each level of inclusiveness or breadth in the hierarchies yields different distinctive gains and losses in ways that closely parallel the results for everyday objects; each level is useful for different goals (Cantor & Mischel, 1979).

So far this approach has yielded findings indicating that people have systematic, widely shared rules for assessing prototypicality in the person domain (Cantor, 1978; Cantor & Mischel, 1979); that there are readily accessible orderly person and situation taxonomies with predictable formal properties analogous to those found for everyday objects; that easily retrievable prototypes are shared for social situations; and, perhaps most interesting, that social situations often are characterized by the typical person–action combinations expected in them (Cantor, Mischel, & Schwartz, 1982). For example, people have detailed expectations about the kinds of behaviors and persons that are "best suited" and "worst suited" for different classes of situations. And they tend to describe social life in terms of the interactions between different types of persons and different types of contexts, thus practicing spontaneously the kind of interactionism now incorporated into contemporary personality theory (e.g., Magnusson & Endler, 1977). At first, the cognitive prototype approach to personality was aimed at clarifying how perceivers form and use person and situation categories and how these categories are organized. It was intended to provide an alternative to traits as units in everyday social perception. The challenging next steps are to apply the approach to study not only the perceiver's categories but also their links to the actions of the perceived.

With that goal, my associates and I have been investigating the patterning of the individual's social behavior, its construction by the perceiver, and the links between the two. We have begun to form a data pool in which objectively measured behaviors within selected social domains are systematically and reliably assessed over time and across a set of relevant contexts (Mischel & Peake, 1982; Wright, 1983; Wright & Mischel, in preparation). Such a data pool is a necessary beginning for a comprehensive assessment of stability and consistency at the behavior level—the level at which the consistency issue has been most hotly debated, but least closely researched, in the last few decades. This behavioral data pool is also the necessary base for further aggregations to more molar levels and for theory-guided categorizations and analyses of consistency. Using the first waves of such data, we have begun to assess how the temporal stability and cross-situational consistency of behavior in a domain are related to the perception and judgment of stability, consistency, and prototypicality in the same domain (e.g., Mischel & Peake, 1982, 1983).

ANALYZING THE CONSISTENCY PARADOX

A first question we addressed is the so-called "consistency paradox" (e.g., Bem & Allen, 1974), that is, the notion that while intuition seems to support the belief that people are characterized by broad dispositions resulting in extensive cross-situational consistency, the research in the area has persistently failed to support that intuition. Bem and Allen proposed a potential resolution of this paradox, suggesting that the low consistency coefficients usually found in research on this problem reflect the fallacy of assuming that all traits are relevant to all people. They urged, instead, that the search for behavioral consistency be limited to that subset of people for whom a given trait is relevant by separating subjects into self-perceived low and high variability groups on that trait. They predicted that cross-situational consistency in behavior would be found but only for the self-perceived low variability people.

To explore this promising proposal, our studies of the consistency paradox, begun in collaboration with Neil Lutsky (Peake & Lutsky, in preparation), as a first step replicated Bem and Allen's 1974 study, greatly extending the behav-ioral referents and battery of measures employed (Mischel & Peake, 1982). Specifically, 63 Carleton College undergraduates volunteered to participate in extensive self-assessments relevant to their conscientiousness and friendliness. (The results for the two dimensions generally paralleled each other; discussion here will be confined to conscientiousness.) They were rated by their parents and a close friend and were observed systematically in various situations relevant to the traits of interest in the college setting. The behavioral referents of conscientiousness in this work consisted of 19 different behavior measures, including, for example, class attendance, study session attendance, assignment neatness, assignment punctuality, reserve reading punctuality for course sessions, room neatness, and personal appearance neatness. To obtain referents for the trait constructs as perceived by the subjects, the specific behaviors selected as relevant to each trait were supplied by the subjects themselves as part of the pretesting at Carleton College. This procedure contrasts with the more typical one in which the assessors, not the subjects, exclusively select the referents. Behavior observations were aggregated over repeated occasions (with a mean of 3.74) to enhance reliability. In addition, self-ratings of perceived consistency (versus variability) for each trait were also obtained from the subjects following the Bem and Allen procedures, as described in Mischel and Peake (1982).

Congruent with earlier findings in the literature (Bem & Allen, 1974), raters agreed well with each other about the overall conscientiousness of people who see themselves as generally consistent (as opposed to variable) from situation to situation. These raters also agreed much less well about the conscientiousness of people who view themselves as highly variable on that dimension. In our efforts to understand the consistency paradox, we found it more surprising and challenging that the students' perceptions of their own overall consistency or variability on conscientiousness were not related closely to the observed cross-situational consistency of their behavior (as assessed by mean pairwise correlation coefficients across the 19 behavioral measures). Although interjudge agreement was greater for those students who saw themselves overall as consistent in conscientiousness, their average behavioral consistency across the measures was not significantly greater than that of students who saw themselves as variable. In sum, people who see themselves as consistent on a dimension seem to be seen with greater interjudge agreement by others, but their overall behavior is not necessarily more cross-situationally consistent. This finding directly contradicts the expectation that behavioral cross-situational consistency would be demonstrable at the level of specific situations, but only for that subset of people who view themselves as consistent on the particular dimension (Bem & Allen, 1974).

Thus in our attempt to understand the consistency paradox and to test the Bem and Allen proposal for its resolution, we found still another puzzle. If the self-perception of consistency is not related to the level of cross-situational consistency in the referent behaviors, on what is it based? To try to answer this question, we turned to the cognitive prototype approach. Applied to the consistency paradox, the cognitive prototype approach suggests that people judge their consistency not by seeking the average of all the observable features of a category, but by noting the reliable occurrence of some features that are central to the category or are more prototypic. Accordingly, Mischel and Peake (1982) proposed that consistency judgments rely heavily on the observation of central (prototypic) features so that the impression of consistency will derive not from average levels of consistency across all the possible features of the category but rather from the observation that some central features are reliably (stably) present. This perspective suggests that extensive cross-situational consistency may not be a basic ingredient for either the organization or the perception of personal consistency in a domain.

Guided by the cognitive prototype view, we hypothesized that the impression that one is consistent with regard to a trait is not based mostly on the observation of average cross-situational consistency in all the potentially relevant behaviors, such as punctuality for classes, punctuality for appointments, desk neatness, and so on. We proposed, instead, that when people try to assess their variability (versus consistency) with regard to a category of behavior, they scan the temporal stability of a limited number of behaviors that for them are most relevant (prototypic) to that category. That is, we proposed that the impression of consistency is based extensively on the observation of *temporal* stability in those behaviors that are highly relevant to the prototype but is independent of the temporal stability of behaviors that are not highly relevant to the prototype. And we further proposed that the impression of high consistency versus variability would be unrelated to overall cross-situational consistency.

The linkage between the global self-perception of consistency (versus variability) and the temporal stability of more (rather than less) prototypic behaviors was of most interest for our hypothesis. (Ratings of prototypicality were available for 17 of the 19 Carleton behavior measures and allowed us to divide these measures into the "more" and "less" prototypical halves.) We examined the links between the global self-perception of consistency and the behavioral data, divided into more prototypic versus less prototypic behaviors. The data pattern supported our expectations (as summarized in Table 2). Those students who saw themselves as highly consistent in conscientiousness were significantly more temporally stable on these prototypic behaviors than were those who viewed themselves as more variable from situation to situation. And the effect was replicated in the domain of friendliness within the same sample of students (Peake, 1982). In contrast to the clear and consistent differences in temporal stability for the prototypic behaviors, the self-perceived low and high variability groups did not differ in mean temporal stability for the less prototypic behaviors. Finally, as expected, self-perceived consistency and behavioral cross-

TABLE 2   Links Between Self-Perceived Consistency and Behavior

BEHAVIORAL DATA	Self-Perceived Consistency	
	LOW VARIABILITY	HIGH VARIABILITY
Cross-situational consistency		
More prototypical	.15	.13
Less prototypical	.09	.14
Temporal stability		
More prototypical	.71	.47
Less prototypical	.65	.64

Note. The coefficients reported are mean correlation coefficients across all possible comparisons of the designated type. (From "Beyond Deja vu in the Search for Cross-Situational Consistency," by W. Mischel and P. Peake, 1982, *Psychological Review, 89,* p. 751. Copyright 1982 by the American Psychological Association.)

situational consistency were unrelated as measured in that study.

If these results prove to be robust and widely replicable, they have intriguing implications. They suggest that people's intuitions of their cross-situational consistency are based on data, but these data may not be highly generalized cross-situational consistencies in what they do. Individuals' intuitions about their consistency may arise, instead, from the observation of temporal stability in prototypical behaviors. That is hardly an illusory or fictitious construction of consistency. The "error" would be to confuse the temporal stability of key behaviors with pervasive cross-situational consistency and then to overestimate the latter. But although the correlational results were suggestive and seem provocative, a more conclusive analysis of the process underlying self-perceptions of consistency awaits an experimental as well as a correlational attack on the problem.

IN PURSUIT OF SPECIFIC (LOCAL) CONSISTENCIES

The search for cross-situational consistencies that characterize persons now seems to be pursued in two different directions. One route is a continua-

tion of the classic trait strategy; it essentially treats situations as if they were error and seeks to cancel their effects by aggregating across them to eliminate their role and to demonstrate stable individual differences (e.g., Epstein, 1979). The strengths and limitations of this strategy were appreciated as early as Hartshorne and May (1928) and have recently been restated in detail (e.g., Mischel, 1983; Mischel and Peake, 1983). In a second direction, the search continues for consistencies by linking the behavior of interest to a circumscribed set of contexts, thus pursuing consistency on a more local and specific (rather than global) level. Both approaches seem to accept the fact that average levels of consistency in behavior from situation to situation tend to be modest, even after aggregation over multiple occasions (e.g., Dudycha, 1936; Hartshorne & May, 1928; Mischel & Peake, 1982, 1983; Newcomb, 1929). Advocates of the traditional trait strategy propose circumventing this constraint by abandoning attempts to predict behavior from situation to situation altogether (e.g., Epstein, 1979, 1983) and confining their predictive efforts to aggregates over multiple situations. Such a strategy can enhance the resulting coefficients dramatically (as the Spearman-Brown formula has long recognized). But it bypasses rather than resolves the classic problems found in the search for consistency from situation to situation by "averaging out" the situation rather than predicting behavior in it (as discussed in Mischel & Peake, 1982, 1983).

Following a different strategy, my associates and I have continued to pursue the search for consistencies from situation to situation but at more specific or "local" levels (e.g., Wright, 1983; Wright & Mischel, in preparation). In particular, we have been trying to specify when consistency from situation to situation might be obtained and when individual differences will and will not make a difference. The critique of global trait and state theories suggests that even when situations allow extensive individual differences to occur, most social behavior may be characterized by discriminative, adaptive, flexible patterns of behavior across contexts. Greater consistency may be displayed by individuals who are functioning poorly or immaturely and thus are characterized as maladaptive or less competent (e.g., Mischel, 1968, 1973; Moos, 1973; Olweus, 1977; Rausch, Dittman, & Taylor, 1959). That is, when individuals are not able to cope appropriately with the challenges and requirements of specific situations, more generalized, rigid modes of behavior may occur. It has been suggested that such relatively indiscriminate responding across situations may be indicative of disadvantageous or immature forms of coping (Mischel, 1973). For example, analyses of hyperaggressive children in therapy indicate "a trend for social behavior to become more related to situational influences with ego development. . . . The children seem to have gained in the ability to discriminate between situations." (Rausch, Dittman & Taylor, 1959, p. 368). In sum, when the behaviors required in the situation for appropriate, competent functioning are not available, more rigid, generalized types of maladaptive responses to the resulting stress may occur. Under such conditions, relatively cross-situationally consistent "characteristic" behavior patterns that are less context-sensitive become more likely. This increased consistency of problematic, disadvanta-

geous behavior should be seen when competency requirements for appropriate functioning exceed the individual's available competence. Such rigidity may be expected especially in highly stressful situations (e.g., Moos, 1973; Bandura & Walters, 1959).

We investigated these expectations with regard to children characterized as generally aggressive or withdrawn. In this project, conducted by Jack Wright, the subjects are samples of emotionally disturbed children, observed extensively in a summer camp residential facility over the course of several summers (Wright, 1983; Wright & Mischel, in preparation). These children, living in groups of eight to ten same-age peers, were selected for intensive daily observations. For example, in one data set, observations were conducted daily by staff over a 40-day period. Observations of 89 boys and girls were made repeatedly during the summer in 21 distinct situations (e.g., music, athletics, cabin group meeting) in the daily schedule. The mean number of repeated observations for each situation for each child was 4.6. A behavior tracking system was developed for rating the children's behavior for categories previously found to be of greatest relevance for this population (Horowitz, Wright, Lowenstein, & Parad, 1981). Multiple-feature prototypicality scales were developed for three categories: aggression, withdrawal, and prosocial behavior. The children's behavior was rated on these dimensions at the end of each observation period.

We anticipated that a child's representative or "typical" levels of inappropriate (problematic, disadvantageous) behavior will occur in situations whose cognitive and self-regulatory competence requirements exceed the child's competence level. Thus, when competence requirements are moderate or low, cross-situational consistency of the child's problematic behavior will be modest, consistency will be greater when competence requirements (for the situationally expected or appropriate behavior) exceed the subjects' available competencies. In such stressful situations, children characterized as generally aggressive will indeed show relatively consistent levels of aggression; those characterized as tending to withdraw will be relatively consistent in their levels of withdrawal. In sum, consistencies in problematic behavior should be more evident in those situations in which more adaptive, task-appropriate behavior required by the context is beyond the subjects' available competencies. In this sample, major individual differences were not expected in prosocial behavior as a response to excessive situational competence requirements. Therefore, with regard to prosocial behavior, no specific prediction of increased consistency was made and our hypothesis was limited to aggression and withdrawal.

To test this hypothesis, the cognitive and self-regulatory competency requirements of each of the situations sampled in two consecutive summers were rated. We also obtained parallel assessments of the childrens' competencies to meet those requirements. Examples of the 20 items for rating situations include: "This situation emphasizes delay of gratification, patience"; "This situation emphasizes listening carefully to instructions, explanations"; and "This situation emphasizes the ability to focus, concentrate, maintain good attention span." The items for the children were matched closely to those for the situations (e.g., "is unable to delay gratification, to be patient"). At the end of each summer program, three independent ratings were obtained on these scales for each situation and two to three separate, independent assessments of each child.

Using these ratings, we grouped the situations into those requiring the highest versus the lowest cognitive and self-regulatory competence in relation to the competence levels of the subjects. We then compared the mean level of cross-situational consistency in children's behavior obtained in the three highest and three lowest situations. Briefly, the data base for these comparisons consisted of 89 boys and girls in 1981 observed in 21 situations on 3 to 26 occasions per situation, and 79 boys in 1982 observed in 18 situations on 6 to 32 occasions per situation. The sit-

uations were regularly scheduled daily camp activities (e.g., art, music, athletics, cabin group meeting). In each, ratings for the categories (aggression, withdrawal, prosocial behavior) were obtained at the conclusion of each observation period and aggregated over repeated occasions in each situation. To assess cross-situational consistency, pairwise comparisons among specific situations were computed for each behavior category. The resulting mean cross-situational consistency coefficients for behavior for high versus low competence requirement situations are summarized in Table 3.

As Table 3 shows, in both samples and for both the aggression and withdrawal behavior categories the hypothesis was supported. Significantly higher ($p < .05$) levels of cross-situational consistency were obtained for those situations in which competency requirements were higher (rather than lower) relative to the subjects' available competence. For prosocial behavior there were no significant differences. Considering the

TABLE 3   Mean Cross-Situational Consistency Coefficients as a Function of Situation's Cognitive and Self-Regulatory Competency Requirements

BEHAVIOR CATEGORY	Situation Competency Requirements	
	LOW	HIGH
1981		
Aggression	.37	.73
Withdrawal	.27	.69
Prosocial	.28	.46
1982		
Aggression	.32	.61
Withdrawal	.06	.37
Prosocial	.34	.43

Note. Based on data from *The Structure and Perception of Behavioral Consistency* by J. C. Wright, 1983, unpublished doctoral dissertation (used by permission of J. C. Wright) and from *Predicting Cross-Situational Consistency: The Role of Person Competencies and Situation Requirements* by J. C. Wright and W. Mischel, manuscript in preparation.

mean levels of cross-situational consistency that have characterized this literature since the beginnings of the search more than half a century ago, the results obtained, especially for aggression, seem encouraging. They provide evidence of relative behavioral consistency across a predictable set of situations and behaviors without requiring any aggregation across situations. Although predictability coefficients of this magnitude (e.g., from ratings to behavior) are not new in the personality literature (e.g., Mischel, 1973, in press-a), mean consistency coefficients from situation to situation at this level have been pursued for years but have generally remained elusive.

The finding that children characterized as maladaptive become relatively consistent in their problematic behavior across situations in which they are excessively stressed supports an earlier thesis (Mischel, 1973). Namely, whereas discriminative facility from situation to situation is adaptive and functional, more indiscriminative responding may indicate ineffective coping and inadequate competence for dealing more appropriately with the specific situation. Personologists have long searched for behavioral consistencies from situation to situation as if such consistency were the essence of personality. Perhaps that form of consistency will prove to be more characteristic of rigid, maladaptive, incompetent social functioning than of the integrated individual.

The cognitive social learning approach to personality assumes areas of consistency in what people do but attempts to incorporate into descriptions of those consistencies the psychological conditions under which the behavior will and will not be expected to occur (Mischel, 1973). The obtained results seem illustrative of such context-bound consistencies, of regularities in representative or typical forms of coping at seemingly "middle" levels of abstraction (Cantor & Mischel, 1979) that become observable under predictable conditions. They show interactions in the form of predictable consistencies for some types of behavior by some types of persons under some types of situations. It should be challenging to explore the degree to which such "if _____ then _____" regularities in behavior also can be identified in other domains and for subjects who are neither extreme in the domain nor characterized as maladaptive.

LINKS BETWEEN CATEGORY JUDGMENTS AND PROTOTYPIC MOLECULAR BEHAVIOR

The results presented so far are based on ratings, judgments of how the child behaved with regard to the category of interest, recorded at the conclusion of each observation period. The value of judgments of this sort, even when made carefully by well-trained observers, continues to be controversial in the current literature. This is another problem on which oversimplifications are both tempting and common. The critique of traditional trait and state assessments called attention to the role of the observers' theories and constructs and to the many possible sources of bias and oversimplification in the judgment process (e.g., Mischel, 1968; Peterson, 1968). It stressed that trait categories may reflect the constructs of perceivers rather than faithfully mirror the behavior of the perceived. Hence memory-based global ratings, while of interest in their own right and as encodings at a molar level, cannot substitute for direct moment-by-moment observation of behavior. Unfortunately the view of traits as constructs easily leads to the premature conclusion that category judgments are perceptual illusions with little or no basis in the behavior of the perceived. To address this problem empirically, we have begun to explore the links between the perceiver's judgments of what other people "are like" and the prototypic behaviors that actually are displayed.

Consider the question: Where do the attributes that are associated in the head of the perceiver with one type of object or person actually reside? On this question, I have long believed that structure exists neither all in the head of the perceiver (cf. Shweder, 1975) nor all in the person perceived (cf. Epstein, 1977). Instead, it is a function of an interaction between the beliefs of observers and the characteristics of the observed, in the person domain as well as in the common object domain (e.g., Cantor & Mischel, 1979; Mischel, 1977). Such a view suggests that while ratings on trait dimensions are influenced by rater's expectations, they have roots in the behavior of the perceived. While I have held this view as an article of faith, data relevant to it have been difficult to obtain and interpret. Until recently, researchers generally studied either the categories of the perceiver or the behavior of the perceived; they rarely considered the fit between the two (e.g., Hoffman, Mischel, & Mazze, 1981). The challenge is not simply to demonstrate the existence of some connection between ratings and behavior but to specify its nature. In this effort, we again turned to the cognitive prototype approach (Buss & Craik, 1983; Cantor & Mischel, 1979), drawing on the data collected by Jack Wright (1983; Wright & Mischel, in preparation) with the children at the summer camp residential treatment facility.

In one analysis, observers' overall judgments of the children with regard to each category were correlated with the childrens' [sic] independently coded molecular behavior for that category, using codes based on the work of Patterson, Reid, Jones, and Conger (1975). The molecular acts were recorded during 6-second intervals of a 5-minute continuous tracking observation period on 15 separate occasions distributed across three camp situations during the summer. The result was some 1,200 six-second behavior codes obtained for each of 64 children. Examples of the code for aggression are: "I'm gonna punch your face" or "Let's go beat up . . . ," which are scored as *threat*; "Your father is a sissy" or "you stink," which are scored as *provoke*; and destroying another child's toy or other object, which is scored as *destructive*. Independent raters rated how often the prototypical or "ideal" aggressive, withdrawn, and prosocial child would exhibit each of the 32 behaviors in the molecular level codes. The 10 most distinctive features for each of the three types of children were combined into an aggregated criterion of prototypic molecular behavior. The question

was: Do raters' judgments of the child's overall aggression, for example, relate to the actual frequency of the child's molecular prototypic aggressive acts as coded by other independent observers as the behavior occurs? For aggression, the mean correlation between the ratings and the aggregate of 10 prototypic molecular behaviors was .52; for withdrawal and for prosocial behavior the coefficients were .40 and .35 respectively (Wright, 1983, p. 64). In other words, children who are construed by independent observers as more aggressive, for example, actually tend to display prototypic aggressive molecular acts more frequently. For instance, they yell and provoke more.

In sum, category judgments seem to have some links to the molecular structure of behavior; they are constructions but not illusions, with a reality base related to the prototypical actions of the perceived, even at a molecular level. Most interesting, similar levels of correlations were obtained between observer judgments and molecular level behaviors when only the single most prototypical feature for each category served as the behavioral criterion (see Table 4). Judgments of aggression, for example, were linked to the frequency of the child's single most prototypic aggressive act as much as they were to an aggregate of multiple aggressive acts that vary in their degree of prototypicality and incorporate the 10 best indicators of category membership. (Similar

TABLE 4   Mean Correlations Between Category Judgments and Frequency of Molecular Behavioral Features

CATEGORY	AGGREGATE OF 10 PROTOTYPIC FEATURES	MOST PROTOTYPIC SINGLE FEATURES
Aggression	.52	.53
Withdrawal	.40	.43
Prosocial	.35	.48

Note. Based on data from *The Structure and Perception of Behavioral Consistency* by J. C. Wright, 1983, unpublished doctoral dissertation. Used by permission of J. C. Wright.

results occurred for smaller aggregates, e.g., of 3 best and 6 best features.)

This opens many interesting possibilities. Does the occurrence of the single best indicator of category membership—for example, provoking—carry as much weight for the judge as an aggregate that also includes many additional prototypic acts, such as being destructive and ridiculing? Does the frequency of even a single behavioral feature, if it is extremely prototypic for the category, influence the dispositional judgment as much as does the frequency of a larger set of relevant prototypic behaviors? Is there a functional interchangeability among the essential features that serve to define a person category? It will be most challenging to pursue the possibility that the links between the observation of behavioral episodes and the inference of the relevant disposition involve a disjunctive rather than an additive or conjunctive relationship of the sort generally assumed. It will be especially interesting if differences can be identified in the formation of person categories compared to natural object categories.

OVERVIEW

Two decades ago, a critical reexamination of personality assessment practices raised questions about their utility and challenged the basic global dispositional assumptions that guided them. A search ensued for more circumscribed, context-bound units, for more direct assessment methods, and for conceptual alternatives that could bring the study of persons into alignment with developments in the study of cognition and social learning. One result was a focus on the power of situations, which until then had received some lip service but little serious attention in personality psychology. Intense debate followed about the comparative power of situations versus persons. A close analysis of how the psychological situation influences behavior in the delay of gratification paradigm illustrates the tenuousness of a rigid person–situation dichotomy. The situation affects how the subject

cognitively represents the crucial elements that make delay relatively difficult or easy; the subjective representation of the external situation, in turn, can transform and reverse its impact. Delay behavior can be predicted with considerable accuracy from knowledge of the specific psychological situation, and experimental analyses of the situation suggest a basic competence that underlies the ability to overcome "stimulus control" through effective self-control. At the same time, the child's early delay behavior is a feature of a long-term cognitive and social competence, reflected in significant links with ratings made more than a decade later. The competencies suggested by these ratings converge with and complement results from the experimental analysis of the cognitive activities underlying the delay process and the ability to overcome the temptations within the waiting situation. These stable competencies coexist with highly discriminative functioning cross-situationally.

In related research, we also have begun to explore the cross-situational structure of behavior and its links to perceived consistency, guided by a cognitive prototype approach. In one direction, with college students as subjects, the results suggest relations between the self-perception of cross-situational consistency and the occurrence of temporal stability of prototypic behaviors. A theory of personality structure does not require a person to be characterizable by high levels of pervasive cross-situational consistency in everything he or she does. It does assume the existence of a structure for behavior and a way to find it. We are now trying to pursue more deeply the proposal that some of the roots of such structure are prototypic features that are temporally stable but cross-situationally discriminative. Instead of seeking high levels of consistency from situation to situation for many behaviors in a wide range of contexts or looking for broad averages, one might try to identify unique "bundles" or sets of temporally stable prototypic behaviors, key features, that characterize the person even over long periods of time but not necessarily across most or all possibly relevant situations.

Although context-sensitivity and discriminativeness across situations may be the rule rather than the exception for most social behavior, areas of consistency can be identified under predictable conditions at least for less adaptive individuals and behaviors. In studies with emotionally disturbed children, we have identified zones of relative consistency from situation to situation, without resorting to aggregation across situations. Such "local" consistencies were found at least in extreme situations that require cognitive and self-regulatory competencies that exceed the person's available competence, and at least with regard to some categories of disadvantageous behavior (aggression, withdrawal) for people characterized as extreme on those dimensions. Moreover, significant links were found between ratings on these dimensions and the individual's actual behavior at relatively molecular episodic levels of observation, even without benefit of aggregating across different behavioral features.

It will be exciting to explore closely the nature of the links between such behavioral episodes at the molecular level and the attribution of dispositions. Even single features of behavior, if they are highly prototypic, may be sufficient to activate in the observer the larger dispositional category of which they are a part and which they represent. The analysis of how those behavioral features are organized and linked to the perception of personality seems an exciting step in the search for personality structure. That task is sure to be long and much less simple than I have suggested. But in the continuing pursuit of the locus of personal consistency and uniqueness in the individual, it may from time to time be worth remembering Paul Valery's observation: "Seeing is forgetting the name of the thing one sees."

REFERENCES

Bandura, A. (1969). *Principles of behavior modification.* New York: Holt, Rinehart & Winston.

Bem, D. J., & Allen, A. (1974). On predicting some of the people some of the time: The search for cross-situational consistencies in behavior. *Psychological Review, 81,* 506–520.

Cantor, N., & Mischel, W. (1979) Prototypes in person perception. In L. Berkowitz (Ed.), *Advances in experimental social psychology* (Vol. 12, pp. 3–52). New York: Academic Press.

Hunt, J. McV. (1965). Traditional personality theory in the light of recent evidence. *American Scientist, 53,* 80–96.

Mischel, W. (1968). *Personality and assessment.* New York: Wiley.

Mischel, W. (1973). Toward a cognitive social learning reconceptualization of personality. *Psychological Review, 80,* 252–283.

Mischel, W., & Peake, P. K. (1982). Beyond deja vu in the search for cross-situational consistency. *Psychological Review, 89,* 730–755.

Peterson, D. R. (1968) *The clinical study of social behavior.* New York: Appleton-Century-Crofts.

Vernon, P. E. (1964). *Personality assessment: A critical survey.* New York: Wiley.

KEY POINTS:

1. In the 1960s personality assessments focused on a few basic indicators. These indicators were believed to predict what individuals would do in new situations. Studies showed, however, that in order to see how people will react to specific situations, one also must study how they reacted to similar situations in the past.

2. How a situation influences people depends on how they think about it (ideation).

3. The delay process is the ability to divert and control attention, focusing it away from the frustration of waiting and the "hot" arousing stimulus pull of rewards while maintaining a "cool" representation of the rewards.

4. It is important to notice the patterning of individual social behavior, its cognitive construction by the perceiver, and the links between the two.

5. People who see themselves as consistent on a dimension often tend to be seen that way by others, but their overall behaviors are not necessarily highly cross-situationally consistent. People judge consistency not by seeking the average of all observable features of a category, but by noting the reliable occurrence of some features that are central to the category.

6. When individuals are not able to cope appropriately with the challenges and requirements of specific situations, more generalized, rigid modes of behavior may occur. Consistencies in problematic behavior should be more evident in those situations in which more adaptive, task-appropriate behavior required by the context is beyond the subjects' available competencies.

QUESTIONS TO THINK ABOUT

1. How does ideation affect the consistency of behavior?

2. Why is it important to take the perceiver into account as well as the perceived? What are some qualities that an efficient perceiver (observer) should possess?

3. Is consistency a desirable characteristic?

4. How should modern personality psychology conceptualize consistency of behavior, given that the eliciting situation is so important?

32

Global Traits: A Neo-Allportian Approach to Personality*

DAVID C. FUNDER

David C. Funder (1953–) focuses his research on personality judgment. He also considers the process by which people come to those judgments on personality. His focus combines psychologists' judgments about personality with personality assessment done by everyday people. That is, he studies a variety of influences on personality assessment. He is also interested in finding out how people acquire the personalities that they have.

Funder received his Ph.D. from Stanford University and was a psychology professor at the University of Illinois and Harvard University before joining the University of California, Riverside. Growing out of the "person-situation controversy," this selection lays out a case for the validity of global personality traits, along with a series of caveats.

But let us not join the camp of skeptics who say an individual's personality is "a mere construct tied together with a name"—that there is nothing outer and objectively structured to be assessed. No scientist, I think, could survive for long if he heeded this siren song of doubt, for it leads to shipwreck. (Allport, 1958, p. 246)

One of the most widely used concepts of intuitive psychology is the global personality trait. Almost everyone is accustomed to thinking about and describing the people one knows using terms like "conscientious," "sociable," and "aggressive." Traits like these are *global* because each refers not just to one or a few specific behaviors, but to *patterns* of behavior presumed to transcend time and specific situations. Historically, the global trait used to be an important part of formal psychological theory as well. Gordon Allport (1931, 1937) wrote extensively about

traits more than a half century ago, and for a time many research programs either developed general trait theories (Cattell, 1946), or investigated in detail specific traits (Witkin et al., 1954).

In recent years, however, theorizing about dispositional constructs such as global traits has been at a relative standstill. As Buss and Craik (1983) pointed out, "the field of personality appears to have set its theoretical gears into neutral" (p. 105). One cause of this inactivity may have been the field's two decades of immersion in a distracting debate over whether significant individual differences in social behavior exist at all (Mischel, 1968). Although, in the end, the existence of important individual regularities was reaffirmed (Kenrick & Funder, 1988), a lingering effect of the controversy seems to be an image of traits—most especially global ones—as old-fashioned, rather quaint ideas not relevant for modern research in personality. Indeed, when global

*Funder, D. C. (1991). Global traits: A Neo-Allportian approach to personality. *Psychological Science, 2*, 31–38. Reprinted by permission. [Ed. note: All citations in the text of this selection have been left intact from the original, but the list of references includes only those sources that are the most relevant and important. Readers wishing to follow any of the other citations can find the full references in the original work or in an online database.]

traits do appear in the literature nowadays, it is usually to play the role of straw man. The recent literature has seen a plethora of "reconceptualizations" of personality each of which begins, typically, by announcing its intention to replace global traits.

Modern reconceptualizations differ from global traits in at least three ways. First and most obviously, many constructs of the new personality psychology go out of their way not to be global. The range of life contexts to which they are relevant is specified narrowly and specifically, and this narrowness is touted as an important virtue. For instance, the recently promulgated "social intelligence" view of personality "guides one away from generalized assessments . . . towards more particular conclusions about the individual's profile of expertise in the life-task domains of central concern at that point in time" (Cantor & Kihlstrom, 1987, p. 241).

Second, and just as importantly, many modern personality variables are relatively *esoteric*—they are deliberately nonintuitive or even counterintuitive. For instance, in the place of trait terms found in ordinary language, one prominent investigator has offered person variables such as "self regulatory systems," "encoding strategies," and the like (Mischel, 1973).

Third, some modern reconceptualizations go so far as to eschew an explanatory role for personality variables altogether. For instance, the act frequency approach treats personality dispositions as little more than frequency counts of "topographically" (i.e., superficially) similar acts (Buss & Craik, 1983).

The intent of these reconceptualizations is laudable. Each is designed to correct one or more of the problems of overgenerality, vagueness, and even philosophical confusion to which trait psychology has sometimes been prone. The present article, however, is motivated by a belief that the movement away from global traits, however fashionable it may be, entails several dangers that are not usually acknowledged.

Briefly, the dangers are these. First, when we use dispositional terms that are framed *narrowly*, we discard any possibility of generating statements about individual differences that have real explanatory power. Second, when we use dispositional terms that are *esoteric,* we fail to make contact with traits as used in everyday social discourse, lose any basis for understanding and evaluating lay trait judgments, and discard the vast lore of common sense and wisdom that they embody. And third, when we are content to define traits as *frequencies* of superficially similar behaviors, we run the risk of being fundamentally deceived when, as often happens, the causes of behavior turn out to be complex. Each of these points will be expanded later in this article.

What follows is a brief outline of a modern, *neo-Allportian* theory of global traits, presented in the form of 17 assertions. The term "neo-Allportian" is meant to emphasize that this approach to personality is fundamentally based on the seminal writings of Gordon Allport (especially Allport, 1937), but also to acknowledge that his basic theory was published more than a half-century ago and so is ripe for updating and reinvigoration (Zuroff, 1986). As it turns out, Allport's basic ideas look remarkably sound even with 53 years of hindsight, and yield a large number of implications for conceptualization and research in modern personality psychology.

DEFINITIONAL ASSERTIONS

Traits Are Real

This assertion is the most fundamental of Allport's assumptions, one he believed was essential for subsequent research to be meaningful. He held this position in the face of objections that it was philosophically naive and arguments (still heard today) that traits should be regarded not as entities that have objective reality, but merely as hypothetical constructs (Carr & Kingsbury, 1938). Allport believed that this idea made about as much sense as astronomers regarding stars as hypothetical constructs rather than astronomical objects. He failed to see how any science, including personality psychology, could proceed without assuming its subject of study to be real.

More specifically, Allport (1931, 1966) said traits are "neurodynamic structures" (1966, p. 3) that have "more than nominal existence" (1966, p. 1). If it is obvious that all behavior originates in the neurons of the brain, and that does seem obvious, then it follows that stable individual differences in behavior—to the extent they exist—must similarly be based on stable individual differences in neural organization.

Unfortunately, a method to assess the neural basis of personality is not yet in sight. The presence of a trait can only be inferred on the basis of overt behavior. For all practical purposes, therefore, a global trait must refer to two things at the same time: (a) a complex pattern of behavior from which the trait is *inferred*, and (b) the psychological structures and processes that are the source of the pattern. When we call someone "friendly" or "aggressive" or "generous," we are saying something both about how the person behaves (or would behave) in certain kinds of situations *and* about the functioning of his or her mind. The next assertion follows as a consequence.

Traits Are More than Just Summaries

A viewpoint prominently expressed in recent years is that "dispositions" (a.k.a. traits) should be considered as no more than summaries of behavioral frequencies, or "act trends" (Buss & Craik, 1983). An individual's generosity then becomes the frequency, over a specified unit of time, of his or her superficially generous acts.

This definition deliberately abdicates any explanatory role. Dispositions are treated as circular constructs in which a generous act implies generosity, and the attribution of generosity is used to predict future generous acts *solely* "on actuarial grounds" (Buss & Craik, 1983, p. 106).

However, the appearance of behavior can be misleading (Block, 1988). As Allport pointed out:

> *A bearer of gifts may not be, in spite of all appearances, a truly generous person: he may be trying to buy favor. . . . Pseudo-traits, then, are errors of inference, misjudgments that come from fixing attention solely upon appearances. The best way to*

> *avoid such errors is to find the genotype that underlies the conduct in question. What is the individual trying to do when he brings his gifts? (Allport, 1937, p. 326)*

The Meaning of a Behavior Depends on Two Kinds of Context

A single behavior, considered out of context, is frequently ambiguous. Depending on the intention with which the act was performed, there may be multiple possible and plausible alternatives for the traits that might be relevant. This is not to deny that there are interpretational defaults. The act of gift-giving might be interpreted as generous, all other things being equal. All other things are seldom equal, however, so the gift-giving might also reflect insecurity, Machiavellianism, or even anger, depending on the situational circumstances, the gift-giver's behavior in other situations, and what together they imply about the gift-giver's inner state and motives.

Two kinds of context help disambiguate an act. The first is the immediate situation. The giving of a gift becomes more interpretable if one knows whether it was given to a subordinate who performed a job well, or to a superior considering the promotion of the gift-giver. The usefulness of this kind of situational information has been discussed in detail by attribution theorists within social psychology (Heider, 1958; Kelley, 1967), but has been taken into account less often by personality psychologists.

The other kind of context is just as important, but is mentioned even more rarely. Acts become less ambiguous to the extent they fit into a pattern of the individual's other acts. A consistent pattern of generous behavior provides a more plausible context in which to infer that generosity is the trait underlying the gift-giving than does a consistent pattern of mean, nasty, and sneaky behavior. (Indeed, an act that seems inconsistent with the actor's past patterns of behavior is commonly called suspicious.) A pattern of sneaky behavior might lead to an attribution of Machiavellianism that would explain, in turn, why the person gave a lavish gift to his worst enemy.

DEVELOPMENTAL ASSERTIONS

Traits Are Learned

Global traits are manifest by patterns of perception and action in the social world; therefore, they must be a product of how one has learned to interact with that world. The process of learning that produces a trait almost certainly involves an interaction between one's experience (in one's particular social environment) and one's genetic endowment (Scarr & McCartney, 1983). Thus, two people with identical environments, or two people with identical genes, could and often do have very different traits.

Because traits are learned, they are not necessarily immutable. Anything learned can in principle be unlearned. Global trait theory is not necessarily pessimistic about possibilities for either personal or social change.

However, traits are relatively stable. Presumably, the difficulty in unlearning a trait (the amount of retaining or new experience required) will be proportional to the amount and salience of the experience through which it was learned in the first place. Genetic predispositions, and perhaps even species-specific characteristics, may also make some traits easier to learn and harder to unlearn than others (Buss, 1984). But the present analysis asserts that because all traits are, in the final analysis, learned, all traits can, in theory if not always in practice, be unlearned.

The Process of Learning a Trait is Complex

Such learning is far more than a simple matter of reward and punishment or S and R. That simple kind of learning can produce, at most, the narrow patterns of behavior that Allport (1931) called "habits." Traits are the result of complex patterns of experience and of higher-order inductions the person makes from that experience. Kelly (1955) believed that *any* pattern of experience could lead a person to any of at least a large number of behavioral outcomes (just as any pattern of data can always lead a scientist to more than one interpretation). Kelly believed that the ability to choose between these alternative outcomes provided a

basis for free will. The comedian Bill Cosby has described his childhood neighborhood as a place where adolescents were all on the verge of deciding whether to be killers or priests. The point is that similar patterns of past experience do not necessarily produce similar outcomes.

When *fully* analyzed, every person's pattern of behavior will be every bit as complex as the unique pattern of endowment and experience that produced it. Again, in Allport's (1937, p. 295) words: "Strictly speaking, no two persons ever have precisely the same trait. . . . What else could be expected in the view of the unique hereditary endowment, the different developmental history, and the never-repeated external influences that determine each personality?"

But there are commonalities among people that are useful for characterizing individual differences. A trait like sociability is relevant to behavior in a set of situations regarded as functionally equivalent by people in general: specifically, situations with other people in them. Hence, it is *generally* meaningful to rank-order people on their overall sociability. Allport acknowledged this point as well: "The case for the ultimate individuality of every trait is indeed invincible, but . . . for all their ultimate differences, normal persons within a given culture-area tend to develop a limited number of roughly comparable modes of adjustment" (1937, pp. 297-298).

Still, the list of social situations that are functionally equivalent for people in general is unlikely to fully capture the situations that are regarded as functionally equivalent by any *single* individual. To capture general trends or gists, and to detect things that are true of people in general, one always loses the details of each individual case. This tradeoff between nomothetic and idiographic analyses can be and often has been lamented, but it is inevitable.

FUNCTIONAL ASSERTIONS

A Behavior May Be Affected by Several Traits At Once

The chief danger in the concept of trait is that, through habitual and careless use, it may come to stand for an assembly of separate and self-active faculties, thought to govern behavior all by themselves, without interference. We must cast out this lazy interpretation of the concept. . . . The basic principle of behavior is its continuous flow, each successive act representing a convergent mobilization of all energy available at the moment. (Allport, 1937, pp. 312-313)

The fact that every behavior is the product of multiple traits implies that disentangling the relationship between a given trait and a given behavior is extremely difficult. It also implies that the ability of any particular trait to predict behavior by itself is limited. Ahadi and Diener (1989) showed that if a behavior is totally caused by only four traits whose influence combines additively, the maximum correlation between any one trait and behavior that could be expected is .45. If different traits combine multiplicatively, which seems plausible, the ceiling is even lower.

A third implication is that modern research on traits should conduct a renewed examination of the way traits combine in the determination of behavior. Investigators should more often look beyond the traditional research question of how single traits affect single behaviors, to how multiple traits interact within persons (Carlson, 1971).

Traits Are Situational Equivalence Classes

In a trenchant phrase, Allport wrote that traits have the capacity "to render many stimuli functionally equivalent" (1937, p. 295). The tendency to view different situations as similar causes a person to respond to them in a like manner, and the patterns of behavior that result are the overt manifestations of traits.

The template-matching technique (Bem & Funder, 1978) provides one empirical approach to the study of situational equivalence classes. The technique looks for empirical ties between behavior in real-life situations that subjects' acquaintances have viewed and interpreted, and laboratory situations in which subjects' behavior is measured directly. To the extent higher-order similarity or functional equivalence exists, correlations will be found. The experimental situations are then interpreted, or in Bem and Funder's words, the subjects' "personalities assessed," based on the equivalence classes thus established.

For instance, in one of Bem and Funder's first studies (1978), the parents of nursery school children provided judgments of the degree to which their children were cooperative with adults. These ratings of cooperativeness turned out to correlate highly with minutes and seconds of delay time measured directly in our delay-of-gratification experiment. We inferred that our experimental situation must have been in some way functionally equivalent to the situations at home from which the parents had judged cooperativeness. Our final conclusion was that delay time in our experiment was a symptom of such cooperativeness as much as it was of self control or anything like it. The equivalence class to which the delay experiment seemed to belong consisted of other cooperation situations, not necessarily other self-control situations.

Access to One's Own Traits Is Indirect

The interpretation of a trait as a subjective, situational-equivalence class offers an idea about phenomenology—about what it feels like to have a trait, to the person who has it. It doesn't feel like anything, directly. Rather, the only subjective manifestation of a trait *within* a person will be his or her tendency to react and feel similarly across the situations to which the trait is relevant. As Allport wrote, "For some the world is a hostile place where men are evil and dangerous; for others it is a stage for fun and frolic. It may appear as a place to do one's duty grimly; or a pasture for cultivating friendship and love" (1961, p. 266).

Certainly a friendly person (ordinarily) does nothing like say to him- or herself, "I am a friendly person; therefore, I shall be friendly now." Rather, he or she responds in a natural way to the situation as he or she perceives it. Similarly, a bigoted person does not decide, "I'm going to acted [sic] bigoted now." Rather, his or her bigoted behavior is the result of his or her perception of a targeted group as threatening, inferior, or both (Geis, 1978).

But on reflection one can indeed begin to come to opinions about one's own traits (Bem, 1972; Thome, 1989). One might realize that one is always happy when there are other people around, or always feels threatened, and therefore conclude that one must be "sociable" or "shy," respectively. But again, this can only happen retrospectively, and probably under unusual circumstances. Psychotherapy might be one of these: when "on the couch," one is encouraged to relate past experiences, and the client and therapist together come up with interpretations. Whether called that or not, these interpretations often involve the discovery of the client's situational equivalence classes, or traits. Certain profound life experiences might also stimulate conscious introspection.

In rare cases, explicit, volitional self-direction toward a trait-relevant behavior might take place. For example, one might say to oneself (before going to an obligatory party attended by people one detests), "now, I'm going to be *friendly* tonight," or, before asking one's boss for a raise, self-instruct "be *assertive*." As a matter of interesting psychological fact, however, in such circumstances the resulting behavior is *not* authentically a product of the trait from which it might superficially appear to emanate. The other people at the party, or the boss, probably would interpret the behavior very differently if they knew about the individual's more general behavior patterns and certainly would interpret it differently if they knew about the self-instruction.

Traits Influence Perceptions of Situations Through Dynamic Mechanisms

Different situations may be rendered functionally equivalent through at least three kinds of mechanism. One kind is *motivational*. A person who is hungry arranges situations along a continuum defined by the degree to which food is offered. A person who is dispositionally fearful sees situations in terms of potential threat. A person with a high degree of sociability approaches most situations where other people are present in a positive frame of mind. Another way to say this is that one's perception of the world is partially structured by one's goals (Cantor & Kihlstrom, 1987).

A second kind of mechanism concerns *capacities* and *tendencies*. A person with great physical strength will respond to the world in terms of situational equivalence classes that are different than those experienced by one who is weak. Situations containing physical obstacles may appear interesting and challenging rather than discouraging. Similarly, a person with a tendency to overcontrol motivational impulses will behave differently across a variety of motivationally involving situations than a person whose tendency is towards undercontrol. The overcontroller will restrain his or her impulses, whereas the undercontroller will tend to express them (Funder & Block, 1989).

A third kind of mechanism is *learning*. Perhaps one has been rewarded consistently in athletic settings. Then one will approach most new athletic-like settings with an expectation of reward, with direct consequences for behavior. (This learning experience might itself be a function of one's physical prowess, an example of how these mechanisms can interact.) Perhaps one has been consistently punished for risk-taking. Such an individual is likely to perceive situations involving risk as threatening, and behave across them in a consistently cautious manner.

An important direction for future research is to specify further the dynamic mechanisms through which global traits influence behavior. Several modern approaches bypass trait concepts on the way to examining goals, perceptions, or abilities. Instead, or at least additionally, it might be helpful to ascertain how people with different traits perceive and categorize situations. In turn, it might be useful to explore how these perceptions and categorizations can be explained through motivational mechanisms, abilities and capacities, and learning.

ASSESSMENT ASSERTIONS

Self-report Is a Limited Tool for Personality Assessment

Because people are not directly aware of the operation of their own traits, their self-reports cannot always be taken at face value. Such reports might be wrong because of errors in retrospective behavioral analysis—including failures of memory and failures of insight. Both kinds of failure are very common. Self-reports are also subject to self-presentation effects, the desire to portray oneself in the most favorable possible light.

This is one point where the present analysis diverges from previous and traditional presentations of trait theory. Self-reports have been and continue to be the most widely used tool for trait measurement (see McClelland, 1984, and Block & Block, 1980, for notable exceptions). This is unfortunate because, according to the present analysis, the person is in a relatively poor position to observe and report accurately his or her own traits, except under exceptional circumstances. Indeed, certain important traits may be almost invisible to the persons who have them. Imagine a chronic repressor asked to rate him- or herself on the item, "tends to deny one's own shortcomings."

This analysis helps account for one of the best known findings of attribution research. Observers of a person's behavior are more likely to report that it was influenced by traits than is the person him- or herself. Traditional accounts of this finding have assumed this is because the observers are, simply, wrong (Jones & Nisbett, 1972). The present analysis views the actor–observer effect as a natural result of the person being in a relatively poor position to observe his or her own traits. A more objective, external point of view is necessary. This leads to the next assertion.

The Single Best Method of Trait Assessment Is Peer Report

As was discussed above, traits are manifest by complex patterns of behavior the precise nature of which have by and large gone unspecified, as personality psychologists focused their attention elsewhere. However, our intuitions daily utilize complex *implicit* models of how traits are manifest in behavior. Making explicit these implicit understandings is an important but almost untouched area for further research. In the meantime, such intuitions are there to be used.

The intuitions available are those of the person being assessed, and those of the people who know him or her in daily life. Self-judgments of personality are easy to gather, and research suggests that by and large they agree well with judgments by peers (Funder & Colvin, in press). Nonetheless, self-reports are also suspect for a number of reasons, as was discussed earlier.

The impressions a person makes on those around him or her may provide a more reliable guide for how he or she can be accurately characterized. Peers' judgments have the advantage of being based on large numbers of behaviors viewed in realistic daily contexts, and on the filtering of these behavioral observations through an intuitive system capable of adjusting for both immediate situational and long-term individual contexts (Funder, 1987). Moreover, as Hogan and Hogan (in press) have observed, "personality has its social impact in terms of the qualities that are ascribed to individuals by their friends, neighbors, employers, and colleagues" (p. 12). For social traits at least, it is hard to imagine a higher court of evidential appeal that could over-rule peers' judgments, *assuming the peers have had ample opportunity to observe the target's behavior in daily life.* If everyone you meet decides you are sociable, for instance, then you are *(Allport & Allport, 1921).*

This assertion implies that an important direction for future research is to find out more about how judges of personality perform (Neisser, 1980). A better understanding of the cues that are used by everyday acquaintances in judging personality, and the circumstances under which those cues are accurate, will lead to progress regarding two important issues: (a) how personality is manifest in behavior, and (b) how personality can most accurately be judged. My own current research focuses on these topics (Funder, 1987, 1989).

EPISTEMOLOGICAL ASSERTIONS

For Purposes of Explanation, the Most Important Traits Are Global (but for Purposes of Prediction, the Narrower the Better)

It appears to have become fashionable in the personality literature to eschew generality by constructing individual difference variables that are as narrow as possible. Cantor and Kihlstrom (1987) espouse a theory of "social intelligence" that regards the attribute as central to personality but *not* a general individual difference. Rather, it is viewed as a collection of relatively discrete, independent, and narrow social capacities, each relevant to performance only within a specific domain of life. A related viewpoint is that of Sternberg and Smith (1985), who suggest that different kinds of social skill are relevant only to extremely narrow classes of behavior, and that as a general construct "social skill" has little or no validity (but see Funder & Harris, 1986).

The use of narrow constructs may well increase correlations when predicting single behaviors, just as at the same time (and equivalently) it decreases the range of behaviors that can be predicted (Fishbein & Ajzen, 1974). But beyond whatever predictive advantages narrowly construed variables may have, they are often presented as if they were somehow *conceptually* superior as well. They are not. Indeed, explaining behavior in terms of a narrow trait relevant to it and little else represents an extreme case of the circularity problem sometimes (unfairly) ascribed to trait psychology in general. If "social skill at parties" is a trait detected by measuring social skill at parties, and is then seen as a *predictor* or even *cause* of social skill at parties, it is obvious that psychological understanding is not getting anywhere.

Global traits, by contrast, have real explanatory power. The recognition of a pattern of behavior is a *bona fide* explanation of each of the behaviors that comprise it. Indeed, the more global a trait is, the more explanatory power it has. Connections between apparently distal phenomena are the most revealing of the deep structure of nature. For instance, if a general trait of social skill exists (see Funder & Harris, 1986), then to explain each of various, diverse behavioral outcomes with that trait is not circular at all. Instead, such an explanation relates a specific behavioral observation to a complex and general pattern of behavior. Such movement from the specific to the general is what explanation is all about.

This is not to say the explanatory task is then finished—it never is. These general patterns called traits should be the targets of further explanatory effort. One might want to investigate the developmental history of a trait, or its dynamic mechanisms, or its relationships with other traits, or the way it derives from even more general personality variables. But traits remain important stopping points in the explanatory regress. To *any* explanation, one can always ask "why?" (as every 4-year-old knows). Still, between each "why" is a legitimate step towards understanding.

The Source of Trait Constructs Should Be Life and Clinical Experience, as Filtered by Insightful Observers

It has often been argued that personality constructs should be formulated independently of, or even in explicit avoidance of, the constructs used by ordinary intuition. Indeed, this is one point upon which investigators as diverse as R. B. Cattell and Walter Mischel have found common ground. Often, mechanical procedures (e.g., factor analysis, behavioral analysis) have been touted as ways to construct personality variables uncontaminated by erroneous preconceptions. The results can be quite esoteric, having ranged from Cattell's (1946) favored variables of "alexia," "praxernia," and the like, to Mischel's (1973) cognitive social-learning variables of "subjective expected values," "encoding strategies," and so forth.

However, the theory of global traits asserts that trait constructs *should* be intuitively meaningful, for three reasons. First, intuitively discernible traits are likely to have greater social utility. Many global traits describe directly the kinds of relationships people have or the impacts they have on each other. More esoteric variables, by and large, do not.

Second, psychology's direct empirical knowledge of human social behavior incorporates only a small number of behaviors, and those only under certain specific and usually artificial circumstances. Restricting the derivation of individual difference variables to the small number of behaviors that have been measured in the laboratory (or the even smaller number that have been measured in field settings) adds precision to their meaning, to be sure, but inevitably fails to incorporate the broader patterns of behaviors and contexts that make up daily life. Our intuitions, by contrast, leapfrog ahead of painstaking research. The range of behaviors and contexts immediately brought to mind by a trait like "sociable" goes far beyond anything research could directly address in the foreseeable future. Of course, our intuitions am unlikely to be completely accurate, so traits as we think of them informally and as they actually exist in nature may not be identical. However, to be useful in daily life our intuitions must provide at least roughly accurate organizations of behavior, and provide a logical starting point for research (Clark, 1987). Corrections and refinements can come later, but to begin analysis of individual differences by eschewing intuitive insight seems a little like beginning a race before the starting line.

Third, the omission of intuitively meaningful concepts from personality psychology makes study of the *accuracy* of human judgments of personality almost meaningless. People make global trait judgments of each other all the time, and the accuracy of such judgments is obviously important (Funder, 1987). However, unless one wishes to finesse the issue by studying only agreement between *perceptions* of personality (Kenny & Albright, 1987), research on accuracy requires a psychology of personality assessment to which informal, intuitive judgments can be compared. Gibson (1979) has persuasively argued that the study of perception cannot proceed without knowledge about the stimulus array and, ultimately, the reality that confronts the perceiver. This point applies equally to person perception. A theory of personality will be helpful in understanding judgments of people for the same reason that a theory of the physics of light is helpful in understanding judgments of color.

EMPIRICAL ASSERTIONS

Global Traits Interact with Situations in Several Ways

Every global trait is situation specific, in the sense that it is relevant to behavior in some (perhaps many), but not all, life situations. Sociability is relevant only to behavior in situations with other people present, aggressiveness when there is the potential for interpersonal confrontation, friendliness when positive interaction is possible, and so forth. Our intuitions handle this sort of situational delimitation routinely and easily.

The delimitation of the situational relevance of a trait is sometimes called a "person-situation interaction." The empirical and conceptual development of this idea is an important achievement of the past two decades of personality research, and a valuable byproduct of the consistency controversy (Kenrick & Funder, 1988). The kind of interaction just described has been called the ANOVA or "passive" form (Buss, 1977). All that is meant is that different traits are relevant to the prediction of behavior in different situations. A child whose cooperativeness leads her to delay gratification in a situation with an adult present may be the first to quit if left alone (Bem & Funder, 1978).

At least two other, more active kinds of interaction are also important. The first is situation selection. Personality traits affect how people choose what situations to enter (Snyder & Ickes, 1985). A party might contain strong, general pressures to socialize, pressures that affect the behavior of nearly everyone who attends. But sociable people are more likely to have chosen to go the party in the first place. Thus, the trait of sociability influences behavior in part by affecting the situational influences to which the individual is exposed.

Traits can also magnify their influence on behavior through another kind of interaction. Most situations are changed to some extent by the behavior of the people in it. The presence of a sociable person can cause a situation to become more sociability-inducing. An aggressive child can turn a previously peaceful playground into a scene of general mayhem.

However, certain situations are *not* freely chosen, being imposed arbitrarily, and some situations will *not* change, no matter what the people in them may do. By short-circuiting the two kinds of person-situation interactions just discussed, such situations limit severely the influence traits can have on behavior. A prototypic example is the psychological experiment. Experiments assign subjects to conditions randomly, and the experimenter works from a set script. The subject's personality then cannot influence which situation he or she is exposed to, nor can his or her actions change the nature of the situation into which he or she is thrust (Wachtel, 1973).

But even in experiments like this, the influence of global traits is frequently detected; many examples could be cited. Consider the delay-of-gratification experiment already discussed (Bem & Funder, 1978). Nearly all the children who happened to be enrolled in a certain nursery school class entered this situation, and the experimenter worked from a set script that did not vary as a function of what the child did. Even so, the children's delay-of-gratification behavior had many and meaningful ties to their global personality traits, as assessed by their parents.

Evidence Concerning Personality Correlates of Behavior Supports the Existence of Global Traits

Findings such as those summarized in the preceding paragraph have been obtained again and again. Numerous studies report correlations between behavior in arbitrarily imposed, implacable situations, and personality traits judged on the basis of behavior observed in real life. These correlations constitute powerful evidence of the important influence of personality traits on behavior, even under circumstances where one would expect their influence to be weakened.

Most of this evidence has accumulated since 1937, and so was not available to Allport, but has been summarized many times in the course of the person-situation debate. Reviews can be found in articles by Funder (1987), Kenrick and Funder (1988), and many others.

Evidence Concerning Interjudge Agreement Supports the Existence of Global Traits

Another form of evidence for the existence of global traits is the good agreement that can be obtained between judgments of traits rendered by peers who know the subject in diverse life situations, and between such judgments and the subject's own self-judgments. Allport regarded evidence of this sort as especially persuasive:

> *What is most noteworthy in research on personality is that different observers should agree as well as they do in judging any one person. This fact alone proves that there must be something really there, something objective in the nature of the individual himself that compels observers, in spite of their own prejudices, to view him in essentially the same way. (Allport, 1937, p. 288)*

Fifty-three years later, the evidence is even stronger. Acquaintances who are well-acquainted with the people they judge can provide personality ratings that agree with ratings provided by other acquaintances as well as by the targets themselves (see Funder & Colvin, in press, for a review). This issue being settled, more recent work has focused on the circumstances that make interjudge agreement higher and lower, including level of acquaintanceship and the nature of the specific trait being judged (Funder, 1989).

Evidence Concerning the Stability of Personality across the Lifespan Supports the Existence of Global Traits

Allport lacked access to well-designed longitudinal studies that examined the stability of personality over time. Today, a vast body of research convincingly demonstrates that general traits of personality can be highly stable across many years. Data showing how behaviors can be predicted from measures of traits taken years before, or "post-dicted" by measures taken years later, have been reported by Funder, Block, and Block (1983), Funder and Block (1989), and Shedler and Block (1990). Similar findings from other longitudinal studies have been reported by Block (1971), Caspi (1987), McCrae and Costa (1984), and others.

DIRECTIONS FOR RESEARCH

As a fruitful theory should, the theory of global traits raises a host of unanswered questions that deserve to be the focus of future research. They include matters of definition, origin, function, and implication.

Definition. How many global traits are there? Allport (1937, p. 305) reported finding 17,953 terms in an unabridged dictionary. Fortunately, these can be partially subsumed by more general constructs. Personality psychology seems to be achieving a consensus that most trait lists boil down to about five overarching terms (Digman, 1990). This does not mean there are "only" five traits, but rather that five broad concepts can serve as convenient, if very *general,* summaries of a wide range of the trait domain. They are Surgency (extraversion), Neuroticism, Openness (or culture), Agreeableness, and Conscientiousness.

Global traits may also be partially reducible to more narrow constructs. Perhaps friendliness is a blend of social potency and positive affect, for instance. The reduction of global traits into more specific (and possibly more factorially pure) constructs is a worthwhile direction for research. But the position taken here is that the appropriate level of analysis at which investigation should *begin,* and which more specific investigations should always remember to *inform,* is the level of intuitively accessible, global traits.

Origin. Developmental psychology has been dominated in recent years by studies of cognitive development, with the term "cognitive" sometimes construed rather narrowly. The theory of global traits draws renewed attention to the importance of investigations, especially longitudinal investigations, into the genetic and environmental origins of personality traits.

Function. The dynamic mechanisms through which global traits influence behavior remain poorly understood. As Allport hinted, they seem to involve the way individuals perceive situations and group them into equivalence classes. But the exact learning, motivational, and perceptual mechanisms involved, the way that different traits interact within individuals, and the circumstances under which a person can become consciously aware of his or her own traits are all issues needing further empirical examination.

Implication. Given that a person has a given level of a global trait, what kinds of behavioral predictions can be made accurately, into what kinds of situations? This *deductive* question will require further and more detailed examination of person-situation interactions. And, given that a person has performed a certain pattern of behavior across a certain set of situations, what can we conclude about his or her global traits? This *inductive* question will require close attention to the behavioral cues that laypersons use in their intuitive judgments of personality, and an empirical examination of the validity of these cues. Progress toward answering this question will help to provide a valid basis by which human social judgment can be evaluated and, therefore, improved (Funder, 1987).

In the current literature, these issues receive much less attention than they deserve. A neo-Allportian perspective may lead not only to a renewed examination of these central issues, but to progress in the study of personality's historic mission of integrating the various subfields of psychology into an understanding of whole, functioning individuals.

REFERENCES

Allport, G. W. (1931). What is a trait of persoanlity? *Journal of Abnormal and Social Psychology, 25,* 368–372.

Allport, G. W. (1937). *Personality: A psychological interpretation.* New York: Henry Holt & Co.

Allport, G. W. (1958). What units shall we employ? In G. Lindzey (Ed.), *Assessment of human motives* (pp. 239–260). New York: Rinehart.

Cantor, N., & Kihlstrom, J. F. (1987). *Personality and social intelligence.* Englewood CLiffs, NJ: Prentice-Hall.

Funder, D. C. (1987). Errors and mistakes: Evaluating the accuracy of social judgment. *Psychological Bulletin, 101,* 75–90

Funder, D. C. (1989). Accuracy in personality judgment and the dancing bear. In D. M. Buss & N. Cantor (Eds.), *Personality psychology: Recent trends and emerging directions* (pp. 210–223). New York: Springer-Verlag.

Zuroff, D. C. (1986). Was Gordon Allport a trait theorist? *Journal of Personality and Social Psychology, 51,* 993–1000.

KEY POINTS

1. Global traits refer to patterns of behaviors presumed to transcend time and specific situations. Funder asserts that modern personality theory should return to a focus on global traits.

2. There are three main dangers to movement away from global traits: new trait concepts will be framed too narrowly, will lose contact with traits as people understand them in everyday life, and will be misleading if they rely on frequencies of superficially similar behaviors.

3. The meaning of a behavior depends on context. A single behavior is ambiguous when taken out of context. Actions become less ambiguous in the context of the individual's other acts. Since every behavior is the product of multiple traits, however, disentangling the relationship between a given trait and a given behavior is extremely difficult.

4. Because global traits are manifested by patterns of perception and action in the social world, they must be a product of how one has learned to interact with that world. Traits can be unlearned as well.

5. The theory of global traits asserts that trait constructs should be intuitively meaningful because intuitively discernible traits are likely to have great social utility.

QUESTIONS TO THINK ABOUT

1. How might Allport have viewed the Neo-Allportian approach to personality?

2. Global traits have a central role in everyday, intuitive understanding of personality. Does the field of personality psychology benefit from this, or suffer because of it?

3. What are some dangers in moving away from global traits? How do these dangers affect our view of people and their behaviors?

4. What is the role of learning in the development of personality traits in Funder's view?

5. Do global traits have better explanatory power than narrower dispositional terms? How can global traits be used to explain situations, personalities, and behavior?

33

The Science and Politics of Comparing Women and Men*

ALICE H. EAGLY

A social psychologist, Alice Eagly (1938–) has not been satisfied with traditional socialization theories and trait theories regarding sex differences. Eagly offers her own theory, which describes the functions of social roles as the determinants of sex differences. According to this theory, the social-behavioral differences between the sexes are embedded in social roles, which include gender roles and roles pertaining to work and family life. She has conducted research in areas such as differences in leadership roles and differences in aggression between males and females.

A professor at Northwestern University, Eagly has critiqued evolutionary psychology from the perspective of social role theory. If sex differences are seen as determined by evolution, politicians may be quick to argue that it is "natural" that men should dominate political and economic systems. By showing that roles give us a parsimonious and less speculative explanation, Eagly provides an alternative theory for the origin of sex differences.

This selection focuses on how sex-difference research has been conducted, reported, and evaluated and on how those processes are influenced by societal trends and researchers' political agendas.

When psychologists publish research that compares the behavior of women and men, they face political as well as scientific issues. The political relevance of this work becomes apparent when it attracts media attention and is quickly incorporated into discourse on the status of women in society. Despite the intense interest on the part of journalists and the public, some psychologists have become uneasy about research that compares the sexes and now believe that such work ought to be discouraged (e.g., Ashmore, 1990; Baumeister, 1988). However, other psychologists welcome such research (e.g., Scarr, 1988). Although on the surface these disparate reactions can seem complex and confusing, they make sense in terms of the political and scientific issues that are entwined in comparing women and men. To elucidate these issues, in this article I review contemporary scientific research on sex-related differences, consider the political context of this research, and discuss the specific sources of the current

*Eagly, A. H. (1995). The science and politics of comparing women and men. *American Psychologist, 50*, 145–158. [Ed. note: All citations in the text of this selection have been left intact from the original, but the list of references includes only those sources that are the most relevant and important. Readers wishing to follow any of the other citations can find the full references in the original work or in an online database.]

stresses between the science and the politics of the research area.

CONTEMPORARY SCIENCE OF COMPARING THE SEXES

Although research psychologists have compared the sexes throughout the 20th century (see Morawski & Agronick, 1991; Rosenberg, 1982; Scarborough & Furumoto, 1987; Shields, 1975a, 1975b), systematic attempts to draw conclusions about differences and similarities did not move to center stage in psychology until the 1970s. Maccoby and Jacklin's (1974) book *The Psychology of Sex Differences* was a major force in bringing the research area to prominence. This volume represented an ambitious effort to synthesize all psychological research that had reported sex comparisons. This task was formidable by the early 1970s because many psychological studies had used participants of both sexes and included a statistical comparison of the two groups, although often as a minor feature.

On the basis of their catalog and evaluation of the extant research, Maccoby and Jacklin (1974) maintained that the sexes differed in several aspects of intellectual abilities (namely, verbal, quantitative, and spatial abilities) and in aggression. They concluded that evidence was insufficient to draw a definitive conclusion about some other aspects of social behavior. They also argued that there were no differences in still other classes of behaviors, despite cultural stereotypes that the sexes differ in these ways. Yet, aside from their generally skeptical conclusions about sex differences, Maccoby and Jacklin showed psychologists the richness of the research base available for examining sex differences empirically and raised many new questions about gender.

Inspired in large part by Maccoby and Jacklin's (1974) synthesis of the then-existing research, other psychologists turned to the available data to explore some of these questions more thoroughly. In the late 1970s and the 1980s some psychologists who used the same narrative reviewing strategy as Maccoby and Jacklin expressed even greater skepticism about the presence of sex differences in psychological findings. For example, Frodi, Macaulay, and Thome (1977) questioned Maccoby and Jacklin's claim that the sex difference in aggressive behavior is relatively clear-cut, and Caplan, MacPherson, and Tobin (1985) contested their claim that males have greater spatial ability than females.

Maccoby and Jacklin's (1974) book happened to appear a few years before the modern metamorphosis in synthesizing psychological research, the change from narrative to quantitative methods. Until late in the 1970s, synthesizing research had been a fairly informal process. Like Maccoby and Jacklin, most reviewers summarized studies and classified them by whether they obtained statistically significant findings. Reviewers typically stated a general conclusion based on what appeared to be the overall trend of findings, with this trend identified on the basis of a rough majority rule.

In contrast to these informal methods of drawing conclusions from research findings, quantitative or meta-analytic techniques provide statistically justified methods for synthesizing research (Cooper & Hedges, 1994; Hedges & Olkin, 1985; Rosenthal, 1991). Meta-analysts typically represent the comparison between male and female behavior for each relevant study in terms of its effect size (or *d*), which expresses the sex difference in units of the study's standard deviation. With each finding represented in this common metric, studies that compared women and men can be collectively represented by taking an average of their effect sizes. This central tendency is located somewhere along a quantitative continuum that runs from no difference to large differences and thus does not provide a simple yes or no answer to the question of whether the sexes differed in general in the available studies. By implying that a continuum is the best metaphor for thinking about sex differences and similarities, meta-analytic methods thus allow psychologists to escape the more simplistic debate about sameness versus difference. After the central tendency of the findings is placed along this continuum, a reviewer must interpret its meaning in terms of the specific research literature that has thereby been aggregated. Only then can questions about sex-related differences in a domain begin to be answered.

In interpreting the meaning of the central tendency of the effect sizes, the reviewer needs to take into account the entire distribution of the effect sizes and be particularly attentive to the consistency of the effect sizes across the studies. When an appropriate statistical test shows that the findings are inconsistent, the meta-analyst attempts to explain why they differ. This task, which can be described as a search for moderator variables, requires additional statistical analyses relating the characteristics of the studies to their effect sizes. Careful application of the methods of quantitative synthesis thus induces reviewers to scrutinize the particular ways in which the studies in a research literature differ from one another. Reviewers code the studies according to their varying characteristics and determine the extent to which studies with different attributes are associated with differing findings. This scrutiny of studies' characteristics ordinarily includes an evaluation of their quality, especially focusing on attributes of studies that could produce artifactual findings.

Although quantitative synthesis has various limitations and can do little to compensate for pervasive deficiencies in the underlying research literature (see Matt & Cook, 1994), it offers substantial gains over informal, narrative reviewing procedures. Most obviously, quantitative reviewers do not rely on statistical significance (i.e., p values) to interpret findings but invoke effect size metrics that are independent of studies' sample sizes. Also, descriptive and inferential statistics, rather than impressionistic techniques, are used to aggregate and integrate findings. In addition, major gains follow from quantitative reviewers' compliance with general procedural rules; for example, the rules that searches for relevant studies should be extremely thorough and that studies should be eliminated from a review

only by criteria that are explicitly stated and uniformly applied.

Even though quantitative synthesis is a rule-bound activity, it entails many subjective decisions, for example, in the selection of criteria for including and excluding studies from the sample and in the subsequent implementation of these criteria. In primary research too, researchers make many subjective decisions in designing a study and analyzing and presenting its data. Yet, primary researchers are expected to describe their methods and findings with precision to enable their decisions to be examined and criticized by the scientific community. Similarly, quantitative reviewers are expected to provide a detailed statement of their methods and findings. Just as in primary research careful replication of a study's procedures with participants from the same population should yield comparable findings, in quantitative synthesis careful replication of a reviewer's procedures should yield comparable findings.

Quantitative Syntheses of Sex-Related Differences in Cognitive Abilities

Research psychologists energetically applied these new methods to examine the performance of males and females on tests of cognitive abilities and intellectual achievement. The first of such efforts was Hyde's (1981) article, which appeared in the *American Psychologist* and covered the same studies of abilities that Maccoby and Jacklin (1974) had included in their narrative review. Subsequent reviewers examined not merely whether the sexes differ but whether any sex differences change in magnitude over the life cycle or over the decades for which research data were available (e.g., Feingold, 1988, 1993; Friedman, 1989; Hyde, Fennema, & Lamon, 1990; Hyde & Linn, 1988; Linn & Petersen, 1985, 1986; Masters & Sanders, 1993). Moreover, reviewers analyzed archival norms from standardized ability and achievement tests administered to millions of Americans, for example, the Preliminary Scholastic Aptitude Test (PSAT) and Scholastic Achievement Tests (SAT), the Wechsler Intelligence Scales, and the California Achievement Tests (e.g., Feingold, 1993; Marsh, 1989; see review by Wilder & Powell, 1989). Also, some quantitative syntheses explored the generalizability of sex-related differences in intellectual abilities to nations other than the United States (Born, Bleichrodt, & Van der Flier, 1987; Stumpf & Klieme, 1989), and others examined the generalizability of overall U.S. findings to various ethnic groups within the United States (Burton, Lewis, & Robertson, 1988; Hyde, Fennema, & Lamon, 1990). Finally, one synthesis examined male and female students' attitudes toward mathematics and their affect related to performance in this area (Hyde, Fennema, Ryan, Frost, & Hopp, 1990).

Considerable controversy surrounds the proper interpretation of these syntheses of cognitive abilities. Some psychologists have argued that their meta-analyses challenge Maccoby and Jacklin's (1974) conclusions by showing that sex differences in cognitive abilities are negligible in magnitude and moreover decrease in magnitude over time (e.g., Hyde, 1981, 1990, 1994). However, other psychologists have maintained that the available findings show some important sex differences (e.g., Halpern, 1989, 1992). In particular, sex differences in quantitative problem-solving remain nontrivial in populations of older adolescents and adults, despite clear-cut decreases in the magnitude of sex differences on general tests of verbal and quantitative ability in adolescent populations. Other researchers have emphasized that the representation of males and females can differ strongly in the tails of the distribution, consistent with the overrepresentation of boys in groups of gifted children and adolescents who are selected for high quantitative skills (e.g., Benbow, 1988; Benbow & Lubinski, 1993). This disproportionate representation of the sexes in highly selected samples appears to be a product of group differences in test score variability as well as central tendency (see Feingold, 1992b, 1994a, 1994c).

Syntheses that have examined how the characteristics of particular tests of intellectual abil-

ity affect the magnitude of sex differences have pinpointed certain aspects of verbal, spatial, and quantitative abilities for which sex differences are larger, even in adolescent populations. For example, differences in favor of males are more substantial on aspects of visuospatial ability, particularly on tests involving the mental rotation of three-dimensional figures (Linn & Petersen, 1985; Masters & Sanders, 1993). Differences in favor of females are more substantial on measures of verbal fluency, particularly on tests requiring that respondents produce words or sentences meeting certain requirements of meaning or form and on tests of speech production requiring rapid and accurate speech (Halpern, 1992; Hyde & Linn, 1988). Such findings have led some psychologists to treat sex differences in aspects of cognitive abilities as consequential (see Halpern, 1992; Hines, 1993; Kimura, 1992).

Quantitative Syntheses of Sex-Related Differences in Social Behavior and Personality

Social psychologists were very quick to take up quantitative reviewing after Maccoby and Jacklin's (1974) work raised new questions about whether aspects of social behavior are sex related. Most of the early meta-analyses examined large research literatures from experimental social psychology. Hall's (1978) pioneering meta-analysis on decoding nonverbal cues was followed by her numerous quantitative syntheses on other nonverbal behaviors as well as vocal behaviors (Hall, 1984; Hall & Halberstadt, 1986; Stier & Hall, 1984). Meta-analyses on conformity and influenceability followed rapidly (Becker, 1986; Cooper, 1979; Eagly & Carli, 1981; Lockheed, 1985). Female and male behavior was carefully examined in studies of empathy (Eisenberg & Lennon, 1983). Reviewers examined prosocial and antisocial tendencies of women and men, with quantitative syntheses devoted to helping behavior and aggressive behavior (Eagly & Crowley, 1986; Eagly & Steffen, 1986; Hyde, 1984). Meta-analyses of social interaction in task-oriented small groups investigated whether women were friendlier and more social than men and whether men were more narrowly task oriented than women (Anderson & Blanchard, 1982; Carli, 1982), whether men were more likely than women to emerge as leaders (Eagly & Karau, 1991), and whether group performance differed between all-male and all-female groups (Wood, 1987). In syntheses that included both organizational and laboratory studies, meta-analysts examined whether the style and the effectiveness of leaders and managers differed according to their sex (Eagly & Johnson, 1990; Eagly, Karau, & Makhijani, 1995).

Quantitative reviewers have examined whether men differ from women in other tendencies important to social behavior, for example, in the qualities they prefer in mates (Feingold, 1990, 1991, 1992a) and their disclosure of personal concerns to others (Dindia & Allen, 1992). Other meta-analyses concerned sexual behavior and attitudes (Oliver & Hyde, 1993; Whitley & Kite, 1995), the life satisfaction or happiness that women and men report in surveys (Wood, Rhodes, & Whelan, 1989), and the incidence of mental illnesses, especially depression, in populations of women and men (Nolen-Hoeksema, 1987). Syntheses have examined female and male personality traits, as assessed by personality tests and inventories (Feingold, 1994b), and personality growth in adolescence and adulthood (Cohn, 1991). Finally, other syntheses have concerned sex-related differences in activity level and in motor behaviors, such as reaction time, flexibility, throw distance, and grip strength (Eaton & Enns, 1986; J. R. Thomas & French, 1985).

The databases that reviewers have synthesized from social, personality, organizational, clinical, and sport psychology have various limitations. Some research areas, especially those produced mainly by experimental social psychologists, overrepresent samples of college students. In addition, the span of years over which studies were conducted is too limited in some domains to allow secular trends to be adequately investigated. Nonetheless, the available analyses suggest no consistent tendency for sex differences in social behavior and personality to have eroded or increased over time. Fortunately, there is some evidence concerning the generalizability of findings to other than U.S. and Canadian populations (Buss et al., 1990; Feingold, 1994b; Nolen-Hoeksema, 1987), but the studies available to reviewers rarely allow them to examine the generalizability of overall findings to subcultures in the United States and Canada. Nonetheless, an extraordinarily large amount of psychological data on male and female social behavior and personality has been systematically integrated in recent years.

The psychologists who have conducted most of these syntheses of sex-related differences in social behavior and personality are in general agreement that their meta-analytic findings yield evidence of differences. A major theme of much of the interpretive writing based on these new syntheses is that empirical research has provided evidence for numerous nontrivial differences (e.g., Eagly, 1987, 1993; Eagly & Wood, 1991; Hall, 1984, 1987; Wood & Rhodes, 1992). In general, conclusions based on these new syntheses usually depart from Maccoby and Jacklin's (1974) description of sex differences in the direction of claiming considerably more evidence that important aspects of social interaction and personality are differentiated by sex. In agreement with these conclusions, other social scientists have used societal data (i.e., crime statistics) to demonstrate that social behavior is differentiated by sex (e.g., Daly & Wilson, 1988; Kenrick & Trost, 1993).

Theories of Sex Differences and Similarities

There was something of a hiatus in the development of theories about sex-related differences in the decade after Maccoby and Jacklin's (1974) book was published because the zeitgeist among research psychologists was one of doubting the existence of these phenomena. In view of the tentative consensus among research psychologists in the 1970s that sex-related differences are generally null or small, it is understandable that contemporary investigators have directed much of their attention to the narrow question of whether there are any manifest differences in intellectual performance, social behavior, and personality. Because research syntheses of the 1980s and 1990s provided increasing evidence of differences, especially in social behavior and personality, psychologists began to develop theories to explain these differences. It is of course true that empirical findings take on meaning and importance to the extent that they become interpretable within theories that explain the antecedents of the findings. Reflecting a shift from description to explanation, the question of whether sex differences exist has evolved into the more demanding question of why the sexes sometimes differ considerably and at other times differ moderately or minimally or do not differ at all.

Favored by social psychologists are several theories that feature status, social roles, and gender-based expectancies about one's own and others' behavior. Status theorists emphasize the higher social status that follows from being male rather than female in society and argue that many sex differences are thinly disguised status differences (e.g., Geis, 1993; Ridgeway & Diekema, 1992). In status theories, the mechanism by which men's higher social status produces behavioral sex differences is that people expect more competent and authoritative behavior from higher status people and constrain social interaction in ways that foster these outcomes. Social role theory also emphasizes shared expectations that apply differentially to women and men but highlights a wider set of expectancies than those associated with status (Eagly, 1987). For example, the expectations that women are warm, friendly, nurturant, and emotionally supportive do not follow in simple fashion from women's lower status. According to social-role theory, the root cause of sex-correlated expectations about behavior is that women and men are differently distributed into family and occupational roles in the society. Other social psychologists, especially Deaux and Major (1987), have analyzed the detailed features

of social interaction and of people's self-concepts that determine the extent to which expectancies about women and men are translated into gendered behavior.

Currently popular among developmental psychologists (and some other social scientists) is the "separate cultures" idea that children learn rules for social interaction from experience in largely sex-segregated peer groups in childhood and then carry this teaming into adult social interaction (e.g., Maccoby, 1990; Maltz & Borker, 1982; Tannen, 1990). Other developmental psychologists continue to pursue perspectives such as social learning theory, cognitive developmental theory, and gender schema theory (e.g., see review by Jacklin & Reynolds, 1993).

Another highly visible class of theories of sex-correlated differences is evolutionary psychology, which features principles of evolution—especially sexual selection—and predicts that female behavior and male behavior differ in domains in which the sexes have faced different adaptive problems. Although evolutionary theory was once applied mainly to nonhuman species (see Daly & Wilson, 1983), recent work by psychologists has focused on testing hypotheses about human social behavior (Buss & Schmitt, 1993; Kenrick, 1994).

The discourse surrounding these theories is sometimes contentious, especially across the divide between theories that give primacy to biological factors and those that give primacy to environmental factors. Although scientists committed to biological or environmentalist theories often pay lip service to interactionist perspectives that take both positions into account, generally these theorists do not take sophisticated versions of the other type of theory into account. Theories can be divided along different lines, however. Biological and developmental theories treat sex differences as arising mainly from essential qualities that are built into the person, whereas social psychological theories generally regard sex differences as arising constructively as a byproduct of social interaction (Bohan, 1993; Kahn & Yoder, 1989; Ridgeway, 1992). Although all of these theories can predict that certain sex differences should be prevalent, different theories tend to focus on different classes of behaviors. For example, evolutionary psychology focuses primarily on behaviors closely related to reproduction (e.g., mate selection), whereas social psychological and developmental theories focus on a wider variety of behaviors.

All theories of sex differences have the task of explaining not just overall differences in various behaviors but also the patterning of these differences across studies and therefore across social settings. Thus, for most general classes of behaviors such as aggression, some studies produce large differences, most produce smaller differences, and a few may yield reversals of the typical direction of the difference. Because quantitative syntheses describe sex differences in each domain by a set of effect sizes, each representing a particular study, the variation that sex comparisons show across contexts is clearly discernible and invites the testing and refinement of theories.

THE POLITICAL CONTEXT OF RESEARCH THAT COMPARES THE SEXES

So far, this article has presented a rather dispassionate description of research psychologists' efforts to understand whether and why female behavior and male behavior differ. The story is like many other stories that could be told about research in psychology. There have been repeated efforts to establish or discount various phenomena, with increasingly sophisticated methods applied. After phenomena were discovered in abundance, theories have bloomed. Yet this description of scientific progress has left out the larger cultural and ideological context of this research. Placing this research area in context produces a political story, the story of why research psychologists have taken so much interest in comparing the sexes and why some now suggest that this interest is misplaced.

Understood in its cultural context, this research area should be viewed as intertwined with the history of feminism as a social and intellec-

tual movement in American society. Just as feminist empiricists active in the early decades of the century were important contributors to the intellectual side of the first women's movement of the 20th century (see Rosenberg, 1982; Scarborough & Furumoto, 1987), it was as part of a broader feminist movement that contemporary researchers have challenged assumptions about women's inferiority. The timing of Maccoby and Jacklin's (1974) book was hardly accidental but reflected the emergence of the modern feminist movement in the United States. As the society and the media questioned traditional assumptions about women's roles, feminist researchers in psychology questioned their discipline's assumptions about women's abilities and behavior.

Maccoby and Jacklin's (1974) skeptical message about the existence of sex differences should be understood in the context of the larger critique that feminism provided of psychologists' rather limited efforts to understand gender. One central target of feminist criticism was research and writing on sex differences. Feminists argued that psychologists' claims about sex differences falsely portrayed women as inferior to men. Some of the rhetoric was heated: Bernard (1974), for example, called studies of sex differences "battle weapons against women" (p. 13). Shields (1975a), in a widely read article, exposed the sexist biases in early writing about maternal instinct and sex differences in the size and structure of the human brain. Feminist writing of the 1970s generally portrayed research purportedly demonstrating sex differences as largely prescientific and obviously faulty or, if the research was more modern, as riddled with artifacts, methodological deficiencies, and unexplained inconsistencies in findings (e.g., Sherif, 1979).

Many psychologists, for the most part women, then started studying sex differences and similarities from a feminist perspective. Implicit or explicit in much of this work was the expectation that methodologically sound comparisons of women and men would raise women's status by dispelling people's stereotypes about women. In fact, much gender research reflected two missions: revealing people's damaging stereotypes and attitudes concerning women and displaying the absence of stereotypic sex differences in behavior, traits, and abilities (see Eagly, 1987). Much feminist research on sex differences was (and still is) intended to shatter stereotypes about women's characteristics and change people's attitudes by proving that women and men are essentially equivalent in their personalities, behavioral tendencies, and intellectual abilities (e.g., Caplan et al., 1985; Fischer, 1993). Caught up in the passions of a burgeoning social movement, many feminist psychologists, including the author of this article (Eagly, 1978), had a relatively uncomplicated vision of what empirical research on sex differences would yield. Properly analyzed to remove artifacts, this research would yield null findings or, at least, differences that could be described as trivially small.

Null findings were congenial to many feminist psychologists not only because they would challenge gender stereotypes but also because sameness was thought to increase women's chances for equal opportunity in the society. To the extent that the "gender-neutral" strategy of making no distinctions between women and men leads to gender equality (see Bem, 1993), scientific research showing that women are not different from men should help ensure women equal access to a variety of roles from which they were excluded. In contrast, evidence of differences might be seen as disqualifying women in relation to certain roles and opportunities and as justifying unequal treatment under the law. For other psychologists, scientific demonstrations that women and men differ seemed to conflict with the ideals of egalitarianism (e.g., Baumeister, 1988). Indeed, the equalitarianism issue can be raised in relation to virtually all research examining differences between social groups.

Despite most feminist empiricists' advocacy of the view that sex differences are small or null, psychology has offered a countertheme in the writings of other feminists who have accepted the existence of certain sex-related differences, primarily those that display women's nurturance and concern for other people. Much of this writing has reflected mainly qualitative methods of producing and examining evidence and thus reflects a different tradition than the formal empiricism that underlies the writing of feminist empiricists. For example, Gilligan (1982) argued that the moral reasoning of women and men differs, with women tending to adopt a care perspective and men a justice perspective. Chodorow (1978) maintained that women's relational skills and desire to form close relationships follow from their experiences as mothers and their successful re-creation of these aspects of personality in their daughters. Other feminist writers have similarly argued that behavior is sex differentiated and praised those aspects of behavior that they ascribed to women (e.g., Helgesen, 1990; Ruddick, 1989). Indeed, the disjunction between those feminist psychologists who have argued in favor of difference and the feminist empiricists, who generally have argued in favor of similarity, led Hare-Mustin and Marecek (1988) to describe the psychology of gender in terms of contrasting biases, which they named *alpha bias*, a preference to exaggerate differences, and *beta bias*, a preference to minimize them.

QUESTIONS UNDERLYING THE CONTEMPORARY STRESSES BETWEEN SCIENCE AND POLITICS

The flood of scientific research on sex differences that followed the modern reemergence of the feminist movement has failed to present psychologists with an absence of differences between the sexes but instead has provided considerably more varied and challenging outcomes. The new wave of research on sex-related differences has encountered a negative reaction from many feminist psychologists (see Hare-Mustin & Marecek, 1988; Kahn & Yoder, 1989; Matlin, 1993a; Mednick, 1991), and this lack of enthusiasm should not be surprising. During the 1970s research psychologists had already enjoyed some success in shaping a scientific consensus about the triviality of sex differences. Indeed, this view has become quite widely accepted in the scientific community and strongly influences contemporary textbook presentations of gender research.

Despite the meta-analytic evidence (and other types of evidence) showing many consequential sex differences, many feminist empiricists have worked energetically to preserve the 1970s scientific consensus that sex-related differences are null or small. Such a reaction is routine in science: Mere research findings rarely displace an entrenched consensus. To examine the means by which the 1970s consensus has been protected, it is useful to examine the specific points most commonly made by critics when countering the onslaught of contemporary research documenting sex-differentiated behavior.

Are Sex Differences Small?

One very popular argument is that virtually all sex differences have been shown to be small (e.g., Archer, 1987; Deaux, 1984; Lott, 1991; Matlin, 1993b). The extent to which sex-correlated differences warrant description as small, medium, or large is an issue that has begun to receive detailed and careful analysis. Any sensible perspective for judging the magnitude of research findings requires that magnitude be regarded as a relative matter. This relativity stems from the influence that particular traditions of measurement and observation have on the magnitude of findings. Factors such as unreliability and invalidity of measures lower the magnitude of findings, and the percentage of variability that can be explained by systematic factors is usually far less than 100. Therefore, to judge the size of sex-difference findings, methodological features of a research area ought to be carefully evaluated. To help gauge the impact that these methodological features have on effect magnitude, differences produced by comparing women and men should be judged in relation to other known findings, preferably on the same classes of dependent variables.

Even though the magnitude of effects should be given careful evaluation in relation to the specific features of each area of empirical research, it is somewhat helpful to keep in mind some general benchmarks or standards of comparison. One such baseline follows from Lipsey and Wilson's (1993) survey of 302 separate meta-analyses on the efficacy of psychological, educational, and behavioral treatments (e.g., psychotherapy, smoking-cessation programs, and computer-aided instruction). These meta-analyses encompassed a very wide range of outcome variables, including many of the dependent variables that have been examined in syntheses of sex differences. Although the mean effects produced by the individual meta-analyses varied considerably in magnitude, their overall average was about 0.5 in terms of the d metric. In other words, the typical treatment designed and carried out by psychologists and other experts improved the status of the treatment group over the control group by about one half of a standard deviation on appropriate outcome measures. Lipsey and Wilson argued persuasively that effects of this size have considerable practical and clinical significance.

Cohen (1977) suggested some guidelines for interpreting the magnitude of effects in psychology, and quantitative reviewers have frequently invoked these general benchmarks, even though they were not derived in a formal way from empirical research. Cohen's guidelines, expressed in terms of the d metric, are that 0.20 is a small effect, 0.50 is a moderate effect, and 0.80 is a large effect. Cohen argued that small effect sizes are generally found in new research areas lacking good experimental or measurement control, that medium effect sizes correspond to group differences that people would normally notice in daily life ("visible to the naked eye" p. 26), and that large differences correspond to group differences that are very readily perceived ("grossly perceptible" p. 27). For differences labeled *small* by Cohen's criteria, the distributions of scores in the two groups that are compared are 15% nonoverlapping and 85% overlapping. For medium differences the distributions are 33% nonoverlapping and 67% overlapping, and for large differences the distributions are 47% nonoverlapping and 53% overlapping. It is thus important to note that even findings that are relatively large in the general domain of psychological findings produce distributions that substantially overlap.

Baselines for particular types of research would be more useful than general guidelines such as Lipsey and Wilson's (1993) treatment effect and Cohen's (1977) benchmarks. More specialized baselines for judging sex-related differences can be generated by examining mean effect sizes produced by specific quantitative syntheses examining the effects of independent variables other than sex. For example, Eagly's (1987) review of a number of such syntheses from various areas of social psychology suggested that modal effects are small to moderate by Cohen's standards, even for well-known and widely accepted phenomena such as the effects of mood on helping behavior and the social facilitation of task performance. In summary, a best guess, informed by findings of quantitative syntheses and less formal observations of research, is that in most areas of psychological research mean effect sizes are often in some moderate range of around one half of a standard deviation or less; considerably larger effect sizes are relatively unusual.

How do sex differences fare relative to these very rough standards for magnitude? Ashmore (1990, Table 19.1) presented mean effect sizes from many quantitative reviews of sex-related differences. Subsequent to Ashmore's survey, Oliver and Hyde (1993, Table 2) presented mean effect sizes for many aspects of sexual behavior and attitudes, and Feingold (1994b, Tables 5 and 6) presented mean effect sizes for performance on numerous personality tests and inventories. Ashmore conveniently classified the mean effect sizes he reviewed in relation to Cohen's (1977) benchmarks for small, medium, and large effects and found that substantial numbers of mean effect sizes fell into each of the resulting magnitude categories. Oliver and Hyde also reported effect sizes in all three ranges of magnitude, as did Feingold.

Consistent with these summaries, it is clear that some sex-difference findings warrant being described as large—substantially larger than the 5% of the variance figure ($d = 0.46$) that Deaux (1984) suggested is an upper boundary for sex differences. These large effects, which should be considered large relative to typical phenomena examined by psychologists, occur with respect to at least one test of cognitive abilities (e.g., Shepard-Metzler test of mental rotation), some social behaviors (e.g., facial expressiveness and frequency of filled pauses in speech), some sexual behaviors (e.g., incidence of masturbation and attitudes toward casual sexual intercourse), one class of personality traits (tenderminded and nurturant tendencies), and some physical abilities (e.g., the velocity, distance, and accuracy of throwing a ball). Yet, most aggregated sex-difference findings appear to be in the small-to-moderate range that appears to be more typical of psychological research. Therefore, when research that has compared the sexes is judged in relation to reasonable benchmarks for judging psychological findings, it does not support descriptions of sex-related differences as routinely small or as generally smaller than other types of findings of interest to psychologists.

Although it would be accurate to describe sex differences and similarities as located along a continuum of magnitude, the writers of psychology textbooks often accompany any reports of sex comparisons by the warning that the differences are small. They seem not to realize that many of these differences are on the whole comparable to the other findings they have reviewed in their textbooks, findings not accompanied by any warnings about their small magnitude or about overlapping distributions. Some psychologists have even recommended that all sex comparisons should be accompanied by a percentage variance "tag" attached to them (McHugh, Koeske, & Frieze, 1986). Unless these tags are added to all effects that are reported for a study (or in a textbook), such a practice would trivialize a particular class of findings because most readers would be unaware that the percentage of variance accounted for by any one variable is ordinarily a small number in psychological research.

The percentage of variance metric that is often applied to sex differences frequently misleads psychologists into discounting findings that have considerable practical importance, as many methodologists have explained (Abelson, 1985; Prentice & Miller, 1992; Rosenthal, 1990; Rosenthal & Rubin, 1979; Sechrest & Yeaton, 1982). Unfortunately, few psychologists, including experienced researchers, have an adequate understanding of the practical significance of effect sizes when they are expressed in terms of percentage of variance (e.g., r^2, η^2, and Ω^2). For example, to illustrate this point, Abelson calculated that in major league baseball the percentage of variance in any single batting performance that is explained by batting skill is approximately 0.3. Yet, the effects of individual batters' skill cumulate over time and across players, producing a much larger effect of batting skill on team success. Similarly, Rosenthal (1990) noted that an experiment on the effects of aspirin on reducing heart attacks was ended prematurely because aspirin's demonstrated effectiveness made it unethical to withhold the treatment from the placebo control group. Yet the aspirin treatment accounted for only 0.1% of the variance in heart-attack incidence, a percentage that seems exceedingly small. An experiment on the effects of the drug propranolol was terminated with the same rationale, despite the fact that the treatment accounted for only 0.2% of the variance in death rates.

Metrics other than percentage of variance provide more intuitive and useful descriptions of the magnitude of effects, including sex differences. For example, Rosenthal and Rubin (1982) advocated use of the binomial effect size display, which translates an effect into a comparison of the percentages of cases that exceed some criterion in two groups. For sex-related differences, the binomial effect size display would compare the percentage of women who are above the overall median of the combined female and male distribution with the percentage of men who are above this median. For example, a researcher might be tempted to dismiss the sex difference in social smiling reported in one of Hall's (1984) meta-analyses as unimportant because it accounted for a mere 9% of the variability in smiling. However, description in terms of the more intuitively meaningful metric of the binomial effect size display indicates that above-average amounts of smiling occurred for 65% of women and 35% of men.

Another useful metric, the common language effect size statistic, was presented by McGraw and Wong (1992). This metric indexes the percentage of occasions on which a score randomly sampled from one distribution exceeds a score randomly sampled from another distribution. For example, McGraw and Wong reported data from the American College Testing Program's (ACT) test of math achievement showing that sex accounted for 5.4% of the variation in performance, with boys scoring higher than girls. Although this percentage may seem trivially small, repeated comparisons of randomly selected boys and girls would show that on 63% of the occasions the boy's score would exceed the girl's score. Descriptions of group differences in terms of the common language effect size indicator thus convey the meaning of the findings in everyday terms. In sum, whereas metrics that assess percentage of variance fail to convey the practical importance of effects and have contributed to the perception that sex-related differences are routinely small, alternative metrics foster more accurate understanding of how these group differences would appear in daily life.

The evaluation of the meaning and importance of sex-related differences should not end with the translation of them into metrics that are easily understood. In practical terms, the importance of a difference depends on the consequences of the behavior in natural settings (see Eagly, 1987). A behavioral difference represented by an extremely small effect size could be very important if people value and closely monitor performance of that behavior, as Abelson's (1985) baseball example illustrates. A difference represented by a very large effect size could be unimportant because little value is attached to relative performance of the behavior. These vital issues have received very little systematic analysis. Readers who learn, for example, that boys would score higher than girls in 63% of randomly selected pairs of girls and boys who took the ACT test of math achievement may be left to their own devices to figure out the implications of this description (e.g., for the distribution of funds for college scholarships).

Are Sex Differences Especially Inconsistent Across Studies?

Another theme in contemporary feminist writing is that sex differences are context dependent and inconsistent (e.g., Archer, 1987; Deaux, 1984; Lott, 1991; Matlin, 1993b). Although this point is in accord with contemporary evidence, it does not necessarily follow that sex-related differences are unusually inconsistent across studies. The extent of these inconsistencies should be judged in relation to other psychological research, just as effect magnitude should be judged in relation to other research.

To provide a formal analysis of the inconsistency of research findings across studies, quantitative reviewers calculate a statistical index that expresses the degree of homogeneity versus heterogeneity of the findings in the sample of studies (Hedges & Olkin, 1985). In syntheses of research on psychological hypotheses, this index ordinarily shows that the findings are inconsistent. In the presence of inconsistency, an additional analysis that a reviewer may perform is to identify outliers among the effect sizes and sequentially remove them until consistency (i.e., homogeneity) is attained according to a statistical standard. Hedges (1987) calculated such outlier analyses for a variety of domains of psychological research and found that removal of fewer than 20% of the effect sizes ordinarily produced a homogeneous set of effect sizes. Meta-analyses of sex differences that have used these techniques have found that the proportions of out-

liers among the effect sizes could be considered quite moderate, that is, within the bounds that Hedges's analyses suggested may be typical of psychological research (see Eagly & Johnson, 1990; Eagly & Karau, 1991; Eagly et al., 1995). This lack of extreme inconsistency in findings, despite evidence that social context is important to female and male behavior, could reflect many factors, especially the tendency for certain contexts to be much more common than others, in research and in daily life.

The idea that sensitivity to context does not set sex-difference findings apart from other classes of findings agrees with observations that variability across studies is a typical feature of psychological research. As Rosnow and Rosenthal (1989) noted, "there is growing awareness in psychology that just about everything under the sun is context dependent in one way or another" (p. 1280). Examples of the context dependence of research abound in all areas of psychological research. For example, research on attitude change has established that the impact of message recipients' involvement on the persuasiveness of messages depends on the particular type of involvement activated and the quality of the arguments contained in the message (Johnson & Eagly, 1989). Under some circumstances involvement increases the persuasiveness of messages, whereas in other circumstances it decreases their persuasiveness. Many well-known theories in psychology are in fact built around contextual factors, for example, contingency theories of leadership, which hold that relations between leadership style and leaders' effectiveness are moderated by situational variables (e.g., Fiedler & Chemers, 1984; House, 1971).

Inconsistencies in sex-related differences are not random but generally prove to be explicable, at least to some extent, in terms of methodological dissimilarities between studies (e.g., differences in measuring instruments, stimulus materials, and social settings). Quantitative reviewers routinely test hypotheses about inconsistencies in sex-difference findings by calculating statistical models that use study characteristics to predict effect size. For example, Eagly and Crowley's (1986) synthesis of helping behavior studies determined that effect magnitude varied with several features of the studies, such as the presence versus absence of an audience of people who could observe research participants' helpful behavior. Syntheses of research on intellectual performance have found that test content explains some of the variability in sex differences (e.g., for mathematics, the cognitive level and mathematics content of tests are important; see Hyde, Fennema, & Lamon, 1990). The identification of such moderator variables fosters the development of theories of sex-related differences and allows psychologists to produce generalizations that take context into account.

Are Sex-Difference Findings Artifactual?

Other arguments discounting differences consist of various hypotheses about artifacts. One idea is that there is a publication bias in favor of statistically significant comparisons between the sexes (e.g., Hyde, 1991; Unger & Crawford, 1992). Yet, in many research areas sex comparisons have typically been peripheral to the studies' main hypotheses and therefore not relevant to publishability. Therefore, what particularly deserves further study is the willingness of researchers to report comparisons between the sexes. Although one conventional rule in reporting research is to mention only significant findings, the null hypothesis has many good friends in research comparing the sexes. To some researchers, nonsignificant sex comparisons may thus seem more worthy of inclusion in a research report than other classes of nonsignificant findings.

Some critics think that research on sex-related differences takes insufficient account of a whole range of other potential artifacts (e.g., Basow, 1986). For example, in experimental social psychology, some studies have confounded the sex of the subject with the sex of the stimulus person (or experimenter or interaction partner) by creating only same-sex combinations. Such designs would leave unresolved the issue of whether any sex-correlated differences are produced by the sex of the study participant (see Harris, 1994). Another criticism is that some sex-difference findings are based on people's ratings of themselves and others and therefore may reflect biases of observers, who were influenced by demand characteristics or stereotypic assumptions about behavior (see Eisenberg & Lennon, 1983).

Analysis of study quality, including these sources of potential artifact, is one of the most distinctive features of the quantitative syntheses that have become increasingly important in discussions of sex differences (see Wortman, 1994). Typically, studies that are completely uninterpretable are excluded from meta-analyses at the outset. Reviewers usually code the remaining studies on numerous quality-relevant features to empirically assess the impact of each component of study quality. Because of the power that meta-analytic techniques give reviewers to examine study quality empirically, potential methodological deficiencies receive more systematic consideration than in the past.

Quantitative syntheses have also raised some new issues about potential research artifacts. An example of such an issue is Eagly and Carli's (1981) discovery of a relation between the sex of the authors of studies on conformity and persuasion and the sex-difference outcomes of their research. This provocative finding is open to various interpretations, some of which were then explored in a subsequent meta-analysis of these studies (Becker, 1986). In addition, the relation between authors' sex and the findings they report has been examined in meta-analyses of other behaviors (e.g., Eagly & Johnson, 1990; Eagly & Karau, 1991; Thomas & French, 1985; Wood, 1987). The attention given to the impact of authors' sex on research findings reflects the concern that quantitative reviewers have about the possibility of artifacts in research findings.

The definition of *artifact* is itself a critical issue in research comparing the sexes. Most researchers interpret *artifact* in terms of features of research methods (e.g., stimulus materials and test items) that would bias study outcomes. For example, respondents' performance on general tests of intellectual performance can be improved through familiarity with the particular situations described in the test items (e.g., the situations used to construct math story problems; see Wilder & Powell, 1989). Researchers would presumably agree that a test including a larger proportion of items whose content is familiar to one sex could produce an artifactual sex difference. A different issue is whether the groups of female and male participants who are compared in a study should be equated on background variables on which they ordinarily differ if control of these variables would diminish a sex difference (see Parlee, 1981). For example, boys take somewhat more mathematics courses than girls, and this difference in academic background accounts for some but not all of the sex difference in performance on mathematics tests such as the PSAT and SAT (see Wilder & Powell, 1989). If boys' and girls' performances on such tests are compared without controlling for courses taken, should any difference favoring boys be deemed a partial artifact of courses taken? The most appropriate interpretation would be that courses taken is causally relevant to the manifest difference in test performance, not that differences in courses taken produce an artifact.

Do Sex-Difference Findings Disconfirm Gender Stereotypes?

The outcomes of empirical research on sex differences pose a special challenge to psychologists who wish to claim that this research has disconfirmed people's stereotypes about gender or at least exposed gender stereotypes as exaggerations of reality (e.g., Matlin, 1993b; Unger & Crawford, 1992). The hope that research would counter cultural stereotypes was central to the endeavor of many feminist empiricists because of the power that gender stereotypes possess to foster traditional roles for women (see Eagly &

Mladinic, 1994; Jost & Banaji, 1994). Contrary to this hope, the results of quantitative syntheses have produced findings that conform to people's ideas about the sexes. For example, thematic analysis of demonstrated sex differences in social behavior suggests that they conform to stereotypic expectations that women are communal and men are agentic (see Eagly, 1987, 1993; Eagly & Wood, 1991). In general, women tend to manifest behaviors that can be described as socially sensitive, friendly, and concerned with others' welfare, whereas men tend to manifest behaviors that can be described as dominant, controlling, and independent.

More formal empirical evidence of the general accuracy of people's gender stereotypes was provided by Swim's (1994) demonstration that subjects' estimates of differences between the sexes predicted with considerable success the mean effect sizes that had been obtained in available meta-analyses (e.g., on cognitive abilities, nonverbal behaviors, and social behaviors such as aggression and helping). Moreover, in most instances, Swim's subjects tended either to be accurate about the magnitude of sex differences or to underestimate them. Swim's conclusion about accuracy can be contrasted with Martin's (1987) earlier claim that gender stereotypes exaggerate actual differences. Yet Martin's research examined study participants' estimates of the proportions of men and women who have various characteristics and compared these estimates with male and female participants' self-reports of whether they possessed the characteristics. Unfortunately, self-reports may be poor indicants of the behavioral sex differences that underlie gender stereotypes because social pressures often cause people to behave gender stereotypically even when such behavior is not consistent with their self-concepts.

Also relevant to the accuracy of gender stereotypes are several quantitative syntheses that obtained judges' estimates of female and male behavior for each of the reviewed studies (Eagly & Crowley, 1986; Eagly & Karau, 1991;

Eagly & Steffen, 1986). Specifically, to provide data relevant to stereotype accuracy, student judges estimated male and female behavior after reading a brief description of the particular behavior examined in each of the studies that had provided a comparison of men's and women's behavior. The correlations between these estimates, which represented students' gender stereotypes, and the actual behavioral sex differences in the studies, assessed by their effect sizes, were positive and significant (e.g., Eagly & Crowley, 1986, Table 5; Eagly & Karau, 1991, Table 6; Eagly & Steffen, 1986, Table 5). In showing that the student judges were successful in taking the particular characteristics of the studies into account in making their estimates of female and male behavior, these findings demonstrate some of the detail and subtlety of people's ideas about women and men.

One reason that Swim's (1994) conclusion that, on the whole, people generally do not exaggerate sex differences may seem surprising is that many discussions of gender stereotypes seem to presume that stereotypes portray women and men as very different, that is, as polar opposites. Because empirical research on male and female behavior finds overlapping distributions of men and women, this research might be thought to disconfirm gender stereotypes. Given these assumptions, gender stereotypes would be exaggerations of true differences between the sexes, consistent with the idea that the categorization of people into groups accentuates the perception of differences between the groups (e.g., Tajfel, 1981). However, people's beliefs have been shown to represent the sexes as partially overlapping groups, possessing different average levels of various attributes (Deaux, 1984; Eagly, 1987; Swim, 1994). In general, although the issue of stereotype accuracy invites further analysis (see Judd & Park, 1993), considerable evidence suggests that laypeople, once maligned as misguided holders of gender stereotypes, are fairly accurate observers of female and male behavior. The assumption that gender stereotypes exag-

gerate reality has yet to receive convincing empirical support.

In view of the substantial match that has been demonstrated between people's gender stereotypes and actual behavioral differences between the sexes, psychologists should now worry that research on sex differences confirms gender stereotypes; it tells people that there is at least a kernel of truth in many of their ideas. This dawning realization is no doubt one source of the heightened tension that surrounds research that compares the sexes. Those who have immersed themselves in this area of science have begun to realize that it is not cultural stereotypes that have been shattered by contemporary psychological research but the scientific consensus forged in the feminist movement of the 1970s. Perhaps the idea that people's ideas about the sexes would be very misguided probably never should have seemed so plausible to psychologists, given the large amount of information that people process about women and men on a daily basis (see Jussim, 1991).

The Persistence of Unsupported Claims About the Findings of Studies That Have Compared the Sexes

Four popular generalizations about sex-difference research—that findings are small, especially inconsistent, often artifactual, and inconsistent with stereotypic differences—have received close empirical examination in recent years. This scrutiny suggests that these generalizations are in need of revision. A more accurate interpretation of the results of empirical research would be that the magnitude and the consistency across studies of sex-difference findings show a range of values that is probably fairly typical of the range of values produced for many other areas of inquiry in psychology. Potential artifacts have been increasingly taken into account before conclusions have been drawn about sex differences. In addition, demonstrated sex differences have proven to be generally consistent with gender stereotypes.

Nonetheless, an outdated scientific consensus on these issues continues to be reiterated in contemporary psychology textbooks (e.g., Lips, 1993; Matlin, 1993b; Morris, 1993; Santrock, 1994; Wade & Tavris, 1990) and in some of the trade books on gender that draw on psychological research (e.g., Tavris, 1992).

CONCLUSION

The common description of empirical research as showing that sex-related differences are small, unusually unstable across studies, very often artifactual, and inconsistent with gender stereotypes arose in part from a feminist commitment to gender similarity as a route to political equality. It also arose from piecemeal and inadequate interpretations of the relevant empirical research. These interpretations failed to place research on sex-related differences in the context of other psychological research and often implied that findings that were very ordinary (in terms of magnitude, consistency, etc.) were rather exceptional. Given the new understanding of empirical findings that is evolving, research psychologists should think more deeply about the purposes for which their research may be used. Is psychological research that compares the sexes beneficial or harmful? Does this research foster or hinder the social change that would increase gender equality? These are many-sided questions that are addressed only in preliminary fashion in this article to stimulate debate.

The fear is often expressed in feminist writing that differences become deficiencies for women because women are an oppressed group (e.g., Unger & Crawford, 1992). Anxiety about sex differences is especially strong to the extent that scientists favor biological explanations, because this approach might produce a portrayal of women as innately inferior to men. Yet, contemporary research that has systematically examined whether the traits and behaviors ascribed to women are regarded as inferior to those ascribed to men has not found evidence for this generalized unfavorable perception of women

(Eagly & Mladinic, 1994; Eagly, Mladinic, & Otto, 1991). This research has shown that the stereotype of women is more positive overall than the stereotype of men, at least in contemporary samples of U.S. and Canadian college students. To the extent that behavioral differences truly do mirror people's stereotypes, scientific research may thus reveal a pattern of differences that shows both sexes to have strengths and deficiencies but that portrays women somewhat more favorably than men, on the whole. Nonetheless, the favorability of the female stereotype may be a mixed blessing because the particular kinds of positive characteristics most often ascribed to women, primarily "niceness–nurturance" qualities, probably contribute to the exclusion of women from certain kinds of high-status roles (e.g., those that are thought to require toughness and aggressiveness). At any rate, the sex differences that scientists have documented do not tell a simple tale of female inferiority.

The possible uses for findings that have demonstrated sex-differentiated behavior will be enhanced to the extent that psychologists understand the causes of the differences. For example, a case has been made for the biological mediation of sex differences in spatial skills (e.g., Gaulin, 1993; H. Thomas & Kail, 1991). If this position is correct, women should prefer a different cue system for negotiating spatial tasks, as Kimura (1992) has argued. If so, gender-informed programs to train women in tasks that have an important spatial component could take account of these female preferences. Alternatively, to the extent that sex differences in spatial ability arise from experience (Baenninger & Newcombe, 1989), psychologists might help devise ways to give girls and women more equal access to experiences that train high spatial ability. Still, despite these possibilities of positive outcomes, knowledge of sex differences in spatial ability could decrease women's access to jobs and professions for which excellent spatial ability is a prerequisite.

Another example of the potential usefulness of research on sex differences can be found in social psychological investigations of small group behavior. This research documents in exquisite detail how men take charge in task-oriented groups (e.g., Eagly & Karau, 1991; Wood & Rhodes, 1992). Women who learn about the specific behaviors that mediate male dominance and the causal factors that underlie these behaviors may be prepared to find the points in the sequence of processes where they can intervene to produce a more equal sharing of power. Some women may even seek out specific training programs designed to increase their dominance (e.g., assertiveness training). Nonetheless, knowledge of men's more dominant behavior could contribute to exclusion of women from some kinds of leadership roles. Which type of outcome would predominate would depend on many factors, including the strength of the women's desire to change their status, their political power, and their interest in using psychological research to help them effect change.

In concert with Scarr's (1988) optimistic analysis, social scientific knowledge of sex differences could enhance women's ability to understand the antecedents of inequality and to improve their status in society. Nonetheless, the aura of danger surrounds research on sex differences. Some critics urge psychologists to stop this dangerous work or at least censor it in various ways (e.g., Baumeister, 1988; McHugh et al., 1986). Each researcher must of course weigh the potential costs and potential benefits. If enough research psychologists conclude that the costs outweigh the benefits, research comparing the sexes will recede once again because it is too politically relevant. However, the scientific work now possesses a momentum of its own, as more investigators become caught up in the sheer excitement of discovery and theory testing.

Contemporary psychology has produced a large amount of research revealing that behavior is sex differentiated to varying extents. The knowledge produced in this area of science can be beneficial both in helping women and men to understand their natures and their society and in suggesting ways to enhance gender equality. Yet there surely are dangers that the new research will be used in far less beneficial ways by the misogynist forces of the society. Therefore, the stresses between gender politics and the science of gender are not going to disappear. Never before in the history of psychology has such a formidable body of scientific information encountered such a powerful political agenda. The results of this encounter should be instructive to all psychologists who believe that psychology should serve human welfare as it advances scientific understanding.

REFERENCES

Bem, S. L. (1993). *The lenses of gender.* New Haven, CT: Yale University Press.

Eagley, A. H. (1987). *Sex differences in social behavior: A social-role interpretation.* Hillsdale, NJ: Erlbaum.

Halpern, D. F. (1989). The disappearance of cognitive gender differences: What you see depends on where you look. *American Psychologist, 44,* 1156–1158.

Jacklin, C. N., & Reynolds, C. (1993). Gender and childhood socialization. In A. E. Beall & R. J. Sternberg (Eds.), *The psychology of gender* (pp. 197–214). New York: Guilford Press.

Maccoby, E. E., & Jacklin, C. N. (1974). *The psychology of sex differences.* Stanford, CA: Stanford University Press.

Scarr, S. (1988). Race and gender as psychological variables: Social and ethical issues. *American Psychologist, 43,* 56–59.

Sherif, C. W. (1979). Bias in psychology. In J. A. Sherman & E. T. Beck (Eds.), *The prism of sex: Essays in the sociology of knowledge* (pp. 93–133). Madison: University of Wisconsin Press.

Shields, S. A. (1975a). Functionalism, Darwinism, and the psychology of women. *American Psychologist, 30,* 739–754.

Unger, R., & Crawford, M. (1992). *Women and gender: A feminist psychology.* New York: McGraw-Hill.

KEY POINTS

1. Psychology research that compares men and women brings to light many political and scientific issues.

2. Research psychologists have examined performance of males and females on tests of cognitive abilities and intellectual achievement. There is controversy regarding the interpretation of these results: Some argue that sex differences in cognitive abilities are negligible, whereas other researchers say that there are some important differences.

3. Psychologists who have conducted syntheses of sex-related differences in social behavior are in general agreement that there are differences in important aspects of social interaction and personality. There are, however, competing explanations. Status theorists argue that many sex differences are due to the fact that higher social status results from being male rather than female in society. Developmental psychologists emphasize the "separate cultures" idea that children learn rules for social interaction from sex-segregated peer groups in childhood and carry this learning into adulthood. Evolutionary psychologists claim that differences in male and female behavior arose as responses to different adaptive problems.

4. Research on sex differences is intertwined with the history of feminism in America. Much feminist research on sex differences is intended to shatter stereotypes about women's characteristics and prove that women and men are essentially equal in their personalities, behavioral tendencies, and intellectual abilities.

5. Moving away from findings of the 1970s, current results of empirical research and quantitative synthesis suggest that males and females do in fact conform to stereotypic expectations. In general, women tend to show behaviors that are socially sensitive, friendly, and concerned with others' welfare. Men tend to show behaviors that can be described as dominant, controlling, and independent.

QUESTIONS TO THINK ABOUT

1. How plausible are the various theories that attempt to explain sex differences and similarities?

2. How might research on sex differences be disentangled from the biases and political agendas of the researchers?

3. Why might self-reports be poor indicators of behavioral sex differences that underlie gender stereotypes?

4. What are possible uses for results of research regarding sex-differentiated behaviors?

5. Should researchers be concerned about how their findings might be used, and should that influence how they conduct or present their work?

34

Psychosocial and Behavioral Predictors of Longevity: The Aging and Death of the "Termites"*

HOWARD S. FRIEDMAN, JOAN S. TUCKER, JOSEPH E. SCHWARTZ,
CAROL TOMLINSON-KEASEY, LESLIE R. MARTIN,
DEBORAH L. WINGARD, AND MICHAEL H. CRIQUI

Howard S. Friedman (1950–) is professor of psychology at the University of California, Riverside. He is the recipient of the career award for "Outstanding Contributions to Health Psychology" from the American Psychological Association. He has authored or edited many books and articles in health psychology and in personality. Co-editor of this readings book and co-author of the textbook, *Personality: Classic Theories and Modern Research*, Professor Friedman is also a recipient of UCR's Distinguished Teaching Award.

For many years, Friedman and his associates have been studying the psychosocial predictors of longevity among 1,538 participants first studied by psychologist Lewis Terman in 1922. Joan Tucker completed her doctoral work with Friedman working on this longevity project. Joseph E. Schwartz is a sociologist and biostatistician at the State University of New York at Stony Brook. Carol Tomlinson-Keasey was a professor of developmental psychology at the University of California, Riverside when this project began, and became the founding Chancellor of the University of California, Merced. Leslie Martin also completed her doctoral work at the University of California, Riverside on this project and became a professor at La Sierra University. Deborah Wingard and Michael Criqui are professors at the University of California, San Diego Medical School.

In 1921, Lewis Terman began one of the most comprehensive and best-known studies in psychology. To investigate his genetic theories of intelligence, Terman recruited 1,528 bright California boys and girls, intensively studied their psychosocial and intellectual development, and followed them into adulthood. These clever participants nicknamed themselves the "Termites." About half of the Termites are now dead, and we have gathered most of their death certificates and

*Friedman, H. S., Tucker, J. S., Schwartz, J. E., Tomlinson-Keasey, C., Martin, L. R., Wingard, D. L., & Criqui, M. H. (1995). Psychosocial and behavioral predictors of longevity: The aging and death of the "Termites." *American Psychologist, 50,* 69–78. Copyright © 1995 by the American Psychological Association. Reprinted with permission. [Ed. note: All citations in the text of this selection have been left intact from the original, but the list of references includes only those sources that are the most relevant and important. Readers wishing to follow any of the other citations can find the full references in the original work or in an online database.]

coded their dates and causes of death. These life span data provide a unique opportunity to address intriguing questions about the role of psychosocial variables in physical health and longevity through a life span prospective design.

Although there is little doubt that psychosocial factors such as stress and coping play some role in the development or progression of many chronic diseases and in premature death, there is quite a bit of uncertainty about the nature of the causal pathways. Are aspects of personality and social stress related to longevity in general and to heart disease or cancer in particular across the life span? If so, what is the nature of the links? To address these matters, we studied Terman's archives and our new follow-up data to focus on psychosocial disturbance and mortality. We considered three types of variables. First, we examined two major sources of social stress: the divorce of one's parents (during childhood) and the instability of one's own marriage. Second, we looked at patterns of personality evident in childhood and general psychological stability in adulthood. Finally, we considered the possible role of certain unhealthy habits in mediating the influence of stress and personality on longevity. This article integrates the key findings uncovered thus far, in a search for synthesis. A common thread does indeed emerge—a psychosocial risk pattern for premature mortality. Our more technical articles should be consulted for details that cannot be included here.

THE "TERMITES"

The Terman Life-Cycle Study (formerly called the Genetic Studies of Genius or Gifted Children Study) began in 1921–1922, when most of the children were preadolescents (Terman & Oden, 1947). Terman's aim was to secure a reasonably random sample of bright California children, and so most public schools in the San Francisco and Los Angeles areas were searched for bright kids, nominated by their teachers and tested by Terman to have an IQ of at least 135. There were 856 boys and 672 girls in the study; they have been followed at 5- to 10- year intervals ever

since. In addition to Terman, many other researchers, including Melita Oden and Robert Sears (himself a Termite), contributed heavily to the archives, and we are certainly in their debt. Our own contribution has been to gather and code death certificates, to gather and refine certain data about smoking, and to develop the many new indexes necessary for studying longevity and cause of death effects.

In this remarkable study, only small percentages (fewer than 10%) of participants are unaccounted for. (Size varies somewhat with the subsample of each analysis.) We generally restricted our analyses to those who were of school age in 1922 ($M = 11$ years old), who lived at least until 1930, and for whom there were no substantial missing data. Our childhood personality measures were derived from information obtained by Terman in 1922, and our adult health behaviors, adult marriage information, and adult adjustment measures derived from midlife follow-ups (usually 1950, but ranging from 1940–1960). This typically resulted in a sample size of between 1,100 and 1,300. Analyses by Terman's researchers as well as our own comparisons indicated that those lost from study did not differ systematically.

In our sample, women significantly outlived men. As of 1991, 50% of the men but only 35% of the women were known to have died. Statistical survival analyses produce a ratio called a relative hazard, which is the relative probability that a person will die at any given time. The hazard rate for women was more than one third lower than that for men, confirming what is of course generally true in the population. Because women in this sample live about six years longer than men, all our analyses examined or controlled for gender differences.

The Termites were a bright, well-educated group, integrated into American society (but none grew up to win a Nobel prize or to be identified as an obvious genius). They had regular contact with Stanford University. Certain confounds common to other psychosocial health studies are therefore not likely in this sample. The Termites could understand medical advice and prescription, had adequate nutrition, and had access to medical care. Explanations of poor health involving poverty, ignorance, or discrimination are generally not applicable to this sample, and so the sample is valuable for focusing on certain personality and social stress variables. The Termites were successful in public school, at least to the extent that they made it through teachers' nominations and Terman's tough screening for intellectual talent; this is important to keep in mind because it helps rule out certain competing explanations for longevity. The sample is certainly not, however, representative of the U.S. population as a whole (e.g., it contains less than 1% Asian, African, or Native Americans); results are not necessarily generalizable to subpopulations that are different on health-relevant dimensions.

During the past several years, we have hunted down and gathered up hundreds of death certificates for the dead Termites, often from resistant state bureaucracies (Friedman, Tucker, & Martin, 1994). Following established epidemiologic procedures, we coded underlying cause of death according to the *International Classification of Diseases* (9th rev., U.S. Department of Health and Human Services, 1980), with the assistance of a certified nosologist supervised by our team's physician–epidemiologist. As in the general population, the leading cause of death was cardiovascular disease, followed by cancer.

DIVORCE

Divorce of Parents

It has been well established that the divorce of one's parents during childhood can have ill effects on one's future mental health. Although some questions remain about the causal processes, there is good longitudinal evidence that children of divorce, especially boys, are at greater risk for observable behavior and adjustment problems (Amato & Keith, 1991; J. Block, Block, & Gjerde, 1988; J. H. Block, Block, & Gjerde, 1986; Hetherington, 1991; Jellinek & Slovik, 1981; Shaw, Emery, & Tuer, 1993; Zill, Morrison, &

Coiro, 1993). Most of the conceptual analyses concern a lack of social dependability or ego control (i.e., impulsivity and nonconformity), although neuroticism or low emotional stability have also often been implicated.

There has never before been a lifelong prospective study of family stress predictors of mortality and cause of death. Even physical health effects of family stress have been the object of little research attention, although some physiological differences among children have been documented (e.g., Gerra et al., 1993; Weidner, Hutt, Connor, & Mendell, 1992). Family stress (particularly parental divorce) has been found to predict unhealthy behaviors such as smoking and drug use in adolescence as well as poor psychological adjustment (Amato & Keith, 1991; Chassin, Presson, Sherman, Corty, & Olshavsky, 1984; Conrad, Flay, & Hill, 1992; Hawkins, Catalano, & Miller, 1992), but the further consequential links to physical health have rarely been studied from long-term longitudinal data. Can these detrimental effects of parental divorce reach across the life span and affect longevity? Do they differentially affect cause of death?

We looked at the children ($N = 1,285$) whose parents either did or did not divorce before the child reached age 21, who were of school age in 1922, and who lived at least until 1930 (Schwartz et al., in press). We used hazard regression analyses (survival analyses) to predict longevity, controlling for gender.

Children of divorced parents faced a one third greater mortality risk than people whose parents remained married at least until they reached age 21 ($p < .01$). Among men whose parents divorced while they were children, the predicted median age of death was 76 years old; for men whose parents remained married, the predicted age of death was 80 years old. For women, the corresponding predicted ages of death were 82 and 86 years (Schwartz et al., in press).

This striking finding raises many important questions about causal mechanisms. Only 13% of the people in the Terman sample had faced the divorce of their parents during childhood, a situation different from that faced by children today.

The estimates of the size of the effects on mortality may not be directly comparable for today's children. Still, in light of the overwhelming evidence from other studies indicating damaging psychological effects of parental divorce, this finding does provoke serious concern. Death of a parent had very little effect, consistent with other research indicating that parental strife and divorce is a greater influence on subsequent psychopathology than is parental death (Tennant, 1988). In the Terman sample, our analyses suggested that parental divorce was the key early social predictor of premature mortality, throughout the life span.

We used the information we gathered and coded from the death certificates to examine whether divorce of one's parents related differentially to cause of death. We found that parental divorce was not associated with whether one is more likely to die of cancer or heart disease or other disease. Also, the overall higher mortality risk cannot be explained away by a higher injury rate, although the possibility of an especially increased risk of injury death cannot be ruled out, because of the small sample.

Instability of One's Own Marriage

There is substantial epidemiological evidence that marriage is correlated with longer life (e.g., House, Robbins, & Metzner, 1982; Hu & Goldman, 1990; Kotler & Wingard, 1989). This is often viewed as a protective effect of the social support of marriage. "Get married" appears on pop lists of health recommendations. However, embedded in this relation are several distinct issues too rarely discussed. Should we assume that it is the marriage itself that is protective? Marriage brings the risk of marital dissolution. Death of spouse, divorce, and marital separation are the top three most stressful events on the classic Social Readjustment Rating Scale (Holmes & Rahe, 1967), and there seems little doubt that marital dissolution is the most significant common social stressor in American society (with the possible exception of abject poverty). Furthermore, is it

possible that an unstable marital history is the result of other psychological and behavioral problems rather than itself being a primary cause of premature mortality?

As of 1950 (when they were about 40 years old), the vast majority of the Termites were alive, mature, and had married if they were ever going to marry. We classified them as currently and steadily married ($N = 829$), married but not in their first marriage (inconsistently married; $N = 142$), never married ($N = 102$), or currently separated, widowed, or divorced ($N = 70$). Very few Termites had been widowed by this point. Controlling for gender and self-reported health, we found (in survival analyses) that the inconsistently married people were at higher risk for premature mortality than the steadily married people and that the currently separated, widowed, or divorced people were at even higher risk. Inconsistently married men had a relative hazard of mortality of almost 1.4 (40% greater risk), and separated or divorced men had a relative hazard of 2.2. For women, the relative hazards were 1.4 and 1.8, respectively. Those who had never married had less of an increased risk and resembled the steadily married when their other social ties were taken into account (men's relative hazard = 1.05 and women's relative hazard = 1.00 when controlling for social ties; Tucker, 1993; Tucker, Friedman, & Wingard, 1994). This last finding concerning the long life of the never marrieds may be particular to the bright, career-oriented nature of the sample. Note that we have purposely considered marital history at a relatively stable, healthy, and mature time of life; the effects might be different in the very young or in much older people.

The steadily married people and the inconsistently married people were all married in 1950, yet they had significantly different life expectancies. This dramatic finding suggests that it may not be marriage's effect as a buffer against stress that is always important. Rather, there seems to be a detrimental effect of previous divorce that is not eliminated when the individuals remarry. Furthermore, additional analyses revealed that part of the association between marital status and mortality risk seems to be due to a selection into steady marriages—Termites who were impulsive children grew up both more likely to be inconsistently married and more likely to die younger ($p < .05$; Tucker, 1993).

Parental Divorce and One's Own Divorce

Is the increased mortality risk of children of divorce due in part to these people's own subsequent divorce? People whose parents divorced were indeed more likely to face divorce themselves ($p < .05$). Furthermore, individuals who were divorced or remarried reported that their childhoods were significantly more stressful than did those who stayed married ($p < .05$). In other words, Terman study participants who experienced a marital breakup were more likely to have seen the divorce of their own parents, and they were more likely to report having experienced a stressful home environment as children, such as marked friction among family members.

Given that parental divorce is associated with one's own future divorce, and given that one's divorce is predictive of increased mortality risk, it is indeed the case that one's unstable adult relations "explain" some of the detrimental effects of parental divorce. However, after controlling for one's (adult) divorce, parental divorce during childhood remained a significant predictor of premature mortality ($p < .05$), suggesting that it has additional adverse consequences in adulthood.

In summary, in this sample, marriage itself was not fully health protective. On the other hand, a stable marriage history was indeed predictive of increased longevity. Advice to get married to promote health seems unjustified. Advice to stay in a satisfactory marriage seems somewhat better, as there are hints of negative health consequences of divorce. Most surprising in light of previous research is the appearance of a psychosocial selection factor: Some people make poor marriage partners and are also prone to die prematurely (Tucker, 1993; Tucker, Friedman, & Wingard, 1994). All in all, family instabilities—

parental and one's own divorce—are clearly predictive of premature mortality.

PERSONALITY AND ADJUSTMENT

Childhood Personality

There is a long history of research and theory arguing that certain patterns of psychological responding are damaging to physical health—that is, that certain personalities are disease-prone or self-healing (see overviews by Friedman, 1990, 1991, 1992; Pennebaker, 1990). The theorists and researchers have generally argued that resilient personalities—high in stability, sociability, and optimism—are prone to health, whereas aggressive, excitable, impulsive, and neurotic people are prone to disease and mortality.

In 1922, Terman collected trait ratings about the participants from their parents and teachers. The scales he used were remarkably modern in their appearance and provide a better assessment than the primitive personality tests that were available at the time. It is reasonable to expect that parents and teachers have a good idea of whether an 11-year-old child is sociable, popular, conscientious, self-confident, and so on. We constructed six personality dimensions and used them to predict longevity and cause of death through 1986, using survival analyses (see Friedman et al., in press; Friedman et al., 1993). We used both Cox proportional hazards and Gompertz regressions; they yielded the same results.

Did childhood personality predict premature mortality decades later? The most striking finding in these and follow-up analyses was that childhood social dependability or conscientiousness predicted longevity. Children, especially boys, who were rated as prudent, conscientious, truthful, and free from vanity (four separate ratings, which we averaged, $\alpha = .76$) lived significantly longer. They were about 30% less likely to die in any given year.

The finding that certain aspects of personality predicted survival across the life span raises many fascinating questions concerning causal mechanisms. Why are conscientious, dependable children who live to adulthood more likely to reach old age than their less conscientious peers? Our survival analyses ($N = 1,215$) suggested that the protective effect of conscientiousness was not primarily due to a reduction in the risk of injury: Although there is some tendency for the unconscientious to be more likely to die a violent death, conscientiousness is also protective against early death from cardiovascular disease and cancer. A focus on unhealthy behaviors showed them to be somewhat relevant as explanatory mechanisms (see below), but a significant effect of conscientiousness remained after controlling for drinking ($p < .01$) and for smoking and other aspects of personality ($p < .05$; Friedman et al., in press).

We have found no evidence so far that the personality trait of sociability or other elements of extraversion were strongly related to health and longevity in this sample. This is somewhat surprising, given that biological and social theories of psychosocial factors and health generally predict such effects. Rather, the locus of health-relevant effects seems to be centered in such traits as impulsivity, egocentrism, toughmindedness, and undependability. For example, childhood ratings on such variables as popularity and preference for playing with other people did not predict longevity. To further explore the lifelong effects of sociability, we followed up on Terman's (1954) study of scientists. Terman had found that the Termites who grew up to be scientists (broadly construed) were much less sociable early in life than the nonscientists. (Terman studied only male scientists.) In fact, Terman considered the differences in sociability to be quite remarkable. Using the Stanford archives, we recreated Terman's groups (Ns 288 and 326) and compared their longevity through 1991. However, our survival analyses found that the scientists did not die at a younger age. In fact, the scientists tended to live longer (relative hazard = 1.26, $p < .09$; Friedman et al., 1994).

What about neuroticism? Although the traits of neuroticism—emotional instability, depres-sion, and hostility—are thought to be correlated with poor health, we have found mixed results in this sample. On the childhood measures, there is some hint that neuroticism may be unhealthy. For example, for men, permanency of mood (as rated in childhood) tended to be associated with increased longevity. Effects of maladjustment appeared in adulthood (see the following section). In general, it has proved challenging to create valid measures of neuroticism because it is desirable to take various elements of the Termites' reaction patterns into account. This is a focus of our ongoing efforts.

Finally, we have been examining childhood cheerfulness—rated optimism and a sense of humor. Contrary to our expectations, we have found that childhood cheerfulness is inversely related to longevity. Survival analyses showed that the cheerful kids grew up to be adults who died younger (about 22% increased risk, $p < .01$, Friedman et al., 1993). Puzzled, we followed up on those Termites rated as cheerful in childhood. We found that they grew up to be more likely to smoke, drink, and take risks (all $ps < .05$, comparing upper and lower quartiles), although these habits do not fully explain their increased risk of premature mortality (Martin et al., 1994). It might be the case that cheerfulness is helpful when facing a stress such as surgery, but harmful if it leads one to be careless or carefree throughout one's life (Tennen & Affleck, 1987; Weinstein, 1984). In other words, the health relevance of such traits as optimism may need to be more carefully conceptualized (cf. Wortman, Sheedy, Gluhoski, & Kessler, 1992).

Personality, Parents' Divorce, and Longevity

Children of divorced parents were somewhat less likely to have been seen as conscientious children, $r(1283) = -.14$, but controlling for parental divorce did not change the relations between childhood personality and longevity. Other correlations of parental divorce with personality characteristics were even smaller. In our

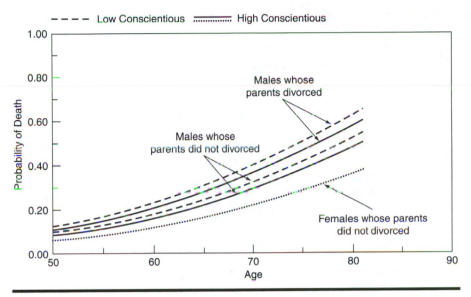

FIGURE 1 Survival Functions for a 20-year-old, by Conscientiousness and Parental Divorce

Note. High and low conscientiousness represent the 75th versus the 25th percentiles. Fitted curves were based on Gompertz hazard function estimates. Copyright 1994, Joseph E. Schwartz and Howard S. Friedman.

sample, personality and parental divorce are independent predictors of longevity (Schwartz et al., in press).

Survival functions for a 20-year-old Termite are shown in Figure 1. It shows the probability of death as a function of age. The top four curves are for males in the sample. The topmost curve is for men who were rated as unconscientious in childhood and whose parents divorced during childhood; their probability of dying by age 70 was 40%. In contrast, for conscientious males whose parents did not divorce, the probability of dying by age 70 was less than 30%.

The bottom curve shows the longest-living women—those rated as conscientious and whose parents did not divorce. The difference between this curve and the bottom curve for men represents the gender effect—the longer lives of women. Note that the difference between these two curves at age 70 is smaller than the difference between the highest and lowest male curves.

This means that the combined effect of the two psychosocial variables is greater than the well-known major effect of gender on longevity. Although we have purposely selected these two strong psychosocial predictors for this figure, there is (as noted above) excellent theoretical and empirical reason to believe that these childhood factors are highly relevant to subsequent unhealthy psychological functioning and behavior. The fact that childhood psychosocial information about personality and family stress does as well as gender in predicting longevity is dramatic evidence of the importance of psychosocial factors for understanding premature mortality.

Adult Psychosocial Adjustment

The relation between psychological adjustment and premature mortality has not been much studied in long-term prospective population research. Although special groups such as the clinically depressed or criminals are more likely to face early death (e.g., from suicide or homicide), the more general question has received surprisingly little study. It could be argued that psychosocial maladjustment is implicit in the Type A disease-prone pattern, but only the psychosomatic theorists have focused intensively on psychotherapy as a means of promoting general physical health (Dunbar, 1943; see also Berry & Pennebaker, 1993).

In 1950, the Termites were asked about tendencies toward nervousness, anxiety, or nervous breakdown; there had also been personal conferences with participants and with family members. On the basis of this and previous related information in the files dating back a decade, Terman's team then categorized each on a 3-point scale of mental difficulty: *satisfactory adjustment, some maladjustment,* or *serious maladjustment.* (Almost one third experienced at least some mental difficulty by this stage.) Survival analyses show that for men, mental difficulty as of 1950 significantly predicted mortality risk through 1991, in the expected direction (relative hazard = 1.30, $p <$ .01, for men and 1.12, *ns*, for women). Similar results were found on a measure we constructed of poor psychological adjustment as self-reported in 1950 on six 11-point scales that included items like *moodiness* (significant risk for men, $p < .05$, but not for women).

Further analyses revealed that the consistently married Termites had the fewest mental difficulties; alternatively, this could be stated as a finding that those with the fewest mental difficulties were most likely to remain married. It is interesting that controlling for mental difficulty weakened but did not eliminate the relation between marital history and longevity. In other words, although mental distress seemed to play the expected role in poor health, a significant detrimental effect of divorce remained, even after taking psychological health in 1950 into account.

In analyses thus far on cause of death, there have been no dramatic differences as a function of psychological adjustment. A general survival analysis model testing for differences among cause of death (cardiovascular disease, cancer, injury, and other diseases) has shown no significant difference. That is, poorly adjusted men are more likely to die from all causes. There is some indication that poorly adjusted participants are especially more likely to die from injury (including suicide), as would be expected. However, because so few people died from injury in this sample, such differences cannot (and do not) account for the main effect of adjustment on longevity. There is also a hint that poorly adjusted men may have an extra risk of dying from cardiovascular disease.

HEALTH BEHAVIORS

Cigarette smoking and heavy use of alcohol (which often occur together) are well established as behavioral causes of significant morbidity and premature mortality. Thus, it is of significant interest to ascertain the extent to which such behaviors can be predicted from childhood and the extent to which they might account for differences in longevity. It is important, however, to keep in mind the time periods in which the various predictors were measured as well as the nature of the Terman sample. We deem it inadvisable to attempt precise effect size comparisons; rather, these data are best suited for uncovering stable, robust patterns.

Terman collected very good contemporaneous data on alcohol consumption. We used information collected in 1950 and 1960 to classify the Termites as heavy drinkers (N = 226 men and 87 women), as moderate drinkers (seldom or never intoxicated; N = 339 men and 302 women), or as rarely (or never) taking a drink (N = 99 men and 128 women). Alcohol use was quite stable across decades. Because moderate drinking may be protective of heart disease, we also looked for U-shaped effects on mortality, but none were found. Information about smoking was poorly documented in the files, so we collected as much smoking information as possible during 1991–1992. We contacted those Termites who could be found, and we attempted to contact relatives of the rest. We gathered smoking data on over 900 Termites, but some of them were missing data on other key variables. Unlike the other measures, there was some evidence of bias in this subsample. Those who died young seemed more likely to have had very unhealthy behaviors and also were less likely to have locatable families. Thus, the mediating effect of smoking may be underestimated.

As expected, smoking and drinking each predicted premature mortality. Did they mediate the relations reported above? Conscientious children grew up to drink and smoke less, but cheerful kids grew up to drink and smoke more (all $ps < .05$; Tucker et al., 1994; cf. J. Block, Block, & Keyes, 1988). However, conscientiousness remained a strong predictor of longevity in various survival analyses, controlling for smoking and drinking (decreased hazard of 20%–30%). Cheerfulness remained predictive when alcohol use was controlled, but the effects of cheerfulness changed when smoking was controlled; because the sample size dropped by one third, what this means is problematic. Termites (especially girls) who faced parental divorce grew up to smoke a little more ($p < .05$), but not drink more (possibly due to Prohibition during adolescence).

Analyses of obesity (body mass index in young to mid-adulthood) showed little systematic relationship to either psychosocial variables or mortality in this intelligent sample, perhaps because obesity was measured in 1940, when few participants were heavily overweight, or because obesity was unusual in bright people of this cohort. What about exercise, hobbies, and other such potentially important mediators? Although there is of course no simple exercise variable per se among the thousands of variables in the data set, information on activity levels and hobbies at various ages is scattered throughout and can eventually be pieced into the puzzle.

It might be the case that psychosocial factors affect a whole host of health behaviors in addition to drinking and smoking—exercise patterns, diet, use of prophylactics, adherence to medication regimens, avoidance of environmental toxins, and more—which, when put together, may explain most of the associations between psychology and longevity. Surprisingly, there has been little prospective study of psychosocial predictors of unhealthy lifestyle patterns across long time periods and how they subsequently and consequently affect health, longevity, and cause of death.

In summary, the data concerning unhealthy behaviors are tantalizing but not definitive. Personal and social factors evident in childhood were predictive of smoking and excessive drinking in adulthood, and these unhealthy behaviors predicted premature mortality in this sample. Yet these behaviors did not come close to fully accounting for the effects of childhood predictors on longevity. It may be the case that more reliable and more extensive measurement of health behaviors could have a major impact in explaining the psychosocial predictors of longevity, without resorting to psychosomatic explanations involving stress. Given the documented associations of stress with both cardiovascular disease mechanisms and suppression of the immune system, however, it is likely that there are multiple pathways linking psychosocial factors to longevity. Our guess is that personality and stress variables have both direct (psychosomatic) and behaviorally mediated effects on health, but ascertaining their relative importance is a difficult empirical question.

DISCUSSION

A number of intriguing new findings have emerged from efforts thus far in studying longevity and cause of death in the Terman cohort. These enduring patterns could emerge only from a lifelong comprehensive study such as the one that Terman and his colleagues worked so hard to establish.

First, and most basically, the results leave little doubt that aspects of individual psychology are significantly linked to longevity, across the life span. In particular, we found confirmation in the physical health arena of the importance of what psychologists have typically seen as ego strength—dependability, trust, and lack of impulsivity. This pattern of results unites and extends the various related sorts of findings by other researchers.

Second, we found evidence that both personality and social stress factors are independent predictors of longevity. Past findings of psychopathological sequelae of divorce and family conflict can now be extended to the arena of long-term health effects. In both childhood and adulthood, the trauma of divorce clearly predicted premature mortality—but so did personality. Yet the effect of each was substantially independent of the other. Further examination of Figure 1 reveals that unconscientious males whose parents divorced crossed the 50th percentile of survival at (i.e., lived on average to) 74 years. For conscientious males from stable families, the average survival was to 81 years. (The figures were analogous for females.) Although these numbers probably represent the maximum size of effect that is likely to be found in such a sample, their dramatic nature nevertheless should promote substantial future research focused on this area.

Third, we have not, as yet, found striking associations with specific disease causes of death. Our careful, physician-supervised collection and coding of underlying cause of death from death certificates makes us confident of the reliability of this variable. The fact that personality and social factors predicted all causes of death suggests either that a general homeostasis is critical to good health (Selye, 1976) or that a group of unhealthy behaviors mediates a wide variety of health problems. This is not to say that a specific psychosocial influence cannot further raise the risk of a particular disease. However, to the extent that specific disease-prone patterns do exist (such as a coronary-prone personality), they probably depend on the co-occurence of more than one factor; in other words, interaction effects are likely involved. This could explain why such phenomena have proved so hard to capture.

How large are these effects? Because genetic hardiness, exposure to microbes and toxins, and many random factors affect longevity, researchers should not normally expect an overwhelming effect of psychosocial influences. Yet, where life and death are concerned, an influence that leaves 55% of the people alive compared with only 45% alive in an uninfluenced comparison group is of great interest. The effects discussed would generally translate into a relative hazard of between 1.2 and 1.5, a correlation of between 0.1 and 0.2, or a decreased life expectancy of two to four years (comparing upper and lower quartiles; cf. Friedman & Booth-Kewley, 1987; Lipsey & Wilson, 1993; Rosenthal, 1991; Schwartz et al., in press). These effects are smaller than the influences of gender or smoking on longevity, but comparable to common biological risk factors such as systolic blood pressure and serum cholesterol and to common behavioral risks such as exercise and diet, as they affect all-cause mortality. Nevertheless, caution should be used in making inferences about the magnitude of the effects in other socioeconomic groups and in other historical times; the Terman data are best suited for uncovering robust psychosocial variables that predict longevity rather than for ruling out complex pathways or explicating a full causal model.

Women significantly outlive men in this sample. Consistent with previous research, most of the psychosocial effects were more pronounced for the men (e.g., greater effects for childhood conscientiousness, adult mental difficulties, and self-reported early family stress). Like other researchers (Wingard, 1984), we have not yet been able to account for the gender differences in longevity, nor for the greater psychological effects in males, but this is a focus of ongoing efforts.

As in the general population, the significant mortality in this sample occurs after age 55. The important questions that remain unanswered revolve around the mechanisms that lead from seemingly physically healthy but psychosocially impaired middle-aged adulthood to premature mortality. We have seen that smoking and excessive drinking likely play some causal role, but perhaps not a dominant role. Our analyses of cause of death have thus far not provided any dramatic insights into this question. We of course are studying this matter in the Terman sample, but insights will also be gleaned from cross-sectional and other shorter-term studies that now can be focused on these issues.

Especially interesting is the importance of stable individual patterns of responding. In light of the current findings, a model that focused on socioenvironmental stress would be clearly inadequate. It is not the case that most people are equally likely to die prematurely until some of them happen to encounter divorce, job loss, or other unexpected stress. Although such factors do play a significant role, it is also the case that personality—a stable individual pattern of responding—is highly relevant. Furthermore, this effect of personality was maintained when we controlled for childhood socioeconomic status and for childhood health (i.e., parents' reports of health and illnesses in infancy and childhood).

Could it be the case that biological factors are a primary cause of both personality and health, as Eysenck (1985, 1991) has argued? At this point, the evidence is not totally inconsistent with such an explanation. Surprisingly, however, it is what Eysenck termed *psychoticism*, not neuroticism or introversion, that seems most relevant. (People high on psychoticism are impulsive, cruel, hostile, foolhardy, impersonal, and troublesome.) That is, the unhealthy patterns that have emerged thus far in our study predominantly involved being impulsive, imprudent, and arrogant rather than anxious, shy, pessimistic, and unsociable. This may change somewhat as more complex approaches are taken to these data; there is of course good evidence from other studies that the latter traits are indeed also relevant. More complex models of causality are also plausible. In addition to underlying biology predisposing an individual to both certain styles of behaving and excessive sympathetic reactivity, individuals undoubtedly play some role in selecting their own healthy or unhealthy environments (Magnus, Diener, Fujita, & Payot, 1993; Scarr & McCartney, 1983; also see work on testosterone, Dabbs & Morris, 1990).

Previous notions of a disease-prone personality (Friedman & Booth-Kewley, 1987) and a self-healing personality (Friedman, 1991) seem

viable in light of the current findings. Indeed, the long-term predictive value of psychosocial factors, across decades, confirms the utility of thinking in terms of stable individual differences. The past emphasis on emotional reaction patterns, however, must be supplemented by significantly increased attention to behavioral correlates and mediators. For those researchers with a psychodynamic bent, the healthy pattern might be termed *mature ego defenses* (Vaillant, 1993). For those more focused on behavior, key issues may involve dependability and addictions. In either case, the same sorts of variables emerge—the destructiveness of impulsiveness and substance abuses, and the healthiness of maturity and social stability.

The longitudinal design of the present study points out the importance of not focusing too heavily on short-term coping with stress to the exclusion of lifelong habits and patterns. Although other research gives reason to believe that aspects of personality such as sociability and optimism are related not only to feelings of psychological well-being but also to good health, such influences may be heavily context dependent. For example, it may be helpful to be optimistic when one is facing trauma and it may be helpful to have friends when one is bereaved, but these things may not necessarily be generally health protective by themselves across the life span. Impaired social support can sometimes occur as a result of (as well as be a cause of) psychological maladjustment.

This line of thinking points to the fascinating speculation that problems in psychosocial adjustment that revolve around an egocentric impulsivity are a key general risk factor for all-cause mortality. In terms of healthy aspects of the so-called "Big Five" dimensions of personality, this would probably involve elements of Agreeableness such as trust and straightforwardness, and elements of Conscientiousness such as achievement striving, competence, and deliberation (see McCrae & Costa, 1991; Ones, Viswesvaran, & Schmidt, 1993; Watson & Clark, 1992); closely related are stable interpersonal ties. It has been pointed out that such a pattern might be seen to define "character" (Costa, McCrae, & Dembroski, 1989). Although common wisdom might argue that a selfish, self-indulgent boor may prosper by stepping on others, this does not seem to be the case. Nor do we find a triumph of the lazy, pampered dropout. In terms of the rush toward death, the encouraging news may be that good guys finish last.

The size of the effects we have uncovered, their fit with previous theory, and their support by ancillary lines of research point to the possibility of major public health implications for these psychosocial variables. Although bright children growing up in California in the 1920s obviously faced some unique challenges and one should not carelessly generalize the results to other groups of people in other historical contexts, it is also the case that the findings fit quite well with what is already known about the correlates of better or worse mental health. Indeed, if such patterns of findings were found concerning toxic associations with insecticides, electromagnetic fields, or diets (even in a nonrandom sample), it is likely that a public health emergency would be perceived.

Although improvements in longevity are often assumed to be a function of medical technology, a good case can be made that most of the increase has come from changes in public health—sewage handling, food supply, inoculation, lessened crowding, and so on (McKeown, 1979, makes a cogent case; of course, there are many particular exceptions where medical cures have been discovered). The psychosocial and behavioral variables we have been discussing fit well into such a public health framework—major, lifelong, psychosocial patterns seem highly relevant to longevity. On the other hand, the effects of successful social intervention are not necessarily so clear, as the casual pathways have not been proved. For example, the effects of early psychological and social interventions on subsequent longevity have not been studied, much less documented. Still, given the other known benefits of a society with socially dependable individuals and stable families, the findings of significant relations with longevity should lend a new sense of urgency to addressing these complex issues.

Terman died in 1956. He was almost 80. His wife had died earlier that same year, after more than 50 years of marriage. Terman had set out in 1921 to study the simple bases of intelligence and success, but he came to recognize that it was much more complicated than he had imagined. The same might now be said about our understanding of the psychosocial bases of longevity.

REFERENCES

Amato, P. R., & Keith, B. (1991). Parental divorce and the well-being of children: A meta-analysis. *Psychological Bulletin, 110,* 26–46.

Block, J. H., Block, J., & Gjerde, P. F. (1986). The personality of children prior to divorce: A prospective study. *Child Development, 57,* 827–840.

Eysenck, H. J. (1991). Personality, stress, and disease: An interactionist perspective. *Psychological Inquiry, 2,* 221–232.

Friedman, H. S. (1990) (Ed.). *Personality and Disease.* New York: Wiley & Sons.

Friedman, H. S. (1991). *The Self-Healing Personality: Why Some People Achieve Health and Others Succumb to Illness.* New York: Henry Holt. (Republished by <Iuniverse.com>, 2000).

Friedman, H. S., & Booth-Kewley, S. (1987). The "disease-prone personality": A meta-analytic view of the construct. *American Psychologist, 42,* 539–555.

Hetherington, E. M. (1991). Families, lies, and videotapes: Presidential Address of the Society for Research in Adolescence. *Journal of Research on Adolescence, 1,* 323–348.

Magnus, K., Diener, E. Fujita, F., & Payot, W. (1993). Extraversion and neuroticism as predictors of objective life events: A longitudinal analysis. *Journal of Personality & Social Psychology, 65,* 1046–1053.

Tennant, C. (1988). Parental loss in childhood: Its effect in adult life. *Archives of General Psychiatry, 45,* 1045–1050.

Vaillant, G. E. (1993). *The wisdom of the ego.* Cambridge: Harvard University Press.

KEY POINTS

1. The role played by personality in health and longevity can best be studied and understood by examining its effects across many years, in a longitudinal study.

2. Children, especially boys, who were prudent, conscientious, truthful, and free from vanity were at significantly lower risk of premature mortality across many decades.

3. Personality appears to affect health through multiple pathways. These include both direct, psychosomatic pathways, and behaviorally mediated pathways.

QUESTIONS TO THINK ABOUT

1. Because no single approach to personality and longevity seems adequate, which combinations of personality perspectives and theories are most likely to prove suitable for understanding the complex relations between personality and health?

2. Why should such issues as conscientiousness, mature ego defenses, lack of impulsiveness, and social stability prove so important to health and longevity?

3. Should efforts to promote health focus primarily on changing the individual (as is now often done), or should significantly more attention be given to changing the society and culture?

35

The Roots of Evil:
Social Conditions, Culture,
Personality, and Basic Human Needs*

ERVIN STAUB

Ervin Staub (1938–) is a psychology professor at the University of Massachusetts who studies the psychology of good and evil. He applies theories and research from personality and social psychology to the understanding of hate, mass violence, and genocide. He is also interested in exploring methods of raising nonviolent children.

Staub's interest in evil (and especially in genocide) becomes more understandable in the context of his own life experiences. As a young child in Hungary in the 1940s, he and his family—all Jews—barely escaped death at the hands of the Nazis. When Staub later moved to the United States and completed his doctorate at Stanford, he remained fascinated by both the genocidal evil of the Nazis and the failure of many millions of ordinary citizens to oppose the killing of their neighbors.

In this selection, Staub addresses how individuals and groups become genocidal and the influence and status of those who could intervene but do not.

The focus of this article is on the origins of evil, in several domains. An important domain is *genocide*, the attempt to exterminate a whole group of people. This is a form of violence that seems "obviously" evil. Another domain is individual violence. What are the origins of aggression in children, and how does the kind of violence that may be regarded as evil develop out of it? A number of elements in the generation of evil are evident as these two domains are explored: the system in which individuals operate—whether constituted by a culture and social conditions, the nature of a family or a classroom, and relationships among people; personal characteristics and the behavior of bystanders; the evolution of increasingly harmful acts over time; and the frustration of basic human needs and their "destructive" fulfillment. To exemplify further how these elements operate, father–daughter incest and, very briefly, bullying in schools also are discussed. Space limitations do not allow a detailed examination of "cures" or prevention, but the discussion of origins at times implies, and at other times I briefly explore ways to stop or prevent evil.

*Staub, E. (1999). The roots of evil: Social conditions, culture, personality, and basic human needs. *Personality and Social Psychology Review, 3,* 179–192. Reprinted by permission. [Ed. note: All citations in the text of this selection have been left intact from the original, but the list of references includes only those sources that are the most relevant and important. Readers wishing to follow any of the other citations can find the full references in the original work or from an online database.]

IS EVIL A USEFUL CONCEPT FOR PSYCHOLOGISTS?

One focus of my work for many years has been the exploration of the roots of violence, especially of genocide and mass killing, which I referred to as *evil* (Staub, 1989). How does a group, a culture, as well as a person evolve so that they come to engage in "evil" actions or even develop a tendency for them? In recent years, I have also been greatly concerned with the prevention of genocide (Staub, 1996b, 1998b, in press-b). Genocide and mass killing may seem obviously evil to most of us. However, because the concept of evil is becoming increasingly used in the social-psychological literature (Baumeister, 1997; Darley, 1992; Staub, 1989), it is important to ask whether it has useful meaning for psychologists. How would the meaning of evil be differentiated from the meaning of "violence"? Is evil the end point in the evolution of violence? In genocide, a plan is formulated to destroy a group. Usually, a decision is made to do this. Reactions to events and psychological and social processes turn into a plan. However, a conscious intention of extreme destructiveness does not seem a necessary aspect of evil. The real motivation is often unconscious, and a group's or person's habitual, spontaneous reactions to certain kinds of events can become highly destructive.

Evil has been a religious concept. The word also has been used as a secular term to describe, explain, or express aversion to certain actions and the human beings or natural forces from which they originate. The notion of a nonhuman force and origin often has been associated with evil, such as the devil, Satan, or Mephistopheles. Some have seen the forces of nature, when manifested in the destruction they sometimes bring, as evil. From a psychological standpoint, the forces of nature are surely neutral: They do, at times, cause harm but without conscious or unconscious intention.

The word *evil* is emotionally expressive for people: It communicates horror over some deed.

People often romanticize evil. They want to see the abhorrent acts or events to which the word refers as having mythic proportions. Designating something as evil is sometimes used to suggest that the actions are not comprehensible in an ordinary human framework: They are outside the bounds of morality or even of human agency. However, evil is the outcome of basic, ordinary psychological processes and their evolution. Arendt's (1963) concept of the "banality of evil" seems to recognize this. However, the notion of the banality of evil also makes it seem as if its ordinariness diminishes the significance of evil.

I originally used the term *evil* to denote extreme human destructiveness, as in cases of genocide and mass killing (Staub, 1989), but evil may be defined by a number of elements. One of these is *extreme harm.* The harm can be pain, suffering, loss of life, or the loss of personal or human potential. Violent actions tend to arise from difficult, threatening circumstances and the psychological reactions of people to them. They are elicited by varied instigators, such as attack, threat, or frustration. Not all people react to such conditions with violence, but some do. Some individuals or groups engage in extremely harmful acts that are not commensurate with any *instigation* or *provocation* (Darley, 1992), another defining element of evil. Finally, some individuals, groups, or societies evolve in a way that makes destructive acts by them likely. The repetition or *persistence of greatly harmful acts* may be another defining element of evil. It is most appropriate to talk of evil when all these defining elements are present: intensely harmful actions, which are not commensurate with instigating conditions, and the persistence or repetition of such actions. A series of actions also can be evil when any one act causes limited harm, but with repetition, these acts cause great harm.

An important question, which this article in part addresses, is what might be the nature of the actor, whether a society or a person, that makes such acts probable. By "nature of the actor," whether a person or society, I do not refer to psychopathology. The evil I focus on and explore in this article arises out of ordinary psychological processes and characteristics, although usually extreme forms or degrees of them: seeing people as hostile, devaluing certain groups of people, having an overly strong respect for authority, and others.

When a person or group is attacked, they have a right to defend themselves. If someone begins to shoot at me and I pull out a gun and kill the person, my action is not evil. Whether self-defense is justified can get complicated very fast, however. What if someone has threatened me, and I then lie in wait for him and shoot him when he leaves his house? If this person in a moment of anger has threatened to kill me, most of us would not see this as sufficient provocation to justify killing him, unless perhaps we know that this person has threatened other people in similar ways and then actually killed them.

A particular person, at a particular time, for idiosyncratic reasons, may take a threat extremely seriously and respond by killing another. This extremely violent act may not be evil: It may be peculiar to the circumstances and emotional state of the person at that time. Not arising from this person's personality, or from a combination of personality and the ongoing of circumstances, it is unlikely to be repeated. Evil usually has a more enduring quality. Thus, it might be best not to regard as evil a single act of intense harm that is out of balance with provocation. However, violence evolves, and individuals and groups change as a result of their actions (see subsequent discussion). As a person or group commits an intensely harmful act, there is an increased likelihood that they will do so again.

As well as action, omission may be evil, especially when it causes extreme harm, there is no strong justification for it in circumstances (such as lack of clarity of events or very high cost of action), and when it persists. Consider an extreme example: A person standing at the edge of a lake, taking no action while witnessing a child drowning in shallow water. Passivity in such an extreme

situation is likely to arise from this person's nature, predicting other evil acts (or from this person's relationship to that particular child).

Evil acts are mainly directed at other human beings, although the destruction of animals or nature may also be considered evil. These actions often cause material harm: death, injury, pain, or severe deprivation and injustice. Persistent neglect or belittling of a child that causes physical harm, psychological pain, or psychological injury that diminishes the capacity for growth and satisfaction are also appropriately regarded as evil.

It may be most appropriate to regard it evil when destructive actions are intentional. However, intention is highly complicated psychologically because a person's real motive is often unconscious; individuals and groups tend to justify their actions, even to themselves; and various belief systems develop that propagate harmful actions in the service of some presumed good. Persons or groups who act destructively tend to claim self-defense or to claim that their victims are morally bad and dangerous or stand in the way of human betterment and, therefore, deserve suffering or death. They may simply use this as justification or may genuinely believe it even when it is completely untrue.

An example of a belief system leading people to act cruelly in the service of what they see as a good cause is the way children were treated in many societies (Greven, 1991; Miller, 1983). In many places, including Germany, England, and the United States, children were seen as inherently willful. Obedience by them was seen as a high virtue and important goal and it was believed that children's will had to be broken early if they were to become good people. Such thinking often had religious roots (Greven, 1991). Any and all means, such as threatening children with the devil and in other ways scaring them, as well as physically punishing them or depriving them, were seen appropriate to break their will and teach them obedience and respect (Miller, 1983).

In the case of genocide, it is usually clear to outside observers that it is not justified by provocations even if it is a response to real violence by the other group. However, frequently the victim group has done nothing to justify violence against them, except in the perpetrators' minds. The Jews engaged in no destructive actions against Germans. Many of the intellectuals and educated people in Cambodia who were killed or worked to death by the Khmer Rouge did no harm that would justify such actions in the minds of most people. According to the Khmer Rouge ideology, however, these intellectuals had participated in an unjust system that favored them at the expense of others and were incapable of participating in a system of total social equality. To fulfill a "higher" ideal, to create total social equality, was the motivation to kill them or to reduce them to slaves working in the "killing fields" (Staub, 1989).

There is the same absence of provocation in many cases of recurrent violence against a spouse, or severe neglect, harsh verbal and physical treatment, and persistent physical violence against children. Some parents blame their children all the time: for having been noisy, thereby causing the car accident in which the parents were involved; for needing things that cost money, thereby depriving the family of other things; for anything and everything (L. Huber, school psychologist, personal communication, June 1997). Peck (1983) gave this as a primary example of evil. Such parents may completely lack awareness of what in themselves leads to their blaming and scapegoating, seeing their actions as justifiable reactions to the child.

Frequently, there are two levels of motivation in harmful behavior, including evil acts. One is to "harm" a person or a group, and another is to fulfill some goal that the harmful act supposedly serves. Perpetrators may present and often actually see their actions as in the service of higher ideals and of beneficial outcomes, even to the victims themselves (raising a good child), to society (creating social equality), or to all of humanity (creating a better world).

My discussion of the concept of evil suggests that it could be a useful concept for psychologists. It could lead, for example, to more focused exploration of the characteristics of persons, cultures, and situations that lead to harmdoing that represents an overreaction to circumstances (provocation), is extreme and/or recurrent. It also could lead to more focused work on how cultures that promote such responses and who respond in these ways develop. Time will tell whether evil will be a comfortable concept for psychologists and whether it will become used.

Although the starting point for evil is usually the frustration of basic human needs (see subsequent discussion), evil actions are made possible by some or all of the following: lack or loss of concern with the welfare of other people; a lack of empathy with people, both lack of empathic feelings and lack of understanding how others feel; lack of self-awareness, the ability to understand one's own motives; having a negative view of others; a sense of entitlement, a focus on one's own rights; and devaluation, fear of, and hostility toward some or all human beings. How do the psychological tendencies that contribute to evil actions come about? How do motivations to intensely harm others arise? How do inhibitions decline?

THE ORIGINS OF EVIL

Both in groups and individuals, the evolution of evil starts with the frustration of basic human needs and the development of destructive modes of need fulfillment. Evil usually begins when profoundly important needs of human beings are not fulfilled, either in the course of growing up or later in life, and especially when early frustration of basic needs is combined with later frustration. We human beings have certain shared psychological needs that must be fulfilled if we are to lead reasonably satisfying lives: We need to feel secure; we need to develop a positive identity; we need to feel effective and to have reasonable control over what is essential to us; we need both deep connections to other people and autonomy or independence; we need to understand the world and our place in it (see Staub, 1989, 1996b, 1998a; for additional views on basic needs, see Burton, 1990; Kelman, 1990; Maslow, 1971).

Basic needs press for satisfaction. If people cannot fulfill them constructively, they will engage in destructive psychological processes and actions to satisfy them. Destructive need satisfaction means one of two things. First, people will satisfy some basic need in ways that in the long run interfere with the satisfaction of other needs. One example is a child who blames himself for harsh parental treatment, in part at least because this increases a sense of security: "If I am at fault, I have a chance to avoid punishment by acting differently." This self-blaming, however, interferes with the need for a positive identity, as well as the ability to create positive connections. Another example is a person who so intensely focuses on the satisfaction of one need, such as feeling effective and being in control, that in the process alienates other people and has difficulty fulfilling the need for positive connection. Second, people may satisfy needs in ways that interfere with the fulfillment of other people's needs or harm others. The need for security, a feeling of effectiveness, or a positive identity may be satisfied by power over other people and the use of force.

EVIL IN GROUPS:
GENOCIDE AND MASS KILLING

I start with an exploration of group behavior, particularly genocide and mass killings, as manifestations of evil. This exploration is relevant to the understanding of lesser harmdoing within societies, such as discrimination. The conception that I briefly describe has been applied to and supported by an examination of the Holocaust, the genocide of the Armenians, the "autogenocide" in Cambodia, and the disappearances in Argentina (Staub, 1989); by a brief examination of the mass killing in Bosnia (Staub, 1996b) and the genocide in Rwanda (Staub, in press-b); and by a brief exploration of the mass killing of native Americans in the United States (Staub, in press-a). Its description (see subsequent discussion) draws on all of these sources, but especially on Staub (1989).

In understanding violence in a group, whether the group is a society or a smaller community such as a school, gang, or family, it is important to consider both influences at the level of the group (culture, political system and processes, the role of leaders, group psychological processes) and individual psychology. The abstract identification of relevant social and psychological or other principles has somewhat limited value. The specification of how psychological and social processes arise from societal conditions and culture and how they join is required. In other words, the generation of violence in the group is best studied and understood as a systemic process.

Instigating Conditions and the Psychological and Social Processes They Give Rise To

Difficult conditions of life in a society are one important starting point for the evolution of mass killing and genocide. Intense economic problems or political conflict, great social changes, or their combination profoundly frustrate basic needs. People usually do not know how to deal with the material deprivation, chaos, and social disorganization these conditions create. They do not join together to deal with them effectively. Instead, the life problems in society give rise to psychological and social processes that turn subgroups of society against each other.

Individuals, feeling helpless on their own, turn to their group for identity and connection. They scapegoat some other groups. They adopt or create destructive ideologies—hopeful visions of social arrangements but visions that also identify enemies who supposedly stand in the way of the fulfillment of these visions. Such psychological and social processes help affirm identity and connection within the group, offer the possibility of effectiveness and control, and provide a new understanding of reality. Ideological movements are especially effective vehicles for the fulfillment of basic needs. Ideologies are almost always part of the generation of genocide and other collective violence.

Other instigators include real conflicts of interest, of varied kinds. These can be conflicts of vital interests, such as the need for living space, as between the Israelis and the Palestinians. However, these real conflicts are intractable because they have essential psychological and cultural components, such as attachment to a territory that is part of the self-definition of a group, or mistrust and fear of the other. Conflict between dominant groups and subordinate groups with little access to resources, power, or privilege, can also instigate violence.

In the latter instances as well, the issue of frustration of basic needs and psychological reactions to their frustration are important, so is the presence, almost invariably, of ideology. When subordinate groups demand more, they threaten not only privilege but also the feeling of security, identity, and worldview of dominant groups. They threaten the "legitimizing ideologies" (Sidanius, in press) that such groups have long employed. When dominant groups engage in increasingly harsh acts to defend their dominance, one of the primary sources of genocide since World War II (Fein, 1993), they usually are guided by such ideologies.

The Evolution of Collective Violence

Great violence, and certainly group violence, usually evolves over time. Individuals and groups change as a result of their own actions. Acts that harm others, without restraining forces, bring about changes in perpetrators, other members of the group, and the whole system that makes further and more harmful acts probable. In the course of this evolution, the personality of individuals, social norms, institutions, and culture change in ways that make further and greater violence easier and more likely.

People justify their actions by blaming the victims. As their initial devaluation intensifies, they come to see their victims as less than human and to exclude them from the moral realm (Opotow, 1990; Staub, 1990). The usual moral principles and values that prohibit violence and protect people from being harmed become inapplicable to the victims. They are replaced by higher values derived from an ide-

ology, such as protecting the purity, goodness, life, and well-being of one's own group and creating a better society or improving all of humanity by destroying the victims.

Progressively, the norms of the group change. Behavior toward the victims that would have been inconceivable becomes accepted and "normal." Institutions are changed or created to serve violence. The society is transformed. In the end, there may be a *reversal of morality*. Killing the victims becomes the right, moral thing to do. This has been advocated and has become accepted by at least some of the perpetrators, and often by many in the society, in many instances ranging from Nazi Germany to Rwanda (Gourevich, 1998). As violence evolves, it frequently expands to include other groups as victims.

Often, this process takes place over a long historical period. For example, in Turkey, Armenians were persecuted for a long time, with occasionally intense violence against them, long before the government that perpetrated the genocide came to power (Staub, 1989). At times, the process seems to unfold fast, but there are usually significant cultural and historical elements that prepare the ground. Past violence between groups and unhealed wounds in perpetrators may be especially likely to contribute to a speedy evolution, as they did in Bosnia. Intense propaganda by leaders and the creation of paramilitary groups also facilitate a speedy evolution to intense violence (Staub, in press-b).

Cultural Preconditions

Evil is the outcome of normal psychological processes in groups (and individuals): the frustration of basic needs, scapegoating and ideologies that serve to fulfill these needs, harming others and the evolution that follows from this. This evolution normally has begun long before a group (or individual) engages in extreme, persistently destructive acts. In the end, a society (or person) may become evil, in the sense that its characteristics make intensely harmful actions probable. Often, groups develop cultures and social institutions that are not themselves evil, but they create the preconditions or enhance the potential for the generation and speedy evolution of evil.

Cultural Devaluation

Perhaps the most important source of evil is the way the "other" is seen, or the devaluation of others. The devaluation of certain groups and their members often becomes part of a culture. Devaluation can vary in form and intensity (Staub, 1989). A milder form is not liking the other, seeing the other as lazy, unintelligent, and generally inferior. A more intense form—which often arises when a devalued group is relatively successful, such as the Jews in Germany, the Armenians in Turkey, or the Tutsis in Rwanda—is to see the other as manipulative, exploitative, dishonest, and generally morally deficient, characteristics that are claimed to have brought members of that group wrongful gains at the expense of the dominant group. This latter form of devaluation easily evolves into seeing the other as a threat to the survival of one's own group, as Hitler (1923/1943) saw the Jews, an especially intense form of devaluation.

The human tendency to differentiate between ingroup and outgroup, us and them, has been extensively demonstrated. The devaluation of a whole group arises out of this tendency. It has several origins (Staub, 1996b). One of them is social stratification: A subgroup of society has become poor or less privileged, which is justified by devaluation. The differentness of a group that may create discomfort or fear or may threaten identity is another source. A further source is exploitation of a group, which may result from prior devaluation but is then justified by further devaluation, as in the case of African Americans.

The need to create a separate identity is a further origin. This seems to have played a role in giving rise to Christian anti-Semitism (Staub, 1989) and may have played a role among Serbs, Croats, and Muslims in Yugoslavia. Difficult life conditions that require a scapegoat, the strengthening of identity and connection within a group

through enmity, and real conflicts of interest all can lead to intense devaluation of another that becomes part of a group's culture.

A past history of conflict, antagonism, and violence between two groups can give rise to an especially intense form of devaluation, which I have called an *ideology of antagonism*. This is a perception of the other as an enemy and a group identity in which enmity to the other is an integral component. When an ideology of antagonism exists, anything good that happens to the other inflames hostility. The ideology makes the world seem a better place without the other.

Once devaluation becomes part of a culture, its literature, art, and media are perpetuated in social institutions, and, especially once it gives rise to discrimination or other institutionalized forms of antagonism, it becomes highly resistant to change. Even when its public expression is relatively quiescent for a period of time, as it was in the first decade of this century in Germany or during the Tito era in the fomer Yugoslavia, it often remains part of the deep structure of the culture and can reemerge when instigating conditions for violence are present.

Orientation to Authority

All societies foster some degree of respect for and obedience to authority. Without that, group life is impossible. However, when respect and unquestioning obedience are overemphasized, the potential for destructive social processes intensifies. Observation and research indicate that, in many cases of genocide or mass killing, the society has been characterized by strong respect for authority (Gourevich, 1998; Kressel, 1996; Staub, 1989).

Such an orientation to authority has at least three problematic consequences. First, when instigation to violence arises, such as difficult life conditions or group conflict, people who have relied on leaders for guidance and protection will find it more difficult to bear the threat, anxiety, and frustration of basic needs they experience. Second, when policies and practices are instituted in a group that harms others, people will be less willing to speak out to oppose the authorities and the rest of the group. As a result, the evolution is less likely to stop. Third, such strong respect for authority makes obedience to immoral orders by authorities more likely.

Other Cultural Characteristics

There are several other predisposing cultural characteristics. One is a pluralistic rather than monolithic culture. Well-established democracies (Rummel, 1994; Staub, in press-b) that are genuinely pluralistic are unlikely to engage in genocide. Pluralistic societies not only allow a broad range of beliefs and views but are likely to be more self-correcting. Societal self-concepts—both of superiority and of weakness or inferiority—are also important.

I recently suggested "unhealed wounds" in a society as an important predisposing characteristic. When a group has experienced great suffering, especially due to persecution and violence at the hand of others, and is therefore deeply wounded, it is more likely to respond to a renewed threat with violence. People who experience trauma are deeply affected (Janoff-Bulman, 1992; McCann & Pearlman, 1990). The resulting self-focus makes it difficult for them to consider the needs of others in case of conflict. Their feeling of insecurity in the world will make members of victimized groups see the world as a dangerous place and experience threat as more intense than it is. They are more likely to engage, therefore, in what they see as defensive aggression (Staub, 1998b).

Healing following victimization makes it less likely that a group turns against another and perpetrates violence. Others acknowledging the group's suffering, expressing caring and empathy, providing emotional and material support, all contribute to healing. The group engaging with its past experience, including certain kinds of memorials and rituals of mourning and remembrance, also can promote healing (Staub, 1998b).

Followers, Leaders, and the Elite

Milgram's (1974) research on and theorizing about obedience has implicated obedience as an important contributor to genocide. I suggested previously the wide-ranging implications of a group's orientation to authority on the evolution of genocidal processes, as well as the importance of direct obedience by perpetrators. Reports from Rwanda indicate that orders by authorities to kill had a powerful influence (Gourevich, 1998).

However, obedience is not a primary cause of genocide. The conception advanced here suggests that instigating conditions and cultural preconditions lead people to be open to, join, and even seek and create leadership that turns the group against others. It suggests that the inclinations of followers are extremely important in a genocidal process.

Still, except under the most extreme conditions, leaders and the elite in a society have some latitude in the direction they take. The political leadership and economic elite of a country, or a segment of them, frequently spearhead the evolution toward violence. They propagate a destructive ideology, intensify historical antagonisms, work to maintain differences in power and status, and create organizations that are potential instruments of violence. Paramilitary-type organizations, broadly defined, have become in many instances tools of collective violence in Rwanda, Argentina and other South American countries, Turkey, Germany, and elsewhere.

Such behavior by leaders frequently is interpreted as the desire to gain followers, to maintain power and influence with followers, or both. These can be and often are part of leaders' motives. However, leaders are also members of their groups and are affected by instigating conditions and culture. Their own basic needs are frustrated; they and their families have unhealed wounds. A more complex psychology of leaders is important both for understanding the origins and developing effective methods of preventing group violence.

Bystander Actions

The passivity of bystanders allows the continued evolution that ends in intense collective violence. Passivity by internal bystanders, by members of the population where the violence is occurring, and by external bystanders, outside groups, and nations, encourages perpetrators. Such passivity is common (Staub, 1989, 1993). External bystanders frequently continue commercial, cultural, and other relations with a country that engages in violence against an internal group, thereby expressing tacit acceptance. Often, some external bystanders actively support the perpetrator group. When instigators and predisposing cultural characteristics have existed but violence has remained limited in scope, as in South Africa, Israel, or Northern Ireland, usually bystanders have taken an active role (Cairns & Darby, 1998; Staub, in press-b).

BYSTANDERS AS EVIL: THE EXAMPLE OF RWANDA

I return to the question of whether bystanders can be seen as evil and examine bystander actions in Rwanda and some complexities surrounding bystander behavior. The circumstances bystanders face in a situation such as Rwanda are different from those of witnesses who see in front of them a person who is in great distress and needs help (DesForges, 1999). Even then, circumstances are usually ambiguous: There is pluralistic ignorance, diffusion of responsibility, and the diffidence of many people to step forward (Latane & Darley, 1970; Staub, 1974). However, circumstances preceding collective violence are often more ambiguous. Perpetrators usually claim self-defense or other good reasons for what they do. When there is mob violence against a victim group, which often is instigated by authorities, participants and the authorities usually claim that it was the spontaneous response of the population to threat, danger, and violent actions by others.

In this spirit, perhaps, France sent troops to help the Rwandan government in 1990, when a small rebel group that called itself the Rwandan Patriotic Front (RPF) entered the country from Uganda. This group consisted primarily of Tutsi refugees who had lived in Uganda since they escaped earlier waves of violence against Tutsis, beginning in 1959. The French help temporarily stopped the RPF, but its activities intensified again after massacres of Tutsi peasants by Hutus, who make up about 85% of the population in Rwanda. France did not complain to the government about these massacres and continued to help militarily (Gourevich, 1998; Prunier, 1995). In 1993, the government and the RPF agreed, in the Arusha accords, to a multiparty government that would include the RPF. The accord prohibited the acquisition of more arms by the parties, but France continued to send arms to the government.

Bystanders often respond to events on the basis of a history of relationships they have had with the parties involved. They refrain from assessing and making decisions on the basis of actual events, moral principles, and human suffering. They either do not exercise prudence or good judgment, which the ancient Greeks regarded an essential element of morality (Staub, 1978), or they act on the basis of sentiments and what they regard as their interests. France may have acted as it did, in part, because of a friendship between President Mitterand of France and the President of Rwanda, Habyarimana. France also may have acted as it did because the RPF came from Uganda, which in the colonial era was ruled by England, and France feared that an Anglophile influence would spread into an area of Africa they considered their domain (Gourevich, 1998; Prunier, 1995).

However, France was not the only culprit. Information about impending violence and later about the ongoing genocide against Tutsis had come to the rest of the world from many quarters. Human Rights Watch issued alarming reports. The commanding general of the United Nations peacekeeping force, Major General Dallaire, received information from a person within the Rwandan president's circle of plans for a genocide against the Tutsis. He was not allowed to take action but was told by his superiors within the United Nations to communicate this information to President Habyarimana, whose circle prepared the plans for genocide (DesForges, 1999).

As the violence began in April 1994, some Belgian peacekeepers were killed. Belgium withdrew its contingent of peacekeepers, and the United Nations followed, withdrawing most of them. As the genocidal proportions of this violence emerged, General Dallaire claimed, and many now believe, that he could have stopped it all with 5,000 troops. However, no one was interested in such action. Within a few months as many as 800,000 people were killed (some estimate 1 million; see Gourevich, 1998), most of them Tutsis, but also more than 50,000 Hutus who were seen as politically "moderate" or who were from the South in contrast to the group in power, which came from the Northwest. (For an application of the conception of the origins in genocide to Rwanda, see Staub, in press-b.)

The United States was a passive bystander but also acted in ways that made a response by others less likely. The United Nations, other nations, and the United States resisted calling the violence genocide, so that the genocide convention, which requires or at least creates strong pressure for a response, would not be invoked. The United States resisted and slowed down a vote in the Security Council on sending back peacekeepers, even though U.S. troops were not required. The United States refused to provide equipment but insisted on leasing it to the United Nations. The United States and the United Nations haggled over the amount to be paid for the equipment, while every day many thousands of people were killed (Gourevich, 1998).

Does it make sense to call the passivity and at times complicity by bystander nations "evil" in the face of information about impending violence, and especially in the face of actual, very large-scale violence? The previous analysis suggests both that such passivity (and, of course, even more support or complicity) makes the evolution toward genocide more likely by encouraging and affirming perpetrators and that bystander nations have great potential influence in inhibiting this evolution. In addition, at times, the need for action is clear and there are low-cost ways to

at least attempt to exert influence (see also Staub, 1989, 1996b, 1996c, in press-a, in press-b).

Passivity and various forms of support for perpetrators by outside nations contributes to extreme harm. Often, there is no provocation to justify even limited violence against the victims, much less genocide—or passivity in the face of it. The passivity and complicity often persist. In its physical properties, the situation is highly dissimilar from allowing a young child to drown while one is watching, but in its meaning, it is similar. Perhaps it is also like passively watching while someone is drowning the child, without even calling out to the person to stop. Although passivity is different from action, in terms of the definition of evil offered previously, the kind of passivity and complicity I discuss here is comparable in its effects to the actions that may be called evil. Even passivity in this case involved action—as torturous contortions by a spokeswoman for the U.S. State Department in avoiding the use of the term *genocide* in relation to Rwanda indicated, together with other actions to stop the international community from responding. Calling certain kinds of passivity and especially complicity evil might have influence on the behavior of nations, which is important for the prevention of future genocides.

Highly questionable actions on the part of international humanitarian organizations and the United Nations followed the genocide. The RPF defeated the government army and stopped the genocide. Elements of this army, together with paramilitary groups—the *interahamwe*—were the prime perpetrators of the genocide. These "genocidaires," together with huge numbers of Hutus—who either participated in the genocide, were pressured or forced by the genocidaires, or frightened by the propaganda about the Tutsis' murderous intentions—fled into neighboring countries. The 1.5 million to 2 million refugees lived in camps, the largest ones in Zaire, very near the Rwandan border. These camps were run by the former army and the *interahamwe*. They ruled over the refugees, stopped those who were so inclined from returning home, used the aid they received as a source of income, and bought large shipments of arms that were delivered to the camps. After awhile, they began incursions into Rwanda, killing many Tutsis and some Hutus who were regarded as sympathetic to Tutsis, and destroying and stealing property. The humanitarian organizations and international community did nothing to deal with this situation, allowing not only ongoing violence but the buildup of the capacity for continuing the genocide. Although some humanitarian organizations, aware of what was happening, pulled out, others immediately took their place.

Part of the problem seemed to be systemic. Humanitarian organizations have a mandate, which is to provide assistance. They do not ask why people need help or make policy judgments as to who should or should not receive help. Under these circumstances, a split self may develop, as in the hero of George Orwell's *1984* (1949) who opposes the totalitarian system and understands the absurdity of the government declaring the friend of yesterday an enemy and the enemy of yesterday a friend, but nonetheless goes about his job with great enthusiasm, erasing written information about the past and replacing it with a false history that is consistent with current circumstance (Staub, 1989). However, part of the problem also may have been what Gourevich (1998) described as a well-known syndrome, "clientitis," the tendency by humanitarian organizations to see only, and be taken in by, the perspective of their client.

The reason for the United Nations and the international community to do nothing about the situation in the camps may have been similar to their usual reasons for inaction: a difficult situation, the absence of clear national interest to motivate action, and a disregard of the human costs of passivity. Besides, action was already taken—people in the camps were being helped. Perhaps there is also some truth to more sinister motives seen by Kegame, the vice president of Rwanda (Gourevich, 1998): Africans, like the Tutsi-led RPF, took events into their own hands, in Rwanda and in Zaire, without guidance and influence by the international community. Moreover, these actions defeated the aims of major international actors, particularly France, who supported the Hutu genocidaires until the very end.

Passivity was certainly not all due to blindness. In the first few months after the genocide, there was discussion within the United Nations of assembling an international force to disarm the "militants" in the camp and separate out from the rest of the refugees the criminal elements and the political forces planning a continuation of the genocide. However, in response to a request for volunteers by the United Nations Secretary-General, no country was willing to provide troops.

The Individual in Group Violence

I address, briefly, the question of the characteristics of participants in group violence at this point, rather than earlier, for two reasons. First, although past study of instances of group violence has provided substantial information of the roots of such violence, individual perpetrators have relatively rarely been studied. Second, the discussion of individual perpetrators relates to the next topic. However, this is not a simple relation: Group violence is a societal process, and some of those who are perpetrators of it would be unlikely to become violent as individuals.

In the conception I advanced, the personalities of people who, in the course of the evolution of group violence become perpetrators, are likely to be primarily the expression of the culture. They may carry the cultural characteristics identified previously, perhaps to a greater extent than the rest of the population. For example, members of the paramilitary group important in bringing the Nazis to power were probably about as anti-Semitic as the German people in general. However, those in leadership positions were intensely anti-Semitic (Merkl, 1980).

The limited evidence also indicates that perpetrators of the Holocaust (Steiner, 1980) and of torture in Greece (Haritos-Fatouros, 1988) were strongly authority-oriented (Staub, 1989). People who have developed strong respect for authority usually like to be part of a hierarchical system. They enjoy being led as well as having authority over others lower in the hierarchy. They prefer order and predictability. Their preference for and reliance on authority, hierarchy, and structure make social conditions under which effective leadership and the protective role of the leaders break down, and when uncertainty about the future and about how to deal with the present is great (Soeters, 1996), it makes it especially difficult for them.

People whose basic needs in childhood were frustrated to a greater extent also may be especially affected by social conditions and group conflict that frustrate basic needs. Individuals with personal wounds, or with hostility toward other people that is kept in check under normal conditions, or both, may be activated by conditions that instigate group violence. All such persons may find a clear and well-defined ideology and involvement with an ideological movement highly appealing. Perpetrators tend to show early ideological affinity with the violent groups they come to serve (Lifton, 1986).

Personality appears to be a source of selection of people by those in authority for perpetrator roles. It also seems to be a source of "self-selection," not initially for destroying others but for roles that later may become violent. Needs for identity and connection, low self-esteem (as in the case of hate groups in the United States; Staub, in press-a), the desire to find leaders, and the need for a clear-cut ideological vision, all may lead people to "join." However, once a group is formed, a system of *careerism*—the desire to advance in the system—can also enter (Steiner, 1980). To gain respect from like-minded others, to be a good member of the group, is probably also an important motivation.

Once they are part of an ideological-perpetrator group and participating in behavior that harms others, important changes seem to take place in people, including a progressive desensitization to others' suffering. This might develop into pleasure in harming others. The boundaries of the self are loosened and the usual internalized prohibitions and controls are lost, as in mobs (Staub & Rosenthal, 1994), but also progressively in individual conduct in relation to devalued others.

THE DEVELOPMENT OF AGGRESSION IN CHILDREN AND ADOLESCENTS

In discussing collective violence, I have focused on instigating conditions, already existing characteristics of the culture and psychological and social processes in the course of the evolution of increasing violence. In exploring the origins of aggression in youth and then commenting on an evolution toward evil, I start with socialization and experience that develops certain characteristics in children.

Neglect and harsh treatment are probably the primary source of aggression in children and youth (Coie & Dodge, 1997; Staub, 1996a, 1996b). When children are neglected and harshly treated, all their basic needs are frustrated. As a result, they come to fear, mistrust, and dislike people. At the least, these feelings easily arise in them in response to threat or the stresses of life (Staub, 1998a).

Children who are treated harshly also learn that aggression is normal, acceptable, or even right, rather than deplorable or unacceptable (Huesmann & Eron, 1984). In addition to experiencing aggression against themselves, they often see it among the adults in their lives, whether it is in their homes or the community around them. This further shows that the world is dangerous and people are hostile. It further models aggression as a way of dealing with conflict and acting in interpersonal situations.

Boys who grow up in such environments are also likely to watch a substantial amount of aggressive television, which provides information consistent with their already evolving understanding of the world and of how to behave in it (Eron, Walder, & Lefkowitz, 1971; Huesmann & Eron, 1984). The experiences of such boys limit opportunities for learning social skills (Weiss, Dodge, Bates, & Pettit, 1992), especially prosocial modes of connecting to and engaging with their peers (Friedrich & Stein, 1973).

Aggressive boys see other people as hostile, especially to themselves. They see others as intending to harm. For example, when they see pictures showing boys playing and one boy kicking another while trying to get the ball away from the him, they interpret this as intentional harmdoing (Coie & Dodge, 1997). Aggressive adults, both college students and prison inmates, also see other people as hostile (Galvin & Spielman, 1999). However, intentional rather than accidental harm caused by others is especially likely to provoke retaliatory aggression (Mallick & McCandless, 1966). Boys who are not aggressive assume that such acts are accidental. Some children who are badly treated, given their specific circumstances, may come to feel hostility and even hatred toward people. However, the need for connection to other people is profound, and even such children and the adults they grow into will desire and seek connection to some others.

Negative beliefs and hostility, as they come to be expressed in behavior, create a self-fulfilling prophecy. Reacting to others as if they had aggressed against us makes them respond aggressively. A group of unfamiliar boys, after spending a period of time with an aggressive boy, becomes aggressive toward him (Dodge, 1980). Our early experiences shape us, but we, in turn, tend to create circumstances that further develop our personalities in the same direction, a form of "self-socialization."

Both in youth and later in life, the characteristics such boys develop lead to expressively violent behavior, apart from any tendency for instrumental violence they may develop. Later in life, they also aggress against their children (Huesmann, Eron, Lefkowitz, & Walder, 1984). It is estimated that about 30% of children who have received harsh physical punishment treat their children the same way, in contrast to 2% to 3% of physical abuse in the general population (Ziegler, Taussig, & Black, 1992).

Harsh treatment also leads to difficulty in liking and accepting oneself. As Freud has proposed, rather than seeing, examining, and accepting conflicting, problematic aspects of oneself, one projects them into other people. Alternatively, it becomes extremely important to affirm one's own value, relative to other people. Because in many parts of our society and in the world men are supposed to be strong and powerful, affirming one's value becomes showing that one is strong and powerful. Many men who have been imprisoned for violent crimes report that they used to pick fights either to feel good about themselves or to look good in others' eyes (Toch, 1969).

Self-Esteem and Aggression

How does this picture fit the recent evidence and debate on self-esteem and aggression in youth? Olweus (1979, 1993) found that bullies, who tend to pick on and repeatedly victimize other children, do not have low self-esteem. Coie and Dodge (1997), in reviewing research on aggression in children, reported that aggressive boys do not have low self-concepts and that they tend to blame others rather than themselves for "negative outcomes." Baumeister (1997) proposed that it is high self-esteem and injured narcissism that are associated with aggression.

However, the background and experience of boys I described make it unlikely that they have "genuinely" high self-esteem, as does further information I describe later. How might we understand the evidence, then? First, such boys, and later the men they become, may compensate for their sense of vulnerability and social and academic difficulties by proclaiming their own worth, thereby affirming themselves to others and even themselves. Related to such a compensatory self-esteem may be projection, seeing weakness, vulnerability, and various bad qualities in others, rather than themselves, and blaming others for negative outcomes.

Second, there may be important, alternative avenues in the development of aggression. One of these is permissiveness and lack of punishment for aggression. Another is an environment that may or may not be harsh and punitive but encourages aggression, so that children, youth, and the adults they grow into feel when they aggress that they are doing the right thing. In fact, although many aggressive children are in-effective, and although their aggressive behavior is disorganized, with limited self-control and easy flare-up of anger (Rausch, 1965), others are effective aggressors. Although the former are unpopular among their peers, among the latter, aggression is unrelated to popularity (Coie & Dodge, 1997).

A group of peers, for example, antisocial friends or members of a gang, may also help to maintain self-esteem. Often a seeming focus in such groups, and probably the most important function of the group for its members, is to help create and maintain positive identity and con-nection to like-minded others. Thus, members of such groups would have a heightened sense of self, at least while they are members.

Perhaps another important issue is not sim-ply the level of self-esteem but what it is based on and how stable and reliable rather than how frag-ile it is. Many boys who become aggressive do not have the socially valued means to gain a positive image through competence and good perfor-mance in school and good relationships with peers. Therefore, they organize their self-esteem around strength, power, and physical superiority over others. Their early experiences as victims, the models of aggression around them, and the culture's focus on male strength and superiority all facilitate this. It is how self-esteem is consti-tuted, what self-esteem is based on, that may mat-ter. However, the self-esteem of aggressive boys and of aggressive men (Baumeister, 1997) appears to be very vulnerable and fragile. Its maintenance may require the continued feeling of and perhaps use of strength and power over others.

Thus, the level of self-esteem, how it is con-stituted, and its fragility and sources may all matter. As I have written elsewhere

> *In groups and in individuals very high self-evaluation often masks self-doubt. Persistent life difficulties may contradict the high self-evaluation and bring self-doubt to the surface. Even when there is no underly-ing self-doubt, a very high self-evaluation may be associated with limited concern for others. Among in-dividuals, a* moderately *positive self concept is most strongly associated with sensitivity and responsive-*

> *ness to other people. (Staub, 1989, p. 55; see also Jary-mowitz, 1977; Reese, 1961)*

People have to value themselves to value other people, but not value themselves so strongly that others do not matter.

"High self-esteem" for some people (but not for many others) may include a sense of superi-ority that must be defended. When it is frustrated, it is likely to lead to aggression. Low self-esteem may lead some people to affirm themselves in their own and others' eyes by aggression or to have a greater sense of insecurity in the world and feel that they must defend themselves. I have suggested that both "group self-concepts" of superiority and of weakness and vulnerabil-ity (and sometimes their combination) are cul-tural elements that may make genocide more likely (Staub, 1989).

However, in many instances of violence or with many actors, self-esteem may not have a primary role. Instead, orientations to people and the world—perceptions of hostility, valuing or devaluing people, and feelings of hostility—may have strong influence, even though the experi-ences that have affected these orientations also have had an impact on self-esteem.

The Evolution of Evil

I have implied and partially described an evolu-tion of aggressive children. Such children and the adults they become see others as hostile, and many of them may come to feel hostile toward people. They develop a cognitive structure, inter-nal dialogue, and behavioral skills (Meichen-baum, 1980) that move them to aggressive actions. The reactions they receive further shape them.

Given their limited social skills and aggres-sive behavior, they are often unpopular with their peers. However, they lack self-awareness. They do not know that they are unpopular. Nonag-gressive kids who are unpopular tend to know this, which makes it more likely that they will change their behavior and become more popular over time (Zakriski, Jacobs, & Coie 1997). Aggres-sive boys often have academic difficulties as well.

They are, on the whole, disconnected from peers and from school in general, a disconnection that seems to increase over time. Their aggressive behavior tends to deteriorate and become more intense (Coie & Dodge, 1997). All along, they tend to have a few other antisocial youth as associates. Over time, they may join a gang.

As a result of this evolution, some of them may come to engage in persistently aggressive behavior that creates great harm to others. They may become highly and predictably reactive in their aggression. Given such an evolution, it is reasonable to assume that some youth, as they grow into adults, develop the intention to harm others. Harming others may be a way for them to affirm their identity, to gain a feeling of security, to feel effective and in control, to develop and maintain connections with aggressive peers or associates, and to maintain the understanding of the world they have developed. In other words, they come to fulfill their basic needs in aggressive ways (Staub, 1998a).

Preventing Violence and Evil in Youth: The Case of Bullying

Warm, affectionate parenting, positive guidance, leading children and youth to learn caring and helping by engaging in such behavior, make the development of aggression unlikely and the development of caring about others' welfare probable (Eisenberg, 1992; Staub, 1979, 1996a). However, children who have had harsh, punitive experiences at home or other experiences that create aggression need not continue to develop in the direction they started. Research on resilience shows, for example, that significant human connections—to teachers, counselors, relatives outside the home, friends of the family (Butler, 1997) and, I believe, to peers as well (Staub, 1979, 1999)—can ameliorate the effects of negative experiences.

Schools can be important places for either allowing and furthering or preventing the evolution of violence. Substantial recent evidence indicates that there is a tremendous amount of bullying or repeated victimization of students in schools by physical or verbal means or by exclusion (Farrington, 1993; Olweus 1993). Such victimization starts in the earliest school years. Some of the victims are themselves not aggressive. Others are aggressive; they also bully, although usually not those who have bullied them (Farrington, 1993).

Bullying contributes to the evolution of perpetrators into even more aggressive people. Although various characteristics of bullies as well as victims have been identified (Farrington, 1993; Olweus, 1993), bullying is not simply a matter of personality, but also of culture and system. Although not well explored as yet, the frequency of bullying differs by school and neighborhood. Variation in the "climate" of the classroom and school, the extent of guidance, and fairness in contrast to punitiveness contribute to school violence (Goldstein & Conoley, 1997) and are likely to contribute to bullying as well.

Teachers are frequently passive, as are peers, in the face of bullying. As with other forms of violence, this affirms perpetrators and must contribute to a feeling of insecurity and mistrust by victims. Bullying and aggression in school may be diminished by creating a community in the classroom that includes all students, a community in which students are participating members and in which respecting others is an important value and harming others is not accepted (Staub, 1999).

Bullying may help us further examine the meaning of the concept of evil. Extensive bullying creates significant harm. In recent years, I have been asking students to write about their personal experiences in relation to theory and research they read and discuss in my classes. The most frequent topic is the experience and painful effects of taunting, exclusion, and being picked on. Although some children and youth who bully may realize how much pain they create, many probably do not. Their motivation may be to get something from the other person, to look good in front of others, to create an alliance with others to feel powerful, or to respond to a differentness in another child that makes them uncomfortable. However, even though they lack awareness, their repeated actions, usually without provocation, create severe psychological pain, with long-term effects. If we are to use the concept, the identification of actions as evil cannot depend on the intentions or motivation of the actors.

Sexual Abuse in the Home: Revisiting Personality and System

A parent or parent substitute sexually engaging the child may be seen as evil, even if there is no physical force or overt intimidation. A child cannot freely give or withdraw consent. Engaging sexually with a child is a form of abuse that involves breaking a moral barrier and, in a large percentage of cases, creates significant long-term harm (McCann & Pearlman, 1990).

I analyze the influences that lead to such behavior with one type of perpetrator I call *needy–dependent* (Staub, 1991). The purpose of this analysis is to clarify further the origins of violence, to show how personality and system join in leading to the destructive fulfillment of basic needs. The analysis that follows is an application of the approach presented for group violence to a form of individual violence.

Gelinas (1983) described the kind of perpetrator I focus on here as a person who has difficulty acting in the world and taking care of his needs. Such a person meets a woman who was a "parentified child," someone who was put into the role of a caretaker of parents and siblings in her family of origin. As a good caretaker, she is good at responding to the needs of this man. They marry and have children. However, at some point, her long history of taking care of others catches up with her. She begins to withdraw. She may become ill or find other ways to pull back from physical and emotional caretaking of her family. She also pulls back from her sexual relationship with her husband. A daughter progressively becomes the parentified child in this family, assuming the burdens of physical as well as emotional caretaking.

In the course of this, warmth and affection may grow between the father and this daughter. They may watch television or do other things together. The father does not have the personal strength and skills needed to take action and satisfy his needs for connection or to feel worthwhile and significant and fulfill other emotional and sexual needs in legitimate ways. Instead, he breaks the moral barrier and sexually engages his daughter. The withdrawal and passivity of his wife also means that she is likely to remain passive as a bystander.

In the case of such a needy–dependent perpetrator, the family system as it interacts with personality is very important. In contrast, there is another type of perpetrator in which personality seems to have primary importance. He treats his family as his property, as chattel. His sexual abuse of his children is one expression of his personality and orientation to his family (Staub, 1991).

Sexually abusing fathers often rationalize and justify their actions. Therapists report absurd claims, such as having sexually engaged a daughter to protect her from the sexual dangers of the outside world (Staub, 1991).

CONCLUSIONS

Even evil actions by individuals are often the joint outcome of culture, whether of the society or a family; of a system of relationships among individuals including the passivity or encouragement of bystanders; of specific or nonspecific (systemic) instigators; and of the personality of perpetrators. Culture, social conditions, and how the system functions are more important in the case of group violence. Attention to the levels of influence, of predisposing conditions, instigators, and personality, are essential both to understand and prevent such violence, whether we call it evil or not.

Considering both individuals and collections of individuals, evil is usually the end result of an evolution. This is not necessarily a smooth, continuous evolution. It can progress to a point, halt, and then evolve further. Depending on where the evolution has progressed, individuals or groups may respond to "instigation" with intense violence. Alternatively, once the evolution has been set into motion, it may continue and lead to intense violence without further instigation.

Evil actions may serve the satisfaction of basic, profound, human needs that have an imperative character. When such needs are frustrated in the life of individuals and groups, destructive modes of need satisfaction are likely to develop. The nature of the individual or of the culture and social system of a group may lead to a heightened probability of violence by them. At the extreme, such individuals and groups also may develop the intention to harm or destroy others that habitually expresses itself in action. The absence of consideration for others' welfare also allows intense instrumental violence as well as wanton, seemingly motiveless violence. Further research and theory are needed on these developed forms of evil.

REFERENCES

Baumeister, R. F. (1997). *Evil: Inside human violence and cruelty.* New York: Freeman.

Latané, B., & Darley, J. (1970). *The unresponsive bystander: Why doesn't he help?* New York: Appleton-Century-Crofts.

Lifton, R. J. (1986). *The Nazi doctors: Medical killing and the psychology of genocide.* New York: Basic Books.

Milgram, S. (1974). *Obedience to authority: An experimental view.* New York: Harper & Row.

Staub, E. (1989). *The roots of evil: The origins of genocide and other group violence.* New York: Cambridge University Press.

Staub, E. (1993). The psychology of bystanders, perpetrators and heroic helpers. *International Journal of Intercultural Relations, 17,* 315–341.

Steiner, J. M. (1980). The SS yesterday and today: A sociopsychological view. In J. Dimsdale (Ed.), *Survivors, victims and perpetrators: Essays on the Nazi Holocaust* (pp. 405–457). Washington, DC: Hemisphere.

KEY POINTS

1. Genocide, the attempt to exterminate (murder) a whole ethnic group of people, is not as uncommon as is usually imagined.

2. Designating something as evil is sometimes used to suggest that the actions are not comprehensible in an ordinary human framework. They seem outside the bounds of morality or even of human agency, but evil behaviors can be studied.

3. Evil intentions are highly complicated because a person's real motive is often unconscious; individuals and groups tend to justify their actions, even to themselves, and various belief systems develop that propagate harmful actions in the service of some presumed good.

4. Evil actions are often caused by frustrations of basic human needs, lack or loss of concern with the welfare of others, a lack of empathy (both lack of empathic feelings and lack of understanding how others feel), lack of self-awareness, a negative view of others, a sense of entitlement, and devaluation of others.

5. Difficult conditions in a society can lead to mass killing and genocide. Helpless individuals may turn to their group for identity and connection, and scapegoat other groups.

6. A past history of conflict, antagonism, and violence between two groups can give rise to an especially intense form of devaluation. Staub calls this *ideology of antagonism.*

7. All societies foster some degree of respect for and obedience to authority. The potential for destructive social processes intensifies when unquestioning obedience is overemphasized. Neglect and harsh treatment are probably the primary source of aggression in children and youth.

QUESTIONS TO THINK ABOUT

1. What social conditions in present-day society might encourage violence and evil? How might our society change, so as to reduce violence?

2. Consider some of the roots of evil that Staub talks about in this article. How can family, peers, and society in general create an "evil" individual?

3. Staub goes into detail about the development of aggression in children, particularly boys. How should we change the way boys are raised?

4. What does Staub mean by a needy–dependent perpetrator? What kind of people fall into this category? What personality characteristics do people of this category have? How do they acquire these personality characteristics?

36

Training to Recognize Individual Differences in Collectivism and Individualism within Culture*

HARRY C. TRIANDIS AND THEODORE M. SINGELIS

Western cultures tend to emphasize the centrality of the autonomous individual. Eastern cultures, on the other hand, tend to emphasize the centrality of the collective (or group). Thus, for example, people in Calcutta tend to be very hospitable, whereas people in New York City tend to be very individualistic. Culture plays a very important, but often overlooked, role in personality and behavior. This article describes a self-administered questionnaire that allows individuals to determine their own tendencies toward individualism and collectivism.

Harry Triandis (1926–) received his Ph.D. from Cornell University and is psychology professor emeritus in the Personality-Social-Organizational division at the University of Illinois. His research focuses on the links of attitudes, norms, roles, and other elements of subjective culture to behavior, in different kinds of cultures such as the individualistic cultures found in Europe and North America, and the collectivist cultures found in most other parts of the world. Theodore M. Singelis, a professor at the California State University, is especially interested in teaching about culture, ethnicity, and diversity. He argues for the introduction of non-Western constructs and theories into psychology.

Triandis, Brislin and Hui (1988) described how individuals from collectivist cultures can be trained to interact more effectively with individuals from individualistic cultures and how individuals from individualistic cultures can be trained to interact more effectively with individuals from collectivist cultures. When such training is given, or when individuals naturally have the skills to place themselves into the framework of the other culture, they are interpersonally more effective (Bhawuk & Brislin, 1992; Singelis, 1994).

When an individual is presented with a scenario where one option is to maintain harmony and another to "tell it as it is," the "correct" response depends on where and with whom the interaction occurs. For example, East Asian collectivists are especially eager to maintain harmonious relationships while individualists from the U.S.A. are more concerned with clearly giving opinions. When a person selects the first option in the scenario with reference to Japan the response is scored as "correct" and the second option is

*Triandis, H. C. & Singelis, T. M. (1998). Training to recognize individual differences in collectivism and individualism within culture. *International Journal of Intercultural Relations, 22*, 35–47. Reprinted with permission from Elsevier Science. [Ed. note: All citations in the text of this selection have been left intact from the original, but the list of references includes only those sources that are the most relevant and important. Readers wishing to follow any of the other citations can find the full references in the original work or in an online database.]

scored as "incorrect." But when referencing the U.S.A. the reverse scoring is applied and it would be more "correct" to "tell it like it is." This type of generalization is well supported in the literature (for reviews see Triandis, 1994, 1995). Of course, there is great variation in the extent to which any individual is representative of the culture.

Triandis (1994, 1995) has stressed that within any culture there are individuals who are more or less allocentric (or idiocentric), the personality attributes that correspond to collectivism (and individualism) at the cultural level. Briefly, in collectivist cultures there will be some countercultural individuals, who will be idiocentric, and will want to escape from what they see as "the oppression" of their ingroups, and in individualistic cultures there will be some counter-cultural individuals, who will be allocentric, and will want to join communes and other collectives.

Thus, while cultural differences may be the most important consideration when making a "first-best guess" about an individual, within culture differences are also important. Demographics, especially social class, are also very important: Daab (1991) found that the more educated, in Poland, were more individualistic than the less educated; those who lived in cities were more individualistic than rural samples; men more than women; the young more than the old. Noricks et al. (1987) found that Americans over age 56 assigned greater importance to context than to content in making judgments about the attributes of individuals. This pattern is more typical of collectivist cultures than of individualist cultures. On the other hand, Americans who were younger than 56 did do this task the way people in individualistic cultures usually do it.

Individuals are subject to diverse experiences that need to be considered when interacting with them. For example, a 33-year-old Japanese business person with a Harvard MBA, who spent three years in France, is almost certain to have become more idiocentric than a 55-year-old Japanese, who owns a small business and has never left Japan. Similarly, an American who has married a Chinese and spent two years in Taiwan is likely to have become more allocentric than an American who has lived exclusively in Wyoming.

This mixing of backgrounds and experiences is increasingly a reality of the modern world. It is therefore not enough to know the culture of the person with whom we are interacting. We need to know a good deal more, and take it into account when formulating our behavior. A more sophisticated approach is to temper cultural knowledge with demographic and life-experience information, such as the type that we will present below. In sum, people should learn to make a "first-best guess" according to culture, and then adjust it in various ways according to demographics, life experiences, and other information revealed as interactions unfold.

We will present below an approach that can help trainees understand both cultural and individual differences. As it is now, the individual aspects are emphasized, but this is really a second step for those trainees who are already familiar with cultural differences. The items can be used at both levels—to introduce the concepts and then to expand the constructs to include individual (within culture) differences.

The nature of the self does vary across cultures (Triandis, 1989; Markus & Kitayama, 1991). Although all individuals will have both tendencies (Triandis, 1989; Singelis & Brown, 1995), in some cultures the self tends to be more independent of groups and in others more interdependent. The life experiences of allocentrics allowed them to maintain the interdependence they developed in their family life, and to transfer it to other ingroups. The life experiences of idiocentrics separated them from their family and other groups, and encouraged them to do "their own thing."

Training an individual to recognize such variations, within culture, will be of great value. After such training, an individual, by asking a few questions concerning the demographics of the person with whom she/he is interacting, will be able to "place" the other person much more accurately along the dimensions of individualism and collectivism and guess that the other person's personality will be more or less allocentric.

One way of providing such training is to ask a trainee to respond to a questionnaire that measures the "subjective individualism and collectivism" (SINDCOL) of individuals. In this paper we will present this questionnaire, and report that in fact it does measure tendencies toward idiocentrism or allocentrism. To simplify the terminology, we will use the words individualism and collectivism, but mean that these terms apply at the individual level (i.e., reflect the way the culture, demographics, and experiences have influenced the individual).

This questionnaire can be used in training. For example, one way would be for the trainer to discuss each section of the questionnaire, and have the trainee challenge the assumptions behind the questionnaire. Questioning the assumptions will make clear how the items reflect the individualism and collectivism cultural orientations as well as show trainees how individual experiences may shape each person's orientation towards social situations.

In sum, we present in the appendix an instrument that can be used to increase the sensitivity of trainees to individual differences in tendencies toward collectivism and individualism within cultures. This instrument happens to be enjoyable to respond to because many people (Americans at least) like to talk about the most important topic: themselves. Aside from training purposes, the questionnaire can also be used to measure tendencies toward collectivism and individualism in multimethod batteries that assess these constructs, because it correlates as expected with other such measures.

METHOD

Instrument Development

While reviewing the relevant literature Triandis (1995) realized that there are many factors that can influence an individual's individualism and collectivism. They were included in that book. They were also formulated into the 24 items composing the SINDCOL instrument shown in the appendix.

Participants

Ninety-six undergraduates, from the University of Illinois and 171 from the University of Hawaii at Manoa, responded to the instrument. The sample was quite diverse, including both men ($n = 109$) and women ($n = 156$) from a wide variety of ethnic backgrounds. The four most frequently reported ethnic backgrounds were: East Asian ($n = 87$), West European ($n = 59$), North European ($n = 46$), and Pacific Islander ($n = 45$).

Procedure

Participants were asked to complete a questionnaire containing the 24 item SINDCOL, attitude items measuring the horizontal and vertical dimensions of individualism and collectivism (see Singelis, Triandis, Bhawuk, & Gelfand, 1995), and the Self-Construal Scale (Singelis, 1994). Finally, we obtained the usual demographics such as sex, age, social class, ethnic background, and religion. Students took the questionnaire home, and returned it to an instructor in exchange for "extra credit points."

Analyses

To eliminate the influence of the social desirability of the terms "individualism" and "collectivism," subjects were randomly assigned to a condition in which they read a page that indicated that each construct had many highly undesirable aspects (e.g. individualists are more likely than collectivists to die of heart attacks; collectivists are more likely than individualists to die of cancer), while the other half of the subjects did not see that page. Results indicated no difference in the scores. Informal interviews with the subjects, suggested that most of them did not read the page. As one subject put it: "I know what these constructs mean. I did not need to read about them."

Initially, the 24 items of the SINDCOL (see appendix) were divided into their individualism and collectivism components. Items with low (below .25) item total correlations were dropped from their respective scales. This yielded a subjective individualism scale containing 9 items (numbers 3, 4, 7, 12, 13, 19, 21, 22, and 23) with an alpha of .71 and a subjective collectivism scale containing 11 items (numbers 1, 2, 5, 6, 9, 11, 15, 17, 18, 20, and 24) with an alpha of .69.

Attitude items measuring horizontal and vertical individualism–collectivism described by Singelis et al. (1995) and the Self-Construal Scale (Singelis, 1994) were used to determine the convergent validity of the Subjective Individualism and Collectivism measures (SINDCOL). Horizontat collectivism (HC) includes perceiving the self as a part of the collective, but seeing all members of the collective as the same, thus equality is stressed. Vertical collectivism (VC) includes perceiving the self as a part (or an aspect) of a collective and accepting inequalities within the collective. Horizontal individualism (HI) includes the conception of an autonomous individual and emphasis on equality. Vertical individualism (VI) includes the conception of an autonomous individual and acceptance of inequality. In short, the horizontal aspects emphasize equality while vertical dimensions accept the existence of inequalities.

Subjective individualism was related to H-I ($r = .39, p < .001$), V-I ($r = −.02, p = $ NS), H-C ($r = −.17, p < .01$), and V-C ($r = −.23, p < .001$). Subjective collectivism was correlated with H-I ($r = −.28, p < .001$), V-I ($r = .07, p = $ NS), H-C ($r = .24, p < .001$), and V-C ($r = .49, p < .001$). In multiple regressions the four vertical and horizontal scales accounted for 23% of the variance in subjective individualism and 31% of the variance in subjective collectivism.

The SINDCOL measures also showed the expected associations with self-construal. Subjective collectivism correlated positively with interdependence ($r = .53, p < .001$) and negatively with independence ($r = −.33, p < .001$) while the opposite pattern was observed for the relationship of subjective individualism with interdependence ($r = −.32, p < .001$) and independence ($r = .46, p < .001$).

Singelis et al. (1995) reported considerable convergence among various methods of mea-surement and the horizontal–vertical, individualism and collectivism constructs. In addition, subjects whose cultural background was from East Asia were significantly higher ($p < .001$) in collectivism than subjects whose background was European. Such convergence suggests the validity of the SINDCOL.

DISCUSSION

The data suggest that subjective individualism is related to being young (item 3), having traveled (item 4), having grandparents from Western cultures (item 7), having traveled overseas alone (item 12), having lived abroad for more than 6 months (item 13), having a job that requires one to work alone (item 19), having the tendency to do "own thing" (item 21), valuing privacy (item 22), and having an occupation that allows one to make own decisions while ignoring the needs and views of others (item 23).

Subjective collectivism is related to choosing family over personal goals (item 1), feeling close to groups (item 2), living in a small community (item 5), being heavily influenced by one's parents' and grandparents' traditions (item 6), being interdependent in one's finances (item 9), having had much formal traditional education, such as Sunday School (item 11), growing up in large families (item 15), disapproving of the story plots often found in the media (item 17), having a job that requires taking into account the views of others (item 18), needing others to be around in order to have fun (item 20), and having an occupation that requires paying attention to the needs of others (item 24).

An obvious problem with this approach is that it can produce data distorted by social desirability. But, [it] is very useful if a trainee learns what is socially desirable in another culture. For example, the data suggest that horizontal individualism is socially desirable, because those who provided high subjective individualism scores also provided high horizontal individualism scores.

In future research we should explore how subjects present themselves on the individualism and collectivism dimensions in more detail. Self-presentations can have important implications for understanding the social desirability of the constructs. Specifically, Triandis' (1995) analysis of horizontal and vertical individualism and collectivism suggested that the U.S. is a more vertical individualist culture than most Scandinavian countries; Sweden or Australia are the typical horizontal individualist cultures. The argument is based on the observations of the way these cultures react to the idea of using the tax structure to re-distribute income. Americans are more resistant than Swedes or Australians to such re-distributions. Furthermore, they tolerate 15% of the population being below the poverty line. Americans do not feel that unsuccessful minority members are "really" a part of their community that must be helped to come out of poverty in every way possible, even if that means much personal sacrifice. On the contrary, Americans are very competitive, concerned with individual success, and feel good when they "beat" others in the game of status. Thus, perhaps, vertical individualism is a better label for the U.S., and probably most of the Western democracies, than horizontal individualism. But our subjects tell us that they are horizontal individualists. This is an important observation. We see here the ambivalence that Myrdal (1944) identified as the American dilemma: How can we argue that we are equal and treat African Americans the way we do?

Subjective collectivism, in our measures, is more strongly related to vertical collectivism than horizontal collectivism. Given that we have a substantial number of Asian Americans in our sample, this may be an accurate reflection of their collectivism.

The items that determined individualism and collectivism in this sample would be useful in training people from collectivist cultures to recognize possible individual differences and to interact more effectively with Americans. A replication of this study in collectivist cultures would provide the data for training Americans to interact effectively with people from collectivist cultures. Until such replications are available, we can provisionally train both Americans and others to pay attention to the topics in the SINDCOL.

Once trainees are familiar with the topics, they can easily be included in ordinary conversation: e.g., How large was your family when you were a child? Do you like to spend some leisure time alone or do you simply have to have others around? Such questions do not appear too intrusive for conversations involving relative strangers across cultures, yet they can "place" the other on the individualism–collectivism continuum, much more accurately than the mere information that the person comes from France or China.

The questionnaire can be used initially to help introduce the constructs to novices, through self assessment and discussion. It could also be used to train more sophisticated audiences in the art of "sizing up" individuals.

Another use would be within the U.S. in diversity training. There is evidence that U.S. Hispanics and Asians (see Triandis, 1994 for summary of studies) are more collectivist than most Americans. But there are undoubtedly individual differences, and working through the categories of the subjective individualism–collectivism scale (SINDCOL) can provide the necessary clues for the differentiation of Hispanics and Asians.

REFERENCES

Markus, H., & Kitayama, S. (1991). Culture and self: Implications for cognition, emotion, and motivation. *Psychological Review, 98,* 224–253.

Myrdal, G. (1944). *An American dilemma: The Negro problem and modern democracy.* New York: Harper.

Noricks, J. S. Agler, L. H., Bartholomew, M., Howard-Smith, S., Martin, D., Pyles, S., & Shapiro, W.

(1987). Age, abstract thinking, and the American concept of person. *American Anthropologist, 89,* 667–675.

Singelis, T. M. (1994). The measurement of independent and interdependent self-construals. *Personality and Social Psychology Bulletin, 20,* 580–591.

Singelis, T. M., & Brown, W. J. (1995). Culture, self, and collectivist communication: Linking culture to individual behavior. *Human Communication Research, 21,* 354–389.

Triandis, H. C. (1989). The self and social behavior in differing cultural contexts. *Psychological Review, 96,* 506–520.

Triandis, H. C. (1995). *Individualism and collectivism.* Boulder, CO: Westview Press.

Triandis, H. C., Brislin, R., & Hui, C. H. (1988). Cross cultural training across the individualism-collectivism divide. *International Journal of Intercultural Relations, 12,* 269–289.

APPENDIX

The SINDCOL Instrument

Are You an Individualist or a Collectivist? Cultures differ in their emphasis on collectivism and individualism. Collectivists place some collective (family, workgroup, country) in a central position regulating social life. Individualists place the individual in the center of things. For example, when there is a conflict between the goals of a collective and an individual, in collectivist cultures it is obvious that the collective should "win" while in individualist cultures it is obvious that the individual *should* "win."

In this questionnaire we wish to help you find out for yourself if you are a collectivist or an individualist, by asking you to answer questions about your own circumstances and life style.

We will help you find out where you stand on these tendencies by summing "points." Under C (collectivism) and I (individualism) you should enter a rating on a 0 to 10 scale, following the instructions under each question.

For example, suppose we ask you: Do you feel a part of any group, so that if you were expelled by that group you would feel that your life has ended? If the answer is "Yes, very definitely, absolutely true," you would enter 10 under C. On the other hand, if it is not at all true, you might use a zero.

We will ask you questions that either reflect individualism, so you should enter a number between 0 and 10 next to I = , or collectivism, so you should enter a number between 0 and 10 next to C = . After you answer all the questions, add all the points you have given to C and separately the points you have given to I. You will then get an idea of how high you are in these tendencies.

This activity is cooperative between you and the researchers. We will give you the theoretical rationale for each question, and then you will make your own judgment concerning whether you are high in C or in I.

We suggest that you simply add the various influences in the collectivist and individualistic direction to get your total scores.

Please follow the instructions carefully and faithfully, so you will get an accurate estimate of your individualism and collectivism.

1. Individualists tend to be concerned with their personal success, even if that does not help their family. Collectivists often choose family over personal goals. On the whole how close do you feel to your family? The closer you feel, the higher should be your collectivism rating.

C =

2. There are probably other groups to which you feel very close. These might be co-workers, neighbors; people of your own religion, race, nationality, political orientation, civil rights views, personal rights view, environmental views, social standing, people with similar aesthetic standards, etc.

Now select the three or four groups that you feel closest to and enter an average collectivism rating, indicating how close you feel to these groups.

C =

3. The younger people are, the more they like to explore new ideas, and do things that do not necessarily fit what their groups want them to do. But that is not constant with age. Young children often want to do what their parents want them to do; in some cultures teenagers want to do what their friends want them to do; old people often want to do what their own children and grand-children want them to do. Now think how free you are from group influences. If you feel totally free enter a 10. Otherwise use a lower number.

I =

4. Individuals who travel a lot, change residences frequently, do not feel that they must necessarily do what their neighbors want them to do. How free do you feel from the influences of your neighbors? If you feel totally free enter a 10.

I =

5. The smaller the community in which you live, the more people (fellow villagers, neighbors) know what you are doing, and you may feel that you must pay attention to their ideas about your life style. If you feel that you are paying maximum attention to the ideas that people in your community have about your life style enter a 10 below.

C =

6. You have probably picked up a lot of ideas about how you should live from your parents, and they from their parents. So, it is likely that traditions that were in the families of your grand-parents are still very influential in your own life. If these traditions are maximally influential in your life use a 10.

C =

7. Think of your grandparents and parents in terms of how much they have been influenced by individualistic cultures, such as the United States, England, Canada, Australia, New Zealand or collectivist cultures such Africa, East Asia, Latin America.

One clue is the kind of child-rearing. When the child-rearing you have experienced was warm-controlling, in other words your parents

adored you as long as you did what they told you to do, you are most likely to have become a collectivist; on the other hand, if the child-rearing was warm-independent, that is your parents adored you and encouraged you to be independent, self-reliant, exploratory, it was okay to get into trouble and they would help you get out of trouble, you are likely to have become an individualist.

If your child-rearing was cold and neglected, you would also be an individualist; if it was cold and controlling you would be a collectivist, but these relationships are weaker, so do not give too many points in this rating.

Try to estimate how individualistic you are, taking into account who your parents and other important influences (e.g. relatives, teachers) were, and also how influential each of them was while you were growing up. If you feel you were influenced so as to become an extreme individualist enter a 10; if on the other hand, you were influenced not to be individualistic enter a 0.

I =

8. Think of the people you socialized (e.g. close friends) with when you were growing up. In the previous question the influences from the different cultures were present but they did not necessarily influence you directly. Now we are talking about direct influence. Did the people you socialized with come from different cultures and traditions? The more diverse they were the more likely it is that you are an individualist. Rate yourself on I = by giving yourself a 10 if most of your friends and influential adults (e.g. teachers), when you were growing up, were from different ethnic groups.

I =

To remind you:
Enter numbers from 0 to 10.

0 = no trace, 5 = quite a bit,
10 = the maximum possible.

9. How interdependent are you in your finances? Some people cannot make any deci-

sions about how to spend their money without consulting others, either because they have too little money or because they have important financial obligations. If you can not spend even small amounts of money without considering what that will do to other people, give yourself a 10.

$$C =$$

10. How much education do you have? The more education you have the more you can consider different points of view, from different parts of the world, and you have to decide for yourself what is right and wrong, and so you become more of an individualist. Rate the maximum a 10.

$$I =$$

11. How much formal traditional education did you have? This is education about your ethnic group (e.g., Sunday School, language school) covering the language, religion, history, rituals, and traditions of your ethnic group? The more traditional education you have had the higher you should rate yourself on $C =$.

$$C =$$

12. How much have you travelled alone abroad? If you have travelled that way a lot enter $I = 10$, because you have seen many countries and met people from all over the world, and you had to decide for yourself what life style is best for you, and so you must have become more of an individualist. If you travelled with your own group, you maintained your home culture while you were abroad, so you did not have to face the question of life styles. In that case, give few points or a zero.

$$I =$$

13. Did you live abroad for more than 6 months? The chances are that if you did that you had to decide for yourself whether the way of life of the host people was the kind of life you wanted for yourself, and so you would have become more individualistic. If you have not lived abroad enter a 0; if you lived in different countries every few years enter $I = 10$.

$$I =$$

14. Are you married? Generally married people have to live in a way that pays attention to the needs of their spouse and that makes them more collectivist. How collectivist do you feel because of your marital status? If you are not married enter a 0.

$$C =$$

15. Did you grow up in a large family, with many siblings and other relatives, in which you had to pay attention to the needs of others? In that case you may have become a collectivist. Rate yourself accordingly.

$$C =$$

16. Television, movies and magazines often expound an individualistic viewpoint (e.g. boy meets girl, they fall in love and get married, though sometimes this upsets their family and friends). How much exposure to such media did you experience? The more exposure the greater the I.

$$I =$$

17. Do you approve or disapprove of the stories in the media mentioned in the previous question? The more you disapprove, the more collectivist you may be. If you strongly condemn these stories enter a 10 below.

$$C =$$

18. Are your jobs or most of your activities allowing you to do your own thing (e.g. you are writing novels as you see fit) or do you have to act so as to take into account the needs and views of others? The more you have to take into account other people the more collectivist you are likely to be.

$$C =$$

19. What percent of your time do you work alone? If you work alone almost all the time, you do not have to pay attention to the needs of others, thus enter a 10 under I.

I =

20. Do you enjoy doing fine things alone (e.g. taking a walk alone) or you must do things with others? The more you must have others with you in order to have fun, the more of a collectivist you are. Rate yourself on that.

C =

21. Would you say that most of the time you do "your own thing" paying no attention to whether or not it fits customs and "proper" behavior? If you do your own thing all the time enter a 10.

I =

22. How much do you value your privacy? If you value your privacy very much, enter a 10 below; if you think that privacy is unimportant rate I = 0.

I =

23. Is your occupation or job such that you can make decisions while ignoring the needs and views of others? The more you can do that the larger should be the number below.

I =

24. Finally, in your occupation or job do you generally pay a lot of attention to the views and needs of others? The more you pay such attention the higher the score.

C =

Self Scoring. Now add all the C and I scores and look at your grand total.

A score of 60 is average. The more you deviate from 60 the more (or less) of that quality you have.

ENTER HERE C =   I =

It would help us if you told us something about your demographic status.

1. Are you a MAN or a WOMAN? (Please circle one)

2. Your age is _____

3. Do you consider yourself to be: (Please circle one of the sentences below)

Upper upper class (e.g. rich, influential, highly educated, you live in the very best neighborhoods, you travel all over the world when you feel like it).

Lower upper (e.g. professionals, such as physicians, lawyers; owner of a major industry).

Upper middle (professionals such as teachers, social workers; owner of a good business; owner of large farm).

Lower middle (clerical, small entrepreneurs; farmer).

Upper Lower (skilled worker, small farmer).

Lower lower (unskilled, unemployed).

4. What is the most important source of your ethnic background? (Please circle one or more of the categories that apply, use your own judgment to mark only the ones that made a difference in your life)

East Asia	North Asia
South Asia	West Asia
North Africa	Africa South of the Sahara
North Europe	South Europe
West Europe	East Europe
Mexico	Caribbean
Hispanic	Pacific Islander
Native American	South and Central America.

5. The most important source of your religious beliefs can be traced to: (Please circle one or more, as you see it)

Christianity	Islam	Judaism
Buddhism	Hinduism	Confucius
Shinto	Animism	Rationalism: Skeptical view of religion or no religion.

Thank you very much for your help.

KEY POINTS

1. As a means of understanding one another, people need to make a "first-best guess" according to culture, and then modify it based on demographics, life experiences, and other information revealed through interaction with the person.

2. The nature of the self varies across cultures.

3. Social desirability is a major concern associated with measuring collectivism and individualism.

QUESTIONS TO THINK ABOUT

1. In what ways could a personality psychologist from an individualistic culture benefit from training about a collectivist culture?

2. What are some fundamental differences between collectivist and individualistic cultures?

3. What are some possible difficulties in conducting or interpreting cross-cultural personality studies? What are some ways to potentially overcome such problems?

INDEX